WASHINGTON IRVING

WASHINGTON IRVING

THREE WESTERN NARRATIVES

A Tour on the Prairies
Astoria
The Adventures of Captain Bonneville

THE LIBRARY OF AMERICA

The paper used in this publication meets the
minimum requirements of the American National Standard for
Information Sciences—Permanence of Paper for Printed
Library Materials, ANSI Z39.48—1984.

Distributed to the trade
in the United States by Penguin Putnam Inc.
and in Canada by Penguin Books Canada Ltd.

Library of Congress Catalog Number: 2003044202
For cataloging information, see end of Notes.
ISBN 1–931082–53–7

—————

First Printing
The Library of America—146

Manufactured in the United States of America

JAMES P. RONDA
WROTE THE NOTES FOR THIS VOLUME

Contents

A TOUR ON THE PRAIRIES

Contents

INTRODUCTION

"As I saw the last blue line of my native land fade away, like a cloud in the horizon, it seemed as if I had closed one volume of the world and its concerns, and had time for meditation, before I opened another. That land, too, now vanishing from my view, which contained all that was most dear to me in life; what vicissitudes might occur in it—what changes might take place in me, before I should visit it again! Who can tell, when he sets forth to wander, whither he may be driven by the uncertain currents of existence; or when he may return; or whether it may ever be his lot to revisit the scenes of his childhood!"*

Such were the dubious thoughts that passed like a shade across my mind many years since, as I lost sight of my native land, on my voyage to Europe. Yet, I had every reason for bright anticipations. I was buoyant with health, had enough of the "world's geer" for all my wants, was on my way to visit the fairest scenes of Europe, with the prospect of returning home in a couple of years, stored with recollections for the remainder of my life.

The boding doubts, however, which had beclouded my mind at the moment of departure, threatened to prove prophetic. Years and years elapsed, yet I remained a voluntary exile from my home. Why did I so?—The question has often been asked; for once I will make a brief reply.

It was my lot, almost on landing in Europe, to experience a reverse of fortune, which cast me down in spirit, and altered the whole tenor of my life. In the midst of perplexities and humiliations, I turned to my pen for solace and support. I had hitherto exercised it for amusement; I now looked to it as my main dependence, resolving, if successful, never to abandon it for any prospect of worldly gain, nor to return to my friends, until, by my literary exertions, I had placed myself above their pity, or assistance.

Such are the main reasons that unexpectedly beguiled me into a long protracted absence. How and why that absence

---

* Sketch Book, Vol. I.

was thus protracted, would involve a story of baffled plans and deferred hopes, which led me on from month to month, and year to year, and left me where they found me; would involve, in short, the chequered story of my humble concerns and precarious feelings—and I have a shrinking repugnance to such an exposure.

Suffice it to say, that my path, which many are apt to think was a flowery one, was too often beset by thorns; and that at times when I was supposed beguiled by the pleasures and splendours of Europe, and "treading the primrose path of dalliance," I was in fact shut up from society, battling with cares and perplexities, and almost struggling for subsistence.

In the mean time, my lengthened exile subjected me to painful doubts and surmises. Some, who really valued me, supposed that I was dazzled by the factitious splendours around me, and was leading a life of epicurean indulgence. Others, who knew me not, or chose to judge harshly, accused me of a want of affection for my native land; I met with imputations of the kind in the public papers, and I received anonymous letters, reiterating them, and basely endeavouring to persuade me that I had lost the good will of my countrymen.

I should have treated these imputations with little regard, but they reached me in desponding moments, when other circumstances had produced a morbid state of feelings, and they sunk deeply in my mind. The literary undertakings in which I was engaged, and on which I depended for my maintainance, required a further absence from my country, yet I found that absence attributed to motives abhorrent to my feelings, and wounding to my pride.

By degrees I was led to doubt the entire sentiment of my countrymen towards me. Perhaps I was rendered more sensitive on this head by the indulgent good will I had ever experienced from them. They had always cherished me beyond my deserts, excusing my many deficiencies, taking my humours and errors in good part, and exaggerating every merit. Their cordial kindness had in a manner become necessary to me. I was like a spoiled child, that could not bear the glance of an altered eye. I cared even less for their good opinion than their good will, and felt indignant at being elbowed into a position with respect to them, from which my soul revolted.

I was repeatedly urged by those who knew the workings of my feelings, to lay them before my countrymen, and to repel the doubts that had been cast upon my patriotism. I declined to follow their advice. I have generally been content, in all matters relating to myself, to suffer the truth to work its own way to light. If the conduct and concerns of an individual are worthy of public attention, they will sooner or later be accurately known and appreciated; and it is that ultimate opinion that alone constitutes true reputation: all transient popularity is little worth struggling for.

Beside, what was I asked to vindicate myself from—a want of affection to my native country? I should as soon think of vindicating myself from the charge of a want of love to the mother that bore me! I could not reply to such an imputation;—my heart would swell in my throat, and keep me silent.

Yet I will confess, that the arrow which had been planted in my heart, rankled and festered there. The corroding doubt that had been infused in my waking thoughts, affected my sleeping fancies. The return to my country, so long anticipated, became the constant subject of harassing dreams. I would fancy myself arrived in my native city, but the place would be so changed that I could not recognize it. I would wander through strange streets, meet with strange faces, and find every thing strange around me: or, what was worse, I would meet with those I loved, with my kindred, and the companions of my youth, but they no longer knew me, or passed me by with neglect. I cannot tell how often I have awakened from such dreary dreams, and felt a sadness at heart for hours afterwards.

At length the long anticipated moment arrived. I again saw the "blue line of my native land" rising like a cloud in that horizon where, so many years before, I had seen it fade away. I again saw the bright city of my birth rising out of its beautiful bay; its multiplied fanes and spires, and its prolonged forest of masts, proclaiming its augmented grandeur. My heart throbbed with pride and admiration as I gazed upon it—I gloried in being its son.

But how was the wanderer to be received, after such an absence? Was he to be taken, as a favoured child, to its bosom; or repulsed as a stranger, and a changeling?

My old doubts recurred as I stepped upon land. I could scarcely realize that I was indeed in my native city, among the haunts of my childhood. Might not this be another of those dreams that had so often beguiled me? There were circumstances enough to warrant such a surmise. I passed through places that ought to be familiar to me, but all were changed. Huge edifices and lofty piles had sprung up in the place of lowly tenements; the old landmarks of the city were gone; the very streets were altered.

As I passed on, I looked wistfully in every face: not one was known to me—not one! Yet I was in haunts where every visage was once familiar to me. I read the names over the door: all were new. They were unassociated with any early recollection. The saddening conviction stole over my heart that I was a stranger in my own home! Alas! thought I, what had I to expect after such an absence!

Let not the reader be mistaken. I have no doleful picture to draw; no sorrowful demand to make upon his sympathies. It has been the lot of many a wanderer, returning after a shorter lapse of years, to find the scenes of his youth gone to ruin and decay. If I had any thing to deplore, it was the improvement of my home. It had outgrown my recollection from its very prosperity, and strangers had crowded into it from every clime, to participate in its overflowing abundance. A little while was sufficient to reconcile me to a change, the result of prosperity. My friends, too, once clustered in neighboring contiguity, in a moderate community, now scattered widely asunder, over a splendid metropolis, soon gathered together to welcome me; and never did wanderer, after such an absence, experience such a greeting. Then it was that every doubt vanished from my mind. Then it was that I felt I was indeed at home—and that it was a home of the heart! I thanked my stars that I had been born among such friends; I thanked my stars, that had conducted me back to dwell among them while I had yet the capacity to enjoy their fellowship.

It is the very reception I met with that has drawn from me these confessions. Had I experienced coldness or distrust— had I been treated as an alien from the sympathies of my countrymen, I should have buried my wounded feelings in my bosom, and remained silent. But they have welcomed me home with their old indulgence; they have shown that, notwithstanding my long absence, and the doubts and suggestions to which it had given rise, they still believe and trust in me. And now, let them feel assured, that I am heart and soul among them.

I make no boast of my patriotism; I can only say, that, as far as it goes, it is no blind attachment. I have sojourned in various countries; have been treated in them above my deserts; and the remembrance of them is grateful and pleasant to me. I have seen what is brightest and best in foreign lands, and have found, in every nation, enough to love and honour; yet, with all these recollections living in my imagination and kindling in my heart, I look round with delightful exultation upon my native land, and feel that, after all my ramblings about the world, I can be happiest at home.

And now a word or two with respect to the volume here presented to the reader. Having, since my return to the United States, made a wide and varied tour, for the gratification of my curiosity, it has been supposed that I did it for the purpose of writing a book; and it has more than once been intimated in the papers, that such a work was actually in the press, containing scenes and sketches of the Far West.

These announcements, gratuitously made for me, before I had put pen to paper, or even contemplated any thing of the kind, have embarrassed me exceedingly. I have been like a poor actor, who finds himself announced for a part he had no thought of playing, and his appearance expected on the stage before he has committed a line to memory.

I have always had a repugnance, amounting almost to disability, to write in the face of expectation; and, in the present instance, I was expected to write about a region fruitful of wonders and adventures, and which had already been made the theme of spirit-stirring narratives from able pens; yet about which I had nothing wonderful or adventurous to offer.

Since such, however, seems to be the desire of the public, and that they take sufficient interest in my wanderings to deem them worthy of recital, I have hastened, as promptly as possible, to meet in some degree, the expectation which others have excited. For this purpose, I have, as it were, plucked a few leaves out of my memorandum book, containing a month's foray beyond the outposts of human habitation, into the wilderness of the Far West. It forms, indeed, but a small portion of an extensive tour; but it is an episode, complete as far as it goes. As such, I offer it to the public, with great diffidence. It is a simple narrative of every day occurrences; such as happen to every one who travels the prairies. I have no wonders to describe, nor any moving accidents by flood or field to narrate; and as to those who look for a marvellous or adventurous story at my hands, I can only reply in the words of the weary knifegrinder: "Story! God bless you, I have none to tell, sir."

Chapter I

I N THE often vaunted regions of the Far West, several hundred miles beyond the Mississippi, extends a vast tract of
uninhabited country, where there is neither to be seen the log
house of the white man, nor the wigwam of the Indian. It consists of great grassy plains, interspersed with forests and groves
and clumps of trees, and watered by the Arkansas, the grand
Canadian, the Red River, and all their tributary streams. Over
these fertile and verdant wastes still roam the Elk, the Buffalo,
and the wild horse in all their native freedom. These, in fact,
are the hunting grounds of the various tribes of the Far West.
Thither repair the Osage, the Creek, the Delaware, and other
tribes that have linked themselves with civilization, and live
within the vicinity of the white settlements. Here resort also
the Pawnees, the Comanches, and other fierce and as yet independent tribes, the nomades of the prairies, or the inhabitants
of the skirts of the Rocky Mountains. The region I have mentioned forms a debateable ground of these warring and vindictive tribes. None of them presume to erect a permanent
habitation within its borders. Their hunters and "braves" repair thither in numerous bodies during the season of game,
throw up their transient hunting camps, consisting of light
bowers, covered with bark and skins, commit sad havoc among
the innumerable herds that graze the prairies, and having
loaded themselves with venison and Buffalo meat, warily retire
from the dangerous neighborhood. These expeditions partake,
always, of a warlike character; the hunters are all armed for action offensive and defensive, and are bound to incessant vigilance. Should they in their excursions meet the hunters of an
adverse tribe, savage conflicts take place. Their encampments
too are always subject to be surprised by wandering war parties, and their hunters when scattered in pursuit of game, to be
captured or massacred by lurking foes. Mouldering skulls and

skeletons bleaching in some dark ravine, or near the traces of a hunting camp, occasionally mark the scene of a foregone act of blood, and let the wanderer know the dangerous nature of the region he is traversing. It is the purport of the following pages to narrate a month's excursion to these noted hunting grounds through a tract of country which had not, as yet, been explored by white men.

It was early in October 1832, that I arrived at Fort Gibson, a frontier post of the Far West, situated on the Neosho, or Grand River, near its confluence with the Arkansas. I had been travelling for a month past with a small party, from St. Louis, up the banks of the Missouri, and along the frontier line of agencies and missions, that extends from the Missouri to the Arkansas. Our party was headed by one of the commissioners appointed by the government of the United States to superintend the settlement of the Indian tribes migrating from the East to the West of the Mississippi. In the discharge of his duties he was thus visiting the various outposts of civilization.

And here let me bear testimony to the merits of this worthy leader of our little band. He was a native of one of the towns of Connecticut, a man in whom a course of legal practice and political life had not been able to vitiate an innate simplicity and benevolence of heart. The greater part of his days had been passed in the bosom of his family and the society of deacons, elders and select men, on the peaceful banks of the Connecticut; when suddenly he had been called to mount his steed, shoulder his rifle and mingle among stark hunters, back woodsmen and naked savages, on the trackless wilds of the Far West.

Another of my fellow travellers was Mr. L——, an Englishman by birth, but descended from a foreign stock; and who had all the buoyancy and accommodating spirit of a native of the Continent. Having rambled over many countries he had become, to a certain degree, a citizen of the world, easily adapting himself to any change. He was a man of a thousand occupations; a botanist, a geologist, a hunter of beetles and butterflies, a musical amateur, a sketcher of no mean pretensions, in short a complete virtuoso; added to which he was a very indefatigable, if not always a very successful sportsman.

Never had a man more irons in the fire, and, consequently, never was man more busy or more cheerful.

My third fellow traveller was one who had accompanied the former from Europe, and travelled with him as his Telemachus; being apt, like his prototype, to give occasional perplexity and disquiet to his mentor. He was a young Swiss Count, scarce twenty one years of age, full of talent and spirit, but galliard in the extreme, and prone to every kind of wild adventure.

Having made this mention of my comrades, I must not pass over unnoticed a personage of inferior rank, but of all pervading and all prevalent importance: the squire, the groom, the cook, the tent man, in a word the factotum, and I may add the universal meddler and marplot of our party. This was a little swarthy, meagre, wiry French Creole, named Antoine, but familiarly dubbed Tonish: a kind of Gil Blas of the frontiers, who had passed a scrambling life sometimes among white men, sometimes among Indians. Sometimes in the employ of traders, missionaries and Indian agents; sometimes mingling with the Osage hunters. We picked him up at St. Louis, near which he has a small farm, an Indian wife and a brood of half blood children. According to his own account, however, he had a wife in every tribe: in fact, if all this little vagabond said of himself were to be believed, he was without morals, without caste, without creed, without country, and even without language; for he spoke a jargon of mingled French, English and Osage. He was, withal, a notorious braggart and a liar of the first water. It was amusing to hear him vapour and gasconade about his terrible exploits and hair breadth escapes in war and hunting. In the midst of his volubility, he was prone to be seized by a spasmodic gasping, as if the springs of his jaws were suddenly unhinged, but I am apt to think it was caused by some falsehood that stuck in his throat, for I generally remarked that immediately afterwards there bolted forth a lie of the first magnitude.

Our route had been a pleasant one, quartering ourselves occasionally at the widely separated establishments of the Indian missionaries, but in general camping out in the fine groves that border the streams, and sleeping under cover of a tent. During the latter part of our tour we had pressed forward in hopes of arriving in time at Fort Gibson to accompany the Osage hunters on their autumnal visit to the Buffalo prairies. Indeed the imagination of the young Count had become completely excited on the subject. The grand scenery and wild habits of the prairies had set his spirits madding, and the stories that little Tonish told him of Indian braves and Indian beauties, of hunting buffaloes and catching wild horses, had set him all agog for a dash into savage life. He was a bold and hard rider, and longed to be scouring the hunting grounds. It was amusing to hear his youthful anticipations of all that he was to see, and do, and enjoy, when mingling among the Indians and participating in their hardy adventures; and it was still more amusing to listen to the gasconadings of little Tonish, who volunteered to be his faithful squire in all his perilous undertakings: to teach him how to catch the wild horse, bring down the buffalo, and win the smiles of Indian princesses:— "And if we can only get sight of a prairie on fire!" said the young Count—"By gar—I'll set one on fire myself!" cried the little Frenchman.

Chapter II

THE ANTICIPATIONS of a young man are prone to meet with disappointment. Unfortunately for the Count's scheme of wild campaigning, before we reached the end of our journey we heard that the Osage hunters had set forth upon their expedition to the buffalo grounds. The young Count still determined, if possible, to follow on their track and overtake them; and, for this purpose stopped short at the Osage Agency, a few miles distant from Fort Gibson, to make enquiries and preparations. His travelling companion Mr. L. stopped with him; while the Commissioner and myself proceeded to Fort Gibson, followed by the faithful and vera-cious Tonish. I hinted to him his promises to follow the count in his campaignings, but I found the little varlet had a keen eye to self interest. He was aware that the Commissioner, from his official duties, would remain for a long time in the country, and be likely to give him permanent employment, while the sojourn of the count would but be transient. The gasconading of the little braggart, was suddenly, therefore, at an end. He spake not another word to the young count about Indians, Buffalos and wild horses, but putting himself tacitly in the train of the commissioner, jogged silently after us to the garrison.

On arriving at the fort, however, a new chance presented it-self for a cruise on the prairies. We learnt that a company of mounted rangers, or riflemen had departed but three days pre-vious, to make a wide exploring tour, from the Arkansas to the Red river, including a part of the Pawnee hunting grounds where no party of white men had as yet penetrated. Here, then, was an opportunity of ranging over those dangerous and inter-esting regions under the safeguard of a powerful escort; pro-tected too by privilege, for the Commissioner in virtue of his office, could claim the service of this newly raised corps of riflemen, and the very country they were to explore, was

destined for the settlement of some of the migrating tribes connected with his mission.

Our plan was promptly formed and put into execution. A
couple of Creek Indians were sent off express by the commander of Fort Gibson to overtake the rangers and bring
them to a halt until the Commissioner and his party should
be able to join them. As we should have a march of three or
four days through a wild country, before we could overtake
the company of rangers, an escort of fourteen mounted riflemen, under the command of a lieutenant, was assigned us.

We sent word to the young count and Mr. L. at the Osage
Agency, of our new plan and prospects, and invited them to
accompany us. The Count, however, could not forego the delights he had promised himself in mingling with absolutely
savage life. In reply he agreed to keep with us until we should
come upon the trail of the Osage hunters, when, it was his
fixed resolve to strike off into the wilderness in pursuit of
them; and his faithful mentor, though he grieved at the madness of the scheme was too staunch a friend to desert him. A
general rendezvous of our party and escort was appointed, for
the following morning, at the Agency.

We now made all arrangements for prompt departure. Our
baggage had hitherto been transported on a light waggon,
but we were now to break our way through an untravelled
country, cut up by rivers, ravines and thickets, where a vehicle
of the kind would be a complete impediment. We were to
travel on horseback, in hunters' style, and with as little en-
cumbrance as possible. Our baggage, therefore, underwent a
rigid and most abstemious reduction. A pair of saddlebags,
and those by no means crammed, sufficed for each man's
scanty wardrobe, and, with his great coat, were to be carried
upon the steed he rode. The rest of the luggage was placed
on pack horses. Each one had a bear skin and a couple of
blankets for bedding, and there was a tent to shelter us in case
of sickness or bad weather. We took care to provide ourselves
with flour, coffee, and sugar, together with a small supply of
salt pork for emergencies; for our main subsistence we were to
depend upon the chase.

Such of our horses as had not been tired out in our recent
journey, were taken with us as pack horses, or supernumer-

aries: but as we were going on a long and rough tour, where there would be occasional hunting, and where, in case of meeting with hostile savages, the safety of the rider might depend upon the goodness of his steed, we took care to be well mounted. I procured a stout silver grey; somewhat rough, but staunch and powerful; and retained a hardy pony, which I had hitherto ridden, and which, being somewhat jaded, was suffered to ramble along with the pack horses, to be mounted only in case of emergency.

All these arrangements being made we left Fort Gibson on the morning of the tenth of October, and crossing the river in the front of it, set off for the rendezvous at the Agency. A ride of a few miles brought us to the ford of the Verdigris, a wild rocky scene overhung with forest trees. We descended to the bank of the river and crossed in straggling file, the horses stepping cautiously from rock to rock, and in a manner feeling about for a foothold beneath the rushing and brawling stream.

Our little Frenchman Tonish brought up the rear with the pack horses. He was in high glee having experienced a kind of promotion. In our journey hitherto he had driven the waggon, which he seemed to consider a very inferior employ; now he was master of the horse. He sat perched like a monkey behind the pack on one of the horses; he sang, he shouted, he yelped like an Indian and ever and anon blasphemed the loitering pack horses in his jargon of mingled French, English and Osage, which not one of them could understand.

As we were crossing the ford we saw on the opposite shore a Creek Indian on horseback. He had paused to reconnoitre us from the brow of a rock, and formed a picturesque object, in unison with the wild scenery around him. He wore a bright blue hunting shirt trimmed with scarlet fringe; a gaily coloured handkerchief was bound round his head something like a turban, with one end hanging down beside his ear; he held a long rifle in his hand and looked like a wild Arab on the prowl. Our loquacious and ever meddling little Frenchman called out to him in his Babylonish jargon, but the savage having satisfied his curiosity tossed his hand in the air, turned the head of his steed, and gallopping along the shore soon disappeared among the trees.

Chapter III

An Indian agency—Riflemen—Osages, Creeks, trappers,
dogs, horses, half breeds—Beatte the huntsman.

HAVING crossed the ford we soon reached the Osage
Agency where Col. Choteau has his offices and magazines for the despatch of Indian affairs, and the distribution of
presents and supplies. It consisted of a few loghouses on the
banks of the river, and presented a motley frontier scene. Here
was our escort awaiting our arrival—some were on horseback,
some on foot, some seated on the trunks of fallen trees, some
shooting at a mark. They were a heterogeneous crew, some in
frock coats made of green blankets; others in leathern hunting
shirts, but the most part in marvellously ill cut garments, much
the worse for wear, and evidently put on for rugged service.

Near by these was a groupe of Osages: stately fellows; stern
and simple in garb and aspect. They wore no ornaments, and
their dress consisted merely of blankets, leathern leggings, and
moccasins. Their heads were bare, their hair was cropped close
excepting a bristling ridge on top like the crest of a helmet,
with a long scalp lock hanging behind. They had fine Roman
countenances, and broad deep chests, and, as they generally
wore their blankets wrapped round their loins, so as to leave
the bust and arms bare, they looked like so many noble bronze
figures. The Osages are the finest looking Indians I have ever
seen in the West. They have not yielded sufficiently, as yet, to
the influence of civilization to lay by their simple Indian garb,
or to lose the habits of the hunter and the warrior, and their
poverty prevents their indulging in much luxury of apparel.

In contrast to these was a gaily dressed party of Creeks.
There is something, at the first glance, quite oriental in the
appearance of this tribe. They dress in calico hunting shirts of
various brilliant colours, decorated with bright fringes: and
belted with broad girdles embroidered with beads: they have
leggings of dressed deer skins or of green or scarlet cloth,
with embroidered knee bands and tassels: their moccasins are
fancifully wrought and ornamented, and they wear gaudy
handkerchiefs tastefully bound round their heads.

Beside these there was a sprinkling of trappers, hunters, half breeds, creoles, negroes of every hue; and all that other rabble rout of nondescript beings that keep about the frontiers, between civilized and savage life, as those equivocal birds the bats, hover about the confines of light and darkness.

The little hamlet of the agency was in a complete bustle; the blacksmith's shed in particular was a scene of preparation. A strapping negro was shoeing a horse; two half breeds were fabricating iron spoons in which to melt lead for bullets. An old trapper in leathern hunting frock and moccasins, had placed his rifle against a work bench, while he superintended the operation and gossipped about his hunting exploits; several large dogs were lounging in and out of the shop or sleeping in the sunshine, while a little cur, with head cocked on one side and one ear erect, was watching, with that curiosity common to little dogs, the process of shoeing the horse, as if studying the art, or waiting for his turn to be shod.

We found the Count and his companion the Virtuoso ready for the march. As they intended to overtake the Osages and pass some time in hunting the Buffalo and the wild horse, they had provided themselves accordingly; having, in addition to the steeds which they used for travelling, others of prime quality, which were to be led when on the march, and only to be mounted for the chase.

They had, moreover, engaged the services of a young man named Antoine, a half breed of French and Osage origin. He was to be a kind of jack of all work; to cook, to hunt, and to take care of the horses, but he had a vehement propensity to do nothing, being one of the worthless brood engendered and brought up among the missions. He was, moreover, a little spoiled by being really a handsome young fellow, an Adonis of the frontier, and still worse by fancying himself highly connected, his sister being concubine to an opulent white trader!

For our own parts, the commissioner and myself were desirous, before setting out, to procure another attendant well versed in wood craft, who might serve us as a hunter; for our little Frenchman would have his hands full when in camp, in cooking, and on the march, in taking care of the pack horses. Such a one presented himself, or rather was recommended to us, in Pierre Beatte, a half breed of French and

Osage parentage. We were assured that he was acquainted with all parts of the country, having traversed it in all directions, both in hunting and war parties; that he would be of use both as guide and interpreter, and that he was a first rate hunter.

I confess I did not like his looks when he was first presented to me. He was lounging about, in an old hunting frock and metasses or leggings, of deer skin, soiled and greased and almost japanned by constant use. He was apparently about thirty six years of age, square and strongly built. His features were not bad, being shaped not unlike those of Napoleon, but sharpened up, with high Indian cheek bones. Perhaps the dusky greenish hue of his complexion aided his resemblance to an old bronze bust I had seen of the Emperor. He had, however, a sullen saturnine expression, set off by a slouched woolen hat, and elf locks that hung about his ears.

Such was the appearance of the man, and his manners were equally unprepossessing. He was cold and laconic; made no promises nor professions; stated the terms he required for the services of himself and his horse, which we thought rather high, but shewed no disposition to abate them, nor any anxiety to secure our employ. He had altogether more of the red than the whiteman in his composition; and, as I had been taught to look upon all half breeds with distrust, as an uncertain and faithless race, I would gladly have dispensed with the services of Pierre Beatte. We had no time, however, to look about for any one more to our taste, and had to make an arrangement with him on the spot. He then set about making his preparations for the journey, promising to join us at our evenings encampment.

One thing was yet wanting to fit me out for the prairies: a thoroughly trust worthy steed. I was not yet mounted to my mind. The grey I had bought, though strong and serviceable, was rough. At the last moment I succeeded in getting an excellent animal; a dark bay; powerful, active, generous spirited, and in capital condition. I mounted him with exultation and transferred the silver grey to Tonish who was in such extacies at finding himself so completely *en Cavalier*, that I feared he might realize the ancient and well known proverb of "a beggar on horseback."

Chapter IV

The departure

THE LONG drawn notes of a bugle at length gave the signal for departure. The rangers filed off in a straggling line of march through the woods: we were soon on horseback and following on, but were detained by the irregularity of the pack horses. They were unaccustomed to keep the line and straggled from side to side among the thickets, in spite of all the pesting and bedevilling of Tonish; who, mounted on his gallant grey, with a long rifle on his shoulder, worried after them, bestowing a superabundance of dry blows and curses.

We soon, therefore, lost sight of our escort, but managed to keep on their track, thridding lofty forests and entangled thickets, and passing by Indian wigwams, and negro huts until towards dusk we arrived at a frontier farm house, owned by a settler of the name of Berryhill. It was situated on a hill, below which the rangers had encamped in a circular grove, on the margin of a stream. The master of the house received us civilly, but could offer us no accommodation, for sickness prevailed in his family. He appeared, himself, to be in no very thriving condition for though bulky in frame, he had a sallow unhealthy complexion, and had a whiffling double voice, shifting abruptly from a treble to a thorough bass.

Finding his log house was a mere hospital, crowded with invalids, we ordered our tent to be pitched in the farm yard.

We had not been long encamped when our recently engaged attendant, Beatte, the Osage half breed, made his appearance. He came mounted on one horse and leading another which seemed to be well packed with supplies for the expedition. Beatte was evidently an "old soldier," as to the art of taking care of himself and looking out for emergencies. Finding that he was in government employ, being engaged by the commissioner, he had drawn rations of flour and bacon, and put them up so as to be weather proof. In addition to the horse for the road, and for ordinary service, which was a rough hardy animal, he had another for hunting. This was of a mixed breed like himself, being a cross of the domestic stock with the wild horse of the prairies; and a noble steed it was, of generous spirit, fine action and admirable bottom. He had taken care to have his horses well shod at the Agency. He came prepared at all points for war or hunting: his rifle on his shoulder, his powder horn and bullet pouch at his side, his hunting knife stuck in his belt, and coils of cordage at his saddle bow, which we were told were lariats, or noosed cords, used in catching the wild horse.

Thus equipped and provided, an Indian hunter on a prairie, is like a cruiser on the ocean, perfectly independent of the world, and competent to self protection and self maintenance. He can cast himself loose from every one, shape his own course, and take care of his own fortunes. I thought Beatte seemed to feel his independence, and to consider himself superior to us all, now that we were launching into the wilderness. He maintained a half proud, half sullen look, and a great taciturnity; and his first care was to unpack his horses, and put them in safe quarters for the night. His whole demeanour was in perfect contrast to our vapouring, chattering, bustling little Frenchman. The latter, too, seemed jealous of this new comer. He whispered to us that these half breeds were a touchy, capricious people, little to be depended upon. That Beatte had evidently come prepared to take care of himself, and that, at any moment in the course of our tour, he would be liable to take some sudden disgust or affront, and abandon us at a moments warning: having the means of shifting for himself, and being perfectly at home on the prairies.

Chapter V

O N THE following morning (Oct. 11) we were on the march by half past seven o'clock, and rode through deep rich bottoms of alluvial soil, overgrown with redundant vegetation, and trees of an enormous size. Our route lay parallel to the west bank of the Arkansas, on the borders of which river, near the confluence of the Red Fork, we expected to overtake the main body of Rangers. For some miles the country was sprinkled with Creek villages and farm houses; the inhabitants of which appeared to have adopted, with considerable facility, the rudiments of civilization, and to have thriven in consequence. Their farms were well stocked and their houses had a look of comfort and abundance.

We met with numbers of them returning from one of their grand games of ball, for which their nation is celebrated. Some were on foot, some on horseback; the latter, occasionally, with gaily dressed females behind them. They are a well made race, muscular and closely knit, with well turned thighs and legs. They have a gipsey fondness for brilliant colours, and gay decorations, and are bright and fanciful objects when seen at a distance on the prairies. One had a scarlet handkerchief bound round his head surmounted with a tuft of black feathers like a cock's tail. Another had a white handkerchief, with red feathers; while a third, for want of a plume, had stuck in his turban a brilliant bunch of sumach.

On the verge of the wilderness we paused to enquire our way at a log house, owned by a white settler or squatter, a tall raw boned old fellow, with red hair, a lank lanthorn visage, and an inveterate habit of winking with one eye, as if every thing he said was of knowing import. He was in a towering passion. One of his horses was missing, he was sure it had been stolen in the night by a straggling party of Osages encamped in a neighboring swamp—but he would have satisfaction! He would make an example of the villains. He had accordingly caught down his rifle from the wall, that invariable enforcer of right or wrong upon the frontiers, and having saddled his steed was about to sally forth on a foray into the swamp; while a brother squatter, with rifle in hand, stood ready to accompany him.

We endeavored to calm the old campaigner of the prairies, by suggesting that his horse might have strayed into the neighboring woods; but he had the frontier propensity to charge every thing to the Indians, and nothing could dissuade him from carrying fire and sword into the swamp.

After riding a few miles further we lost the trail of the main body of rangers, and became perplexed by a variety of tracks made by the Indians and settlers. At length coming to a log house, inhabited by a white man, the very last on the frontier, we found that we had wandered from our true course. Taking us back for some distance he again brought us to the right trail; putting ourselves upon which, we took our final departure and launched into the broad wilderness.

The trail kept on like a straggling foot path, over hill and dale, through bush and brake, and tangled thicket, and open prairie. In traversing the wilds it is customary for a party either of horse or foot to follow each other in single file like the Indians: so that the leaders break the way for those who follow and lessen their labour and fatigue. In this way, also, the number of a party is concealed, the whole leaving but one narrow well trampled track to mark their course.

We had not long regained the trail, when, on emerging from a forest, we beheld our raw boned, hard winking, hard riding knight errant of the frontier, descending the slope of a hill, followed by his companion in arms. As he drew near to us the gauntness of his figure and ruefulness of his aspect, reminded me of the descriptions of the hero of La Mancha, and he was equally bent on affairs of doughty enterprise, being about to penetrate the thickets of the perilous swamp, within which the enemy lay ensconced.

While we were holding a parley with him on the slope of the hill, we descried an Osage on horseback, issuing out of a skirt of wood about half a mile off, and leading a horse by a halter. The latter was immediately recognized by our hard winking friend as the steed of which he was in quest. As the Osage drew near I was struck with his appearance. He was about nineteen or twenty years of age but well grown; with the fine Roman countenance common to his tribe, and as he rode with his blanket wrapped round his loins his naked bust would have furnished a model for a statuary. He was mounted on a beautiful piebald horse, a mottled white and brown, of the wild breed of the prairies, decorated with a broad collar from which hung in front a tuft of horse hair dyed of a bright scarlet.

The youth rode slowly up to us with a frank open air, and signified, by means of our interpreter Beatte, that the horse he was leading had wandered to their camp and he was now on his way to conduct him back to his owner.

I had expected to witness an expression of gratitude on the part of our hard favoured cavalier, but to my surprize the old fellow broke out into a furious passion. He declared that the Indians had carried off his horse in the night, with the intention of bringing him home in the morning, and claiming a reward for finding him; a common practice, as he affirmed, among the Indians. He was, therefore, for tying the young Indian to a tree and giving him a sound lashing; and was quite surprized at the burst of indignation which this novel mode of requiting a service drew from us. Such, however, is too often the administration of law on the frontier, "Lynch's law," as it is technically termed, in which the plaintiff is apt to be witness, jury, judge and executioner, and the defendant to be convicted and punished on mere presumption: and in this way I am convinced, are occasioned many of those heart burnings and resentments among the Indians, which lead to retaliation, and end in Indian wars. When I compared the open, noble countenance and frank demeanour of the young Osage, with the sinister visage and high handed conduct of the frontiers-man, I felt little doubt on whose back a lash would be most meritoriously bestowed.

Being thus obliged to content himself with the recovery of his horse, without the pleasure of flogging the finder into the bargain, the old Lycurgus, or rather Draco of the frontier set off growling on his return homeward, followed by his brother squatter.

As for the youthful Osage, we were all prepossessed in his favour; the young count especially, with the sympathies proper to his age and incident to his character, had taken quite a fancy to him. Nothing would suit but he must have the young Osage as a companion and squire in his expedition into the wilderness. The youth was easily tempted, and, with the prospect of a safe range over the buffalo prairies and the promise of a new blanket, he turned his bridle, left the swamp and the encampment of his friends behind him, and set off to follow the count in his wanderings in quest of the Osage hunters. Such is the glorious independence of man in a savage state. This youth with his rifle, his blanket and his horse was ready at a moments warning to rove the world; he carried all his worldly effects with him; and in the absence of artificial wants, possessed the great secret of personal freedom. We of society are slaves not so much to others, as to ourselves; our superfluities are the chains that bind us, impeding every movement of our bodies and thwarting every impulse of our souls. Such at least were my speculations at the time though I am not sure but that they took their tone from the enthusiasm of the young Count, who seemed more enchanted than ever with the wild chivalry of the prairies, and talked of putting on the Indian dress and adopting the Indian habits during the time he hoped to pass with the Osages.

Chapter VI

I N the course of the morning the trail we were pursuing was
crossed by another, which struck off through the forest to
the west in a direct course for the Arkansas river. Beatte, our
half breed, after considering it for a moment, pronounced it
the trail of the Osage Hunters; and that it must lead to the
place where they had forded the river on their way to the
hunting grounds.

Here then the young Count and his companion came to a
halt and prepared to take leave of us. The most experienced
frontiers men in the troop remonstrated on the hazard of the
undertaking. They were about to throw themselves loose in
the wilderness, with no other guides, guards or attendants
than a young, ignorant half breed and a still younger Indian.
They were embarrassed by a pack horse and two led horses,
with which they would have to make their way through matted forests, and across rivers and morasses. The Osages and
Pawnees were at war and they might fall in with some warrior
party of the latter, who are ferocious foes; besides, their small
number, and their valuable horses would form a great temptation to some of the straggling bands of Osages loitering
about the frontier, who might rob them of their horses in the
night, and leave them destitute and on foot in the midst of
the prairies.

Nothing, however, could restrain the romantic ardour of the
Count for a campaign of Buffalo hunting with the Osages, and
he had a game spirit that seemed always stimulated by the idea
of danger. His travelling companion, of discreeter age and
calmer temperament, was convinced of the rashness of the enterprize, but he could not control the impetuous zeal of his
youthful friend, and he was too loyal to leave him to pursue his
hazardous scheme alone. To our great regret, therefore, we saw
them abandon the protection of our escort, and strike off on
their haphazard expedition. The old hunters of our party shook

their heads, and our half breed Beatte predicted all kinds of trouble to them; my only hope, was that they would soon meet with perplexities enough to cool the impetuosity of the young count, and induce him to rejoin us. With this idea we travelled slowly and made a considerable halt at noon. After resuming our march we came in sight of the Arkansas. It presented a broad and rapid stream bordered by a beach of fine sand, over-grown with willows and cotton wood trees. Beyond the river the eye wandered over a beautiful champaign country, of flow-ery plains and sloping uplands, diversified by groves and clumps of trees, and long screens of woodland; the whole wearing the aspect of complete, and even ornamental cultivation, instead of native wildness. Not far from the river, on an open eminence, we passed through the recently deserted camping place of an Osage war party. The frames of the tents or wigwams remained, consisting of poles bent into an arch with each end stuck into the ground: these are intertwined with twigs and branches, and covered with bark, and skins. Those experienced in Indian lore can ascertain the tribe, and whether on a hunting, or a warlike expedition, by the shape and disposition of the wigwams. Beatte pointed out to us, in the present skeleton camp, the wig-wam in which the chiefs had held their consultations round the council fire; and an open area, well trampled down, on which the grand war dance had been performed.

Pursuing our journey, as we were passing through a forest we were met by a forlorn half famished dog, who came ram-bling along the trail, with inflamed eyes, and bewildered look. Though nearly trampled upon by the foremost rangers he took notice of no one, but rambled heedlessly among the horses. The cry of "mad dog" was immediately raised, and one of the rangers levelled his rifle, but was stayed by the ever ready humanity of the Commissioner. "He is blind!" said he, "it is the dog of some poor Indian, following his master by the scent. It would be a shame to kill so faithful an animal." The ranger shouldered his rifle, the dog blundered blindly through the cavalcade unhurt; and, keeping his nose to the ground continued his course along the trail, affording a rare instance of a dog surviving a bad name.

About three o'clock we came to a recent camping place of the company of rangers: the brands of one of their fires were still smoking; so that, according to the opinion of Beatte, they could not have passed on above a day previously. As there was a fine stream of water close by, and plenty of pea vine for the horses, we encamped here for the night.

We had not been here long when we heard a halloo from a distance and beheld the young count and his party advancing through the forest. We welcomed them to the camp with heartfelt satisfaction; for their departure upon so hazardous an expedition had caused us great uneasiness. A short experiment had convinced them of the toil and difficulty of inexperienced travellers like themselves making their way through the wilderness with such a train of horses, and such slender attendance. Fortunately they determined to rejoin us before nightfall; one night's camping out might have cost them their horses. The Count had prevailed upon his protegee and esquire the young Osage to continue with him, and still calculated upon achieving great exploits with his assistance, on the Buffalo prairies.

Chapter VII

In the morning early (Oct. 12) the two Creeks who had been sent express by the Commander of Fort Gibson, to stop the Company of rangers, arrived at our encampment on their return. They had left the company encamped about fifty miles distant in a fine place on the Arkansas abounding in game, where they intended to await our arrival. This news spread animation throughout our party and we set out on our march at sunrise, with renewed spirit.

In mounting our steeds the young Osage attempted to throw a blanket upon his wild horse. The fine, sensitive animal took fright, reared and recoiled. The attitudes of the wild horse and the almost naked savage would have formed studies for a painter or a statuary.

I often pleased myself in the course of our march with noticing the appearance of the young count, and his newly enlisted follower, as they rode before me. Never was preux chevalier better suited with an esquire. The count was well mounted, and, as I have before observed, was a bold and graceful rider. He was fond too of caracolling his horse, and dashing about in the buoyancy of youthful spirits. His dress was a gay Indian hunting frock of dressed deer skin, setting well to the shape, dyed of a beautiful purple and fancifully embroidered with silks of various colours; as if it had been the work of some Indian beauty to decorate a favorite chief. With this he wore leathern pantaloons and moccasins, a foraging cap, and a double barrelled gun slung by a bandaleer athwart his back: so that he was quite a picturesque figure as he managed gracefully his spirited steed.

The young Osage would ride close behind him on his wild and beautifully mottled horse, which was decorated with crimson tufts of hair. He rode with his finely shaped head and bust naked; his blanket being girt round his waist. He carried his rifle in one hand and managed his horse with the other, and seemed ready to dash off at a moments warning, with his youthful leader on any mad cap foray or scamper. The count, with the sanguine anticipations of youth, promised himself many hardy adventures and exploits in company with his youthful "brave," when we should get among the buffaloes, in the Pawnee hunting grounds.

After riding some distance we crossed a narrow deep stream upon a solid bridge, the remains of an old beaver dam; the industrious community which had constructed it had all been destroyed. Above us a streaming flight of wild geese, high in air, and making a vociferous noise, gave note of the waning year.

About half past ten o'clock we made a halt in a forest where there was abundance of the pea vine. Here we turned the horses loose to graze. A fire was made, water procured from an adjacent spring, and in a short time our little Frenchman Tonish had a pot of coffee prepared, for our refreshment. While partaking of it we were joined by an old Osage, one of a small hunting party who had recently passed this way. He was in search of his horse which had wandered away or been stolen. Our half breed Beatte made a wry face on hearing of Osage hunters in this direction. "Until we pass those hunters," said he, "we shall see no buffalos. They frighten away every thing, like a prairie on fire."

The morning repast being over the party amused themselves in various ways. Some shot with their rifles at a mark, others lay asleep half buried in the deep bed of foliage, with their heads resting on their saddles; others gossipped round the fire at the foot of a tree, which sent up wreaths of blue smoke among the branches. The horses banquetted luxuriously on the pea vine, and some lay down and rolled amongst them.

We were overshadowed by lofty trees, with straight smooth trunks, like stately columns, and as the glancing rays of the sun shone through the transparent leaves, tinted with the many coloured hues of autumn, I was reminded of the effect of sunshine among the stained windows and clustering columns of a Gothic cathedral. Indeed there is a grandeur and solemnity in some of our spacious forests of the West that awaken in me the same feeling I have experienced in those vast and venerable piles, and the sound of the wind sweeping through them, supplies occasionally the deep breathings of the organ.

About noon the bugle sounded to horse, and we were again on the march, hoping to arrive at the encampment of the rangers before night, as the old Osage had assured us it was not above ten or twelve miles distant. In our course through a forest we passed by a lonely pool covered with the most magnificent water lilies that I had ever beheld; among which swam several wood ducks, one of the most beautiful of water fowl, remarkable for the gracefulness and brilliancy of its plumage.

After proceeding some distance farther we came down upon the banks of the Arkansas at a place where tracks of numerous horses all entering the water, shewed where a party of Osage hunters had recently crossed the river on their way to the buffalo range. After letting our horses drink in the river we continued along its bank for a space, and then across prairies where we saw a distant smoke, which we hoped might proceed from the encampment of the rangers. Following what we supposed to be their trail we came to a meadow in which were a number of horses grazing. They were not, however, the horses of the troop. A little further on, we reached a straggling Osage village on the banks of the Arkansas. Our arrival created quite a sensation. A number of old men came forward and shook hands with us all severally: while the women and children huddled together in groupes, staring at us wildly, chattering and laughing among themselves. We found that all the young men of the village had departed on a hunting expedition, leaving the women and children and old men behind. Here the Commissioner made a speech from horseback; informing his hearers of the purport of his mission to promote a general peace among the tribes of the West, and urging them to lay aside all warlike and bloodthirsty notions and not to make any wanton attacks upon the Pawnees. This speech being interpreted by Beatte, seemed to have a most pacifying effect upon the multitude who promised faithfully that as far as in them lay, the peace should not be disturbed; and indeed their age and sex gave some reason to hope that they would keep their word.

Still hoping to reach the encampment of the rangers before nightfall, we pushed on until twilight, when we were obliged to halt on the borders of a ravine. The rangers bivouacked

under trees, at the bottom of the dell, while we pitched our
tent on a rocky knoll near a running stream. The night came
on dark and overcast, with flying clouds, and much appearance of rain. The fires of the rangers burnt brightly in the
dell, and threw strong masses of light upon the robber looking groups that were cooking, eating and drinking around
them. To add to the wildness of the scene, several Osage
Indians, visitors from the village we had passed, were mingled
among the men. Three of them came and seated themselves
by our fire. They watched every thing that was going on
round them in silence, and looked like figures of monumen-
tal bronze. We gave them food, and, what they most relished,
coffee: for the Indians partake in the universal fondness for
this beverage which pervades the West. When they had made
their supper they stretched themselves, side by side, before
the fire and began a low nasal chaunt, drumming with their
hands upon their breasts by way of accompaniment. Their
chaunt seemed to consist of regular staves, every one terminating, not in a melodious cadence, but in the abrupt interjec-
tion huh! uttered almost like a hiccup. This chaunt, we were
told by our interpreter Beatte related to ourselves; our appearance, our treatment of them, and all that they knew of our
plans. In one part they spoke of the young count, whose animated character and eagerness for Indian enterprize had stuck
their fancy, and they indulged in some waggery about him
and the young Indian beauties that produced great merryment
among our half breeds.

This mode of improvising is common throughout the savage tribes; and in this way with a few simple inflections of the
voice, they chaunt all their exploits in war and hunting, and
occasionally indulge in a vein of comic humour and dry satire,
to which the Indians appear to me much more prone than is
generally imagined.

In fact the Indians that I have had an opportunity of seeing
in real life are quite different from those described in poetry.
They are by no means the stoics that they are represented; taciturn, unbending, without a tear or a smile. Taciturn they are,
it is true, when in company with white men, whose good
will they distrust, and whose language they do not understand;
but the white man is equally taciturn under like circumstances.

When the Indians are among themselves, however, there cannot be greater gossips. Half their time is taken up in talking
over their adventures in war and hunting, and in telling whimsical stories. They are great mimics and buffoons, also, and entertain themselves excessively at the expense of the whites, with
whom they have associated, and who have supposed them impressed with profound respect for their grandeur and dignity.
They are curious observers, noting every thing in silence, but
with a keen and watchful eye; occasionally exchanging a glance
or a grunt with each other, when any thing particularly strikes
them: but reserving all comments until they are alone. Then it
is that they give full scope to criticism, satire, mimicry and
mirth.

In the course of my journey along the frontier I have had
repeated opportunities of noticing their excitability and boisterous merryment at their games, and have occasionally noticed a groupe of Osages sitting round a fire until a late hour
of the night, engaged in the most animated and lively conversation, and at times making the woods resound with peals
of laughter.

As to tears, they have them in abundance both real and affected; for at times they make a merit of them. No one weeps
more bitterly or profusely at the death of a relative or friend:
and they have stated times when they repair to howl and
lament at their graves. I have heard doleful wailings at daybreak in the neighborhood of Indian villages, made by some
of the inhabitants, who go out at that hour into the fields, to
mourn and weep for the dead: at such times, I am told, the
tears will stream down their cheeks in torrents.

As far as I can judge, the Indian of poetical fiction is like
the shepherd of pastoral romance, a mere personification of
imaginary attributes.

The nasal chaunt of our Osage guests gradually died away,
they covered their heads with their blankets and fell fast asleep
and in a little while all was silent, excepting the pattering of
scattered rain drops upon our tent.

In the morning our Indian visitors breakfasted with us, but
the young Osage, who was to act as esquire to the Count in
his knight errantry on the prairies, was no where to be found.
His wild horse too was missing, and, after many conjectures

we came to the conclusion that he had taken "Indian leave" of us in the night. We afterwards ascertained that he had been persuaded so to do by the Osages we had recently met with, who had represented to him the perils that would attend him on an expedition to the Pawnee hunting grounds, where he might fall into the hands of the implacable enemies of his tribe; and, what was scarcely less to be apprehended, the annoyances to which he would be subjected from the capricious and overbearing conduct of the white men; who, as I have witnessed in my own short experience, are prone to treat the poor Indians as little better than brute animals. Indeed he had had a specimen of it himself in the narrow escape he made from the infliction of Lynch's law, by the hard winking worthy of the frontier, for the flagitious crime of finding a stray horse.

The disappearance of the youth was generally regretted by our party, for we had all taken a great fancy to him from his handsome, frank and manly appearance, and the easy grace of his deportment. He was indeed a native born gentleman. By none, however, was he so much lamented as by the young count, who thus suddenly found himself deprived of his esquire. I regretted the departure of the Osage for his own sake, for we should have cherished him throughout the expedition, and I am convinced from the munificent spirit of his patron, he would have returned to his tribe laden with wealth of beads and trinkets and Indian blankets.

Chapter VIII

The honey camp.

THE WEATHER, which had been rainy in the night, having held up; we resumed our march at seven o'clock in the morning, in confident hope of soon arriving at the encampment of the rangers. We had not ridden above three or four miles when we came to a large tree, which had recently been felled by an axe, for the wild honey contained in the hollow of its trunk, several broken flakes of which still remained. We now felt sure that the camp could not be far distant. About a couple of miles further some of the rangers set up a shout and pointed to a number of horses grazing in a woody bottom. A few paces brought us to the brow of an elevated ridge whence we looked down upon the encampment. It was a wild bandit, or Robin Hood scene. In a beautiful open forest, traversed by a running stream, were booths of bark and branches, and tents of blankets, temporary shelters from the recent rain, for the rangers commonly bivouack in the open air. There were groupes of rangers in every kind of uncouth garb. Some were cooking at huge fires made at the feet of trees; some were stretching and dressing deer skins; some were shooting at a mark and some lying about on the grass. Venison jerked, and hung on frames—was drying over the embers in one place; in another lay carcasses recently brought in by the hunters. Stacks of rifles were leaning against the trunks of the trees and saddles bridles and powder horns hanging above them, while horses were grazing here and there among the thickets.

Our arrival was greeted with acclamation. The rangers crowded about their comrades to enquire the news from the fort: for our own part, we were received in frank simple hunter's style by Capt. Bean the commander of the company; a man about forty years of age, vigorous and active. His life had been chiefly passed on the frontier, occasionally in Indian warfare, so that he was a thorough woodsman, and a first rate hunter. He was equipped in character; in leathern hunting shirt and leggings, and a leathern foraging cap.

While we were conversing with the Captain a veteran hunts-man approached whose whole appearance struck me. He was of the middle size, but tough and weather proved; a head partly bald and garnished with loose iron grey locks, and a fine black eye, beaming with youthful spirit. His dress was similar to that of the Captain, a rifle shirt and leggings of dressed deer skin, that had evidently seen service; a powder horn was slung by his side, a hunting knife stuck in his belt, and in his hand was an ancient and trusty rifle, doubtless as dear to him as a bosom friend. He asked permission to go hunting which was readily granted. "That's Old Ryan," said the captain, when he had gone. "There's not a better hunter in the camp. He's sure to bring in game."

In a little while our pack horses were unloaded and turned loose to revel among the pea vines. Our tent was pitched; our fire made; the half of a deer had been sent to us from the Captain's lodge; Beatte brought in a couple of wild turkeys; the spits were laden and the camp kettle crammed with meat, and to crown our luxuries, a basin filled with great flakes of delicious honey, the spoils of a plundered bee tree, was given us by one of the rangers. Our little Frenchman Tonish was in an extacy, and tucking up his sleeves to the elbows, set to work to make a display of his culinary skill, on which he prided himself almost as much as upon his hunting, his riding and his warlike prowess.

Chapter IX

A bee hunt.

THE BEAUTIFUL FOREST in which we were encamped abounded in bee trees; that is to say trees in the decayed trunks of which wild bees had established their hives. It is surprizing in what countless swarms the bees have overspread the Far West within but a moderate number of years. The Indians consider them the harbinger of the white man, as the Buffalo is of the red man; and say that, in proportion as the bee advances, the Indian and the Buffalo retire. We are always accustomed to associate the hum of the bee hive with the farm house and the flower garden, and to consider those industrious little animals as connected with the busy haunts of man, and I am told that the wild bee is seldom to be met with at any great distance from the frontier. They have been the heralds of civilization, steadfastly preceding it as it advanced from the Atlantic borders, and some of the ancient settlers of the West pretend to give the very year when the honey bee first crossed the Mississippi. The Indians with surprize found the mouldering trees of their forests suddenly teeming with ambrosial sweets, and nothing, I am told, can exceed the greedy relish with which they banquet for the first time upon this unbought luxury of the wilderness.

At present the honey bee swarms in myriads in the noble groves and forests that skirt and intersect the prairies and extend along the alluvial bottoms of the rivers. It seems to me as if these beautiful regions answer literally to the description of the land of promise, "a land flowing with milk and honey;" for the rich pasturage of the prairies is calculated to sustain herds of cattle as countless as the sands upon the sea shore, while the flowers with which they are enamelled render them a very paradise for the nectar seeking bee.

We had not been long in the camp when a party set out in quest of a bee tree: and, being curious to witness the sport, I gladly accepted an invitation to accompany them. The party was headed by a veteran bee hunter, a tall lank fellow, in homespun garb that hung loosely about his limbs, and a straw hat shaped not unlike a bee hive; a comrade, equally uncouth in garb, and without a hat, straddled along at his heels, with a long rifle on his shoulder. To these succeeded half a dozen others, some with axes and some with rifles, for no one stirs far from the camp without fire arms, so as to be ready either for wild deer or wild Indian.

After proceeding some distance we came to an open glade on the skirts of the forest. Here our leader halted, and then advanced quietly to a low bush on the top of which I perceived a piece of honey comb. This I found was the bait or lure for the wild bees. Several were humming about it, and diving into its cells. When they had laden themselves with honey they would rise into the air, and dart off in a straight line, almost with the velocity of a bullet. The hunters watched attentively the course they took, and then set off in the same direction, stumbling along over twisted roots and fallen trees, with their eyes turned up to the sky. In this way they traced the honey laden bees to their hive, in the hollow trunk of a blasted oak, where after buzzing about for a moment they entered a hole about sixty feet from the ground.

Two of the Bee hunters now plied their axes vigorously at the foot of the tree to level it with the ground. The mere spectators and amateurs, in the mean time, drew off to a cautious distance, to be out of the way of the falling of the tree and the vengeance of its inmates. The jarring blows of the axe seemed to have no effect in alarming or disturbing this most industrious community. They continued to ply at their usual occupations, some arriving full freighted into port, others sallying forth on new expeditions, like so many merchantmen in a money making metropolis, little suspicious of impending bankruptcy and downfall. Even a loud crack which announced the disrupture of the trunk failed to divert their attention from the intense pursuit of gain; at length down came the tree with a tremendous crash, bursting open from end to end, and displaying all the hoarded treasures of the commonwealth.

One of the hunters immediately ran up with a whisp of lighted hay as a defence against the bees. The latter, however, made no attack and sought no revenge; they seemed stupified by the catastrophe and unsuspicious of its cause, and remained crawling and buzzing about the ruins without offering us any molestation. Every one of the party now fell to, with spoon and hunting knife, to scoop out the flakes of honey comb with which the hollow trunk was stored. Some of them were of old date and a deep brown colour, others were beautifully white, and the honey in their cells was almost limpid. Such of the combs as were entire were placed in camp kettles to be conveyed to the encampment; those which had been shivered in the fall were devoured upon the spot. Every stark bee hunter was to be seen with a rich morsel in his hand, dripping about his fingers, and disappearing as rapidly as a cream tart before the holiday appetite of a schoolboy.

Nor was it the bee hunters alone that profited by the downfall of this industrious community; as if the bees would carry through the similitude of their habits with those of laborious and gainful man, I beheld numbers from rival hives, arriving on eager wing, to enrich themselves with the ruins of their neighbors. These busied themselves as eagerly and cheerily as so many wreckers on an Indiaman that has been driven on shore: plunging into the cells of the broken honey combs, banquetting greedily on the spoil, and then winging their way full freighted to their homes. As to the poor proprictors of the ruin they seemed to have no heart to do any thing, not even to taste the nectar that flowed around them; but crawled backwards and forwards, in vacant desolation, as I have seen a poor fellow with his hands in his breeches pocket, whistling vacantly and despondingly about the ruins of his house that had been burnt.

It is difficult to describe the bewilderment and confusion of the bees of the bankrupt hive who had been absent at the time of the catastrophe, and who arrived from time to time, with full cargoes from abroad. At first they wheeled about in the air, in the place where the fallen tree had once reared its head, astonished at finding it all a vacuum. At length, as if comprehending their disaster, they settled down in clusters on a dry branch of a neighboring tree, whence they seemed to contemplate the prostrate ruin and to buzz forth doleful lamentations over the downfall of their republic. It was a scene on which the "Melancholy Jacques" might have moralized by the hour.

We now abandoned the place, leaving much honey in the hollow of the tree. "It will be all cleared off by varmint," said one of the rangers.

"What vermin?" asked I.

"Oh Bears, and skunks, and raccoons and 'possums. The bears is the knowingest varmint for finding out a bee tree in the world. They'll gnaw for days together at the trunk till they make a hole big enough to get in their paws, and then they'll haul out honey, bees and all."

Chapter X

O N RETURNING to the camp we found it a scene of the
greatest hilarity. Some of the rangers were shooting at a
mark, others were leaping, wrestling and playing at prison
bars. They were mostly young men, on their first expedition,
in high health and vigour, and buoyant with anticipations;
and I can conceive nothing more likely to set the youthful
blood into a flow than a wild wood life of the kind and the
range of a magnificent wilderness abounding with game and
fruitful of adventure. We send our youth abroad to grow luxurious and effeminate in Europe; it appears to me that a previous tour on the prairies would be more likely to produce
that manliness, simplicity and self dependence most in unison
with our political institutions

While the young men were engaged in these boisterous
amusements a graver set, composed of the Captain the Doctor and other sages and leaders of the camp were seated or
stretched out on the grass, round a frontier map, holding a
consultation about our position, and the course we were to
pursue.

Our plan was to cross the Arkansas just above where the
Red Fork falls into it then to keep westerly, until we should
pass through a grand belt of open forest, called the Cross
Timber, which ranges nearly north and south from the
Arkansas to Red river, after which we were to keep a southerly
course towards the latter river.

Our half breed Beatte, being an experienced Osage hunter,
was called into the consultation. "Have you ever hunted in
this direction?" said the Captain.

"Yes," was the laconic reply.

"Perhaps then you can tell us in which direction lies the
Red Fork."

"If you keep along yonder, by the edge of the prairie you
will come to a bald hill, with a pile of stones upon it."

"I have noticed that hill as I was hunting," said the Captain.

"Well! those stones were set up by the Osages as a land mark: from that spot you may have a sight of the Red Fork."

"In that case," cried the Captain, "we shall reach the Red Fork tomorrow; then cross the Arkansas above it, into the Pawnee country, and then in two days we shall crack Buffalo bones!"

The idea of arriving at the adventurous hunting grounds of the Pawnees and of coming upon the traces of the buffaloes, made every eye sparkle with animation. Our further conversation was interrupted by the sharp report of a rifle at no great distance from the camp.

"That's Old Ryan's rifle," exclaimed the Captain, "there's a buck down I'll warrant." Nor was he mistaken, for, before long, the veteran made his appearance, calling upon one of the younger rangers to return with him and aid in bringing home the carcass.

The surrounding country in fact, abounded with game, so that the camp was overstocked with provisions, and, as no less than twenty bee trees had been cut down in the vicinity every one revelled in luxury. With the wasteful prodigality of hunters there was a continual feasting, and scarce any one put by provision for the morrow. The cooking was conducted in hunters' style. The meat was stuck upon tapering spits of dog wood, which were thrust perpendicularly into the ground, so as to sustain the joint before the fire, where it was roasted or broiled with all its juices retained in it in a manner that would have tickled the palate of the most experienced gourmand. As much could not be said in favour of the bread. It was little more than a paste made of flour and water and fried like fritters, in lard; though some adopted a ruder style, twisting it round the ends of sticks and thus roasting it before the fire. In either way I have found it extremely palatable on the prairies. No one knows the true relish of food until he has a hunter's appetite.

Before sunset we were summoned by little Tonish to a sumptuous repast. Blankets had been spread on the ground near to the fire, upon which we took our seats. A large dish or bowl, made from the root of a maple tree, and which we had purchased at the Indian village, was placed on the ground before us, and into it were emptied the contents of one of the camp kettles, consisting of a wild turkey hashed, together with slips of bacon and lumps of dough. Beside it was placed another bowl of similar ware, containing an ample supply of fritters. After we had discussed the hash, two wooden spits, on which the ribs of a fat buck were broiling before the fire, were removed and planted in the ground before us, with a triumphant air, by little Tonish. Having no dishes we had to proceed in hunters' style, cutting off strips and slices with our hunting knives, and dipping them in salt and pepper. To do justice to Tonish's cookery, however, and to the keen sauce of the prairies, never have I tasted venison so delicious. With all this our beverage was coffee, boiled in a camp kettle sweetened with brown sugar, and drank out of tin cups: and such was the style of our banquetting throughout this expedition, whenever provisions were plenty, and as long as flour and coffee and sugar held out.

As the twilight thickened into night the centinels were marched forth to their stations around the camp, an indispensable precaution in a country infested by Indians. The encampment now presented a picturesque appearance. Camp fires were blazing and smouldering here and there among the trees, with groups of rangers around them; some seated or lying on the ground, others standing in the ruddy glare of the flames, or in shadowy relief.

At some of the fires there was much boisterous mirth, where peals of laughter were mingled with loud ribald jokes and uncouth exclamations, for the troop was evidently a raw undisciplined band; levied among the wild youngsters of the frontier, who had enlisted, some for the sake of roving adventure, and some for the purpose of getting a knowledge of the country. Many of them were the neighbors of their officers and accustomed to regard them with the familiarity of equals and companions. None of them had any idea of the restraint and decorum of a camp, or ambition to acquire a name for exactness in a profession in which they had no intention of continuing.

While this boisterous merriment prevailed at one of the fires, there suddenly rose a strain of nasal melody from another, at which a choir of "vocalists" were uniting their voices

in a most lugubrious psalm tune. This was led by one of
the lieutenants; a tall spare man, who we were informed had
officiated as schoolmaster, singing master and occasionally
as methodist preacher in one of the villages of the frontier.
The chaunt rose solemnly and sadly in the night air, and
reminded me of the description of similar canticles in the
camps of the Covenanters; and, indeed, the strange medley
of figures and faces and uncouth garbs congregated together
in our troop would not have disgraced the banners of Praise
God Barebones.

In one of the intervals of this nasal psalmody, an amateur
owl, as if in competition, began his dreary hooting. Immediately there was a cry throughout the camp of "Charley's owl!
Charley's owl!" It seems this "obscure bird" had visited the
camp every night and had been fired at by one of the centinels, a half witted lad, named Charley, who on being called
up for firing when on duty, excused himself by saying that he
understood that owls made uncommonly good soup.

One of the young rangers mimicked the cry of this bird of
wisdom, who, with a simplicity little consonant with his character, came hovering within sight and alighted on the naked
branch of a tree lit up by the blaze of our fire. The young
Count immediately seized his fowling piece, took fatal aim
and in a twinkling the poor bird of ill omen came fluttering
to the ground. Charley was now called upon to make and eat
his dish of owl soup, but declined as he had not shot the bird.

In the course of the evening I paid a visit to the Captain's
fire. It was composed of huge trunks of trees and of sufficient
magnitude to roast a buffalo whole. Here were a number of
the prime hunters and leaders of the camp, some sitting, some
standing, and others lying on skins or blankets before the fire,
telling old frontier stories about hunting and Indian warfare.

As the night advanced we perceived above the trees to the
west, a ruddy glow flushing up the sky.

"That must be a prairie set on fire by the Osage hunters,"
said the Captain.

"It is at the Red Fork," said Beatte, regarding the sky. "It
seems but three miles distant, yet it perhaps is twenty."

About half past eight o'clock a beautiful pale light gradually sprang up in the East, a precursor of the rising moon.

Drawing off from the captain's lodge I now prepared for the nights repose. I had determined to abandon the shelter of the tent and henceforth to bivouack like the rangers. A bear skin spread at the foot of a tree was my bed, with a pair of saddle bags for a pillow. Wrapping myself in blankets I stretched myself on this hunter's couch, and soon fell into a sound and sweet sleep, from which I did not awake until the bugle sounded at day break.

Chapter XI

OCT. 14. At the signal note of the bugle the sentinels and patrols marched in from their stations around the camp and were dismissed. The rangers were roused from their nights repose and soon a bustling scene took place. While some cut wood, made fires and prepared the mornings meal others struck their foul weather shelters of blankets, and made every preparation for departure while others dashed about, through brush and brake catching the horses and leading or driving them into camp.

During all this bustle the forest rang with whoops, and shouts, and peals of laughter. When all had breakfasted, packed up their effects and camp equipage and loaded the pack horses, the bugle sounded to saddle and mount. By eight o'clock the whole troop set off in a long straggling line, with whoop and halloo, intermingled with many an oath at the loitering pack horses, and in a little while the forest which for several days had been the scene of such unwonted bustle and uproar relapsed into its primeval solitude and silence. It was a bright sunny morning with that pure transparent atmosphere that seems to bathe the very heart with gladness. Our march continued parallel to the Arkansas, through a rich and varied country; sometimes we had to break our way through alluvial bottoms matted with redundant vegetation where the gigantic trees were entangled with grape vines, hanging like cordage from their branches. Sometimes we coasted along sluggish brooks whose feebly trickling current just served to link together a succession of glassy pools, embedded like mirrors in the quiet bosom of the forest, reflecting its autumnal foliage, and patches of the clear blue sky. Sometimes we scrambled up broken and rocky hills from the summits of which we had wide views stretching on one side over distant prairies diversified by groves and forests and on the other ranging along a line of blue and shadowy hills beyond the waters of the Arkansas.

The appearance of our troop was suited to the country; stretching along in a line of upwards of half a mile in length, winding among brakes and bushes, and up and down the defiles of the hills: the men in every kind of uncouth garb, with long rifles on their shoulders, and mounted on horses of every colour. The pack horses too would incessantly wander from the line of march to crop the surrounding herbage and were banged and beaten back by Tonish and his half breed compeers, with vollies of mongrel oaths. Every now and then the notes of the bugle from the head of the column, would echo through the woodlands and along the hollow glens, summoning up stragglers and announcing the line of march. The whole scene reminded me of the descriptions given of bands of buccaneers penetrating the wilds of South America on their plundering expeditions against the Spanish settlements.

At one time we passed through a luxuriant bottom or meadow bordered by thickets where the tall grass was pressed down into numerous "deer beds," where those animals had couched the preceding night. Some oak trees also bore signs of having been clambered by bears, in quest of acorns, the marks of their claws being visible in the bark. As we opened a glade of this sheltered meadow we beheld several deer bounding away in wild affright, until, having gained some distance, they would stop and gaze back, with the curiosity common to this animal, at the strange intruders into their solitudes. There was immediately a sharp report of rifles in every direction, from the young huntsmen of the troop, but they were too eager to aim surely, and the deer, unharmed, bounded away into the depths of the forest.

In the course of our march we struck the Arkansas but found ourselves still below the Red Fork, and, as the river made deep bends, we again left its banks and continued through the woods until nearly three o'clock, when we encamped in a beautiful basin bordered by a fine stream, and shaded by clumps of lofty oaks.

The horses were now "hobbled," that is to say their fore legs were fettered with cords or leathern straps, so as to impede their movements, and prevent their wandering far from the camp; they were then turned loose to graze. A number of rangers, prime hunters, started off in different directions in search of game. There was no whooping or laughing about the camp as in the morning; all were either busy about the fires preparing the evenings repast or reposing upon the grass. Shots were soon heard in various directions. After a time a huntsman rode into the camp with the carcass of a fine buck hanging across his horse. Shortly after came in a couple of stripling hunters on foot, one of whom bore on his shoulders the body of a doe. He was evidently proud of his spoil, being probably one of his first achievements, though he and his companion were much bantered by their comrades, as young beginners who hunted in partnership.

Just as the night set in there was a great shouting at one end of the camp, and immediately afterwards a body of young rangers came parading round the various fires bearing one of their comrades in triumph on their shoulders. He had shot an elk for the first time in his life, and it was the first animal of the kind that had been killed on this expedition. The young hunts- man, whose name was M'Lellan, was the hero of the camp for the night, and was the "father of the feast" into the bargain; for portions of his Elk were soon roasting at every fire.

The other hunters returned without success. The Captain had observed the tracks of a buffalo, which must have passed within a few days, and had tracked a bear for some distance until the foot prints had disappeared. He had seen an Elk too on the banks of the Arkansas, which walked out on a sand bar of the river, but before he could steal round through the bushes to get a shot it had re entered the woods.

Our own hunter Beatte returned, silent and sulky, from an unsuccessful hunt. As yet he had brought us in nothing, and we had depended for our supplies of venison upon the cap- tain's mess. Beatte was evidently mortified, for he looked down with contempt upon the rangers, as raw and inexperi- enced woodmen, but little skilled in hunting lore. They, on the other hand, regarded Beatte with no very complacent eye, as one of an evil breed, and always spoke of him as "the Indian."

Our little Frenchman Tonish also, by his incessant boasting and chattering and gasconading, in his balderdashed dialect, had drawn upon himself the ridicule of many of the wags of the troop, who amused themselves at his expense in a vein of raillery by no means remarkable for its delicacy; but the little varlet was so completely fortified by vanity and self conceit that he was invulnerable to every joke. I must confess, however, that I felt a little mortified at the sorry figure our retainers were making among these moss troopers of the frontier. Even our very equipments came in for a share of unpopularity, and I heard many sneers at the double barreled guns with which we were provided against smaller game; the lads of the West holding "shot guns" as they call them in great contempt, thinking grouse, partridges, and even wild turkeys as beneath their serious attention, and the rifle the only fire arm worthy of a hunter.

I was awakened before daybreak the next morning by the mournful howling of a wolf, who was skulking about the purlieus of the camp attracted by the scent of venison. Scarcely had the first grey streak of dawn appeared when a youngster at one of the distant lodges, shaking off his sleep crowed in imitation of a cock with a loud clear note and prolonged cadence that would have done credit to the most veteran chanticleer. He was immediately answered from another quarter, as if from a rival rooster. The chaunt was echoed from lodge to lodge, and followed by the cackling of hens, quacking of ducks, gobbling of turkeys and grunting of swine, until we seemed to have been transported into the midst of a farm yard, with all its inmates in full concert around us.

After riding a short distance this morning we came upon a well worn Indian track and following it scrambled to the summit of a hill, whence we had a wide prospect over a country diversified by rocky ridges and waving lines of upland, and enriched by groves and clumps of trees of varied tint and foliage. At a distance to the west, to our great satisfaction we beheld the Red Fork rolling its ruddy current to the Arkansas, and found that we were above the point of junction. We now descended and pushed forward, with much difficulty, through the rich alluvial bottom that borders the Arkansas. Here the trees were interwoven with enormous grapevines, forming a kind of cordage, from trunk to trunk and limb to limb; there was a thick undergrowth also of bush and bramble, and such an abundance of hops, fit for gathering, that it was difficult for our horses to force their way through.

The soil was imprinted in many places with the tracks of deer, and the claws of bears were to be traced on various trees. Every one was on the look out in the hope of starting some game, when suddenly there was a bustle and a clamour of voices in a distant part of the line. A bear! A bear! was the cry. We all pressed forward to be present at the sport, when, to my infinite, though whimsical chagrin, I found it to be our two worthies Beatte and Tonish, perpetrating a foul murder on a pole cat, or skunk! The animal had ensconced itself beneath the trunk of a fallen tree, whence it kept up a vigorous defence in its peculiar style, until the surrounding forest was in a high state of fragrance.

Gibes and jeers now broke out on all sides at the expense of the Indian hunter and he was advised to wear the scalp of the skunk as the only trophy of his prowess. When they found, however, that he and Tonish were absolutely bent upon bearing off the carcass as a peculiar dainty there was a universal expression of disgust; and they were regarded as little better than cannibals.

Mortified at this ignominious debut of our two hunters, I insisted upon their abandoning their prize and resuming their march. Beatte complied, with a dogged discontented air, and lagged behind muttering to himself. Tonish, however, with his usual buoyancy consoled himself by vociferous eulogies on the richness and delicacy of a roasted pole cat, which he swore was considered the daintiest of dishes by all experienced Indian gourmands. It was with difficulty I could silence his loquacity by repeated and peremptory commands. A Frenchman's vivacity however, if repressed in one way will break out in another, and Tonish now eased off his spleen by bestowing vollies of oaths and dry blows on the pack horses. I was likely to be no gainer in the end by my opposition to the humours of these varlets, for after a time Beatte, who had lagged behind, rode up to the head of the line to resume his station as a guide, and I had the vexation to see the carcass of his prize, stripped of its skin, and looking like a fat sucking pig, dangling behind his saddle. I made a solemn vow, however, in secret that our fire should not be disgraced by the cooking of that pole cat.

Chapter XII

The crossing of the Arkansas.

WE HAD now arrived at the river about a quarter of a
mile above the junction of the Red Fork, but the banks
were steep and crumbling, and the current was deep and
rapid. It was impossible, therefore, to cross at this place, and
we resumed our painful course through the forest, despatching Beatte ahead in search of a fording place. We had proceeded about a mile further when he rejoined us bringing
intelligence of a place hard by, where the river, for a great part
of its breadth, was rendered fordable by sand bars, and the remainder might easily be swam by the horses.

Here then we made a halt. Some of the rangers set to work
vigorously with their axes felling trees on the edge of the
river, wherewith to form rafts for the transportation of the
baggage and camp equipage. Others patrolled the banks of
the river farther up, in hopes of finding a better fording place;
being unwilling to risk their horses in the deep channel.

It was now that our worthies Beatte and Tonish had an opportunity of displaying their Indian adroitness and resource.
At the Osage village which we had passed a day or two before, they had procured a dried buffalo skin. This was now
produced; cords were passed through a number of small eye-
let holes with which it was bordered, and it was drawn up until it formed a kind of deep trough. Sticks were then placed
athwart it on the inside to keep it in shape; our camp
equipage and a part of our baggage were placed within and
the singular bark was carried down the bank and set afloat. A
cord was attached to the prow which Beatte took between his
teeth and, throwing himself into the water, went ahead towing the bark after him, while Tonish followed behind, to keep
it steady and to propel it. Part of the way they had foot hold
and were enabled to wade, but in the main current they were
obliged to swim. The whole way they whooped and yelled in
the Indian style until they landed safely on the opposite shore.

The commissioner and myself were so well pleased with this
Indian mode of ferriage that we determined to trust ourselves

in the buffalo hide. Our companions the Count and Mr. L. had proceeded with the horses along the river bank, in search of a ford which some of the rangers had discovered about a mile and a half distant. While we were waiting for the return of our ferry men, I happened to cast my eyes upon a heap of luggage under a bush, and descried the sleek carcass of the pole cat, snugly trussed up and ready for roasting before the evening fire. I could not resist the temptation to plump it into the river, where it sank to the bottom like a lump of lead, and thus our lodge was relieved from the bad odour which this savoury viand had threatened to bring upon it.

Our men having recrossed with their cockleshell bark, it was drawn on shore, half filled with saddles, saddle bags and other luggage amounting to at least a hundred weight and being again placed in the water I was invited to take my seat. It appeared to me pretty much like the embarcation of the wise men of Gotham who went to sea in a bowl: I stepped in, however, without hesitation, though as cautiously as possible, and sat down on top of the luggage, the margin of the hide sinking to within a hands breadth of the water's edge. Rifles, fowling pieces and other articles of small bulk were then handed in until I protested against receiving any more freight. We then launched forth upon the stream, the bark being towed and propelled as before.

It was with a sensation half serious half comic that I found myself thus afloat, on the skin of a buffalo, in the midst of a wild river, surrounded by wilderness and towed along by a half savage whooping and yelling like a devil incarnate. To please the vanity of little Tonish I discharged the double barrelled gun to the right and left when in the centre of the stream. The report echoed along the woody shores and was answered by shouts from some of the rangers to the great exultation of the little Frenchman, who took to himself the whole glory of this Indian mode of navigation.

Our voyage was accomplished happily; the Commissioner was ferried across with equal success, and all our effects were brought over in the same manner. Nothing could equal the vain glorious vapouring of little Tonish, as he strutted about the shore and exulted in his superior skill and knowledge to the rangers. Beatte, however, kept his proud saturnine look, without a smile. He had a vast contempt for the ignorance of the rangers and felt that he had been undervalued by them. His only observation was, "Dey now see de Indian good for something—any how!"

The broad sandy shore where we had landed was intersected by innumerable tracks of elk, deer, bears, raccoons, turkeys and waterfowl. The river scenery at this place was beautifully diversified presenting long shining reaches bordered by willows and cotton wood trees; rich bottoms with lofty forests among which towered enormous plane trees, and the distance was closed in by high embowered promontories. The foliage had a yellow autumnal tint which gave to the sunny landscape the golden tone of one of the landscapes of Claude Lorraine. There was animation given to the scene by a raft of logs and branches on which the Captain, and his prime companion the Doctor were ferrying their effects across the stream, and by a long line of rangers on horseback fording the river obliquely along a series of sand bars about a mile and a half distant.

Chapter XIII

THE CAMP OF THE GLEN

*Camp gossip—Pawnees and their habits—A hunter's
adventure—Horses found and men lost.*

BEING JOINED by the Captain and some of the rangers, we
struck into the woods for about half a mile and then entered a wild rocky dell, bordered by two lofty ridges of lime
stone which narrowed as we advanced, until they met and
united making almost an angle. Here a fine spring of water
rose from among the rocks and fed a silver rill that ran the
whole length of the dell freshening the grass with which it
was carpeted.

In this rocky nook we encamped among tall trees. The
rangers gradually joined us; straggling through the forest
singly or in groupes; some on horseback, some on foot driving
their horses before them heavily laden with baggage some
dripping wet, having fallen into the river; for they had experienced much fatigue and trouble from the length of the ford,
and the depth and rapidity of the stream. They looked not
unlike banditti returning with their plunder, and the wild dell
was a retreat worthy to receive them. The effect was heightened after dark, when the light of the fires was cast upon
rugged looking groupes of men and horses; with baggage
tumbled in heaps, rifles piled against the trees and saddles,
bridles and powderhorns hanging about their trunks.

At the encampment we were joined by the young count,
and his companion and the young half breed Antoine, who
had all passed successfully by the ford. To my annoyance, however, I discovered that both of my horses were missing. I had
supposed them in the charge of Antoine, but he with characteristic carelessness, had paid no heed to them and they had
probably wandered from the line on the opposite side of the
river. It was arranged that Beatte and Antoine should recross
the river at an early hour of the morning in search of them.

A fat buck and a number of wild turkeys being brought
into the camp, we managed, with the addition of a cup of coffee to make a comfortable supper: after which I repaired to

the captain's lodge, which was a kind of council fire and gossipping place for the veterans of the camp.

As we were conversing together we observed, as on former nights, a dusky red glow in the west, above the summits of the surrounding cliffs; it was again attributed to Indian fires on the prairies; and supposed to be on the western side of the Arkansas. If so it was thought they must be made by some party of Pawnees, as the Osage hunters seldom ventured in that quarter. Our half breeds, however, pronounced them Osage fires, and that they were on the opposite side of the Arkansas.

The conversation now turned upon the Pawnees, into whose hunting grounds we were about entering. There is always some wild untamed tribe of Indians who form for a time the terror of a frontier, and about whom all kinds of fearful stories are told. Such at present was the case with the Pawnees who rove the regions between the Arkansas and the Red River, and the prairies of Texas. They were represented as admirable horsemen, and always on horseback; mounted on fleet and hardy steeds, the wild race of the prairies. With these they roam the great plains that extend about the Arkansas, the Red River, and through Texas to the Rocky Mountains, sometimes engaged in hunting the deer and buffalo, sometimes in warlike and predatory expeditions, for like their counterparts, the sons of Ishmael their hand is against every one, and every one's hand against them. Some of them have no fixed habitation, but dwell in tents of skins, easily packed up and transported so that they are here to day and away, no one knows where, tomorrow.

One of the veteran hunters gave several anecdotes of their mode of fighting. Luckless, according to his account, is the band of weary traders or hunters descried by them in the midst of a prairie. Sometimes they will steal upon them by stratagem hanging with one leg over the saddle and their bodies concealed, so that their troop at a distance has the appearance of a gang of wild horses. When they have thus gained sufficiently upon the enemy they will suddenly raise themselves in their saddles and come like a rushing blast all fluttering with feathers, shaking their mantles, brandishing their weapons and making hideous yells. In this way they seek to strike a panic into the horses and put them to the scamper, when they will pursue and carry them off in triumph.

The best mode of defence, according to this veteran wood-man, is to get into the covert of some wood or thicket, or if there be none at hand, to dismount, tie the horses firmly head to head in a circle, so that they cannot break away and scat-ter, and resort to the shelter of a ravine, or make a hallow in the sand, where they may be screened from the shafts of the Pawnees. The latter chiefly use the bow and arrow and are dexterous archers, circling round and round their enemy and launching their arrows when at full speed. They are chiefly formidable on the prairies where they have free career for their horses and no trees to turn aside their arrows. They will rarely follow a flying enemy into the forest.

Several anecdotes also were given of the secrecy and cau-tion with which they will follow and hang about the camp of an enemy, seeking a favorable moment for plunder or attack.

"We must now begin to keep a sharp look out," said the cap-tain. "I must issue written orders that no man shall hunt with-out leave or fire off a gun, on pain of riding a wooden horse with a sharp back. I have a wild crew of young fellows, unac-customed to frontier service. It will be difficult to teach them caution. We are now in the land of a silent, watchful, crafty peo-ple, who, when we least suspect it may be around us spying out all our movements and ready to pounce upon all stragglers."

"How will you be able to keep your men from firing, if they see game while strolling round the camp?" asked one of the rangers.

"They must not take their guns with them, unless they are on duty or have permission."

"Ah Captain!" cried the ranger, "that will never do for me. Where I go my rifle goes. I never like to leave it behind. It's like a part of myself. There's no one will take such care of it as I, and there's nothing will take such care of me as my rifle."

"There's truth in all that," said the captain touched by a true hunter's sympathy. "I've had my rifle pretty nigh as long as I have had my wife, and a faithful friend it has been to me."

Here the Doctor, who is as keen a hunter as the Captain, joined in the conversation. "A neighbor of mine says, next to my rifle I'd as leave lend you my wife."

"There's few," observed the Captain, "that take care of their rifles as they ought to be taken care of."

"Or of their wives either," replied the Doctor, with a wink.

"That's a fact," rejoined the Captain.

Word was now brought that a party of four rangers headed by "Old Ryan" were missing. They had separated from the main body, on the opposite side of the river, when searching for a ford, and had straggled off no body knew whither. Many conjectures were made about them and some apprehensions expressed for their safety.

"I should send to look after them," said the Captain, "but Old Ryan is with them and he knows how to take care of himself and of them too. If it were not for him I would not give much for the rest, but he is as much at home in the woods or on a prairie as he would be in his own farm yard. He's never lost wherever he is. There's a good gang of them to stand by one another; four to watch and one to take care of the fire."

"It's a dismal thing to get lost at night in a strange and wild country," said one of the younger rangers.

"Not if you have one or two in company," said an older one. "For my part I could feel as cheerful in this hollow as in my own home if I had but one comrade to take turns to watch and keep the fire going. I could lie here for hours and gaze up to that blazing star there, that seems to look down into the camp as if it were keeping guard over it."

"Aye, the stars are a kind of company to one, when you have to keep watch alone. That's a cheerful star too, some how, that's the evening star, the planet Venus they call it, I think."

"If that's the planet Venus," said one of the council, who I believe was the psalm singing school master, "it bodes us no good, for I recollect reading in some book that the Pawnees worship that star and sacrifice their prisoners to it. So I should not feel the better for the sight of that star in this part of the country."

"Well," said the sergeant, a thorough bred woodman, "star or no star, I have passed many a night alone in a wilder place than this, and slept sound too, I'll warrant you. Once however I had rather an uneasy time of it. I was belated in passing through a tract of wood near the Tombigbee river; so I struck a light, made a fire, and turned my horse loose while I stretched myself to sleep. By and bye I heard the wolves howl. My horse came crowding near me for protection; for he was terribly frightened. I drove him off but he returned, and drew nearer and nearer, and stood looking at me and at the fire, and dozing and nodding and tottering on his fore feet, for he was powerful tired. After a while I heard a strange dismal cry. I thought at first it might be an owl. I heard it again, and then I knew it was not an owl but must be a panther. I felt rather awkward, for I had no weapon but a double bladed pen knife. I, however, prepared for defence in the best way I could, and piled up small brands from the fire, to pepper him with should he come nigh. The company of my horse now seemed a comfort to me; the poor creature laid down beside me and soon fell asleep, being so tired. I kept watch and nodded and dozed, and started awake, and looked round expecting to see the glaring eyes of the panther close upon me; but some how or other fatigue got the better of me and I fell asleep outright. In the morning I found the tracks of a panther within sixty paces. They were as large as my two fists. He had evidently been walking backwards and forwards, trying to make up his mind to attack me: but luckily he had not courage."

Oct. 16. I awoke before day break. The moon was shining feebly down into the glen from among light drifting clouds, the camp fires were nearly burnt out, and the men lying about them, wrapped in blankets. With the first streak of day our huntsman Beatte, with Antoine the young half breed set off to recross the river in search of the stray horses, in company with several rangers who had left their rifles and baggage on the opposite shore. As the ford was deep and they were obliged to cross in a diagonal line, against a rapid current, they had to be mounted on the tallest and strongest horses.

By eight o'clock Beatte returned. He had found both horses but had lost Antoine. The latter he said was a boy, a green horn, that knew nothing of the woods. He had wandered out of sight of him and got lost. However there were plenty more for him to fall in company with, as some of the rangers had gone astray also, and Old Ryan and his party had not returned.

We waited until the morning was somewhat advanced, in hopes of being rejoined by the stragglers but they did not make their appearance. The Captain observed that the Indians on the opposite side of the river were all well disposed to the whites, so that no serious apprehensions need be entertained for the safety of the missing; the greatest danger was that their horses might be stolen in the night by straggling Osages. He determined, therefore, to proceed leaving a rear guard in the camp to await their arrival.

I sat on a rock that overhung the spring at the upper part of the dell, and amused myself by watching the changing scene before me. First the preparations for departure. Horses driven in from the purlieus of the camp; rangers riding about among rocks and bushes in quest of others that had strayed to a distance; the bustle of packing up camp equipage and the clamour after kettles and frying pans borrowed by one mess from another, mixed up with oaths and exclamations at restive horses, or others that had wandered away to graze after being packed: among which the voice of our little Frenchman Tonish was particularly to be distinguished.

The bugle sounded the signal to mount and march. The troop filed off in irregular line down the glen and through the open forest, winding and gradually disappearing among the trees, though the clamour of voices, and the notes of the bugle could be heard for some time afterwards. The rear guard remained under the trees in the lower part of the dell, some on horseback with their rifles on their shoulders; others seated by the fire or lying on the ground gossiping in a low lazy tone of voice, their horses unsaddled, standing and dozing around: while one of the rangers profiting by this interval of leisure, was shaving himself before a pocket mirror stuck against the trunk of a tree.

The clamour of voices and the notes of the bugle at length died away, and the glen relapsed into quiet and silence, broken occasionally by the low murmuring tones of the groupe around the fire, the pensive whistle of some laggard among the trees, or the rustling of the yellow leaves which the lightest breath of air brought down in wavering showers; a sign of the departing glories of the year.

Chapter XIV

HAVING PASSED through the skirt of woodland bordering the river, we ascended the hills, taking a westerly course through an undulating country, of "oak openings" where the eye stretched at times over wide tracts of hill and dale, diversified by forests, groves, and clumps of trees. As we were proceeding at a slow pace those who were at the head of the line descried four deer grazing on a grassy slope about half a mile distant. They apparently had not perceived our approach and continued to graze in perfect tranquility. A young ranger obtained permission from the Captain to go in pursuit of them, and the troop halted in lengthened line, watching him in silence. Walking his horse slowly and cautiously he made a circuit until a skreen of wood intervened between him and the deer. Dismounting then he left his horse among the trees, and creeping round a knoll, was hidden from our view. We now kept our eyes intently fixed on the deer, which continued grazing, unconscious of their danger. Presently there was the sharp report of a rifle; a fine buck made a convulsive bound and fell to the earth, his companions scampered off. Immediately our whole line of march was broken; there was a helter skelter galloping of the youngsters of the troop, eager to get a shot at the fugitives; and one of the most conspicuous personages in the chase was our little Frenchman, Tonish, on his silver grey; having abandoned his pack horses at the first sight of the deer. It was some time before our scattered forces could be recalled by the bugle and our march resumed.

Two or three times in the course of the day we were interrupted by hurry scurry scenes of the kind. The young men of the troop were full of excitement on entering an unexplored country abounding in game, and they were too little accustomed to discipline or restraint to be kept in order. No one, however, was more unmanageable than Tonish. Having an intense conceit of his skill as a hunter and an irrepressible passion for display he was continually sallying forth, like an ill broken hound, whenever any game was started, and had as often to be whipped back.

At length his curiosity got a salutary check. A fat doe came bounding along in full sight of the whole line. Tonish dismounted, levelled his rifle and had a fair shot. The doe kept on. He sprang upon his horse, stood up on the saddle like a posture master and continued gazing after the animal as if certain to see it fall. The doe, however, kept on its way rejoicing: a laugh broke out along the line, the little Frenchman slipt quietly into his saddle, began to belabour and blaspheme the wandering pack horses, as if they had been to blame, and for some time we were relieved from his vaunting and vapouring.

In one part of our march we came to the remains of an old Indian encampment, on the banks of a fine stream, with the moss grown sculls of deer lying here and there, about it. As we were in the Pawnee country it was supposed, of course, to have been a camp of those formidable rovers; the Doctor, however, after considering the shape and disposition of the lodges pronounced it the camp of some bold Delawares, who had probably made a brief and dashing excursion into these dangerous hunting grounds.

Having proceeded some distance further we observed a couple of figures on horseback, slowly moving parallel to us along the edge of a naked hill about two miles distant; and apparently reconnoitering us. There was a halt and much gazing and conjecturing. Were they Indians? If Indians, were they Pawnees? There is something exciting to the imagination and stirring to the feelings, while traversing these hostile plains, in seeing a horseman prowling along the horizon. It is like descrying a sail at sea in time of war, when it may be either a privateer or a pirate. Our conjectures were soon set at rest by reconnoitering the two horsemen through a small spy glass when they proved to be two of the men we had left at the camp, who had set out to rejoin us and had wandered from the track.

Our march this day was animating and delightful. We were in a region of adventure; breaking our way through a country hitherto untrodden by white men, excepting perchance by some solitary trapper. The weather was in its perfection, temperate, genial and enlivening; a deep blue sky with a few light feathery clouds; an atmosphere of perfect transparency, an air pure and bland, and a glorious country spreading out far and wide in the golden sunshine of an autumnal day; but all silent, lifeless, without a human habitation and apparently without a human inhabitant!

It was as if a ban hung over this fair but fated region. The very Indians dared not abide here but made it a mere scene of perilous enterprize, to hunt for a few days and then away.

After a march of about fifteen miles west we encamped in a beautiful peninsula made by the windings and doublings of a deep, clear and almost motionless brook, and covered by an open grove of lofty and magnificent trees. Several hunters immediately started forth in quest of game before the noise of the camp should frighten it from the vicinity. Our man Beatte also took his rifle and went forth alone, in a different course from the rest.

For my own part, I laid on the grass under the trees, and built castles in the clouds, and indulged in the very luxury of rural repose. Indeed I can scarcely conceive a kind of life more calculated to put both mind and body in a healthful tone. A mornings ride of several hours diversified by hunting incidents, an encampment in the afternoon under some noble grove on the borders of a stream; an evening banquet of venison fresh killed; roasted, or broiled on the coals; turkeys just from the thickets and wild honey from the trees: and all relished with an appetite unknown to the gourmets of the cities. And then at night—such sweet sleeping in the open air; or waking and gazing at the moon and stars, shining between the branches of the trees!

On the present occasion, however, we had not much reason to boast of our larder. But one deer had been killed during the day, and none of that had reached our lodge. We were fain, therefore, to stay our keen appetites by some scraps of turkey brought from the last encampment, eked out with a slice or two of salt pork. This scarcity, however, did not continue long. Before dark a young hunter returned well laden with spoil. He had shot a deer, cut it up in an artist like style, and, putting the meat in a kind of sack made of the hide, had slung it across his shoulder and trudged with it to camp.

Not long after, Beatte made his appearance with a fat doe across his horse. It was the first game he had brought in, and I was glad to see him with a trophy that might efface the memory of the pole cat. He laid the carcass down by our fire without saying a word, and then turned to unsaddle his horse: nor could any questions from us about his hunting draw from him more than laconic replies. If Beatte however observed this Indian taciturnity about what he had done, Tonish made up for it by boasting of what he meant to do. Now that we were in a good hunting country he meant to take the field, and, if we would take his word for it, our lodge would henceforth be overwhelmed with game. Luckily his talking did not prevent his working, the doe was skilfully dissected, several fat ribs roasted before the fire, the coffee kettle replenished, and in a little while we were enabled to indemnify ourselves luxuriously for our late meagre repast.

The Captain did not return until late and he returned empty handed. He had been in pursuit of his usual game the deer, when he came upon the tracks of a gang of about sixty Elk. Having never killed an animal of the kind, and the elk being at this moment an object of ambition among all the veteran hunters of the camp, he abandoned his pursuit of the deer, and followed the newly discovered track. After some time he came in sight of the elk and had several fair chances of a shot, but was anxious to bring down a large buck which kept in the advance. Finding at length, that there was danger of the whole gang escaping him he fired at a doe. The shot took effect, but the animal had sufficient strength to keep on for a time with its companions. From the tracks of blood he felt confident it was mortally wounded, but evening came on, he could not keep the trail and had to give up the search until morning.

Old Ryan and his little band had not yet rejoined us, neither had our young half breed Antoine made his appearance. It was determined therefore to remain at our encampment for the following day, to give time for all stragglers to arrive.

The conversation, this evening, among the old huntsmen turned upon the Delaware tribe, one of whose encampments we had passed in the course of the day; and anecdotes were given of their prowess in war and dexterity in hunting. They used to be deadly foes of the Osages who stood in great awe of their desperate valour though they were apt to attribute it to a whimsical cause. "Look at dem Delawares," would they say, "dey got short leg—no can run—must stand and fight a great heap." In fact the Delawares are rather short legged while the Osages are remarkable for length of limb.

The expeditions of the Delawares whether of war or hunting are wide and fearless; a small band of them will penetrate far into these dangerous and hostile wilds, and will push their encampments even to the Rocky Mountains. This daring temper may be in some measure encouraged by one of the superstitions of their creed. They believe that a guardian spirit, in the form of a great eagle, watches over them, hovering in the sky, far out of sight. Sometimes, when well pleased with them, he wheels down into the lower regions and may be seen circling with wide spread wings against the white clouds: at such times the seasons are propitious the corn grows finely, and they have great success in hunting. Sometimes however, he is angry, and then he vents his rage in the thunder, which is his voice, and the lightning, which is the flashing of his eye, and strikes dead the object of his displeasure.

The Delawares make sacrifices to this spirit, who occasionally lets drop a feather from his wing in token of satisfaction. These feathers render the wearer invincible, and invulnerable. Indeed the Indians generally consider the feathers of the eagle possessed of occult and sovereign virtues.

At one time a party of Delawares, in the course of a bold incursion into the Pawnee hunting grounds were surrounded on one of the great plains, and nearly destroyed. The remnant took refuge on the summit of one of those isolated and conical hills that rise almost like artificial mounds, from the midst of the prairies. Here the chief warrior, driven almost to despair, sacrificed his horse to the tutelar spirit. Suddenly an enormous eagle rushing down from the sky bore off the victim in his talons and mounting into the air, dropped a quill feather from his wing. The chief caught it up with joy, bound it to his forehead and, leading his followers down the hill, cut his way through the enemy with great slaughter, and without any one of his party receiving a wound.

Chapter XV

THE ELK CAMP

The search for the elk—Pawnee stories.

WITH THE morning dawn the prime hunters of the camp were all on the alert, and set off in different directions to beat up the country for game. The Captain's brother, Sergeant Bean, was among the first, and returned before breakfast with success, having killed a fat doe almost within the purlieus of the camp.

When breakfast was over the Captain mounted his horse to go in quest of the Elk which he had wounded on the preceding evening, and which, he was persuaded, had received its death wound. I determined to join him in the search and we accordingly sallied forth together, accompanied also by his brother the sergeant and a lieutenant. Two rangers followed on foot, to bring home the carcass of the doe which the sergeant had killed. We had not ridden far when we came to where it lay on the side of a hill, in the midst of a beautiful woodland scene. The two rangers immediately fell to work, with true hunters' skill, to dismember it, and prepare it for transportation to the camp, while we continued on our course. We passed along sloping hill sides, among skirts of thicket and scattered forest trees until we came to a place where the long herbage was pressed down with numerous elk beds. Here the captain had first roused the gang of elks, and, after looking about diligently for a little while, he pointed out their "trail," the foot prints of which were as large as those of horned cattle. He now put himself upon the track and went quietly forward, the rest of us following him in Indian file. At length he halted at the place where the elk had been when shot at. Spots of blood on the surrounding herbage shewed that the shot had been effective. The wounded animal had evidently kept for some distance with the rest of the herd, as could be seen by sprinklings of blood here and there on the shrubs and weeds bordering the trail. These at length suddenly disappeared. "Somewhere hereabout," said the Captain, "the elk must have turned off from the gang. Whenever they feel themselves mortally wounded they will turn aside, and seek some out of the way place to die alone."

There was something in this picture of the last moments of a wounded deer to touch the sympathies of one not hardened to the gentle disports of the chase; such sympathies, however, are but transient. Man is naturally an animal of prey, and, however changed by civilization, will readily relapse into his instinct for destruction. I found my ravenous and sanguinary propensities daily growing stronger upon the prairies.

After looking about for a little while the captain succeeded in finding the separate trail of the wounded elk, which turned off almost at right angles from that of the herd and entered an open forest of scattered trees. The traces of blood became more faint and rare, and occurred at greater distances: at length they ceased altogether, and the ground was so hard and the herbage so much parched and withered, that the foot prints of the animal could no longer be perceived.

"The elk must lie some where in this neighborhood," said the Captain, "as you may know by those turkey buzzards wheeling about in the air: for they always hover in that way above some carcass. However, the dead elk cannot get away, so let us follow the trail of the living ones: they may have halted at no great distance and we may find them grazing and get another crack at them."

We accordingly returned and resumed the trail of the Elks which led us a straggling course over hill and dale covered with scattered oaks. Every now and then we would catch a glimpse of a deer bounding away across some glade of the forest, but the Captain was not to be diverted from his elk hunt by such inferior game. A large flock of wild turkeys too were roused by the trampling of our horses, some scampered off as fast as their long legs could carry them: others fluttered up into the trees, where they remained with outstretched necks, gazing at us. The Captain would not allow a rifle to be discharged at them, lest it should alarm the elk which he hoped to find in the vicinity. At length we came to where the forest ended in a steep bank, and the Red Fork wound its way below us, between broad sandy shores. The trail descended the bank and we could trace it, with our eyes, across the level sands until it terminated in the river, which, it was evident, the gang had forded on the preceding evening.

"It is needless to follow on any further," said the Captain. "The elk must have been much frightened, and, after crossing the river may have kept on for twenty miles without stopping."

Our little party now divided, the lieutenant and sergeant making a circuit in quest of game, and the Captain and myself taking the direction of the camp. On our way we came to a buffalo track more than a year old. It was not wider than an ordinary foot path and worn deep into the soil; for these animals follow each other in single file. Shortly afterwards we met two rangers on foot, hunting. They had wounded an elk, but he had escaped; and in pursuing him had found the one shot by the captain on the preceding evening. They turned back and conducted us to it. It was a noble animal, as large as a yearling heifer, and lay in an open part of the forest about a mile and a half distant from the place where it had been shot. The turkey buzzards which we had previously noticed were wheeling in the air above it. The observation of the captain seemed verified. The poor animal, as life was ebbing away, had apparently abandoned its unhurt companions, and turned aside to die alone.

The Captain and the two rangers forthwith fell to work, with their hunting knives, to flay and cut up the carcass. It was already tainted on the inside, but ample collops were cut from the ribs and haunches, and laid in a heap on the outstretched hide. Holes were then cut along the border of the hide, raw thongs were passed through them, and the whole drawn up like a sack, which was swung behind the Captain's saddle. All this while the turkey buzzards were soaring over head, waiting for our departure, to swoop down and banquet on the carcass.

The wreck of the poor Elk being thus dismantled the captain and myself mounted our horses and jogged back to the camp, while the two rangers resumed their hunting.

On reaching the camp I found there our young half breed Antoine. After separating from Beatte, in the search after the stray horses on the other side of the Arkansas, he had fallen upon a wrong track which he followed for several miles; when he overtook Old Ryan and his party and found he had been following their traces.

They all forded the Arkansas about eight miles above our crossing place, and found their way to our late encampment in the glen, where the rear guard we had left behind was waiting for them. Antoine being well mounted and somewhat impatient to rejoin us had pushed on alone following our trail to our present encampment, and bringing the carcass of a young bear which he had killed.

Our camp during the residue of the day presented a mingled picture of bustle and repose. Some of the men were busy round the fires jerking and roasting venison and bear's meat, to be packed up as a future supply. Some were stretching and dressing the skins of the animals they had killed, others were washing their clothes in the brook and hanging them on the bushes to dry, while many were lying on the grass and lazily gossipping in the shade. Every now and then a hunter would return, on horseback or on foot, laden with game, or empty handed. Those who brought home any spoil deposited it at the captain's fire, and then filed off to their respective messes to relate their days exploits to their companions. The game killed at this camp consisted of six deer, one elk, two bears and six or eight turkeys.

During the last two or three days, since their wild Indian achievement in navigating the river, our retainers had risen in consequence among the rangers, and now I found Tonish making himself a complete oracle among some of the raw and inexperienced recruits, who had never been in the wilderness. He had continually a knot hanging about him and listening to his extravagant tales about the Pawnees, with whom he pretended to have often had fearful encounters. His representations, in fact, were calculated to inspire his hearers with an awful idea of the foe into whose lands they were intruding. According to his accounts the rifle of the white man was no match for the bow and arrow of the Pawnee. When the rifle was once discharged, it took time and trouble to load it again, and in the mean time the enemy could keep on launching his shafts as fast as he could draw his bow. Then the Pawnee, according to Tonish, could shoot with unerring aim three hundred yards, and send his arrow clean through and through a buffalo; nay he had known a Pawnee shaft pass through one buffalo and wound another. And then the way the Pawnees sheltered themselves from the shots of their enemy: they would hang with one leg over the saddle crouching their bodies along the opposite side of their horse, and would shoot their arrows from under his neck, while at full speed!

If Tonish was to be believed there was peril at every step in these debateable grounds of the Indian tribes. Pawnees lurked unseen among the thickets and ravines. They had their scouts and sentinels on the summit of the mounds which command a view over the prairies, where they lay crouched in the tall grass only now and then raising their heads to watch the movements of any war or hunting party that might be passing in lengthened line below. At night they would lurk round an encampment; crawling through the grass, and imitating the movements of a wolf, so as to deceive the centinel on the outpost, until, having arrived sufficiently near, they would speed an arrow through his heart, and retreat undiscovered. In telling his stories Tonish would appeal from time to time to Beatte for the truth of what he said; the only reply would be a nod or shrug of the shoulders; the latter being divided in mind between a distaste for the gasconading spirit of his comrade, and a sovereign contempt for the inexperience of the young rangers in all that he considered true knowledge.

Chapter XVI

*A sick camp—The march—The disabled horse—Old Ryan
and the stragglers—Symptoms of change of weather and
change of humours.*

OCT. 18. We prepared to march at the usual hour but word was brought to the Captain that three of the rangers, who had been attacked with the meazles, were unable to proceed, and that another one was missing. The last was an old frontiers man, by the name of Sawyer, who had gained years without experience; and having sallied forth to hunt on the preceding day, had probably lost his way on the prairies. A guard of ten men was, therefore, left to take care of the sick, and wait for the straggler. If the former recovered sufficiently in the course of two or three days they were to rejoin the main body, other wise to be escorted back to the garrison.

Taking our leave of the sick camp we shaped our course westward along the heads of small streams, all wandering, in deep ravines, towards the Red Fork. The land was high and undulating, or "rolling" as it is termed in the West; with a poor hungry soil mingled with the sandstone, which is universal in this part of the country, and checquered with harsh forests of post oak and black jack.

In the course of the morning I received a lesson on the importance of being chary of one's steed on the prairies. The one I rode surpassed in action most horses of the troop, and was of great mettle and a generous spirit. In crossing the deep ravines he would scramble up the steep banks like a cat, and was always for leaping the narrow runs of water. I was not aware of the imprudence of indulging him in such exertions, until, in leaping him across a small brook, I felt him immediately falter beneath me. He limped forward a short distance but soon fell stark lame, having sprained his shoulder. What was to be done? He could not keep up with the troop, and was too valuable to be abandoned on the prairie. The only alternative was to send him back to join the invalids in the sick camp, and to share their fortunes. Nobody, however, seemed disposed to lead him back, although I offered a liberal reward.

Either the stories of Tonish about the Pawnees had spread an apprehension of lurking foes, and imminent perils on the prairies; or there was a fear of missing the trail and getting lost. At length two young men stepped forward and agreed to go in company, so that, should they be benighted on the prairies, there might be one to watch while the other slept.

The horse was accordingly consigned to their care, and I looked after him with a rueful eye as he limped off, for it seemed as if, with him, all strength and buoyancy had departed from me.

I looked round for a steed to supply his place and fixed my eye upon the gallant grey which I had transferred at the Agency to Tonish. The moment, however, that I hinted about his dismounting and taking up with the supernumerary pony the little varlet broke out into vociferous remonstrances and lamentations, gasping and almost strangling, in his eagerness to give vent to them. I saw that to unhorse him would be to prostrate his spirit and cut his vanity to the quick. I had not the heart to inflict such a wound, or to bring down the poor devil from his transient vain glory: so I left him in possession of his gallant grey; and contented myself with shifting my saddle to the jaded pony.

I was now sensible of the complete reverse to which a horseman is exposed on the prairies. I felt how completely the spirit of the rider depends upon his steed. I had hitherto been able to make excursions at will from the line, and to gallop in pursuit of any object of interest or curiosity. I was now reduced to the tone of the jaded animal I bestrode, and doomed to plod on patiently and slowly after my file leader. Above all, I was made conscious how unwise it is, in expeditions of the kind, where a man's life may depend upon the strength and speed, and freshness of his horse, to task the generous animal by any unnecessary exertion of his powers.

I have observed that the wary and experienced huntsman and traveller of the prairies is always sparing of his horse, when on a journey; never, except in emergency, putting him off of a walk. The regular journeyings of frontiers men and Indians when on a long march seldom exceed above fifteen miles a day, and are generally about ten or twelve, and they never indulge in capricious gallopping. Many of those, however, with whom I was travelling, were young and inexperienced and full of excitement at finding themselves in a country abounding with game. It was impossible to retain them in the sobriety of a march, or to keep them to the line. As we broke our way through the coverts and ravines, and the deer started up and scampered off to the right and left, the rifle balls would whiz after them and our young hunters dash off in pursuit. At one time they made a grand burst after what they supposed to be a gang of bears, but soon pulled up on discovering them to be black wolves, prowling in company.

After a march of about twelve miles we encamped, a little after mid day, on the borders of a brook which loitered through a deep ravine. In the course of the afternoon "Old Ryan" the Nestor of the camp made his appearance followed by his little band of stragglers. He was greeted with joyful acclamations, which shewed the estimation in which he was held by his brother woodmen. The little band came laden with venison; a fine haunch of which the veteran hunter laid, as a present, by the Captain's fire.

Our men Beatte and Tonish both sallied forth early in the afternoon, to hunt. Towards evening the former returned with a fine buck across his horse. He laid it down, as usual, in silence, and proceeded to unsaddle and turn his horse loose. Tonish came back without any game, but with much more glory; having made several capital shots, though unluckily the wounded deer had all escaped him.

There was an abundant supply of meat in the camp; for, beside other game, three elk had been killed. The wary and veteran woodmen were all busy jerking meat against a time of scarcity; the less experienced revelled in present abundance leaving the morrow to provide for itself.

On the following morning (Oct. 19) I succeeded in changing my pony and a reasonable sum of money for a strong and active horse. It was a great satisfaction to find myself once more tolerably well mounted. I perceived, however, that there would be little difficulty in making a selection from among the troop, for the rangers had all that propensity for "swapping" or, as they term it "trading" which pervades the West. In the course of our expedition, there was scarce a horse, rifle, powder horn, or blanket that did not change owners several times; and one keen "trader" boasted of having by dint of frequent bargains changed a bad horse into a good one and put a hundred dollars in his pocket.

The morning was lowering and sultry with low muttering of distant thunder. The change of weather had its effect upon the spirits of the troop. The camp was unusually sober and quiet; there was none of the accustomed farm yard melody of crowing and cackling at day break; none of the bursts of merriment, the loud jokes and banterings that had commonly prevailed during the bustle of equipment. Now and then might be heard a short strain of a song, a faint laugh or a solitary whistle, but in general every one went silently and doggedly about the duties of the camp, or the preparations for departure.

When the time arrived to saddle and mount five horses were reported as missing although all the woods and thickets had been beaten up for some distance round the camp. Several rangers were dispatched to "skir" the country round in quest of them. In the mean time the thunder continued to growl and we had a passing shower. The horses, like their riders, were affected by the change of weather. They stood here and there about the camp, some saddled and bridled, others loose, but all spiritless and dozing, with stooping head, one hind leg partly drawn up so as to rest on the point of the hoof, and the whole hide reeking with the rain and sending up wreaths of vapour. The men, too, waited in listless groupes the return of their comrades who had gone in quest of the horses, now and then turning up an anxious eye to the drifting clouds, which boded an approaching storm. Gloomy weather inspires gloomy thoughts. Some expressed fears that we were dogged by some party of Indians who had stolen the horses in the night. The most prevalent apprehension, however, was, that they had returned on their traces to our last encampment, or had started off on a direct line for Fort Gibson. In this respect the instinct of horses is said to resemble that of the pigeon. They will strike for home by a direct course, passing through tracts of wilderness which they have never before traversed.

After delaying until the morning was somewhat advanced, a lieutenant with a guard was appointed to await the return of the rangers and we set off on our days journey; considerably reduced in numbers, much as I thought to the discomposure of some of the troop who intimated that we might prove too weak handed in case of an encounter with the Pawnees.

Chapter XVII

*Thunder storm on the prairies—The storm encampment—
Night scene —Indian stories—A frightened horse.*

OUR MARCH for a part of the day, lay a little to the south of west, through straggling forests of the kind of low scrubbed trees already mentioned, called "post oaks" and "black jacks." The soil of these "oak barrens" is loose and unsound, being little better at times than a mere quicksand in which, in rainy weather the horse's hoof slips from side to side, and now and then sinks in a rotten spongy turf to the fetlock. Such was the case at present in consequence of successive thundershowers, through which we draggled along in dogged silence. Several deer were roused by our approach and scudded across the forest glades, but no one, as formerly, broke the line of march to pursue them. At one time we passed the bones and horns of a buffalo, and at another time a Buffalo track, not above three days old. These signs of the vicinity of this grand game of the prairies had a reviving effect on the spirits of our huntsmen, but it was of transient duration.

In crossing a prairie of moderate extent, rendered little better than a slippery bog by the recent showers, we were overtaken by a violent thundergust. The rain came rattling upon us in torrents and spattered up like steam along the ground; the whole landscape was suddenly wrapped in gloom that gave a vivid effect to the intense sheets of lightning, while the thunder seemed to burst over our very heads, and was reverberated by the groves and forests that checquered and skirted the prairie. Man and beast were so pelted, drenched and confounded that the line was thrown in complete confusion; some of the horses were so frightened as to be almost unmanageable, and our scattered cavalcade looked like a tempest tost fleet, driven hither and thither at the mercy of wind and wave.

At length, at half past two o'clock, we came to a halt, and, gathering together our forces, encamped in an open and lofty grove with a prairie on one side and a stream on the other. The forest immediately rung with the sound of the axe, and the crash of falling trees. Huge fires were soon blazing; blankets were stretched before them by way of tents; booths were hastily reared of bark and skins; every fire had its groupe drawn close round it, drying and warming themselves or preparing a comforting meal. Some of the rangers were discharging and cleaning their rifles which had been exposed to the rain, while the horses, relieved from their saddles and burthens, rolled in the wet grass.

The showers continued from time to time until late in the evening. Before dark our horses were gathered in and tethered about the skirts of the camp, within the outposts through fear of Indian prowlers; who are apt to take advantage of stormy nights for their depredations and assaults. As the night thickened the huge fires became more and more luminous lighting up masses of the overhanging foliage, and leaving other parts of the grove in deep gloom. Every fire had its goblin groupe around it, while tethered horses were dimly seen, like spectres, among the thickets excepting that here and there a grey one stood out in bright relief.

The grove thus fitfully lighted up by the ruddy glare of the fires resembled a vast leafy dome, walled in by opaque darkness; but every now and then two or three quivering flashes of lightning in quick succession would suddenly reveal a vast champaign country where fields and forests and running streams, would start as it were into existence for a few brief seconds, and, before the eye could ascertain them, vanish again into gloom.

A thunder storm on a prairie as upon the ocean, derives grandeur and sublimity from the wild and boundless waste over which it rages and bellows. It is not surprizing that these awful phenomena of nature should be objects of superstitious reverence to the poor savages, and that they should consider the thunder the angry voice of the great spirit. As our half breeds sat gossipping round the fire, I drew from them some of the notions entertained on the subject by their Indian friends. The latter declare that extinguished thunder bolts are sometimes picked up by hunters on the prairies, who use them for the heads of arrows and lances, and that any warrior, thus armed, is invincible. Should a thunder storm occur, however, during battle he is liable to be carried away by the thunder and never heard of more.

A warrior of the Konza tribe, hunting on a prairie was overtaken by a storm, and struck down senseless by the thunder.
On recovering he beheld the thunder bolt lying on the ground
and a horse standing beside it. Snatching up the bolt he sprang
upon the horse but found, too late that he was astride of the
lightning. In an instant he was whisked away over prairies, and
forests, and streams, and deserts until he was flung senseless at
the foot of the Rocky Mountains, whence, on recovering, it
took him several months to return to his own people.

This story reminded me of an Indian tradition, related by a
traveller, of the fate of a warrior who saw the thunder lying
upon the ground with a beautifully wrought moccasin on
each side of it. Thinking he had found a prize he put on the
moccasins; but they bore him away to the land of spirits,
whence he never returned.

These are simple and artless tales, but they had a wild and
romantic interest heard from the lips of half savage narrators,
round a hunter's fire, in a stormy night with a forest on one
side and a howling waste on the other: and, where peradventure savage foes might be lurking in the outer darkness.

Our conversation was interrupted by a loud clap of thunder, followed immediately by the sound of a horse gallopping
off madly into the waste. Every one listened in mute silence.
The hoofs resounded vigorously for a time but grew fainter
and fainter, until they died away in remote distance.

When the sound was no longer to be heard the listeners
turned to conjecture what could have caused this sudden
scamper. Some thought the horse had been startled by the
thunder; others that some lurking Indian had mounted and
gallopped off with him. To this it was objected, that the usual
mode with the Indians is to steal quietly upon the horse, take
off his fetters, mount him gently, and walk him off as silently
as possible, leading off others, without any unusual stir or
noise to disturb the camp.

On the other hand, it was stated as a common practice with
the Indians to creep among a troop of horses when grazing at
night, mount one quietly and then start off suddenly at full
speed. Nothing is so contagious among horses as a panic, one
sudden break away of this kind will sometimes alarm the whole
troop, and they will set off, helter skelter, after the leader.

Every one who had a horse grazing on the skirts of the camp was uneasy lest his should be the fugitive, but it was impossible to ascertain the fact until morning. Those who had tethered their horses felt more secure, though horses thus tied up and limited to a short range at night are apt to fall off in flesh and strength, during a long march; and many of the horses of the troop already gave signs of being way worn.

After a gloomy and unruly night the morning dawned bright and clear, and a glorious sunrise transformed the whole landscape, as if by magic. The late dreary wilderness brightened into a fine open country with stately groves and clumps of oaks of a gigantic size, some of which stood singly as if planted for ornament and shade in the midst of rich meadows, while our horses scattered about and grazing under them gave to the whole the air of a noble park. It was difficult to realize the fact that we were so far in the wilds beyond the residence of man. Our encampment, alone, had a savage appearance; with its rude tents of skins and blankets; and its columns of blue smoke rising among the trees.

The first care in the morning was to look after our horses. Some of them had wandered to a distance but all were fortunately found: even the one whose clattering hoofs had caused such uneasiness in the night. He had come to a halt about a mile from the camp and was found quietly grazing near a brook.

The Bugle sounded for departure about half past eight. As we were in greater risk of Indian molestation the farther we advanced, our line was formed with more precision than heretofore. Every one had his station assigned him and was forbidden to leave it in pursuit of game without special permission. The pack horses were placed in the centre of the line and a strong guard in the rear.

Chapter XVIII

*A grand prairie—Cliff Castle—Buffalo tracks—Deer
hunted by wolves—Cross Timber.*

A FTER a toilsome march of some distance through a country cut up by ravines and brooks, and entangled by
thickets, we emerged upon a grand prairie. Here one of the
characteristic scenes of the Far West broke upon us. An immense extent of grassy undulating, or as it is termed, rolling
country with here and there a clump of trees, dimly seen in
the distance like a ship at sea; the landscape deriving sublimity from its vastness and simplicity. To the south west on the
summit of a hill was a singular crest of broken rocks resembling
a ruined fortress. It reminded me of the ruin of some Moorish
castle crowning a height in the midst of a lonely Spanish landscape. To this hill we gave the name of Cliff Castle.

The prairies of these great hunting regions differed in the
character of their vegetation from those through which I had
hitherto passed. Instead of a profusion of tall flowering plants
and long flaunting grasses, they were covered with a shorter
growth of herbage called Buffalo grass, somewhat coarse, but,
at the proper seasons, affording excellent and abundant pasturage. At present it was growing wiry, and in many places
was too much parched for grazing.

The weather was verging into that serene but somewhat
arid season called The Indian Summer. There was a smoky
haze in the atmosphere that tempered the brightness of the
sunshine into a golden tint, softening the features of the landscape and giving a vagueness to the outlines of distant objects.
This haziness was daily increasing and was attributed to the
burning of distant prairies by the Indian hunting parties.

We had not gone far upon the prairie before we came to
where deeply worn footpaths were seen traversing the country: sometimes two or three would keep on parallel to each
other and but a few paces apart. These were pronounced to
be traces of buffalos, where large droves had passed. There
were tracks also of horses, which were observed with some attention by our experienced hunters. They could not be the

82

tracks of wild horses, as there were no prints of the hoofs of colts, all were full grown. As the horses evidently were not shod, it was concluded they must belong to some hunting party of Pawnees. In the course of the morning the tracks of a single horse, with shoes, were discovered. This might be the horse of a Cherokee hunter; or perhaps a horse stolen from the whites of the frontier. Thus in traversing these perilous wastes every foot print and dint of hoof becomes matter of cautious inspection and shrewd surmise; and the question continually is, whether it be the trace of friend or foe; whether of recent or ancient date, and whether the being that made it be out of reach, or liable to be encountered.

We were getting more and more into the game country: as we proceeded we repeatedly saw deer to the right and left, bounding off for the coverts; but their appearance no longer excited the same eagerness to pursue. In passing along a slope of the prairie between two rolling swells of land we came in sight of a genuine natural hunting match. A pack of seven black wolves and one white one were in full chase of a buck which they had nearly tired down. They crossed the line of our march without apparently perceiving us; we saw them have a fair run of nearly a mile, gaining upon the buck until they were leaping upon his haunches when he plunged down a ravine. Some of our party galloped to a rising ground commanding a view of the ravine. The poor buck was completely beset, some on his flanks, some at his throat: he made two or three struggles and desperate bounds but was dragged down, overpowered and torn to pieces. The black wolves in their ravenous hunger and fury took no notice of the distant group of horsemen, but the white wolf, apparently less game, abandoned the prey and scampered over hill and dale, rousing various deer that were crouched in the hollows, and which bounded off likewise in different directions. It was altogether a wild scene, worthy of the "hunting grounds."

We now came once more in sight of the Red Fork, winding its turbid course between well wooded hills and through a vast and magnificent landscape. The prairies, bordering on the rivers, are always varied, in this way, with woodland, so beautifully interspersed as to appear to have been laid out by the hand of taste; and they only want here and there a village spire, the battlements of a castle, or the turrets of an old family mansion rising from among the trees, to rival the most ornamented scenery of Europe.

About midday we reached the edge of that scattered belt of forest land, about forty miles in width, which stretches across the country from north to south, from the Arkansas to the Red River, separating the upper from the lower prairies, and commonly called the "Cross Timber." On the skirts of this forest land, just on the edge of a prairie, we found traces of a Pawnee Encampment of between one and two hundred lodges, shewing that the party must have been numerous. The scull of a buffalo lay near the camp, and the moss which had gathered on it shewed that the encampment was at least a year old. About half a mile off we encamped in a beautiful grove watered by a fine spring and rivulet. Our days journey had been about fourteen miles.

In the course of the afternoon we were rejoined by two of Lieutenant King's party which we had left behind a few days before, to look after stray horses. All the horses had been found, though some had wandered to the distance of several miles. The lieutenant, with seventeen of his companions, had remained at our last nights encampment to hunt, having come upon recent traces of buffalo. They had also seen a fine wild horse which, however, had gallopped off with a speed that defied pursuit.

Confident anticipations were now indulged that on the following day we should meet with buffalo, and perhaps with wild horses, and every one was in spirits. We needed some excitement of the kind, for our young men were growing weary of marching and encamping under restraint, and provisions this day were scanty. The captain and several of the rangers went out hunting but brought home nothing but a small deer and a few turkeys. Our two men Beatte and Tonish likewise went out. The former returned with a deer athwart his horse, which as usual he laid down by our lodge and said nothing: Tonish returned with no game but with his customary budget of wonderful tales. Both he and the deer had done marvels. Not one had come within the level of his rifle without being hit in a mortal part, yet strange to say every one had kept on his way without flinching. We all determined that from the wonderful accuracy of his aim Tonish must have shot with charmed balls, but that every deer had a charmed life. The most important intelligence brought by him, however, was, that he had seen the fresh tracks of several wild horses. He now considered himself upon the eve of great exploits, for there was nothing upon which he glorified himself more than his skill in horse catching.

Chapter XIX

Hunters' anticipations—The rugged ford—A wild horse.

OCT. 21. This morning the camp was in a bustle at an early hour: the expectation of falling in with buffalo in the course of the day roused every one's spirit. There was a continual cracking off of rifles, that they might be reloaded: the shot was drawn off from double barrelled guns and balls were substituted. Tonish, however, prepared chiefly for a campaign against wild horses.

He took the field with a coil of cordage hung at his saddle bow, and a couple of white wands something like fishing rods, eight or ten feet in length, with forked ends. The coil of cordage thus used in hunting the wild horse, is called a lariat, and answers to the laso of South America. It is not flung, however, in the graceful and dexterous Spanish style. The hunter after a hard chase, when he succeeds in getting almost head and head with the wild horse, hitches the running noose of the lariat over his head by means of the forked stick, then letting him have the full length of the cord, plays him like a fish, and chokes him into subjection.

All this Tonish promised to exemplify to our full satisfaction; we had not much confidence in his success, and feared he might knock up a good horse for us, in a headlong gallop after a bad one, for, like all the French Creoles, he was a merciless hard rider. It was determined, therefore, to keep a sharp eye upon him and check his sallying propensities.

We had not proceeded far on our mornings march when we were checked by a deep stream, running along the bottom of a thickly wooded ravine. After coasting it for a couple of miles we came to a fording place; but to get down to it was the difficulty, for the banks were steep and crumbling, and overgrown with forest trees, mingled with thickets, brambles and grape vines. At length the leading horseman broke his way through the thicket, and his horse putting his feet together, slid down the black crumbling bank, to the narrow margin of the stream; then floundering across, with mud and water up to the saddle girths, he scrambled up the opposite bank and

arrived safe on level ground. The whole line followed pell
mell after the leader, and pushing forward in close order, Indian file, they crowded each other down the bank and into
the stream. Some of the horsemen missed the ford and were
soused over head and ears; one was unhorsed and plumped
head foremost into the middle of the stream; for my own
part, while pressed forward and hurried over the bank by
those behind me I was interrupted by a grape vine, as thick as
a cable, which hung in a festoon as low as the saddle bow,
and, dragging me from the saddle, threw me among the feet
of the trampling horses. Fortunately I escaped without injury,
regained my steed, crossed the stream without further difficulty, and was enabled to join in the merriment occasioned by
the ludicrous disasters of the fording.

It is at passes like this that occur the most dangerous ambuscades and sanguinary surprises of Indian warfare. A party
of savages, well placed among the thickets, might have made
sad havoc among our men while entangled in the ravine.

We now came out upon a vast and glorious prairie, spreading out beneath the golden beams of an autumnal sun. The
deep and frequent traces of buffalo shewed it to be one of
their favorite grazing grounds yet none were to be seen. In
the course of the morning we were overtaken by the lieutenant and seventeen men who had remained behind, and
who came laden with the spoils of buffalos having killed three
on the preceding day. One of the rangers, however, had little
luck to boast of, his horse having taken fright at sight of the
buffalos, thrown his rider, and escaped into the woods.

The excitement of our hunters both young and old, now
rose almost to fever height, scarce any of them having ever
encountered any of this farfamed game of the prairies. Accordingly, when in the course of the day, the cry of Buffalo!
Buffalo! rose from one part of the line, the whole troop were
thrown in agitation. We were just then passing through a
beautiful part of the prairie, finely diversified by hills and
slopes, and woody dells, and high stately groves. Those who
had given the alarm pointed out a large black looking animal,
slowly moving along the side of a rising ground about two
miles off. The ever ready Tonish jumped up and stood with
his feet on the saddle, and his forked sticks in his hands, like

a posture master or scaramouch at a circus just ready for a feat of horsemanship. After gazing at the animal for a moment, which he could have seen full as well without rising from his stirrups he pronounced it a wild horse, and dropping again into his saddle, was about to dash off full tilt in pursuit, when, to his inexpressible chagrin, he was called back, and ordered to keep to his post in rear of the baggage horses.

The captain and two of his officers now set off to reconnoitre the game. It was the intention of the captain, who was an admirable marksman, to endeavour to crease the horse; that is to say, to hit him with a rifle ball in the ridge of the neck. A wound of this kind paralyzes a horse for a moment, he falls to the ground, and may be secured before he recovers. It is a cruel expedient however, for an ill directed shot may kill or maim the noble animal.

As the Captain and his companions moved off laterally and slowly, in the direction of the horse we continued our course forward; watching intently, however, the movements of the game. The horse moved quietly over the profile of the rising ground and disappeared behind it. The Captain and his party were likewise soon hidden by an intervening hill.

After a time the horse suddenly made his appearance to our right, just a head of the line emerging out of a small valley on a brisk trot, having evidently taken the alarm. At sight of us he stopped short, gazed at us for an instant with surprize, then tossing up his head trotted off in fine style, glancing at us first over one shoulder then over the other, his ample mane and tail streaming in the wind. Having dashed through a skirt of thicket that looked like a hedge row, he paused in the open field beyond, glanced back at us again with a beautiful bend of the neck, snuffed the air and then, tossing his head again, broke into a gallop and took refuge in a wood.

It was the first time I had ever seen a horse scouring his native wilderness in all the pride and freedom of his nature. How different from the poor, mutilated, harnessed, checked, reined-up victim of luxury, caprice and avarice in our cities!

After travelling about fifteen miles we encamped about one o'clock, that our hunters might have time to procure a supply of provisions. Our encampment was in a spacious grove of lofty oaks and walnuts, free from underwood, on the border of a brook. While unloading the pack horses our little French-man was loud in his complaints at having been prevented from pursuing the wild horse, which he would certainly have taken. In the mean time I saw our halfbreed Beatte quietly saddle his best horse, a powerful steed of a half savage race, hang a lariat at the saddle bow, take a rifle and forked stick in hand, and, mounting, depart from the camp without saying a word. It was evident he was going off in quest of the wild horse, but was disposed to hunt alone.

Chapter XX

W E HAD encamped in a good neighborhood for game, as the reports of rifles in various directions speedily gave notice. One of our hunters soon returned with the meat of a doe tied up in the skin and slung across his shoulders. Another brought a fat buck across his horse. Two other deer were brought in and a number of turkeys. All the game was thrown down in front of the captain's fire to be portioned out among the various messes. The spits and camp kettles were soon in full employ and throughout the evening there was a scene of hunters' feasting and profusion.

We had been disappointed this day in our hopes of meeting with buffalo, but the sight of the wild horse had been a great novelty and gave a turn to the conversation of the camp for the evening. There were several anecdotes told of a famous grey horse that has ranged the prairies of this neighborhood for six or seven years setting at naught every attempt of the hunters to capture him. They say he can pace and rack (or amble) faster than the fleetest horses can run. Equally marvellous accounts were given of a black horse on the Brasis, who grazed the prairies on that river's banks in the Texas. For years he outstripped all pursuit. His fame spread far and wide; offers were made for him to the amount of a thousand dollars; the boldest and most hard riding hunters tried incessantly to make prize of him but in vain. At length he fell a victim to his gallantry, being decoyed under a tree by a tame mare, and a noose dropped over his head by a boy perched among the branches.

The capture of the wild horse is one of the most favorite achievements of the prairie tribes, and indeed it is from this source that the Indian hunters chiefly supply themselves. The wild horses which range those vast grassy plains extending from the Arkansas to the Spanish settlements are of various forms and colours, betraying their various descents. Some resemble the common English stock, and are probably descended from horses which have escaped from our border settlements. Others are of a low but strong make, and are supposed to be of the Andalusian breed, brought out by the Spanish discoverers.

Some fanciful speculatists have seen in them descendants of the Arab stock brought into Spain from Africa and thence transferred to this country, and have pleased themselves with the idea, that their sires may have been of the pure coursers of the desert, that once bore Mahomet and his warlike disciples across the sandy plains of Arabia.

The habits of the Arab seem to have come with the steed. The introduction of the horse on the boundless prairies of the Far West changed the whole mode of living of their inhabitants. It gave them that facility of rapid motion and of sudden and distant change of place so dear to the roving propensities of man. Instead of lurking in the depths of gloomy forests, and patiently threading the mazes of a tangled wilderness on foot, like his brethren of the North, the Indian of the West is a rover of the plain; he leads a brighter and more sunshiny life, almost always on horseback, on vast flowery prairies and under cloudless skies.

I was lying by the Captain's fire late in the evening, listening to stories about these coursers of the prairies, and weaving speculations of my own, when there was a clamour of voices and a loud cheering at the other end of the camp, and word was passed that Beatte the half breed had brought in a wild horse.

In an instant every fire was deserted; the whole camp crowded to see the Indian and his prize. It was a colt about two years old, well grown, finely limbed, with bright prominent eyes and a spirited yet gentle demeanour. He gazed about him with an air of mingled stupefaction and surprize, at the men the horses and the camp fires; while the Indian stood before him with folded arms, having hold of the other end of the cord which noosed his captive, and gazing on him with a most imperturbable aspect. Beatte as I have before observed has a greenish olive complexion, with a strongly marked countenance not unlike the bronze casts of Napoleon; and as he stood before his captive horse, with folded arms and fixed aspect, he looked more like a statue than a man.

If the horse, however, manifested the least restiveness Beatte would immediately worry him with the lariat, jerking him first on one side, then on the other so as almost to throw him on the ground; when he had thus rendered him passive he would resume his statue like attitude and gaze at him in silence.

The whole scene was singularly wild; the tall grove partially illumined by the flashing fires of the camp, the horses tethered here and there among the trees; the carcasses of deer hanging around; and in the midst of all, the wild huntsman and his wild horse, with an admiring throng of rangers, almost as wild.

In the eagerness of their excitement several of the young rangers sought to get the horse by purchase or barter, and even offered extravagant terms, but Beatte declined all their offers. "You give great price now," said he—"tomorrow you be sorry, and take back—and say d——d Indian!"

The young men importuned him with questions about the mode in which he took the horse, but his answers were dry and laconic; he evidently retained some pique at having been undervalued and sneered at by them, and at the same time looked down upon them with contempt as green horns; little versed in the noble science of wood craft.

Afterwards, however, when he was seated by our fire I readily drew from him an account of his exploit, for, though taciturn among strangers, and little prone to boast of his actions, yet his taciturnity like that of all Indians, had its times of relaxation.

He informed me that on leaving the camp he had returned to the place where we had lost sight of the wild horse. Soon getting upon its track he followed it to the banks of the river. Here, the prints being more distinct in the sand, he perceived that one of the hoofs was broken and defective, so he gave up the pursuit.

As he was returning to the camp he came upon a gang of six horses, which immediately made for the river. He pursued them across the stream, left his rifle on the river bank, and putting his horse to full speed, soon came up with the fugitives. He attempted to noose one of them, but the lariat hitched on one of his ears and he shook it off. The horses dashed up a hill, he followed hard at their heels, when, of a sudden, he saw their tails whisking in the air and they plunging down a precipice. It was too late to stop. He shut his eyes, held in his breath and went over with them—neck or nothing.

The descent was between twenty and thirty feet but they all came down safe upon a sandy bottom.

He now succeeded in throwing his noose round a fine young horse. As he galloped along side of him the two horses passed each side of a sapling and the end of the lariat was jerked out of his hand. He regained it, but an intervening tree obliged him again to let it go. Having once more caught it, and coming to a more open country, he was enabled to play the young horse with the line until he gradually checked and subdued him, so as to lead him to the place where he had left his rifle.

He had another formidable difficulty in getting him across the river, where both horses stuck for a time in the mire and Beatte was nearly unseated from his saddle by the force of the current and the struggles of his captive. After much toil and trouble, however, he got across the stream and brought his prize safe into the camp.

For the remainder of the evening the camp remained in a high state of excitement; nothing was talked of but the capture of wild horses; every youngster of the troop was for this harum scarum kind of chase; every one promised himself to return from the campaign in triumph, bestriding one of these wild coursers of the prairies. Beatte had suddenly risen to great importance; he was the prime hunter, the hero of the day; offers were made him by the best mounted rangers to let him ride their horses in the chase provided he would give them a share of the spoil. Beatte bore his honours in silence and closed with none of the offers. Our stammering, chattering, gasconading little Frenchman however, made up for his taciturnity by vaunting as much upon the subject as if it were he that had caught the horse. Indeed he held forth so learnedly in the matter, and boasted so much of the many horses he had taken, that he began to be considered an oracle and some of the youngsters were inclined to doubt whether he were not superior even to the taciturn Beatte.

The excitement kept the camp awake later than usual. The hum of voices, interrupted by occasional peals of laughter was heard from the groupes around the various fires, and the night was considerably advanced before all had sunk to sleep.

With the morning dawn the excitement revived and Beatte and his wild horse were again the gaze and talk of the camp.

The captive had been tied all night to a tree among the other horses. He was again led forth by Beatte by a long halter or lariat, and, on his manifesting the least restiveness, was, as before, jerked and worried into passive submission. He appeared to be gentle and docile by nature and had a beautifully mild expression of the eye. In his strange and forlorn situation the poor animal seemed to seek protection and companionship in the very horse which had aided to capture him.

Seeing him thus gentle and tractable, Beatte, just as we were about to march, strapped a light pack upon his back, by way of giving him the first lesson in servitude. The native pride and independence of the animal took fire at this indignity. He reared, and plunged and kicked, and tried in every way to get rid of the degrading burthen. The Indian was too potent for him. At every paroxysm he renewed the discipline of the halter, until the poor animal, driven to despair, threw himself prostrate on the ground, and lay motionless, as if acknowledging himself vanquished. A stage hero, representing the despair of a captive prince, could not have played his part more dramatically. There was absolutely a moral grandeur in it.

The imperturbable Beatte folded his arms and stood for a time looking down in silence upon his captive; until, seeing him perfectly subdued, he nodded his head slowly, screwed his mouth into a sardonic smile of triumph, and, with a jerk of the halter, ordered him to rise. He obeyed and, from that time forward, offered no resistance. During that day he bore his pack patiently and was led by the halter, but in two days he followed voluntarily at large among the supernumerary horses of the troop.

I could not but look with compassion upon this fine young animal whose whole course of existence had been so suddenly reversed. From being a denizen of these vast pastures, ranging at will from plain to plain and mead to mead, cropping of every herb and flower and drinking of every stream, he was suddenly reduced to perpetual and painful servitude, to pass his life under the harness and the curb amid, perhaps the din and dust and drudgery of cities. The transition in his lot was such as sometimes takes place in human affairs, and in the fortunes of towering individuals.—One day a prince of the prairies—the next day a pack horse!

Chapter XXI

WE LEFT the Camp of the Wild Horse about a quarter before eight and, after steering nearly south for three or four miles, arrived on the banks of the Red Fork at as we supposed about seventy five miles above its mouth. The river was about three hundred yards wide, wandering among sand bars and shoals. Its shores, and the long sandy banks that stretched out into the stream, were printed, as usual, with the traces of various animals that had come down to cross it, or to drink its waters.

Here we came to a halt and there was much consultation about the possibility of fording the river with safety as there was an apprehension of quicksands. Beatte, who had been somewhat in the rear came up while we were debating. He was mounted on his horse of the half wild breed, and leading his captive by the bridle. He gave the latter in charge to Tonish and, without saying a word, urged his horse into the stream, and crossed it in safety. Every thing was done by this man in a similar way, promptly, resolutely and silently, without a previous promise or an after vaunt.

The troop now followed the lead of Beatte and reached the opposite shore without any mishap, though one of the pack horses wandering a little from the track, came near being swallowed up in a quicksand, and was with difficulty dragged to land.

After crossing the river we had to force our way, for nearly a mile, through a thick cane brake, which, at first sight, appeared an impervious mass of reeds and brambles. It was a hard struggle, our horses were often to the saddle girths in mire and water, and both horse and horseman harassed and torn by bush and briar. Falling however, upon a Buffalo track we at length extricated ourselves from this morass and ascended a ridge of land, where we beheld a beautiful open country before us; while to our right the belt of forest land called The Cross Timber, continued stretching away to the southward, as far as the eye could reach. We soon abandoned the open country and struck into the forest land. It was the intention of the Captain to keep on south west by south and traverse the Cross Timber diagonally, so as to come out upon the edge of the great Western Prairie. By thus maintaining something of a southerly direction he trusted, while he crossed the belt of forest, he would at the same time approach the Red River.

The plan of the Captain was judicious, but he erred from not being informed of the nature of the country. Had he kept directly west a couple of days would have carried us through the forest land, and we might then have had an easy course along the skirts of the upper prairies to Red River, by going diagonally we were kept for many weary days toiling through a dismal series of rugged forests.

The cross timber is about forty miles in breadth, and stretches over a rough country of rolling hills, covered with scattered tracts of post oak and black jack; with some intervening valleys that at proper seasons would afford good pasturage. It is very much cut up by deep ravines, which, in the rainy seasons, are the beds of temporary streams, tributary to the main rivers, and thence called "branches." The whole tract may present a pleasant aspect in the fresh time of the year when the ground is covered with herbage; when the trees are in their green leaf, and the glens are enlivened by running streams. Unfortunately we entered it too late in the season. The herbage was parched; the foliage of the scrubby forests was withered, the whole woodland prospect, as far as the eye could reach, had a brown and arid hue. The fires made on the prairies by the Indian hunters had frequently penetrated these forests, sweeping in light transient flames along the dry grass, scorching and calcining the lower twigs and branches of the trees, and leaving them black and hard, so as to tear the flesh of man and horse that had to scramble through them. I shall not easily forget the mortal toil, and the vexations of flesh and spirit that we underwent occasionally, in our wanderings through the cross timber. It was like struggling through forests of cast iron.

After a tedious ride of several miles we came out upon an open tract of hill and dale interspersed with woodland. Here we were roused by the cry of Buffalo! Buffalo! The effect was something like that of the cry of a sail! a sail! at sea. It was not a false alarm. Three or four of those enormous animals were visible to our right, grazing on the slope of a distant hill.

There was a general movement to set off in pursuit and it was with some difficulty that the vivacity of the younger men of the troop could be restrained. Leaving orders that the line of march should be preserved, the Captain and two of his officers departed at a quiet pace accompanied by Beatte, and by the ever forward Tonish, for it was impossible any longer to keep the little Frenchman in check, being half crazy to prove his skill and prowess in hunting the Buffalo.

The intervening hills soon hid from us both the game and the huntsmen. We kept on our course in quest of a camping place, which was difficult to be found, almost all the channels of the streams being dry, and the country being destitute of fountain heads.

After proceeding some distance there was again a cry of Buffalo, and two were pointed out on a hill to the left. The Captain being absent it was no longer possible to restrain the ardour of the young hunters. Away several of them dashed full speed and soon disappeared among the ravines. The rest kept on, anxious to find a proper place for encampment.

Indeed we now began to experience the disadvantages of the season. The pasturage of the prairies was scanty and parched; the pea vines which grew in the woody bottoms were withered, and most of the "branches" or streams were dried up. While wandering in this perplexity we were overtaken by the Captain and all his party except Tonish. They had pursued the Buffalo for some distance without getting within shot, and had given up the chase, being fearful of fatiguing their horses, or being led off too far from camp. The little Frenchman, however had galloped after them at headlong speed, and the last they saw of him—he was engaged, as it were, yard arm and yard arm with a great Buffalo bull, firing broadsides into him. "I tink dat little man crazy—some how," observed Beatte dryly.

Chapter XXII

The alarm camp.

W E NOW came to a halt and had to content ourselves with an indifferent encampment. It was in a grove of scrub oaks, on the borders of a deep ravine, at the bottom of which were a few scanty pools of water. We were just at the foot of a gradually sloping hill covered with half withered grass that afforded meagre pasturage. In the spot where we had encamped the grass was high and parched. The view around us was circumscribed and much shut in by gently swelling hills.

Just as we were encamping Tonish arrived all glorious from his hunting match, his white horse hung all round with buffalo meat. According to his own account he had laid low two mighty bulls. As usual we deducted one half from his boastings; but now that he had something real to vaunt about, there was no restraining the valour of his tongue.

After having in some measure appeased his vanity by boasting of his exploit, he informed us that he had observed the fresh track of horses, which, from various circumstances he suspected to have been made by some roving band of Pawnees. This caused some little uneasiness. The young men who had left the line of march in pursuit of the two buffalo had not yet rejoined us. Apprehensions were expressed that they might be waylayed and attacked. Our veteran hunter "Old Ryan" also, immediately on our halting to encamp had gone off on foot in company with a young disciple. "Dat old man will have his brains knocked out by de Pawnees yet," said Beatte. "He tink he know every ting, but he don't know Pawnees—any how."

Taking his rifle, the Captain repaired on foot to reconnoitre the country from the naked summit of one of the neighboring hills. In the mean time the horses were hobbled and turned loose to graze in the adjacent fields; and wood was cut, and fires made, to prepare the evenings repast.

Suddenly there was an alarm of fire in the camp! The flame from one of the kindling fires had caught to the tall dry grass: a breeze was blowing; there was danger that the camp would soon be wrapped in a light blaze. "Look to the horses!" cried one; "drag away the baggage!" cried another. "Take care of the rifles and powder horns!" cried a third. All was hurry scurry and uproar. The horses dashed wildly about—some of the men snatched away rifles and powder horns, others dragged off saddles and saddle bags: mean time no one thought of quelling the fire, nor indeed knew how to quell it. Beatte, however, and his comrades attacked it in the Indian mode, beating down the edges of the fire, with blankets and horse cloths, and endeavoring to prevent its spreading among the grass; the rangers followed their example, and in a little while the flames were happily quelled.

The fires were now properly kindled on places from which the dry grass had been cleared away. The horses were scattered about a small valley and on the sloping hill side, cropping the scanty herbage. Tonish was preparing a sumptuous evenings meal from his buffalo meat, promising us a rich soup and a prime piece of roast beef: but we were doomed to experience another and more serious alarm.

There was an indistinct cry from some rangers on the summit of the hill of which we could only distinguish the words, "The horses! the horses! get in the horses!"

Immediately a clamour of voices arose; shouts, enquiries, replies were all mingled together so that nothing could be clearly understood, and every one drew his own inference.

"The Captain has started buffalos," cried one, "and wants horses for the chase." Immediately a number of rangers seized their rifles and scampered for the hill top. "The prairie is on fire beyond the hill," cried another. "I see the smoke—the captain means we shall drive the horses beyond the brook."

By this time a ranger from the hill had reached the skirts of the camp. He was almost breathless and could only say that the Captain had seen Indians at a distance.

"Pawnees! Pawnees!" was now the cry among our wild headed youngsters. "Drive the horses into the camp!" cried one. "Saddle the horses!" cried another. "Form the line!" cried a third. There was now a scene of clamour and confusion that baffles all description. The rangers were scampering about the adjacent field in pursuit of their horses. One might be seen tugging his steed along by a halter, another, without a hat, riding bare backed; another driving a hobbled horse before him that made awkward leaps like a Kangaroo.

The alarm increased. Word was brought from the lower end of the camp that there was a band of Pawnees in a neighboring valley. They had shot Old Ryan through the head, and were chasing his companion! "No, it was not Old Ryan that was killed—it was one of the hunters that had been after the two buffalos." "There are three hundred Pawnees just beyond the hill," cried one voice. "More—more!" cried another.

Our situation shut in among hills prevented our seeing to any distance and left us a prey to all these rumours. A cruel enemy was supposed to be at hand; and an immediate attack apprehended. The horses by this time were driven into the camp and were dashing about among the fires and trampling upon the baggage. Every one endeavored to prepare for action; but here was the perplexity. During the late alarm of fire the saddles, bridles, rifles, powder horns and other equipments had been snatched out of their places and thrown helter skelter among the trees.

"Where is my saddle?" cried one. "Has any one seen my rifle?" cried another.

"Who will lend me a ball?" cried a third who was loading his piece. "I have lost my bullet pouch."

"For God's sake help me to girth this horse!" cried another, "he's so restive I can do nothing with him."—In his hurry and worry he had put on the saddle the hind part before!

Some affected to swagger and talk bold. Others said nothing, but went on steadily preparing their horses and weapons, and on these I felt the most reliance. Some were evidently excited and elated with the idea of an encounter with Indians, and none more so than my young Swiss fellow traveller, who had a passion for wild adventure. Our man, Beatte, led his horses in the rear of the camp, placed his rifle against a tree, then seated himself by the fire in perfect silence. On the other hand little Tonish, who was busy cooking, stopped every moment from his work to play the fanfaron, singing, swearing, and affecting an unusual hilarity, which made me strongly suspect that there was some little fright at bottom, to cause all this effervescence.

About a dozen of the rangers, as soon as they could saddle their horses, dashed off in the direction in which the Pawnees

were said to have attacked the hunters. It was now determined, in case our camp should be assailed, to put our horses
in the ravine in rear, where they would be out of danger from
arrow or rifle ball, and to take our stand within the edge of the
ravine. This would serve as a trench, and the trees and thickets with which it was bordered would be sufficient to turn
aside any shaft of the enemy. The Pawnees, beside, are wary of
attacking any covert of the kind; their warfare, as I have already observed, lies in the open prairies where mounted upon
their fleet horses they can swoop like hawks upon their enemy
or wheel about him and discharge their arrows. Still I could
not but perceive, that, in case of being attacked by such a
number of these well mounted and warlike savages as were
said to be at hand, we should be exposed to considerable risk
from the inexperience and want of discipline of our newly
raised rangers, and from the very courage of many of the
younger ones, who seemed bent on adventure and exploit.

By this time the Captain reached the camp and every one
crowded round him for information. He informed us that he
had proceeded some distance on his reconnoitering expedition and was slowly returning towards the camp, along the
brow of a naked hill, when he saw something on the edge of
a parallel hill that looked like a man. He paused and watched
it, but it remained so perfectly motionless that he supposed it
a bush, or the top of some tree beyond the hill. He resumed
his course, when it likewise began to move in a parallel direction. Another form now rose beside it, of some one who had
either been lying down, or had just ascended the other side of
the hill. The captain stopped and regarded them; they likewise stopped. He then lay down upon the grass and they began to walk. On his rising they again stopped, as if watching
him. Knowing that the Indians are apt to have their spies and
centinels thus posted on the summit of naked hills, commanding extensive prospects, his doubts were increased by
the suspicious movements of these men. He now put his foraging cap on the end of his rifle and waved it in the air. They
took no notice of the signal. He then walked on until he entered the edge of a wood which concealed him from their
view. Stepping out of sight for a moment, he again looked
forth, when he saw the two men passing swiftly forward. As

the hill on which they were walking made a curve toward that on which he stood, it seemed as if they were endeavouring to head him before he should reach the camp. Doubting whether they might not belong to some large party of Indians either in ambush, or moving along the valley beyond the hill, the Captain hastened his steps homeward, and descrying some rangers on an eminence between him and the camp he called out to them to pass the word to have the horses driven in, as these are generally the first objects of Indian depredation.

Such was the origin of the alarm which had thrown the camp in commotion. Some of those who heard the Captain's narrative had no doubt that the men on the hill were Pawnee scouts, belonging to the band that had waylaid the hunters. Distant shots were heard at intervals, which were supposed to be fired by those who had sallied out to rescue their comrades. Several more rangers, having completed their equipments, now rode forth in the direction of the firing; others looked anxious and uneasy.

"If they are as numerous as they are said to be," said one, "and as well mounted as they generally are, we shall be a bad match for them with our jaded horses."

"Well," replied the captain, "we have a strong encampment and can stand a siege."

"Aye, but they may set fire to the prairie in the night and burn us out of our encampment."

"We will then set up a counter fire."

The word was now passed that a man on horseback approached the camp.

"It is one of the hunters!"—"It is Clements!"—"He brings buffalo meat!" was announced by several voices as the horseman drew near.

It was, in fact, one of the rangers who had set off in the morning in pursuit of the two buffaloes. He rode into the camp with the spoils of the chase hanging round his horse and followed by his companions, all sound and unharmed and equally well laden. They proceeded to give an account of a grand gallop they had had after the two buffalos, and how many shots it had cost them to bring one to the ground—

"Well, but the Pawnees—the Pawnees—where are the Pawnees?"

"What Pawnees—?"

"The Pawnees that attacked you—?"

"No one attacked us."

"But have you seen no Indians on your way?"

"Oh yes, two of us got to the top of a hill to look out for the camp, and saw a fellow on an opposite hill cutting queer antics, who seemed to be an Indian."

"Pshaw! That was I!" cried the captain.

Here the bubble burst. The whole alarm had risen from this mutual mistake of the Captain and the two rangers. As to the report of the three hundred Pawnees and their attack on the hunters, it proved to be a wanton fabrication, of which no further notice was taken; though the author deserved to have been sought out and severely punished.

There being no longer any prospect of fighting every one now thought of eating; and here the stomachs throughout the camp were in unison. Tonish served up to us his promised regale of Buffalo soup and Buffalo beef. The soup was peppered most horribly, and the roast beef proved the Bull to have been one of the patriarchs of the prairies: never did I have to deal with a tougher morsel. However, it was our first repast on buffalo meat, so we ate it with a lively faith, nor would our little Frenchman allow us any rest until he had extorted from us an acknowledgment of the excellence of his cookery; though the pepper gave us the lie in our throats.

The night closed in without the return of Old Ryan and his companion; we had become accustomed, however, to the aberrations of this old Cock of the Woods and no further solicitude was expressed on his account.

After the fatigues and agitations of the day the camp soon sunk into a profound sleep, excepting those on guard; who were more than usually on the alert, for the traces recently seen of Pawnees, and the certainty that we were in the midst of their hunting grounds excited to constant vigilance. About half past ten o'clock we were all startled from sleep by a new alarm. A centinel had fired off his rifle and run into camp, crying that there were Indians at hand.

Every one was on his legs in an instant. Some seized their rifles; some were about to saddle their horses; some hastened to the captain's lodge, but were ordered back to their respective fires. The centinel was examined. He declared he had seen an Indian approach, crawling along the ground; whereupon he had fired upon him and run into camp. The captain gave it as his opinion that the supposed Indian was a wolf, he reprimanded the centinel for deserting his post and obliged him to return to it. Many seemed inclined to give credit to the story of the sentinel; for the events of the day had predisposed them to apprehend lurking foes and sudden assaults during the darkness of the night. For a long time they sat round their fires, with rifle in hand, carrying on low murmuring conversations and listening for some new alarm. Nothing further, however, occurred; the voices gradually died away; the gossippers nodded and dozed and sunk to rest, and by degrees silence and sleep once more stole over the camp.

Chapter XXIII

Beaver dam—Buffalo and horse tracks—A Pawnee trail—
Wild horses—The young hunter and the bear—Change
of route.

O N MUSTERING our forces in the morning (Oct. 23) Old
Ryan and his comrade were still missing, but the captain
had such perfect reliance on the skill and resources of the veteran woodsman that he did not think it necessary to take any
measures with respect to him.

Our march this day lay through the same kind of rough
rolling country checquered by brown dreary forests of post
oak, and cut up by deep dry ravines. The distant fires were evidently increasing on the prairies: the wind had been at north
west for several days, and the atmosphere had become so
smoky, as in the height of Indian summer, that it was difficult
to distinguish objects at any distance.

In the course of the morning we crossed a deep stream
with a complete beaver dam above three feet high making a
large pond, and doubtless containing several families of that
industrious animal, though not one shewed his nose above
water. The Captain would not permit this amphibious commonwealth to be disturbed.

We now were continually coming upon the tracks of buffalos and wild horses, those of the former tended invariably to
the south, as we could perceive by the direction of the trampled grass. It was evident we were on the great high way of
these migratory herds but that they had chiefly passed to the
southward.

Beatte, who generally kept a parallel course several hundred
yards distant from our line of march, to be on the look out
for game, and who regarded every track with the knowing eye
of an Indian, reported that he had come upon a very suspicious "trail." There were the tracks of men who wore Pawnee
moccasins. He had scented the smoke of mingled sumach and
tobacco, such as the Indians use. He had observed tracks of
horses, mingled with those of a dog; and a mark in the dust
where a cord had been trailed along, probably the long bridle

one end of which the Indian horsemen suffer to trail after them on the ground. It was evident, they were not the tracks of wild horses.

My anxiety began to revive about the safety of our veteran hunter Ryan, for I had taken a great fancy to this real old Leatherstocking; every one expressed a confidence, however, that wherever Ryan was, he was safe, and knew how to take care of himself.

We had accomplished the greater part of a weary days march and were passing through a glade of the oak openings when we came in sight of six wild horses, among which I especially noticed two very handsome ones, a grey and a roan. They pranced about, with heads erect and long flaunting tails, offering a proud contrast to our poor, spiritless, travel tired steeds. Having reconnoitered us for a moment they set off at a gallop, passed through a woody dingle, and in a little while emerged once more to view trotting up a slope about a mile distant.

The sight of these horses was again a sore trial to the vapouring Tonish, who had his lariat and forked stick ready, and was on the point of launching forth in pursuit, on his jaded horse, when he was again ordered back to the pack horses.

After a days journey of fourteen miles in a southwest direction, we encamped on the banks of a small clear stream, on the northern border of the Cross Timbers, and on the edge of those vast prairies that extend away to the foot of the Rocky Mountains. In turning loose the horses to graze their bells were stuffed with grass to prevent their tinkling, lest it might be heard by some wandering horde of Pawnees.

Our hunters now went out in different directions but without much success as but one deer was brought into the camp. A young ranger had a long story to tell of his adventures. In skirting the thickets of a deep ravine he had wounded a buck which he plainly heard to fall among the bushes. He stopped to fix the lock of his rifle, which was out of order, and to reload it: then advancing to the edge of the thicket in quest of his game he heard a low growling. Putting the branches aside, and stealing silently forward he looked down into the ravine and beheld a huge bear dragging the carcass of the deer along the dry channel of a brook and growling and snarling at four or five officious wolves who seemed to have dropped in to take supper with him.

The ranger fired at the bear, but missed him. Bruin maintained his ground and his prize and seemed disposed to make battle. The wolves too, who were evidently sharp set, drew off to but a small distance. As night was coming on the young hunter felt dismayed at the wildness and darkness of the place, and the strange company he had fallen in with, so he quietly withdrew and returned empty handed to the camp, where having told his story, he was heartily bantered by his more experienced comrades.

In the course of the evening Old Ryan came straggling into the camp followed by his disciple, and as usual was received with hearty gratulations. He had lost himself yesterday when hunting and camped out all night, but had found our trail in the morning and followed it up. He had passed some time at the beaver dam admiring the skill and solidity with which it had been constructed. "These beavers," said he, "are industrious little fellows. They are the knowingest varment as I know; and I'll warrant the pond was stocked with them."

"Aye," said the captain, "I have no doubt most of the small rivers we have passed are full of beaver. I should like to come and trap on these waters all winter."

"But would you not run the chance of being attacked by Indians?" asked one of the company.

"Oh, as to that, it would be safe enough here in the winter time. There would be no Indians here until spring. I should want no more than two companions. Three persons are safer than a larger number for trapping beaver. They can keep quiet and need seldom fire a gun. A Bear would serve them for food for two months, taking care to turn every part of it to advantage."

A consultation was now held as to our future progress. We had thus far pursued a western course, and, having traversed the Cross Timber, were on the skirts of the Great Western Prairie. We were still, however, in a very rough country where food was scarce. The season was so far advanced that the grass was withered and the prairies yielded no pasturage. The peavines of the bottoms, also, which had sustained our horses for some part of the journey, were nearly gone, and for several

days past the poor animals had fallen off woefully both in
flesh and spirit. The Indian fires on the prairies were approaching us from north and south, and west; they might
spread also from the east, and leave a scorched desert between
us and the frontier, in which our horses might be famished.

It was determined, therefore, to advance no further to the
westward, but to shape our course more to the east so as to
strike the north fork of the Canadian as soon as possible
where we hoped to find abundance of young cane; which, at
this season of the year affords the most nutritious pasturage
for the horses, and, at the same time, attracts immense quantities of game. Here then we fixed the limits of our tour to
the Far West, being within little more than a days march of
the boundary line of Texas.

Chapter XXIV

THE MORNING broke bright and clear, but the camp had nothing of its usual gaiety. The concert of the farm yard was at an end; not a cock crew nor dog barked; nor was there either singing or laughing; every one pursued his avocations quietly and gravely. The novelty of the expedition was wearing off; some of the young men were getting as way worn as their horses, and most of them unaccustomed to the hunter's life, began to repine at its privations. What they most felt was the want of bread, their rations of flour having been exhausted for several days. The old hunters, who had often experienced this want, made light of it: and Beatte, accustomed when among the Indians to live for months without it, considered it a mere article of luxury. "Bread," he would say scornfully, "is only fit for a child."

About a quarter before eight o'clock we turned our backs upon the Far West, and set off in a south east course, along a gentle valley. After riding a few miles Beatte, who kept parallel with us along the ridge of a naked hill to our right called out and made signals, as if something was coming round the hill to intercept us. Some who were near me cried out that it was a party of Pawnees. A skirt of thickets hid the approach of the supposed enemy from our view. We heard a trampling among the brush wood. My horse looked toward the place, snorted and pricked up his ears, when presently a couple of huge Buffalo bulls who had been alarmed by Beatte came crashing through the brake and making directly towards us. At sight of us they wheeled round and scuttled along a narrow defile of the hills. In an instant half a score of rifles cracked off; there was a universal whoop and halloo, and away went half the troop helter skelter in pursuit, and myself among the number. The most of us soon pulled up and gave over a chase which led through bush and briar and break neck ravines. Some few of the rangers persisted for a time; but eventually rejoined the line slowly lagging one after another.

One of them returned on foot, he had been thrown while in full chase; his rifle had been broken in the fall, and his horse, retaining the spirit of the rider, had kept on after the buffalo. It was a melancholy predicament to be reduced to; to be without horse or weapon in the midst of the Pawnee hunting grounds.

For my own part—I had been fortunate enough recently by a further exchange to get possession of the best horse in the troop; a full blooded sorrel, of excellent bottom, beautiful form and most generous qualities. In such a situation it almost seems as if a man changes his nature with his horse. I felt quite like another being now that I had an animal under me spirited yet gentle, docile to a remarkable degree, and easy, elastic and rapid in all his movements. In a few days he became almost as much attached to me as a dog; would follow me when I dismounted, would come to me in the morning to be noticed and caressed; and would put his muzzle between me and my book as I sat reading at the foot of a tree. The feeling I had for this my dumb companion of the prairies gave me some faint idea of that attachment the Arab is said to entertain for the horse that has borne him about the deserts.

After riding a few miles further we came to a fine meadow with a broad clear stream winding through it, on the banks of which there was excellent pasturage. Here we at once came to a halt, in a beautiful grove of elms, on the site of an old Osage encampment. Scarcely had we dismounted when a universal firing of rifles took place upon a large flock of turkeys scattered about the grove, which proved to be a favorite roosting place for these simple birds. They flew to the trees and sat perched upon their branches stretching out their long necks and gazing in stupid astonishment until eighteen of them were shot down.

In the height of the carnage word was brought that there were four buffaloes in a neighboring meadow. The turkeys were now abandoned for nobler game. The tired horses were again mounted and urged to the chase. In a little while we came in sight of the Buffaloes, looking like brown hillocks among the long green herbage. Beatte endeavored to get ahead of them and turn them towards us, that the inexperienced hunters might have a chance. They ran round the base of a rocky hill that hid us from the sight. Some of us endeavored to cut across the hill but became entrapped in a thick wood, matted with grape vines. My horse who, under his former rider had hunted the buffalo, seemed as much excited as myself and endeavored to force his way through the bushes. At length we extricated ourselves, and, galloping over the hill, I found our little Frenchman Tonish curvetting on horseback round a great buffalo which he had wounded too severely to fly, and which he was keeping employed until we should come up. There was a mixture of the grand and the comic in beholding this tremendous animal and his fantastic assailant. The Buffalo stood with his shagged front always presented to his foe, his mouth open, his tongue parched, his eyes like coals of fire and his tail erect with rage; every now and then he would make a faint rush upon his foe, who easily evaded his attack, capering and cutting all kinds of antics before him.

We now made repeated shots at the Buffalo, but they glanced into his mountain of flesh without proving mortal. He made a slow and grand retreat into the shallow river, turning upon his assailants whenever they pressed upon him; and when in the water took his stand there as if prepared to sustain a siege. A rifle ball, however, more fatally lodged, sent a tremour through his frame. He turned and attempted to wade across the stream but, after tottering a few paces, slowly fell upon his side and expired. It was the fall of a hero, and we felt somewhat ashamed of the butchery that had effected it; but, after the first shot or two, we had reconciled it to our feelings by the old plea of putting the poor animal out of his misery.

Two other buffalos were killed this evening, but they were all bulls, the flesh of which is meagre and hard at this season of the year. A fat buck yielded us much more savory meat for our evenings repast.

Chapter XXV

Ringing the wild horse.

W E LEFT the Buffalo Camp about eight o'clock, and had
a toilsome and harassing march of two hours over ridges
of hills covered with a ragged meagre forest of scrub oaks and
broken by deep gullies. Among the oaks I observed many of
the most diminutive size, some not above a foot high, yet
bearing abundance of small acorns. The whole of the cross
timbers, in fact, abound with mast. There is a pine oak which
produces an acorn pleasant to the taste, and ripening early in
the season.

About ten o'clock in the morning we came to where this
line of rugged hills swept down into a valley through which
flowed the north fork of the Red river. A beautiful meadow
about half a mile wide, enameled with yellow autumnal flowers, stretched for two or three miles along the foot of the
hills, bordered on the opposite side by the river, whose banks
were fringed with cotton wood trees, the bright foliage of
which refreshed and delighted the eye, after being wearied by
the contemplation of monotonous wastes of brown forest.

The meadow was finely diversified by groves and clumps of
trees, so happily disposed that they seemed as if set out by the
hand of art. As we cast our eyes over this fresh and delightful
valley we beheld a troop of wild horses quietly grazing on a
green lawn about a mile distant to our right, while to our left
at nearly the same distance, were several buffaloes, some feeding, others reposing and ruminating among the high rich
herbage, under the shade of a clump of cotton wood trees. The
whole had the appearance of a broad beautiful tract of pasture
land, on the highly ornamented estate of some gentleman
farmer, with his cattle grazing about the lawns and meadows.

A council of war was now held, and it was determined to
profit by the present favorable opportunity, and try our hand
at the grand hunting maneuvre which is called ringing the
wild horse. This requires a large party of horsemen well
mounted. They extend themselves in each direction singly at
certain distances apart, and gradually form a ring of two or

three miles in circumference, so as to surround the game. This has to be done with extreme care, for the wild horse is the most readily alarmed inhabitant of the prairie and can scent a hunter at a great distance if to windward.

The ring being formed, two or three hunters ride towards the horses who start off in an opposite direction. Wherever they approach the bounds of the ring, however, a huntsman presents himself and turns them from their course. In this way they are checked and driven back at every point, and kept galloping round and round this magic circle until being completely tired down, it is easy for the hunters to ride up beside them and throw the lariat over their heads. The prime horses of most speed, courage and bottom, however, are apt to break through and escape so that, in general, it is the second rate horses that are taken.

Preparations were now made for a hunt of the kind. The pack horses were taken into the woods and firmly tied to trees lest, in a rush of the wild horses, they should break away with them. Twenty five men were then sent, under the command of a lieutenant, to steal along the edge of the valley within the strip of woods that skirted the hills. They were to station themselves about fifty yards apart within the edge of the woods, and not to advance or shew themselves, until the horses dashed in that direction. Twenty five men were sent across the valley to steal in like manner, along the river bank that bordered the opposite side, and to station themselves among the trees. A third party of about the same number, was to form a line stretching across the lower part of the valley, so as to connect the two wings. Beatte and our other half breed Antoine, together with the ever officious Tonish, were to make a circuit through the woods so as to get to the upper part of the valley in the rear of the horses, and to drive them forward into the kind of sack that we had formed, while the two wings should join behind them and make a complete circle.

The flanking parties were quietly extending themselves, out of sight, on each side of the valley and the residue were stretching themselves, like the links of a chain, across it, when the wild horses gave signs that they scented an enemy: snuffing the air, snorting and looking about. At length they pranced off slowly toward the river and disappeared behind a green bank. Here,

had the regulations of the chase been observed, they would
have been quietly checked and turned back by the advance of a
hunter from among the trees: unluckily, however, we had our
wild fire Jack o lantern little Frenchman to deal with. Instead
of keeping quietly up the right side of the valley, to get above
the horses, the moment he saw them move toward the river he
broke out of the covert of woods and dashed furiously across
the plain in pursuit of them; being mounted on one of the led
horses belonging to the Count. This put an end to all system.
The half breeds and half a score of rangers joined in the chase.
Away they all went over the green bank; in a moment or two
the wild horses reappeared and came thundering down the valley with Frenchman, half breeds and rangers gallopping and
yelling like devils behind them. It was in vain that the line
drawn across the valley attempted to check and turn back the
fugitives. They were too hotly pressed by their pursuers; in
their panic they dashed through the line and clattered down
the plain. The whole troop joined in the headlong chase, some
of the rangers without hats or caps, their hair flying about their
ears, others with handkerchiefs tied round their heads. The
Buffalos who had been calmly ruminating among the herbage
heaved up their huge forms, gazed for a moment with astonishment at the tempest that came scouring down the meadow,
then turned and took to heavy rolling flight. They were soon
overtaken, the promiscuous throng were pressed together by
the contracting sides of the valley, and away they went pell
mell—hurry scurry—wild buffalo, wild horse, wild huntsman,
with clang and clatter and whoop and halloo that made the
forests ring.

    At length the Buffalos turned into a green brake on the river
bank, while the horses dashed up a narrow defile of the hills
with their pursuers close at their heels. Beatte passed several of
them having fixed his eye upon a fine Pawnee horse that had
his ears slit and saddle marks on his back. He pressed him gallantly, but lost him in the woods. Among the wild horses was
a fine black mare far gone with foal. In scrambling up the defile she tripped and fell. A young ranger sprang from his horse
and seized her by the mane and muzzle. Another ranger dismounted and came to his assistance. The mare struggled
fiercely, kicking and biting and striking with her forefeet, but a

noose was slipped over her head and her struggles were in vain. It was some time, however, before she gave over rearing and plunging and lashing out with her feet on every side. The two rangers then led her along the valley by two long lariats, which enabled them to keep at a sufficient distance on each side to be out of the reach of her hoofs, and whenever she struck out in one direction she was jerked in the other. In this way her spirit was gradually subdued.

As to little Scaramouch Tonish, who had marred the whole scheme by his precipitancy, he had been more successful than he deserved, having managed to catch a beautiful cream coloured colt, about seven months old, which had not strength to keep up with its companions. The mercurial little Frenchman was beside himself with exultation. It was amusing to see him with his prize. The colt would rear and kick, and struggle to get free, while Tonish would take him about the neck, wrestle with him, jump on his back, and cut as many antics as a monkey with a kitten. Nothing surprised me more, however, than to witness how soon these poor animals, thus taken from the unbounded freedom of the prairie, yielded to the dominion of man. In the course of two or three days the mare and colt went with the led horses and became quite docile.

Chapter XXVI

*Fording of the North Fork—Dreary scenery of the Cross
Timber—Scamper of horses in the night—Osage war
party—Effects of a peace harangue—Buffalo—Wild horse.*

RESUMING our march we forded the North Fork, a rapid
stream, and of a purity seldom to be found in the rivers
of the prairies. It evidently had its sources in high land, well
supplied with springs. After crossing the river we again ascended among hills, from one of which we had an extensive
view over this belt of cross timber, and a cheerless prospect it
was, hill beyond hill, forest beyond forest, all of one sad rus-
set hue, excepting that here and there a line of green cotton
wood trees, sycamores and willows marked the course of
some streamlet through a valley. A procession of buffalos
moving slowly up the profile of one of those distant hills,
formed a characteristic object in the savage scene. To the left
the eye stretched beyond this rugged wilderness of hills, and
ravines and ragged forests, to a prairie about ten miles off, extending in a clear blue line along the horizon. It was like
looking from among rocks and breakers upon a distant tract
of tranquil ocean. Unluckily our route did not lie in that direction, we still had to traverse many a weary mile of the
"cross timber."

We encamped towards evening in a valley beside a scanty
pool, under a scattered grove of elms the upper branches of
which were fringed with tufts of the mystic mistletoe. In the
course of the night the wild colt whinnied repeatedly; and
about two hours before day there was a sudden *stampedo*, or
rush of horses along the purlieus of the camp, with a snorting and neighing, and a clattering of hoofs, that startled
most of the rangers from their sleep, who listened in silence
until the sound died away like the rushing of a blast. As usual
the noise was at first attributed to some party of marauding
Indians: but as the day dawned a couple of wild horses were
seen in a neighboring meadow, which scoured off on being
approached. It was now supposed that a gang of them had
dashed through our camp in the night. A general mustering

of our horses took place, many were found scattered to a considerable distance and several were not to be found. The prints of their hoofs, however, appeared deeply dinted in the soil, leading off at full speed into the waste, and their owners, putting themselves on the trail, set off in weary search of them.

We had a ruddy day break, but the morning gathered up grey and lowering with indications of an autumnal storm. We resumed our march silently and seriously, through a rough and cheerless country, from the highest points of which we could descry large prairies stretching indefinitely westward. After travelling for two or three hours, as we were traversing a withered prairie, resembling a great brown heath, we beheld seven Osage warriors approaching at a distance. The sight of any human being in this lonely wilderness was interesting; it was like speaking a ship at sea. One of the Indians took the lead of his companions and advanced towards us with head erect, chest thrown forward, and a free and noble mien. He was a fine looking fellow, dressed in scarlet frock and fringed leggings of deer skin; his head was decorated with a white tuft and he stepped forward with something of a martial air, swaying his bow and arrows in one hand.

We held some conversation with him through our interpreter Beatte, and found that he and his companions had been with the main part of their tribe hunting the buffalo and had met with great success, and he informed us that in the course of another days march we would reach the prairies on the banks of the Grand Canadian and find plenty of game. He added that, as their hunt was over, and the hunters on their return homeward, he and his comrades had set out on a war party, to waylay and hover about some Pawnee camp, in hopes of carrying off scalps or horses.

By this time his companions, who at first stood aloof, joined him. Three of them had indifferent fowling pieces the rest were armed with bows and arrows. I could not but admire the finely shaped heads and busts of these savages, and their graceful attitudes and expressive gestures, as they stood conversing with our interpreter and surrounded by a cavalcade of rangers. We endeavoured to get one of them to join us, as we were desirous of seeing him hunt the buffalo with his bow and arrow. He seemed at first somewhat inclined to do so, but was dissuaded by his companions.

The worthy Commissioner now remembered his mission as Pacificator and made a speech, exhorting them to abstain from all offensive acts against the Pawnees; informing them of the plan of their Father at Washington to put an end to all war among his Red children; and assuring them that he was sent to the frontier to establish a universal peace. He told them therefore to return quietly to their homes with the certainty that the Pawnees would no longer molest them, but would soon regard them as brothers.

The Indians listened to the speech with their customary silence and decorum: after which exchanging a few words among themselves they bade us farewell and pursued their way across the prairie.

Fancying that I saw a lurking smile in the countenance of our interpreter Beatte I privately enquired what the Indians had said to each other after hearing the speech. The leader he said had observed to his companions, that, as their great Father intended so soon to put an end to all warfare, it behooved them to make the most of the little time that was left them. So they had departed with redoubled zeal to pursue their project of horse stealing!

We had not long parted from the Indians before we discovered three Buffalos among the thickets of a marshy valley to our left. I set off with the captain and several rangers in pursuit of them. Stealing through a straggling grove the captain, who took the lead, got within rifle shot and wounded one of them in the flank. They, all three, made off in headlong panic, through thickets and brush wood, and swamp and mire, bearing down every obstacle by their immense weight. The captain and rangers soon gave up a chase which threatened to knock up their horses; I had got upon the traces of the wounded bull, however, and was in hopes of getting near enough to use my pistols, the only weapons with which I was provided; but before I could effect it, he reached the foot of a rocky hill covered with post oak and brambles, and plunged forward, dashing and crashing along with neck or nothing fury, where it would have been madness to follow him.

The chase had led me so far on one side that it was some time before I regained the trail of our troop. As I was slowly ascending a hill a fine black mare came prancing round the summit and was close to me before she was aware. At sight of me she started back, then turning, swept at full speed down into the valley and up the opposite hill, with flowing mane and tail and action free as air. I gazed after her as long as she was in sight, and breathed a wish that so glorious an animal might never come under the degrading thraldom of whip and curb, but remain a free rover of the prairies.

Chapter XXVII

Foul weather encampment—Anecdotes of bear hunting—
Indian notions about omens—Scruples respecting the dead.

O N OVERTAKING the troop I found it encamping in a rich
bottom of wood land, traversed by a small stream, running between deep crumbling banks. A sharp cracking off of
rifles was kept up for some time in various directions, upon a
numerous flock of turkeys, scampering among the thickets, or
perched upon the trees. We had not been long at a halt when
a drizzling rain ushered in the autumnal storm that had been
brewing. Preparations were immediately made to weather it.
Our tent was pitched, and our saddles, saddlebags, packages of
coffee, sugar, salt and every thing else that could be damaged
by the rain were gathered under its shelter. Our men Beatte,
Tonish and Antoine drove stakes with forked ends into the
ground, laid poles across them for rafters, and thus made a
shed or penthouse, covered with bark and skins, sloping towards the wind, and open towards the fire. The rangers formed
similar shelters of bark and skins, or of blankets stretched on
poles, supported by forked stakes, with great fires in front.

These precautions were well timed. The rain set in sullenly
and steadily and kept on, with slight intermissions, for two
days. The brook which flowed peaceably on our arrival
swelled into a turbid and boiling torrent, and the forest became little better than a mere swamp. The men gathered under their shelters of skins and blankets, or sat cowering round
their fires; while columns of smoke curling up among the
trees, and diffusing themselves in the air, spread a blue haze
through the woodland. Our poor way worn horses, reduced
by weary travel and scanty pasturage, lost all remaining spirit,
and stood, with drooping head, flagging ears and half closed
eyes, dozing and steaming in the rain; while the yellow autumnal leaves, at every shaking of the breeze, came wavering
down around them.

Notwithstanding the bad weather, however our hunters were
not idle, but during the intervals of the rain, sallied forth on
horseback to prowl through the woodland. Every now and

then the sharp report of a distant rifle boded the death of a deer. Venison in abundance was brought in. Some busied themselves under the sheds flaying and cutting up the carcasses, or round the fires with spits and camp kettles, and a rude kind of feasting or rather gormandizing prevailed throughout the camp. The axe was continually at work and wearied the forest with its echoes. Crash! some mighty tree would come down; in a few minutes its limbs would be blazing and crackling on the huge camp fires, with some luckless deer roasting before it, that had once sported beneath its shade.

The change of weather had taken sharp hold of our little Frenchman. His meagre frame composed of bones and whip cord, was racked with rheumatic pains and twinges. He had the tooth ache—the ear ache, his face was tied up, he had shooting pains in every limb: yet all seemed but to increase his restless activity and he was in an incessant fidget about the fire, roasting and stewing, and groaning and scolding and swearing.

Our man Beatte returned grim and mortified from hunting. He had come upon a bear of formidable dimensions and wounded him with a rifle shot. The bear took to the brook which was swollen and rapid. Beatte dashed in after him and assailed him in the rear with his hunting knife. At every blow the bear turned furiously upon him, with a terrific display of white teeth. Beatte, having a foot hold in the brook, was enabled to push him off with his rifle, and when he turned to swim would flounder after, and attempt to hamstring him. The bear, however, succeeded in scrambling off among the thickets, and Beatte had to give up the chase.

His adventure, if it produced no game, brought up at least several anecdotes round the evening fire, relative to bear hunting, in which the grizzly bear figured conspicuously. This powerful and ferocious animal, is a favorite theme of hunters' story, both among red and white men; and his enormous claws are worn round the neck of an Indian brave as a trophy more honorable than a human scalp. He is now rarely seen below the upper prairies and the skirts of the Rocky Mountains. Other bears are formidable when wounded and provoked, but seldom make battle when allowed to escape. The grizzly bear alone, of all the animals of our western wilds, is prone to unprovoked hostility. His prodigious size and strength make him a formidable opponent, and his great tenacity of life often baffles the skill of the hunter, withstanding repeated shots of the rifle and wounds of the hunting knife.

One of the anecdotes related on this occasion gave a picture of the accidents and hard shifts to which our frontier rovers are enured. A hunter while in pursuit of a deer fell into one of those deep funnel shaped pits formed on the prairies by the settling of the waters after heavy rains, and known by the name of sink holes. To his great horror he came in contact, at the bottom, with a huge grizzly bear. The monster grappled him; a deadly contest ensued in which the poor hunter was severely torn and bitten and had a leg and an arm broken, but succeeded in killing his rugged foe. For several days he remained at the bottom of the pit, too much crippled to move, and subsisting on the raw flesh of the bear, during which time he kept his wounds open that they might heal gradually and effectually. He was at length enabled to scramble to the top of the pit and so out upon the open prairie. With great difficulty he crawled to a ravine formed by a stream, then nearly dry. Here he took a delicious draught of water, which infused new life into him; then dragging himself along from pool to pool, he supported himself by small fish and frogs.

One day he saw a wolf hunt down and kill a deer in the neighboring prairie. He immediately crawled forth from the ravine, drove off the wolf, and, lying down beside the carcass of the deer remained there until he had made several hearty meals, by which his strength was much recruited.

Returning to the ravine he pursued the course of the brook until it grew to be a considerable stream. Down this he floated until he came to where it emptied into the Mississippi. Just at the mouth of the stream he found a forked tree which he launched with some difficulty, and, getting astride of it, committed himself to the current of the mighty river. In this way he floated along until he arrived opposite the fort at Council Bluffs. Fortunately he arrived there in the day time, otherwise he might have floated unnoticed past this solitary post and perished in the idle waste of waters. Being descried from the fort a canoe was sent to his relief and he was brought to shore more dead than alive, where he soon recovered from his wounds, but remained maimed for life.

Our man Beatte had come out of his contest with the bear, very much worsted and discomfited. His drenching in the brook, together with the recent change of weather had brought on rheumatic pains in his limbs to which he is subject. Though ordinarily a fellow of undaunted spirit, and above all hardship, yet he now sat down by the fire gloomy and dejected and for once gave way to repining. Though in the prime of life, and of a robust frame and apparently iron constitution yet, by his own account he was little better than a mere wreck. He was, in fact, a living monument of the hardships of wild frontier life. Baring his arm, he shewed it warped and contracted by a former attack of rheumatism; a malady with which the Indians are often afflicted; for their exposure to the vicissitudes of the elements, does not produce that perfect hardihood and insensibility to the changes of the seasons that many are apt to imagine. He bore the scars of various maims and bruizes, some received in hunting, some in Indian warfare. His right arm had been broken by a fall from his horse, at another time his steed had fallen with him, and crushed his left leg.

"I am all broke to pieces and good for nothing;" said he— "I no care now what happen to me any more—" "However," added he, after a moments pause, "for all that—it would take a pretty strong man to put me down—any how."

I drew from him various particulars concerning himself which served to raise him in my estimation. His residence was on the Neosho, in an Osage hamlet or neighborhood, under the superintendence of a worthy missionary from the banks of the Hudson, by the name of Requa who was endeavoring to instruct the savages in the art of agriculture, and to make husbandmen and herdsmen of them. I had visited this agricultural mission of Requa in the course of my recent tour along the frontier, and had considered it more likely to produce solid advantages to the poor Indians, than any of the mere praying and preaching missions along the border.

In this neighborhood Pierre Beatte had his little farm, his Indian wife, and his halfbreed children: and aided Mr. Requa in his endeavors to civilize the habits and meliorate the condition of the Osage tribe. Beatte had been brought up a Catholic, and was inflexible in his religious faith; he could not pray with Mr. Requa, he said, but he could work with him, and he evinced a great zeal for the good of his savage relatives and neighbors. Indeed, though his father had been French, and he himself, had been brought up in communion with the whites, he evidently was more of an Indian in his tastes, and his heart yearned towards his mother's nation. When he talked to me of the wrongs and insults that the poor Indians suffered in their intercourse with the rough settlers on the frontiers; when he described the precarious and degraded state of the Osage tribe, diminished in numbers, broken in spirit, and almost living on sufferance in the land where they once figured so heroically, I could see his veins swell and his nostrils distend with indignation: but he would check the feeling with a strong exertion of Indian self command, and, in a manner, drive it back into his bosom.

He did not hesitate to relate an instance wherein he had joined his kindred Osages, in pursuing and avenging themselves on a party of white men who had committed a flagrant outrage upon them; and I found, in the encounter that took place, Beatte had shown himself the complete Indian.

He had more than once accompanied his Osage relatives in their wars with the Pawnees, and related a skirmish which took place on the borders of these very hunting grounds, in which several Pawnees were killed. We should pass near the place, he said, in the course of our tour, and the unburied bones and sculls of the slain were still to be seen there.

The Surgeon of the troop, who was present at our conversation, pricked up his ears at this intelligence. He was something of a phrenologist, and offered Beatte a handsome reward if he would procure him one of the sculls.

Beatte regarded him for a moment with a look of stern surprize.

"No!" said he at length—"Dat too bad! I have heart strong enough—I no care kill—but—*let the dead alone!*"

He added that once in travelling with a party of white men he had slept in the same tent with a Doctor and found that he had a Pawnee scull among his baggage: he at once renounced the Doctor's tent, and his fellowship. "He try to coax me," said Beatte—"but I say no—we must part—I no keep such company."

In the temporary depression of his spirits Beatte gave way to those superstitious forebodings to which Indians are prone. He had sat for some time, with his cheek upon his hand, gazing into the fire. I found his thoughts were wandering back to his humble home on the banks of the Neosho; he was sure, he said, that he should find some one of his family ill, or dead, on his return: his left eye had twitched and twinkled for two days past; an omen which always boded some misfortune of the kind. Such are the trivial circumstances which, when magnified into omens, will shake the souls of these men of iron. The least sign of mystic and sinister portent is sufficient to turn a hunter or a warrior from his course, or to fill his mind with apprehensions of impending evil. It is this superstitious propensity, common to the solitary and savage rovers of the wilderness that gives such powerful influence to the prophet and the dreamer.

The Osages with whom Beatte had passed much of his life, retain these superstitious fancies and rites in much of their original force. They all believe in the existence of the soul after its separation from the body, and that it carries with it all its mortal tastes and habitudes. At an Osage village in the neighborhood of Beatte, one of the chief warriors lost an only child a beautiful girl of a very tender age. All her play things were buried with her. Her favorite little horse, also, was killed and laid in the grave beside her, that she might have it to ride in the land of spirits.

I will here add a little story which I picked up in the course of my tour through Beatte's country, and which illustrates the superstitions of his Osage kindred. A large party of Osages had been encamped for some time on the borders of a fine stream, called the Nick a nansa. Among them was a young hunter one of the bravest and most graceful of the tribe, who was to be married to an Osage girl, who for her beauty was called the Flower of the Prairies. The young hunter left her for a time among her relatives in the encampment and went to St. Louis to dispose of the products of his hunting, and purchase ornaments for his bride.

After an absence of some weeks he returned to the banks of the Nickanansa, but the camp was no longer there: the bare frames of the lodges and the brands of extinguished fires alone marked the place. At a distance he beheld a female seated, as if weeping, by the side of the stream. It was his affianced bride. He ran to embrace her but she turned mournfully away. He dreaded lest some evil had befallen the camp.

"Where are our people?" cried he.

"They are gone to the banks of the Wagrushka."

"And what art thou doing here alone?"

"Waiting for thee."

"Then let us hasten to join our people on the banks of the Wagrushka."

He gave her his pack to carry, and walked ahead, according to Indian custom.

They came to where the smoke of the distant camp was seen rising from the woody margin of the stream. The girl seated herself at the foot of a tree. "It is not proper for us to return together;" said she. "I will wait here."

The young hunter proceeded to the camp alone, and was received by his relatives with gloomy countenances.

"What evil has happened," said he, "that ye are all so sad."

No one replied.

He turned to his favorite sister, and bade her go forth, seek his bride and conduct her to the camp.

"Alas!" cried she, "how shall I seek her? She died a few days since."

The relatives of the young girl now surrounded him weeping and wailing; but he refused to believe the dismal tidings. "But a few moments since," cried he, "I left her alive and in health—Come with me and I will conduct you to her."

He led the way to the tree where she had seated herself, but she was no longer there, and his pack lay on the ground. The fatal truth struck him to the heart: he fell to the ground dead.

I give this simple little story almost in the words in which it was related to me as I lay by the fire in an evening encampment on the banks of the haunted stream where it is said to have happened.

Chapter XXVIII

A secret expedition—Deer bleating—Magic balls.

ON THE following morning we were rejoined by the rangers who had remained at the last encampment to seek for the stray horses. They had tracked them for a considerable distance through bush and brake and across streams, until they found them cropping the herbage on the edge of a prairie. Their heads were in the direction of the fort and they were evidently grazing their way homewards, heedless of the unbounded freedom of the prairie so suddenly laid open to them.

About noon the weather held up and I observed a mysterious consultation going on between our half breeds and Tonish: it ended in a request that we would dispense with the services of the latter for a few hours, and permit him to join his comrades in a grand foray. We objected that Tonish was too much disabled by aches and pains for such an undertaking; but he was wild with eagerness for the mysterious enterprize, and, when permission was given him, seemed to forget all his ailments in an instant.

In a short time the trio were equipped and on horseback; with rifles on their shoulders and handkerchiefs twisted round their heads, evidently bound for a grand scamper. As they passed by the different lodges of the camp, the vainglorious little Frenchman could not help boasting to the right and left, of the great things he was about to achieve; though the taciturn Beatte, who rode in advance, would every now and then check his horse, and look back at him with an air of stern rebuke. It was hard, however, to make the loquacious Tonish play "Indian."

Several of the hunters likewise sallied forth, and the prime old woodman Ryan came back early in the afternoon with ample spoil, having killed a buck and two fat does. I drew near to a groupe of rangers that had gathered round him as he stood by the spoil, and found they were discussing the merits of a stratagem sometimes used in deer hunting. This consists in imitating, with a small instrument called a bleat, the cry of the faun, so as to lure the doe within reach of the rifle. There are bleats of various kinds, suited to calm or windy weather, and to the age of the faun. The poor animal, deluded by them, in its anxiety about its young, will sometimes advance close up to the hunter. "I once bleated a doe," said a young hunter, "until it came within twenty yards of me and presented a sure mark. I levelled my rifle three times, but had not the heart to shoot, for the poor doe looked so wistfully that it in a manner made my heart yearn. I thought of my own mother and how anxious she used to be about me when I was a child; so to put an end to the matter, I gave a halloo and started the doe out of rifle shot in a moment."

"And you did right," cried honest Old Ryan: "for my part I never could bring myself to bleating deer. I've been with hunters who had bleats, and have made them throw them away. It is a rascally trick to take advantage of a mother's love for her young."

Towards evening our three worthies returned from their mysterious foray. The tongue of Tonish gave notice of their approach long before they came in sight; for he was vociferating at the top of his lungs, and rousing the attention of the whole camp. The lagging gait and reeking flanks of their horses gave evidence of hard riding, and on nearer approach we found them hung round with meat like a butcher's shambles. In fact they had been scouring an immense prairie that extended beyond the forest, and which was covered with herds of buffalo. Of this prairie, and the animals upon it, Beatte had received intelligence a few days before, in his conversation with the Osages; but had kept the information a secret from the rangers, that he and his comrades might have the first dash at the game. They had contented themselves with killing four, though, if Tonish might be believed, they might have slain them by scores.

These tidings, and the buffalo meat brought home in evidence, spread exultation through the camp, and every one looked forward with joy to a Buffalo hunt on the prairies. Tonish was again the oracle of the camp and held forth by the hour to a knot of listeners, crouched round the fire with their shoulders up to their ears. He was now more boastful than ever of his skill as a marksman. All his want of success in the early part of our march he attributed to being "out of luck," if not "spell bound," and finding himself listened to with apparent credulity, gave an instance of the kind, which he declared had happened to himself, but which was evidently a tale picked up among his relatives the Osages.

According to this account, when about fourteen years of age, as he was one day hunting he saw a white deer come out from a ravine. Crawling near to get a shot, he beheld another, and another, come forth until there were seven, all as white as snow. Having crept sufficiently near he singled one out and fired but without effect; the deer remained unfrightened. He loaded and fired again, and again he missed. Thus he continued firing and missing until all his ammunition was expended, and the deer remained without a wound. He returned home despairing of his skill as a marksman but was consoled by an old Osage hunter. "These white deer," said he, "have a charmed life and can only be killed by bullets of a particular kind."

The old Indian cast several balls for Tonish, but would not suffer him to be present on the occasion, nor inform him of the ingredients and mystic ceremonials.

Provided with these balls Tonish again set out in quest of the white deer and succeeded in finding them. He tried at first with ordinary balls, but missed as before. A magic ball, however, immediately brought a fine buck to the ground. Whereupon the rest of the herd immediately disappeared and were never seen again.

Oct. 29th. The morning opened gloomy and lowering; but, towards eight o'clock the sun struggled forth and lighted up the forest, and the notes of the bugle gave signal to prepare for marching. Now began a scene of bustle and clamour and gaiety. Some were scampering and bawling after their horses, some were riding in bare backed, and driving in the horses of their comrades. Some were stripping the poles of the wet blankets that had served for shelters, others packing up with all possible despatch, and loading the baggage horses as they arrived, while others were cracking off their damp rifles and charging them afresh, to be ready for the sport.

About ten o'clock we began our march. I loitered in the rear of the troop as it forded the turbid brook and defiled through the labyrinths of the forest. I always felt disposed to linger until the last straggler disappeared among the trees and the distant note of the bugle died upon the ear, that I might behold the wilderness relapsing into silence and solitude. In the present instance the deserted scene of our late bustling encampment had a forlorn and desolate appearance. The surrounding forest had been in many places trampled into a quagmire. Trees felled and partly hewn in pieces and scattered in huge fragments; tent poles stripped of their covering; smouldering fires, with great morsels of roasted venison and Buffalo meat, standing on wooden spits before them, hacked and slashed by the knives of hungry hunters; while around were strewed the hides, the horns, the antlers and bones of buffalos and deer, with uncooked joints and unplucked turkeys, left behind with that reckless improvidence and wastefulness which young hunters are apt to indulge when in a neighborhood where game abounds. In the mean time a score or two of turkey buzzards, or vultures, were already on the wing, wheeling their magnificent flight high in the air, and preparing for a descent upon the camp as soon as it should be abandoned.

Chapter XXIX

The Grand Prairie—A buffalo hunt.

AFTER PROCEEDING about two hours, in a southerly direction, we emerged towards midday from the dreary belt of the Cross Timber, and to our infinite delight beheld "The Great Prairie" stretching to the right and left before us. We could distinctly trace the meandering course of the Main Canadian and various smaller streams, by the strips of green forest that bordered them. The landscape was vast and beautiful. There is always an expansion of feeling in looking upon these boundless and fertile wastes; but I was doubly conscious of it after emerging from our "close dungeon of innumerable boughs."

From a rising ground Beatte pointed out to us the place where he and his comrades had killed the Buffaloes; and we beheld several black objects moving in the distance, which he said were part of the herd. The Captain determined to shape his course to a woody bottom about a mile distant and to encamp there, for a day or two by way of having a regular buffalo hunt and getting a supply of provisions. As the troop defiled along the slope of the hill towards the camping ground, Beatte proposed to my mess mates and myself that we should put ourselves under his guidance, promising to take us where we should have plenty of sport. Leaving the line of march, therefore, we diverged towards the prairie; traversing a small valley and ascending a gentle swell of land. As we reached the summit we beheld a gang of wild horses about a mile off. Beatte was immediately on the alert, and no longer thought of buffalo hunting. He was mounted on his powerful, half wild horse, with a lariat coiled at the saddle bow, and set off in pursuit: while we remained on a rising ground watching his maneuvres with great solicitude. Taking advantage of a strip of wood land he stole quietly along so as to get close to them before he was perceived. The moment they caught sight of him a grand scamper took place. We watched him skirting along the horizon like a privateer in full chase of a merchantman; at length he passed over the brow of a ridge and down into a shallow valley; in a few moments he was on the opposite hill and close upon one of the horses. He was soon head and head, and appeared to be trying to noose his prey, but they both disappeared again below the hill and we saw no more of them. It turned out afterwards that he had noosed a powerful horse but could not hold him, and had lost his lariat in the attempt.

While we were waiting for his return we perceived two buffalo bulls descending a slope towards a stream which wound through a ravine fringed with trees. The young count and myself endeavored to get near them under covert of the trees. They discovered us while we were yet three or four hundred yards off, and, turning about, retreated up the rising ground. We urged our horses across the ravine and gave chase. The immense weight of head and shoulders causes the buffalo to labour heavily up hill, but it accelerates his descent. We had the advantage, therefore, and gained rapidly upon the fugitives, though it was difficult to get our horses to approach them, their very scent inspiring them with terror. The Count, who had a double barrelled gun loaded with ball, fired but missed. The bulls now altered their course, and gallopped down hill with headlong rapidity. As they ran in different directions we each singled one and separated. I was provided with a brace of veteran brass barrelled pistols which I had borrowed at Fort Gibson, and which had evidently seen some service. Pistols are very effective in Buffalo hunting, as the hunter can ride up close to the animal and fire at it while at full speed; whereas the long heavy rifles used on the frontier cannot be easily managed, nor discharged with accurate aim from horseback. My object, therefore, was to get within pistolshot of the Buffalo. This was no very easy matter. I was well mounted, on a horse of excellent speed and bottom, that seemed eager for the chase and soon overtook the game, but the moment he came nearly parallel he would keep sheering off with ears forked and pricked forward, and every symptom of aversion and alarm. It was no wonder. Of all animals a Buffalo, when close pressed by the hunter, has an aspect the most diabolical. His two short black horns curve out of a huge frontlet of shaggy hair, his eyes glow like coals; his mouth is open, his tongue parched and drawn up into a half crescent, his tail is erect and the tufted end whisking about in the air, he is a perfect picture of mingled rage and terror.

It was with difficulty I urged my horse sufficiently near, when taking aim, to my chagrin both pistols missed fire. Unfortunately the locks of these veteran weapons were so much worn that, in the gallop, the priming had been shaken out of the pans. At the snapping of the last pistol I was close upon the buffalo when, in his despair he turned round with a sudden snort and rushed upon me. My horse wheeled about as if on a pivot, made a convulsive spring, and as I had been leaning on one side with pistol extended I came near being thrown at the feet of the buffalo.

Three or four bounds of the horses carried us out of reach of the enemy, who, having merely turned in desperate self defence, quickly resumed his flight. As soon as I could gather in my panic stricken horse, and prime the pistols afresh, I again spurred in pursuit of the Buffalo, who had slackened his speed to take breath. On my approach he again set off full tilt, heaving himself forward with a heavy rolling gallop, dashing with headlong precipitation through brakes and ravines, while several deer and wolves startled from their coverts by his thundering career ran helter skelter to right and left across the waste.

A gallop across the prairies in pursuit of game is by no means so smooth a career as those may imagine, who have only the idea of an open level plain. It is true the prairies of the hunting grounds are not so much entangled with flowering plants and long herbage as the lower prairies, and are principally covered with short buffalo grass; but they are diversified by hill and dale, and where most level are apt to be cut up by deep rifts and ravines, made by torrents after rains, and which, yawning from an even surface, are almost like pitfalls in the way of the hunter, checking him suddenly, when in full career, or subjecting him to the risk of limb and life. The plains, too, are beset by burrowing holes of small animals, in which the horse is apt to sink to the fet lock, and throw both himself and his rider. The late rain had covered some parts of the prairie, where the ground was hard, with a thin sheet of water, through which the horse had to splash his way. In other parts there were innumerable shallow hollows, eight or ten feet in diameter, made by the buffalos, who wallow in sand and mud like swine. These being filled with water shone like mirrors, so that the horse was continually leaping over them or springing on one side. We had reached, too, a rough part of the prairie, very much broken and cut up; the buffalo, who was running for life, took no heed to his course plunging down break neck ravines, where it was necessary to skirt the borders in search of a safer descent. At length he came to where a winter stream had torn a deep chasm across the whole prairie; laying open jagged rocks and forming a long glen bordered by steep crumbling cliffs of mingled stone and clay. Down one of these the buffalo flung himself half tumbling half leaping, and then scuttled off along the bottom, while I, seeing all further pursuit useless, pulled up, and gazed quietly after him from the border of the cliff, until he disappeared amidst the windings of the ravine.

Nothing now remained but to turn my steed and rejoin my companions. Here at first was some little difficulty. The ardour of the chase had betrayed me into a long heedless gallop. I now found myself in the midst of a lonely waste in which the prospect was bounded by undulating swells of land, naked and uniform, where, from the deficiency of land marks and distinct features an inexperienced man may become bewildered and lose his way as readily as in the wastes of the ocean. The day too was overcast, so that I could not guide myself by the sun; my only mode was to retrace the track my horse had made in coming, though this I would often lose sight of, where the ground was covered with parched herbage.

To one unaccustomed to it there is something inexpressibly lonely in the solitude of a prairie. The loneliness of a forest seems nothing to it. There the view is shut in by trees, and the imagination is left free to picture some livelier scene beyond. But here we have an immense extent of landscape without a sign of human existence. We have the consciousness of being far, far beyond the bounds of human habitation; we feel as if moving in the midst of a desert world. As my horse lagged slowly back over the scenes of our late scamper, and the delirium of the chase had passed away, I was peculiarly sensible to these circumstances. The silence of the waste was now and then broken by the cry of a distant flock of pelicans stalking like spectres about a shallow pool. Sometimes by the sinister croaking of a raven in the air, while occasionally a scoundrel wolf would scour off from before me and having attained a safe distance, would sit down and howl and whine with tones that gave a dreariness to the surrounding solitude.

After pursuing my way for some time I descried a horseman on the edge of a distant hill and soon recognized him to be the Count. He had been equally unsuccessful with myself; we were shortly afterwards rejoined by our worthy comrade the Virtuoso, who, with spectacles on nose, had made two or three ineffectual shots from horseback.

We determined not to seek the camp until we had made one more effort. Casting our eyes about the surrounding waste we descried a herd of buffalo about two miles distant, scattered apart and quietly grazing near a small strip of trees and bushes. It required but little stretch of fancy to picture them so many cattle grazing on the edge of a common and that the grove might shelter some lowly farmhouse.

We now formed our plan to circumvent the herd, and by getting on the other side of them to hunt them in the direction where we knew our camp to be situated: otherwise the pursuit might take us to such a distance as to render it impossible for us to find our way back before nightfall. Taking a wide circuit therefore, we moved slowly and cautiously, pausing occasionally, when we saw any of the herd desist from grazing. The wind fortunately set from them, otherwise they might have scented us and have taken the alarm. In this way we succeeded in getting round the herd without disturbing it. It consisted of about forty head, bulls, cows and calves. Separating to some distance from each other, we now approached slowly in a parallel line, hoping by degrees to steal near without exciting attention. They began however to move off quietly, stopping at every step or two to graze, when suddenly a bull that, unobserved by us, had been taking his siesta under a clump of trees to our left, roused himself from his lair, and hastened to join his companions. We were still at a considerable distance but the game had taken the alarm. We quickened our pace, they broke into a gallop and now commenced a full chase.

As the ground was level they shouldered along with great speed, following each other in a line; two or three bulls bringing up the rear, the last of whom, from his enormous size and venerable frontlet and beard of sunburnt hair, looked like the patriarch of the herd and as if he might long have reigned the monarch of the prairie.

There is a mixture of the awful and the comic in the look of these huge animals as they heave their great bulk forwards, with an up and down motion of the unwieldy head and shoulders; their tail cocked up like the queue of pantaloon in a pantomime, the end whisking about in a fierce yet whimsical style, and their eyes glaring venomously with an expression of fright and fury.

For some time I kept parallel with the line without being able to force my horse within pistolshot, so much had he been alarmed by the assault of the Buffalo in the preceding chase. At length I succeeded, but was again balked by my pistols missing fire. My companions, whose horses were less fleet, and more way worn, could not overtake the herd; at length Mr. L—, who was in the rear of the line, and losing ground levelled his double barrelled gun and fired a long raking shot. It struck a buffalo just above the loins, broke its back bone and brought it to the ground. He stopped and alighted to despatch his prey, when borrowing his gun which had yet a charge remaining in it, I put my horse to his speed, again overtook the herd which was thundering along pursued by the Count. With my present weapon there was no need of urging my horse to such close quarters; gallopping along parallel, therefore, I singled out a buffalo and by a fortunate shot brought it down on the spot. The ball had struck a vital part; it could not move from the place where it fell but lay there struggling in mortal agony: while the rest of the herd kept on their headlong career across the prairie.

Dismounting I now fettered my horse to prevent his straying and advanced to contemplate my victim. I am nothing of a sportsman: I had been prompted to this unwonted exploit by the magnitude of the game and the excitement of an adventurous chase. Now that the excitement was over I could not but look with commiseration upon the poor animal that lay struggling and bleeding at my feet. His very size and importance, which had before inspired me with eagerness, now increased my compunction. It seemed as if I had inflicted pain in proportion to the bulk of my victim, and as if there were a hundred fold greater waste of life than there would have been in the destruction of an animal of inferior size.

To add to these after qualms of conscience the poor animal lingered in his agony. He had evidently received a mortal wound, but death might be long in coming. It would not do to leave him here to be torn piece meal while yet alive, by the wolves that had already snuffed his blood, and were skulking and howling at a distance and waiting for my departure and by the ravens that were flapping about and croaking dismally in the air. It became now an act of mercy to give him his quietus, and put him out of his misery. I primed one of the pistols therefore and advanced close up to the buffalo. To inflict a wound thus in cool blood I found a totally different thing from firing in the heat of the chase. Taking aim, however, just behind the foreshoulder my pistol for once proved true; the ball must have passed through the heart, for the animal gave one convulsive throe and expired.

While I stood meditating and moralizing over the wreck I had so wantonly produced, with my horse grazing near me I was rejoined by my fellow sportsman the Virtuoso, who, being a man of universal adroitness and withal more experienced and hardened in the gentle art of "venerie," soon managed to carve out the tongue of the buffalo, and delivered it to me to bear back to the camp as a trophy.

Chapter XXX

A comrade lost—A search for the camp—The commissioner,
the wild horse and the buffalo—A wolf serenade.

OUR SOLICITUDE was now awakened for the young
Count. With his usual eagerness and impetuosity he
had persisted in urging his jaded horse in pursuit of the herd,
unwilling to return without having likewise killed a buffalo.
In this way he had kept on following them hither and thither,
and occasionally firing an ineffectual shot, until by degrees
horseman and herd became indistinct in the distance, and at
length swelling ground and strips of trees and thickets hid
them entirely from sight.

By the time my friend the Amateur joined me the young
count had been long lost to view. We held a consultation on
the matter. Evening was drawing on. Were we to pursue him it
would be dark before we should overtake him granting we did
not entirely lose trace of him in the gloom. We should then be
too much bewildered to find our way back to the encampment;
even now our return would be difficult. We determined, therefore, to hasten to the camp as speedily as possible and send out
our half breeds and some of the veteran hunters, skilled in
cruizing about the prairies, to search for our companion.

We accordingly set forward in what we supposed to be the
direction of the camp. Our weary horses could hardly be
urged beyond a walk. The twilight thickened upon us; the
landscape grew gradually indistinct; we tried in vain to recognize various land marks which we had noted in the morning.
The features of the prairies are so similar as to baffle the eye of
any but an Indian or a practised woodsman. At length night
closed in. We hoped to see the distant glare of camp fires; we
listened to catch the sound of the bells about the necks of the
grazing horses. Once or twice we thought we distinguished
them. We were mistaken. Nothing was to be heard but a monotonous concert of insects, with now and then the dismal
howl of wolves mingling with the night breeze. We began to
think of halting for the night and bivouacking under the lea of
some thicket. We had implements to strike a light; there was

plenty of fire wood at hand, and the tongues of our buffaloes would furnish us with a repast.

Just as we were preparing to dismount we heard the report of a rifle, and shortly after the notes of the bugle calling up the night guard. Pushing forward in that direction the camp fires soon broke upon our sight, gleaming at a distance from among the thick groves of an alluvial bottom.

As we entered the camp we found it a scene of rude hunters' revelry and wassail. There had been a grand days sport in which all had taken a part. Eight buffaloes had been killed. Roaring fires were blazing on every side; all hands were feasting upon roasted joints, broiled marrow bones, and the juicy hump, farfamed among the epicures of the prairies. Right glad were we to dismount and partake of the sturdy cheer, for we had been on our weary horses since morning without tasting food.

As to our worthy friend the commissioner, with whom we had parted company at the outset of this eventful day, we found him lying in a corner of the tent, much the worse for wear in the course of a successful hunting match.

It seems that our man Beatte, in his zeal to give the Commissioner an opportunity of distinguishing himself and gratifying his hunting propensities, had mounted him upon his half wild horse, and started him in pursuit of a huge buffalo bull that had already been frightened by the hunters. The horse, which was fearless as his owner, and like him had a considerable spice of devil in his composition, and who, beside, had been made familiar with the game, no sooner came in sight and scent of the buffalo, than he set off at full speed, bearing the involuntary hunter hither and thither and whither he would not—up hill, and down hill, leaping pools and brooks, dashing through glens and gullies; until he came up with the game. Instead of sheering off he crowded upon the buffalo. The Commissioner almost in self defence, discharged both barrels of a double barrelled gun into the enemy. The broad side took effect, but was not mortal. The Buffalo turned furiously upon his pursuer. The horse as he had been taught by his owner, wheeled off. The Buffalo plunged after him. The worthy commissioner, in great extremity, drew his sole pistol from his holster, fired it off as a stern chaser, shot the buffalo full in the breast, and brought him lumbering forward to the earth.

The commissioner returned to camp, lauded on all sides for his signal exploit; but grievously battered and way worn. He had been a hard rider per force, and a victor in spite of himself. He turned a deaf ear to all compliments and congratulations; had but little stomach for the hunter's fare placed before him and soon retreated to stretch his limbs in the tent, declaring that nothing should tempt him again to mount that half devil Indian horse, and that he had enough of buffalo hunting for the rest of his life.

It was too dark now to send any one in search of the young count. Guns, however, were fired and the bugle sounded from time to time, to guide him to the camp, if by chance he should straggle within hearing, but the night advanced without his making his appearance; there was not a star visible to guide him, and we concluded that, wherever he was, he would give up wandering in the dark and bivouack until day break.

It was a raw overcast night. The carcasses of the buffaloes killed in the vicinity of the camp had drawn about it an unusual number of wolves, who kept up the most forlorn concert of whining yells prolonged into dismal cadences and inflexions, literally converting the surrounding waste into a howling wilderness. Nothing is more melancholy than the midnight howl of a wolf on a prairie. What rendered the gloom and wildness of the night and the savage concert of the neighboring waste the more dreary to us, was the idea of the lonely and exposed situation of our young and inexperienced comrade. We trusted, however, that on the return of daylight he would find his way back to the camp, and then all the events of the night would be remembered only as so many savoury gratifications of his passion for adventure.

Chapter XXXI

A hunt for a lost comrade.

The morning dawned and an hour or two passed with out any tidings of the Count. We began to feel uneasiness lest, having no compass to aid him, he might perplex himself and wander in some opposite direction. Stragglers are thus often lost for days; what made us the more anxious about him was, that he had no provisions with him, was totally unversed in "wood craft," and liable to fall into the hands of some lurking or straggling party of savages.

As soon as our people, therefore, had made their breakfast we beat up for volunteers for a cruize in search of the count. A dozen of the rangers, mounted on some of the best and freshest horses, and armed with rifles were soon ready to start; our half breeds Beatte and Antoine also, with our little mongrel Frenchman were zealous in the cause, so Mr. L— and myself, taking the lead, to shew the way to the scene of our late hunt, where we had parted company with the count, we all set out across the prairie.

A ride of a couple of miles brought us to the carcasses of the two buffalos we had killed. A legion of ravenous wolves were already gorging upon them. At our approach they reluctantly drew off, skulking with a caitiff look to the distance of a few hundred yards, and there awaiting our departure that they might return to their banquet.

I conducted Beatte and Antoine to the spot whence the young count had continued the chase alone. It was like putting hounds upon the scent. They immediately distinguished the track of his horse amidst the trampings of the buffalos, and set off at a round pace, following with the eye in nearly a straight course, for upwards of a mile when they came to where the herd had divided and run hither and thither about a meadow. Here the track of the horse's hoofs wandered, and doubled and often crossed each other; our half breeds were like hounds at fault. While we were all at a halt, waiting until they should unravel the maze, Beatte suddenly gave a short Indian whoop or rather yelp, and pointed to a

141

distant hill. On regarding it attentively we perceived a horse-man on the summit. "It is the Count!" cried Beatte, and set off at full gallop, followed by the whole company. In a few moments he checked his horse. Another figure on horseback had appeared on the brow of the hill. This completely altered the case. The count had wandered off alone; no other person had been missing from the camp. If one of these horsemen was indeed the count, the other must be an Indian. If an Indian, in all probability a Pawnee. Perhaps they were both Indians; scouts of some party lurking in the vicinity. While these and other suggestions were hastily discussed, the two horsemen glided down from the profile of the hill and we lost sight of them. One of the rangers suggested that there might be a straggling party of Pawnees behind the hill, and that the count might have fallen into their hands. The idea had an electric effect upon the little troop. In an instant every horse was at full speed, the half breeds leading the way; the young rangers as they rode set up wild yelps of exultation at the thoughts of having a brush with Indians. A neck or nothing gallop brought us to the skirts of the hill, and revealed our mistake. In a ravine we found the two horsemen standing by the carcass of a buffalo which they had killed. They proved to be two rangers who, unperceived, had left the camp a little before us, and had come here in a direct line, while we had made a wide circuit about the prairie.

This episode being at an end and the sudden excitement being over, we slowly and cooly retraced our steps to the meadow, but it was some time before our halfbreeds could again get on the track of the count. Having at length found it, they succeeded in following it through all its doublings, until they came to where it was no longer mingled with the tramp of buffalos, but became single and separate, wandering here and there about the prairies, but always tending in a di-rection opposite to that of the camp. Here the count had ev-idently given up the pursuit of the herd and had endeavored to find his way to the encampment, but had become bewil-dered as the evening shades thickened around him, and had completely mistaken the points of the compass.

In all this quest our halfbreeds displayed that quickness of eye, in following up a track, for which Indians are so noted.

Beatte especially, was as staunch as a veteran hound. Sometimes he would keep forward on an easy trot, his eyes fixed on the ground a little a head of his horse, clearly distinguishing prints in the herbage, which to me were invisible excepting on the closest inspection. Sometimes he would pull up and walk his horse slowly, regarding the ground intensely, where, to my eye nothing was apparent. Then he would dismount, lead his horse by the bridle and advance cautiously, step by step, with his face bent towards the earth, just catching, here and there, a casual indication of the vaguest kind to guide him onward. In some places where the soil was hard and the grass withered, he would lose the track entirely and wander backwards and forwards and right and left in search of it; returning occasionally to the place where he had lost sight of it, to take a new departure. If this failed he would examine the banks of the neighboring streams, or the sandy bottoms of the ravines, in hopes of finding tracks where the count had crossed. When he again came upon the track he would remount his horse and resume his onward course. At length, after crossing a stream, in the crumbling banks of which the hoofs of the horse were deeply dinted we came upon a high dry prairie, where our halfbreeds were completely baffled. Not a foot print was to be discerned, though they searched in every direction, and Beatte at length coming to a pause, shook his head most despondingly.

Just then a small herd of deer, roused from a neighboring ravine came bounding by us. Beatte sprang from his horse, levelled his rifle and wounded one slightly, but without bringing it to the ground. The report of the rifle was almost immediately followed by a long halloo from a distance. We looked around but could see nothing. Another long halloo was heard and at length a horseman was descried emerging out of a skirt of forest. A single glance shewed him to be the young count; there was a universal shout and scamper, every one setting off full gallop to greet him. It was a joyful meeting to both parties, for much anxiety had been felt by us all on account of his youth and inexperience, and for his part, with all his love of adventure, he seemed right glad to be once more among his friends.

As we supposed, he had completely mistaken his course on the preceding evening, and had wandered about until dark, when he thought of bivouacking. The night was cool yet he feared to make a fire lest it might betray him to some lurking party of Indians. Hobbling his horse with his pockethandkerchief, and leaving him to graze on the margin of the prairie, he clambered into a tree, fixed his saddle in the fork of the branches, and, placing himself securely with his back against the trunk, prepared to pass a dreary and anxious night, regaled occasionally with the howlings of the wolves. He was agreeably disappointed. The fatigue of the day soon brought on a sound sleep; he had delightful dreams about his home in Switzerland, nor did he awake until it was broad day light.

He then descended from his roosting place, mounted his horse and rode to the naked summit of a hill, whence he beheld a trackless wilderness around him, but at no great distance the Grand Canadian, winding its way between borders of forest land. The sight of this river consoled him with the idea that, should he fail in finding his way back to the camp, or in being found by some party of his comrades, he might follow the course of the stream which could not fail to conduct him to some frontier post or Indian hamlet.

So closed the events of our haphazard buffalo hunt.

Chapter XXXII

A republic of prairie dogs.

ON RETURNING from our expedition in quest of the young Count I learned that a burrow, or village, as it is termed, of prairie dogs had been discovered on the level summit of a hill about a mile from the camp. Having heard much of the habits and peculiarities of these little animals I determined to pay a visit to the community. The prairie dog is, in fact, one of the curiosities of the Far West, about which travellers delight to tell marvellous tales, endowing him at times, with something of the politic and social habits of a rational being, and giving him systems of civil government and domestic economy almost equal to what they used to bestow upon the beaver.

The Prairie Dog is an animal of the coney kind and about the size of a rabbit. He is of a sprightly, mercurial nature, quick, sensitive and somewhat petulant. He is very gregarious, living in large communities, sometimes of several acres in extent, where innumerable little heaps of earth shew the entrances to the subterranean cells of the inhabitants, and the well beaten tracks, like lanes and streets, shew their mobility and restlessness. According to the accounts given of them they would seem to be continually full of sport, business and public affairs; whisking about hither and thither, as if on gossipping visits to each other's houses, or congregating in the cool of the evening, or after a shower, and gambolling together in the open air. Sometimes, especially when the moon shines, they pass half the night in revelry, barking or yelping with short, quick yet weak tones, like those of very young puppies. While in the height of their playfulness and clamour, however, should there be the least alarm, they all vanish into their cells in an instant, and the village remains blank and silent. In case they are hard pressed by their pursuers, without any hope of escape, they will assume a pugnacious air, and a most whimsical look of impotent wrath and defiance.

The Prairie Dogs are not permitted to remain sole and undisturbed inhabitants of their own homes. Owls and rattlesnakes are said to take up their abodes with them, but whether as

invited guests or unwelcome intruders, is a matter of contro-
versy. The owls are of a peculiar kind and would seem to partake of the character of the hawk, for they are taller and more
erect on their legs, more alert in their looks and rapid in their
flight, than ordinary owls, and do not confine their excursions
to the night, but sally forth in broad day.

Some say that they only inhabit cells which the prairie dogs
have deserted and suffer to go to ruin, in consequence of the
death in them of some relative, for they would make out this
little animal to be endowed with keen sensibilities, that will
not permit it to remain in the dwelling where it has witnessed
the death of a friend. Other fanciful speculators represent the
owl as a kind of housekeeper to the prairie dog, and, from
having a note very similar, insinuate that it acts, in a manner,
as family preceptor, and teaches the young litter to bark.

As to the rattle snake, nothing satisfactory has been ascertained of the part he plays in this most interesting household,
though he is considered as little better than a sycophant and
sharper, that winds himself into the concerns of the honest
credulous little dog, and takes him in most sadly. Certain it is,
if he acts as toad eater, he occasionally solaces himself with
more than the usual perquisites of his order, as he is now and
then detected with one of the younger members of the family
in his maw.

Such are a few of the particulars that I could gather about
the domestic economy of this little inhabitant of the prairies,
who, with his pigmy republic, appears to be a subject of
much whimsical speculation and burlesque remark among
the hunters of the Far West.

It was towards evening that I set out with a companion to
visit the village in question. Unluckily it had been invaded in
the course of the day by some of the rangers, who had shot
two or three of its inhabitants, and thrown the whole sensitive
community in confusion. As we approached we could perceive numbers of the inhabitants seated at the entrances of
their cells, while centinels seemed to have been posted on the
outskirts, to keep a look out. At sight of us the picket guards
scampered in and gave the alarm; whereupon every inhabitant
gave a short yelp or bark and dived into his hole, his heels
twinkling in the air as if he had thrown a summerset.

We traversed the whole village, or republic, which covered an area of about thirty acres, but not a whisker of an inhabitant was to be seen. We probed their cells as far as the ramrods of our rifles would reach, but could unearth neither dog, nor owl nor rattlesnake. Moving quietly to a little distance we lay down upon the ground and watched for a long time silent and motionless. By and bye a cautious old burgher would slowly put forth the end of his nose but instantly draw it in again. Another, at a greater distance would emerge entirely, but, catching a glance of us would throw a summerset and plunge back again into his hole. At length some who resided on the opposite side of the village, taking courage from the continued stillness, would steal forth and hurry off to a distant hole, the residence possibly of some family connexion or gossipping friend, about whose safety they were solicitous, or with whom they wished to compare notes about the late occurrences.

Others, still more bold, assembled in little knots, in the streets and public places, as if to discuss the recent outrages offered to the commonwealth, and the atrocious murders of their fellow burghers. We rose from the ground and moved forward to take a nearer view of these public proceedings when, yelp! yelp! yelp!—there was a shrill alarm passed from mouth to mouth; the meetings suddenly dispersed; feet twinkled in the air in every direction, and in an instant all had vanished into the earth.

The dusk of the evening put an end to our observations, but the train of whimsical comparisons produced in my brain by the moral attributes which I had heard given to these little politic animals, still continued after my return to camp; and late in the night, as I lay awake after all the camp was asleep, and heard in the stillness of the hour, a faint clamour of shrill voices from the distant village, I could not help picturing to myself the inhabitants gathered together in noisy assemblage, and windy debate, to devise plans for the public safety, and to vindicate the invaded rights and insulted dignity of the republic.

Chapter XXXIII

WHILE BREAKFAST was preparing a council was held as to our future movements. Symptoms of discontent had appeared for a day or two past among the rangers, most of whom, unaccustomed to the life of the prairies, had become impatient of its privations, as well as of the restraints of the camp. The want of bread had been felt severely, and they were wearied with constant travel. In fact the novelty and excitement of the expedition were at an end. They had hunted the deer, the bear, the elk, the buffalo and the wild horse, and had no further object of leading interest to look forward to. A general inclination prevailed, therefore, to turn homewards.

Grave reasons disposed the captain and his officers to adopt this resolution. Our horses were generally much jaded by the fatigues of travelling and hunting, and had fallen away sadly for want of good pasturage, and from being tethered at night, to protect them from Indian depredations. The late rains, too, seemed to have washed away the nourishment from the scanty herbage that remained, and since our encampment during the storm our horses had lost flesh and strength rapidly. With every possible care, horses, accustomed to grain, and to the regular and plentiful nourishment of the stable and the farm, lose heart and condition in travelling on the prairies. In all expeditions of the kind we were engaged in, the hardy Indian horses, which are generally mustangs, or a cross of the wild breed, are to be preferred. They can stand all fatigues, hardships and privations, and thrive on the grasses and wild herbage of the plains.

Our men, too, had acted with little fore thought; galloping off whenever they had a chance, after the game that we encountered while on the march. In this way they had strained and wearied their horses, instead of husbanding their strength and spirits. On a tour of the kind, horses should as seldom as possible be put off of a quiet walk: and the average days journey should not exceed ten miles.

We had hoped by pushing forward, to reach the bottoms of the Red River, which abound with young cane, a most nourishing forage for cattle at this season of the year. It would now take us several days to arrive there, and in the meantime many of our horses would probably give out. It was the time, too, when the hunting parties of Indians set fire to the prairies; the herbage, throughout this part of the country, was in that parched state favorable to combustion, and there was daily more and more risk that the prairies between us and the fort would be set on fire by some of the return parties of Osages, and a scorched desert left for us to traverse. In a word we had started too late in the season or loitered too much in the early part of our march, to accomplish our originally intended tour; and there was imminent hazard, if we continued on, that we should lose the greater part of our horses, and, beside suffering various other inconveniences, be obliged to return on foot. It was determined, therefore, to give up all further progress, and turning our faces to the southeast, to make the best of our way back to Fort Gibson.

This resolution being taken there was an immediate eagerness to put it into operation. Several horses, however, were missing, and among others those of the captain and the Surgeon. Persons had gone in search of them, but the morning advanced without any tidings of them. Our party in the mean time, being all ready for a march, the commissioner, determined to set off in the advance, with his original escort of a lieutenant and fourteen rangers, leaving the captain to come on, at his convenience, with the main body. At ten o'clock, we accordingly started, under the guidance of Beatte; who had hunted over this part of the country and knew the direct route to the garrison.

For some distance we skirted the prairie, keeping a south east direction, and in the course of our ride we saw a variety of wild animals, deer, white and black wolves, Buffalos and wild horses. To the latter our half breeds and Tonish gave ineffectual chase, only serving to add to the weariness of their already jaded steeds. Indeed it is rarely that any but the weaker and least fleet of the wild horses are taken in these hard racings; while the horse of the huntsman is prone to be knocked up. The latter, in fact, risks a good horse to catch a bad one. On this occasion Tonish, who was a perfect imp on horseback, and noted for ruining every animal he bestrode, succeeded in laming and almost disabling the powerful grey, on which we had mounted him at the outset of our tour.

After proceeding a few miles we left the prairie and struck to the east, taking what Beatte pronounced an old Osage war track. This led us through a rugged tract of country, over-grown with scrubbed forests and entangled thickets, and in-tersected by deep ravines, and brisk running streams, the sources of Little River. About three o'clock we encamped by some pools of water in a small valley, having come about four-teen miles. We had brought on a supply of provisions from our last camp, and supped heartily upon stewed buffalo meat, roasted venison, beignets, or fritters of flour fried in bear's lard, and tea made of a species of the golden rod, which we had found, throughout our whole route, almost as grateful a beverage as coffee. Indeed our coffee, which, as long as it held out, had been served up with every meal, according to the cus-tom of the West, was by no means a beverage to boast of. It was roasted in a frying pan, without much care, pounded in a leathern bag, with a round stone, and, boiled in our prime and almost only kitchen utensil, the camp kettle, in "branch" or brook water, which, on the prairies, is deeply coloured by the soil, of which it always holds abundant particles in a state of solution and suspension. In fact in the course of our tour we had tasted the quality of every variety of soil, and the draughts of water we had taken might vie in diversity of colour, if not of flavour, with the tinctures of an apothecary's shop. Pure, limpid water, is a rare luxury on the prairies, at least at this season of the year.

Supper over, we placed sentinels about our scanty and dimin-ished camp, spread our skins and blankets under the trees, now nearly destitute of foliage, and slept soundly until morning.

We had a beautiful day break. The camp again resounded with cheerful voices; every one was animated with the thoughts of soon being at the fort; and revelling on bread and vegeta-bles. Even our saturnine man Beatte seemed inspired on the occasion and, as he drove up the horses for the march, I heard him singing in nasal tones, a most forlorn Indian ditty. All this transient gaiety, however, soon died away amidst the fatigues of our march, which lay through the same kind of rough, hilly, thicketed country as that of yesterday. In the course of the morning we arrived at the valley of Little River where it wound through a broad bottom of alluvial soil. At present it had over-flowed its banks and inundated a great part of the valley. The difficulty was to distinguish the stream from the broad sheets of water it had formed, and to find a place where it might be forded; for it was in general deep and miry, with abrupt crum-bling banks. Under the pilotage of Beatte, therefore, we wan-dered for some time among the links made by this winding stream, in what appeared to us a trackless labyrinth of swamps, thickets and standing pools. Sometimes our jaded horses dragged their limbs forward with the utmost difficulty, having to toil for a great distance, with the water up to the stirrups, and beset at the bottom with roots and creeping plants. Some-times we had to force our way through dense thickets of bram-bles and grape vines, which almost pulled us out of our saddles. In one place one of the pack horses sank in the mire and fell on his side, so as to be extricated with great difficulty. Wherever the soil was bare, or there was a sand bank, we beheld innu-merable tracks of bears, wolves, buffaloes wild horses, turkeys and water fowl, shewing the abundant sport this valley might afford to the huntsman: our men, however, were sated with hunting, and too weary to be excited by these signs, which in the outset of our tour, would have put them in a fever of antic-ipation. Their only desire at present was to push on doggedly for the fortress.

At length we succeeded in finding a fording place where we all crossed Little River, with the water and mire to the saddle girths, and then halted for an hour and a half, to overhaul the wet baggage, and give the horses time to rest.

On resuming our march we came to a pleasant little meadow, surrounded by groves of elms and cotton wood trees, in the midst of which was a fine black horse grazing. Beatte, who was in the advance, beckoned us to halt, and, being mounted on a mare, approached the horse gently, step by step, imitating the whinny of the animal with admirable exactness. The noble courser of the prairie gazed for a time, snuffed the air, neighed, pricked up his ears, and pranced round and round the mare, in gallant style but keeping at too great a distance for Beatte to throw the lariat. He was a magnificent object, in all the pride and glory of his nature. It was admirable to see the lofty and airy carriage of his head; the freedom of every movement; the elasticity with which he trod the meadow. Finding it impossible to get within noosing distance, and seeing that the horse was receding and growing alarmed, Beatte slid down from his saddle, levelled his rifle across the back of his mare and took aim with the evident intention of creasing him. I felt a throb of anxiety for the safety of the noble animal, and called out to Beatte to desist. It was too late; he pulled the trigger as I spoke; luckily he did not shoot with his usual accuracy, and I had the satisfaction to see the coal black steed dash off unharmed into the forest.

On leaving this valley we again ascended among broken hills and rugged, ragged forests equally harassing to horse and rider. The ravines too were of red clay and often so steep that in descending the horses would put their feet together and fairly slide down, and then scramble up the opposite side like cats. Here and there among the thickets in the valleys, we met with sloes and persimmon, and the eagerness with which our men broke from the line of march, and ran to gather these poor fruits shewed how much they craved some vegetable condiment after living so long exclusively on animal food.

About half past three we encamped near a brook in a meadow where there was some scanty herbage for our half famished horses. As Beatte had killed a fat doe in the course of the day, and one of our company a fine turkey, we did not lack for provisions.

It was a splendid autumnal evening. The horizon after sunset, was of a clear apple green, rising into a delicate lake, which gradually lost itself in a deep purple blue. One narrow streak of cloud of a mahogany colour edged with amber and gold, floated in the west, and just beneath it was the evening star, shining with the pure brilliancy of a diamond. In unison with this scene there was an evening concert of insects of various kinds, all blended and harmonized into one sober and somewhat melancholy note, which I have always found to have a soothing effect upon the mind, disposing it to quiet musings.

The night that succeeded was calm and beautiful. There was a faint light from the moon, now in its second quarter, and after it had set, a fine star light, with shooting meteors. The wearied rangers after a little murmuring conversation round their fires sank to rest at an early hour, and I seemed to have the whole scene to myself. It is delightful, in thus bivouacking on the prairies, to lie awake and gaze at the stars; it is like watching them from the deck of a ship at sea, when at one view we have the whole cope of heaven. One realizes, in such lonely scenes, that companionship with these beautiful luminaries which made astronomers of the eastern shepherds, as they watched their flocks by night. How often, while contemplating their mild and benignant radiance, I have called to mind the exquisite text of Job: "Canst thou bind the sweet influences of the Pleiades, or loose the bands of Orion?" I do not know why it was, but I felt this night unusually affected by the solemn magnificence of the firmament, and seemed, as I lay thus under the open vault of heaven, to inhale with the pure untainted air, an exhilarating buoyancy of spirit, and as it were, an ecstasy of mind. I slept and waked alternately, and when I slept my dreams partook of the happy tone of my waking reveries. Towards morning one of the centinels, the oldest man in the troop, came and took a seat near me: he was weary and sleepy and impatient to be relieved. I found he had been gazing at the heavens also, but with different feelings.

"If the stars don't deceive me," said he, "it is near day break."

"There can be no doubt of that," said Beatte, who lay close by. "I heard an owl just now."

"Does the owl, then, hoot towards day break?" asked I.

"Aye, sir, just as the cock crows."

This was a useful habitude of the bird of wisdom of which I was not aware. Neither the stars nor owl deceived their votaries. In a short time there was a faint streak of light in the east.

Chapter XXXIV

*Old Creek encampment—Scarcity of provisions—Bad
weather—Weary marching—A hunter's bridge.*

THE COUNTRY through which we passed this morning
(Nov. 2) was less rugged, and of more agreeable aspect
than that we had lately traversed. At eleven o'clock we came
out upon an extensive prairie, and about six miles to our left,
beheld a long line of green forest, marking the course of the
north fork of the Canadian. On the edge of the prairie and in
a spacious grove of noble trees which overshadowed a small
brook, were the traces of an old Creek hunting camp. On the
bark of the trees were rude delineations of hunters and squaws,
scrawled with charcoal; together with various signs and hiero-
glyphics which our half breeds interpreted as indicating that
from this encampment the hunters had returned home.

In this beautiful camping ground we made our midday
halt. While reposing under the trees we heard a shouting
at no great distance, and presently the Captain and the
main body of rangers, whom we had left behind two days
before, emerged from the thicket and, crossing the brook,
were joyfully welcomed into the camp. The Captain and
the Doctor had been unsuccessful in the search after their
horses, and were obliged to march for the greater part of
the time on foot; yet they had come on with more than
ordinary speed.

We resumed our march about one o'clock, keeping easterly
and approaching the north fork obliquely: it was late before
we found a good camping place; the beds of the streams were
dry, the prairies, too, had been burnt in various places by
Indian hunting parties: at length we found water in a small
alluvial bottom where there was tolerable pasturage.

On the following morning there were flashes of lightning in
the east with low rumbling thunder, and clouds began to
gather about the horizon. Beatte prognosticated rain, and that
the wind would veer to the north. In the course of our march
a flock of brant were seen over head, flying from the north.
"There comes the wind!" said Beatte, and in fact it began to

blow from that quarter almost immediately with occasional flurries of rain.

About half past nine o'clock we forded the north fork of the Canadian and encamped about one, that our hunters might have time to beat up the neighborhood for game. In fact a serious scarcity began to prevail in the camp. Most of the rangers were young, heedless and inexperienced, and could not be prevailed upon, while provisions abounded, to provide for the future, by jerking meat or carrying away any on their horses. On leaving an encampment they would leave quantities of meat lying about, trusting to providence and their rifles for a future supply. The consequence was that any temporary scarcity of game, or ill luck in hunting produced almost a famine in the camp. In the present instance they had left loads of buffalo meat at the camp on the great prairie, and having ever since been on a forced march, leaving no time for hunting, they were now destitute of supplies and pinched with hunger. Some had not eaten any thing since the morning of the preceding day. Nothing would have persuaded them when revelling in the abundance of the buffalo encampment, that they would so soon be in such famishing plight.

The hunters returned with indifferent success. The game had been frightened away from this part of the country by Indian hunting parties which had preceded us. Ten or a dozen wild turkeys were brought in, but not a deer had been seen. The rangers began to think turkeys and even prairie hens deserving of attention; game which they had hitherto considered unworthy of their rifles.

The night was cold and windy, with occasional sprinklings of rain, but we had roaring fires to keep us comfortable. In the night a flight of wild geese passed over the camp, making a great cackling in the air; symptoms of approaching winter.

We set forward at an early hour the next morning in a north east course and came upon the trace of a party of Creek Indians, which enabled our poor horses to travel with more ease. We entered upon a fine champaign country. From a rising ground we had a noble prospect over extensive prairies finely diversified by groves and tracts of wood land and bounded by long lines of distant hills all clothed with the rich mellow tints of autumn. Game too was more plenty. A fine buck sprang up from among the herbage on our right and dashed off at full speed; but a young ranger by the name of Childers who was on foot levelled his rifle, discharged a ball that broke the neck of the bounding deer and sent him tumbling head over heels forward. Another buck and a doe, beside several turkeys were killed before we came to a halt, so that the hungry mouths of the troop were once more supplied.

About three o'clock we encamped in a grove after a forced march of twenty five miles, that had proved a hard trial to the horses. For a long time after the head of the line had encamped the rest kept straggling in, two and three at a time; one of our pack horses had given out, about nine miles back, and a poney belonging to Beatte shortly after. Many of the other horses looked so gaunt and feeble that doubts were entertained of their being able to reach the fort. In the night there was heavy rain, and the morning dawned cloudy and dismal. The camp resounded, however, with something of its former gaiety. The rangers had supped well, and were renovated in spirits anticipating a speedy arrival at the garrison. Before we set forward on our march Beatte returned and brought his poney to the camp with great difficulty. The pack horse, however, was completely knocked up and had to be abandoned. The wild mare too had cast her foal, through exhaustion, and was not in a state to go forward. She and the poney, therefore, were left at this encampment, where there was water and good pasturage, and where there would be a chance of their reviving, and being afterwards sought out and brought to the garrison.

We set off about eight o'clock, and had a day of weary and harassing travel part of the time over rough hills, and part over rolling prairies. The rain had rendered the soil slippery and plashy so as to afford unsteady foot hold. Some of the rangers dismounted, their horses having no longer strength to bear them. We made a halt in the course of the morning, but the horses were too tired to graze. Several of them laid down, and there was some difficulty in getting them on their feet again. Our troop presented a forlorn appearance, straggling slowly along, in a broken and scattered line that extended over hill and dale for three miles and upwards, in groupes of three and four widely apart; some on horseback some on foot, with a few laggards far in the rear. About four o'clock we halted for the night in a spacious forest, beside a deep narrow river called the Little North Fork or Deep Creek. It was late before the main part of the troop straggled into the encampment: many of the horses having given out. As the stream was too deep to be forded we waited until the next day to devise means to cross it; but our half breeds swam the horses of our party to the other side in the evening as they would have better pasturage, and the stream was evidently swelling. The night was cold and unruly; the wind sounding hoarsely through the forest and whirling about the dry leaves. We made long fires of great trunks of trees, which diffused something of consolation, if not cheerfulness around.

The next morning there was general permission given to hunt until twelve o'clock, the camp being destitute of provisions. The rich woody bottom in which we were encamped abounded with wild turkeys, of which a considerable number were killed. In the mean time preparations were made for crossing the river, which had risen several feet during the night; and it was determined to fell trees for the purpose, to serve as bridges.

The captain and Doctor and one or two other leaders of the camp, versed in wood craft, examined with learned eye the trees growing on the river bank, until they singled out a couple of the largest size, and most suitable inclinations. The axe was then vigorously applied to their roots in such way as to ensure their falling directly across the stream. As they did not reach to the opposite bank, it was necessary for some of the men to swim across and fell trees on the other side to meet them. They at length succeeded in making a precarious foot way across the deep and rapid current, by which the baggage could be carried over: but it was necessary to grope our way, step by step, along the trunks and main branches of the trees, which for a part of the distance were completely submerged, so that we were to our waists in water. Most of the horses were then swam across, but some of them were too weak to brave the current; and evidently too much knocked up to bear any further travel.

Twelve men, therefore, were left at the encampment to guard these horses until by repose and good pasturage they should be sufficiently recovered to complete their journey, and the Captain engaged to send the men a supply of flour and other necessaries as soon as we should arrive at the fort.

Chapter XXXV

A look out for land—Hard travelling and hungry
halting—A frontier farm house—Arrival at the garrison.

I T WAS a little after one o'clock when we again resumed our
weary wayfaring. The residue of that day and the whole of
the next were spent in toilsome travel. Part of the way was
over stoney hills, part across wide prairies, rendered spongy
and mirey by the recent rain, and cut up by brooks swollen
into torrents. Our poor horses were so feeble that it was with
difficulty we could get them across the deep ravines and turbulent streams. In traversing the miry plains they slipped and
staggered at every step, and most of us were obliged to dismount and walk for the greater part of the way. Hunger prevailed throughout the troop; every one began to look anxious
and haggard; and to feel the growing length of each additional mile. At one time in crossing a hill Beatte climbed a
high tree commanding a wide prospect, and took a look out
like a mariner from the mast head at sea. He came down with
cheering tidings. To the left he had beheld a line of forest
stretching across the country which he knew to be the woody
border of the Arkansas; and at a distance he had recognized
certain land marks from which he concluded that we could
not be above forty miles distant from the fort. It was like the
welcome cry of land to tempest tost mariners.

In fact we soon after saw smoke rising from a woody glen
at a distance. It was supposed to be made by a hunting party
of Creek or Osage Indians from the neighborhood of the
Fort, and was joyfully hailed as a harbinger of man. It was
now confidently hoped that we would soon arrive among the
frontier hamlets of Creek Indians, which are scattered along
the skirts of the uninhabited wilderness; and our hungry
rangers trudged forward with reviving spirit, regaling themselves with savory anticipations of farm house luxuries, and
enumerating every article of good cheer, until their mouths
fairly watered at the shadowy feasts thus conjured up.

A hungry night, however, closed in upon a toilsome day.
We encamped on the border of one of the tributary streams

of the Arkansas, amidst the ruins of a stately grove that had
been riven by a hurricane. The blast had torn its way through
the forest in a narrow column, and its course was marked by
enormous trees shivered and splintered and upturned with
their roots in the air: all lay in one direction, like so many
brittle reeds broken and trodden down by the hunter.

Here was fuel in abundance without the labour of the axe:
we had soon immense fires blazing and sparkling in the frosty
air and lighting up the whole forest, but alas! we had no meat
to cook at them. The scarcity in the camp almost amounted
to famine. Happy was he who had a morsel of jerked meat, or
even the half picked bones of a former repast. For our part,
we were more lucky at our mess than our neighbors; one of
our men having shot a turkey. We had no bread to eat with it,
nor salt to season it withal. It was simply boiled in water; the
latter was served up as soup, and we were fain to rub each
morsel of the turkey on the empty salt bag, in hopes some
saline particle might remain to relieve its insipidity.

The night was biting cold; the brilliant moon light sparkled
on the frosty chrystals which covered every object around us.
The water froze beside the skins on which we bivouacked,
and in the morning I found the blanket in which I was
wrapped covered with a hoar frost; yet I had never slept more
comfortably.

After a shadow of a breakfast, consisting of turkey bones and
a cup of coffee without sugar, we decamped at an early hour,
for hunger is a sharp quickener on a journey. The prairies were
all gemmed with frost, that covered the tall weeds and glis-
tened in the sun. We saw great flights of prairie hens, or grouse,
that hovered from tree to tree, or sat in rows along the naked
branches, waiting until the sun should melt the frost from the
weeds and herbage. Our rangers no longer despised such humble game, but turned from the ranks in pursuit of a prairie hen
as eagerly as they formerly would go in pursuit of a deer.

Every one now pushed forward anxious to arrive at some
human habitation before night. The poor horses were urged
beyond their strength in the thought of soon being able to
indemnify them for present toil, by rest and ample provender.
Still the distances seemed to stretch out more than ever,
and the blue hills pointed out as landmarks on the horizon to

recede as we advanced. Every step became a labour: every now and then a miserable horse would give out and lie down. His owner would rouse him by main strength; force him forward to the margin of some stream where there might be a scanty border of herbage and then abandon him to his fate. Among those that were thus left on the way was one of the led horses of the Count, a prime hunter, that had taken the lead of every thing in the chase of the wild horses. It was intended, however, as soon as we should arrive at the fort, to send out a party provided with corn, to bring in such of the horses as should survive.

In the course of the morning we came upon Indian tracks, crossing each other in various directions, a proof that we must be in the neighborhood of human habitations. At length, on passing through a skirt of woods we beheld two or three log houses, sheltered under lofty trees on the border of a prairie, the habitations of Creek Indians, who had small farms adjacent. Had they been sumptuous villas abounding with the luxuries of civilization, they could not have been hailed with greater delight.

Some of the rangers rode up to them in quest of food; the greater part, however, pushed forward in search of the habitation of a white settler, which we were told was at no great distance. The troop soon disappeared among the trees and I followed slowly in their track, for my once fleet and generous steed faltered under me and was just able to drag one foot after the other, yet I was too weary and exhausted to spare him.

In this way we crept feebly on until, on turning a thick clump of trees a frontier farm house suddenly presented itself to view. It was a low tenement of logs overshadowed by great forest trees, but it seemed as if a very region of Cocaigne prevailed around it. Here was a stable and barn and granaries teeming with abundance, while legions of grunting swine, gobbling turkeys, cackling hens and strutting roosters swarmed about the farm yard.

My poor jaded and half famished horse raised his head and pricked up his ears at the well known sights and sounds. He gave a chuckling inward sound, something like a dry laugh; whisked his tail, and made great lee way toward a corn crib, filled with golden ears of maize, and it was with some difficulty that I could control his course, and steer him up to the door of the cabin.

A single glance within was sufficient to rouse every gastronomic faculty. There sat the Captain of the rangers and his officers round a three legged table crowned by a broad and smoking dish of boiled beef and turnips. I sprang off of my horse in an instant, cast him loose to make his way to the corn crib, and entered this palace of plenty. A fat good humoured negress received me at the door. She was the mistress of the house, the spouse of the white man, who was absent. I hailed her as some swart fairy of the wild, that had suddenly conjured up a banquet in a desert: and a banquet was it in good sooth. In a twinkling she lugged from the fire a huge iron pot that might have rivalled one of the famous flesh pots of Egypt, or the witches' cauldron in Macbeth. Placing a brown earthen dish on the floor she inclined the corpulent cauldron on one side, and out leaped sundry great morsels of beef, with a regiment of turnips tumbling after them, and a rich cascade of broth overflowing the whole. This she handed me with an ivory smile that extended from ear to ear; apologizing for her humble fare and the humble style in which it was served up. Humble fare! humble style! Boiled beef and turnips—and an earthen dish to eat them from! To think of apologizing for such a treat to a half starved man from the prairies—and then such magnificent slices of bread and butter! Head of Apicius, what a banquet!

"The rage of hunger" being appeased I began to think of my horse. He, however, like an old campaigner, had taken good care of himself. I found him paying assiduous attention to the crib of Indian corn, and dexterously drawing forth and munching the ears that protruded between the bars. It was with great regret that I interrupted his repast, which he abandoned with a heavy sigh, or rather a rumbling groan. I was anxious, however, to rejoin my travelling companions, who had passed by the farm house without stopping, and proceeded to the banks of the Arkansas; being in the hopes of arriving before night at the Osage Agency. Leaving the Captain and his troop, therefore, amidst the abundance of the farm, where they had determined to quarter themselves for the night, I bade adieu to our sable hostess, and again pushed forward.

A ride of about a mile brought me to where my comrades were waiting on the banks of the Arkansas, which here poured along between beautiful forests. A number of Creek Indians, in their brightly coloured dresses, looking like so many gay tropical birds, were busy aiding our men to transport the baggage across the river in a canoe. While this was doing, our horses had another regale from two great cribs heaped up with ears of Indian corn, which stood near the edge of the river. We had to keep a check upon the poor half famished animals, lest they should injure themselves by their voracity.

The baggage being all carried to the opposite bank, we embarked in the canoe, and swam our horses across the river. I was fearful, lest in their enfeebled state, they should not be able to stem the current; but their banquet of Indian corn had already infused fresh life and spirit into them, and it would appear as if they were cheered by the instinctive consciousness of their approach to home, where they would soon be at rest and in plentiful quarters; for no sooner had we landed and resumed our route, than they set off on a hand gallop, and continued so for a great part of seven miles that we had to ride through the woods.

It was an early hour in the evening when we arrived at the Agency on the banks of the Verdigris river, whence we had set off about a month before. Here we passed the night comfortably quartered; yet, after having been accustomed to sleep in the open air, the confinement of a chamber was, in some respects, irksome. The atmosphere seemed close, and destitute of freshness; and when I woke in the night and gazed about me upon complete darkness, I missed the glorious companionship of the stars.

The next morning after breakfast, I again set forward in company with the worthy Commissioner for Fort Gibson where we arrived much tattered, travel stained and weather beaten, but in high health and spirits—and thus ended my foray into the Pawnee Hunting Grounds.

THE END

ASTORIA

or
Anecdotes of an Enterprize
Beyond the Rocky Mountains

Contents

INTRODUCTION

In the course of occasional visits to Canada many years since, I became intimately acquainted with some of the principal partners of the great North West Fur Company, who at that time lived in genial style at Montreal, and kept almost open house for the stranger. At their hospitable boards I occasionally met with partners, and clerks, and hardy fur traders from the interior posts; men who had passed years remote from civilized society, among distant and savage tribes, and who had wonders to recount of their wide and wild peregrinations, their hunting exploits, and their perilous adventures and hairbreadth escapes among the Indians. I was at an age when the imagination lends its coloring to every thing, and the stories of these Sindbads of the wilderness made the life of a trapper and fur trader perfect romance to me. I even meditated at one time a visit to the remote posts of the company in the boats which annually ascended the lakes and rivers, being thereto invited by one of the partners; and I have ever since regretted that I was prevented by circumstances from carrying my intention into effect. From those early impressions, the grand enterprizes of the great fur companies, and the hazardous errantry of their associates in the wild parts of our vast continent, have always been themes of charmed interest to me; and I have felt anxious to get at the details of their adventurous expeditions among the savage tribes that peopled the depths of the wilderness.

About two years ago, not long after my return from a tour upon the prairies of the far west, I had a conversation with my friend Mr. John Jacob Astor, relative to that portion of our country, and to the adventurous traders to Santa Fé and the Columbia. This led him to advert to a great enterprize set on foot and conducted by him, between twenty and thirty years since, having for its object to carry the fur trade across the Rocky Mountains, and to sweep the shores of the Pacific.

Finding that I took an interest in the subject, he expressed a regret that the true nature and extent of his enterprize and its national character and importance had never been understood, and a wish that I would undertake to give an account of it. The suggestion struck upon the chord of early associations, already vibrating in my mind. It occurred to me that a work of this kind might comprise a variety of those curious details, so interesting to me, illustrative of the fur trade; of its remote and adventurous enterprizes, and of the various people, and tribes, and castes, and characters, civilized and savage, affected by its operations. The journals, and letters also, of the adventurers by sea and land employed by Mr. Astor in his comprehensive project, might throw light upon portions of our country quite out of the track of ordinary travel, and as yet but little known. I therefore felt disposed to undertake the task, provided documents of sufficient extent and minuteness could be furnished to me. All the papers relative to the enterprize were accordingly submitted to my inspection. Among them were journals and letters narrating expeditions by sea, and journeys to and fro across the Rocky Mountains by routes before untravelled, together with documents illustrative of savage and colonial life on the borders of the Pacific. With such materials in hand, I undertook the work. The trouble of rummaging among business papers, and of collecting and collating facts from amidst tedious and commonplace details, was spared me by my nephew, Pierre M. Irving, who acted as my pioneer, and to whom I am greatly indebted for smoothing my path and lightening my labors.

As the journals, on which I chiefly depended, had been kept by men of business, intent upon the main object of the enterprize, and but little versed in science, or curious about matters not immediately bearing upon their interests, and as they were written often in moments of fatigue or hurry, amid the inconveniences of wild encampments, they were often meagre in their details, furnishing hints to provoke rather than narratives to satisfy inquiry. I have, therefore, availed myself occasionally of collateral lights supplied by the published journals of other travellers who have visited the scenes described: such as Messrs. Lewis and Clarke, Bradbury, Breckenridge, Long, Franchere, and Ross Cox, and make a general acknowledgment of aid received from these quarters.

The work I here present to the public, is necessarily of a rambling and somewhat disjointed nature, comprising various

expeditions and adventures by land and sea. The facts, however, will prove to be linked and banded together by one
grand scheme, devised and conducted by a master spirit; one
set of characters, also, continues throughout, appearing occasionally, though sometimes at long intervals, and the whole
enterprize winds up by a regular catastrophe; so that the
work, without any labored attempt at artificial construction,
actually possesses much of that unity so much sought after in
works of fiction, and considered so important to the interest
of every history.

Chapter I

Objects of American enterprize—Gold hunting and fur trading—Their effect on colonization—Early French Canadian settlers—Ottawa and Huron hunters—An Indian trading camp—Coureurs des bois or Rangers of the woods—Their roaming life—Their revels and excesses—Licenced traders—Missionaries—Trading posts—Primitive French Canadian merchant; his establishment and dependents—British Canadian fur merchant—Origin of the North West Company—Its constitution—Its internal trade—A candidate for the Company—Privations in the wilderness—North West clerks—North West partners—A North West nabob—Feudal notions in the forests—The lords of the Lakes—Fort William, its parliamentary hall and banqueting room—Wassailing in the wilderness.

Two leading objects of commercial gain have given birth to wide and daring enterprize in the early history of the Americas; the precious metals of the south, and the rich peltries of the north. While the fiery and magnificent Spaniard, inflamed with the mania for gold, has extended his discoveries and conquests over those brilliant countries scorched by the ardent sun of the tropics, the adroit and buoyant Frenchman and the cool and calculating Briton have pursued the less splendid, but no less lucrative, traffic in furs amidst the hyperborean regions of the Canadas, until they have advanced even within the Arctic circle.

These two pursuits have thus in a manner been the pioneers and precursors of civilization. Without pausing on the borders, they have penetrated at once, in defiance of difficulties and dangers, to the heart of savage continents: laying open the hidden secrets of the wilderness; leading the way to remote regions of beauty and fertility that might have remained unexplored for ages, and beckoning after them the slow and pausing steps of agriculture and colonization.

It was the fur trade, in fact, which gave early sustenance and vitality to the great Canadian provinces. Being destitute of the precious metals, at that time the leading object of American enterprize, they were long neglected by the parent country.

The French adventurers, however, who had settled on the banks of the S' Lawrence, soon found that in the rich peltries of the interior, they had sources of wealth that might almost rival the mines of Mexico and Peru. The Indians, as yet unacquainted with the artificial value given to some descriptions of furs, in civilized life, brought quantities of the most precious kinds and bartered them away for European trinkets and cheap commodities. Immense profits were thus made by the early traders, and the traffic was pursued with avidity.

As the valuable furs soon became scarce in the neighborhood of the settlements, the Indians of the vicinity were stimulated to take a wider range in their hunting expeditions; they were generally accompanied on these expeditions by some of the traders or their dependents, who shared in the toils and perils of the chase, and at the same time made themselves acquainted with the best hunting and trapping grounds, and with the remote tribes, whom they encouraged to bring their peltries to the settlements. In this way the trade augmented and was drawn from remote quarters to Montreal. Every now and then a large body of Ottawas, Hurons, and other tribes who hunted the countries bordering on the Great lakes, would come down in a squadron of light canoes, laden with beaver skins, and other spoils of their year's hunting. The canoes would be unladen, taken on shore, and their contents disposed in order. A camp of birch bark would be pitched outside of the town, and a kind of primitive fair opened with that grave ceremonial so dear to the Indians. An audience would be demanded of the Governor General, who would hold the conference with becoming state, seated in an elbow chair, with the Indians ranged in semicircles before him, seated on the ground and silently smoking their pipes. Speeches would be made, presents exchanged and the audience would break up in universal good humour.

Now would ensue a brisk traffic with the merchants, and all Montreal would be alive with naked Indians running from shop to shop bargaining for arms, kettles, knives, axes, blankets, bright colored cloths and other articles of use or fancy; upon all which, says an old French writer, the merchants were sure to clear at least two hundred per cent. There was no money used in this traffic, and, after a time, all payment in

spirituous liquors was prohibited, in consequence of the frantic and frightful excesses and bloody brawls which they were
apt to occasion.

Their wants and caprices being supplied, they would take
leave of the governor, strike their tents, launch their canoes,
and ply their way up the Ottawa to the lakes.

A new and anomalous class of men gradually grew out of
this trade. These were called *Coureurs des bois*, Rangers of the
woods; originally men who had accompanied the Indians in
their hunting expeditions and made themselves acquainted
with remote tracts and tribes, and who now became, as it
were, pedlars of the wilderness. These men would set out
from Montreal with canoes well stocked with goods, with
arms and ammunition, and would make their way up the
mazy and wandering rivers that interlace the vast forests of
the Canadas, coasting the most remote lakes, and creating
new wants and habitudes among the natives. Sometimes they
sojourned for months among them, assimilating to their tastes
and habits with the happy facility of Frenchmen; adopting in
some degree the Indian dress, and not unfrequently taking to
themselves Indian wives.

Twelve, fifteen, eighteen months would often elapse without any tidings of them, when they would come sweeping
their way down the Ottawa in full glee, their canoes laden
down with packs of beaver skins. Now came their time for
revelry and extravagance. "You would be amazed," says an
old writer already quoted, "if you saw how lewd these pedlars
are when they return; how they feast and game and how
prodigal they are not only in their clothes, but upon their
sweethearts. Such of them as are married have the wisdom to
retire to their own houses; but the bachelors act just as our
East India men and pirates are wont to do; for they lavish,
eat, drink, and play all away as long as the goods hold out;
and when these are gone, they e'en sell their embroidery,
their lace and their clothes. This done they are forced upon a
new voyage for subsistence."*

Many of these *Coureurs des bois* became so accustomed to
the Indian mode of living, and the perfect freedom of the

*La Hontan. V. 1. Let. 4.

wilderness, that they lost all relish for civilization, and identified themselves with the savages among whom they dwelt, or could only be distinguished from them by superior licentiousness. Their conduct and example gradually corrupted the natives, and impeded the works of the Catholic missionaries, who were at this time prosecuting their pious labors in the wilds of Canada.

To check these abuses, and to protect the fur trade from various irregularities practised by these loose adventurers, an order was issued by the French government prohibiting all persons, on pain of death, from trading into the interior of the country without a licence.

These licences were granted in writing by the Governor General, and at first were given only to persons of respectability; to gentlemen of broken fortunes; to old officers of the Army who had families to provide for; or to their widows. Each licence permitted the fitting out of two large canoes with merchandize for the lakes and no more than twenty five licences were to be issued in one year. By degrees, however, private licences were also granted and the number rapidly encreased. Those who did not choose to fit out the expeditions themselves, were permitted to sell them to the merchants; these employed the *Coureurs des bois*, or Rangers of the woods, to undertake the long voyages on shares, and thus the abuses of the old system were revived and continued.*

* The following are the terms on which these expeditions were commonly undertaken. The merchant holding the licence would fit out the two canoes with a thousand crowns worth of goods and put them under the conduct of six *Coureurs des bois*, to whom the goods were charged at the rate of fifteen per cent above the ready money price in the Colony. The *Coureurs des bois* in their turn dealt so sharply with the Savages, that they generally returned at the end of a year or so, with four canoes well laden, so as to ensure a clear profit of seven hundred per cent, insomuch that the thousand crowns invested produced eight thousand. Of this extravagant profit the merchant had the lion's share. In the first place he would set aside six hundred crowns for the cost of his licence; then a thousand crowns for the cost of the original merchandize. This would leave 6400 crowns from which he would take forty per cent for bottomry, amounting to 2560 crowns. The residue would be equally divided among the six wood rangers, who would thus receive little more than 600 crowns, for all their toils and perils.

The pious missionaries employed by the Roman Catholic church to convert the Indians, did every thing in their power to counteract the profligacy carried and propagated by these men in the heart of the wilderness. The Catholic chapel might often be seen planted beside the trading house, and its spire surmounted by a cross, towering from the midst of an Indian village on the banks of a river or a lake. The missions had often a beneficial effect on the simple sons of the forest, but had little power over the renegades from civilization.

At length it was found necessary to establish fortified posts at the confluence of the rivers and the lakes for the protection of the trade, and the restraint of these profligates of the wilderness. The most important of these was at Michilimackinac, situated at the strait of the same name, which connects Lakes Huron and Michigan. It became the great interior mart and place of deposit, and some of the regular merchants, who prosecuted the trade in person, under their licences, formed establishments here. This too was a rendezvous for the Rangers of the woods, as well those who came up with goods from Montreal as those who returned with peltries from the interior. Here new expeditions were fitted out and took their departure for Lake Michigan and the Mississippi; Lake Superior and the north west; and here the peltries brought in return were embarked for Montreal.

The French merchant at his trading post, in those primitive days of Canada, was a kind of commercial patriarch. With the lax habits and easy familiarity of his race, he had a little world of self indulgence and misrule around him. He had his clerks, canoemen and retainers of all kinds, who lived with him on terms of perfect sociability, always calling him by his christian name; he had his harem of Indian beauties, and his troop of halfbreed children; nor was there ever wanting a louting train of Indians, hanging about the establishment, eating and drinking at his expense in the intervals of their hunting expeditions.

The Canadian traders for a long time had troublesome competitors in the British merchants of New York, who inveigled the Indian hunters and the *Coureurs des bois*, to their posts, and traded with them on more favorable terms. A still more formidable opposition was organized in the Hudson's Bay Company, chartered by Charles II in 1670 with the exclusive

privilege of establishing trading houses on the shores of that
bay and its tributary rivers; a privilege which they have maintained to the present day. Between this British Company and
the French merchants of Canada feuds and contests arose
about alleged infringements of territorial limits, and acts of violence and bloodshed occurred between their agents.

In 1762 the French lost possession of Canada and the trade
fell principally into the hands of British subjects. For a time,
however, it shrunk within narrow limits. The old *Coureurs des
bois* were broken up and dispersed, or, where they could be
met with, were slow to accustom themselves to the habits and
manners of their British employers. They missed the freedom,
indulgence, and familiarity of the old French trading houses,
and did not relish the sober exactness, reserve and method of
the new comers. The British traders, too, were ignorant of the
country and distrustful of the natives. They had reason to be
so. The treacherous and bloody affairs of Detroit and Michilimackinac shewed them the lurking hostility cherished by the
Savages, who had too long been taught by the French to regard them as enemies.

It was not until the year 1766 that the trade regained its old
channels; but it was then pursued with avidity and emulation
by individual merchants, and soon transcended its former
bounds. Expeditions were fitted out by various persons from
Montreal and Michilimackinac and rivalships and jealousies of
course ensued. The trade was injured by their artifices to out-
bid and undermine each other; the Indians were debauched
by the sale of spirituous liquors, which had been prohibited
under the French rule. Scenes of drunkenness, brutality and
brawl were the consequence, in the Indian villages and
around the trading houses, while bloody feuds took place between rival trading parties when they happened to encounter
each other in the lawless depths of the wilderness.

To put an end to these sordid and ruinous contentions several of the principal merchants of Montreal entered into a
partnership in the winter of 1783, which was augmented by
amalgamation with a rival company in 1787. Thus was created
the famous "North West Company" which for a time held a
lordly sway over the wintry lakes and boundless forests of the
Canadas, almost equal to that of the East India Company

over the voluptuous climes and magnificent realms of the Orient.

The Company consisted of twenty three share holders, or partners, but held in its employ about two thousand persons as clerks, guides, interpreters and "voyageurs" or boatmen. These were distributed at various trading posts, established far and wide on the interior lakes and rivers, at immense distances from each other, and in the heart of trackless countries and savage tribes.

Several of the partners resided in Montreal and Quebec, to manage the main concerns of the Company. These were called agents, and were personages of great weight and importance; the other partners took their stations at the interior posts, where they remained throughout the winter, to superintend the intercourse with the various tribes of Indians. They were thence called wintering partners.

The goods destined for this wide and wandering traffic were put up at the warehouses of the Company in Montreal, and conveyed in batteaux, or boats, and canoes, up the river Attawa, or Ottawa, which falls into the S' Lawrence near Montreal, and by other rivers and portages to Lake Nipising, Lake Huron, Lake Superior, and thence by several chains of great and small lakes to Lake Winipeg, Lake Athabasca and the great Slave lake. This singular and beautiful system of internal seas which renders an immense region of wilderness so accessible to the frail bark of the Indian or the trader, was studded by the remote posts of the Company, where they carried on their traffic with the surrounding tribes.

The Company, as we have shown, was at first a spontaneous association of merchants; but, after it had been regularly organized, admission into it became extremely difficult. A candidate had to enter, as it were, "before the mast," to undergo a long probation, and to rise slowly by his merits and services. He began, at an early age, as a clerk, and served an apprenticeship of seven years, for which he received one hundred pounds sterling, was maintained at the expense of the Company, and furnished with suitable clothing and equipments. His probation was generally passed at the interior trading posts; removed for years from civilized society, leading a life almost as wild and precarious as the savages around him, exposed to the severities of a northern winter, often suffering from scarcity of food, and sometimes destitute for a long time of both bread and salt. When his apprenticeship had expired he received a salary according to his deserts, varying from eighty to one hundred and sixty pounds sterling, and was now eligible to the great object of his ambition, a partnership in the Company, though years might yet elapse before he attained to that enviable station.

Most of the clerks were young men of good families, from the highlands of Scotland, characterised by the perseverance, thrift and fidelity of their country and fitted by their native hardihood to encounter the rigorous climates of the north and to endure the trials and privations of their lot; though it must not be concealed that the constitutions of many of them became impaired, by the hardships of the wilderness, and their stomachs injured by occasional famishing, and especially by the want of bread and salt. Now and then, at an interval of years, they were permitted to come down on a visit to the establishment at Montreal, to recruit their health and to have a taste of civilized life; and these were brilliant spots in their existence.

As to the principal partners, or agents, who resided in Montreal and Quebec, they formed a kind of commercial aristocracy, living in lordly and hospitable style. Their early associations, when clerks at the remote trading posts, and the pleasures, dangers, adventures and mishaps which they had shared together in their wild wood life, had linked them heartily to each other, so that they formed a convivial fraternity. Few travellers that have visited Canada some thirty years since, in the days of the M'Tavishes, the MacGillivrays, the MacKenzies, the Frobishers and the other magnates of the north west, when the Company was in all its glory, but must remember the round of feasting and revelry kept up among these hyperborean nabobs.

Sometimes one or two partners recently from the interior posts, would make their appearance in New York, in the course of a tour of pleasure and curiosity. On these occasions there was always a degree of magnificence of the purse about them, and a peculiar propensity to expenditure at the goldsmiths and jewellers, for rings, chains, brooches, necklaces, jewelled watches, and other rich trinkets, partly for their own wear, partly for presents to their female acquaintances: a gorgeous prodigality, such as was often to be noticed in former times in Southern planters and West India creoles, when flush with the profits of their plantations.

To behold the North West Company in all its state and grandeur, however, it was necessary to witness an annual gathering at the great interior place of conference, established at Fort William, near what is called the Grand Portage, on Lake Superior. Here two or three of the leading partners from Montreal proceeded once a year, to meet the partners from the various trading posts of the wilderness, to discuss the affairs of the Company during the preceding year, and to arrange plans for the future.

On these occasions might be seen the change since the unceremonious times of the old French traders; now the aristocratical character of the Briton shone forth magnificently, or rather the feudal spirit of the highlander. Every partner who had charge of an interior post, and a score of retainers at his command, felt like the chieftain of a highland clan, and was almost as important in the eyes of his dependants as of himself. To him a visit to the grand conference at Fort William was a most important event; and he repaired there as to a meeting of parliament.

The partners from Montreal, however, were the lords of the ascendant; coming from the midst of luxurious and ostentatious life, they quite eclipsed their compeers from the woods, whose forms and faces had been battered and hardened by hard living and hard service, and whose garments and equipments were all the worse for wear. Indeed the partners from below considered the whole dignity of the Company as represented in their persons and conducted themselves in suitable style. They ascended the rivers in great state, like sovereigns making a progress: or rather like highland chieftains navigating their subject lakes. They were wrapped in rich furs, their huge canoes freighted with every convenience and luxury and manned by Canadian voyageurs, as obedient as highland clansmen. They carried up with them cooks, and bakers, together with delicacies of every kind, and abundance of choice wines for the banquets which attended this great convocation. Happy were they, too, if they could meet with some distinguished stranger, above all some titled member of the British nobility, to accompany them on this stately occasion, and grace their high solemnities.

Fort William, the scene of this important annual meeting, was a considerable village on the banks of Lake Superior. Here, in an immense wooden building, was the great Council Hall, as also the banqueting chamber, decorated with Indian arms and accoutrements and the trophies of the Fur trade. The house swarmed at this time, with traders and voyageurs, some from Montreal, bound to the interior posts; some from the interior posts, bound to Montreal. The councils were held in great state, for every member felt as if sitting in parliament, and every retainer and dependant looked up to the assemblage with awe, as to the House of Lords. There was a vast deal of solemn deliberation, and hard Scottish reasoning with an occasional swell of pompous declamation.

These grave and weighty councils were alternated by huge feasts and revels like some of the old feasts described in highland castles. The tables in the great banqueting room groaned under the weight of game of all kinds; of venison from the woods, and fish from the lakes, with hunters' delicacies, such as buffalo tongues and beavers' tails: and various luxuries from Montreal, all served up by experienced cooks brought for the purpose. There was no stint of generous wine, for it was a hard drinking period, a time of loyal toasts, and bacchanalian songs and brimming bumpers.

While the chiefs thus revelled in hall, and made the rafters resound with bursts of loyalty and old Scottish songs chaunted in voices cracked and sharpened by the northern blast, their merriment was echoed and prolonged by a mongrel legion of retainers; Canadian voyageurs, half breeds, Indian hunters and vagabond hangers on, who feasted sumptuously without on the crumbs that fell from their table and made the welkin ring with old French ditties, mingled with Indian yelps and yellings.

Such was the North West Company in its powerful and prosperous days, when it held a kind of feudal sway over a vast domain of lake and forest. We are dwelling too long, perhaps, upon these individual pictures, endeared to us by the associations of early life, when, as yet a stripling youth, we have sat at the hospitable boards of the "Mighty North Westers," then lords of the ascendant at Montreal, and gazed with wondering and inexperienced eye at their baronial wassailing, and listened with astonished ear to their tales of hardships and adventures. It is one object of our task, however, to present scenes of the rough life of the wilderness, and we are tempted to fix these few memorials of a transient state of things fast passing into oblivion;—for for the feudal state of Fort William is at an end; its council chamber is silent and deserted; its banquet hall no longer echoes to the burst of loyalty or the "auld world" ditty; the lords of the lakes and forests have passed away; and the hospitable magnates of Montreal—where are they!

Chapter II

*Rise of the Mackinaw Company—Attempts of the American
Government to counteract foreign influence over the Indian
tribes—John Jacob Astor—His birth place—His arrival in
the United States—What first turned his attention to the Fur
trade—His character, enterprizes and success—His communications with the American Government—Origin of the
American Fur Company.*

THE SUCCESS of the North West Company stimulated further enterprize in this opening and apparently boundless
field of profit. The traffic of that company lay principally in
the high northern latitudes, while there were immense regions to the south and west known to abound with valuable
peltries, but which as yet had been but little explored by the
fur trader. A new association of British merchants was therefore formed, to prosecute the trade in this direction. The
chief factory was established at the old emporium of Michilimackinac, from which place the association took its name;
and was commonly called the Mackinaw Company.

While the North Westers continued to push their enterprizes into the hyperborean regions from their strong hold at
Fort William, and to hold almost sovereign sway over the
tribes of the upper lakes and rivers; the Mackinaw Company
sent forth their light pirogues and barks, by Green bay, Fox
River, and the Wisconsin, to that great artery of the West, the
Mississippi; and down that stream to all its tributary rivers. In
this way they hoped soon to monopolize the trade with all the
tribes on the southern and western waters, and of those vast
tracts comprized in ancient Louisiana.

The Government of the United States began to view with
a wary eye the growing influence, thus acquired by combinations of foreigners, over the aboriginal tribes inhabiting its
territories, and endeavored to counteract it. For this purpose,
as early as 1796, the government sent out agents to establish
rival trading houses on the frontiers, so as to supply the wants
of the Indians; to link their interests and feelings with those
of the people of the United States, and to divert this important branch of trade into national channels.

The expedient, however, was unsuccessful; as most commercial expedients are prone to be, where the dull patronage of government is counted upon to outvie the keen activity of private enterprize. What Government failed to effect, however, with all its patronage and all its agents, was at length brought about by the enterprize and perseverance of a single merchant, one of its adopted citizens; and this brings us to speak of the individual whose enterprize is the especial subject of the following pages; a man whose name and character are worthy of being enrolled in the history of Commerce, as illustrating its noblest aims and soundest maxims. A few brief anecdotes of his early life and of the circumstances which first determined him to the branch of Commerce of which we are treating cannot but be interesting.

John Jacob Astor, the individual in question, was born in the honest little German village of Waldorf near Heidelberg, on the banks of the Rhine. He was brought up in the simplicity of rural life, but, while yet a mere stripling, left his home and launched himself amid the busy scenes of London, having had, from his very boyhood, a singular presentiment that he would ultimately arrive at great fortune.

At the close of the American Revolution he was still in London and scarce on the threshold of active life. An elder brother had been for some few years resident in the United States, and Mr. Astor determined to follow him and to seek his fortunes in the rising country. Investing a small sum which he had amassed since leaving his native village, in merchandize suited to the American market, he embarked, in the month of November 1783 in a ship bound to Baltimore, and arrived in Hampton Roads in the month of January. The winter was extremely severe, and the ship, with many others, was detained by the ice in and about Chesapeak bay for nearly three months.

During this period the passengers of the various ships used occasionally to go on shore, and mingle sociably together. In this way Mr. Astor became acquainted with a countryman of his, a furrier by trade. Having had a previous impression that this might be a lucrative trade in the new world he made many enquiries of his new acquaintance on the subject, who cheerfully gave him all the information in his power as to the quality and value of different furs, and the mode of carrying on the traffic. He subsequently accompanied him to New York, and by his advice Mr. Astor was induced to invest the proceeds of his merchandize in furs. With these he sailed from New York to London in 1784, disposed of them advantageously, made himself further acquainted with the course of the trade and returned the same year to New York, with a view to settle in the United States.

He now devoted himself to the branch of Commerce with which he had thus casually been made acquainted. He began his career, of course, on the narrowest scale, but he brought to the task a persevering industry, rigid economy and strict integrity. To these were added an aspiring spirit that always looked upward, a genius bold, fertile and expansive, a sagacity quick to grasp and convert every circumstance to its advantage, and a singular and never wavering confidence of signal success.*

As yet trade in peltries was not organized in the United States, and could not be said to form a regular line of business. Furs and skins were casually collected by the country traders in their dealings with the Indians or the white hunters, but the main supply was derived from Canada. As Mr. Astor's means encreased he made annual visits to Montreal, where he purchased furs from the houses at that place engaged in the trade. These he shipped from Canada to London, no direct trade being allowed from that colony to any but the mother country.

In 1794 or 5 a treaty with Great Britain removed the restrictions imposed upon the trade with the Colonies and opened a direct commercial intercourse between Canada and the United States. Mr. Astor was in London at the time and immediately made a contract with the agents of the North West Company for furs. He was now enabled to import them

* An instance of this buoyant confidence, which no doubt aided to produce the success it anticipated, we have from the lips of Mr. A. himself. While yet almost a stranger in the city, and in very narrow circumstances, he passed by where a row of houses had just been erected in Broad way, and which from the superior style of their architecture, were the talk and boast of the city. "I'll build, one day or other, a greater house than any of these, in this very street" said he to himself. He has accomplished his prediction.

from Montreal into the United States for the home supply, and to be shipped thence to different parts of Europe, as well as to China, which has ever been the best market for the richest and finest kinds of peltry.

The treaty in question provided, likewise, that the military posts occupied by the British within the territorial limits of the United States should be surrendered. Accordingly Oswego, Niagara, Detroit, Michilimackinac and other posts on the American sides of the lakes were given up. An opening was thus made for the American merchant to trade on the confines of Canada, and within the territories of the United States. After an interval of some years, about 1807, Mr. Astor embarked in this trade on his own account. His capital and resources had by this time greatly augmented, and he had risen from small beginnings to take his place among the first merchants and financiers of the country. His genius had ever been in advance of his circumstances prompting him to new and wider fields of enterprize beyond the scope of ordinary merchants. With all his enterprize and resources, however, he soon found the power and influence of the Michilimackinac (or Mackinaw) Company too great for him, having engrossed most of the trade within the American borders.

A plan had to be devised to enable him to enter into successful competition. He was aware of the wish of the American Government, already stated, that the fur trade within its boundaries should be in the hands of American citizens, and of the ineffectual measures it had taken to accomplish that object. He now offered, if aided and protected by government, to turn the whole of that trade, into American channels. He was invited to unfold his plans to Government, and they were warmly approved, though the Executive could give no direct aid.

Thus countenanced, however, he obtained in 1809, a charter from the legislature of the state of New York, incorporating a company under the name of "The American Fur Company" with a capital of One Million of Dollars, with the privilege of encreasing it to Two millions. The capital was furnished by himself; he, in fact, constituted the Company; for though he had a board of directors, they were merely nominal; the whole business was conducted on his plans, and with his resources, but he preferred to do so under the imposing and formidable aspect of a corporation, rather than in his individual name; and his policy was sagacious and effective.

As the Mackinaw Company still continued its rivalry, and as the fur trade would not advantageously admit of competition, he made a new arrangement in 1811 by which, in conjunction with certain partners of the North West Company, and other persons engaged in the Fur trade, he bought out the Mackinaw Company, and merged that and the American Fur Company into a new association, to be called "The South West Company." This he likewise did with the privity and approbation of the American government.

By this arrangement Mr. Astor became proprietor of one half of the Indian establishments and goods which the Mackinaw Company had within the territory of the Indian country in the United States, and it was understood that the whole was to be surrendered into his hands at the expiration of five years, on condition that the American company would not trade within the British dominions.

Unluckily the war which broke out in 1812 between Great Britain and the United States suspended the association; and, after the war, it was entirely dissolved: Congress having passed a law prohibiting British fur traders from prosecuting their enterprizes within the territories of the United States.

Chapter III

Fur trade in the Pacific—American coasting voyages—Russian enterprizes—Discovery of the Columbia River—Carver's project to found a settlement there—MacKenzie's expedition —Lewis and Clarke's journey across the Rocky Mountains— Mr. Astor's grand commercial scheme—His correspondence on the subject with Mr. Jefferson—His negotiations with the North West Company—His steps to carry his scheme into effect.

WHILE the various companies we have noticed were pushing their enterprizes far and wide in the wilds of Canada, and along the course of the great western waters, other adventurers, intent on the same objects, were traversing the watery wastes of the Pacific and skirting the North West Coast of America. The last voyage of that renowned but unfortunate discoverer, Captain Cook, had made known the vast quantities of the sea otter to be found along that coast, and the immense prices to be obtained for its fur in China. It was as if a new gold coast had been discovered. Individuals from various countries dashed into this lucrative traffic, so that in the year 1792 there were twenty one vessels under different flags, playing along the coast and trading with the natives. The greater part of them were American and owned by Boston merchants. They generally remained on the coast, and about the adjacent seas for two years, carrying on as wandering and adventurous a commerce on the water as did the traders and trappers on land.

Their trade extended along the whole coast from California to the high northern latitudes. They would run in near shore, anchor, and wait for the natives to come off in their canoes with peltries. The trade exhausted at one place, they would up anchor and off to another. In this way they would consume the summer and when autumn came on, would run down to the Sandwich islands and winter in some friendly and plentiful harbour. In the following year they would resume their summer trade, commencing at California and proceeding north; and, having in the course of the two seasons, collected a sufficient cargo of peltries, would make the best of their way to China. Here they would sell their furs, take in teas, nankeens and other merchandize, and return to Boston after an absence of two or three years.

The people however who entered most extensively and effectively in the fur trade of the Pacific were the Russians. Instead of making casual voyages, in transient ships, they established regular trading houses in the high latitudes, along the North West Coast of America and upon the chain of the Aleutian islands between Kamtschatka and the promontory of Alaska.

To promote and protect these enterprizes a company was incorporated by the Russian Government with exclusive privileges and a capital of two hundred and sixty thousand pounds sterling; and the sovereignty of that part of the American continent, along the coast of which the posts had been established, was claimed by the Russian crown, on the plea that the land had been discovered and occupied by its subjects.

As China was the grand mart for the furs collected in these quarters the Russians had the advantage over their competitors in the trade. The latter had to take their peltries to Canton, which, however, was a mere receiving mart, from whence they had to be distributed over the interior of the empire and sent to the northern parts, where there was the chief consumption. The Russians, on the contrary, carried their furs, by a shorter voyage, directly to the northern parts of the Chinese Empire, thus being able to afford them in the market without the additional cost of internal transportation.

We now come to the immediate field of operation of the great enterprize we have undertaken to illustrate.

Among the American ships which traded along the North West Coast in 1792 was the Columbia, Captain Gray, of Boston. In the course of her voyage she discovered the mouth of a large river in Lat. 46° 19′ north. Entering it with some difficulty, on account of sand bars and breakers, she came to anchor in a spacious bay. A boat was well manned, and sent on shore to a village on the beach, but all the inhabitants fled excepting the aged and infirm. The kind manner in which these were treated and the presents given to them gradually lured back the others, and a friendly intercourse took place.

They had never seen a ship or a white man. When they had first described the Columbia they had supposed it a floating island; then some monster of the deep; but when they saw the boat putting for shore, with human beings on board, they considered them cannibals sent by the great Spirit to ravage the country and devour the inhabitants.

Captain Gray did not ascend the river farther than the bay in question, which continues to bear his name. After putting to sea he fell in with the celebrated discoverer Vancouver, and informed him of his discovery, furnishing him with a chart which he had made of the river. Vancouver visited the river, and his Lieutenant Broughton explored it by the aid of Captain Gray's chart; ascending it upwards of one hundred miles, until within view of a snowy mountain to which he gave the name of Mount Hood, which it still retains.

The existence of this river, however, was known long before the visits of Gray and Vancouver, but the information concerning it was vague and indefinite, being gathered from the reports of Indians. It was spoken of by travellers as The Oregon and as the great River of the West. A Spanish ship is said to have been wrecked at its mouth, several of the crew of which lived for some time among the natives. The Columbia, however, is believed to be the first ship that made a regular discovery and anchored within its waters, and it has since generally borne the name of that vessel.

As early as 1763, shortly after the acquisition of the Canadas by Great Britain, Captain Jonathan Carver, who had been in the British provincial army, projected a journey across the continent between the forty third and forty sixth degrees of northern latitude, to the shores of the Pacific Ocean. His objects were to ascertain the breadth of the continent at its broadest part, and to determine on some place on the shores of the Pacific, where government might establish a post to facilitate the discovery of a northwest passage, or a communication between Hudson's Bay and the Pacific Ocean. This place he presumed would be somewhere about the Straits of Annian, at which point he supposed the Oregon disembogued itself. It was his opinion, also, that a settlement on this extremity of America would disclose new sources of trade, promote many useful discoveries, and open a more direct

communication with China and the English settlements in the
East Indies, than that by the Cape of Good Hope or the
Straits of Magellan.*

This enterprizing and intrepid traveller was twice baffled in
individual efforts to accomplish this great journey. In 1774 he
was joined in the scheme by Richard Whitworth, a member of
Parliament, and a man of wealth. Their enterprize was projected on a broad and bold plan. They were to take with them
fifty or sixty men, artificers and mariners. With these they
were to make their way up one of the branches of the Missouri, explore the mountains for the source of the Oregon or
River of the West, and sail down that river to its supposed exit
near the Straits of Annian. Here they were to erect a fort, and
build the vessels necessary to carry their discoveries by sea
into effect. Their plan had the sanction of the British government, and grants and other requisites were nearly completed,
when the breaking out of the American revolution once more
defeated the undertaking.†

The expedition of Sir Alexander MacKenzie in 1793 across
the continent to the Pacific Ocean which he reached in
Lat. 52° 20′ 48″ again suggested the possibility of linking
together the trade of both sides of the continent. In Lat. 52°
30′ he had descended a river for some distance which flowed
toward the south and was called by the natives Tacoutche
Tesse, and which he erroneously supposed to be the Columbia. It was afterwards ascertained that it emptied itself in Lat.
49°, whereas the mouth of the Columbia is about three degrees further south.

When MacKenzie some years subsequently published an account of his expeditions he suggested the policy of opening
an intercourse between the Atlantic and Pacific oceans, and
forming regular establishments through the interior and at
both extremes as well as along the coasts and islands. By this
means, he observed, the entire command of the Fur trade of
North America might be obtained from Latitude 48° north,
to the pole, excepting that portion held by the Russians, for
as to the American adventurers who had hitherto enjoyed the

* Carver's Travels. Introd. p. iii. Phila. 1796.
† Carver's Travels. P. 360. Phila. 1796.

traffic along the North West Coast, they would instantly disappear, he added, before a well regulated trade.

A scheme of this kind, however, was too vast and hazardous for individual enterprize; it could only be undertaken by a company, under the sanction and protection of a government: and as there might be a clashing of claims between the Hudson's Bay and North West companies, the one holding by right of charter, the other by right of possession, he proposed that the two companies should coalesce in this great undertaking. The long cherished jealousies of these two companies, however, were too deep and strong to allow them to listen to such council.

In the mean time the attention of the American Government was attracted to the subject and the memorable expedition under Messrs. Lewis and Clark fitted out. These gentlemen, in 1804, accomplished the enterprize which had been projected by Carver and Whitworth in 1774. They ascended the Missouri, passed through the stupendous gates of the Rocky Mountains, hitherto unknown to white man; discovered and explored the upper waters of the Columbia, and followed that river down to its mouth, where their countryman Gray had anchored about twelve years previously. Here they passed the winter and returned across the Mountains in the following spring. The reports published by them of their expedition, demonstrated the practicability of establishing a line of communication across the continent from the Atlantic to the Pacific ocean.

It was then that the idea presented itself to the mind of Mr. Astor of grasping with his individual hand, this great enterprize, which for years had been dubiously yet desirously contemplated by powerful associations and national governments. For some time he revolved the idea in his mind, gradually extending and maturing his plans as his means of executing them augmented. The main feature of his scheme was to establish a line of trading posts along the Missouri and the Columbia, to the mouth of the latter: where was to be founded the chief trading house or mart. Inferior posts would be established in the interior, and on all the tributary streams of the Columbia, to trade with the Indians; these posts would draw their supplies from the main establishment and bring to it the peltries they collected. Coasting craft would be built and fitted out, also, at the mouth of the Columbia, to trade, at favorable seasons, all along the north west coast, and return with the proceeds of their voyages, to this place of deposit. Thus all the Indian trade, both of the interior and the coast, would converge to this point, and thence derive its sustenance.

A ship was to be sent annually from New York to this main establishment with reinforcements and supplies, and with merchandize suited to the trade. It would take on board the furs collected during the preceding year, carry them to Canton, invest the proceeds in the rich merchandize of China, and return thus freighted to New York.

As, in extending the American trade along the coast to the northward, it might be brought into the vicinity of the Russian Fur Company, and produce a hostile rivalry, it was part of the plan of Mr. Astor to conciliate the good will of that company by the most amicable and beneficial arrangements. The Russian establishment was chiefly dependent for its supplies upon transient trading vessels from the United States. These vessels, however, were often of more harm than advantage. Being owned by private adventurers on casual voyages who cared only for present profit and had no interest in the permanent prosperity of the trade, they were reckless in their dealings with the natives, and made no scruple of supplying them with fire arms. In this way several fierce tribes in the vicinity of the Russian posts, or within the range of their trading excursions, were furnished with deadly means of warfare, and rendered troublesome and dangerous neighbors.

The Russian government had made representations to that of the United States of these malpractices on the part of its citizens, and urged to have this traffic in arms prohibited; but, as it did not infringe any municipal law, our government could not interfere. Still it regarded, with solicitude, a traffic which, if persisted in, might give offense to Russia, at that time almost the only power friendly to us. In this dilemma the government had applied to Mr. Astor, as one conversant in this branch of trade, for information that might point out a way to remedy the evil. This circumstance had suggested to him the idea of supplying the Russian establishment regularly by means of the annual ship that should visit the settlement at the mouth of the Columbia (or Oregon); by this means the casual trading vessels would be excluded from those parts of the coast, where their malpractices were so injurious to the Russians.

Such is a brief outline of the enterprize projected by Mr. Astor, but which continually expanded in his mind. Indeed it is due to him to say that he was not actuated by mere motives of individual profit. He was already wealthy beyond the ordinary desires of man, but he now aspired to that honorable fame which is awarded to men of similar scope of mind, who by their great commercial enterprizes have enriched nations, peopled wildernesses and extended the bounds of empire. He considered his projected establishment at the mouth of the Columbia as the emporium to an immense commerce; as a colony that would form the germ of a wide civilization; that would, in fact, carry the American population across the Rocky Mountains and spread it along the shores of the Pacific, as it already animated the shores of the Atlantic.

As Mr. Astor by the magnitude of his commercial and financial relations, and the vigour and scope of his self taught mind, had elevated himself into the consideration of Government and the communion and correspondence with leading statesmen, he, at an early period, communicated his schemes to President Jefferson, soliciting the countenance of Government. How highly they were esteemed by that eminent man we may judge by the following passage written by him some time afterwards, to Mr. Astor.

"I remember well having invited your proposition on this subject,* and encouraged it with the assurance of every facility and protection which the Government could properly afford. I considered as a great public acquisition the commencement of a settlement on that point of the Western Coast of America, and looked forward with gratification to the time when its descendants should have spread themselves thro' the whole length of that coast, covering it with free and independent Americans, unconnected with us but by the ties

---

* On this point Mr. Jefferson's memory was in error. The proposition alluded to was the one, already mentioned, for the establishment of an American Fur Company in the Atlantic states. The great enterprize beyond the Mountains, that was to sweep the shores of the Pacific, originated in the mind of Mr. Astor, and was proposed by him to the Government.

of blood and interest, and enjoying like us the rights of self government."

The cabinet joined with Mr. Jefferson in warm approbation of the plan, and held out assurance of every protection that could, consistently with general policy, be afforded.

Mr. Astor now prepared to carry his scheme into prompt execution. He had some competition however to apprehend and guard against. The North West Company, acting feebly and partially upon the suggestions of its former agent Sir Alexander MacKenzie, had pushed one or two advanced trading posts across the Rocky Mountains, into a tract of country visited by that enterprizing traveller, and since named New Caledonia. This tract lay about two degrees north of the Columbia, and intervened between the territories of the United States and those of Russia. Its length was about 550 miles and its breadth from the Mountains to the Pacific, from 300 to 350 geographical miles.

Should the North West Company persist in extending their trade in that quarter their competition might be of serious detriment to the plans of Mr. Astor. It is true they would contend with him to a vast disadvantage, from the checks and restrictions to which they were subjected. They were straitened on one side by the rivalry of the Hudson's Bay Company. Then they had no good port on the Pacific where they could receive supplies by sea for their establishments beyond the mountains; nor, if they had one, could they ship their furs thence to China, that great mart for peltries; the Chinese trade being comprized in the monopoly of the East India Company. Their posts beyond the mountains had to be supplied, in yearly expeditions, like caravans, from Montreal, and the furs conveyed back in the same way, by long, precarious and expensive routes across the continent. Mr. Astor, on the contrary, would be able to supply his proposed establishment at the mouth of the Columbia by sea, and to ship the furs collected there directly to China, so as to undersell the North West Company in the great Chinese market.

Still the competition of two rival companies west of the Rocky Mountains could not but prove detrimental to both, and fraught with those evils, both to the trade and to the Indians, that had attended similar rivalries in the Canadas. To prevent any contest of the kind, therefore, he made known his plan to the agents of the North West Company, and proposed to interest them, to the extent of one third, in the trade thus to be opened.

Some correspondence and negotiation ensued; the Company were aware of the advantages which would be possessed by Mr. Astor should he be able to carry his scheme into effect; but they anticipated a monopoly of the trade beyond the mountains, by their establishments in New Caledonia, and were loth to share it with an individual who had already proved a formidable competitor in the Atlantic trade. They hoped, too, by a timely move, to secure the mouth of the Columbia before Mr. Astor would be able to put his plans into operation, and, that key to the internal trade once in their possession, the whole country would be at their command. After some negotiation and delay, therefore, they declined the proposition that had been made to them; but subsequently despatched a party for the mouth of the Columbia, to establish a post there, before any expedition sent out by Mr. Astor might arrive.

In the mean time Mr. Astor, finding his overtures rejected, proceeded fearlessly to execute his enterprize in face of the whole power of the North West Company. His main establishment once planted at the mouth of the Columbia, he looked with confidence to ultimate success. Being able to reinforce and supply it amply by sea, he would push his interior posts in every direction up the rivers and along the coast; supplying the natives at a lower rate, and thus gradually obliging the North West Company to give up the competition, relinquish New Caledonia, and retire to the other side of the mountains. He would then have possession of the trade, not merely of the Columbia and its tributaries, but of the regions farther north, quite to the Russian possessions. Such was a part of his brilliant and comprehensive plan.

He now proceeded, with all diligence, to procure proper agents and coadjutors, habituated to the Indian trade and to the life of the wilderness. Among the clerks of the North West Company were several of great capacity and experience, who had served out their probationary terms, but who, either through lack of interest and influence, or a want of vacancies, had not been promoted. They were consequently much dissatisfied, and ready for any employment in which their talents and acquirements might be turned to better account.

Mr. Astor made his overtures to several of these persons and three of them entered into his views. One of these, Mr. Alexander M'Kay, had accompanied Sir Alexander MacKenzie in both of his expeditions to the North West Coast of America in 1789 and 1793. The other two were Duncan M'Dougall and Donald M'Kenzie. To these was subsequently added Mr. Wilson Price Hunt of New Jersey. As this gentleman was a native born citizen of the United States, and a person of great probity and worth, he was selected by Mr. Astor to be his chief agent and to represent him in the contemplated establishment.

On the 23d of June 1810 articles of agreement were entered into between Mr. Astor and those four gentlemen, acting for themselves and for the several persons who had already agreed to become, or should thereafter become, associated under the firm of The Pacific Fur Company.

According to these articles Mr. Astor was to be at the head of the Company and to manage its affairs in New York. He was to furnish vessels, goods, provisions, arms, ammunition and all other requisites for the enterprize at first cost and charges, provided that they did not, at any time, involve an advance of more than four hundred thousand dollars.

The stock of the Company was to be divided into a hundred equal shares with the profits accruing thereon. Fifty shares were to be at the disposition of Mr. Astor, and the other fifty to be divided among the partners and their associates.

Mr. Astor was to have the privilege of introducing other persons into the connexion, as partners, two of whom, at least, should be conversant with the Indian trade and none of them entitled to more than three shares.

A general meeting of the Company was to be held annually at Columbia River, for the investigation and regulation of its affairs; at which absent members might be represented and might vote by proxy under certain specified conditions.

The association, if successful, was to continue for twenty years; but the parties had full power to abandon and dissolve it within the first five years, should it be found unprofitable.

For this term Mr. Astor covenanted to bear all the loss that might be incurred; after which it was to be borne by all the partners in proportion to their respective shares.

The parties of the second part were to execute faithfully such duties as might be assigned to them by a majority of the Company on the North West Coast, and to repair to such place or places as the majority might direct.

An agent, appointed for the term of five years, was to reside at the principal establishment on the North West Coast, and Wilson Price Hunt was the one chosen for the first term. Should the interests of the concern at any time require his absence, a person was to be appointed, in general meeting, to take his place.

Such were the leading conditions of this association; we shall now proceed to relate the various hardy and eventful expeditions, by sea and land, to which it gave rise.

Chapter IV

Two expeditions set on foot—The Tonquin and her crew—
Captain Thorn, his character—The partners and clerks—
Canadian voyageurs, their habits, employments, dress,
character, songs—Expedition of a Canadian boat and its
crew by land and water—Arrival at New York—Prepara-
tions for a sea voyage—North West braggarts—Under hand
precautions—Letter of instructions.

IN PROSECUTING his great scheme of commerce and colonization, two expeditions were devised by Mr. Astor, one
by sea, the other by land. The former was to carry out the
people, stores, ammunition and merchandize requisite for establishing a fortified trading post at the mouth of Columbia
River. The latter, conducted by Mr. Hunt, was to proceed up
the Missouri and across the Rocky Mountains, to the same
point, exploring a line of communication across the continent, and noting the places where interior trading posts might
be established. The expedition by sea is the one which comes
first under consideration.

A fine ship was provided called the Tonquin, of two hundred
and ninety tons burthen, mounting ten guns, with a crew of
twenty men. She carried an assortment of merchandize for
trading with the natives of the sea board and of the interior, together with the frame of a schooner to be employed in the
coasting trade. Seeds also were provided for the cultivation of
the soil, and nothing was neglected for the necessary supply of
the establishment. The command of the ship was entrusted to
Jonathan Thorn, of New York, a lieutenant in the United
States Navy, on leave of absence. He was a man of courage and
firmness who had distinguished himself in our Tripolitan war,
and from being accustomed to naval discipline was considered
by Mr. Astor as well fitted to take charge of an expedition of
the kind. Four of the partners were to embark in the ship,
namely, Messrs. M'Kay, M'Dougall, David Stuart, and his
nephew Robert Stuart. Mr. M'Dougall was empowered by
Mr. Astor to act as his proxy in the absence of Mr. Hunt, to

vote for him and in his name, on any question that might come before any meeting of the persons interested in the voyage.

Beside the partners there were twelve clerks to go out in the ship, several of them natives of Canada, who had some experience in Indian trade. They were bound to the service of the company for five years at the rate of one hundred dollars a year, payable at the expiration of the term, and an annual equipment of clothing to the amount of forty dollars. In case of ill conduct they were liable to forfeit their wages and be dismissed; but, should they acquit themselves well, the confident expectation was held out to them of promotion, and partnership. Their interests were thus, to some extent, identified with those of the Company.

Several artizans were likewise to sail in the ship, for the supply of the colony; but the most peculiar and characteristic part of this motley embarcation consisted of thirteen Canadian "voyageurs," who had enlisted for five years. As this class of functionaries will continually recur in the course of the following narrations and as they form one of those distinct and strongly marked castes or orders of people, springing up in this vast continent, out of geographical circumstances, or the varied pursuits, habitudes and origins of its population, we shall sketch a few of their characteristics for the information of the reader.

The "voyageurs" form a kind of confraternity in the Canadas, like the Arrieros, or Carriers of Spain, and like them are employed in long internal expeditions of travel and traffic: with this difference that the Arrieros travel by land, the voyageurs by water; the former with mules and horses, the latter with batteaux and canoes. The voyageurs may be said to have sprung up out of the Fur trade, having originally been employed by the early French merchants in their trading expeditions through the labyrinth of rivers and lakes of the boundless interior. They were coeval with the "*Coureurs des bois*" or Rangers of the woods, already noticed, and like them, in the intervals of their long, arduous and laborious expeditions, were prone to pass their time in idleness and revelry about the trading posts or settlements; squandering their hard earnings in heedless conviviality, and rivalling their neighbors the

Indians in indolent indulgence and an imprudent disregard of the morrow.

When Canada passed under British domination, and the old French trading houses were broken up, the voyageurs, like the *Coureurs des bois*, were for a time disheartened and disconsolate, and with difficulty could reconcile themselves to the service of the new comers, so different in habits, manners and language from their former employers. By degrees, however, they became accustomed to the change, and at length came to consider the British fur traders and especially the members of the North West Company, as the legitimate lords of creation.

The dress of these people is generally half civilized half savage. They wear a capot or surcoat, made of a blanket, a striped cotton shirt, cloth trowsers, or leathern leggings, moccasins of deer skin and a belt of variegated worsted, from which are suspended the knife, tobacco pouch and other implements. Their language is of the same pyebald character, being a French patois, embroidered with Indian and English words and phrases.

The lives of the voyageurs are passed in wild and extensive rovings, in the service of individuals, but more especially of the Fur traders. They are generally of French descent, and inherit much of the gaiety and lightness of heart of their ancestors, being full of anecdote and song and ever ready for the dance. They inherit, too, a fund of civility and complaisance; and instead of that hardness and grossness which men in laborious life are apt to indulge towards each other, they are mutually obliging and accommodating; interchanging kind offices, yielding each other assistance and comfort in every emergency, and using the familiar appellations of "cousin" and "brother," when there is in fact no relationship. Their natural good will is probably heightened by a community of adventure and hardship in their precarious and wandering life.

No men are more submissive to their leaders and employers, more capable of enduring hardship, or more good humoured under privations. Never are they so happy as when on long and rough expeditions, toiling up rivers or coasting lakes; encamping at night on the borders, gossipping round their fires, and bivouacking in the open air. They are dextrous boatmen, vigorous and adroit with the oar and paddle, and will row from morning until night without a murmur. The steersman often sings an old traditionary French song, with some regular burden in which they all join, keeping time with their oars; if at any time they flag in spirits or relax in exertion, it is but necessary to strike up a song of the kind to put them all in fresh spirits and activity. The Canadian waters are vocal with these little French chansons, that have been echoed from mouth to mouth and transmitted from father to son, from the earliest days of the Colony; and it has a pleasing effect, in a still golden summer evening, to see a batteau gliding across the bosom of a lake and dipping its oars to the cadence of these quaint old ditties, or sweeping along, in full chorus on a bright sunny morning, down the transparent current of one of the Canada rivers.

But we are talking of things that are fast fading away! The march of mechanical invention is driving every thing poetical before it. The steamboats which are fast dispelling the wildness and romance of our lakes and rivers and aiding to subdue the world into commonplace, are proving as fatal to the race of the Canadian voyageurs as they have been to that of the boatmen of the Mississippi. Their glory is departed. They are no longer the lords of our internal seas and the great navigators of the wilderness. Some of them may still occasionally be seen coasting the lower lakes with their frail barks and pitching their camps and lighting their fires upon the shores; but their range is fast contracting to those remote waters and shallow and obstructed rivers unvisited by the steamboat. In the course of years they will gradually disappear: their songs will die away like the echoes they once awakened, and the Canadian voyageurs will become a forgotten race, or remembered, like their associates the Indians, among the poetical images of past times, and as themes for local and romantic associations.

An instance of the buoyant temperament and the professional pride of these people was furnished in the gay and braggart style in which they arrived at New York to join the enterprize. They were determined to regale and astonish the people of the "States" with the sight of a Canadian boat and a Canadian crew. They accordingly fitted up a large but light bark canoe, such as is used in the fur trade; transported it in

a waggon from the banks of the S' Lawrence to the shores of
Lake Champlain; traversed the lake in it, from end to end;
hoisted it again on a waggon and wheeled it off to Lansing-
burgh and there launched it upon the waters of the Hudson.
Down this river they plied their course merrily on a fine summer's day, making its banks resound for the first time with
their old French boat songs; passing by the villages with
whoop and halloo, so as to make the honest Dutch farmers
mistake them for a crew of savages. In this way they swept, in
full song, and with regular flourish of the paddle, round New
York, in a still summer evening, to the wonder and admiration
of its inhabitants, who had never before witnessed on their
waters, a nautical apparition of the kind.

Such was the variegated band of adventurers about to embark in the Tonquin on this arduous and doubtful enterprize.
While yet in port and on dry land, in the bustle of preparation
and the excitement of novelty, all was sunshine and promise.
The Canadians especially, who, with their constitutional vivacity, have a considerable dash of the Gascon, were buoyant
and boastful and great braggarts as to the future; while all
those who had been in the service of the North West Company, and engaged in the Indian trade, plumed themselves
upon their hardihood and their capacity to endure privations.
If Mr. Astor ventured to hint at the difficulties they might
have to encounter, they treated them with scorn. They were
"north westers," men seasoned to hardships, who cared for
neither wind nor weather. They could live hard, lie hard, sleep
hard, eat dogs!—in a word they were ready to do and suffer
any thing for the good of the enterprize. With all this profession of zeal and devotion, Mr. Astor was not over confident
of the stability and firm faith of these mercurial beings. He
had received information, also, that an armed brig from
Halifax, probably at the instigation of the North West Company, was hovering on the coast, watching for the Tonquin,
with the purpose of impressing the Canadians on board of
her, as British subjects, and thus interrupting the voyage. It
was a time of doubt and anxiety, when the relations between
the United States and Great Britain were daily assuming a
more precarious aspect, and verging towards that war which
shortly ensued. As a precautionary measure, therefore, he re-

quired that the voyageurs, as they were about to enter into the service of an American Association, and to reside within the limits of the United States, should take the oaths of naturalization, as American citizens. To this they readily agreed, and shortly afterward assured him that they had actually done so. It was not until after they had sailed that he discovered that they had entirely deceived him in the matter.

The confidence of Mr. Astor was abused in another quarter. Two of the partners, both of them Scotchmen, and recently in the service of the North West Company, had misgivings as to an enterprize which might clash with the interests and establishments protected by the British flag. They privately waited upon the British Minister, Mr. Jackson, then in New York, laid open to him the whole scheme of Mr. Astor, though entrusted to them in confidence, and dependent, in a great measure, upon secrecy at the outset for its success, and enquired whether they, as British subjects, could lawfully engage in it. The reply satisfied their scruples, while the information they imparted excited the surprize and admiration of Mr. Jackson, that a private individual should have conceived and set on foot at his own risk and expense, so great an enterprize.

This step on the part of those gentlemen was not known to Mr. Astor until sometime afterwards or it might have modified the trust and confidence reposed in them.

To guard against any interruption to the voyage by the armed brig said to be off the harbour, Mr. Astor applied to Commodore Rogers, at that time commanding at New York, to give the Tonquin safe convoy off the coast. The Commodore having received from a high official source assurance of the deep interest which the government took in the enterprize, sent directions to Captain Hull, at that time cruizing off the harbour, in the Frigate Constitution, to afford the Tonquin the required protection when she should put to sea.

Before the day of embarcation, Mr. Astor addressed a letter of instruction to the four partners who were to sail in the ship. In this he enjoined them, in the most earnest manner, to cultivate harmony and unanimity, and recommended that all differences of opinions on points connected with the objects and interests of the voyage should be discussed by the whole, and decided by a majority of votes. He, moreover, gave them especial caution as to their conduct on arriving at their destined port; exhorting them to be careful to make a favorable impression upon the wild people among whom their lot and the fortunes of the enterprize would be cast. "If you find them kind," said he, "as I hope you will, be so to them. If otherwise, act with caution and forbearance and convince them that you come as friends."

With the same anxious forethought he wrote a letter of instructions to Captain Thorn in which he urged the strictest attention to the health of himself and his crew, and to the promotion of good humour and harmony on board his ship. "To prevent any misunderstanding," added he, "will require your particular good management." His letter closed with an injunction of wariness in his intercourse with the natives, a subject on which Mr. Astor was justly sensible he could not be too earnest. "I must recommend you," said he, "to be particularly careful on the coast, and not to rely too much on the friendly disposition of the natives. All accidents which have as yet happened there arose from too much confidence in the Indians."

The reader will bear these instructions in mind as events will prove their wisdom and importance, and the disasters which ensued in consequence of the neglect of them.

Chapter V

Sailing of the Tonquin—A rigid commander and a reckless crew—Landsmen on shipboard—Fresh water sailors at sea —Lubber nests—Ship fare—A Labrador veteran—Literary clerks—Curious travellers—Robinson Crusoe's island— Quarter deck quarrels—Falkland islands—A wild goose chase—Port Egmont—Epitaph hunting—Old Mortality— Penguin shooting—Sportsmen left in the lurch—A hard pull—Further altercations—Arrival at Owyhee.

O N THE EIGHTH of September 1810, the Tonquin put to sea where she was soon joined by the Frigate Constitution. The wind was fresh and fair from the south west, and the ship was soon out of sight of land and free from the apprehended danger of interruption. The Frigate, therefore, gave her "God speed" and left her to her course.

The harmony so earnestly enjoined by Mr. Astor on this heterogeneous crew, and which had been so confidently promised in the buoyant moments of preparation, was doomed to meet with a check at the very outset.

Captain Thorn was an honest, straight forward, but somewhat dry and dictatorial commander who, having been nurtured in the system and discipline of a ship of war and in a sacred opinion of the supremacy of the quarter deck, was disposed to be absolute lord and master on board of his ship. He appears, moreover, to have had no great opinion from the first, of the persons embarked with him. He had stood by with surly contempt while they vaunted so bravely to Mr. Astor of all they could do and all they could undergo, how they could face all weathers, put up with all kinds of fare, and even eat dogs with a relish, when no better food was to be had. He had set them down as a set of land lubbers and braggadocios, and was disposed to treat them accordingly. Mr. Astor was, in his eyes, his only real employer, being the father of the enterprize, who furnished all funds and bore all losses. The others were mere agents and subordinates, who lived at his expense. He evidently had but a narrow idea of the scope and nature of the enterprize, limiting his views merely to his part of it;

every thing beyond the concerns of his ship was out of his sphere; and any thing that interfered with the routine of his nautical duties put him in a passion.

The partners, on the other hand, had been brought up in the service of the North West Company, and in a profound idea of the importance, dignity and authority of a partner. They already began to consider themselves on a par with the M'Tavishes, the MacGillivrays, the Frobishers and the other magnates of the North West, whom they had been accustomed to look up to as the Great ones of the Earth, and they were a little disposed, perhaps, to wear their suddenly acquired honours, with some air of pretension. Mr. Astor, too, had put them on their mettle with respect to the Captain, describing him as a gun powder fellow who would command his ship in fine style, and, if there was any fighting to do, would "blow all out of the water."

Thus prepared to regard each other with no very cordial eye, it is not to be wondered at that the parties soon came into collision. On the very first night Captain Thorn began his man of war discipline by ordering the lights in the cabin to be extinguished at eight o'clock.

The pride of the partners was immediately in arms. This was an invasion of their rights and dignities not to be borne. They were on board of their own ship, and entitled to consult their ease and enjoyment. M'Dougall was the champion of their cause. He was an active, irritable, fuming, vain glorious little man, and elevated in his own opinion, by being the proxy of Mr. Astor. A violent altercation ensued in the course of which Thorn threatened to put the partners in irons should they prove refractory; upon which M'Dougall seized a pistol and swore to be the death of the Captain should he ever offer such an indignity. It was some time before the irritated parties could be pacified by the more temperate bystanders.

Such was the Captain's outset with the partners: Nor did the clerks stand much higher in his good graces; indeed he seems to have regarded all the landsmen on board his ship as a kind of live lumber, continually in the way. The poor voyageurs, too, continually irritated his spleen by their "lubberly" and unseemly habits, so abhorrent to one accustomed to the cleanliness of a man of war. These poor fresh water sailors, so vainglorious on shore, and almost amphibious when on lakes and rivers, lost all heart and stomach the moment they were at sea. For days they suffered the doleful rigours and retchings of seasickness, lurking below in their berths in squalid state, or emerging now and then like spectres from the hatch ways, in capotes and blankets; with dirty night cap, grizly beard, lanthorn visage and unhappy eye, shivering about the deck, and ever and anon crawling to the sides of the vessel, and offering up their tributes to the windward, to the infinite annoyance of the Captain.

His letters to Mr. Astor, wherein he pours forth the bitterness of his soul, and his seamanlike impatience of, what he considers, the "*lubberly*" character and conduct of those around him, are before us, and are amusingly characteristic. The honest Captain is full of vexation on his own account, and solicitude on account of Mr. Astor, whose property he considers at the mercy of a most heterogeneous and wasteful crew.

As to the clerks, he pronounces them mere pretenders, not one of whom had ever been among Indians, nor farther to the north west than Montreal, nor of higher rank than bar keeper of a tavern or marker of a billiard table, excepting one, who had been a schoolmaster, and whom he emphatically sets down for "as foolish a pedant as ever lived."

Then as to the artizans and laborers who had been brought from Canada and shipped at such expense, the three most respectable, according to the Captain's account, were culprits who had fled from Canada on account of their misdeeds: the rest had figured in Montreal as draymen, barbers, waiters and carriole drivers, and were the most helpless worthless beings "that ever broke sea biscuit."

It may easily be imagined what a series of misunderstandings and cross purposes would be likely to take place between such a crew and such a commander. The Captain in his zeal for the health and cleanliness of his ship, would make sweeping visitations to the "lubber nests" of the unlucky "voyageurs" and their companions in misery, ferret them out of their berths, make them air and wash themselves and their accoutrements, and oblige them to stir about briskly and take exercise.

Nor did his disgust and vexation cease when all hands had recovered from seasickness, and become accustomed to the ship, for now broke forth an alarming keenness of appetite that threatened havoc to the provisions. What especially irritated the Captain was the daintiness of some of his cabin passengers. They were loud in their complaints of the ship's fare, though their table was served with fresh pork, hams, tongues, smoked beef and puddings. "When thwarted in their cravings for delicacies," said he, "they would exclaim that it was d——d hard they could not live as they pleased upon their own property, being on board of their own ship, freighted with their own merchandize.—And these," added he, "are the fine fellows who made such boast that they could 'eat dogs.' "

In his indignation at, what he termed, their effeminacy, he would swear that he would never take them to sea again "without having Fly Market on the fore castle, Covent Garden on the poop and a cool spring from Canada in the main top."

As they proceeded on their voyage and got into the smooth seas and pleasant weather of the tropics, other annoyances occurred to vex the spirit of the Captain. He had been crossed by the irritable moods of one of the partners, he was now excessively annoyed by the good humour of another. This was the elder Stuart, who was an easy soul and of a social disposition. He had seen life in Canada, and on the coast of Labrador, had been a fur trader in the former and a fisherman on the latter; and, in the course of his experience had made various expeditions with voyageurs. He was accustomed, therefore, to the familiarity which prevails between that class and their superiors, and the gossippings which take place among them when seated round a fire at their encampments. Stuart was never so happy as when he could seat himself on the deck with a number of these men round him, in camping style, smoke together, passing the pipe from mouth to mouth after the manner of the Indians, sing old Canadian boat songs, and tell stories about their hardships and adventures, in the course of which he rivalled Sindbad in his long tales of the sea, about his fishing exploits on the coast of Labrador.

This gossipping familiarity shocked the Captain's notions of rank and subordination, and nothing was so abhorrent to him as the community of pipe between master and man, and their mingling in chorus in the outlandish boat songs.

Then there was another whimsical source of annoyance to him. Some of the young clerks, who were making their first voyage, and to whom every thing was new and strange, were, very rationally, in the habit of taking notes and keeping journals. This was a sore abomination to the honest Captain who held their literary pretensions in great contempt. "The collecting of materials for long histories of their voyage and travels," said he, in his letter to Mr. Astor, "appears to engross most of their attention." We can conceive what must have been the crusty impatience of the worthy navigator, when, on any trifling occurrence in the course of the voyage, quite commonplace in his eyes, he saw these young landsmen running to record it in their journals; and what indignant glances he must have cast to right and left, as he worried about the deck, giving out his orders for the management of the ship, surrounded by singing, smoking, gossipping, scribbling groupes, all, as he thought, intent upon the amusement of the passing hour, instead of the great purpose and interests of the voyage.

It is possible the Captain was in some degree right in his notions. Though some of the passengers had much to gain by the voyage, none of them had any thing positively to lose; they were mostly young men, in the heyday of life, and having got into fine latitudes, upon smooth seas, with a well stored ship under them and a fair wind in the shoulder of the sail, they seemed to have got into a holyday world, and were disposed to enjoy it. That craving desire, natural to untravelled men of fresh and lively minds, to see strange lands, and to visit scenes famous in history or fable, was expressed by some of the partners and clerks, with respect to some of the storied coasts and islands that lay within their route. The Captain, however, who regarded every coast and island with a matter of fact eye, and had no more associations connected with them than those laid down in his sea chart, considered all this curiosity as exceedingly idle and childish. "In the first part of the voyage," says he in his letter, "they were determined to have it said they had been in Africa, and therefore insisted on my stopping at the Cape de Verds.—Next they said the ship should stop on the coast of Patagonia for they must see the large and uncommon inhabitants of that place. Then they must go to the island where Robinson Crusoe had so long lived. And lastly they were determined to see the handsome inhabitants of Easter Island."

To all these resolves the Captain opposed his peremptory veto, as "contrary to instructions." Then would break forth an unavailing explosion of wrath on the part of certain of the partners, in the course of which they did not even spare Mr. Astor for his act of supererogation in furnishing orders for the control of the ship while they were on board; instead of leaving them to be the judges, where it would be best for her to touch and how long to remain. The choleric M'Dougall took the lead in these railings, being as has been observed, a little puffed up with the idea of being Mr. Astor's proxy.

The Captain, however, became only so much the more crusty and dogged in his adherence to his orders, and techy and harsh in his dealings with his passengers, and frequent altercations ensued. He may in some measure have been influenced by his seamanlike impatience of the interference of landsmen, and his high notions of naval etiquette and quarter deck authority; but he evidently had an honest, trusty concern for the interests of his employer. He pictured to himself the anxious projector of the enterprize, who had disbursed so munificently in its outfit; calculating on the zeal, fidelity and singleness of purpose of his associates and agents; while they, on the other hand, having a good ship at their disposal, and a deep pocket at home, to bear them out, seemed ready to loiter on every coast and amuse themselves in every port.

On the fourth of December they came in sight of the Falkland Islands. Having been for some time on an allowance of water it was resolved to anchor here and obtain a supply. A boat was sent into a small bay to take soundings. Mr. M'Dougall and Mr. M'Kay took this occasion to go on shore, but with a request from the Captain that they would not detain the ship. Once on shore, however, they were in no haste to obey his orders, but rambled about in search of curiosities. The anchorage proving unsafe, and water difficult to be procured, the Captain stood out to sea, and made repeated signals for those on shore to rejoin the ship, but it was not until nine at night that they came on board.

The wind being adverse the boat was again sent on shore on the following morning, and the same gentlemen again landed, but promised to come off at a moment's warning; they again forgot their promise in their eager pursuit of wild geese and sea wolves. After a time the wind hauled fair and signals were made for the boat. Half an hour elapsed but no boat put off. The Captain reconnoitered the shore with his glass and, to his infinite vexation, saw the loiterers in the full enjoyment of their "wild goose chase." Nettled to the quick he immediately made sail. When those on shore saw the ship actually under way they embarked with all speed, but had a hard pull of eight miles before they got on board, and then experienced but a grim reception, notwithstanding that they came well laden with the spoils of the chase.

Two days afterwards, on the 7th of December, they anchored at Port Egmont in the same island, where they remained four days taking in water and making repairs. This was a joyous time for the landsmen. They pitched a tent on shore, had a boat at their command and passed their time merrily in rambling about the island, and coasting along the shores shooting sea lions, seals, foxes, geese, ducks and penguins. None were keener in pursuit of this kind of game than M'Dougall and David Stuart; the latter was reminded of aquatic sports on the coast of Labrador, and his hunting exploits in the north west.

In the meantime the Captain addressed himself steadily to the business of his ship, scorning the holyday spirit and useless pursuits of his emancipated messmates, and warning them, from time to time, not to wander away nor be out of hail. They promised, as usual, that the ship should never experience a moment's detention on their account, but, as usual, forgot their promise.

On the morning of the 11th, the repairs being all finished, and the water casks replenished, the signal was given to embark, and the ship began to weigh anchor. At this time several of the passengers were dispersed about the island, amusing themselves in various ways. Some of the young men had found two inscriptions, in English, over a place where two unfortunate mariners had been buried in this desert island. As the inscriptions were nearly worn out by time and weather, they were playing the part of "Old Mortality," and piously renewing them. The signal from the ship summoned them from their labors, they saw the sails unfurled and that she was getting under way. The two sporting partners, however, Mr. M'Dougall and David Stuart, had strolled away to the south of the island in pursuit of penguins. It would never do to put off without them, as there was but one boat to convey the whole.

While this delay took place on shore the Captain was storming on board. This was the third time his orders had been treated with contempt, and the ship wantonly detained, and it should be the last, so he spread all sail and put to sea, swearing he would leave the laggards to shift for themselves. It was in vain that those on board made remonstrances and entreaties and represented the horrors of abandoning men upon a sterile and uninhabited island: the sturdy Captain was inflexible.

In the meantime the penguin hunters had joined the engravers of tombstones but not before the ship was already out at sea. They all, to the number of eight, threw themselves into their boat, which was about twenty feet in length, and rowed with might and main. For three hours and a half did they tug anxiously and severely at the oar, swashed occasionally by the surging waves of the open sea, while the ship inexorably kept on her course and seemed determined to leave them behind.

On board of the ship was the nephew of David Stuart, a young man of spirit and resolution. Seeing, as he thought, the Captain obstinately bent upon abandoning his uncle and the others, he seized a pistol, and in a paroxysm of wrath swore he would blow out the Captain's brains unless he put about or shortened sail.

Fortunately for all parties the wind just then came ahead, and the boat was enabled to reach the ship, otherwise disastrous circumstances might have ensued. We can hardly believe that the Captain really intended to carry his threat into full effect, and rather think he meant to let the laggards off for a long pull and a hearty fright: he declared, however, in his letter to Mr. Astor, that he was serious in his threats; and there is no knowing how far such an iron man may push his notions of authority.

"Had the wind," writes he, "(unfortunately) not hauled ahead soon after leaving the harbour's mouth, I should positively have left them; and indeed I cannot but think it an unfortunate circumstance for you that it so happened, for the first loss in this instance, would, in my opinion, have proved the best, as they seem to have no idea of the value of property nor any apparent regard for your interest, although interwoven with their own."

This it must be confessed was acting with a high hand and carrying a regard to the owner's property to a dangerous length. Various petty feuds occurred also between him and the partners in respect to the goods on board the ship, some articles of which they wished to distribute for clothing among the men, or for other purposes which they deemed essential. The Captain, however, kept a mastiff watch upon the cargo and growled and snapped if they but offered to touch box or bale. It was "contrary to orders"; it would forfeit his insurance; it was out of all rule. It was in vain they insisted upon their right to do so, as part owners, and as acting for the good of the enterprize; the Captain only stuck to his point the more staunchly. They consoled themselves, therefore, by declaring that, as soon as they made land they would assert their rights and do with ship and cargo as they pleased.

Beside these feuds between the Captain and the partners, there were feuds between the partners themselves, occasioned, in some measure, by jealousy of rank. M'Dougall and M'Kay began to draw plans for the fort and other buildings of the intended establishment. They agreed very well as to the outline and dimensions, which were on a sufficiently grand scale, but when they came to arrange the details fierce disputes arose, and they would quarrel by the hour about the distribution of the doors and windows. Many were the hard words and hard names bandied between them on these occasions, according to the Captain's account: each accused the other of endeavoring to assume unwarrantable power and to take the lead, upon which Mr. M'Dougall would vauntingly lay down Mr. Astor's letter constituting him his representative and proxy, a document not to be disputed.

These wordy contests though violent were brief, "and within fifteen minutes," says the Captain, "they would be caressing each other like children."

While all this petty anarchy was agitating the little world within the Tonquin, the good ship prosperously pursued her course, doubled Cape Horn on the 25th of December, careered across the bosom of the Pacific, until, on the 11th of February, the snowy peaks of Owyhee were seen brightening above the horizon.

Chapter VI

OWYHEE, or Hawaii as it is written by more exact orthographers, is the largest of the cluster, ten in number, of the Sandwich islands. It is about ninety seven miles in length and seventy eight in breadth rising gradually into three pyramidal summits or cones, the highest, Mouna Roa, being eighteen thousand feet above the level of the sea, so as to domineer over the whole archipelago, and to be a land mark over a wide extent of ocean. It remains a lasting monument of the enterprizing and unfortunate Captain Cook, who was murdered by the natives of this island.

The Sandwich islanders when first discovered evinced a character superior to most of the Savages of the Pacific isles. They were frank and open in their deportment; friendly and liberal in their dealings, with an apt ingenuity apparent in all their rude inventions. The tragical fate of the discoverer, which for a time brought them under the charge of ferocity, was, in fact, the result of sudden exasperation caused by the seizure of their chief.

At the time of the visit of the Tonquin the islanders had profited in many respects, by occasional intercourse with white men; and had shewn a quickness to observe and cultivate those arts important to their mode of living. Originally they had no means of navigating the seas by which they were surrounded, superior to light pirogues, which were little competent to contend with the storms of the broad ocean. As the islanders are not in sight of each other, there could, therefore, be but casual intercourse between them. The traffic with white men had put them in possession of vessels of superior description; they had made themselves acquainted with their management, and had even made rude advances in the art of ship building.

These improvements had been promoted in a great measure by the energy and sagacity of one man, the famous Tamaahmaah. He had originally been a petty Eri or chief; but, being of an intrepid and aspiring nature, he had risen in rank, and, availing himself of the superior advantages now afforded in navigation, had brought the whole archipelago in subjection to his arms. At the time of the arrival of the Tonquin he had about forty schooners of from twenty to thirty tons burthen, and one old American ship. With these he maintained undisputed sway over his insular domains, and carried on an intercourse with the chiefs or governors whom he had placed in command of the several islands.

The situation of this groupe of islands far in the bosom of the vast Pacific, and their abundant fertility, rendered them important stopping places on the high way to China, or to the North West Coast of America. Here the vessels engaged in the Fur Trade touched to make repairs and procure provisions, and here they often sheltered themselves during the winters that occurred in their long coasting expeditions.

The British navigators were from the first aware of the value of these islands to the purposes of Commerce, and Tamaahmaah, not long after he had attained the sovereign sway, was persuaded by Vancouver, the celebrated discoverer, to acknowledge, on behalf of himself and subjects, allegiance to the King of Great Britain. The reader cannot but call to mind the visit which the royal family and Court of the Sandwich islands was, in late years, induced to make to the Court of S' James; and the serio-comic ceremonials and mock parade which attended that singular travesty of monarchial style.

It was a part of the wide and comprehensive plan of Mr. Astor to establish a friendly intercourse between these islands and his intended colony; which might for a time have occasion to draw supplies thence; and he even had a vague idea of, some time or other, getting possession of one of these islands, as a rendezvous for his ships, and a link in the chain of his commercial establishments.

On the evening of the 12th of February the Tonquin anchored in the bay of Karakakooa, in the island of Owyhee.
The surrounding shores were wild and broken, with overhanging cliffs and precipices of black volcanic rock. Beyond
these, however, the country was fertile and well cultivated,
with enclosures of yams, plantains, sweet potatoes, sugarcanes
and other productions of warm climates and teeming soils;
and the numerous habitations of the natives were pleasantly
sheltered beneath clumps of cocoa nut and breadfruit trees,
which afforded both food and shade. This mingled variety of
garden and grove swept gradually up the sides of the mountains, until succeeded by dense forests, which in turn gave
place to naked and craggy rocks, until the summits rose into
the regions of perpetual snow.

The royal residence of Tamaahmaah was at this time at another island named Woahoo; the island of Owyhee was under
the command of one of his Eris, or chiefs, who resided at the
village of Tocaigh situated on a different part of the coast
from the bay of Karakakooa.

On the morning after her arrival the ship was surrounded
by canoes and pirogues filled with the islanders of both sexes
bringing off supplies of fruits and vegetables, bananas, plantains, water melons, yams, cabbages and taro. The Captain
was desirous, however, of purchasing a number of hogs, but
there were none to be had. The trade in pork was a royal monopoly and no subject of the great Tamaahmaah dared to
meddle with it. Such provisions as they could furnish, however, were brought by the natives in abundance, and a lively
intercourse was kept up during the day, in which the women
mingled in the kindest manner.

The Islanders are a comely race, of a copper complexion. The men are tall and well made with forms indicating
strength and activity: the women with regular and occasionally handsome features, and a lascivious expression, characteristic of their temperament. Their style of dress was nearly
the same as in the days of Captain Cook. The men wore the
Maro, a band one foot in width and several feet in length,
swathed round the loins and formed of tappa, or cloth of
bark; the Kihei or mantle, about six feet square, tied in a
knot over one shoulder, passed under the opposite arm, so

as to leave it bare, and falling in graceful folds before and behind, to the knee, so as to bear some resemblance to a Roman toga.

The female dress consisted of the pau, a garment formed of a piece of tappa, several yards in length and one in width, wrapped round the waist and reaching, like a petticoat, to the knees. Over this a Kihei or mantle larger than that of the men, sometimes worn over both shoulders, like a shawl, sometimes over one only. These mantles were seldom worn by either sex during the heat of the day, when the exposure of their persons was at first very revolting to a civilized eye.

Towards evening several of the partners and clerks went on shore where they were well received and hospitably entertained; a dance was performed for their amusement in which nineteen young women and one man figured very gracefully, singing in concert and moving to the cadence of their song.

All this, however, was nothing to the purpose in the eyes of Captain Thorn, who, being disappointed in his hope of obtaining a supply of pork, or finding good water, was anxious to be off. This it was not so easy to effect. The passengers, once on shore, were disposed, as usual, to profit by the occasion. The partners had many enquiries to make relative to the island, with a view to business, while the young clerks were delighted with the charms and graces of the dancing damsels.

To add to their gratifications and old man offered to conduct them to the spot where Captain Cook was massacred. The proposition was eagerly accepted and all hands set out on a pilgrimage to the place. The veteran islander performed his promise faithfully and pointed out the very spot where the unfortunate discoverer fell. The rocks and cocoa trees around bore record of the fact, in the marks of the balls fired from the boats upon the savages. The pilgrims gathered round the old man and drew from him all the particulars he had to relate respecting this memorable event; while the honest Captain stood by and bit his nails with impatience. To add to his vexation they employed themselves in knocking off pieces of the rocks and cutting off the bark of the trees marked by the balls, which they conveyed back to the ship as precious reliques.

Right glad, therefore, was he to get them and their treasures fairly on board; when he made sail from this unprofitable place and steered for the bay of Tocaigh, the residence of the chief or governor of the island, where he hoped to be more successful in obtaining supplies. On coming to anchor the Captain went on shore, accompanied by Mr. M'Dougall and Mr. M'Kay, and paid a visit to the governor. This dignitary proved to be an old sailor, by the name of John Young; who, after being tossed about the seas like another Sindbad, had, by one of the whimsical freaks of fortune, been elevated to the government of a savage island. He received his visitors with more hearty familiarity than personages in his high station are apt to indulge, but soon gave them to understand that provisions were scanty at Tocaigh, and that there was no good water, no rain having fallen in the neighborhood in three years.

The Captain was immediately for breaking up the conference and departing, but the partners were not so willing to part with the nautical governor, who seemed disposed to be extremely communicative, and from whom they might be able to procure some useful information. A long conversation accordingly ensued in the course of which they made many enquiries about the affairs of the islands, their natural productions and the possibility of turning them to advantage in the way of trade; nor did they fail to enquire into the individual history of John Young, and how he came to be Governor. This he gave with great condescension, running through the whole course of his fortunes "even from his boyish days."

He was a native of Liverpool in England and had followed the sea from his boyhood until, by dint of good conduct, he had risen so far in his profession as to be boatswain of an American ship called the Eleanor, commanded by Captain Metcalf. In this vessel he had sailed in 1789, on one of those casual expeditions to the north west coast, in quest of furs. In the course of the voyage the Captain left a small schooner named the Fair American, at Nootka, with a crew of five men commanded by his son a youth of eighteen. She was to follow on in the track of the Eleanor.

In February 1790 Captain Metcalf touched at the Island of Mowee, one of the Sandwich groupe. While anchored here a boat which was astern of the Eleanor was stolen and a seaman who was in it was killed. The natives generally disclaimed the outrage and brought the shattered remains of the boat and the dead body of the seaman to the ship. Supposing that they had thus appeased the anger of the Captain they thronged as usual in great numbers about the vessel to trade. Captain Metcalf, however, determined on a bloody revenge. The Eleanor mounted ten guns; all these he ordered to be loaded with musket balls, nails and pieces of old iron, and then fired them, and the small arms of the ship, among the natives. The havoc was dreadful; more than a hundred, according to Young's account, were slain.

After this signal act of vengeance Captain Metcalf sailed from Mowee and made for the island of Owyhee: where he was well received by Tamaahmaah. The fortunes of this warlike chief were at that time on the rise; he had originally been of inferior rank, ruling over only one or two districts of Owyhee, but had gradually made himself sovereign of his native island.

The Eleanor remained some few days at anchor here, and an apparently friendly intercourse was kept up with the inhabitants. On the 17th of March, John Young obtained permission to pass the night on shore. On the following morning a signal gun summoned him to return on board.

He went to the shore to embark, but found all the canoes hauled up on the beach and rigorously tabooed, or interdicted. He would have launched one himself, but was informed by Tamaahmaah that if he presumed to do so he would be put to death.

Young was obliged to submit, and remained all day in great perplexity to account for this mysterious taboo, and fearful that some hostility was intended. In the evening he learnt the cause of it, and his uneasiness was increased. It appeared that the vindictive act of Captain Metcalf had recoiled upon his own head. The Schooner Fair American, commanded by his son, following in his track, had fallen into the hands of the natives to the southward of Tocaigh bay, and young Metcalf and four of the crew had been massacred.

On receiving intelligence of this event Tamaahmaah had immediately tabooed all the canoes and interdicted all intercourse with the ship, lest the Captain should learn the fate of the schooner, and take his revenge upon the island. For the same reason he prevented Young from rejoining his countrymen. The Eleanor continued to fire signals from time to time for two days, and then sailed, concluding, no doubt, that the boatswain had deserted.

John Young was in despair when he saw the ship make sail, and found himself abandoned among savages, and savages, too, sanguinary in their character and inflamed by acts of hostility. He was agreeably disappointed, however, in experiencing nothing but kind treatment from Tamaahmaah and his people. It is true, he was narrowly watched whenever a vessel came in sight, lest he should escape and relate what had passed; but at other times he was treated with entire confidence and great distinction. He became a prime favorite, cabinet councellor and active coadjutor of Tamaahmaah, attending him in all his excursions whether of business or pleasure, and aiding in his warlike and ambitious enterprizes. By degrees he rose to the rank of a chief; espoused one of the beauties of the island, and became habituated and reconciled to his new way of life; thinking it better, perhaps, to rule among savages than serve among white men: to be a feathered chief than a tarpawlin boatswain. His favour with Tamaahmaah never declined, and when that sagacious, intrepid and aspiring chieftain had made himself sovereign over the whole groupe of islands, and removed his residence to Woahoo, he left his faithful adherent John Young in command of Owyhee.

Such is an outline of the history of Governor Young as furnished by himself, and we regret that we are not able to give any account of the state maintained by this seafaring worthy, and the manner in which he discharged his high functions, though it is evident he had more of the hearty familiarity of the forecastle than the dignity of the gubernatorial office.

These long conferences were bitter trials to the patience of the Captain; who had no respect either for the governor or his island, and was anxious to push on in quest of provisions and water. As soon as he could get his inquisitive partners once more on board, he weighed anchor and made sail for the island of Woahoo, the royal residence of Tamaahmaah.

This is the most beautiful island of the Sandwich groupe. It is 46 miles in length and 23 in breadth. A ridge of volcanic mountains extends through the centre, rising into lofty peaks and skirted by undulating hills and rich plains, where the cabins of the natives peep out from beneath groves of cocoa nut and other luxuriant trees.

On the 21st of February the Tonquin cast anchor in the beautiful bay, before the village of Waititi, (pronounced Whyteetee) the abode of Tamaahmaah. This village contained about two hundred habitations, composed of poles set in the ground, tied together at the ends and thatched with grass, and was situated in an open grove of cocoa nuts.

The Royal palace of Tamaahmaah was a large house of two stories, the lower of stone the upper of wood. Round this his body guard kept watch, composed of twenty four men, in long blue cassocks turned up with yellow, and each armed with a musket.

While at anchor at this place much ceremonious visiting and long conferences took place between the potentate of the islands and the partners of the Company. Tamaahmaah came on board of the ship in royal style, in his double pirogue. He was between fifty and sixty years of age, above the middle size, large and well made though somewhat corpulent. He was dressed in an old suit of regimentals, with a sword by his side, and seemed somewhat embarrassed by his magnificent attire. Three of his wives accompanied him; they were almost as tall and quite as corpulent as himself; but by no means to be compared with him in grandeur of habiliments, wearing no other garb than the pau. With him, also, came his great favorite and confidential councellor Kraimaker, who from holding a post equivalent to that of prime minister had been familiarly named Billy Pitt, by the British visitors to the islands.

The sovereign was received with befitting ceremonial. The American flag was displayed, four guns were fired, and the partners appeared in scarlet coats, and conducted their illustrious guests to the cabin, where they were regaled with wine. In this interview the partners endeavored to impress the monarch with a sense of their importance, and of the importance of the association to which they belonged. They let him know that they were Eris, or chiefs, of a great company about to be established on the north west coast, and talked of the probability of opening a trade with his islands, and of sending ships there occasionally. All this was gratifying and interesting to him; for he was aware of the advantages of trade and desirous of promoting frequent intercourse with white men. He encouraged Europeans and Americans to settle in his islands and intermarry with his subjects. There were between twenty and thirty white men at that time resident on the island, but many of them were mere vagabonds, who remained there in hopes of leading a lazy and an easy life. For such Tamaahmaah had a great contempt; those only had his esteem and countenance who knew some trade or mechanic art, and were sober and industrious.

On the day subsequent to the monarch's visit the partners landed and waited upon him in return. Knowing the effect of show and dress upon men in savage life and wishing to make a favorable impression as the *Eris* or chiefs of the great American Fur Company, some of them appeared in highland plaids and Kelts to the great admiration of the natives.

While visits of ceremony and grand diplomatic conferences were going on between the partners and the King, the Captain, in his plain, matter of fact way, was pushing, what he considered a far more important negotiation—the purchase of a supply of hogs. He found that the King had profited in more ways than one by his intercourse with white men. Above all other arts he had learnt the art of driving a bargain. He was a magnanimous monarch, but a shrewd pork merchant; and perhaps thought he could not do better with his future allies the American Fur Company, than to begin by close dealing. Several interviews were requisite and much bargaining before he could be brought to part with a bristle of his bacon, and then he insisted upon being paid in hard Spanish dollars; giving as a reason that he wanted money to purchase a frigate from his brother George, as he affectionately termed the King of England.*

At length the royal bargain was concluded; the necessary supply of hogs obtained, beside several goats, two sheep, a quantity of poultry and vegetables in abundance. The partners now urged to recruit their forces from the natives of this island. They declared they had never seen watermen equal to them, even among the voyageurs of the north west, and indeed they are remarkable for their skill in managing their light craft, and can swim and dive like water fowl. The partners were inclined, therefore, to take thirty or forty with them to the Columbia, to be employed in the service of the Company. The Captain, however, objected that there was not room in his vessel for the accommodation of such a number. Twelve only, were therefore enlisted for the Company, and as many more for the service of the ship. The former engaged to serve for the term of three years, during which they were to be fed and clothed, and at the expiration of the time, were to receive one hundred dollars in merchandize.

And now, having embarked his live stock, fruits, vegetables and water, the Captain made ready to set sail. How much the honest man had suffered in spirit by what he considered the freaks and vagaries of his passengers, and how little he had

---

* It appears from the accounts of subsequent voyagers that Tamaahmaah subsequently succeeded in his wish of purchasing a large ship. In this he sent a cargo of sandal wood to Canton, having discovered that the foreign merchants trading with him made large profits on this wood, shipped by them from the islands to the Chinese markets. The ship was manned by natives but the officers were Englishmen. She accomplished her voyage and returned in safety to the islands with the Hawaiian flag floating gloriously in the breeze. The King hastened on board, expecting to find his sandal wood converted into crapes and damasks and other rich stuffs of China but found, to his astonishment, by the legerdemain of traffic his cargo had all disappeared; and, in place of it, remained a bill of charges amounting to *three thousand dollars.* It was some time before he could be made to comprehend certain of the most important items of the bill, such as pilotage, anchorage and Custom House fees; but when he discovered that maritime states in other countries derived large revenues in this manner, to the great cost of the merchant; "Well," cried he, "then I will have harbour fees also." He established them accordingly. Pilotage a dollar a foot on the draft of each vessel. Anchorage from 60 to 70 Dollars. In this way he greatly increased the royal revenue, and turned his China speculation to account.

understood their humours and intentions, is amusingly shewn in a letter written to Mr. Astor from Woahoo, which contains his comments on the scenes we have described.

"It would be difficult," he writes, "to imagine the frantic gambols that are daily played off here; sometimes dressing in red coats, and otherwise very fantastically, and collecting a number of ignorant natives around them, telling them they are the great eares of the northwest, and making arrangements for sending three or four vessels yearly to them from the coast with spars &c.: while those very natives cannot even furnish a hog to the ship. Then dressing in Highland plaids and Kelts and making similar arrangements, with presents of rum, wine, or any thing that is at hand. Then taking a number of clerks and men on shore to the very spot on which Captain Cook was killed, and each fetching off a piece of the rock or tree that was touched by the shot. Then sitting down with some white man or some native who can be a little understood, and collecting the history of those islands, of Tamaahmaah's wars; the curiosities of the islands &c. preparatory to the histories of their voyages;—and the collection is indeed ridiculously contemptible.—To enumerate the thousand instances of ignorance, filth &c., or to particularize all the frantic gambols that are daily practised, would require volumes."

Before embarking, the great Eris of the American Fur Company took leave of their illustrious ally in due style, with many professions of lasting friendship and promises of future intercourse; while the matter of fact Captain anathematized him in his heart for a grasping, trafficking savage; as shrewd and sordid in his dealings as a white man. As one of the vessels of the Company will, in the course of events, have to appeal to the justice and magnanimity of this island potentate, we shall see how far the honest Captain was right in his opinion.

Chapter VII

Departure from the Sandwich islands—Misunderstandings —Miseries of a suspicious man—Arrival at the Columbia —Dangerous service—Gloomy apprehensions—Bars and breakers—Perils of the ship—Disasters of a boat's crew— Burial of a Sandwich islander.

IT WAS on the 28th of February that the Tonquin set sail from the Sandwich islands. For two days the wind was contrary, and the vessel was detained in their neighborhood; at length a favorable breeze sprang up, and in a little while the rich groves, green hills and snowy peaks of those happy islands, one after another sank from sight, or melted into the blue distance, and the Tonquin ploughed her course towards the sterner regions of the Pacific.

The misunderstandings between the Captain and his passengers still continued; or rather, encreased in gravity. By his altercations and his moody humours, he had cut himself off from all community of thought, or freedom of conversation with them; he disdained to ask any questions as to their proceedings, and could only guess at the meaning of their movements, and in so doing indulged in conjectures and suspicions, which produced the most whimsical self torment.

Thus in one of his disputes with them, relative to the goods on board, some of the packages of which they wished to open to take out articles of clothing for the men or presents for the natives, he was so harsh and peremptory that they lost all patience and hinted that they were the strongest party and might reduce him to a very ridiculous dilemma, by taking from him the command.

A thought now flashed across the Captain's mind that they really had a design to depose him, and that, having picked up some information at Owyhee, possibly of war between the United States and England, they meant to alter the destination of the voyage; perhaps to seize upon ship and cargo for their own use.

Once having conceived this suspicion every thing went to foster it. They had distributed fire arms among some of their

men, a common precaution among the fur traders when mingling with the natives. This, however, looked like preparation.
Then several of the partners and clerks and some of the men,
being Scotsmen, were acquainted with the Gaelic, and held
long conversations together in that language. These conversations were considered by the Captain of a "mysterious and
unwarrantable nature," and related no doubt to some foul
conspiracy that was brewing among them. He frankly avows
such suspicions, in his letter to Mr. Astor, but intimates that
he stood ready to resist any treasonous outbreak, and seems
to think that the evidence of preparation on his part had an
effect in overawing the conspirators.

The fact is, as we have since been informed by one of the
parties, it was a mischievous pleasure with some of the partners
and clerks, who were young men, to play upon the suspicions,
temper and splenetic humours of the Captain; to this we may
ascribe many of their whimsical pranks and absurd proposi-
tions, and above all their mysterious colloquys in Gaelic.

In this sore and irritable mood did the Captain pursue his
course, keeping a wary eye on every movement, and bristling
up whenever the detested sound of the Gaelic language grated
upon his ear. Nothing occurred, however, materially to disturb the residue of the voyage excepting a violent storm, and,
on the twenty second of March, the Tonquin arrived at the
mouth of the Oregon, or Columbia River.

The aspect of the river and the adjacent coast was wild and
dangerous. The mouth of the Columbia is upwards of four
miles wide, with a peninsula and promontory on one side,
and a long low spit of land on the other; between which a
sand bar and chain of breakers almost block up the entrance.
The interior of the country rises into successive ranges of
mountains, which, at the time of the arrival of the Tonquin,
were covered with snow.

A fresh wind from the north west sent a rough tumbling
sea upon the coast, which broke upon the bar in furious
surges and extended a sheet of foam almost across the mouth
of the river. Under these circumstances the Captain did not
think it prudent to approach within three leagues, until the
bar should be sounded and the channel ascertained. Mr. Fox,
the chief mate, was ordered to this service in the whale boat,

accompanied by John Martin, an old seaman, who had formerly visited the river, and by three Canadians. Fox requested to have regular sailors to man the boat, but the Captain would not spare them from the service of the ship, and supposed the Canadians, being expert boatmen on lakes and rivers, were competent to the service, especially when directed and aided by Fox and Martin. Fox seems to have lost all firmness of spirit on the occasion, and to have regarded the service with a misgiving heart. He came to the partners for sympathy, knowing their differences with the Captain, and the tears were in his eyes as he represented his case. "I am sent off," said he, "without seamen to man my boat, in boisterous weather and on the most dangerous part of the north west coast. My uncle was lost a few years ago on this same bar and I am now going to lay my bones along side of his." The partners sympathized in his apprehensions and remonstrated with the Captain. The latter, however, was not to be moved. He had been displeased with Mr. Fox in the earlier part of the voyage, considering him indolent and inactive, and probably thought his present repugnance arose from a want of true nautical spirit. The interference of the partners in the business of the ship, also, was not calculated to have a favorable effect on a stickler for authority like himself, especially in his actual state of feeling towards them.

At one o'clock P.M. therefore Fox and his comrades set off in the whaleboat, which is represented as small in size, and crazy in condition. All eyes were strained after the little bark, as it pulled for shore, rising and sinking with the huge rolling waves, until it entered, a mere speck, among the foaming breakers and was soon lost to view. Evening set in, night succeeded and passed away and morning returned, but without the return of the boat.

As the wind had moderated the ship stood near to the land so as to command a view of the river mouth. Nothing was to be seen but a wild chaos of tumbling waves breaking upon the bar and apparently forming a foaming barrier from shore to shore. Towards night the ship again stood out to gain sea room, and a gloom was visible in every countenance. The Captain, himself, shared in the general anxiety, and probably repented of his peremptory orders. Another weary and watchful night succeeded, during which the wind subsided and the weather became serene.

On the following day, the ship, having drifted near the land, anchored in fourteen fathoms water, to the northward of the long peninsula or promontory which forms the north side of the entrance and is called Cape Disappointment. The pinnace was then manned and two of the partners, Mr. David Stuart and Mr. M'Kay, set off in the hope of learning something of the fate of the whaleboat. The surf, however, broke with such violence along the shore, that they could find no landing place. Several of the natives appeared on the beach and made signs to them to row round the cape, but they thought it most prudent to return to the ship.

The wind now springing up the Tonquin got under way and stood in to seek the channel, but was again deterred, by the frightful aspect of the breakers, from venturing within a league. Here she hove to, and Mr. Mumford, the second mate, was despatched with four hands, in the pinnace, to sound across the channel until he should find four fathoms depth. The pinnace entered among the breakers but was near being lost, and with difficulty got back to the ship. The Captain insisted that Mr. Mumford had steered too much to the southward; he now turned to Mr. Aiken, an able mariner destined to command the schooner intended for the coasting trade, and ordered him, together with John Coles, sail maker, Stephen Weekes, armourer, and two Sandwich islanders, to proceed ahead and take soundings, while the ship should follow under easy sail. In this way they proceeded until Aiken had ascertained the channel, when signal was given from the ship for him to return on board. He was then within pistol shot, but so furious was the current, and tumultuous the breakers that the boat became unmanageable, and was hurried away, the crew crying out piteously for assistance. In a few moments she could not be seen from the ship's deck. Some of the passengers climbed to the mizen top, and beheld her, still struggling to reach the ship; but shortly after she broached broadside to the waves, and her case seemed desperate. The attention of those on board of the ship was now called to their own safety. They were in shallow water; the vessel struck repeatedly, the waves broke over her and there was danger of her foundering. At length she got into seven fathoms water, and, the wind lulling and the night coming on, cast anchor. With the darkness their anxieties encreased. The wind whistled, the sea roared, the gloom was only broken by the ghastly glare of the foaming breakers, the minds of the seamen were full of dreary apprehensions, and some of them fancied they heard the cries of their lost comrades mingling with the uproar of the elements. For a time too the rapidly ebbing tide threatened to sweep them from their precarious anchorage. At length its reflux, and the springing up of the wind, enabled them to quit their dangerous situation and take shelter in a small bay within Cape Disappointment, where they rode in safety during the residue of a stormy night, and enjoyed a brief interval of refreshing sleep.

With the light of day returned their cares and anxieties. They looked out from the mast head over a wild coast, and wilder sea, but could discover no trace of the two boats, and their crews, that were missing. Several of the natives came on board with peltries, but there was no disposition to trade. They were interrogated by signs, after the lost boats, but could not understand the enquiries.

Parties now went on shore and scoured the neighborhood. One of these was headed by the Captain. They had not proceeded far when they beheld a person at a distance, in civilized garb. As he drew near he proved to be Weekes the armourer. There was a burst of joy, for it was hoped his comrades were near at hand. His story, however, was one of disaster. He and his companions had found it impossible to govern their boat, having no rudder and being beset by rapid and whirling currents, and boisterous surges. After long struggling they had let her go at the mercy of the waves, tossing about, sometimes with her bow, sometimes with her broad side to the surges, threatened each instant with destruction, yet repeatedly escaping, until a huge sea broke over and swamped her. Weekes was overwhelmed by the boiling waves, but emerging above the surface looked round for his companions. Aikin and Coles were not to be seen; near him were the two Sandwich islanders, stripping themselves of their clothing that they might swim more freely. He did the same, and the boat floating near to him he seized hold of it. The two islanders joined him, and, uniting their forces they succeeded in turning the boat upon her keel. Then bearing down her stern and rocking her, they forced out so much water that she was able to bear the weight of a man without sinking. One of the islanders now got in, and in a little while bailed out the water with his hands. The other swam about and collected the oars and they all three got once more on board.

By this time the tide had swept them beyond the breakers and Weekes called on his companions to row for land: they were so chilled and benumbed by the cold, however, that they lost all heart and absolutely refused. Weekes was equally chilled, but had superior sagacity and self command. He counteracted the tendency to drowsiness and stupor which cold produces, by keeping himself in constant exercise; and seeing that the vessel was advancing, and that every thing depended upon himself, he set to work to scull the boat clear of the bar, and into quiet water.

Towards midnight one of the poor islanders expired: his companion threw himself on his corps and could not be persuaded to leave him. The dismal night wore away amidst these horrors; as the day dawned Weekes found himself near the land. He steered directly for it, and at length, with the aid of the surf, ran his boat high upon a sandy beach.

Finding that one of the Sandwich islanders yet gave signs of life he aided him to leave the boat, and set out with him towards the adjacent woods. The poor fellow, however, was too feeble to follow him, and Weekes was soon obliged to abandon him to his fate and provide for his own safety. Falling upon a beaten path he pursued it and, after a few hours, came to a part of the coast where to his surprise and joy he beheld the ship at anchor, and was met by the Captain and his party.

After Weekes had related his adventures three parties were despatched to beat up the coast in search of the unfortunate islander. They returned at night without success, though they had used the utmost diligence. On the following day the search was resumed, and the poor fellow was at length discovered lying beneath a groupe of rocks, his legs swollen, his feet torn and bloody from walking through bushes and briars, and himself half dead with cold, hunger and fatigue. Weekes and this islander were the only survivors of the crew of the jolly boat, and no trace was ever discovered of Fox and his party. Thus eight men were lost on the first approach to the coast; a commencement that cast a gloom over the spirits of the whole party, and was regarded by some of the superstitious, as an omen that boded no good to the enterprize.

Towards night the Sandwich islanders went on shore to bury the body of their unfortunate countryman who had perished in the boat. On arriving at the place where it had been left, they dug a grave in the sand in which they deposited the corps with a biscuit under one of the arms, some lard under the chin and a small quantity of tobacco, as provisions for its journey in the land of Spirits. Having covered the body with sand and flints they kneeled along the grave in a double row with their faces turned to the East, while one who officiated as a priest sprinkled them with water from a hat. In so doing he recited a kind of prayer or invocation, to which at intervals, the others made responses. Such were the simple rites performed by these poor savages at the grave of their comrade on the shores of a strange land; and when these were done they rose and returned in silence to the ship, without once casting a look behind.

Chapter VIII

*Mouth of the Columbia—The native tribes—Their fishing—
Their canoes—Bold navigators—Equestrian Indians and
Piscatory Indians, difference in their physical organization—
Search for a trading site—Expedition of M'Dougall and
David Stuart—Comcomly the one eyed chieftain—Influence
of wealth in savage life—Slavery among the natives—An
aristocracy of Flatheads—Hospitality among the Chinooks—
Comcomly's daughter, her conquest.*

THE COLUMBIA, or Oregon, for the distance of thirty or
forty miles from its entrance into the Sea, is properly
speaking a mere estuary indented by deep bays so as to vary
from three to seven miles in width; and is rendered extremely
intricate and dangerous by shoals reaching nearly from shore to
shore, on which at times the winds and currents produce foaming and tumultuous breakers. The mouth of the river proper is
but about half a mile wide; formed by the contracting shores of
the estuary. The entrance from the Sea, as we have already observed, is bounded on the south side by a flat sandy spit of land,
stretching into the Ocean. This is commonly called Point
Adams. The opposite or northern side is Cape Disappointment: a kind of peninsula, terminating in a steep knoll or
promontory crowned with a forest of pine trees, and connected
with the main land by a low and narrow neck. Immediately
within this cape is a wide open bay, terminating at Chinook
point, so called from a neighboring tribe of Indians. This was
called Baker's Bay, and here the Tonquin was anchored.

The natives inhabiting the lower part of the river, and
with whom the company was likely to have the most frequent
intercourse, were divided at this time into four tribes, the
Chinooks, Clatsops, Wahkiacums and Cathlamahs. They resembled each other in person, dress, language and manner,
and were probably from the same stock, but broken into tribes,
or rather hordes, by those feuds and schisms frequent among
Indians.

These people generally live by fishing; it is true they occasionally hunt the elk and deer, and ensnare the waterfowl of

their ponds and rivers; but these are casual luxuries; their chief subsistence is derived from the salmon and other fish which abound in the Columbia and its tributary streams; aided by roots and herbs, especially the Wappatoo, which is found on the islands of the river.

As the Indians of the plains who depend upon the chase, are bold and expert riders, and pride themselves upon their horses, so these piscatory tribes of the coast excel in the management of canoes and are never more at home than when riding upon the waves. Their canoes vary in form and size: some are upwards of fifty feet long, cut out of a single tree, either fir or white cedar and capable of carrying thirty persons. They have thwart pieces from side to side about three inches thick, and their gunwales flare outwards so as to cast off the surges of the waves. The bow and stern are decorated with grotesque figures of men and animals sometimes five feet in height.

In managing their canoes they kneel, two and two along the bottom, sitting on their heels, and wielding paddles from four to five feet long, while one sits on the stern and steers with a paddle of the same kind. The women are equally expert with the men in managing the canoe, and generally take the helm.

It is surprizing to see with what fearless unconcern these savages venture in their light barks upon the roughest and most tempestuous seas. They seem to ride upon the waves like sea fowl. Should a surge throw the canoe upon its side and endanger its overturn, those to windward lean over the upper gunwale, thrust their paddles deep into the wave, apparently catch the water and force it under the canoe, and by this action, not merely regain an equilibrium, but give their bark a vigorous impulse forward.

The effect of different modes of life upon the human frame and human character is strikingly instanced in the contrast between the hunting Indians of the prairies and the piscatory Indians of the sea coast. The former, continually on horseback, scouring the plains, gaining their food by hardy exercise and subsisting chiefly on flesh, are generally tall, sinewy, meagre but well formed, and of bold and fierce deportment; the latter, lounging about the river banks, or squatting and curved up in their canoes, are generally low in stature, ill shaped, with crooked legs, thick ancles and broad flat feet. They are inferior also in muscular power and activity, and in *game* qualities and appearance to their hard riding brethren of the prairies.

Having premised these few particulars concerning the neighboring Indians, we will return to the immediate concerns of the Tonquin and her crew.

Further search was made for Mr. Fox and his party but with no better success and they were at length given up as lost. In the mean time the Captain and some of the partners explored the river for some distance in a large boat to select a suitable place for the trading post. Their old jealousies and differences continued; they never could coincide in their choice, and the Captain objected altogether, to any site so high up the river. They all returned, therefore, to Baker's bay in no very good humour. The partners proposed to examine the opposite shore, but the Captain was impatient of any further delay. His eagerness to "get on" had encreased upon him. He thought all these excursions a sheer loss of time, and was resolved to land at once, build a shelter for the reception of that part of his cargo destined for the use of the settlement, and, having cleared his ship of it, and of his irksome ship mates, to depart upon the prosecution of his coasting voyage according to orders.

On the following day, therefore, without troubling himself to consult the partners, he landed in Baker's Bay and proceeded to erect a shed for the reception of the rigging, equipments and stores of the schooner that was to be built for the use of the settlement.

This dogged determination on the part of the sturdy captain gave high offence to Mr. M'Dougall, who now considered himself at the head of the concern, as Mr. Astor's representative and proxy. He set off the same day, (April 5th) accompanied by Mr. David Stuart, for the southern shore, intending to be back by the seventh. Not having the Captain to contend with they soon pitched upon a spot which appeared to them favorable for the intended establishment. It was on a point of land called Point George, having a very good harbour where vessels, not exceeding two hundred tons burthen, might anchor within fifty yards of the shore.

After a day thus profitably spent they re crossed the river, but landed on the northern shore, several miles above the anchoring ground of the Tonquin, in the neighborhood of Chinook, and visited the village of that tribe. Here they were received with great hospitality by the chief who was named Comcomly, a shrewd old savage, with but one eye, who will occasionally figure in this narrative. Each village forms a petty sovereignty governed by its own chief, who however possesses but little authority, unless he be a man of wealth and substance, that is to say, possessed of canoes, slaves and wives. The greater number of these the greater is the chief. How many wives this one eyed potentate maintained we are not told, but he certainly possessed great sway not merely over his own tribe, but over the neighborhood.

Having mentioned slaves, we would observe that slavery exists among several of the tribes beyond the Rocky Mountains. The slaves are well treated, while in good health, but occupied in all kinds of drudgery. Should they become useless however by sickness or old age, they are totally neglected and left to perish; nor is any respect paid to their bodies after death.

A singular custom prevails not merely among the Chinooks, but among most of the tribes about this part of the coast, which is the flattening of the forehead. The process by which this deformity is effected commences immediately after birth. The infant is laid in a wooden trough, by way of cradle. The end on which the head reposes is higher than the rest. A padding is placed on the forehead of the infant, with a piece of bark above it, and is pressed down by cords, which pass through holes on each side of the trough. As the tightening of the padding and the pressing of the head to the board is gradual, the process is said not to be attended with much pain. The appearance of the infant, however, while in this state of compression, is whimsically hideous, and "its little black eyes," we are told, "being forced out by the tightness of the bandages, resemble those of a mouse choked in a trap."

About a year's pressure is sufficient to produce the desired effect, at the end of which time the child emerges from its bandages a complete Flathead, and continues so through life. It must be noted, however, that this flattening of the head has something in it of aristocratical significancy, like the crippling of the feet among Chinese ladies of quality. At any rate, it is a sign of freedom. No slave is permitted to bestow this enviable deformity upon his child; all the slaves, therefore, are roundheads.

With this worthy tribe of Chinooks the two partners passed a part of a day very agreeably. M'Dougall, who was somewhat vain of his official rank, had given it to be understood that they were two chiefs of a great trading company, about to be established here, and the quicksighted, though one eyed chief, who was somewhat practiced in traffic with white men, immediately perceived the policy of cultivating the friendship of two such important visitors. He regaled them, therefore, to the best of his ability, with abundance of salmon and Wappatoo. The next morning, April 7th, they prepared to return to the vessel according to promise. They had eleven miles of open bay to traverse; the wind was fresh, the waves ran high. Comcomly remonstrated with them on the hazard to which they would be exposed.

They were resolute, however, and launched their boat; while the wary chieftain followed at some short distance in his canoe. Scarce had they rowed a mile when a wave broke over their boat and upset it. They were in imminent peril of drowning, especially Mr. M'Dougall, who could not swim. Comcomly, however, came bounding over the waves in his light canoe and snatched them from a watery grave.

They were taken on shore and a fire made at which they dried their clothes, after which Comcomly conducted them back to his village. Here every thing was done that could be devised for their entertainment during three days that they were detained by bad weather. Comcomly made his people perform antics before them; and his wives and daughters endeavored by all the soothing and endearing arts of women, to find favor in their eyes. Some even painted their bodies with red clay and anointed themselves with fish oil to give additional lustre to their charms. Mr. M'Dougall seems to have had a heart susceptible to the influence of the gentler sex; whether or no it was first touched on this occasion we do not learn, but it will be found, in the course of this work, that one of the daughters of the hospitable Comcomly eventually made a conquest of the great Eri of the American Fur Company.

When the weather had moderated and the sea become tranquil the one eyed chief of the Chinooks manned his state canoe and conducted his guests in safety to the ship: where they were welcomed with joy, for apprehensions had been felt for their safety. Comcomly and his people were then entertained on board of the Tonquin and liberally rewarded for their hospitality and services. They returned home highly satisfied, promising to remain faithful friends and allies of the white men.

Chapter IX

Point George—Founding of Astoria—Indian visitors—Their reception—The Captain taboos the ship—Departure of the Tonquin—Comments on the conduct of Captain Thorn.

FROM the report made by the two exploring partners it was determined that Point George should be the site of the trading house. These gentlemen, it is true, were not perfectly satisfied with the place, and were desirous of continuing their search, but Captain Thorn was impatient to land his cargo and continue his voyage, and protested against any more of what he termed "sporting excursions."

Accordingly, on the 12th of April the launch was freighted with all things necessary for the purpose and sixteen persons departed in her to commence the establishment, leaving the Tonquin to follow as soon as the harbor could be sounded.

Crossing the wide mouth of the river the party landed and encamped at the bottom of a small bay within Point George. The situation chosen for the fortified post was on an elevation facing to the north, with the wide estuary, its sand bars and tumultuous breakers spread out before it, and the promontory of Cape Disappointment, fifteen miles distant, closing the prospect to the left. The surrounding country was in all the freshness of spring, the trees were in the young leaf; the weather was superb, and every thing looked delightful to men just emancipated from a long confinement on shipboard. The Tonquin shortly afterwards made her way through the intricate channel and came to anchor in the little bay and was saluted from the encampment with three vollies of musketry and three cheers. She returned the salute with three cheers and three guns.

All hands now set to work cutting down trees, clearing away thickets and marking out the place for the residence, store house and powder magazine, which were to be built of logs and covered with bark: others landed the timbers intended for the frame of the coasting vessel, and proceeded to put them together; while others prepared a garden spot, and sowed the seeds of various vegetables.

The next thought was to give a name to the embryo metropolis: the one that naturally presented itself was that of the projector and supporter of the whole enterprize. It was accordingly named ASTORIA.

The neighboring Indians now swarmed about the place; some brought a few land otter and sea otter skins to barter, but in very scanty parcels; the greater number came prying about to gratify their curiosity, for they are said to be impertinently inquisitive, while not a few came with no other design than to pilfer; the laws of *meum* and *tuum* being but slightly respected among them. Some of them beset the ship in their canoes, among whom was the Chinook chief Comcomly and his liege subjects. These were well received by Mr. M'Dougall, who was delighted with an opportunity of entering upon his functions and acquiring importance in the eyes of his future neighbors. The confusion thus produced on board, and the derangement of the cargo caused by this petty trade, stirred the spleen of the Captain, who had a sovereign contempt for the one eyed chieftain and all his crew. He complained loudly of having his ship lumbered by a host of "Indian ragamuffins" who had not a skin to dispose of, and at length put his positive interdict upon all trafficking on board. Upon this Mr. M'Dougall was fain to land and establish his quarters at the encampment, where he could exercise his rights and enjoy his dignities without control.

The feud, however, between these rival powers still continued, but was chiefly carried on by letter. Day after day and week after week elapsed, yet the store houses requisite for the reception of the cargo were not completed, and the ship was detained in port; while the Captain was teased by frequent requisitions for various articles for the use of the establishment or the trade with the natives. An angry correspondence took place, in which he complained bitterly of the time wasted in "smoking and sporting parties," as he termed the reconnoitering expeditions, and in clearing and preparing meadow ground and turnip patches, instead of despatching his ship. At length all these jarring matters were adjusted, if not to the satisfaction, at least to the acquiescence of all parties. The part of the cargo destined for the use of Astoria was landed, and the ship left free to proceed on her voyage.

As the Tonquin was to coast to the north, to trade for peltries at the different harbours, and to touch at Astoria on her
return in the autumn, it was unanimously determined that
Mr. M'Kay should go in her as supercargo, taking with him
Mr. Lewis as ship's clerk. On the first of June the ship got
under way and dropped down to Baker's Bay, where she was
detained for a few days by a head wind; but early in the morning of the 5th stood out to sea with a fine breeze and swelling
canvas, and swept off gaily on her fatal voyage from which she
was never to return!

On reviewing the conduct of Captain Thorn and examining
his peevish and somewhat whimsical correspondence, the impression left upon our mind is, upon the whole, decidedly in
his favour. While we smile at the simplicity of his heart and
the narrowness of his views, which made him regard every
thing out of the direct path of his daily duty, and the rigid
exigencies of the service as trivial and impertinent, which
inspired him with contempt for the swelling vanity of some
of his coadjutors, and the literary exercises and curious researches of others; we cannot but applaud that strict and conscientious devotion to the interests of his employer and to
what he considered the true objects of the enterprize in which
he was engaged.

He certainly was to blame occasionally for the asperity of his
manners and the arbitrary nature of his measures, yet much
that is exceptionable in this part of his conduct may be traced
to rigid notions of duty acquired in that tyrannical school a
ship of war, and to the construction given by his companions
to the orders of Mr. Astor so little in conformity with his own.
His mind, too, appears to have become almost diseased by the
suspicions he had formed as to the loyalty of his associates and
the nature of their ultimate designs: yet on this point there
were circumstances to in some measure justify him. The relations between the United States and Great Britain were at that
time in a critical state, in fact the two countries were on the
eve of a war. Several of the partners were British subjects, and
might be ready to desert the flag under which they acted,
should a war take place. Their application to the British Minister at New York shews the dubious feeling with which they
had embarked in the present enterprize. They had been in the

employ of the North West Company and might be disposed to rally again under that association, should events threaten the prosperity of this embryo establishment of Mr. Astor. Beside, we have the fact, avowed to us by one of the partners, that some of them who were young and heedless took a mischievous and unwarrantable pleasure in playing upon the jealous temper of the Captain, and affecting mysterious consultations and sinister movements.

These circumstances are cited in palliation of the doubts and surmises of Captain Thorn, which might otherwise appear strange and unreasonable. That most of the partners were perfectly upright and faithful in the discharge of the trust reposed in them we are fully satisfied; still the honest Captain was not invariably wrong in his suspicions; and that he formed a pretty just opinion of the integrity of that aspiring personage Mr. M'Dougall, will be substantially proven in the sequel.

Chapter X

Disquieting rumours from the interior—Reconnoitering party—Preparations for a trading post—An unexpected arrival—A spy in the camp—Expedition into the interior— Shores of the Columbia—Mount Coffin—Indian sepulchres— The land of Spirits—Columbian valley—Vancouver's point —Falls and rapids—A great fishing mart—The village of Wish-ram—Difference between fishing Indians and hunting Indians—Effects of habits of trade on the Indian character— Post established at the Oakinagan.

WHILE the Astorians were busily occupied in completing their factory and fort, a report was brought to them by an Indian from the upper part of the River, that a party of thirty white men had appeared on the banks of the Columbia, and were actually building houses at the Second Rapids. This information caused much disquiet. We have already mentioned that the North West Company had established posts to the west of the Rocky Mountains in a district called by them New Caledonia, which extended from Lat. 52° to 55° north; being within the British territories; it was now apprehended that they were advancing within the American limits, and were endeavoring to seize upon the upper part of the river and forestall the American Fur Company in the surrounding trade, in which case bloody feuds might be anticipated, such as had prevailed between the rival fur companies in former days.

A reconnoitering party was sent up the river to ascertain the truth of the report. They ascended to the foot of the first rapid, about two hundred miles, but could hear nothing of any white men being in the neighborhood.

Not long after their return, however, further accounts were received by two wandering Indians, which established the fact that the North West Company had actually erected a trading house on the Spokan River, which falls into the north branch of the Columbia.

What rendered this intelligence the more disquieting was the inability of the Astorians, in their present reduced state as to numbers, and the exigencies of their new establishment, to furnish detachments to penetrate the country in different directions, and fix the posts necessary to secure the interior trade.

It was resolved, however, at any rate to advance a counter check to this post on the Spokan, and one of the partners, Mr. David Stuart, prepared to set out for the purpose with eight men and a small assortment of goods. He was to be guided by the two Indians, who knew the country, and promised to take him to a place not far from the Spokan River, and in a neighborhood abounding with beaver. Here he was to establish himself and to remain for a time provided he found the situation advantageous and the natives friendly.

On the 15th of July, when Mr. Stuart was nearly ready to embark, a canoe made its appearance standing for the harbour and manned by nine white men. Much speculation took place who these strangers could be; for it was too soon to expect their own people, under Mr. Hunt, who were to cross the Continent. As the canoe drew near the British standard was distinguished: on coming to land, one of the crew stepped on shore, and announced himself as Mr. David Thompson, astronomer, and partner of the North West Company. According to his account he had set out in the preceding year with a tolerably strong party and a supply of Indian goods to cross the Rocky Mountains. A part of his people, however, had deserted him on the eastern side, and returned with the goods to the nearest North West post. He had persisted in crossing the mountains with eight men who remained true to him. They had traversed the higher regions and wintered near the source of the Columbia, where, in the spring, they had constructed a cedar canoe, the same in which they had reached Astoria.

This, in fact, was the party dispatched by the North West Company to anticipate Mr. Astor in his intention of effecting a settlement at the mouth of the Columbia River. It appears from information subsequently derived from other sources that Mr. Thompson had pushed on his course with great haste, calling at all the Indian villages in his march, presenting them with British flags, and even planting them at the forks of the rivers, proclaiming formally that he took possession of the country in the name of the King of Great Britain for the North West Company. As his original plan was defeated by the desertion of his people it is probable that he descended the river simply to reconnoiter and ascertain whether an American settlement had been commenced.

Mr. Thompson was, no doubt, the first white man who descended the northern branch of the Columbia from so near its source. Lewis and Clark struck the main body of the river at the forks, about four hundred miles from its mouth. They entered it from Lewis River, its southern branch, and thence descended.

Though Mr. Thompson could be considered as little better than a spy in the camp, he was received with great cordiality by Mr. M'Dougall, who had a lurking feeling of companionship and good will for all of the North West Company. He invited him to head quarters, where he and his people were hospitably entertained. Nay, further, being somewhat in extremity, he was furnished by Mr. M'Dougall with goods and provisions for his journey back, across the mountains, much against the wishes of Mr. David Stuart, who did not think the object of his visit entitled him to any favor.

On the 23d of July Mr. Stuart set out upon his expedition to the interior. His party consisted of four of the clerks, Messrs. Pillet, Ross, M'Lennon and Montigny, accompanied by two Canadian voyageurs and two natives of the Sandwich Islands. They had three canoes well laden with provisions, and with goods and necessaries for a trading establishment.

Mr. Thompson and his party set out in company with them, it being his intention to proceed direct to Montreal. The partners at Astoria forwarded by him a short letter to Mr. Astor, informing him of their safe arrival at the mouth of the Columbia, and that they had not yet heard of Mr. Hunt.

The little squadron of canoes set sail with a favorable breeze and soon passed Tongue Point, a long, high and rocky promontory, covered with trees and stretching far into the river. Opposite to this on the northern shore is a deep bay, where the Columbia anchored at the time of the discovery, and which is still called Gray's Bay, from the name of her commander.

From hence the general course of the river for about seventy miles was nearly south east; varying in breadth according to its bays and indentations, and navigable for vessels of three hundred tons. The shores were in some places high and rocky, with low marshy islands at their feet, subject to inundation, and covered with willows, poplars, and other trees that love an alluvial soil. Sometimes the mountains receded and gave place to beautiful plains and noble forests. While the river margin was richly fringed with trees of deciduous foliage, the rough uplands were crowned by majestic pines and firs of gigantic size; some towering to the height of between two and three hundred feet, with proportionate circumference. Out of these the Indians wrought their great canoes and pirogues.

At one part of the river they passed on the northern side an isolated rock, about one hundred and fifty feet high, rising from a low marshy soil and totally disconnected with the adjacent mountains. This was held in great reverence by the neighboring Indians, being one of their principal places of sepulture. The same provident care for the deceased that prevails among the hunting tribes of the prairies is observable among the piscatory tribes of the rivers and sea coast. Among the former the favorite horse of the hunter is buried with him in the same funereal mound, and his bow and arrows are laid by his side, that he may be perfectly equipped for the "happy hunting grounds" of the land of Spirits. Among the latter the Indian is wrapped in his mantle of skins, laid in his canoe with his paddle, his fishing spear, and other implements beside him, and placed aloft on some rock or other eminence overlooking the river or bay or lake that he has frequented. He is thus fitted out to launch away upon those placid streams and sunny lakes stocked with all kinds of fish and waterfowl, which are prepared in the next world for those who have acquitted themselves as good sons, good fathers, good husbands and, above all, good fishermen, during their mortal sojourn.

The isolated rock in question presented a spectacle of the kind: numerous dead bodies being deposited in canoes on its summit: while on poles around were trophies, or rather funeral offerings of trinkets, garments, baskets of roots, and other articles for the use of the deceased. A reverential feeling protects these sacred spots from robbery or insult. The friends of the deceased, especially the women, repair here at sunrise and sunset for some time after his death, singing his funeral dirge and uttering loud wailings and lamentations.

From the number of dead bodies in canoes observed upon this rock by the first explorers of the river it received the name of Mount Coffin, which it continues to bear.

Beyond this rock they passed the mouth of a river on the right bank of the Columbia, which appeared to take its rise on a distant mountain covered with snow. The Indian name of this river was the Cowleskee. Some miles further on they came to the great Columbian valley, so called by Lewis and Clark. It is sixty miles in width and extends far to the south southeast between parallel ridges of mountains which bound it on the east and west. Through the centre of this valley flowed a large and beautiful stream called the Wallamot,* which came wandering for several hundred miles through a yet unexplored wilderness. The sheltered situation of this immense valley had an obvious effect upon the climate. It was a region of great beauty and luxuriance, with lakes and pools, and green meadows shaded by noble groves. Various tribes were said to reside in this valley, and along the banks of the Wallamot.

About eight miles above the mouth of the Wallamot the little squadron arrived at Vancouver's point, so called in honor of that celebrated voyager by his lieutenant (Broughton) when he explored the river. This point is said to present one of the most beautiful scenes on the Columbia: a lovely meadow, with a silver sheet of limpid water in the centre, enlivened by wildfowl; a range of hills crowned by forests, while the prospect is closed by Mount Hood, a magnificent mountain rising into a lofty peak and covered with snow; the ultimate land mark of the first explorers of the river.

Point Vancouver is about one hundred miles from Astoria; here the reflux of the tide ceases to be perceptible. To this place vessels of two and three hundred tons burthen may ascend. The party under the command of Mr. Stuart had been three or four days in reaching it, though we have forborne to notice their daily progress and nightly encampments.

From Point Vancouver the river turned towards the north east and became more contracted and rapid with occasional islands and frequent sand banks. These islands are furnished with a number of ponds and at certain seasons abound with

* Pronounced Wallámot, the accent being upon the second syllable.

swan, geese, brandts, cranes, gulls, plover, and other wildfowl. The shores, too, are low and closely wooded, with such an undergrowth of vines and rushes as to be almost impassable.

About thirty miles above Point Vancouver the mountains again approach on both sides of the river, which is bordered by stupendous precipices, covered with the fir and the white cedar, and enlivened occasionally by beautiful cascades leaping from a great height, and sending up wreaths of vapour. One of these precipices or cliffs is curiously worn by time and weather, so as to have the appearance of a ruined fortress, with towers and battlements, beetling high above the river, while two small cascades one hundred and fifty feet in height, pitch down from the fissures of the rocks.

The turbulence and rapidity of the current continually augmenting as they advanced, gave the voyagers intimation that they were approaching the great obstructions of the river, and at length they arrived at Strawberry Island, so called by Lewis and Clark, which lies at the foot of the first rapid. As this part of the Columbia will be repeatedly mentioned in the course of this work, being the scene of some of its incidents, we shall give a general description of it in this place.

The Falls or Rapids of the Columbia are situated about one hundred and eighty miles above the mouth of the river. The first is a perpendicular cascade of twenty feet, after which there is a swift descent for a mile between islands of hard black rock, to another pitch of eight feet, divided by two rocks. About two and a half miles below this the river expands into a wide basin, seemingly dammed up by a perpendicular ridge of black rock. A current, however, sets diagonally to the left of this rocky barrier, where there is a chasm forty five yards in width. Through this the whole body of the river roars along, swelling and whirling and boiling for some distance in the wildest confusion. Through this tremendous channel the intrepid explorers of the river, Lewis and Clark, passed safely in their boats, the danger being, not from the rocks, but from the great surges and whirlpools.

At the distance of a mile and a half from the foot of this narrow channel is a rapid formed by two rocky islands, and two miles beyond is a second great fall, over a ledge of rocks twenty feet high, extending nearly from shore to shore. The river is again compressed into a channel from fifty to a hundred feet wide, worn through a rough bed of hard black rock, along which it boils and roars with great fury for the distance of three miles. This is called "The Long Narrows."

Here is the great fishing place of the Columbia. In the spring of the year, when the water is high, the salmon ascend the river in incredible numbers. As they pass through this narrow strait the Indians, standing on the rocks, or on the end of wooden stages projecting from the banks, scoop them up with small nets distended on hoops and attached to long handles, and cast them on the shore.

They are then cured and packed in a peculiar manner. After having been opened and disembowelled they are exposed to the sun on scaffolds erected on the river banks. When sufficiently dry they are pounded fine between two stones, pressed into the smallest compass and packed in baskets or bales of grass matting, about two feet long and one in diameter, lined with the cured skin of a salmon. The top is likewise covered with fish skins secured by cords passing through holes in the edge of the basket. Packages are then made, each containing twelve of these bales, seven at bottom, five at top, pressed close to each other, with the corded side upward, wrapped in mats and corded. These are placed in dry situations and again covered with matting. Each of these packages contains from ninety to a hundred pounds of dried fish, which in this state will keep sound for several years.*

We have given this process at some length, as furnished by the first explorers, because it marks a practised ingenuity in preparing articles of traffic for a market, seldom seen among our aboriginals. For like reasons we would make especial mention of the Village of Wish-ram at the head of the Long Narrows, as being a solitary instance of an aboriginal trading mart, or emporium. Here the salmon caught in the neighboring rapids were "ware housed" to await customers. Hither the tribes from the mouth of the Columbia repaired with the fish of the sea coast, the roots, berries and especially the Wappatoo, gathered in the lower parts of the river, together with goods and trinkets obtained from the ships which casu-

* Lewis and Clark. V. II. P. 32.

ally visited the coast. Hither also the tribes from the Rocky
Mountains brought down horses, bear grass, Quamash and
other commodities of the interior. The merchant fishermen at
the Falls acted as middle men or factors: and passed the objects of traffic as it were cross handed, trading away part of
the wares received from the mountain tribes, to those of the
river and the plains, and vice versa: their packages of pounded
salmon entered largely into the system of barter, and being
carried off in opposite directions, found their way to the savage hunting camps far in the interior, and to the casual white
traders who touched upon the coast.

We have already noticed certain contrarieties of character
between the Indian tribes, produced by their diet and mode of
life, and no where are they more apparent than about the Falls
of the Columbia. The Indians of this great fishing mart are
represented by the earliest explorers as sleeker and fatter, but
less hardy and active, than the tribes of the mountains and the
prairies, who live by hunting; or of the upper parts of the river,
where fish is scanty and the inhabitants must eke out their subsistence by digging roots or chasing the deer. Indeed, whenever an Indian of the upper country is too lazy to hunt yet is
fond of good living, he repairs to the Falls to live in abundance
without labour.

"By such worthless dogs as these," says an honest trader in
his journal, which now lies before us, "by such worthless dogs
as these are these noted fishing places peopled; which, like our
great cities, may with propriety be called the head quarters of
vitiated principles."

The habits of trade and the avidity of gain have their cor-
rupting effects even in the wilderness, as may be instanced in
the members of this aboriginal emporium, for the same jour-
nalist denounces them as "saucy, impudent rascals, who will
steal when they can, and pillage whenever a weak party falls in
their power."

That he does not belie them will be evidenced hereafter,
when we have occasion again to touch at Wish-ram and navigate the rapids; in the present instance the travellers effected
the laborious ascent of this part of the river, with all its various portages, without molestation, and once more launched
away in smooth water above the high falls.

The two parties continued together, without material impediment, for three or four hundred miles further up the Columbia; Mr. Thompson appearing to take great interest in the success of Mr. Stuart, and pointing out places favorable, as he said, to the establishment of his contemplated trading post.

Mr. Stuart, who distrusted his sincerity, at length pretended to adopt his advice, and, taking leave of him, remained as if to establish himself, while the other proceeded on his course towards the Mountains. No sooner, however, had he fairly departed than Mr. Stuart again pushed forward, under guidance of the two Indians, nor did he stop until he had arrived within about 140 miles of the Spokan River, which he considered near enough to keep the rival establishment in check.

The place which he pitched upon for his trading post was a point of land about three miles in length and two in breadth, formed by the junction of the Oakinagan with the Columbia. The former is a river which has its source in a considerable lake about a hundred and fifty miles west of the point of junction. The two rivers about the place of their confluence are bordered by immense prairies covered with herbage, but destitute of trees. The point itself was enameled with wild flowers of every hue, in which innumerable hummingbirds were "banqueting nearly the livelong day."

The situation of this point appeared to be well adapted for a trading post. The climate was salubrious, the soil fertile, the rivers well stocked with fish, the natives peaceable and friendly. There were easy communications with the interior by the upper waters of the Columbia, and the lateral stream of the Oakinagan, while the downward current of the Columbia furnished a high way to Astoria.

Availing himself, therefore, of the drift wood which had collected in quantities in the neighboring bends of the river Mr. Stuart and his men set to work to erect a house, which in a little while was sufficiently completed for their residence; and thus was established the first interior post of the Company. We will now return to notice the progress of affairs at the mouth of the Columbia.

Chapter XI

THE SAILING of the Tonquin and the departure of
Mr. David Stuart and his detachment had produced a
striking effect on affairs at Astoria. The natives who had
swarmed about the place began immediately to drop off, until
at length not an Indian was to be seen. This at first was attributed to the want of peltries with which to trade; but in a little
while the mystery was explained in a more alarming manner. A
conspiracy was said to be on foot among the neighboring
tribes to make a combined attack upon the white men, now
that they were so reduced in number. For this purpose there
had been a gathering of warriors in a neighboring bay, under
pretext of fishing for sturgeon, and fleets of canoes were expected to join them from the north and south. Even Comcomly the one eyed chief, notwithstanding his professed
friendship for Mr. M'Dougall, was strongly suspected of being
concerned in this general combination.

Alarmed at rumours of this impending danger, the Astorians suspended their regular labour, and set to work, with all
haste, to throw up temporary works for refuge and defence. In
the course of a few days they surrounded their dwelling house
and magazines with a picket fence ninety feet square, flanked
by two bastions on which were mounted four four-pounders.

Every day they exercised themselves in the use of their
weapons, so as to qualify themselves for military duty, and at
night ensconced themselves in their fortress and posted centinels to guard against surprize. In this way they hoped, even in
case of attack, to be able to hold out until the arrival of the party
to be conducted by Mr. Hunt across the Rocky Mountains, or
until the return of the Tonquin. The latter dependance however
was doomed soon to be destroyed. Early in August a wandering
band of Savages from the Strait of Juan de Fuca, made their
appearance at the mouth of the Columbia, where they came
to fish for sturgeon. They brought disastrous accounts of the
Tonquin, which were at first treated as mere fables; but which

were too sadly confirmed by a different tribe that arrived a few days subsequently. We shall relate the circumstances of this mclancholy affair as correctly as the casual discrepancies in the statements that have reached us will permit.

We have already stated that the Tonquin set sail from the mouth of the river on the fifth of June. The whole number of persons on board amounted to twenty three. In one of the outer bays they picked up, from a fishing canoe, an Indian named Lamazee, who had already made two voyages along the coast and knew something of the languages of the various tribes. He agreed to accompany them as interpreter.

Steering to the north Captain Thorn arrived in a few days at Vancouver's island and anchored in the harbour of Neweetie, very much against the advice of his Indian interpreter, who warned him against the perfidious character of the natives of this part of the coast. Numbers of canoes soon came off bringing sea otter skins to sell. It was too late in the day to commence a traffic but Mr. M'Kay, accompanied by a few of the men, went on shore to a large village to visit Wicananish the chief of the surrounding territory, six of the natives remaining on board as hostages. He was received with great professions of friendship, entertained hospitably and a couch of sea otter skins was prepared for him in the dwelling of the chieftain, where he was prevailed upon to pass the night.

In the morning, before Mr. M'Kay had returned to the ship, great numbers of the natives came off in their canoes to trade, headed by two sons of Wicananish. As they brought abundance of sea otter skins, and there was every appearance of a brisk trade, Captain Thorn did not wait for the return of Mr. M'Kay, but spread out his wares upon the deck, making a tempting display of blankets, cloths, knives, beads and fish hooks, expecting a prompt and profitable sale. The Indians, however, were not so eager and simple as he had supposed, having learned the art of bargaining and the value of merchandize from the casual traders along the coast. They were guided too by a shrewd old chief named Nookamis, who had grown gray in traffic with New England skippers and prided himself upon his acuteness. His opinion seemed to regulate the market. When Captain Thorn made what he considered a liberal offer for an otter skin the wily old Indian treated it with scorn and asked more than double. His comrades all took their cue from him and not an otter skin was to be had at a reasonable rate.

The old fellow, however, overshot his mark, and mistook the character of the man he was treating with. Thorn was a plain, straight forward sailor, who never had two minds nor two prices in his dealings, was deficient in patience and pliancy and totally wanting in the chicanery of traffic. He had a vast deal of stern but honest pride in his nature, and, moreover, held the whole savage race in sovereign contempt. Abandoning all further attempts, therefore, to bargain with his shuffling customers, he thrust his hands into his pockets and paced up and down the deck in sullen silence. The cunning old Indian followed him to and fro, holding out a sea otter skin to him at every turn, and pestering him to trade. Finding other means unavailing, he suddenly changed his tone and began to jeer and banter him upon the mean prices he offered. This was too much for the patience of the Captain, who was never remarkable for relishing a joke, especially when at his own expense. Turning suddenly upon his persecutor, he snatched the proffered otter skin from his hands, rubbed it in his face, and dismissed him over the side of the ship with no very complimentary application to accelerate his exit. He then kicked the peltries to the right and left about the deck and broke up the market in the most ignominious manner. Old Nookamis made for shore in a furious passion, in which he was joined by Shewish, one of the sons of Wicananish, who went off breathing vengeance, and the ship was soon abandoned by the natives.

When Mr. M'Kay returned on board the interpreter related what had passed and begged him to prevail upon the Captain to make sail, as, from his knowledge of the temper and pride of the people of the place, he was sure they would resent the indignity offered to one of their chiefs. Mr. M'Kay who himself possessed some experience of Indian character, went to the Captain, who was still pacing the deck in moody humour, represented the danger to which his hasty act had exposed the vessel, and urged him to weigh anchor. The Captain made light of his councils and pointed to his cannon and fire arms as a sufficient safe guard against naked savages. Futher remonstrances only provoked taunting replies and sharp altercations. The day passed away without any signs of hostility, and at night the Captain retired as usual to his cabin, taking no more than the usual precautions.

On the following morning, at day break, while the Captain and Mr. M'Kay were yet asleep, a canoe came along side in which were twenty Indians, commanded by young Shewish. They were unarmed, their aspect and demeanor friendly, and they held up otter skins and made signs indicative of a wish to trade. The caution enjoined by Mr. Astor in respect to the admission of Indians on board of the ship had been neglected for some time past, and the officer of the watch, perceiving those in the canoe to be without weapons, and having received no orders to the contrary, readily permitted them to mount the deck. Another canoe soon succeeded, the crew of which was likewise admitted. In a little while other canoes came off and Indians were soon clambering into the vessel on all sides.

The officer of the watch now felt alarmed, and called to Captain Thorn and Mr. M'Kay. By the time they came on deck it was thronged with Indians. The interpreter noticed to Mr. M'Kay that many of the natives wore short mantles of skins, and intimated a suspicion that they were secretly armed. Mr. M'Kay urged the Captain to clear the ship and get under way. He again made light of the advice, but the augmented swarm of canoes about the ship and the numbers still putting off from shore at length awakened his distrust and he ordered some of the crew to weigh anchor while seven were sent aloft to make sail.

The Indians now offered to trade with the Captain on his own terms, prompted apparently by the approaching departure of the ship. Accordingly a hurried trade was commenced. The main articles sought by the savages in barter, were knives; as fast as some were supplied they moved off and others succeeded. By degrees they were thus distributed about the deck, and all with weapons.

The anchor was now nearly up; the sails were loose and the Captain, in a loud and peremptory tone, ordered the ship to be cleared. In an instant a signal yell was given: it was echoed on every side, knives and war clubs were brandished in every direction, and the savages rushed upon their marked victims.

The first that fell was Mr. Lewis, the ship's clerk. He was leaning with folded arms over a bale of blankets, engaged in bargaining, when he received a deadly stab in the back and fell down the companionway.

Mr. M'Kay, who was seated on the taffrail, sprang on his feet, but was instantly knocked down with a war club and flung backwards into the sea, where he was despatched by the women in the canoes.

In the mean time, Captain Thorn made desperate fight against fearful odds. He was a powerful as well as a resolute man, but he had come upon deck without weapons. Shewish the young chief singled him out as his peculiar prey, and rushed upon him at the first outbreak. The Captain had barely time to draw a clasp knife with one blow of which he laid the young savage dead at his feet. Several of the stoutest followers of Shewish now set upon him. He defended himself vigorously, dealing crippling blows to right and left, and strewing the quarter deck with the slain and wounded. His object was to fight his way to the cabin, where there were fire arms, but he was hemmed in with foes, covered with wounds and faint with loss of blood. For an instant he leaned upon the tiller wheel, when a blow from behind with a war club felled him to the deck, where he was despatched with knives and thrown overboard.

While this was transacting upon the quarter deck a chance medley fight was going on throughout the ship. The crew fought desperately with knives, handspikes, and whatever weapon they could seize upon in the moment of surprize. They were soon, however, overpowered by numbers and mercilessly butchered.

As to the seven who had been sent aloft to make sail, they contemplated with horror the carnage that was going on below. Being destitute of weapons they let themselves down by the running rigging in hopes of getting between decks. One fell in the attempt and was instantly despatched. Another received a death blow in the back as he was descending; a third, Stephen Weekes the armourer, was mortally wounded as he was getting down the hatch way.

The remaining four made good their retreat into the cabin, where they found Mr. Lewis, still alive though mortally wounded. Barricading the cabin door they broke holes through the companion way, and, with the muskets and ammunition which were at hand opened a brisk fire that soon cleared the deck.

Thus far the Indian interpreter, from whom these particulars are derived, had been an eye witness of the deadly conflict. He had taken no part in it, and had been spared by the natives, as being of their race. In the confusion of the moment he took refuge with the rest, in the canoes. The survivors of the crew now sallied forth and discharged some of the deck guns, which did great execution among the canoes and drove all the savages to shore.

For the remainder of the day no one ventured to put off to the ship, deterred by the effects of the fire arms. The night passed away without any further attempt on the part of the natives. When the day dawned the Tonquin still lay at anchor in the bay, her sails all loose and flapping in the wind, and no one apparently on board of her. After a time some of the canoes ventured forth to reconnoiter, taking with them the interpreter. They paddled about her keeping cautiously at a distance, but growing more and more emboldened at seeing her quiet and lifeless. One man at length made his appearance on the deck, and was recognized by the interpreter as Mr. Lewis. He made friendly signs and invited them on board. It was long before they ventured to comply. Those who mounted the deck met with no opposition; no one was to be seen on board; for Mr. Lewis, after inviting them, had disappeared. Other canoes now pressed forward to board the prize; the decks were soon crowded and the sides covered with clambering savages, all intent on plunder. In the midst of their eagerness and exultation the ship blew up with a tremendous explosion. Arms, legs and mutilated bodies were blown into the air, and dreadful havoc was made in the surrounding canoes. The interpreter was in the main chains at the time of the explosion and was thrown unhurt into the water where he succeeded in getting into one of the canoes. According to his statement the bay presented an awful spectacle after the catastrophe. The ship had disappeared, but the bay was covered with fragments of the wreck, with shattered canoes and Indians swimming for their lives or struggling in the agonies of death; while those who had escaped the danger remained aghast and stupified, or made with frantic panic for the shore. Upwards of a hundred savages were destroyed by the explosion; many more were shockingly mutilated, and for days afterwards the limbs and bodies of the slain were thrown up on the beach.

The inhabitants of Neweetie were overwhelmed with consternation at this astounding calamity which had burst upon them in the very moment of triumph. The warriors sat mute and mournful, while the women filled the air with loud lamentations. Their weeping and wailing, however, were suddenly changed into yells of fury at the sight of four unfortunate white men brought captive into the village. They had been driven on shore in one of the ship's boats and taken at some distance along the coast.

The interpreter was permitted to converse with them. They proved to be the four brave fellows who had made such desperate defence from the cabin. The interpreter gathered from them some of the particulars already related. They told him further, that, after they had beaten off the enemy and cleared the ship, Lewis advised that they should slip the cable and endeavor to get to sea. They declined to take his advice, alledging that the wind set too strongly into the bay and would drive them on shore. They resolved as soon as it was dark, to put off quietly in the ship's boat, which they would be able to do unperceived, and to coast along back to Astoria. They put their resolution into effect; but Lewis refused to accompany them; being disabled by his wound, hopeless of escape and determined on a terrible revenge. On the voyage out he had repeatedly expressed a presentiment that he should die by his own hands, thinking it highly probable that he should be engaged in some contest with the natives, and being resolved in case of extremity, to commit suicide, rather than be made a prisoner. He now declared his intention to remain on board of the ship until day light, to decoy as many of the savages on board as possible, then to set fire to the powder magazine and terminate his life by a signal act of vengeance. How well he succeeded has been shewn.

His companions bade him a melancholy adieu and set off on their precarious expedition. They strove with might and main to get out of the bay, but found it impossible to weather a point of land, and were at length compelled to take shelter in a small cove, where they hoped to remain concealed until the wind should be more favorable. Exhausted by fatigue and watching they fell into a sound sleep and in that state were surprized by the savages. Better had it been for these unfortunate men had they remained with Lewis and shared his heroic death: as it was, they perished in a more painful and protracted manner, being sacrificed by the natives to the manes of their friends with all the lingering tortures of savage cruelty. Some time after their death, the interpreter, who had remained a kind of prisoner at large, effected his escape and brought the tragical tidings to Astoria.

Such is the melancholy story of the Tonquin, and such was the fate of her brave but headstrong commander, and her adventurous crew. It is a catastrophe that shows the importance in all enterprizes of moment, to keep in mind the general instructions of the sagacious heads which devise them. Mr. Astor was well aware of the perils to which ships were exposed on this coast from quarrels with the natives, and from perfidious attempts of the latter to surprize and capture them in unguarded moments. He had repeatedly enjoined it upon Captain Thorn, in conversation, and at parting, in his letter of instructions, to be courteous and kind in his dealings with the Savages, but by no means to confide in their apparent friendship, *nor to admit more than a few on board of his ship at a time.*

Had the deportment of Captain Thorn been properly regulated, the insult so wounding to Savage pride would never have been given. Had he enforced the rule to admit but a few at a time the Savages would not have been able to get the mastery. He was too irritable, however, to practice the necessary self command; and having been nurtured in a proud contempt of danger, thought it beneath him to manifest any fear of a crew of unarmed Savages.

With all his faults and foibles we cannot but speak of him with esteem, and deplore his untimely fate, for we remember him well in early life, as a companion in pleasant scenes and joyous hours. When on shore, among his friends, he was a frank, manly, soundhearted sailor. On board ship he evidently assumed the hardness of deportment and sternness of demeanor which many deem essential to naval service. Throughout the whole of the expedition, however, he shewed himself loyal, single minded, straight forward and fearless, and if the fate of his vessel may be charged to his harshness and imprudence we should recollect that he paid for his error with his life.

The loss of the Tonquin was a grievous blow to the infant establishment of Astoria, and one that threatened to bring after it a train of disasters. The intelligence of it did not reach Mr. Astor until many months afterwards. He felt it in all its force and was aware that it must cripple, if not entirely defeat, the great scheme of his ambition. In his letters written at the time he speaks of it as "a calamity the length of which he could not foresee." He indulged, however, in no weak and vain lamentation, but sought to devise a prompt and efficient remedy. The very same evening he appeared at the theatre with his usual serenity of countenance. A friend who knew the disastrous intelligence he had received expressed his astonishment that he could have calmness of spirit sufficient for such a scene of light amusement. "What would you have me do?" was his characteristic reply; "Would you have me stay at home and weep for what I cannot help?"

Chapter XII

Gloom at Astoria—An ingenious stratagem—The small pox chief—Launching of the Dolly—An arrival—A Canadian trapper—A Freeman of the forests—An Iroquois hunter—Winter on the Columbia—Festivities of New Year.

THE TIDINGS of the loss of the Tonquin and the massacre of her crew struck dismay into the hearts of the Astorians. They found themselves a mere handful of men, on a savage coast, surrounded by hostile tribes, who would doubtless be incited and encouraged to deeds of violence by the late fearful catastrophe. In this juncture Mr. M'Dougall, we are told, had recourse to a stratagem by which to avail himself of the ignorance and credulity of the savages, and which certainly does credit to his ingenuity.

The natives of the coast, and indeed of all the regions west of the mountains, had an extreme dread of the small pox; that terrific scourge having a few years previously appeared among them and almost swept off entire tribes. Its origin and nature were wrapped in mystery, and they conceived it an evil inflicted upon them by the Great Spirit or brought among them by the white men. The last idea was seized upon by Mr. M'Dougall. He assembled several of the chieftains whom he believed to be in the conspiracy. When they were all seated around he informed them that he had heard of the treachery of some of their northern brethren towards the Tonquin, and was determined on vengeance. "The white men among you," said he, "are few in number, it is true, but they are mighty in medicine. See here," continued he, drawing forth a small bottle and holding it before their eyes; "—in this bottle I hold the small pox safely corked up; I have but to draw the cork and let loose the pestilence, to sweep man, woman and child from the face of the earth."

The chiefs were struck with horror and alarm. They implored him not to uncork the bottle, since they and all their people were firm friends of the white men, and would always remain so, but, should the smallpox be once let out it would run like wildfire throughout the country, sweeping off the good as well as the bad; and surely he would not be so unjust as to punish his friends for crimes committed by his enemies.

Mr. M'Dougall pretended to be convinced by their reasoning and assured them that, so long as the white people should be unmolested, and the conduct of their Indian neighbors friendly and hospitable, the phial of wrath should remain sealed up; but, on the least act of hostility the fatal cork should be drawn.

From this time, it is added, he was much dreaded by the natives as one who held their fate in his hands, and was called, by way of pre eminence, "the Great Small pox Chief."

All this while the labours at the infant settlement went on with unremitting assiduity, and by the 26th of September a commodious mansion spacious enough to accommodate all hands was completed. It was built of stone and clay, there being no calcarious stone in the neighborhood from which lime for mortar could be procured. The schooner was also finished and launched with the accustomed ceremony on the second of October, and took her station below the fort. She was named the Dolly and was the first American vessel launched on this coast.

On the 5th of October in the evening the little community at Astoria was enlivened by the unexpected arrival of a detachment from Mr. David Stuart's post on the Oakinagan. It consisted of two of the clerks and two of the privates. They brought favorable accounts of the new establishment, but reported that, as Mr. Stuart was apprehensive there might be a difficulty of subsisting his whole party throughout the winter, he had sent one half back to Astoria, retaining with him only Ross, Montigny and two others. Such is the hardihood of the Indian trader. In the heart of a savage and unknown country, seven hundred miles from the main body of his fellow adventurers, Stuart had dismissed half of his little number, and was prepared with the residue to brave all the perils of the wilderness, and the rigours of a long and dreary winter.

With the return party came a Canadian Creole named Regis Brugiere, and an Iroquois hunter, with his wife and two children. As these two personages belong to certain classes which have derived their peculiar characteristics from the fur

trade, we deem some few particulars concerning them perti-
nent to the nature of this work.

Brugiere was of a class of beaver trappers and hunters technically called Freemen, in the language of the traders. They
are generally Canadians by birth, and of French descent, who
have been employed for a term of years by some fur company,
but, their term being expired, continue to hunt and trap on
their own account, trading with the company like the Indians.
Hence they derive their appellation of Freemen, to distinguish
them from the trappers who are bound for a number of years
and receive wages or hunt on shares.

Having passed their early youth in the wilderness, separated
almost entirely from civilized man, and in frequent intercourse with the Indians, they lapse, with a facility common to
human nature, into the habitudes of Savage life. Though no
longer bound by engagements to continue in the interior they
have become so accustomed to the freedom of the forest and
the prairie that they look back with repugnance upon the
restraints of civilization. Most of them intermarry with the
natives, and, like the latter, have often a plurality of wives.
Wanderers of the wilderness, according to the vicissitudes of
the seasons, the migrations of animals, and the plenty or
scarcity of game, they lead a precarious and unsettled existence, exposed to sun and storm and all kinds of hardships,
until they resemble the Indians in complexion as well as in
tastes and habits. From time to time they bring the peltries
they have collected to the trading houses of the company in
whose employ they have been brought up. Here they traffic
them away for such articles of merchandize or ammunition as
they may stand in need of. At the time when Montreal was the
great emporium of the fur trader, one of these Freemen of the
wilderness would suddenly return, after an absence of many
years, among his old friends and comrades. He would be
greeted as one risen from the dead; and with the greater welcome, as he returned flush of money. A short time, however,
spent in revelry would be sufficient to drain his purse and
sate him with civilized life, and he would return with new
relish to the unshackled freedom of the forest.

Numbers of men of this class were scattered throughout
the north west territories. Some of them retained a little of

the thrift and forethought of the civilized man; and became wealthy among their improvident neighbors, their wealth being chiefly displayed in large bands of horses, which covered the prairies in the vicinity of their abodes. Most of them, however, were prone to assimilate to the red man in their heedlessness of the future.

Such was Regis Brugiere, a freeman and rover of the wilderness. Having been brought up in the service of the North West Company, he had followed in the train of one of its expeditions across the Rocky Mountains, and undertaken to trap for the trading post established on the Spokan River. In the course of his hunting excursions he had either accidentally or designedly found his way to the post of Mr. Stuart; and been prevailed upon to descend the Columbia and "try his luck" at Astoria.

Ignace Shonowane the Iroquois hunter was a specimen of a different class. He was one of those Aboriginals of Canada who had partially conformed to the habits of civilization and the doctrines of Christianity, under the influence of the French colonists and the Catholic priests; who seem generally to have been more successful in conciliating, taming, and converting the savages, than their English and Protestant rivals. These half civilized Indians retained some of the good and many of the evil qualities of their original stock. They were first rate hunters and dextrous in the management of the canoe. They could undergo great privations and were admirable for the service of the rivers, lakes and forests provided they could be kept sober and in proper subordination; but, once inflamed with liquor, to which they were madly addicted, all the dormant passions inherent in their nature were prone to break forth, and to hurry them into the most vindictive and bloody acts of violence.

Though they generally professed the Roman Catholic religion, yet it was mixed occasionally with some of their ancient superstitions; and they retained much of the Indian belief in charms and omens. Numbers of these men were employed by the North West Company as trappers, hunters and canoe men, but on lower terms than were allowed to white men. Ignace Shonowane had, in this way, followed the enterprize of the Company to the banks of the Spokan, being probably one of the first of his tribe that had traversed the Rocky Mountains.

Such were some of the motley populace of the wilderness, incident to the fur trade, who were gradually attracted to the new settlement of Astoria.

The month of October now began to give indications of approaching winter. Hitherto the colonists had been well pleased with the climate. The summer had been temperate, the mercury never rising above 80°. Westerly winds had prevailed during the spring and the early part of summer, and been succeeded by fresh breezes from the north west. In the month of October the southerly winds set in, bringing with them frequent rain.

The Indians now began to quit the borders of the Ocean and to retire to their winter quarters in the sheltered bosom of the forests or along the small rivers and brooks. The rainy season, which commences in October, continues with little intermission until April, and though the winters are generally mild, the mercury seldom sinking below the freezing point, yet the tempests of wind and rain are terrible. The sun is sometimes obscured for weeks; the brooks swell into roaring torrents and the country is threatened with a deluge.

The departure of the Indians to their winter quarters gradually rendered provisions scanty, and obliged the colonists to send out foraging expeditions in the Dolly. Still the little handful of adventurers kept up their spirits in their lonely fort at Astoria, looking forward to the time when they should be animated and reinforced by the party under Mr. Hunt that was to come to them across the Rocky Mountains.

The year gradually wore away; the rain which had poured down almost incessantly since the first of October, cleared up towards the evening of the 31st of December, and the morning of the first of January ushered in a day of sunshine.

The hereditary French holyday spirit of the Canadian voyageurs is hardly to be depressed by any adversities, and they can manage to get up a fête in the most squalid situations and under the most untoward circumstances. An extra allowance of rum, and a little flour to make cakes and puddings, constitute a "regale" and they forget all their toils and troubles in the song and the dance.

On the present occasion the partners endeavored to celebrate the New Year with some effect. At sunrise the drums beat to arms; the colours were hoisted, with three rounds of small arms and three discharges of cannon. The day was devoted to games of agility and strength and other amusements; and grog was temperately distributed, together with bread, butter and cheese. The best dinner their circumstances could afford was served up at midday. At sunset the colours were lowered with another discharge of artillery. The night was spent in dancing, and though there was a lack of female partners to excite their gallantry, the voyageurs kept up the ball with true French spirit until three o'clock in the morning. So passed the New Year's festival of 1812 at the infant colony of Astoria.

Chapter XIII

W E HAVE followed up the fortunes of the Maritime part of this enterprize to the shores of the Pacific, and have conducted the affairs of the embryo establishment to the opening of the New Year: let us now turn back to the adventurous band to whom was entrusted the land expedition, and who were to make their way to the mouth of the Columbia up vast rivers, across trackless plains and over the rugged barriers of the Rocky Mountains.

The conduct of this expedition, as has already been mentioned, was assigned to Mr. Wilson Price Hunt, of Trenton, New Jersey, one of the partners of the Company, who was ultimately to be at the head of the establishment at the mouth of the Columbia. He is represented as a man scrupulously upright and faithful in his dealings, amiable in his disposition, and of most accommodating manners, and his whole conduct will be found in unison with such a character. He was not practically experienced in the Indian trade; that is to say, he had never made any expeditions of traffic into the heart of the wilderness; but he had been engaged in Commerce at S' Louis, then a frontier settlement on the Mississippi, where the chief branch of his business had consisted in furnishing Indian traders with goods and equipments. In this way he had acquired much knowledge of the trade at second hand, and of the various tribes and the interior country over which it extended.

Another of the partners, Mr. Donald M'Kenzie, was associated with Mr. Hunt in the expedition and excelled on those points in which the other was deficient, for he had been ten years in the interior, in the service of the North West Company and valued himself on his knowledge of "woodcraft" and the strategy of Indian trade and Indian warfare. He had a frame seasoned to toils and hardships, a spirit not to be intimidated, and was reputed to be a "remarkable shot," which of itself was sufficient to give him renown upon the frontier.

Mr. Hunt and his coadjutor repaired, about the latter part of July (1810) to Montreal, the Ancient Emporium of the fur trade; where every thing requisite for the expedition could be procured. One of the first objects was to recruit a complement of Canadian voyageurs from the disbanded herd usually to be found loitering about the place. A degree of jockeyship, however, is required for this service, for a Canadian voyageur is as full of latent tricks and vices as a horse, and when he makes the greatest external promise, is prone to prove the greatest "take in." Beside, the North West Company, who maintained a long established control at Montreal and knew the qualities of every voyageur, secretly interdicted the prime hands from engaging in this new service, so that, although liberal terms were offered, few presented themselves but such as were not worth having.

From these Mr. Hunt engaged a number sufficient, as he supposed, for present purposes, and having laid in a supply of ammunition, provisions and Indian goods, embarked all on board one of those great canoes at that time universally used by the fur traders, for navigating the intricate and often obstructed rivers. The canoe was between thirty and forty feet long and several feet in width; constructed of birch bark, sewed with fibres of the roots of the spruce tree, and daubed with resin of the pine instead of tar. The cargo was made up in packages, weighing from ninety to one hundred pounds each, for the facility of loading and unloading, and of transportation at portages. The canoe itself, though capable of sustaining a freight of upwards of four tons, could readily be carried on men's shoulders.

Canoes of this size are generally managed by eight or ten men; two of whom are picked veterans, who receive double wages and are stationed, one at the bow and the other at the stern, to keep a look out, and to steer. They are termed the foreman and the steersman. The rest, who ply the paddles, are called middle men. When there is a favorable breeze the canoe is occasionally navigated with a sail.

The expedition took its regular departure, as usual, from S' Anne's, near the extremity of the island of Montreal, the great starting place of the traders to the interior. Here stood the ancient chapel of S' Anne, the patroness of the Canadian voyageurs; where they made confession and offered up their vows previous to departing on any hazardous expedition. The shrine of the saint was decorated with reliques and votive offerings hung up by these superstitious beings, either to propitiate her favor, or in gratitude for some signal deliverance in the wilderness. It was the custom, too, of these devout vagabonds, after leaving the chapel, to have a grand carouse, in honor of the saint and for the prosperity of the voyage. In this part of their devotions the crew of Mr. Hunt proved themselves by no means deficient. Indeed he soon discovered that his recruits enlisted at Montreal were fit to vie with the ragged regiment of Falstaff. Some were able bodied, but inexpert; others were expert but lazy, while a third class were expert and willing, but totally worn out, being broken down veterans, incapable of toil.

With this inefficient crew he made his way up the Ottawa River and by the ancient route of the fur traders along a succession of small lakes and rivers to Michilimackinac. Their progress was slow and tedious. Mr. Hunt was not accustomed to the management of "voyageurs" and he had a crew admirably disposed to play the old soldier, and balk their work, and ever ready to come to a halt; land, make a fire, put on the great pot and smoke, and gossip and sing by the hour.

It was not until the 22d of July that they arrived at Mackinaw, situated on the island of the same name, at the confluence of Lakes Huron and Michigan. This famous old French trading post continued to be a rallying point for a multifarious and motley population. The inhabitants were amphibious in their habits, most of them being, or having been, voyageurs or canoe men. It was the great place of arrival and departure of the South West Fur trade. Here the Mackinaw Company had established its principal post from whence it communicated with the interior and with Montreal.

Hence its various traders and trappers set out for their respective destinations about Lake Superior and its tributary waters or for the Mississippi, the Arkansas, the Missouri, and the other regions of the West. Here, after the absence of a year or more, they returned with their peltries and settled their accounts; the furs rendered in by them, being transmitted in canoes from hence to Montreal. Mackinaw was, therefore, for a great part of the year very scantily peopled, but at certain seasons the traders arrived from all points, with their crews of voyageurs, and the place swarmed like a hive.

Mackinaw at that time was a mere village, stretching along a small bay, with a fine broad beach in front of its principal row of houses, and dominated by the old fort, which crowned an impending height. The beach was a kind of public promenade, where were displayed all the vagaries of a seaport on the arrival of a fleet from a long cruize. Here were voyageurs frolicking away their wages, fiddling and dancing in the booths and cabins; buying all kinds of knick knacks, dressing themselves out finely and parading up and down like arrant braggarts and coxcombs. Sometimes they met with rival coxcombs in the young Indians from the opposite shore, who would appear on the beach painted and decorated in fantastic style, and would saunter up and down, to be gazed at and admired, perfectly satisfied that they eclipsed their palefaced competitors.

Now and then a chance party of "North Westers" appeared at Mackinaw from the Rendezvous at Fort William. These held themselves up as the chivalry of the Fur trade. They were men of iron, proof against cold weather, hard fare and perils of all kinds. Some would wear the North West button, and a formidable dirk and assume something of a military air; they generally wore feathers in their hats; and affected the "brave." "Je suis un homme du Nord"—"I am a man of the North" one of these swelling fellows would exclaim, sticking his arms a kimbo and ruffling by the South Westers, whom he regarded with great contempt, as men softened by mild climates and the luxurious fare of bread and bacon, and whom he stigmatized with the inglorious name of Pork eaters. The superiority assumed by these vainglorious swaggerers was, in general, tacitly admitted; indeed some of them had acquired great notoriety for deeds of hardihood and courage, for the fur trade had its heroes whose names resounded throughout the wilderness.

Such was Mackinaw at the time of which we are treating. It now, doubtless, presents a totally different aspect. The Fur companies no longer assemble there; the navigation of the lakes is carried on by steamboats and various shipping, and the race of traders, and trappers and voyageurs and Indian dandies have vapoured out their brief hour and disappeared— Such changes does the lapse of a handful of years make in this ever changing country.

At this place Mr. Hunt remained for some time to complete his assortment of Indian goods, and to encrease his number of voyageurs, as well as to engage some of a more efficient character than those enlisted at Montreal.

And now commenced another game of jockeyship. There were able and efficient men in abundance at Mackinaw but for several days not one presented himself. If offers were made to any, they were listened to with a shake of the head. Should any one seem inclined to enlist, there were officious idlers and busybodies, of that class who are ever ready to dissuade others from any enterprize in which they themselves have no concern: these would pull him by the sleeve, take him on one side, and murmur in his ear; or would suggest difficulties outright.

It was objected that the expedition would have to navigate unknown rivers and pass through howling wildernesses infested by savage tribes who had already cut off the unfortunate voyageurs that had ventured among them. That it was to climb the Rocky Mountains and descend into desolate and famished regions where the traveller was often obliged to subsist on grasshoppers and crickets, or to kill his own horse for food.

At length one man was hardy enough to engage, and he was used like a "stool pigeon," to decoy others; but several days elapsed before any more could be prevailed upon to join him. A few then came to terms. It was desireable to engage them for five years, but some refused to engage for more than three. Then they must have part of their pay in advance; which was readily granted. When they had pocketed the amount and squandered it in regales or in outfits, they began to talk of pecuniary obligations at Mackinaw which must be

discharged before they would be free to depart; or engagements with other persons, which were only to be cancelled by
a "reasonable consideration."

It was in vain to argue or remonstrate, the money advanced
had already been sacked and spent, and must be lost and the
recruits left behind, unless they could be freed from their
debts and engagements. Accordingly a fine was paid for one;
a judgment for another; a tavern bill for a third, and almost
all had to be bought off from some prior engagement, either
real or pretended.

Mr. Hunt groaned in spirit at the incessant and unreasonable demands of these worthies upon his purse; yet with all
this outlay of funds the number recruited was but scanty; and
many of the most desireable still held themselves aloof and
were not to be caught by a golden bait. With these he tried
another temptation. Among the recruits who had enlisted he
distributed feathers and ostrich plumes; these they put in their
hats, and thus figured about Mackinaw, assuming airs of vast
importance as "voyageurs in a New Company that was to
eclipse the North West." The effect was complete. A French
Canadian is too vain and mercurial a being to withstand the
finery and ostentation of the feather. Numbers immediately
pressed into the service: one must have an ostrich plume; another a white feather with a red end; a third a bunch of cocks'
tails. Thus all paraded about in vain glorious style, more delighted with the feathers in their hats than with the money in
their pockets; and considering themselves fully equal to the
boastful "men of the north."

While thus recruiting the number of rank and file Mr. Hunt
was joined by a person whom he had invited by letter to engage as a partner in the expedition. This was Mr. Ramsay
Crooks, a young man, a native of Scotland, who had served under the North West Company and been engaged in trading expeditions upon his individual account, among the tribes of the
Missouri. Mr. Hunt knew him personally and had conceived a
high and merited opinion of his judgement, enterprize and integrity: he was rejoiced therefore when the latter consented to
accompany him. Mr. Crooks, however, drew from experience a
picture of the dangers to which they would be subjected, and
urged the importance of going with a considerable force. In

ascending the upper Missouri they would have to pass through the country of the Sioux Indians, who had manifested repeated hostility to the white traders and rendered their expeditions extremely perilous; firing upon them from the river banks as they passed beneath in their boats, and attacking them in their encampments. Mr. Crooks himself, when voyaging in company with another trader of the name of M'Lellan, had been interrupted by these marauders, and had considered himself fortunate in escaping down the river without loss of life or property, but with a total abandonment of his trading voyage.

Should they be fortunate enough to pass through the country of the Sioux without molestation they would have another tribe still more savage and warlike beyond, and deadly foes of the white men. These were the Blackfeet Indians, who ranged over a wide extent of country which they would have to traverse.

Under all these circumstances it was thought adviseable to augment the party considerably. It already exceeded the number of thirty to which it had originally been limited, but it was determined, on arriving at S' Louis, to encrease it to the number of sixty.

These matters being arranged they prepared to embark; but the embarcation of a crew of Canadian voyageurs on a distant expedition is not so easy a matter as might be imagined; especially of such a set of vainglorious fellows with money in both pockets and cocks' tails in their hats. Like sailors, the Canadian voyageurs generally preface a long cruise with a carouse. They have their cronies, their brothers, their cousins, their wives, their sweethearts all to be entertained at their expense; they feast, they fiddle, they drink, they sing, they dance, they frolick and fight until they are all as mad as so many drunken Indians. The publicans are all obedience to their commands, never hesitating to let them run up scores without limit, knowing that, when their own money is expended, the pursers of their employers must answer for the bill, or the voyage must be delayed. Neither was it possible at that time to remedy the matter at Mackinaw; in that amphibious community there was always a propensity to wrest the laws in favour of riotous or mutinous boatmen. It was necessary also to keep the recruits in good humour, seeing the novelty and danger of the service into which they were entering, and the ease with which they might at any time escape it, by jumping into a canoe and going down the stream.

Such were the scenes that beset Mr. Hunt and gave him a foretaste of the difficulties of his command. The little cabarets and sutlers' shops along the bay resounded with the scraping of fiddles, with snatches of old French songs, with Indian whoops and yelps; while every plumed and feathered vagabond had his troop of loving cousins and comrades at his heels. It was with the utmost difficulty that they could be extricated from the clutches of the publicans and the embraces of their pot companions, who followed them to the water's edge with many a hug, a kiss on each cheek, and a maudlin benediction in Canadian French.

It was about the 12th of August that they left Mackinaw, and pursued the usual route by Green Bay; Fox and Wisconsin Rivers to Prairie du Chien, and thence down the Mississippi to S' Louis, where they landed on the third of September.

Chapter XIV

S' Louis, which is situated on the right bank of the Mississippi River, a few miles below the mouth of the Missouri, was, at that time, a frontier settlement and the last fitting out place for the Indian trade of the South West. It possessed a motley population, composed of the Creole descendants of the original French colonists; the keen traders from the Atlantic states; the backwoodsmen of Kentucky and Tennessee; the Indians and half breeds of the prairies; together with a singular aquatic race that had grown up from the navigation of the rivers, the "boatmen of the Mississippi," who possessed habits, manners and almost a language, peculiarly their own and strongly technical. They at that time were extremely numerous, and conducted the chief navigation and commerce of the Ohio and the Mississippi, as the voyageurs did of the Canadian waters; but, like them, their consequence and characteristics are rapidly vanishing before the all pervading intrusion of steamboats.

The old French houses engaged in the Indian trade had gathered round them a train of dependents, mongrel Indians and mongrel Frenchmen, who had intermarried with Indians. These they employed in their various expeditions by land and water. Various individuals of other countries had of late years pushed the trade farther into the interior, to the upper waters of the Missouri, and had swelled the number of these hangers on. Several of these traders had, two or three years previously, formed themselves into a company, composed of twelve partners, with a capital of about forty thousand dollars, called the Missouri Fur Company, the object of which was to establish posts along the upper part of that river and monopolize the trade. The leading partner of this Company was Mr. Manuel Lisa, a Spaniard by birth and a man of bold and enterprizing character, who had ascended the Missouri almost to its source, and made himself well acquainted and popular with several of its tribes. By his exertions trading posts had been established in 1808 in the Sioux country and among the Arickara and Mandan tribes; and a principal one, under Mr. Henry, one of the partners, at the forks of the Missouri. This company had in its employ about two hundred and fifty men, partly American hunters and partly creoles and Canadian voyageurs.

All these circumstances combined to produce a population at S' Louis even still more motley than that at Mackinaw. Here were to be seen about the river banks the hectoring, extravagant, bragging boatmen of the Mississippi, with the gay, grimacing, singing, goodhumoured Canadian voyageurs; vagrant Indians of various tribes loitered about the streets; now and then a stark Kentucky hunter, in leathern hunting dress, with rifle on shoulder and knife in belt, strode along. Here and there were new brick houses and shops just set up by bustling, driving and eager men of traffic from the Atlantic states; while on the other hand the old French mansions, with open casements still retained the easy indolent air of the original colonists; and now and then the scraping of a fiddle, a strain of an ancient French song, or the sound of billiard balls, shewed that the happy Gallic turn for gaiety and amusement still lingered about the place.

Such was S' Louis at the time of Mr. Hunt's arrival there; and the appearance of a new Fur company, with ample funds at its command, produced a strong sensation among the Indian traders of the place, and awakened keen jealousy and opposition on the part of the Missouri Company. Mr. Hunt proceeded to strengthen himself against all competition. For this purpose he secured to the interests of the association another of those enterprizing men who had been engaged in individual traffic with the tribes of the Missouri. This was a Mr. Joseph Miller, a gentleman well educated and well informed, and of a respectable family of Baltimore. He had been an officer in the Army of the United States, but had resigned in disgust, on being refused a furlough, and had taken to trapping beaver and trading among the Indians. He was easily induced by Mr. Hunt to join as a partner, and was considered by him, on account of his education and acquirements, and his experience in Indian trade, a valuable addition to the Company.

Several additional men were, likewise, enlisted at S' Louis; some as boatmen and others as hunters. These last were engaged, not merely to kill game for provisions, but also, and indeed chiefly, to trap beaver and other animals of rich furs, valuable in the trade. They enlisted on different terms. Some were to have a fixed salary of three hundred dollars, others were to be fitted out and maintained at the expense of the Company and were to hunt and trap on shares.

As Mr. Hunt met with much opposition on the part of rival traders, especially the Missouri Fur Company, it took him some weeks to complete his preparations. The delays which he had previously experienced at Montreal, Mackinaw, and on the way, added to those at S' Louis, had thrown him much behind his original calculations, so that it would be impossible to effect his voyage up the Missouri in the present year. This river flowing from high and cold latitudes, and through wide and open plains exposed to chilling blasts, freezes early. The winter may be dated from the first of November; there was every prospect, therefore, that it would be closed with ice long before Mr. Hunt could reach its upper waters. To avoid, however, the expense of wintering at S' Louis he determined to push up the river as far as possible to some point above the settlements where game was plenty, and where his whole party could be subsisted by hunting, until the breaking up of the ice in the spring should permit them to resume their voyage.

Accordingly, on the twenty first of October he took his departure from S' Louis. His party was distributed in three boats: One was the barge which he had brought from Mackinaw; another was of a larger size, such as was formerly used in navigating the Mohawk River, and known by the generic name of the Schenectady barge; the other was a large keel boat, at that time the grand conveyance on the Mississippi.

In this way they set out from S' Louis, in buoyant spirits, and soon arrived at the mouth of the Missouri. This vast river, three thousand miles in length, and which, with its tributary streams, drains such an immense extent of country, was as yet but casually and imperfectly navigated by the adventurous bark of the Fur trader. A steamboat had never yet stemmed its turbulent current; sails were but of casual assistance, for it required a strong wind to conquer the force of the stream; the main dependence was on bodily strength and manual dexterity. The boats in general had to be propelled by oars and setting poles, or drawn by the hand and by grappling hooks, from one root or overhanging tree to another; or towed by the long cordelle, or towing line, where the shores were sufficiently clear of woods and thickets to permit the men to pass along the banks.

During this slow and tedious progress the boat would be exposed to frequent danger from floating trees and great masses of drift wood; or to be impaled upon snags and sawyers, that is to say, sunken trees, presenting a jagged or pointed end above the surface of the water. As the channel of the river frequently shifted from side to side, according to the bends and sand banks, the boat had, in the same way, to advance in a zig zag course. Often a part of the crew would have to leap into the water at the shallows, and wade along with the towing line, while their comrades on board toilfully assisted with oar and setting pole. Sometimes the boat would seem to be retained motionless, as if spell bound, opposite some point round which the current set with violence, and where the utmost labour scarce effected any visible progress.

On these occasions it was that the merits of the Canadian voyageurs came into full action. Patient of toil, not to be disheartened by impediments and disappointments, fertile in expedients, and versed in every mode of humouring and conquering the wayward current, they would ply every exertion, sometimes in the boat, sometimes on shore, sometimes in the water, however cold: always alert, always in good humour; and, should they at any time flag or grow weary, one of their popular boatsongs, chanted by a veteran oarsman, and responded to in chorus, acted as a neverfailing restorative.

By such assiduous and persevering labour they made their way about four hundred and fifty miles up the Missouri, by the 16th of November, to the mouth of the Nodawa. As this was a good hunting country, and as the season was rapidly advancing, they determined to establish their winter quarters at this place, and, in fact, two days after they had come to a halt, the river closed just above their encampment.

The party had not been long at this place when they were joined by Mr. Robert M'Lellan, another trader of the Missouri, the same who had been associated with Mr. Crooks in the unfortunate expedition in which they had been intercepted by the Sioux Indians and obliged to make a rapid retreat down the river.

M'Lellan was a remarkable man. He had been a partizan under General Wayne in his Indian wars, where he had distinguished himself by his fiery spirit and reckless daring, and marvellous stories were told of his exploits. His appearance answered to his character. His frame was meagre but muscular; shewing strength, activity and iron firmness. His eyes were dark, deep set and piercing. He was restless, fearless, but of impetuous and sometimes ungovernable temper. He had been invited by Mr. Hunt to enrol himself as a partner and gladly consented; being pleased with the thoughts of passing with a powerful force through the country of the Sioux, and perhaps having an opportunity of revenging himself upon that lawless tribe for their past offences.

Another recruit that joined the camp at Nodawa deserves equal mention. This was John Day, a hunter from the backwoods of Virginia, who had been several years on the Missouri in the service of Mr. Crooks and of other traders. He was about forty years of age, six feet two inches high, straight as an Indian; with an elastic step as if he trod on springs, and a handsome, open, manly countenance. It was his boast that, in his younger days nothing could hurt or daunt him but he had "lived too fast" and injured his constitution by his excesses. Still he was strong of hand, bold of heart, a prime woodman and an almost unerring shot. He had the frank spirit of a Virginian and the rough heroism of a pioneer of the West.

The party were now brought to a halt for several months. They were in a country abounding with deer and wild turkeys, so that there was no stint of provisions, and every one appeared cheerful and contented. Mr. Hunt determined to avail himself of this interval to return to S' Louis and obtain a reinforcement. He wished to procure an interpreter acquainted with the language of the Sioux, as, from all accounts, he apprehended difficulties in passing through the country of that nation. He felt the necessity also of having a greater number of hunters, not merely to keep up a supply of provisions throughout their long and arduous expedition, but also as a protection and defence in case of Indian hostilities. For such service the Canadian voyageurs were little to be depended upon, fighting not being a part of their profession; the proper kind of men were American hunters, experienced in savage life and savage warfare and possessed of the true game spirit of the West.

Leaving, therefore, the encampment in charge of the other partners, Mr. Hunt set off on foot on the first of January (1811) for S' Louis. He was accompanied by eight men as far as Fort Osage, about one hundred and fifty miles below Nodawa. Here he procured a couple of horses and proceeded on the remainder of his journey with two men, sending the other six back to the encampment. He arrived at S' Louis on the 20th of January.

Chapter XV

*Opposition of the Missouri Fur Company—Blackfeet Indians
—Pierre Dorion, a half breed interpreter—Old Dorion and
his hybrid progeny—Family quarrels—Cross purposes between
Dorion and Lisa—Renegadoes from Nodawa—Perplexities
of a commander—Messrs. Bradbury and Nuttall join the expedition—Legal embarrassments of Pierre Dorion—Departure from S' Louis—Conjugal discipline of a half breed—
Annual swelling of the Rivers—Daniel Boon, the patriarch
of Kentucky—John Colter, his adventures among the Indians
—Rumors of danger a head—Fort Osage—An Indian war
feast—Troubles in the Dorion family—Buffalos and turkey
buzzards.*

O N THIS his second visit to S' Louis Mr. Hunt was again
impeded in his plans by the opposition of the Missouri
Fur Company. The affairs of that company were, at this time,
in a very dubious state. During the preceding year their principal establishment at the Forks of the Missouri had been so
much harassed by the Blackfeet Indians, that its commander,
Mr. Henry, one of the partners, had been compelled to abandon the post and cross the Rocky Mountains, with the intention of fixing himself upon one of the upper branches of the
Columbia. What had become of him and his party was unknown; the most intense anxiety was felt concerning them,
and apprehensions that they might have been cut off by
the Savages. At the time of Mr. Hunt's arrival at S' Louis, the
Missouri Company were fitting out an expedition to go in
quest of Mr. Henry. It was to be conducted by Mr. Manuel
Lisa, the enterprizing partner already mentioned.

There being thus two expeditions on foot at the same
moment, an unusual demand was occasioned for hunters and
voyageurs, who accordingly profited by the circumstance and
stipulated for high terms. Mr. Hunt found a keen and subtle
competitor in Lisa, and was obliged to secure his recruits by
liberal advances of pay, and by other pecuniary indulgences.

The greatest difficulty was to procure the Sioux interpreter.
There was but one man to be met with at S' Louis who was
fitted for the purpose but to secure him would require much

management. The individual in question was a half breed, named Pierre Dorion, and as he figures hereafter in this narrative, and is, withal, a striking specimen of the hybrid race on the frontier, we shall give a few particulars concerning him. Pierre was the son of Dorion the French interpreter who accompanied Messrs. Lewis and Clarke in their famous exploring expedition across the Rocky Mountains. Old Dorion was one of those French Creoles, descendants of the ancient Canadian stock, who abound on the Western frontier, and amalgamate or cohabit with the Savages. He had sojourned among various tribes and perhaps left progeny among them all; but his regular, or habitual, wife was a Sioux squaw. By her he had a hopeful brood of halfbreed sons, of whom Pierre was one. The domestic affairs of old Dorion were conducted on the true Indian plan. Father and sons would occasionally get drunk together, and then the cabin was a scene of ruffian brawl and fighting, in the course of which the old Frenchman was apt to get soundly belaboured by his mongrel offspring. In a furious scuffle of the kind one of the sons got the old man upon the ground and was upon the point of scalping him. "Hold! my son," cried the old fellow, in imploring accents,—"you are too brave, too *honorable* to scalp your father!" This last appeal touched the French side of the half breed's heart, so he suffered the old man to wear his scalp unharmed.

Of this hopeful stock was Pierre Dorion, the man whom it was now the desire of Mr. Hunt to engage as an interpreter. He had been employed in that capacity by the Missouri Fur Company during the preceding year, and had conducted their traders in safety through the different tribes of the Sioux. He had proved himself faithful and serviceable while sober, but the love of liquor in which he had been nurtured and brought up, would occasionally break out, and with it the savage side of his character.

It was this love of liquor which had embroiled him with the Missouri Company. While in their service at Fort Mandan on the frontier he had been seized with a whisky mania, and, as the beverage was only to be procured at the Company's store, it had been charged in his account at the rate of ten dollars a quart. This item had ever remained unsettled; and a matter of furious dispute the mere mention of which was sufficient to put him in a passion.

The moment it was discovered by Mr. Lisa that Pierre Dorion was in treaty with the new and rival association, he endeavored by threats as well as promises to prevent his engaging in their service. His promises might perhaps have prevailed, but his threats, which related to the whisky debt, only served to drive Pierre into the opposite ranks. Still he took advantage of this competition for his services to stand out with Mr. Hunt on the most advantageous terms and after a negotiation of nearly two weeks, capitulated to serve in the expedition as hunter and interpreter at the rate of three hundred dollars a year, two hundred of which were to be paid in advance.

When Mr. Hunt had got every thing ready for leaving S' Louis, new difficulties arose. Five of the American hunters from the encampment at Nodawa suddenly made their appearance. They alleged that they had been ill treated by the partners at the encampment, and had come off clandestinely in consequence of a dispute. It was useless at the present moment and under present circumstances, to attempt any compulsory measures with these deserters. Two of them Mr. Hunt prevailed upon, by mild means, to return with him. The rest refused. Nay, what was worse, they spread such reports of the hardships and dangers to be apprehended in the course of the expedition, that they struck a panic into those hunters who had recently engaged at S' Louis, and, when the hour of departure arrived, all, but one, refused to embark. It was in vain to plead or remonstrate, they shouldered their rifles and turned their backs upon the expedition, and Mr. Hunt was fain to put off from shore with the single hunter and a number of voyageurs whom he had engaged. Even Pierre Dorion at the last moment refused to enter the boat until Mr. Hunt consented to take his squaw and two children on board also. But the tissue of perplexities on account of this worthy individual did not end here.

Among the various persons who were about to proceed up the Missouri with Mr. Hunt were two scientific gentlemen: one Mr. John Bradbury, a man of mature age, but great enterprize and personal activity, who had been sent out by the

Linnean Society of Liverpool, to make a collection of American plants; the other a Mr. Nuttall, likewise an Englishman, younger in years, who has since made himself known as the author of "Travels in Arkansas," and a work on the "Genera of American Plants." Mr. Hunt had offered them the protection and facilities of his party, in their scientific researches up the Missouri.

As they were not ready to depart at the moment of embarcation they put their trunks on board of the boat, but remained at S' Louis until the next day for the arrival of the post, intending to join the expedition at S' Charles, a short distance above the mouth of the Missouri.

The same evening, however, they learnt that a writ had been issued against Pierre Dorion for his whiskey debt, by Mr. Lisa as agent of the Missouri Company, and that it was the intention to entrap the mongrel linguist on his arrival at S' Charles. Upon hearing this, Mr. Bradbury and Mr. Nuttall set off a little after midnight, by land; got ahead of the boat as it was ascending the Missouri, before its arrival at S' Charles, and gave Pierre Dorion warning of the legal toil prepared to ensnare him. The knowing Pierre immediately landed and took to the woods, followed by his squaw laden with their pappooses and a large bundle containing their most precious effects; promising to rejoin the party some distance above S' Charles.

There seemed little dependence to be placed upon the promises of a loose adventurer of the kind, who was at the very time playing an evasive game with his former employers; who had already received two thirds of his year's pay, and had his rifle on his shoulder, his family and worldly fortune at his heels, and the wild woods before him. There was no alternative, however, and it was hoped his pique against his old employers would render him faithful to his new ones.

The party reached S' Charles in the afternoon, but the harpies of the law looked in vain for their expected prey. The boats resumed their course on the following morning, and had not proceeded far when Pierre Dorion made his appearance on the shore. He was gladly taken on board, but he came without his squaw. They had quarrelled in the night; Pierre had administered the Indian discipline of the cudgel, whereupon she had taken to the woods, with their children and all their worldly goods. Pierre evidently was deeply grieved and disconcerted at the loss of his wife and his knapsack; wherefore Mr. Hunt dispatched one of the Canadian voyageurs in search of the the fugitive, and the whole party, after proceeding a few miles further, encamped on an island to await his return. The Canadian rejoined the party, but without the squaw, and Pierre Dorion passed a solitary and anxious night, bitterly regretting his indiscretion in having exercised his conjugal authority so near home. Before day break, however, a well known voice reached his ears from the opposite shore. It was his repentant spouse who had been wandering the woods all night in quest of the party and had at length descried it by its fires. A boat was despatched for her; the interesting family was once more united, and Mr. Hunt now flattered himself that his perplexities with Pierre Dorion were at an end.

Bad weather, very heavy rains and an unusually early rise in the Missouri rendered the ascent of the river toilsome, slow and dangerous. The rise of the Missouri does not generally take place until the month of May or June: the present swelling of the river must have been caused by a freshet in some of its more southern branches; it could not have been the great annual flood, as the higher branches must still have been ice bound. And here we cannot but pause to notice the admirable arrangement of nature, by which the annual swellings of the various great rivers which empty themselves into the Mississippi, have been made to precede each other at considerable intervals. Thus the flood of the Red River precedes that of the Arkansas by a month; the Arkansas also, rising in a much more southern latitude than the Missouri, takes the lead of it in its annual excess, and its superabundant waters are disgorged and disposed of long before the breaking up of the icy barriers of the north: otherwise, did all these mighty streams rise simultaneously and discharge their vernal floods into the Mississippi an inundation would be the consequence that would submerge and devastate all the lower country.

On the afternoon of the third day, March 17th, the boats touched at Charette, one of the old villages founded by the original French colonists. Here they met with Daniel Boon, the renowned patriarch of Kentucky, who had kept in the advance of civilization, and on the borders of the wilderness, still leading a hunter's life, though now in his eighty fifth year. He had but recently returned from a hunting and trapping expedition and had brought nearly sixty beaver skins as trophies of his skill. The old man was still erect in form, strong in limb and unflinching in spirit, and as he stood on the river bank, watching the departure of an expedition destined to traverse the wilderness to the very shores of the Pacific, very probably felt a throb of his old pioneer spirit, impelling him to shoulder his rifle and join the adventurous band. Boon flourished several years after this meeting, in a vigorous old age, the nestor of hunters and backwoodsmen, and died full of sylvan honour and renown in 1818 in his ninety second year.

The next morning early, as the party were yet encamped at the mouth of a small stream, they were visited by another of these heroes of the wilderness, one John Colter, who had accompanied Lewis and Clarke in their memorable expedition. He had recently made one of those vast internal voyages so characteristic of this fearless class of men, and of the immense regions over which they hold their lonely wanderings, having come from the head waters of the Missouri to S' Louis, in a small canoe. This distance of three thousand miles he had accomplished in thirty days. Colter kept with the party all the morning. He had many particulars to give them concerning the Blackfeet Indians, a restless and predatory tribe, who had conceived an implacable hostility to the white men, in consequence of one of their warriors having been killed by Captain Lewis, while attempting to steal horses. Through the country infested by these savages the expedition would have to proceed, and Colter was urgent in reiterating the precautions that ought to be observed respecting them. He had himself experienced their vindictive cruelty, and his story deserves particular citation, as shewing the hairbreadth adventures to which these solitary rovers of the wilderness are exposed.

Colter, with the hardihood of a regular trapper, had cast himself loose from the party of Lewis and Clarke in the very heart of the wilderness, and had remained to trap beaver alone on the head waters of the Missouri. Here he fell in with another lonely trapper, like himself, named Potts, and they agreed to keep together. They were in the very region of the terrible Blackfeet, at that time thirsting to revenge the death of their companion, and knew that they had to expect no mercy at their hands. They were obliged to keep concealed all day in the woody margins of the rivers, setting their traps after nightfall and taking them up before day break. It was running a fearful risk for the sake of a few beaver skins; but such is the life of the trapper.

They were on a branch of the Missouri called Jefferson's Fork, and had set their traps at night, about six miles up a small river that emptied into the fork. Early in the morning they ascended the river in a canoe, to examine the traps. The banks on each side were high and perpendicular and cast a shade over the stream. As they were softly paddling along they heard the trampling of many feet upon the banks. Colter immediately gave the alarm of "Indians!" and was for instant retreat. Potts scoffed at him for being frightened by the trampling of a herd of buffalo. Colter checked his uneasiness and paddled forward. They had not gone much farther when frightful whoops and yells burst forth from each side of the river, and several hundred Indians appeared on either bank. Signs were made to the unfortunate trappers to come on shore. They were obliged to comply. Before they could get out of their canoe a savage seized the rifle belonging to Potts. Colter sprang on shore, wrested the weapon from the hands of the Indian and restored it to his companion, who was still in the canoe, and immediately pushed into the stream. There was the sharp twang of a bow, and Potts cried out that he was wounded. Colter urged him to come on shore and submit as his only chance for life, but the other knew there was no prospect of mercy, and determined to die game. Levelling his rifle he shot one of the savages dead on the spot. The next moment he fell himself, pierced with innumerable arrows.

The vengeance of the savages now turned upon Colter. He was stripped naked, and, having some knowledge of the Blackfoot language, overheard a consultation as to the mode of despatching him, so as to derive the greatest amusement from his death. Some were for setting him up as a mark, and having a trial of skill at his expense. The chief, however, was for nobler sport. He seized Colter by the shoulder and demanded if he could run fast. The unfortunate trapper was too well acquainted with Indian customs not to comprehend the drift of the question. He knew he was to run for his life, and to furnish a kind of human hunt to his persecutors. Though in reality he was noted among his brother hunters for swiftness of foot, he assured the chief that he was a very bad runner. His stratagem gained him some vantage ground. He was led by the chief into the prairie about four hundred yards from the main body of savages and then turned loose to save himself if he could. A tremendous yell let him know that the whole pack of bloodhounds were off in full cry. Colter flew rather than ran; he was astonished at his own speed; but he had six miles of prairie to traverse before he should reach the Jefferson fork of the Missouri; how could he hope to hold out such a distance with the fearful odds of several hundred to one against him. The plain, too, abounded with the prickly pear, which wounded his naked feet. Still he fled on, dreading each moment to hear the twang of a bow and to feel an arrow quivering at his heart. He did not even dare to look round lest he should lose an inch of that distance on which his life depended. He had run nearly half way across the plain when the sound of pursuit grew somewhat fainter and he ventured to turn his head. The main body of his pursuers were a considerable distance behind; several of the faster runners were scattered in the advance, while a swiftfooted warrior armed with a spear, was not more than a hundred yards behind him.

Inspired with new hope Colter redoubled his exertions, but strained himself to such a degree that the blood gushed from his mouth and nostrils and streamed down his breast. He arrived within a mile of the river. The sound of footsteps gathered upon him. A glance behind shewed his pursuer within twenty yards, and preparing to launch his spear. Stopping short, he turned round and spread out his arms. The savage, confounded by this sudden action, attempted to stop and to hurl his spear, but fell in the very act. His spear stuck in the ground and the shaft broke in his hand. Colter plucked up the pointed part, pinned the savage to the earth and continued his flight. The Indians, as they arrived at their slaughtered companion, stopped to howl over him.

Colter made the most of this precious delay; gained the skirt of cottonwood bordering the river, dashed through it and plunged into the stream. He swam to a neighboring island, against the upper end of which the drift wood had lodged in such quantities as to form a natural raft. Under this he dived, and swam below water until he succeeded in getting a breathing place between the floating trunks of trees, where branches and bushes formed a covert several feet above the level of the water. He had scarcely drawn breath after all his toils when he heard his pursuers on the river bank whooping and yelling like so many fiends. They plunged in the river and swam to the raft. The heart of Colter almost died within him as he saw them, through the chinks of his concealment, passing and repassing and seeking for him in all directions. They at length gave up the search, and he began to rejoice in his escape when the idea presented itself that they might set the raft on fire. Here was a new source of horrible apprehension, in which he remained until night fall. Fortunately the idea did not suggest itself to the Indians. As soon as it was dark, finding by the silence around that his pursuers had departed, Colter dived again and came up beyond the raft. He then swam silently down the river for a considerable distance, when he landed, and kept on all night, to get as far off as possible from this dangerous neighborhood.

By day break he had gained sufficient distance to relieve him from the terrors of his savage foes; but now new sources of inquietude presented themselves. He was naked and alone, in the midst of an unbounded wilderness; his only chance was to reach a trading post of the Missouri Company, situated on a branch of the Yellow stone River. Even should he elude his pursuers days must elapse before he could reach this post, during which he must traverse immense prairies destitute of shade, his naked body exposed to the burning heat of the sun by day, and the dews and chills of the night season; and his feet lacerated by the thorns of the prickly pear. Though he might see game in abundance around him, he had no means of killing any for his sustenance, and must depend for food upon the roots of the earth. In defiance of these difficulties he pushed resolutely forward, guiding himself on his trackless course by those signs and indications known only to Indians and backwoodsmen, and after braving dangers and hardships enough to break down any spirit but that of a western pioneer, arrived safe at the solitary post in question.*

Such is a sample of the rugged experience which Colter had to relate of Savage life; yet, with all these perils and terrors fresh in his recollection, he could not see the present band on their way to those regions of danger and adventure, without feeling a vehement impulse to join them. A Western trapper is like a sailor; past hazards only stimulate him to further risques. The vast prairie is to the one what the ocean is to the other, a boundless field of enterprize and exploit; however he may have suffered in his last cruize he is always ready to join a new expedition, and the more adventurous its nature, the more attractive is it to his vagrant spirit.

Nothing seems to have kept Colter from continuing with the party to the shores of the Pacific but the circumstance of his having recently married. All the morning he kept with them, balancing in his mind the charms of his bride against those of the Rocky Mountains; the former, however, prevailed, and after a march of several miles he took a reluctant leave of the travellers and turned his face homeward.

Continuing their progress up the Missouri the party encamped on the evening of the 21st of March in the neighborhood of a little frontier village of French Creoles. Here Pierre Dorion met with some of his old comrades with whom he had a long gossip and returned to the camp with rumours of bloody feuds between the Osages and the Ioways, or Ayaways, Potowatomies, Sioux and Saukees. Blood had already been shed and scalps been taken. A war party three hundred strong were prowling in the neighborhood; others might be met with higher up the river; it behoved the travellers, therefore, to be upon their guard against robbery or surprize, for an Indian war party on the march is prone to acts of outrage. In consequence of this report, which was subsequently confirmed by further intelligence, a guard was kept up at night round the encampment, and they all slept on their arms. As they were sixteen in number and well supplied with weapons and ammunition, they trusted to be able to give any marauding party a warm reception. Nothing occurred, however, to

* Bradbury. Travels in America. P. 17.

molest them on their voyage, and on the 8th of April they came in sight of Fort Osage. On their approach the flag was hoisted on the fort, and they saluted it by a discharge of fire arms. Within a short distance of the fort was an Osage village, the inhabitants of which, men, women and children, thronged down to the water side to witness their landing. One of the first persons they met on the river bank was Mr. Crooks, who had come down in a boat, with nine men, from the winter encampment at Nodawa to meet them.

They remained at Fort Osage a part of three days, during which they were hospitably entertained at the garrison by Lieutenant Brownson who held a temporary command. They were regaled also with a war feast at the village; the Osage warriors having returned from a successful foray against the Ioways, in which they had taken seven scalps. These were paraded on poles about the village, followed by the warriors decked out in all their savage ornaments and hideously painted as if for battle.

By the Osage warriors Mr. Hunt and his companions were again warned to be on their guard in ascending the river, as the Sioux tribe meant to lay in wait and attack them.

On the 10th of April they again embarked, their party being now augmented to twenty six by the addition of Mr. Crooks and his boat's crew. They had not proceeded far, however, when there was a great outcry from one of the boats; it was occasioned by a little domestic discipline in the Dorion family. The squaw of the worthy interpreter, it appeared, had been so delighted with the scalp dance and other festivities of the Osage village that she had taken a strong inclination to remain there. This had been as strongly opposed by her liege lord, who had compelled her to embark. The good dame had remained sulky ever since, whereupon Pierre, seeing no other mode of exorcising the evil spirit out of her, and being perhaps a little inspired by whiskey, had resorted to the Indian remedy of the cudgel, and, before his neighbors could interfere had belaboured her so soundly, that there is no record of her having shown any refractory symptoms throughout the remainder of the expedition.

For a week they continued their voyage, exposed to almost incessant rains. The bodies of drowned buffaloes floated past them in vast numbers; many had drifted upon the shore, or against the upper ends of the rafts and islands. These had attracted great flights of turkey buzzards; some were banqueting on the carcasses, others were soaring far aloft in the sky, and others were perched on the trees, with their backs to the sun, and their wings stretched out to dry, like so many vessels in harbour, spreading their sails after a shower.

The turkey buzzard (Vultur Aura, or Golden Vulture) when on the wing is one of the most specious and imposing of birds. Its flight in the upper regions of the air is really sublime, extending its immense wings and wheeling slowly and majestically to and fro, seemingly without exerting a muscle or fluttering a feather, but moving by mere volition, and sailing on the bosom of the air, as a ship upon the ocean. Usurping the empyreal realm of the eagle, he assumes for a time the port and dignity of that majestic bird, and often is mistaken for him by ignorant crawlers upon earth. It is only when he descends from the clouds to pounce upon carrion that he betrays his low propensities and reveals his caitiff character. Near at hand he is a disgusting bird, ragged in plumage, base in aspect, and of loathsome odour.

On the 17th of April Mr. Hunt arrived with his party at the station near the Nodawa River, where the main body had been quartered during the winter.

Chapter XVI

Return of spring—Appearance of snakes—Great flights of wild pigeons—Renewal of the voyage—Night encampments —Platte River—Ceremonials on passing it—Signs of Indian war parties—Magnificent prospect at Papillion creek—Desertion of two hunters—An irruption into the camp of Indian desperadoes—Village of the Omahas—Anecdotes of the tribe—Feudal wars of the Indians—Story of Blackbird the famous Omaha chief.

THE WEATHER continued rainy and ungenial for some days after Mr. Hunt's return to Nodawa, yet spring was rapidly advancing, and vegetation was putting forth with all its early freshness and beauty. The snakes began to recover from their torpor and crawl forth into day, and the neighborhood of the wintering house seems to have been much infested with them. Mr. Bradbury, in the course of his botanical researches, found a surprizing number in a half torpid state, under flat stones upon the banks which overhung the cantonment, and narrowly escaped being struck by a rattle snake, which darted at him from a cleft in the rocks, but fortunately gave him warning by its rattle.

The pigeons too were filling the woods in vast migratory flocks. It is almost incredible to describe the prodigious flights of these birds in the western wildernesses. They appear absolutely in clouds, and move with astonishing velocity, their wings making a whistling sound as they fly. The rapid evolutions of these flocks, wheeling and shifting suddenly as if with one mind and one impulse; the flashing changes of colour they present, as their backs, their breasts, or the under part of their wings are turned to the spectator, are singularly pleasing. When they alight, if on the ground, they cover whole acres at a time; if upon trees, the branches often break beneath their weight. If suddenly startled while feeding in the midst of a forest, the noise they make in getting on the wing is like the roar of a cataract or the sound of distant thunder.

A flight of this kind, like an Egyptian flight of locusts, devours every thing that serves for its food as it passes along.

So great were the numbers in the vicinity of the camp that Mr. Bradbury in the course of a morning's excursion, shot nearly three hundred with a fowling piece. He gives a curious, though apparently a fanciful, account of the kind of discipline observed in these immense flocks, so that each may have a chance at picking up food. As the front ranks must meet with the greatest abundance, and the rear ranks must have scanty pickings, the instant a rank finds itself the hindmost, it rises in the air, flies over the whole flock and takes its place in the advance. The next rank follows in its course, and thus the last is continually becoming first, and all by turns have a front place at the banquet.

The rains having at length subsided, Mr. Hunt broke up the encampment and resumed his course up the Missouri.

The party now consisted of nearly sixty persons; of whom five were partners, one, John Reed, was a clerk, forty were Canadian "voyageurs" or "*engagés*" and there were several hunters. They embarked in four boats, one of which was of a large size, mounting a swivel and two howitzers. All were furnished with masts and sails, to be used when the wind was sufficiently favorable and strong to overpower the current of the river. Such was the case for the first four or five days, when they were wafted steadily up the stream by a strong south easter.

Their encampments at night were often pleasant and picturesque: on some beautiful bank, beneath spreading trees, which afforded them shelter and fuel. The tents were pitched, the fires made and the meals prepared by the voyageurs, and many a story was told and joke passed and song sung round the evening fire. All, however, were asleep at an early hour. Some under the tents; others wrapped in blankets before the fire, or beneath the trees; and some few in the boats and canoes.

On the 28th they breakfasted on one of the islands which lie at the mouth of the Nebraska or Platte River; the largest tributary of the Missouri and about 600 miles above its confluence with the Mississippi. This broad but shallow stream flows for an immense distance through a wide and verdant valley, scooped out of boundless prairies. It draws its main supplies, by several forks or branches, from the Rocky Mountains. The mouth of this river is established as the dividing point between the upper and lower Missouri, and the earlier voyagers, in their toilsome ascent, before the introduction of steamboats, considered one half of their labours accomplished when they reached this place. The passing of the mouth of the Nebraska, therefore, was equivalent among boatmen to the crossing of the line among sailors, and was celebrated with like ceremonials of a rough and waggish nature, practiced upon the uninitiated; among which was the old nautical joke of shaving. The river deities, however, like those of the sea, were to be propitiated by a bribe, and the infliction of these rude honors to be parried by a treat to the adepts.

At the mouth of the Nebraska new signs were met with of war parties which had recently been in the vicinity. There was the frame of a skin canoe, in which the warriors had traversed the river. At night, also, the lurid reflection of immense fires hung in the sky, shewing the conflagration of great tracts of the prairies. Such fires not being made by hunters, so late in the season, it was supposed they were caused by some wandering war parties. These often take the precaution to set the prairies on fire behind them to conceal their traces from their enemies. This is chiefly done when the party has been unsuccessful and is on the retreat, and apprehensive of pursuit. At such time it is not safe even for friends to fall in with them, as they are apt to be in savage humour and disposed to vent their spleen in capricious outrage. These signs, therefore, of a band of marauders on the prowl called for some degree of vigilance on the part of the travellers.

After passing the Nebraska the party halted for part of two days on the bank of the river, a little above Papillion Creek, to supply themselves with a stock of oars and poles from the tough wood of the ash, which is not met with higher up the Missouri. While the voyageurs were thus occupied, the naturalists rambled over the adjacent country, to collect plants. From the summit of a range of bluffs on the opposite side of the river, about two hundred and fifty feet high, they had one of those vast and magnificent prospects which sometimes unfold themselves in these boundless regions. Below them was the valley of the Missouri, about seven miles in breadth, clad in the fresh verdure of spring; enamelled with flowers and interspersed with clumps and groves of noble trees, between which the mighty river poured its turbulent and turbid stream. The interior of the country presented a singular scene; the immense waste being broken up by innumerable green hills, not above eighty feet in height, but extremely steep, and acutely pointed at their summits. A long line of bluffs extended for upwards of thirty miles, parallel to the Missouri, with a shallow lake stretching along their base, which had evidently once formed a bed of the river. The surface of this lake was covered with aquatic plants, on the broad leaves of which numbers of water snakes, drawn forth by the genial warmth of spring, were basking in the sunshine.

On the 2d of May at the usual hour of embarking the camp was thrown into some confusion by two of the hunters, named Harrington, expressing their intention to abandon the expedition and return home. One of these had joined the party in the preceding autumn, having been hunting for two years on the Missouri; the other had engaged at S' Louis in the following March and had come up from thence with Mr. Hunt. He now declared that he had enlisted merely for the purpose of following his brother and persuading him to return; having been enjoined to do so by his mother, whose anxiety had been awakened by the idea of his going on such a wild and distant expedition.

The loss of two stark hunters and prime riflemen was a serious affair to the party, for they were approaching the region where they might expect hostilities from the Sioux; indeed, throughout the whole of their perilous journey, the services of such men would be all important, for little reliance was to be placed upon the valour of the Canadians in case of attack. Mr. Hunt endeavored by arguments, expostulations and entreaties to shake the determination of the two brothers. He represented to them that they were between six and seven hundred miles above the mouth of the Missouri; that they would have four hundred miles to go before they could reach the habitation of a white man, throughout which they would be exposed to all kinds of risks, since, he declared, if they persisted in abandoning him and breaking their faith, he would not furnish them with a single round of ammunition. All was in vain; they obstinately persisted in their resolution; whereupon Mr. Hunt, partly incited by indignation, partly by the

policy of deterring others from desertion, put his threat in execution, and left them to find their way back to the settlements
without, as he supposed, a single bullet or a charge of powder.

The boats now continued their slow and toilsome course,
for several days, against the current of the river. The late signs
of roaming war parties caused a vigilant watch to be kept up
at night when the crews encamped on shore; nor was this vigilance superfluous, for on the night of the Seventh instant,
there was a wild and fearful yell and eleven Sioux warriors,
stark naked with tomahawks in their hands, rushed into the
camp. They were instantly surrounded and seized, whereupon
their leader called out to his followers to desist from any violence, and pretended to be perfectly pacific in his intentions.
It proved, however, that they were a part of the war party the
skeleton of whose canoe had been seen at the mouth of the
river Platte, and the reflection of whose fires had been descried in the air. They had been disappointed or defeated in
their foray, and in their rage and mortification these eleven
warriors had "devoted their clothes to the Medicine." This is
a desperate act of Indian braves, when foiled in war and in
dread of scoffs and sneers. In such case they sometimes throw
off their clothes and ornaments, devote themselves to the
Great Spirit, and attempt some reckless exploit with which to
cover their disgrace. Woe to any defenceless party of white
men that may then fall in their way!

Such was the explanation given by Pierre Dorion, the half
breed interpreter, of this wild intrusion into the camp; and the
party were so exasperated when apprized of the sanguinary intentions of the prisoners that they were for shooting them on
the spot. Mr. Hunt, however, exerted his usual moderation
and humanity, and ordered that they should be conveyed
across the river in one of the boats, threatening them, however, with certain death, if again caught in any hostile act.

On the 10th of May the party arrived at the Omaha (pronounced Omawhaw) village, about eight hundred and thirty
miles above the mouth of the Missouri, and encamped in its
neighborhood. The village was situated under a hill on the
bank of the river and consisted of about eighty lodges. These
were of a circular and conical form and about sixteen feet in
diameter; being mere tents of dressed buffalo skins, sewed

together and stretched on long poles, inclined towards each other so as to cross at about half their height. Thus the naked tops of the poles diverge in such a manner that, if they were covered with skins like the lower ends, the tent would be shaped like an hour glass; and present the appearance of one cone inverted on the apex of another.*

The forms of Indian lodges are worthy of attention, each tribe having a different mode of shaping and arranging them, so that it is easy to tell on seeing a lodge or an encampment at a distance, to what tribe the inhabitants belong. The exterior of the Omaha lodges have often a gay and fanciful appearance, being painted with undulating bands of red or yellow, or decorated with rude figures of horses, deer and buffaloes, and with human faces, painted like full moons, four and five feet broad.

The Omahas were once one of the numerous and powerful tribes of the prairies, vying in warlike might and prowess with the Sioux, the Pawness, the Sauks, the Konzas and the Iatans. Their wars with the Sioux however had thinned their ranks and the small pox in 1802 had swept off two thirds of their number. At the time of Mr. Hunt's visit they still boasted about two hundred warriors and hunters, but they are now fast melting away and, before long, will be numbered among those extinguished nations of the West that exist but in tradition.

In his correspondence with Mr. Astor from this point of his journey, Mr. Hunt gives a sad account of the Indian tribes bordering on the river. They were in continual war with each other; and their wars were of the most harassing kind, consisting, not merely of main conflicts and expeditions of moment, involving the sackings, burnings and massacres of towns and villages, but of individual acts of treachery, murder and cold blooded cruelty: or of vaunting and fool hardy exploits of single warriors, either to avenge some personal wrong, or gain the vain glorious trophy of a scalp. The lonely hunter, the wandering wayfarer, the poor squaw, cutting wood or gathering corn, was liable to be surprized and slaughtered. In this way tribes were either swept away at once, or gradually thinned out and Savage life was surrounded with constant

---

* Bradbury. P. 66.

horrors and alarms. That the race of red men should diminish from year to year, and so few should survive of the numerous nations which evidently once peopled the vast regions of the west, is nothing surprising; it is rather matter of surprize that so many should survive, for the existance of a savage in these parts seems little better than a prolonged and all besetting death. It is, in fact, a caricature of the boasted romance of feudal times; chivalry in its native and uncultured state, and knight errantry run wild.

In their more prosperous days the Omahas looked upon themselves as the most powerful and perfect of human beings, and considered all created things as made for their peculiar use and benefit. It is this tribe of whose chief, the famous Wash-ing-guh-sah-ba, or Black bird, such savage and romantic stories are told. He had died about ten years previous to the arrival of Mr. Hunt's party, but his name was still mentioned with awe by his people. He was one of the first among the Indian chiefs on the Missouri to deal with the white traders, and shewed great sagacity in levying his royal dues. When a trader arrived in his village he caused all his goods to be brought into his lodge and opened. From these he selected whatever suited his sovereign pleasure, blankets, tobacco, whisky, powder, ball, beads and red paint, and laid the articles on one side, without deigning to give any compensation. Then calling to him his herald or crier he would order him to mount on top of the lodge and summon all the tribe to bring in their peltries and trade with the white man. The lodge would soon be crowded with Indians bringing bear, beaver, otter, and other skins. No one was allowed to dispute the prices fixed by the white trader upon his articles; who took care to indemnify himself five times over for the goods set apart by the chief. In this way the Black bird enriched himself, and enriched the white men, and became exceedingly popular among the traders of the Missouri. His people, however, were not equally satisfied by a regulation of trade which worked so manifestly against them, and began to shew signs of discontent. Upon this a crafty and unprincipled trader revealed a secret to the Blackbird, by which he might acquire unbounded sway over his ignorant and superstitious subjects. He instructed him in the poisonous qualities of arsenic, and furnished him with an ample supply of that baneful drug. From this time the Blackbird seemed endowed with supernatural powers, to possess the gift of prophecy and to hold the disposal of life and death within his hands. Woe to any one who questioned his authority or dared to dispute his commands. The Black bird prophesied his death within a certain time, and he had the secret means of verifying his prophecy. Within the fated period the offender was smitten with strange and sudden disease and perished from the face of the earth. Every one stood aghast at these multiplied examples of his superhuman might and dreaded to displease so omnipotent and vindictive a being and the Blackbird enjoyed a wide and undisputed sway.

It was not, however, by terror alone that he ruled his people; he was a warrior of the first order, and his exploits in arms were the theme of young and old. His career had begun by hardships, having been taken prisoner by the Sioux, in early youth. Under his command the Omahas obtained great character for military prowess, nor did he permit an insult or injury to one of his tribe to pass unrevenged. The Pawnee Republicans had inflicted a gross indignity on a favorite and distinguished Omaha brave. The Black bird assembled his warriors, led them against the Pawnee town; attacked it with irresistible fury, slaughtered a great number of its inhabitants and burnt it to the ground. He waged fierce and bloody war against the Otoes for many years, until peace was effected between them by the mediation of the Whites. Fearless in battle, and fond of signalizing himself, he dazzled his followers by his daring acts. In attacking a Konza village he rode singly round it, loading and discharging his rifle at the inhabitants as he gallopped past them. He kept up in war the same idea of mysterious and supernatural power. At one time when pursuing a war party by their tracks across the prairies, he repeatedly discharged his rifle into the prints made by their feet and by the hoofs of their horses, assuring his followers that he would thereby cripple the fugitives so that they would easily be overtaken. He in fact did overtake them, and destroyed them almost to a man; and his victory was considered miraculous, both by friend and foe. By these and similar exploits, he made himself the pride and boast of his people, and became popular among them notwithstanding his death denouncing flat.

With all his savage and terrific qualities he was sensible to the power of female beauty and capable of love. A war party of the Poncas had made a foray into the lands of the Omahas and carried off a number of women and horses. The Black bird was roused to fury, and took the field with all his braves swearing to "eat up the Ponca nation," the Indian threat of exterminating war. The Poncas, sorely pressed, took refuge behind a rude bulwark of earth, but the Black bird kept up so galling a fire that he seemed likely to execute his menace. In their extremity they sent forth a herald bearing the calumet or pipe of peace, but he was shot down by order of the Black bird. Another herald was sent forth in similar guize, but he shared a like fate. The Poncas chief then, as a last hope, arrayed his beautiful daughter in her finest ornaments, and sent her forth with a calumet, to sue for peace. The charms of the Indian maid touched the stern heart of the Black bird; he accepted the pipe at her hand, smoked it, and from that time a peace took place between the Poncas and the Omahas.

This beautiful damsel, in all probability, was the favorite wife whose fate makes so tragic an incident in the story of the Black bird. Her youth and beauty had gained an absolute sway over his rugged heart, so that he distinguished her above all his other wives. The habitual gratification of his vindictive impulses, however, had taken away from him all mastery over his passions, and rendered him liable to the most furious transports of rage. In one of these his beautiful wife had the misfortune to offend him, when suddenly drawing his knife he laid her dead at his feet with a single blow.

In an instant his frenzy was at an end. He gazed for a time in mute bewilderment upon his victim, then drawing his buffalo robe over his head he sat down beside the corpse and remained brooding over his crime and his loss. Three days elapsed, yet the chief continued silent and motionless; tasting no food and apparently sleepless. It was apprehended that he intended to starve himself to death; his people approached him in trembling awe, and entreated him once more to uncover his face and be comforted, but he remained unmoved. At length one of his warriors brought in a small child and, laying it on the ground, placed the foot of the Black bird upon its neck. The heart of the gloomy savage was touched by this appeal: he threw aside his robe; made an harangue upon what he had done; and from that time forward seemed to have thrown the load of grief and remorse from his mind.

He still retained his fatal and mysterious secret and with it his terrific power; but, though able to deal death to his enemies he could not avert it from himself or his friends. In 1802 the smallpox, that dreadful pestilence which swept over the land like a fire over the prairies, made its appearance in the Village of the Omahas. The poor savages saw with dismay the ravages of a malady loathsome and agonizing in its details and which set the skill and experience of their conjurers and medicine men at defiance. In a little while two thirds of the population were swept from the face of the earth, and the doom of the rest seemed sealed. The stoicism of the warriors was at an end: they became wild and desperate. Some set fire to the village as a last means of checking the pestilence; others, in a frenzy of despair, put their wives and children to death, that they might be spared the agonies of an inevitable disease, and "that they might all go to some better country."

When the general horror and dismay was at its height the Blackbird himself was struck down with the malady. The poor savages, when they saw their chief in danger, forgot their own miseries and surrounded his dying bed. His dominant spirit and his love for the white men were evinced in his latest breath, with which he designated his place of sepulture. It was to be on a hill or promontory, upwards of four hundred feet in height overlooking a great extent of the Missouri from whence he had been accustomed to watch for the barks of the white men. The Missouri washes the base of the promontory, and after winding and doubling in many links and mazes in the plain below, returns to within nine hundred yards of its starting place; so that for thirty miles navigating with sail and oar, the voyager finds himself continually near to this singular promontory as if spell bound.

It was the dying command of the Blackbird that his tomb should be upon the summit of this hill, in which he should be interred, seated on his favorite horse, that he might overlook his ancient domain and behold the barks of the white men as they came up the river to trade with his people.

His dying orders were faithfully obeyed. His corpse was placed astride of his war steed, and a mound raised over them on the summit of the hill. On top of the mound was erected a staff from which fluttered the banner of the chieftain and the scalps that he had taken in battle. When the expedition under Mr. Hunt visited that part of the country the staff still remained with the fragments of the banner; and the superstitious rite of placing food from time to time on the mound for the use of the deceased was still observed by the Omahas. That rite has since fallen into disuse, for the tribe itself is almost extinct; yet the hill of the Black bird continues an object of veneration to the wandering savage, and a land mark to the voyager of the Missouri; and as the civilized traveller comes within sight of its spell bound crest, the mound is pointed out to him from afar, which still incloses the grim skeletons of the Indian warrior and his horse.

Chapter XVII

Rumors of danger from the Sioux Tetons—Ruthless character of those savages—Pirates of the Missouri—Their affair with Crooks and M'Lellan—A trading expedition broken up—M'Lellan's vow of vengeance—Uneasiness in the camp—Desertions—Departure from the Omaha village—Meeting with Jones and Carson, two adventurous trappers—Scientific pursuits of Messrs. Bradbury and Nuttall—Zeal of a botanist—Adventure of Mr. Bradbury with a Ponca Indian—Expedient of the pocket compass and microscope—A messenger from Lisa—Motives for pressing forward.

WHILE Mr. Hunt and his party were sojourning at the village of the Omahas, three Sioux Indians of the Yankton Ahna tribe arrived, bringing unpleasant intelligence. They reported that certain bands of the Sioux Tetons, who inhabited a region many leagues further up the Missouri, were near at hand, awaiting the approach of the party, with the avowed intention of opposing their progress.

The Sioux Tetons were at that time a sort of pirates of the Missouri, who considered the wellfreighted bark of the American trader fair game. They had their own traffic with the British merchants of the north west, who brought them regular supplies of merchandize by way of the river S' Peter. Being thus independent of the Missouri traders for their supplies, they kept no terms with them, but plundered them whenever they had an opportunity. It has been insinuated that they were prompted to these outrages by the British merchants, who wished to keep off all rivals in the Indian trade; but others allege another motive, and one savoring of a deeper policy. The Sioux, by their intercourse with the British traders, had acquired the use of fire arms, which had given them vast superiority over other tribes higher up the Missouri. They had made themselves also, in a manner, factors for the upper tribes, supplying them at second hand, and at greatly advanced prices, with goods derived from the white men. The Sioux, therefore, saw with jealousy the American traders pushing their way up the Missouri; foreseeing that the upper tribes would thus be relieved from all dependance on them for supplies; nay, what was worse, would be furnished with fire arms and elevated into formidable rivals.

We have already alluded to a case in which Mr. Crooks and Mr. M'Lellan had been interrupted in a trading voyage by these ruffians of the river, and, as it is in some degree connected with circumstances hereafter to be related, we shall specify it more particularly.

About two years before the time of which we are treating, Crooks and M'Lellan were ascending the river in boats with a party of about forty men, bound on one of their trading expeditions to the upper tribes. In one of the bends of the river where the channel made a deep curve under impending banks, they suddenly heard yells and shouts above them, and beheld the cliffs over head covered with armed savages. It was a band of Sioux warriors upwards of six hundred strong. They brandished their weapons in a menacing manner, and ordered the boats to turn back and land lower down the river. There was no disputing their commands, for they had the power to shower destruction upon the white men, without risk to themselves. Crooks and M'Lellan, therefore, turned back with feigned alacrity; and, landing, had an interview with the Sioux. The latter forbade them, under pain of exterminating hostility, from attempting to proceed up the river, but offered to trade peacefully with them if they would halt where they were. The party, being principally composed of voyageurs, was too weak to contend with so superior a force, and one so easily augmented; they pretended therefore to comply cheerfully with their arbitrary dictation and immediately proceeded to cut down trees and erect a trading house. The warrior band departed for their village which was about twenty miles distant, to collect objects of traffic; they left six or eight of their number, however, to keep watch upon the white men, and scouts were continually passing to and fro with intelligence.

Mr. Crooks saw that it would be impossible to prosecute his voyage without the danger of having his boats plundered, and a great part of his men massacred; he determined, however, not to be entirely frustrated in the objects of his expedition. While he continued, therefore, with great apparent earnestness and assiduity the construction of the trading house, he despatched the hunters and trappers of his party in a canoe, to make their way up the river to the original place of destination, there to busy themselves in trapping and collecting peltries, and to await his arrival at some future period.

As soon as the detachment had had sufficient time to ascend beyond the hostile country of the Sioux, Mr. Crooks suddenly broke up his feigned trading establishment, embarked his men and effects, and, after giving the astonished rear guard of savages a galling and indignant message to take to their countrymen, pushed down the river with all speed, sparing neither oar nor paddle, day nor night, until fairly beyond the swoop of these river hawks.

What encreased the irritation of Messrs. Crooks and M'Lellan at this mortifying check to their gainful enterprize, was the information that a rival trader was at the bottom of it; the Sioux, it is said, having been instigated to this outrage by Mr. Manuel Lisa, the leading partner and agent of the Missouri Fur Company already mentioned. This intelligence, whether true or false, so roused the fiery temper of M'Lellan that he swore, if ever he fell in with Lisa in the Indian country, he would shoot him on the spot; a mode of redress perfectly in unison with the character of the man, and the code of honor prevalent beyond the frontier.

If Crooks and M'Lellan had been exasperated by the insolent conduct of the Sioux Tetons, and the loss which it had occasioned, those freebooters had been no less indignant at being outwitted by the white men, and disappointed of their anticipated gains, and it was apprehended they would be particularly hostile against the present expedition, when they should learn that these gentlemen were engaged in it.

All these causes of uneasiness were concealed as much as possible from the Canadian voyageurs, lest they should become intimidated; it was impossible, however, to prevent the rumours brought by the Indians from leaking out, and they became subjects of gossipping and exaggeration. The chief of the Omahas, too, on returning from a hunting excursion, reported that two men had been killed some distance above, by a band of Sioux. This added to the fears that already began to be excited. The voyageurs pictured to themselves bands of fierce warriors stationed along each bank of the river, by whom they would be exposed to be shot down in their boats: or lurking hordes who would set on them at night and massacre them in their encampments. Some lost heart and proposed to return, rather than fight their way, and, in a manner, run the gauntlet through the country of these piratical marauders. In fact three men deserted while at this village. Luckily their place was supplied by three others who happened to be there, and who were prevailed on to join the expedition by promises of liberal pay and by being fitted out and equipped in complete style.

The irresolution and discontent visible among some of his people, arising at times almost to mutiny, and the occasional desertions which took place while thus among friendly tribes, and within reach of the frontiers, added greatly to the anxieties of Mr. Hunt, and rendered him eager to press forward and leave a hostile tract behind him, so that it would be as perilous to return as to keep on, and no one would dare to desert.

Accordingly, on the 15th of May he departed from the Village of the Omahas and set forward towards the country of the formidable Sioux Tetons. For the first five days they had a fair and fresh breeze, and the boats made good progress. The wind then came ahead, and the river beginning to rise, and to increase in rapidity, betokened the commencement of the annual flood, caused by the melting of the snow on the Rocky Mountains and the vernal rains on the upper prairies.

As they were now entering a region where foes might be lying in wait on either bank, it was determined, in hunting for game, to confine themselves principally to the islands, which sometimes extend to considerable length and are beautifully wooded, affording abundant pasturage and shade. On one of these they killed three buffaloes and two elks; and, halting on the edge of a beautiful prairie, made a sumptuous hunters' repast. They had not long resumed their boats and pulled along the river banks, when they descried a canoe approaching navigated by two men whom, to their surprize, they ascertained to be white men. They proved to be two of those strange and fearless wanderers of the wilderness, the trappers. Their names were Benjamin Jones and Alexander Carson. They had been for two years past hunting and trapping near the head of the Missouri, and were thus floating for thousands of miles

in a cockle shell down a turbulent stream, through regions infested by savage tribes, yet apparently as easy and unconcerned as if navigating securely in the midst of civilization.

The acquisition of two such hardy, experienced and dauntless hunters was peculiarly desirable at the present moment.
They needed but little persuasion. The wilderness is the home
of the trapper; like the sailor, he cares but little to which point
of the compass he steers; and Jones and Carson readily abandoned their voyage to S' Louis and turned their faces towards
the Rocky Mountains and the Pacific.

The two naturalists, Mr. Bradbury and Mr. Nuttall, who had
joined the expedition at S' Louis, still accompanied it and pursued their researches on all occasions. Mr. Nuttall seems to
have been exclusively devoted to his scientific pursuits. He was
a zealous botanist and all his enthusiasm was awakened at beholding a new world, as it were, opening upon him in the
boundless prairies clad in the vernal and variegated robe of unknown flowers. Whenever the boats landed at meal times or
for any temporary purpose he would spring on shore and
set out on a hunt for new specimens. Every plant or flower
of a rare or unknown species was eagerly seized as a prize.
Delighted with the treasures spreading themselves out before
him, he went groping and stumbling along among a wilderness of sweets, forgetful of every thing but his immediate pursuit and had often to be sought after when the boats were
about to resume their course. At such times he would be
found far off in the prairies or up the course of some petty
stream laden with plants of all kinds.

The Canadian voyageurs, who are a class of people that
know nothing out of their immediate line, and with constitutional levity make a jest of any thing they cannot understand,
were extremely puzzled by this passion for collecting what they
considered mere useless weeds. When they saw the worthy
botanist coming back heavy laden with his specimens, and
treasuring them up as carefully as a miser would his hoard,
they used to make merry among themselves at his expense,
regarding him as some whimsical kind of madman.

Mr. Bradbury was less exclusive in his tastes and habits and
combined the hunter and sportsman with the naturalist. He
took his rifle or his fowling piece with him in his geological

researches, conformed to the hardy and rugged habits of the men around him and of course gained favour in their eyes. He had a strong relish for incident and adventure, was curious in observing savage manners and savage life, and ready to join any hunting or other excursion. Even now that the expedition was proceeding through a dangerous neighborhood he could not check his propensity to ramble. Having observed, on the evening of the twenty second of May, that the river a head made a great bend which would take up the navigation of the following day, he determined to profit by the circumstance. On the morning of the 23d, therefore, instead of embarking, he filled his shot pouch with parched corn, for provisions, and set off to cross the neck on foot and meet the boats in the afternoon at the opposite side of the bend. Mr. Hunt felt uneasy at his venturing thus alone and reminded him that he was in an enemy's country; but Mr. Bradbury made light of the danger and started off cheerily upon his ramble. His day was passed pleasantly in traversing a beautiful tract, making botanical and geological researches and observing the habits of an extensive village of prairie dogs, at which he made several in-effectual shots, without considering the risque he ran of at-tracting the attention of any savages that might be lurking in the neighborhood. In fact he had totally forgotten the Sioux Tetons and all the other perils of the country, when, about the middle of the afternoon, as he stood near the river bank, and was looking out for the boat, he suddenly felt a hand laid on his shoulder. Starting and turning round he beheld a naked savage with a bow bent, and the arrow pointed at his breast. In an instant his gun was levelled and his hand upon the lock. The Indian drew his bow still further, but forebore to launch the shaft. Mr. Bradbury, with admirable presence of mind, reflected that the savage, if hostile in his intents, would have shot him without giving him a chance of defence; he paused therefore and held out his hand. The other took it in sign of friendship, and demanded in the Osage language whether he was a "Big Knife," or American. He answered in the affirmative and enquired whether the other were a Sioux. To his great relief he found that he was a Ponca. By this time two other Indians came running up, and all three laid hold of Mr. Bradbury and seemed disposed to compel him to go off with them among the hills. He resisted, and sitting down on a sandhill contrived to amuse them with a pocket compass. When the novelty of this was exhausted they again seized him, but he now produced a small microscope. This new wonder again fixed the attention of the savages, who have far more curiosity than it has been the custom to allow them. While thus engaged, one of them suddenly leaped up and gave a war whoop. The hand of the hardy naturalist was again on his gun and he was prepared to make battle when the Indian pointed down the river and revealed the true cause of his yell. It was the mast of one of the boats appearing above the low willows which bordered the stream. Mr. Bradbury felt infinitely relieved by the sight. The Indians, on their part, now shewed signs of apprehension, and were disposed to run away; but he assured them of good treatment and something to drink if they would accompany him on board of the boats. They lingered for a time, but disappeared before the boats came to land.

On the following morning they appeared at the camp accompanied by several of their tribe. With them came also a white man, who announced himself as a messenger bearing missives for Mr. Hunt. In fact he brought a letter from Mr. Manuel Lisa, partner and agent of the Missouri Fur Company. As has already been mentioned, this gentleman was going in search of Mr. Henry and his party, who had been dislodged from the Forks of the Missouri by the Blackfeet Indians, and had shifted his post somewhere beyond the Rocky Mountains. Mr. Lisa had left S' Louis three weeks after Mr. Hunt, and, having heard of the hostile intentions of the Sioux, had made the greatest exertions to overtake him, that they might pass through the dangerous part of the river together. He had twenty stout oarsmen in his service, and they plied their oars so vigorously, that he had reached the Omaha village just four days after the departure of Mr. Hunt. From this place he despatched the messenger in question, trusting to his overtaking the barges as they toiled up against the stream, and were delayed by the windings of the river. The purport of his letter was to entreat Mr. Hunt to wait until he could come up with him, that they might unite their forces and be a protection to each other in their perilous course through the country of the Sioux. In fact, as it was afterwards ascertained, Lisa was apprehensive that Mr. Hunt would do him some ill office with the Sioux bands, securing his own passage through their country by pretending that he with whom they were accustomed to trade, was on his way to them with a plentiful supply of goods. He feared, too, that Crooks and M'Lellan would take this opportunity to retort upon him the perfidy which they accused him of having used, two years previously among these very Sioux. In this respect, however, he did them signal injustice. There was no such thing as covert design or treachery in their thought; but M'Lellan when he heard that Lisa was on his way up the river, renewed his open threat of shooting him the moment he met him on Indian land.

The representations made by Crooks and M'Lellan of the treachery they had experienced, or fancied, on the part of Lisa, had great weight with Mr. Hunt, especially when he recollected the obstacles that had been thrown in his own way by that gentleman at S' Louis. He doubted, therefore, the fair dealing of Lisa, and feared that, should they enter the Sioux country together, the latter might make use of his influence with that tribe, as he had in the case of Crooks and M'Lellan, and instigate them to oppose his progress up the river.

He sent back, therefore, an answer calculated to beguile Lisa, assuring him that he would wait for him at the Poncas Village, which was but a little distance in advance; but, no sooner had the messenger departed, than he pushed forward with all diligence, barely stopping at the village to procure a supply of dried buffalo meat, and hastening to leave the other party as far behind as possible, thinking there was less to be apprehended from the open hostility of Indian foes, than from the quiet strategy of an Indian trader.

Chapter XVIII

Camp gossip—Deserters—Recruits—Kentucky hunters—A veteran woodman—Tidings of Mr. Henry—Danger from the Blackfeet—Alteration of plans—Scenery of the river— Buffalo roads—Iron ore—Country of the Sioux—A land of danger—Apprehensions of the voyageurs—Indian scouts— Threatened hostilities—A council of war—An array of battle —A parley—The pipe of peace—Speech making.

IT WAS about noon when the party left the Poncas Village, about a league beyond which they passed the mouth of the Quicourt or Rapid River, (called in the original French *L'Eau qui court*). After having proceeded some distance further, they landed and encamped for the night. In the evening camp the voyageurs gossipped, as usual, over the events of the day, and especially over intelligence picked up among the Poncas. These Indians had confirmed the previous reports of the hostile intentions of the Sioux, and had assured them that five tribes, or bands, of that fierce nation were actually assembled higher up the river, and waiting to cut them off. This evening gossip, and the terrific stories of Indian warfare to which it gave rise, produced a strong effect upon the imaginations of the irresolute, and in the morning it was discovered that the two men who had joined the party at the Omaha village and been so bounteously fitted out, had deserted in the course of the night, carrying with them all their equipments. As it was known that one of them could not swim, it was hoped that the banks of the Quicourt River would bring them to a halt; a general pursuit was, therefore, instituted but without success.

On the following morning (May 26th) as they were all on shore breakfasting on one of the beautiful banks of the river, they observed two canoes descending along the opposite side. By the aid of spy glasses, they ascertained that there were two white men in one of the canoes and one in the other. A gun was discharged which called the attention of the voyagers who crossed over. They proved to be three Kentucky hunters of the true "dread nought" stamp. Their names were

Edward Robinson, John Hoback and Jacob Rezner. Robinson
was a veteran backwoodsman, sixty six years of age. He had
been one of the first settlers of Kentucky and engaged in
many of the conflicts of the Indians on "The Bloody Ground."
In one of these battles he had been scalped, and he still wore
a handkerchief bound round his head to protect the part.
These men had passed several years in the upper wilderness.
They had been in the service of the Missouri Company under
Mr. Henry and had crossed the Rocky Mountains with him in
the preceding year when driven from his post on the Missouri
by the hostilities of the Blackfeet. After crossing the mountains Mr. Henry had established himself on one of the head
branches of the Columbia River. There they had remained
with him for some months hunting and trapping, until, having
satisfied their wandering propensities, they felt disposed to return to the families and comfortable homes which they had
left in Kentucky. They had accordingly made their way back
across the mountains, and down the rivers, and were in full
career for S' Louis, when thus suddenly interrupted. The sight
of a powerful party of traders, trappers, hunters and voyageurs,
well armed and equipped, furnished at all points, in high health
and spirits, and banquetting lustily on the green margin of
the river was a spectacle equally stimulating to these veteran
backwoodsmen, with the glorious array of a campaigning
army to an old soldier, but when they learnt the grand scope
and extent of the enterprize in hand, it was irresistible; homes
and families and all the charms of green Kentucky vanished
from their thoughts; they cast loose their canoes to drift
down the stream and joyfully enlisted in the band of adventurers. They engaged on similar terms with some of the other
hunters. The company was to fit them out, and keep them
supplied with the requisite equipments and munitions and
they were to yield one half of the produce of their hunting
and trapping.

The addition of three such staunch recruits was extremely
acceptable at this dangerous part of the river; the knowledge
of the country which they had acquired, also, in their journeys and hunting excursions along the rivers and among the
Rocky Mountains, was all important; in fact the information derived from them induced Mr. Hunt to alter his future

course. He had hitherto intended to proceed by the route taken by Lewis and Clarke in their famous exploring expedition, ascending the Missouri to its forks, and thence going by land, across the mountains. These men informed him, however, that on taking that course he would have to pass through the country infested by the savage tribe of the Blackfeet and would be exposed to their hostilities, they being, as has already been observed, exasperated to deadly animosity against the whites, on account of the death of one of their tribe by the hands of Captain Lewis. They advised him rather to pursue a route more to the southward; being the same by which they had returned. This would carry him over the mountains about where the head waters of the Platte and the Yellow stone take their rise, at a place much more easy and practicable than that where Lewis and Clarke had crossed. In pursuing this course, also, he would pass through a country abounding with game, where he would have a better chance of procuring a constant supply of provisions than by the other route; and would run less risk of molestation from the Blackfeet. Should he adopt this advice it would be better for him to abandon the river at the Arickara town, at which he would arrive in the course of a few days. As the Indians of that town possessed horses in abundance he might purchase a sufficient number of them for the great journey overland which would commence at that place.

After reflecting on this advice and consulting with his associates, Mr. Hunt came to the determination to follow the route thus pointed out, in which the hunters engaged to pilot him.

The party continued their voyage with delightful May weather. The prairies bordering on the river were gaily painted with innumerable flowers, exhibiting the motley confusion of colours of a Turkey carpet. The beautiful islands, also, on which they occasionally halted, presented the appearance of mingled grove and garden.

The trees were often covered with clambering grape vines in blossom, which perfumed the air. Between the stately masses of the groves were grassy lawns and glades studded with flowers, or interspersed with rose bushes in full bloom. These islands were often the resort of the buffalo, the elk and the antilope, who had made innumerable paths among the trees and thickets, which had the effect of the mazy walks and alleys of parks and shrubberies.

Sometimes, where the river passed between high banks and bluffs, the roads, made by the tramp of buffalos for many ages, along the face of the heights looked like so many well travelled high ways. At other places the banks were banded with great veins of iron ore, laid bare by the abrasion of the river. At one place the course of the river was nearly in a straight line for about fifteen miles. The banks sloped gently to its margin, without a single tree: but bordered with grass and herbage of a vivid green. Along each bank, for the whole fifteen miles, extended a stripe one hundred yards in breadth, of a deep rusty brown, indicating an inexhaustible bed of iron through the centre of which the Missouri had worn its way. Indications of the continuance of this bed were afterwards observed higher up the river. It is, in fact, one of the mineral magazines which nature has provided in the heart of this vast realm of fertility, and which, in connexion with the immense beds of coal on the same river, seem garnered up as the elements of the future wealth and power of the mighty west.

The sight of these mineral treasures greatly excited the curiosity of Mr. Bradbury, and it was tantalizing to him to be checked in his scientific researches and obliged to forego his usual rambles on shore; but they were now entering the fated country of the Sioux Tetons in which it was dangerous to wander about unguarded.

This country extends for some days' journey along the river and consists of vast prairies, here and there diversified by swelling hills and cut up by ravines, the channels of turbid streams in the rainy seasons but almost destitute of water during the heats of summer. Here and there, on the sides of the hills, or along the alluvial borders and bottoms of the ravines, are groves and skirts of forest; but for the most part the country presented to the eye a boundless waste, covered with herbage, but without trees.

The soil of this immense region is strongly impregnated with sulphur, copperas, alum and glauber salts; its various earths impart a deep tinge to the streams which drain it, and these, with the crumbling of the banks along the Missouri, give to the waters of that river much of the colouring matter with which they are clouded.

Over this vast tract the roving bands of the Sioux Tetons hold their vagrant sway; subsisting by the chase of the buffalo, the elk, the deer and the antilope, and waging ruthless warfare with other wandering tribes.

As the boats made their way up the stream bordered by this land of danger, many of the Canadian voyageurs, whose fears had been awakened, would regard with a distrustful eye the boundless waste extending on each side. All, however, was silent and apparently untenanted by a human being. Now and then a herd of deer would be seen feeding tranquilly among the flowery herbage, or a line of buffaloes like a caravan on its march, moving across the distant profile of the prairie. The Canadians, however, began to apprehend an ambush in every thicket, and to regard the broad, tranquil plain as a sailor eyes some shallow and perfidious sea, which, though smooth and safe to the eye conceals the lurking rock or treacherous shoal. The very name of a Sioux became a watchword of terror. Not an elk, a wolf or any other animal could appear on the hills, but the boats resounded with exclamations from stem to stern, "*Voila les Sioux!*" "*voila les Sioux!*" (There are the Sioux! there are the Sioux!) Whenever it was practicable, the night encampment was on some island in the centre of the stream.

On the morning of the 31st of May as the travellers were breakfasting on the right bank of the river, the usual alarm was given, but with more reason, as two Indians actually made their appearance on a bluff on the opposite, or north east, side and harangued them in a loud voice. As it was impossible, at that distance, to distinguish what they said, Mr. Hunt, after breakfast, crossed the river with Pierre Dorion the interpreter, and advanced boldly to converse with them, while the rest remained watching, in mute suspense, the movements of the parties. As soon as Mr. Hunt landed, one of the Indians disappeared behind the hill, but shortly reappeared on horseback and went scouring off across the heights. Mr. Hunt held some conference with the remaining savage, and then recrossed the river to his party.

These two Indians proved to be spies or scouts of a large war party encamped about a league off, and numbering two hundred and eighty lodges, or about six hundred warriors, of three different tribes of Sioux: the Yangtons Ahna, the Tetons Bois Brulé and the Tetons Min-na-kine-azzo. They expected daily to be reinforced by two other tribes, and had been waiting eleven days for the arrival of Mr. Hunt's party with a determination to oppose their progress up the river; being resolved to prevent all trade of the white men with their enemies the Arickaras, Mandans and Minatarees. The Indian who had gallopped off on horseback had gone to give notice of the approach of the party, so that they might now look out for some fierce scenes with these piratical savages, of whom they had received so many formidable accounts.

The party braced up their spirits to the encounter, and re embarking, pulled resolutely up the stream. An island for some time intervened between them and the opposite side of the river, but on clearing the upper end they came in full view of the hostile shore. There was a ridge of hills down which the Savages were pouring in great numbers, some on horseback and some on foot. Reconnoitering them with the aid of glasses, they perceived that they were all in warlike array, painted and decorated for battle. Their weapons were bows and arrows, and a few short carbines, and most of them had round shields. Altogether they had a wild and gallant appearance, and taking possession of a point which commanded the river ranged themselves along the bank as if prepared to dispute the passage.

At sight of this formidable front of war, Mr. Hunt and his companions held council together. It was plain that the rumours they had heard were correct; and the Sioux were determined to oppose their progress by force of arms. To attempt to elude them and continue along the river was out of the question. The strength of the mid current was too violent to be withstood, and the boats were obliged to ascend along the river banks. These banks were often high and perpendicular, affording the savages frequent stations from whence, safe themselves, and almost unseen, they might shower down their missiles upon the boats below, and retreat at will, without danger from pursuit. Nothing apparently remained, therefore, but to fight or turn back. The Sioux far out numbered them, it is true, but their own party was about sixty strong, well armed

and supplied with ammunition, and beside their guns and rifles
they had a swivel and two howitzers mounted in the boats.
Should they succeed in breaking this Indian force by one vigorous assault, it was likely they would be deterred from making any future attack of consequence. The fighting alternative
was, therefore, instantly adopted, and the boats pulled to shore
nearly opposite to the hostile force. Here the arms were all
examined and put in order. The swivel and howitzers were
then loaded with powder and discharged, to let the savages
know by the report how formidably they were provided. The
noise echoed along the shores of the river, and must have startled the warriors who were only accustomed to the sharp reports of rifles. The same pieces were then loaded with as many
bullets as they would probably bear; after which the whole
party embarked and pulled across the river. The Indians remained watching them in silence, their painted forms and visages glaring in the sun and their feathers fluttering in the
breeze. The poor Canadians eyed them with rueful glances,
and now and then a fearful ejaculation would escape them.
"Par bleu! this is a sad scrape we are in, brother!" would one
mutter to the next oarsman. "Aye aye," the other would reply,
"we are not going to a wedding, my friend!"

When the boats arrived within rifle shot, the hunters and
other fighting personages on board, seized their weapons and
prepared for action. As they rose to fire a confusion took
place among the savages: they displayed their buffalo robes,
raised them with both hands above their heads and then
spread them before them on the ground. At sight of this,
Pierre Dorion eagerly cried out to the party not to fire, as this
movement was a peaceful signal and an invitation to a parley.
Immediately about a dozen of the principal warriors, separating from the rest, descended to the edge of the river , lighted
a fire, seated themselves in a semi circle round it, and displaying the Calumet, invited the party to land. Mr. Hunt now
called a council of the partners on board of his boat. The
question was, whether to trust to the amicable overtures of
these ferocious people? It was determined in the affirmative;
for, otherwise, there was no alternative but to fight them. The
main body of the party were ordered to remain on board of
the boats, keeping within shot, and prepared to fire in case of

any signs of treachery: while Mr. Hunt and the other partners, (M'Kenzie, Crooks, Miller, and M'Lellan) proceeded to
land, accompanied by the interpreter and Mr. Bradbury. The
chiefs who awaited them on the margin of the river, remained
seated in their semi circle, without stirring a limb or moving
a muscle, motionless as so many statues. Mr. Hunt and his
companions advanced without hesitation and took their seats
on the sand so as to complete the circle. The band of warriors
who lined the banks above stood looking down in silent
groups and clusters, some ostentatiously equipped and decorated, others entirely naked, but fantastically painted, and all
variously armed.

The pipe of peace was now brought forward with due ceremony. The bowl was of a species of red stone resembling
porphyry, the stem was six feet in length decorated with tufts
of horse hair dyed red. The pipe bearer stepped within the circle, lighted the pipe, held it towards the sun, then towards
the different points of the compass, after which he handed it
to the principal chief. The latter smoked a few whiffs, then,
holding the head of the pipe in his hand, offered the other
end to Mr. Hunt and to each one successively in the circle;
when all had smoked it was considered that an assurance of
good faith and amity had been interchanged. Mr. Hunt now
made a speech in French, which was interpreted as he proceeded, by Pierre Dorion. He informed the Sioux of the real
object of the expedition of himself and his companions, which
was not to trade with any of the tribes up the river, but to
cross the Mountains to the great Salt lake in the West, in
search of some of their brothers whom they had not seen for
eleven months. That he had heard of the intention of the
Sioux to oppose his passage, and was prepared, as they might
see, to effect it at all hazards: nevertheless, his feelings towards the Sioux were friendly, in proof of which he had
brought them a present of tobacco and corn. So saying, he
ordered about fifteen carottes of tobacco, and as many bags
of corn to be brought from the boat and laid in a heap near
the council fire.

The sight of these presents mollified the chieftain, who had
doubtless been previously rendered considerate by the resolute conduct of the white men, the judicious disposition of

their little armament, the completeness of their equipments and the compact array of battle which they presented. He made a speech in reply in which he stated the object of their hostile assemblage, which had been merely to prevent supplies of arms and ammunition from going to the Arickaras, Mandans and Minatarees with whom they were at war; but being now convinced that the party were carrying no supplies of the kind, but merely proceeding in quest of their brothers beyond the mountains, they would not impede them in their voyage. He concluded by thanking them for their present, and advising them to encamp on the opposite side of the river, as he had some young men among his warriors for whose discretion he could not be answerable, and who might be troublesome.

Here ended the conference; they all arose, shook hands and parted. Mr. Hunt and his companions re embarked, and the boats proceeded on their course unmolested.

Chapter XIX

The great bend of the Missouri—Crooks and M'Lellan meet with two of their Indian opponents—Wanton outrage of a white man the cause of Indian hostility—Dangers and precautions—An Indian war party—Dangerous situation of Mr. Hunt—A friendly encampment—Feasting and dancing —Approach of Manuel Lisa and his party—A grim meeting between old rivals—Pierre Dorion in a fury—A burst of chivalry.

O N THE AFTERNOON of the following day (June 1st) they arrived at the Great bend, where the river winds for about thirty miles round a circular peninsula, the neck of which is not above two thousand yards across. On the succeeding morning, at an early hour, they descried two Indians standing on a high bank of the river, waving and spreading their buffalo robes in signs of amity. They immediately pulled to shore and landed. On approaching the savages, however, the latter shewed evident symptoms of alarm, spreading out their arms horizontally, according to their mode of supplicating clemency. The reason was soon explained. They proved to be two chiefs of the very war party that had brought Messrs. Crooks and M'Lellan to a stand two years before, and obliged them to escape down the river. They ran to embrace these gentlemen, as if delighted to meet with them; yet they evidently feared some retaliation of their past misconduct, nor were they quite at ease until the pipe of peace had been smoked.

Mr. Hunt having been informed that the tribe to which these men belonged had killed three white men during the preceding summer, reproached them with the crime and demanded their reasons for such savage hostility. "We kill white men," replied one of the chiefs, "because white men kill us. That very man," added he, pointing to Carson, one of the new recruits, "killed one of our brothers last summer. The three white men were slain to avenge his death."

The chief was correct in his reply. Carson admitted that, being with a party of Arickaras on the banks of the Missouri and seeing a war party of Sioux on the opposite side he had fired

with his rifle across. It was a random shot, made without much
expectation of effect, for the river was full half a mile in
breadth. Unluckily it brought down a Sioux warrior, for whose
wanton destruction three fold vengeance had been taken as has
been stated. In this way outrages are frequently committed
on the natives by thoughtless or mischievous white men: the
Indians retaliate according to a law of their code, which requires blood for blood; their act of what with them is pious
vengeance resounds throughout the land and is represented as
wanton and unprovoked; the neighborhood is roused to arms;
a war ensues, which ends in the destruction of half the tribe,
the ruin of the rest and their expulsion from their hereditary
homes. Such is too often the real history of Indian warfare,
which in general is traced up only to some vindictive act of
a savage; while the outrage of the scoundrel white man that
provoked it is sunk in silence.

The two chiefs, having smoked their pipe of peace and
received a few presents, departed well satisfied. In a little
while two others appeared on horseback and road up abreast
of the boats. They had seen the presents given to their comrades, but were dissatisfied with them and came after the
boats to ask for more. Being somewhat peremptory and insolent in their demands, Mr. Hunt gave them a flat refusal and
threatened, if they or any of their tribe followed him with
similar demands, to treat them as enemies. They turned and
rode off in a furious passion. As he was ignorant what force
these chiefs might have behind the hills, and as it was very
possible they might take advantage of some pass of the river
to attack the boats, Mr. Hunt called all stragglers on board
and prepared for such emergency. It was agreed that the large
boat commanded by Mr. Hunt, should ascend along the
north east side of the river, and the three smaller boats along
the south side. By this arrangement each party would command a view of the opposite heights above the heads and out
of the sight of their companions, and could give the alarm
should they perceive any Indians lurking there. The signal of
alarm was to be two shots fired in quick succession.

The boats proceeded for the greater part of the day without seeing any signs of an enemy. About four o'clock in the
afternoon the large boat, commanded by Mr. Hunt, came to

where the river was divided, by a long sand bar, which apparently, however, left a sufficient channel between it and the shore along which they were advancing. He kept up this channel, therefore, for some distance until the water proved too shallow for the boat. It was necessary, therefore, to put about, return down the channel and pull round the lower end of the sand bar into the main stream. Just as he had given orders to this effect to his men, two signal guns were fired from the boats on the opposite side of the river. At the same moment a file of savage warriors was observed pouring down from the impending bank and gathering on the shore at the lower end of the bar. They were evidently a war party, being armed with bows and arrows, battle clubs and carbines and round bucklers of buffalo hide, and their naked bodies were painted with black and white stripes. The natural inference was that they belonged to the two tribes of Sioux which had been expected by the great war party, and that they had been incited to hostility by the two chiefs who had been enraged by the refusal and the menace of Mr. Hunt. Here then was a fearful predicament. Mr. Hunt and his crew seemed caught as it were in a trap. The Indians, to the number of about a hundred, had already taken possession of a point near which the boat would have to pass: others kept pouring down the bank, and it was probable that some would remain posted on the top of the height.

The hazardous situation of Mr. Hunt was perceived by those in the other boats and they hastened to his assistance. They were at some distance above the sand bar, however, and on the opposite side of the river, and saw, with intense anxiety, the number of Savages continually augmenting, at the lower end of the channel, so that the boat would be exposed to a fearful attack before they could render it any assistance. Their anxiety encreased as they saw Mr. Hunt and his party descending the channel and dauntlessly approaching the point of danger, but it suddenly changed into surprize on beholding the boat pass close by the savage horde unmolested, and steer out safely into the broad river.

The next moment the whole band of warriors was in motion. They ran along the bank until they were opposite to the boats, then throwing by their weapons and buffalo robes, plunged into the river, waded and swam off to the boats and surrounded them in crowds, seeking to shake hands with every individual on board, for the Indians have long since found this to be the white man's token of amity, and they carry it to an extreme.

All uneasiness was now at an end. The Indians proved to be a war party of Arickaras, Mandans and Minatarees, consisting of three hundred warriors, and bound on a foray against the Sioux. Their war plans were abandoned for the present and they determined to return to the Arickara town, where they hoped to obtain from the white men arms and ammunition that would enable them to take the field with advantage over their enemies.

The boats now sought the first convenient place for encamping. The tents were pitched, the warriors fixed their camp at about a hundred yards distant, provisions were furnished from the boats sufficient for all parties; there was hearty though rude feasting in both camps, and in the evening the red warriors entertained their white friends with dances and songs that lasted until after midnight.

On the following morning (June 3d) the travellers re embarked and took a temporary leave of their Indian friends, who intended to proceed immediately for the Arickara town where they expected to arrive in three days, long before the boats could reach there. Mr. Hunt had not proceeded far before the chief came gallopping along the shore and made signs for a parley. He said, his people could not go home satisfied unless they had something to take with them to prove that they had met with the white men. Mr. Hunt understood the drift of the speech and made the chief a present of a cask of powder, a bag of balls and three dozen of knives, with which he was highly pleased. While the chief was receiving these presents an Indian came running along the shore and announced that a boat, filled with white men, was coming up the river. This was by no means agreeable tidings to Mr. Hunt, who correctly concluded it to be the boat of Mr. Manuel Lisa, and he was vexed to find that alert and adventurous trader upon his heels, when he had hoped to have out manœuvred and left him far behind. Lisa, however, was too much experienced in the wiles of Indian trade to be lulled by the promise of waiting for him at the Poncas village; on the contrary, he had allowed himself no repose and had strained every nerve to overtake the rival party, and, availing himself of the moonlight, had even sailed during a considerable part of the night. In this he was partly prompted by his apprehensions of the Sioux, having met a boat which had probably passed Mr. Hunt's party in the night, and which had been fired into by these savages.

On hearing that Lisa was so near at hand Mr. Hunt perceived that it was useless to attempt any longer to evade him; after proceeding a few miles further, therefore, he came to a halt and waited for him to come up. In a little while the barge of Lisa made its appearance. It came sweeping gallantly up the river, manned by its twenty stout oarsmen, and armed by a swivel mounted at the bow. The whole number on board amounted to twenty six men; among whom was Mr. Henry Breckenridge, then a young enterprizing man; who was a mere passenger, tempted by motives of curiosity to accompany Mr. Lisa. He has since made himself known by various writings, among which may be noted a narrative of this very voyage.

The approach of Lisa, while it was regarded with uneasiness by Mr. Hunt, roused the ire of M'Lellan; who calling to mind old grievances, began to look round for his rifle as if he really intended to carry his threat into execution and shoot him on the spot; and it was with some difficulty that Mr. Hunt was enabled to restrain his ire, and prevent a scene of outrage and confusion.

The meeting between the two leaders, thus mutually distrustful, could not be very cordial; and as to Messrs. Crooks and M'Lellan; though they refrained from any outbreak, yet they regarded in grim defiance their old rival and underplotter. In truth a general distrust prevailed throughout the party concerning Lisa and his intentions. They considered him artful and slippery, and secretly anxious for the failure of their expedition. There being now nothing more to be apprehended from the Sioux, they suspected that Lisa would take advantage of his twenty oared barge to leave them and get first among the Arickaras. As he had traded with those people and possessed great influence over them it was feared he might make use of it to impede the business of Mr. Hunt and his party. It was resolved therefore to keep a sharp look out upon his movements; and M'Lellan swore that if he saw the least sign of treachery on his part, he would instantly put his old threat into execution.

Notwithstanding these secret jealousies and heart burnings the two parties maintained an outward appearance of civility, and for two days continued forward in company with some degree of harmony. On the third day, however, an explosion took place, and it was produced by no less a personage than Pierre Dorion, the half breed interpreter. It will be recollected that this worthy had been obliged to steal a march from S' Louis, to avoid being arrested for an old whiskey debt which he owed to the Missouri Fur Company, and by which Mr. Lisa had hoped to prevent his enlisting in Mr. Hunt's expedition. Dorion, since the arrival of Lisa, had kept aloof and regarded him with a sullen and dogged aspect. On the fifth of June the two parties were brought to a halt by a heavy rain, and remained encamped about a hundred yards apart. In the course of the day Lisa undertook to tamper with the faith of Pierre Dorion, and, inviting him on board of his boat, regaled him with his favorite whisky. When he thought him sufficiently mellowed he proposed to him to quit the service of his new employers and return to his old allegiance. Finding him not to be moved by soft words, he called to mind his old debt to the company and threatened to carry him off by force, in payment of it. The mention of this debt always stirred up the gall of Pierre Dorion, bringing with it the re-membrance of the whiskey extortion. A violent quarrel arose between him and Lisa, and he left the boat in high dudgeon. His first step was to repair to the tent of Mr. Hunt and reveal the attempt that had been made to shake his faith. While he was yet talking Lisa entered the tent, under the pretext of coming to borrow a towing line. High words instantly ensued between him and Dorion, which ended by the half breed's dealing him a blow. A quarrel in the "Indian Country," how-ever, is not to be settled with fisty cuffs. Lisa immediately rushed to his boat for a weapon. Dorion snatched up a pair of pistols belonging to Mr. Hunt, and placed himself in battle array. The noise had roused the camp and every one pressed to know the cause. Lisa now re appeared upon the field with a knife stuck in his girdle. Mr. Breckenridge, who had tried in vain to mollify his ire, accompanied him to the scene of action. Pierre Dorion's pistols gave him the advantage, and he maintained a most warlike attitude. In the mean time Crooks and M'Lellan had learnt the cause of the affray and were each eager to take the quarrel into their own hands. A scene of uproar and hubbub ensued that defies description. M'Lellan would have brought his rifle into play and settled all old and new grudges by a pull of the trigger had he not been restrained by Mr. Hunt. That gentleman acted as moderator, endeavoring to prevent a general melée; in the midst of the brawl, however, an expression was made use of by Lisa derogatory to his own honour. In an instant the tranquil spirit of Mr. Hunt was in a flame. He now became as eager for fight as any one on the ground and challenged Lisa to settle the dispute on the spot with pistols. Lisa repaired to his boat to arm himself for the deadly feud. He was followed by Messrs. Bradbury and Breckenridge, who, novices in Indian life and the "chivalry" of the frontier, had no relish for scenes of blood and brawl. By their earnest mediation the quarrel was, with great difficulty, brought to a close without blood shed; but the two leaders of the rival camps separated in anger and all personal intercourse ceased between them.

Chapter XX

THE RIVAL PARTIES now coasted along the opposite sides of the river, within sight of each other; the barges of Mr. Hunt always keeping some distance in the advance, lest Lisa should push on and get first to the Arickara village. The scenery and objects as they proceeded gave evidence that they were advancing deeper and deeper into the domains of savage nature. Boundless wastes kept extending to the eye, more and more animated by herds of buffalo. Sometimes these un-wieldy animals were seen moving in long procession across the silent landscape; at other times they were scattered about, singly or in groups, on the broad enameled prairies and green acclivities, some cropping the rich pasturage, others reclining amidst the flowery herbage; the whole scene realizing in a manner the old scriptural descriptions of the vast pastoral countries of the Orient, with "cattle upon a thousand hills."

At one place the shores seemed absolutely lined with buf-falos; many were making their way across the stream, snort-ing, and blowing and floundering. Numbers, in spite of every effort, were borne by the rapid current within shot of the boats, and several were killed. At another place a number were descried on the beach of a small island, under the shade of the trees or standing in the water, like cattle, to avoid the flies and the heat of the day.

Several of the best marksmen stationed themselves in the bow of a barge which advanced slowly and silently, stemming the current with the aid of a broad sail and a fair breeze. The buffalo stood gazing quietly at the barge as it approached, perfectly unconscious of their danger. The fattest of the herd was selected by the hunters, who all fired together and brought down their victim.

Beside the buffaloes they saw abundance of deer, and frequent gangs of stately elks, together with light troops of sprightly antelopes, the fleetest and most beautiful inhabitants of the prairies.

There are two kinds of antelopes in these regions, one nearly the size of the common deer, the other not much larger than a goat. Their colour is a light grey or rather dun, slightly spotted with white; and they have small horns like those of the deer, which they never shed. Nothing can surpass the delicate and elegant finish of their limbs; in which lightness, elasticity and strength are wonderfully combined. All the attitudes and movements of this beautiful animal are graceful and picturesque, and it is altogether as fit a subject for the fanciful uses of the poet, as the oft sung gazelle of the east.

Their habits are shy and capricious; they keep on the open plains, are quick to take the alarm and bound away with a fleetness that defies pursuit. When thus skimming across a prairie in the autumn, their light grey or dun colour blends with the hue of the withered herbage, the swiftness of their motion baffles the eye and they almost seem unsubstantial forms driven like a gossamer before the wind.

While they thus keep to the open plain and trust to their speed they are safe; but they have a prurient curiosity that sometimes betrays them to their ruin. When they have scud for some distance and left their pursuer behind, they will suddenly stop and turn to gaze at the object of their alarm. If the pursuit is not followed up they will, after a time, yield to their inquisitive hankering, and return to the place from whence they have been frightened.

John Day, the veteran hunter already mentioned, displayed his experience and skill in entrapping one of these beautiful animals. Taking advantage of its well known curiosity, he laid down flat among the grass, and putting his handkerchief on the end of his ram rod, waved it gently in the air. This had the effect of the fabled fascination of the rattle snake. The antelope gazed at the mysterious object for some time at a distance, then approached timidly, pausing and reconnoitering with encreased curiosity; moving round the point of attraction in a circle, but still drawing nearer and nearer, until being within the range of the deadly rifle, he fell a victim to his curiosity.

On the 10th of June as the party were making brisk progress with a fine breeze they met a canoe with three Indians descending the river. They came to a parley and brought news from the Arickara village. The war party, which had caused such alarm at the sand bar, had reached the village some days previously, announced the approach of a party of traders, and displayed with great ostentation the presents they had received from them. On further conversation with these three Indians Mr. Hunt learnt the real danger which he had run, when hemmed up within the sand bar. The Mandans, who were of the war party, when they saw the boat so completely entrapped and apparently within their power, had been eager for attacking it, and securing so rich a prize. The Minatarees, also, were nothing loth, feeling in some measure committed in hostility to the whites, in consequence of their tribe having killed two white men above the Fort of the Missouri Fur Company. Fortunately, the Arickaras who formed the majority of the war party, proved true in their friendship to the whites and prevented any hostile act, otherwise a bloody affray, and perhaps a horrible massacre, might have ensued.

On the 11th of June Mr. Hunt and his companions encamped near an island about six miles below the Arickara village. Mr. Lisa encamped, as usual, at no great distance; but the same sullen and jealous reserve and non intercourse continued between them. Shortly after pitching the tents Mr. Breckenridge made his appearance as an ambassador from the rival camp. He came on behalf of his companions, to arrange the manner of making their entrance into the village and of receiving the chiefs; for every thing of the kind is a matter of grave ceremonial among the Indians.

The partners now expressed frankly their deep distrust of the intentions of Mr. Lisa, and their apprehensions, that, out of the jealousy of trade and resentment of recent disputes, he might seek to instigate the Arickaras against them. Mr. Breckenridge assured them that their suspicions were entirely groundless and pledged himself that nothing of the kind should take place. He found it difficult, however, to remove

their distrust; the conference, therefore, ended without producing any cordial understanding; and M'Lellan recurred to
his old threat of shooting Lisa the instant he discovered any
thing like treachery in his proceedings.

That night the rain fell in torrents accompanied by thunder
and lightning. The camp was deluged and the bedding and
baggage drenched. All hands embarked at an early hour and
set forward for the village. About nine o'clock, when half
way, they met a canoe, on board of which were two Arickara
dignitaries. One, a fine looking man, much above the common size, was hereditary chief of the village; he was called the
Left handed, on account of a personal peculiarity. The other,
a ferocious looking savage, was the War chief, or generalis-
simo: who was known by the name of The Big Man, an appellation he well deserved from his size, for he was of a
gigantic frame. Both were of fairer complexion than is usual
with savages.

They were accompanied by an interpreter: a French creole;
one of those haphazard wights of Gallic origin, who abound
upon our frontier, living among the Indians like one of their
own race. He had been twenty years among the Arickaras,
had a squaw and a troop of pie bald children, and officiated
as interpreter to the chiefs. Through this worthy organ the
two dignitaries signified to Mr. Hunt their sovereign intention to oppose the further progress of the expedition up the
river unless a boat were left to trade with them. Mr. Hunt, in
reply, explained the object of his voyage, and his intention of
debarking at their village and proceeding thence by land; and
that he would willingly trade with them for a supply of horses
for his journey. With this explanation they were perfectly satisfied and putting about, steered for their village to make
preparations for the reception of the strangers.

The village of the Ricaras, Arickaras or Ricarees, for the
name is thus variously written, is between the 46th and 47th
parallels of north latitude, and 1430 miles above the mouth
of the Missouri. The party reached it about ten o'clock in
the morning, but landed on the opposite side of the river,
where they spread out their baggage and effects to dry. From
hence they commanded an excellent view of the village. It was
divided into two portions, about eighty yards apart, being

inhabited by two distinct bands. The whole extended about three quarters of a mile along the river bank, and was composed of conical lodges that looked like so many small hillocks, being wooden frames intertwined with osier and covered with earth. The plain beyond the village swept up into hills of considerable height, but the whole country was nearly destitute of trees. While they were regarding the village they beheld a singular fleet coming down the river. It consisted of a number of canoes, each made of a single buffalo hide stretched on sticks, so as to form a kind of circular trough. Each one was navigated by a single squaw, who knelt in the bottom and paddled; towing after her frail bark a bundle of floating wood intended for firing. This kind of canoe is in frequent use among the Indians; the buffalo hide being readily made up into a bundle and transported on horseback; it is very serviceable in conveying baggage across rivers.

The great number of horses grazing around the village, and scattered over the neighboring hills and valleys, bespoke the equestrian habits of the Arickaras, who are admirable horsemen. Indeed in the number of his horses consists the wealth of an Indian of the prairies; who resembles an Arab in his passion for this noble animal, and in his adroitness in the management of it.

After a time the voice of the Sovereign Chief "The left handed" was heard across the river, announcing that the council lodge was preparing, and inviting the white men to come over. The river was half a mile in width, yet every word uttered by the chieftain was heard. This may be partly attributed to the distinct manner in which every syllable of the compound words in the Indian languages is articulated and accented; but in truth a savage warrior might often rival Achilles himself for force of lungs.*

Now came the delicate point of management, how the two rival parties were to conduct their visit to the village with proper circumspection and due decorum. Neither of the leaders had spoken to each other since their quarrel; all communication had been by ambassadors. Seeing the jealousy entertained of Lisa, Mr. Breckenridge in his negotiation had

* Bradbury. P. 110.

arranged that a deputation from each party should cross the river at the same time so that neither would have the first access to the ear of the Arickaras.

The distrust of Lisa, however, had encreased in proportion as they approached the sphere of action, and M'Lellan in particular, kept a viligant eye upon his motions, swearing to shoot him if he attempted to cross the river first.

About two o'clock the large boat of Mr. Hunt was manned and he stepped on board accompanied by Messrs. M'Kenzie and M'Lellan: Lisa at the same time embarked in his barge; the two deputations amounted in all to fourteen persons, and never was any movement of rival potentates conducted with more wary exactness.

They landed amidst a rabble crowd and were received on the bank by the left handed chief, who conducted them into the village with grave courtesy; driving to the right and left the swarms of old squaws, implike boys and vagabond dogs, with which the place abounded. They wound their way between cabins which looked like dirt heaps huddled together without any plan, and surrounded by old pallisades; all filthy in the extreme and redolent of villanous smells.

At length they arrived at the council lodge. It was somewhat spacious, and formed of four forked trunks of trees placed upright, supporting cross beams and a frame of poles interwoven with osiers, and the whole covered with earth. A hole sunken in the centre formed the fire place, and immediately above was a circular hole in the apex of the lodge, to let out the smoke and let in the daylight. Around the lodge were recesses for sleeping, like the berths on board ships, screened from view by curtains of dressed skins. At the upper end of the lodge was a kind of hunting and warlike trophy consisting of two buffalo heads garishly painted, surmounted by shields, bows, quivers of arrows and other weapons.

On entering the lodge the chief pointed to mats or cushions which had been placed around for the strangers and on which they seated themselves, while he placed himself on a kind of stool. An old man then came forward with the pipe of peace or good fellowship, lighted and handed it to the chief, and then falling back, squatted himself near the door. The pipe was passed from mouth to mouth each one taking a whiff, which

is equivalent to the inviolable pledge of faith of taking salt together among the ancient Britons. The chief then made a sign
to the old pipe bearer, who seemed to fill, likewise, the station
of herald, seneschal and public crier, for he ascended to the
top of the lodge to make proclamation. Here he took his post
beside the aperture for the emission of smoke and the admission of light; the chief dictated from within what he was to
proclaim, and he bawled it forth with a force of lungs that
resounded over all the village. In this way he summoned
the warriors and great men to council; every now and then
reporting progress to his chief through the hole in the roof.

In a little while the braves and sages began to enter one by
one as their names were called or announced, emerging from
under the buffalo robe suspended over the entrance instead of
a door, stalking across the lodge to the skins placed on the
floor and crouching down on them in silence. In this way
twenty entered and took their seats, forming an assemblage
worthy of the pencil, for the Arickaras are a noble race of
men, large and well formed, and maintain a savage grandeur
and gravity of demeanour in their solemn ceremonials.

All being seated the old seneschal prepared the pipe of ceremony or council and having lit it, handed it to the chief. He in-
haled the sacred smoke, gave a puff upward to the heaven, then
downward to the earth, then towards the east; after this it
was, as usual, passed from mouth to mouth, each holding it
respectfully until his neighbor had taken several whiffs; and
now the grand council was considered as opened in due form.*

The chief made an harangue welcoming the white men to
his village and expressing his happiness in taking them by the
hand as friends; but at the same time complaining of the
poverty of himself and his people, the usual prelude among
Indians to begging or hard bargaining.

Lisa rose to reply, and the eyes of Hunt and his companions
were eagerly turned upon him, those of M'Lellan glaring like
a basilisk's. He began by the usual expressions of friendship,
and then proceeded to explain the object of his own party.
Those persons, however, said he, pointing to Mr. Hunt and
his companions, are of a different party, and are quite distinct

* Breckenridge.

in their views: but, added he, though we are separate parties we make but one common cause when the safety of either is concerned. Any injury or insult offered to them I shall consider as done to myself, and will resent it accordingly. I trust, therefore, that you will treat them with the same friendship that you have always manifested for me, doing every thing in your power to serve them and to help them on their way.

The speech of Lisa, delivered with an air of frankness and sincerity, agreeably surprized and disappointed the rival party.

Mr. Hunt then spoke declaring the object of his journey to the great Salt Lake beyond the mountains, and that he should want horses for the purpose, for which he was ready to trade, having brought with him plenty of goods. Both he and Lisa concluded their speeches by making presents of tobacco.

The Left handed chieftain in reply promised his friendship and aid to the new comers and welcomed them to his village. He added that they had not the number of horses to spare that Mr. Hunt required, and expressed a doubt whether they should be able to part with any. Upon this another chieftain, called Grey Eyes, made a speech and declared that they could readily supply Mr. Hunt with all the horses he might want, since, if they had not enough in the village, they could easily steal more. This honest expedient immediately removed the main difficulty; but the chief deferred all trading for a day or two, until he should have time to consult with his subordinate chiefs, as to market rates; for the principal chief of a village, in conjunction with his council, usually fixes the prices at which articles shall be bought and sold, and to these the village must conform.

The council now broke up. Mr. Hunt transferred his camp across the river at a little distance below the village and the Left Handed chief placed some of his warriors as a guard to prevent the intrusion of any of his people. The camp was pitched on the river bank just above the boats. The tents and the men wrapped in their blankets and bivouacking on skins in the open air, surrounded the baggage at night. Four sentinels also kept watch within sight of each other outside of the camp until midnight, when they were relieved by four others who mounted guard until day light. Mr. Lisa encamped near to Mr. Hunt, between him and the village.

The speech of Mr. Lisa in the council had produced a pacific effect in the encampment. Though the sincerity of his friendship and good will towards the new company still remained matter of doubt, he was no longer suspected of an intention to play false. The intercourse between the two leaders was, therefore, resumed and the affairs of both parties went on harmoniously.

Chapter XXI

An Indian horse fair—Love of the Indians for horses—Scenes in the Arickara village—Indian hospitality—Duties of Indian women—Game habits of the men—Their indolence—Love of gossipping—Rumours of lurking enemies—Scouts—An alarm—A sallying forth—Indian dogs—Return of a horse stealing party—An Indian deputation—Fresh alarms—Return of a successful war party—Dress of the Arickaras—Indian toilette—Triumphal entry of the war party—Meetings of relatives and friends—Indian sensibility—Meeting of a wounded warrior and his mother—Festivities and lamentations.

A TRADE now commenced with the Arickaras, under the regulation and supervision of their two chieftains. Lisa sent a part of his goods to the lodge of the Left handed dignitary and Mr. Hunt established his mart in the lodge of the Big Man. The village soon presented the appearance of a busy fair; and as horses were in demand, the purlieus and the adjacent plain were like the vicinity of a Tartar encampment; horses were put through all their paces, and horsemen were careering about with that dexterity and grace for which the Arickaras are noted. As soon as a horse was purchased his tail was cropped, a sure mode of distinguishing him from the horses of the tribe; for the Indians disdain to practice this absurd, barbarous and indecent mutilation, invented by some mean and vulgar mind insensible to the merit and perfections of the animal; on the contrary, the Indian horses are suffered to remain in every respect the superb and beautiful animals which nature formed them.

The wealth of an Indian of the Far West consists principally in his horses, of which each chief and warrior possesses a great number, so that the plains about an Indian village or encampment are covered with them. These form objects of traffic or objects of depredation, and in this way pass from tribe to tribe over great tracts of country. The horses owned by the Arickaras were, for the most part, of the wild stock of the prairies; some however had been obtained from the Poncas, Pawnees, and other tribes to the southwest, who had stolen

them from the Spaniards in the course of horse stealing expeditions into the Mexican territories. These were to be known
by being branded; a Spanish mode of marking horses not
practiced by the Indians.

As the Arickaras were meditating another expedition against
their enemies the Sioux, the articles of traffic most in demand
were guns, tomahawks, scalping knives, powder, ball and
other munitions of war. The price of a horse, as regulated by
the chiefs, was commonly ten dollars worth of goods at first
cost. To supply the demand thus suddenly created, parties of
young men and braves had sallied forth on expeditions to steal
horses; a species of service, among the Indians, which takes
precedence of hunting, and is considered a department of
honorable warfare.

While the leaders of the expedition were actively engaged in
preparing for the approaching journey, those who had accompanied it for curiosity or amusement, found ample matter for
observation in the village and its inhabitants. Wherever they
went they were kindly entertained. If they entered a lodge, the
buffalo robe was spread before the fire, for them to sit down;
the pipe was brought, and while the master of the lodge con-
versed with his guests, the squaw put the earthen vessel over
the fire, well filled with dried buffalo meat and pounded corn:
for the Indian in his native state, before he has mingled much
with white men, and acquired their sordid habits, has the hospitality of the Arab: never does a stranger enter his door without having food placed before him, and never is the food thus
furnished made a matter of traffic.

The life of an Indian when at home in his village is a life of
indolence and amusement. To the woman is consigned the
labours of the household and the field; she arranges the lodge;
brings wood for the fire; cooks; jirks venison and buffalo meat;
dresses the skins of the animals killed in the chase; cultivates
the little patch of maize, pumpkins and pulse which furnishes a
great part of their provisions. Their time for repose and recreation is at sunset, when, the labors of the day being ended,
they gather together to amuse themselves with petty games, or
to hold gossiping convocations on the tops of their lodges.

As to the Indian he is a game animal, not to be degraded
by useful or menial toil. It is enough that he exposes himself

to the hardships of the chase and the perils of war; that he brings home food for his family and watches and fights for its protection. Every thing else is beneath his attention. When at home he attends only to his weapons and his horses, preparing the means of future exploit. Or he engages with his comrades in games of dexterity, agility and strength; or in gambling games in which every thing is put at hazard, with a recklessness seldom witnessed in civilized life.

A great part of the idle leisure of the Indians when at home, is passed in groupes, squatted together on the bank of a river, on the top of a mound on the prairie, or on the roof of one of their earth covered lodges, talking over the news of the day, the affairs of the tribe, the events and exploits of their last hunting or fighting expedition; or listening to the stories of old times told by some veteran chronicler; resembling a groupe of our village quidnuncs and politicians, listening to the prosings of some superannuated oracle, or discussing the contents of an ancient newspaper.

As to the Indian women they are far from complaining of their lot. On the contrary, they would despise their husbands could they stoop to any menial office, and would think it conveyed an imputation upon their own conduct. It is the worst insult one virago can cast upon another in a moment of altercation. "Infamous Woman!" will she cry—"I have seen your husband carrying wood into his lodge to make the fire. Where was his squaw, that he should be obliged to make a woman of himself!"

Mr. Hunt and his fellow travellers had not been many days at the Arickara village when rumours began to circulate that the Sioux had followed them up, and that a war party, four or five hundred in number, were lurking somewhere in the neighborhood. These rumours produced much embarrassment in the camp. The white hunters were deterred from venturing forth in quest of game, neither did the leaders think it proper to expose them to such risk. The Arickaras, too, who had suffered greatly in their wars with this cruel and ferocious tribe, were roused to encreased vigilance, and stationed mounted scouts upon the neighboring hills. This, however, is a general precaution among the tribes of the prairies. Those immense plans present a horizon like the Ocean, so that any object of importance can be descried afar, and information communicated to a great distance. The scouts are stationed on the hills, therefore, to look out both for game and for enemies, and are, in a manner, living telegraphs conveying their intelligence by concerted signs. If they wish to give notice of a herd of buffalo in the plain beyond, they gallop backwards and forwards abreast, on the summit of the hill. If they perceive an enemy at hand they gallop to and fro, crossing each other; at sight of which the whole village flies to arms.

Such an alarm was given in the afternoon of the 15th. Four scouts were seen crossing and recrossing each other at full gallop, on the summit of a hill about two miles distant down the river. The cry was up that the Sioux were coming. In an instant the village was in an uproar. Men, women and children were all bawling and shouting; dogs barking, yelping and howling. Some of the warriors ran for the horses to gather and drive them in from the prairie, some for their weapons. As fast as they could arm and equip they sallied forth; some on horseback, some on foot. Some hastily arrayed in their war dress, with coronets of fluttering feathers, and their bodies smeared with paint; others naked and only furnished with the weapons they had snatched up.

The women and children gathered on the tops of the lodges and heightened the confusion of the scene by their vociferation. Old men who could no longer bear arms took similar stations, and harangued the warriors as they passed, exhorting them to valorous deeds. Some of the veterans took arms themselves, and sallied forth with tottering steps. In this way the savage chivalry of the village to the number of five hundred, poured forth, helter skelter, riding and running, with hideous yells and war whoops like so many bedlamites or demoniacs let loose.

After a while the tide of war rolled back, but with far less uproar. Either it had been a false alarm, or the enemy had retreated on finding themselves discovered, and quiet was restored to the village. The white hunters continuing to be fearful of ranging this dangerous neighborhood, fresh provisions began to be scarce in the camp. As a substitute, therefore, for venison and buffalo meat, the travellers had to purchase a number of dogs to be shot and cooked for the supply of the camp. Fortunately, however chary the Indians might be of their horses, they were liberal of their dogs. In fact, these animals swarm about an Indian village as they do about a Turkish town. Not a family but has two or three dozen belonging to it, of all sizes and colours. Some of a superior breed are used for hunting; others to draw the sledge, while others of a mongrel breed, and idle vagabond nature, are fatted for food. They are supposed to be descended from the wolf, and retain something of his savage but cowardly temper, howling rather than barking: shewing their teeth and snarling on the slightest provocation, but sneaking away on the least attack.

The excitement of the village continued from day to day. On the day following the alarm just mentioned several parties arrived from different directions, and were met and conducted by some of the braves to the council lodge; where they reported the events and success of their expeditions, whether of war or hunting, which news was afterwards promulgated throughout the village, by certain old men who acted as heralds or town criers. Among the parties which arrived was one that had been among the Snake nation stealing horses, and returned crowned with success. As they passed in triumph through the village they were cheered by the men, women and children, collected as usual on the tops of the lodges, and were exhorted by the nestors of the village to be generous in their dealings with the white men.

The evening was spent in feasting and rejoicing among the relatives of the successful warriors; but sounds of grief and wailing were heard from the hills adjacent to the village: the lamentations of women who had lost some relative in the foray.

An Indian village is subject to continual agitations and excitements. The next day arrived a deputation of braves from the Cheyenne or Shienne nation; a broken tribe, cut up, like the Arickaras, by wars with the Sioux, and driven to take refuge among the Black Hills, near the sources of the Cheyenne River from which they derive their name. One of these deputies was magnificently arrayed in a buffalo robe, on which various figures were fancifully embroidered with split quills, dyed red and yellow; and the whole was fringed with the slender hoofs of young fawns that rattled as he walked.

The arrival of this deputation was the signal for another of those ceremonials which occupy so much of Indian life; for no being is more courtly and punctilious, and more observant of etiquette and formality than an American Savage.

The object of the deputation was to give notice of an intended visit of the Shienne (or Cheyenne) tribe to the Arickara village in the course of fifteen days. To this visit Mr. Hunt looked forward, to procure additional horses for his journey; all his bargaining being ineffectual in obtaining a sufficient supply from the Arickaras. Indeed nothing could prevail upon the latter to part with their prime horses, which had been trained to buffalo hunting.

As Mr. Hunt would have to abandon his boats at this place, Mr. Lisa now offered to purchase them, and such of his merchandize as was superfluous, and to pay him in horses, to be obtained at a Fort belonging to the Missouri Fur Company situated at the Mandan villages, about a hundred and fifty miles further up the river. A bargain was promptly made, and Mr. Lisa and Mr. Crooks, with several companions, set out for the Fort to procure the horses. They returned after upwards of a fortnight's absence, bringing with them the stipulated number of horses.

Still the cavalry was not sufficiently numerous to convey the party and the baggage and merchandize, and a few days more were required to complete the arrangements for the journey.

On the 9th of July, just before day break, a great noise and vociferation was heard in the village. This being the usual Indian hour of attack and surprize, and the Sioux being known to be in the neighborhood, the camp was instantly on the alert. As the day broke Indians were descried in considerable number, on the bluffs, three or four miles down the river. The noise and agitation in the village continued. The tops of the lodges were crowded with the inhabitants, all earnestly looking towards the hills, and keeping up a vehement chattering. Presently an Indian warrior gallopped past the camp towards the village, and in a little while the legions began to pour forth.

The truth of the matter was now ascertained. The Indians upon the distant hills were three hundred Arickara braves, returning from a foray. They had met the war party of Sioux who had been so long hovering about the neighborhood, had fought them the day before, killed several and defeated the rest with the loss of but two or three of their own men and about a dozen wounded; and they were now halting at a distance until their comrades in the village should come forth to meet them, and swell the parade of their triumphal entry. The warrior who had gallopped past the camp was the leader of the party hastening home to give tidings of his victory.

Preparations were now made for this great martial ceremony. All the finery and equipments of the warriors were sent forth to them, that they might appear to the greatest advantage. Those, too, who had remained at home, tasked their wardrobes and toilettes to do honor to the procession.

The Arickaras generally go naked, but, like all savages, they have their gala dress of which they are not a little vain. This usually consists of a gay surcoat and leggings of the dressed skin of the antelope, resembling chamois leather, and embroidered with porcupine quills brilliantly dyed. A buffalo robe is thrown over the right shoulder, and across the left is slung a quiver of arrows. They wear gay coronets of plumes, particularly those of the swan; but the feathers of the black eagle are considered the most worthy, being a sacred bird among the Indian warriors. He who has killed an enemy in his own land, is entitled to drag at his heels a fox's skin attached to each moccasin; and he who has slain a grizzly bear, wears a necklace of his claws, the most glorious trophy that a hunter can exhibit.

An Indian toilette is an operation of some toil and trouble; the warrior often has to paint himself from head to foot, and is extremely capricious and difficult to please as to the hideous distribution of streaks and colours. A great part of the morning, therefore, passed away before there were any signs of the distant pageant. In the mean time a profound stillness reigned over the village. Most of the inhabitants had gone forth; others remained in mute expectation. All sports and occupations were suspended, excepting that in the lodges the painstaking squaws were silently busied in preparing the repasts for the warriors.

It was near noon that a mingled sound of voices and rude music faintly heard from a distance, gave notice that the procession was on the march. The old men and such of the squaws as could leave their employments hastened forth to meet it. In a little while it emerged from behind a hill, and had a wild and picturesque appearance as it came moving over the summit in measured step, and to the cadence of songs and savage instruments; the warlike standards and trophies flaunting aloft, and the feathers and paint, and silver ornaments of the warriors glaring and glittering in the sunshine.

The pageant had really something chivalrous in its arrangement. The Arickaras are divided into several bands, each bearing the name of some animal or bird, as the buffalo, the bear, the dog, the pheasant. The present party consisted of four of these bands, one of which was the dog, the most esteemed in war, being composed of young men under thirty and noted for prowess. It is engaged on the most desperate occasions. The bands marched in separate bodies under their several leaders. The warriors on foot came first, in platoons of ten or twelve abreast; then the horsemen. Each band bore as an ensign a spear or bow decorated with beads, porcupine quills and painted feathers. Each bore its trophies of scalps, elevated on poles, their long black locks streaming in the wind. Each was accompanied by its rude music and minstrelsy. In this way the procession extended nearly a quarter of a mile. The warriors were variously armed, some few with guns, others with bows and arrows and war clubs; all had shields of buffalo hide, a kind of defence generally used by the Indians of the open prairies, who have not the covert of trees and forests to protect them. They were painted in the most savage style. Some had the stamp of a red hand across their mouths, a sign that they had drunk the life blood of a foe!

As they drew near to the village the old men and the women began to meet them and now a scene ensued that proved the fallacy of the old fable of Indian apathy and stoicism. Parents and children, husbands and wives, brothers and sisters met with the most rapturous expressions of joy; while wailings and lamentations were heard from the relatives of the killed and wounded. The procession, however, continued on with slow and measured step, in cadence to the solemn chaunt, and the warriors maintained their fixed and stern demeanour.

Between two of the principal chiefs rode a young warrior who had distinguished himself in the battle. He was severely wounded so as with difficulty to keep on his horse; but he preserved a serene and steadfast countenance as if perfectly unharmed. His mother had heard of his condition. She broke through the throng and rushing up, threw her arms around him and wept aloud. He kept up the spirit and demeanor of a warrior to the last, but expired shortly after he had reached his home.

The village was now a scene of the utmost festivity and triumph. The banners and trophies and scalps and painted shields were elevated on poles near the lodges. There were war feasts, and scalp dances, with warlike songs and savage music; all the inhabitants were arrayed in their festal dresses; while the old heralds went round from lodge to lodge, promulgating with loud voices the events of the battle and the exploits of the various warriors.

Such was the boisterous revelry of the village; but sounds of another kind were heard on the surrounding hills; piteous wailings of the women, who had retired thither to mourn in darkness and solitude for those who had fallen in battle. There the poor mother of the youthful warrior who had returned home in triumph but to die, gave full vent to the anguish of a mother's heart. How much does this custom among the Indian women of repairing to the hill tops in the night, and pouring forth their wailings for the dead, call to mind the beautiful and affecting passage of Scripture, "In Rama was there a voice heard, lamentation, and weeping and great mourning, Rachel weeping for her children, and would not be comforted, because they are not."

Chapter XXII

WHILE Mr. Hunt was diligently preparing for his arduous journey some of his men began to lose heart at the
perilous prospect before them; but, before we accuse them of
want of spirit, it is proper to consider the nature of the wilderness into which they were about to adventure. It was a region
almost as vast and trackless as the ocean, and, at the time of
which we treat, but little known, excepting through the vague
accounts of Indian hunters. A part of their route would lay
across an immense tract stretching north and south for hundreds of miles along the foot of the Rocky Mountains, and
drained by the tributary streams of the Missouri and the Mississippi. This region, which resembles one of the immeasurable steppes of Asia, has not inaptly been termed "The Great
American desert." It spreads forth into undulating and treeless plains, and desolate sandy wastes, wearisome to the eye
from their extent and monotony, and which are supposed by
geologists, to have formed the ancient floor of the ocean,
countless ages since, when its primeval waves beat against the
granite bases of the Rocky Mountains.

It is a land where no man permanently abides; for, in certain
seasons of the year there is no food either for the hunter or his
steed. The herbage is parched and withered; the brooks and
streams are dried up; the buffalo, the elk and the deer have
wandered to distant parts, keeping within the verge of expiring
verdure, and leaving behind them a vast uninhabited solitude,
seamed by ravines, the beds of former torrents, but now serving only to tantalize and encrease the thirst of the traveller.

Occasionally the monotony of this vast wilderness is interrupted by mountainous belts of sand and lime stone; broken
into confused masses; with precipitous cliffs and yawning

ravines, looking like the ruins of a world; or is traversed by lofty and barren ridges of rock, almost impassable, like those denominated the Black Hills. Beyond these rise the stern barriers of the Rocky Mountains, the limits, as it were, of the Atlantic world. The rugged defiles and deep valleys of this vast chain form sheltering places for restless and ferocious bands of savages, many of them the remnants of tribes, once inhabitants of the prairies, but broken up by war and violence, and who carry into their mountain haunts the fierce passions and reckless habits of desperadoes.

Such is the nature of this immense wilderness of the Far West; which apparently defies cultivation, and the habitation of civilized life. Some portions of it along the rivers may partially be subdued by agriculture, others may form vast pastoral tracts, like those of the east; but it is to be feared that a great part of it will form a lawless interval between the abodes of civilized man, like the wastes of the ocean or the deserts of Arabia; and, like them, be subject to the depredations of the marauder. Here may spring up new and mongrel races, like new formations in geology, the amalgamation of the "debris" and "abrasions" of former races, civilized and savage; the remains of broken and almost extinguished tribes; the descendants of wandering hunters and trappers; of fugitives from the Spanish and American frontiers; of adventurers and desperadoes of every class and country, yearly ejected from the bosom of society into the wilderness. We are contributing incessantly to swell this singular and heterogeneous cloud of wild population that is to hang about our frontier, by the transfer of whole tribes of savages from the east of the Mississippi to the great wastes of the Far West. Many of these bear with them the smart of real or fancied injuries; many consider themselves expatriated beings, wrongfully exiled from their hereditary homes, and the sepulchres of their fathers, and cherish a deep and abiding animosity against the race that has dispossessed them. Some may gradually become pastoral hordes, like those rude and migratory people, half shepherd, half warrior, who, with their flocks and herds, roam the plains of upper Asia; but, others, it is to be apprehended, will become predatory bands, mounted on the fleet steeds of the prairies, with the open plains for their marauding grounds, and the mountains for their retreats and lurking places. Here they may resemble those great hordes of the north, "Gog and Magog with their bands," that haunted the gloomy imaginations of the prophets. "A great company and a mighty host, all riding upon horses, and warring upon those nations which were at rest, and dwelt peaceably, and had gotten cattle and goods."

The Spaniards changed the whole character and habits of the Indians when they brought the horse among them. In Chili, Tucuman and other parts, it has converted them, we are told, into Tartar-like tribes, and enabled them to keep the Spaniards out of their country, and even to make it dangerous for them to venture far from their towns and settlements. Are we not in danger of producing some such state of things in the boundless regions of the Far West? That these are not mere fanciful and extravagant suggestions we have sufficient proofs in the dangers already experienced by the traders to the Spanish mart of Santa Fé, and to the distant posts of the Fur Companies. These are obliged to proceed in armed caravans, and are subject to murderous attacks from bands of Pawnees, Camanches and Blackfeet, that come scouring upon them in their weary march across the plains, or lie in wait for them among the passes of the mountains.

We are wandering, however, into excursive speculations, when our intention was merely to give an idea of the nature of the wilderness which Mr. Hunt was about to traverse; and which at that time was far less known than at present; though it still remains in a great measure an unknown land. We cannot be surprized, therefore, that some of the least resolute of his party should feel dismay at the thoughts of adventuring into this perilous wilderness under the uncertain guidance of three hunters, who had merely passed once through the country and might have forgotten the land marks. Their apprehensions were aggravated by some of Lisa's followers, who, not being engaged in the expedition, took a mischievous pleasure in exaggerating its dangers. They painted in strong colours, to the poor Canadian voyageurs, the risk they would run of perishing with hunger and thirst; of being cut off by war parties of the Sioux who scoured the plains; of having their horses stolen by the Upsarokas or Crows, who infested the skirts of the Rocky Mountains, or of being butchered by the Blackfeet, who lurked among the defiles. In a word, there was little chance of their getting alive across the mountains; and even if they did, those three guides knew nothing of the howling wilderness that lay beyond.

The apprehensions thus awakened in the minds of some of the men came well nigh proving detrimental to the expedition. Some of them determined to desert, and to make their way back to S' Louis. They accordingly purloined several weapons and a barrel of gunpowder, as ammunition for their enterprize, and buried them in the river bank, intending to seize one of the boats and make off in the night. Fortunately their plot was overheard by John Day, the Kentuckyan, and communicated to the partners, who took quiet and effectual means to frustrate it.

The dangers to be apprehended from the Crow Indians had not been over rated by the camp gossips. These savages through whose mountain haunts the party would have to pass, were noted for daring and excursive habits, and great dexterity in horse stealing. Mr. Hunt, therefore, considered himself fortunate in having met with a man who might be of great use to him in any intercourse he might have with the tribe. This was a wandering individual named Edward Rose, whom he had picked up somewhere on the Missouri—one of those anomalous beings found on the frontier who seem to have neither kin nor country. He had lived some time among the Crows so as to become acquainted with their language and customs; and was, withal, a dogged, sullen, silent fellow, with a sinister aspect, and more of the savage than the civilized man in his appearance. He was engaged to serve in general as a hunter, but as guide and interpreter when they should reach the country of the Crows.

On the 18th of July Mr. Hunt took up his line of march by land from the Arikara village, leaving Mr. Lisa and Mr. Nuttall there, where they intended to await the expected arrival of Mr. Henry from the Rocky Mountains. As to Messrs. Bradbury and Breckenridge, they had departed some days previously, on a voyage down the river to S' Louis, with a detachment from Mr. Lisa's party.

With all his exertions Mr. Hunt had been unable to obtain a sufficient number of horses for the accommodation of all his people. His cavalcade consisted of eighty two horses, most of them heavily laden with Indian goods, beaver traps, ammunition, Indian corn, corn meal and other necessaries. Each of the partners was mounted, and a horse was allotted to the interpreter Pierre Dorion, for the transportation of his luggage and his two children. His squaw, for the most part of the time, trudged on foot, like the residue of the party; nor did any of the men shew more patience and fortitude than this resolute woman in enduring fatigue and hardship.

The veteran trappers and voyageurs of Lisa's party shook their heads as their comrades set out, and took leave of them as of doomed men; and even Lisa, himself, gave it as his opinion, after the travellers had departed, that they would never reach the shores of the Pacific, but would either perish with hunger in the wilderness or be cut off by the Savages.

Chapter XXIII

THE COURSE taken by Mr. Hunt was at first to the north
west, but soon turned and kept generally to the south
west, to avoid the country infested by the Blackfeet. His route
took him across some of the tributary streams of the Missouri,
and over emmense prairies, bounded only by the horizon, and
destitute of trees. It was now the height of summer, and these
naked plains would be intolerable to the traveller were it not
for the breezes which sweep over them during the fervour of
the day, bringing with them tempering airs from the distant
mountains. To the prevalence of these breezes, and to the
want of all leafy covert, may we also attribute the freedom
from those flies and other insects so tormenting to man and
beast during the summer months, in the lower prairies, which
are bordered and interspersed with woodland.

The monotony of these immense landscapes, also, would be
as wearisome as that of the ocean, were it not relieved in some
degree by the purity and elasticity of the atmosphere and the
beauty of the heavens. The sky has that delicious blue for
which the sky of Italy is renowned; the sun shines with a splendor unobscured by any cloud or vapour, and a star light night
on the prairies is glorious. This purity and elasticity of atmosphere encreases as the traveller approaches the mountains, and
gradually rises into the more elevated prairies.

On the second day of the journey Mr. Hunt arranged the
party into small and convenient messes, distributing among
them the camp kettles. The encampments at night were as before; some sleeping under tents and others bivouacking in the
open air. The Canadians proved as patient of toil and hardship
on the land as on the water; indeed nothing could surpass the
patience and goodhumour of these men upon the march. They

were the cheerful drudges of the party, loading and unloading the horses, pitching the tents, making the fires, cooking; in short, performing all those household and menial offices which the Indians usually assign to the squaws—and, like the squaws, they left all the hunting and fighting to others. A Canadian has but little affection for the exercise of the rifle.

The progress of the party was but slow for the first few days. Some of the men were indisposed; Mr. Crooks especially was so unwell that he could not keep on his horse. A rude kind of litter was, therefore, prepared for him, consisting of two long poles, fixed one on each side of two horses, with a matting between them on which he reclined at full length, and was protected from the sun by a canopy of boughs.

On the evening of the 23d (July) they encamped on the banks of what they term Big River; and here we cannot but pause to lament the stupid, commonplace, and often ribald names entailed upon the rivers and other features of the Great West, by traders and settlers. As the aboriginal tribes of these magnificent regions are yet in existence the Indian names might easily be recovered; which, beside being in general more sonorous and musical, would remain mementos of the primitive lords of the soil, of whom in a little while scarce any traces will be left. Indeed it is to be wished that the whole of our country could be rescued, as much as possible, from the wretched nomenclature inflicted upon it, by ignorant and vulgar minds, and this might be done, in a great degree, by restoring the Indian names, wherever significant and euphonious. As there appears to be a spirit of research abroad in respect to our aboriginal antiquities, we would suggest, as a worthy object of enterprize, a map, or maps, of every part of our country, giving the Indian names wherever they could be ascertained. Whoever achieves such an object worthily will leave a monument to his own reputation.

To return from this digression. As the travellers were now in a country abounding with buffalo, they remained for several days encamped upon the banks of Big River, to obtain a supply of provisions and to give the invalids time to recruit.

On the second day of their sojourn, as Ben Jones, John Day and others of the hunters were in pursuit of game they came upon an Indian camp on the open prairie, near to a small stream which ran through a ravine. The tents or lodges were of dressed buffalo skins, sewn together and stretched on tapering pine poles, joined at top, but radiating at bottom, so as to form a circle capable of admitting fifty persons. Numbers of horses were grazing in the neighborhood of the camp or straying at large in the prairie, a sight most acceptable to the hunters. After reconnoitering the camp for some time they ascertained it to belong to a band of Cheyenne Indians, the same that had sent a deputation to the Arickaras. They received the hunters in the most friendly manner; invited them to their lodges, which were more cleanly than Indian lodges are prone to be, and set food before them with true uncivilized hospitality. Several of them accompanied the hunters back to the camp, when a trade was immediately opened. The Cheyennes were astonished and delighted to find a convoy of goods and trinkets thus brought into the very heart of the prairie; while Mr. Hunt and his companions were overjoyed to have an opportunity of obtaining a further supply of horses from these equestrian savages.

During a fortnight that the travellers lingered at this place their encampment was continually thronged by the Cheyennes. They were a civil, well behaved people, cleanly in their persons and decorous in their habits. The men were tall, straight and vigorous, with aquiline noses and high cheek bones. Some were almost as naked as ancient statues, and might have stood as models for a statuary; others had leggings and moccasins of deer skin, and buffalo robes, which they threw gracefully over their shoulders. In a little while, however, they began to appear in more gorgeous array, tricked out in the finery obtained from the white men; bright cloths; brass rings; beads of various colours, and happy was he who could render himself hideous with vermillion.

The travellers had frequent occasion to admire the skill and grace with which these Indians managed their horses. Some of them made a striking display when mounted; themselves and their steeds decorated in gala style; for the Indians often bestow more finery upon their horses than upon themselves. Some would hang round the necks, or rather on the breasts of their horses the most precious ornaments they had obtained from the white men; others interwove feathers in their manes and tails. The Indian horses, too, appear to have an attachment to their wild riders, and indeed it is said that the horses of the prairies readily distinguish an Indian from a white man by the smell, and give a preference to the former. Yet the Indians, in general, are hard riders, and, however they may value their horses, treat them with great roughness and neglect. Occasionally the Cheyennes joined the white hunters in pursuit of the elk and buffalo, and when in the ardor of the chase, spared neither themselves nor their steeds, scouring the prairies at full speed, and plunging down precipices and frightful ravines that threatened the necks of both horse and horseman. The Indian steed, well trained to the chase, seems as mad as his rider and pursues the game as eagerly as if it were his natural prey, on the flesh of which he was to banquet.

The history of the Cheyennes is that of many of these wandering tribes of the prairies. They were the remnant of a once powerful people called the Shaways, inhabiting a branch of the Red River which flows into Lake Winnipeg. Every Indian tribe has some rival tribe with which it wages implacable hostility. The deadly enemies of the Shaways were the Sioux, who after a long course of warfare, proved too powerful for them and drove them across the Missouri. They again took root near the Warricanne creek and established themselves there in a fortified village.

The Sioux still followed them with deadly animosity; dislodged them from their village and compelled them to take refuge in the Black Hills, near the upper waters of the Shienne (or Cheyenne) River. Here they lost even their name, and became known among the French colonists by that of the river they frequented.

The heart of the tribe was now broken; its numbers were greatly thinned by their harassing wars. They no longer attempted to establish themselves in any permanent abode that might be an object of attack to their cruel foes. They gave up the cultivation of the fruits of the earth and became a wandering tribe subsisting by the chase and following the buffalo in its migrations.

Their only possessions were horses; which they caught on the prairies, or reared, or captured on predatory incursions into the Mexican territories as has already been mentioned.

With some of these they repaired once a year to the Arickara villages, exchanged them for corn, beans, pumpkins and articles of European merchandize, and then returned into the heart of the prairies.

Such are the fluctuating fortunes of these savage nations. War, famine, pestilence, together or singly, bring down their strength and thin their numbers. Whole tribes are rooted up from their native places, wander for a time about these immense regions, become amalgamated with other tribes, or disappear from the face of the earth. There appears to be a tendency to extinction among all the savage nations, and this tendency would seem to have been in operation among the aboriginals of this country long before the advent of the white men, if we may judge from the traces and traditions of ancient populousness in regions which were silent and deserted at the time of the discovery; and from the mysterious and perplexing vestiges of unknown races, predecessors of those found in actual possession, and who must long since have become gradually extinguished or been destroyed. The whole history of the aboriginal population of this country, however, is an enigma, and a grand one—will it ever be solved?

Chapter XXIV

New distribution of horses—Secret information of treason in the camp—Rose the interpreter, his perfidious character—His plots—Anecdotes of the Crow Indians—Notorious horse stealers—Some account of Rose—A desperado of the frontier.

O<small>N THE SIXTH</small> of August the travellers bade farewell to the friendly band of Cheyennes, and resumed their journey. As they had obtained thirty six additional horses by their recent traffic, Mr. Hunt made a new arrangement. The baggage was made up in smaller loads. A horse was allotted to each of the six prime hunters, and others were distributed among the voyageurs, a horse for every two, so that they could ride and walk alternately. Mr. Crooks being still too feeble to mount the saddle, was carried on a litter.

Their march this day lay among singular hills and knolls of an indurated red earth, resembling brick, about the bases of which were scattered pumice stones and cinders, the whole bearing traces of the action of fire. In the evening they encamped on a branch of Big River.

They were now out of the tract of country infested by the Sioux; and had advanced such a distance into the interior that Mr. Hunt no longer felt apprehensive of the desertion of any of his men. He was doomed, however, to experience new cause of anxiety. As he was seated in his tent after night fall one of the men came to him privately, and informed him that there was mischief brewing in the camp. Edward Rose, the interpreter, whose sinister looks we have already mentioned, was denounced by this secret informer, as a designing, treacherous scoundrel, who was tampering with the fidelity of certain of the men and instigating them to a flagrant piece of treason. In the course of a few days they would arrive at the mountainous district infested by the Upsarokas or Crows, the tribe among which Rose was to officiate as interpreter. His plan was that several of the men should join with him, when in that neighborhood, in carrying off a number of the horses with their packages of goods, and deserting to those savages. He assured them of good treatment among the Crows, the principal chiefs and warriors of whom he knew: they would soon become great men among them and have the finest women, and the daughters of the chiefs for wives, and the horses and goods they carried off would make them rich for life.

The intelligence of this treachery on the part of Rose gave much disquiet to Mr. Hunt, for he knew not how far it might be effective among his men. He had already had proofs that several of them were disaffected to the enterprize, and loth to cross the mountains. He knew also that savage life had charms for many of them, especially the Canadians, who were prone to intermarry and domesticate themselves among the Indians.

And here a word or two concerning the Crows may be of service to the reader, as they will figure occasionally in the succeeding narrative.

The tribe consists of four bands, which have their nestling places in fertile, well wooded valleys lying among the Rocky Mountains, and watered by the Big Horn River and its tributary streams; but, though these are properly their homes, where they shelter their old people, their wives and their children, the men of the tribe are almost continually on the foray and the scamper. They are, in fact, notorious marauders and horse stealers; crossing and re crossing the mountains, robbing on the one side, and conveying their spoils to the other. Hence, we are told, is derived their name, given to them on account of their unsettled and predatory habits; winging their flight, like the crows, from one side of the mountains to the other, and making free booty of every thing that lies in their way. Horses, however, are the especial objects of their depredations, and their skill and audacity in stealing them are said to be astonishing. This is their glory and delight; an accomplished horse stealer fills up their idea of a hero. Many horses are obtained by them, also, in barter from tribes in and beyond the mountains. They have an absolute passion for this noble animal, beside which he is with them an important object of traffic. Once a year they make a visit to the Mandans, Minatarees and other tribes of the Missouri, taking with them droves of horses which they exchange for guns, ammunition, trinkets, vermillion, cloths of bright colours and various other articles of European manufacture. With these they supply their own wants and caprices, and carry on the internal trade for horses already mentioned.

The plot of Rose to rob and abandon his countrymen when in the heart of the wilderness, and to throw himself into the hands of a horde of Savages, may appear strange and improbable to those unacquainted with the singular and anomalous characters that are to be found about the borders. This fellow it appears was one of those desperadoes of the frontier, outlawed by their crimes, who combine the vices of civilized and savage life and are ten times more barbarous than the Indians with whom they consort. Rose had formerly belonged to one of the gangs of pirates who infested the islands of the Mississippi, plundering boats as they went up and down the river, and who sometimes shifted the scene of their robberies to the shore, way laying travellers as they returned by land from New Orleans, with the proceeds of their downward voyage, plundering them of their money and effects, and often perpetrating the most atrocious murders.

These hordes of villains being broken up and dispersed, Rose had betaken himself to the wilderness, associated himself with the Crows, whose predatory habits were congenial with his own, had married a woman of the tribe and, in short, had identified himself with those vagrant savages.

Such was the worthy guide and interpreter, Edward Rose. We give his story, however, not as it was known to Mr. Hunt and his companions at the time, but as it has been subsequently ascertained. Enough was known of the fellow and his dark and perfidious character to put Mr. Hunt upon his guard: still, as there was no knowing how far his plans might have succeeded, and as any rash act might blow the mere smouldering sparks of treason into a sudden blaze, it was thought adviseable by those with whom Mr. Hunt consulted, to conceal all knowledge or suspicion of the meditated treachery, but to keep up a vigilant watch upon the movements of Rose and a strict guard upon the horses at night.

Chapter XXV

THE PLAINS over which the travellers were journeying continued to be destitute of trees or even shrubs; insomuch that they had to use the dung of the buffalo for fuel; as the Arabs of the desert use that of the camel. This substitute for fuel is universal among the Indians of these upper prairies, and is said to make a fire equal to that of turf. If a few chips are added, it throws out a cheerful and kindly blaze.

These plains, however, had not always been equally destitute of wood, as was evident from the trunks of trees which the travellers repeatedly met with, some still standing, others lying about in broken fragments, but all in a fossil state, having flourished in times long past. In these singular remains the original grain of the wood was still so distinct that they could be ascertained to be the ruins of oak trees. Several pieces of the fossil wood were selected by the men to serve as whetstones.

In this part of the journey there was no lack of provisions, for the prairies were covered with immense herds of buffalo. These in general are animals of peaceable demeanour, grazing quietly like domestic cattle, but this was the season when they are in heat, and when the bulls are unusually fierce and pugnacious. There was accordingly a universal restlessness and commotion throughout the plain; and the amorous herds gave utterance to their feelings in low bellowings that resounded like distant thunder. Here and there fierce duellos took place between rival enamorados; butting their huge shagged fronts together, goring each other with their short black horns, and tearing up the earth with their feet in perfect fury.

In one of the evening halts Pierre Dorion the interpreter, together with Carson and Gardpie, two of the hunters, were missing, nor had they returned by morning. As it was supposed they had wandered away in pursuit of buffalo, and would readily find the track of the party, no solicitude was felt on their account. A fire was left burning, to guide them by its column of smoke, and the travellers proceeded on their march. In the evening a signal fire was made on a hill adjacent to the camp, and in the morning it was replenished with fuel so as to last throughout the day. These signals are usual among the Indians, to give warnings to each other, or to call home straggling hunters: and such is the transparency of the atmosphere in these elevated plains that a slight column of smoke can be discerned from a great distance, particularly in the evenings. Two or three days elapsed, however, without the reappearance of the three hunters; and Mr. Hunt slackened his march to give them time to overtake him.

A vigilant watch continued to be kept upon the movements of Rose, and of such of the men as were considered doubtful in their loyalty; but nothing occurred to excite immediate apprehensions. Rose evidently was not a favorite among his comrades, and it was hoped that he had not been able to make any real partizans.

On the 10th of August they encamped among hills, on the highest peak of which Mr. Hunt caused a huge pyre of pine wood to be made which soon sent up a great column of flame that might be seen far and wide over the prairies. This fire blazed all night and was amply replenished at day break; so that the towering pillar of smoke could not but be descried by the wanderers if within the distance of a day's journey.

It is a common occurrence, in these regions, where the features of the country so much resemble each other, for hunters to lose themselves and wander for many days, before they can find their way back to the main body of their party. In the present instance, however, a more than common solicitude was felt in consequence of the distrust awakened by the sinister designs of Rose.

The route now became excessively toilsome over a ridge of steep rocky hills, covered with loose stones. These were intersected by deep valleys formed by two branches of Big River coming from the south of west, both of which they crossed. These streams were bordered by meadows, well stocked with buffalos. Loads of meat were brought in by the hunters; but the travellers were rendered dainty by profusion and would cook only the choice pieces.

They had now travelled for several days at a very slow rate and had made signal fires and left traces of their route at every stage, yet nothing was heard or seen of the lost men. It began to be feared that they might have fallen into the hands of some lurking band of savages. A party numerous as that of Mr. Hunt, with a long train of pack horses, moving across open plains or naked hills, is discernible at a great distance by Indian scouts; who spread the intelligence rapidly to various points, and assemble their friends to hang about the skirts of the travellers, steal their horses, or cut off any stragglers from the main body.

Mr. Hunt and his companions were more and more sensible how much it would be in the power of this sullen and daring vagabond Rose, to do them mischief, when they should become entangled in the defiles of the mountains, with the passes of which they were wholly unacquainted, and which were infested by his freebooting friends the Crows. There, should be succeed in seducing some of the party into his plans, he might carry off the best horses and effects, throw himself among his savage allies and set all pursuit at defiance. Mr. Hunt resolved, therefore, to frustrate the knave, divert him, by management, from his plans, and make it sufficiently advantageous for him to remain honest. He took occasion, accordingly, in the course of conversation, to inform Rose that, having engaged him chiefly as a guide and interpreter through the country of the Crows, they would not stand in need of his services beyond. Knowing therefore his connexion by marriage with that tribe and his predilection for a residence among them, they would put no constraint upon his will, but, whenever they met with a party of that people, would leave him at liberty to remain among his adopted brethren. Furthermore that, in thus parting with him, they would pay him half a year's wages in consideration of his past services, and would give him a horse, three beaver traps and sundry other articles calculated to set him up in the world.

This unexpected liberality, which made it nearly as profitable and infinitely less hazardous for Rose to remain honest than to play the rogue, completely disarmed him. From that time his whole deportment underwent a change. His brow cleared up and appeared more cheerful; he left off his sullen, skulking habits and made no further attempts to tamper with the faith of his comrades.

On the 13th of August Mr. Hunt varied his course and inclined westward, in hopes of falling in with the three lost hunters; who, it was now thought, might have kept to the right hand of Big River. This course soon brought him to a fork of the Little Missouri, about a hundred yards wide, and resembling the great river of the same name in the strength of its current, its turbid water, and the frequency of drift wood and sunken trees.

Rugged mountains appeared ahead, crowding down to the water edge and offering a barrier to further progress on the side they were ascending. Crossing the river, therefore, they encamped on its north west bank, where they found good pasturage and buffalo in abundance. The weather was overcast and rainy and a general gloom pervaded the camp; the voyageurs sat moping in groupes with their shoulders as high as their heads, croaking their forebodings, when suddenly towards evening a shout of joy gave notice that the lost men were found. They came slowly lagging into the camp with weary looks, and horses jaded and way worn. They had, in fact, been for several days incessantly on the move. In their hunting excursion on the prairies they had pushed so far in pursuit of buffalo as to find it impossible to retrace their steps, over plains trampled by innumerable herds; and were baffled by the monotony of the landscape in their attempts to recall land marks. They had ridden to and fro until they had almost lost the points of the compass and become totally bewildered; nor did they once perceive any of the signal fires and columns of smoke made by their comrades. At length, about two days previously, when almost spent by anxiety and hard riding, they came, to their great joy, upon the "trail" of the party, which they had since followed up steadily.

Those only who have experienced the warm cordiality that grows up between comrades in wild and adventurous expeditions of the kind, can picture to themselves the hearty cheering with which the stragglers were welcomed to the camp. Every one crowded round them to ask questions and to hear the story of their mishaps; and even the Squaw of the moody half breed Pierre Dorion, forgot the sternness of his domestic rule and the conjugal discipline of the cudgel in her joy at his safe return.

Chapter XXVI

*The Black Mountains—Haunts of predatory Indians—Their
wild and broken appearance—Superstitions concerning them
—Thunder spirits—Singular noises in the mountains—Secret
mines—Hidden treasures—Mountains in labor—Scientific
explanation—Impassable defiles—Black tailed deer—The Big
horn or Asahta—Prospect from a lofty height—Plain with
herds of buffalo—Distant peaks of the Rocky Mountains—
Alarms in the camp—Tracks of grizly bears—Dangerous nature of this animal—Adventures of William Cannon and
John Day with grizly bears.*

M R. HUNT and his party were now on the skirts of the
Black Hills, or Black Mountains, as they are sometimes called, an extensive chain, lying about a hundred miles
east of the Rocky Mountains and stretching in a north east direction from the south fork of the Nebraska, or Platte River,
to the great north bend of the Missouri. The Sierra or ridge
of the Black Hills, in fact, forms the dividing line between the
waters of the Missouri and those of the Arkansas and the Mississippi, and gives rise to the Cheyenne, the Little Missouri,
and several tributary streams of the Yellow Stone.

The wild recesses of these hills, like those of the Rocky
Mountains, are retreats and lurking places for broken and
predatory tribes, and it was among them that the remnant of
the Cheyenne tribe took refuge, as has been stated, from their
conquering enemies, the Sioux.

The Black Hills are chiefly composed of sand stone, and in
many places are broken into savage cliffs and precipices, and
present the most singular and fantastic forms; sometimes resembling towns and castellated fortresses. The ignorant inhabitants of plains are prone to clothe the mountains that
bound their horizon with fanciful and superstitious attributes.
Thus the wandering tribes of the prairies who often behold
clouds gathering round the summits of these hills and lightning flashing and thunder pealing from them when all the
neighboring plains are serene and sunny, consider them the
abode of the genii or thunder spirits who fabricate storms and
tempests. On entering their defiles, therefore, they often hang

offerings on the trees, or place them on the rocks, to propitiate the invisible "Lords of the mountains," and procure good
weather and successful hunting; and they attach unusual
significancy to the echoes which haunt the precipices.

This superstition may also have arisen, in part, from a natural phenomenon of a singular nature. In the most calm and
serene weather, and at all times of the day or night, successive
reports are now and then heard among these mountains, resembling the discharge of several pieces of artillery. Similar
reports were heard by Messrs. Lewis and Clarke in the Rocky
Mountains, which they say, were attributed by the Indians
to the bursting of the rich mines of silver contained in the
bosom of the mountains.

In fact these singular explosions have received fanciful
explanations from learned men, and have not been satisfactorily accounted for even by philosophers. They are said to
occur frequently in Brazil. Vasconcelles, a Jesuit father, describes one which he heard in the Sierra, or mountain region
of Piratininga, and which he compares to the discharges of a
park of artillery. The Indians told him that it was an explosion
of stones. The worthy father had soon a satisfactory proof of
the truth of their information, for the very place was found
where a rock had burst and exploded from its entrails a stoney
mass, like a bomb shell, and of the size of a bull's heart. This
mass was broken either in its ejection or its fall, and wonderful was the internal organization revealed. It had a shell harder
even than iron; within which were arranged, like the seeds of
a pomegranate, jewels of various colours: some transparent as
chrystal: others of a fine red and others of mixed hues.

The same phenomenon is said to occur occasionally in the
adjacent province of Guayra, where stones of the bigness of a
man's hand are exploded, with a loud noise, from the bosom
of the earth, and scatter about glittering and beautiful fragments that look like precious gems, but are of no value.

The Indians of the Orellano, also, tell of horrible noises
heard occasionally in the Paraguaxo, which they consider the
throes and groans of the mountain endeavoring to cast forth
the precious stones hidden within its entrails. Others have
endeavored to account for these discharges of "mountain artillery" on humbler principles: attributing them to the loud

reports made by the disruption and fall of great masses of rock, reverberated and prolonged by the echoes: others to the disengagement of hydrogen, produced by subterraneous beds of coal in a state of ignition. In whatever way this singular phenomenon may be accounted for, the existence of it appears to be well established. It remains one of the lingering mysteries of nature which throw something of a supernatural charm over her wild mountain solitudes, and we doubt whether the imaginative reader will not rather join with the poor Indian in attributing it to the thunder spirits, or the guardian genii of unseen treasures, than to any commonplace physical cause.

Whatever might be the supernatural influences among these mountains, the travellers found their physical difficulties hard to cope with. They made repeated attempts to find a passage through, or over the chain, but were as often turned back by impassable barriers. Sometimes a defile seemed to open a practicable path, but it would terminate in some wild chaos of rocks and cliffs, which it was impossible to climb. The animals of these solitary regions were different from those they had been accustomed to. The black tailed deer would bound up the ravines on their approach, and the Big horn would gaze fearlessly down upon them from some impending precipice, or skip playfully from rock to rock.

These animals are only to be met with in mountainous regions. The former is larger than the common deer, but its flesh is not equally esteemed by hunters. It has very large ears and the tip of the tail is black, from which it derives its name.

The Big horn is so named from its horns; which are of a great size and twisted like those of a ram. It is called by some the Argali, by others the Ibex, though differing from both of these animals. The Mandans call it the Ahsahta, a name much better than the clumsy appellation which it generally bears. It is of the size of a small elk, or large deer, and of a dun colour, excepting the belly and round the tail, where it is white. In its habits it resembles the goat, frequenting the rudest precipices; cropping the herbage from their edges; and, like the chamois, bounding lightly and securely among dizzy heights, where the hunter dares not venture. It is difficult, therefore, to get within shot of it. Ben Jones the hunter, however, in one of the passes of the Black Hills, succeeded in bringing down a Big horn from the verge of a precipice, the flesh of which was pronounced by the gourmands of the camp to have the flavor of excellent mutton.

Baffled in his attempts to traverse this mountain chain, Mr. Hunt skirted along it to the south west, keeping it on the right; and still in hope of finding an opening. At an early hour one day, he encamped in a narrow valley on the banks of a beautifully clear but rushy pool; surrounded by thickets bearing abundance of wild cherries, currants and yellow and purple gooseberries.

While the afternoon's meal was in preparation Mr. Hunt and Mr. M'Kenzie ascended to the summit of the nearest hill, from whence, aided by the purity and transparency of the evening atmosphere, they commanded a vast prospect on all sides. Below them extended a plain, dotted with innumerable herds of buffalo. Some were lying down among the herbage, others roaming in their unbounded pastures, while many were engaged in fierce contests like those already described, their low bellowings reaching the ear like the hoarse murmurs of the surf on a distant shore.

Far off in the west they descried a range of lofty mountains printing the clear horizon, some of them evidently capped with snow. These they supposed to be the Big Horn mountains, so called from the animal of that name with which they abound. They are a spur of the Great Rocky chain. The hill from whence Mr. Hunt had this prospect was, according to his computation, about two hundred and fifty miles from the Arickara Village.

On returning to the camp Mr. Hunt found some uneasiness prevailing among the Canadian voyageurs. In straying among the thickets they had beheld tracks of grizzly bears in every direction; doubtless attracted thither by the fruit. To their dismay they now found that they had encamped in one of the favorite resorts of this dreaded animal. The idea marred all the comfort of the encampment. As night closed the surrounding thickets were peopled with terrors; insomuch that, according to Mr. Hunt, they could not help starting at every little breeze that stirred the bushes.

The grizzly bear is the only really formidable quadruped of our continent. He is the favorite theme of the hunters of the

Far West, who describe him as equal in size to a common cow and of prodigious strength. He makes battle if assailed, and often, if pressed by hunger, is the assailant. If wounded he becomes furious and will pursue the hunter. His speed exceeds that of a man, but is inferior to that of a horse. In attacking he rears himself on his hind legs and springs the length of his body. Woe to horse or rider that comes within the sweep of his terrific claws, which are sometimes nine inches in length, and tear every thing before them.

At the time we are treating of, the grizzly bear was still frequent on the Missouri, and in the lower country, but like some of the broken tribes of the prairies, he has gradually fallen back before his enemies and is now chiefly to be found in the upland regions, in rugged fastnesses like those of the Black Hills and the Rocky Mountains. Here he lurks in caverns, or holes which he has digged in the sides of hills, or under the roots and trunks of fallen trees. Like the common bear he is fond of fruits and mast and roots, the latter of which he will dig up with his fore claws. He is carnivorous also, and will even attack and conquer the lordly buffalo, dragging his huge carcass to the neighborhood of his den, that he may prey upon it at his leisure.

The hunters, both white and red men, consider this the most heroic game. They prefer to hunt him on horseback and will venture so near as sometimes to singe his hair with the flash of the rifle. The hunter of the grizzly bear, however, must be an experienced hand, and know where to aim at a vital part; for of all quadrupeds, he is the most difficult to be killed. He will receive repeated wounds without flinching, and rarely is a shot mortal unless through the head or heart.

That the dangers apprehended from the grizly bear, at this night encampment, were not imaginary, was proved on the following morning. Among the hired men of the party was one William Cannon, who had been a soldier at one of the frontier posts, and entered into the employ of Mr. Hunt at Mackinaw. He was an inexperienced hunter and a poor shot, for which he was much bantered by his more adroit comrades. Piqued at their raillery he had been practicing ever since he had joined the expedition but without success. In the course of the present afternoon he went forth by himself to take a lesson in venerie and, to his great delight, had the good fortune to kill a buffalo. As he was a considerable distance from the camp, he cut out the tongue and some of the choice bits, made them into a parcel, and, slinging them on his shoulders by a strap passed round his forehead, as the voyageurs carry packages of goods, set out all glorious for the camp, anticipating a triumph over his brother hunters. In passing through a narrow ravine he heard a noise behind him and looking round beheld, to his dismay, a grizzly bear in full pursuit: apparently attracted by the scent of the meat. Cannon had heard so much of the invulnerability of this tremendous animal that he never attempted to fire, but, slipping the strap from his forehead let go the buffalo meat and ran for his life. The bear did not stop to regale himself with the game but kept on after the hunter. He had nearly overtaken him when Cannon reached a tree and, throwing down his rifle, scrambled up it. The next instant Bruin was at the foot of the tree, but, as this species of bear does not climb, he contented himself with turning the chase into a blockade. Night came on. In the darkness Cannon could not perceive whether or not the enemy maintained his station, but his fears pictured him rigorously mounting guard. He passed the night, therefore, in the tree, a prey to dismal fancies. In the morning the bear was gone. Cannon warily descended the tree, gathered up his gun, and made the best of his way back to the camp without venturing to look after his buffalo meat.

While on this theme we will add another anecdote of an adventure with a grizly bear, told of John Day, the Kentucky hunter, but which happened at a different period of the expedition. Day was hunting in company with one of the clerks of the Company, a lively youngster, who was a great favorite with the veteran, but whose vivacity he had continually to keep in check. They were in search of deer, when suddenly a huge grizzly bear emerged from a thicket about thirty yards distant, rearing himself upon his hind legs with a terrific growl and displaying a hideous array of teeth and claws. The rifle of the young man was levelled in an instant, but John Day's iron hand was as quickly upon his arm. "Be quiet boy! be quiet!" exclaimed the hunter, between his clenched teeth and without turning his eyes from the bear.

They remained motionless. The monster regarded them for a time, then, lowering himself on his fore paws, slowly withdrew. He had not gone many paces before he again turned, reared himself on his hind legs and repeated his menace. Day's hand was still on the arm of his young companion, he again pressed it hard, and kept repeating between his teeth "Quiet boy!—keep quiet!—keep quiet!"—though the latter had not made a move since his first prohibition.

The bear again lowered himself on all fours, retreated some twenty yards further, and again turned, reared, shewed his teeth and growled. This third menace was too much for the game spirit of John Day. "By Jove!" exclaimed he, "I can stand this no longer" and in an instant a ball from his rifle whizzed into the foe. The wound was not mortal; but, luckily, it dismayed instead of enraging the animal and he retreated into the thicket.

Day's young companion reproached him for not practicing the caution which he enjoined upon others. "Why boy," replied the veteran, "caution is caution, but one must not put up with too much even from a bear. Would you have me suffer myself to be bullied all day by a varmint!"

Chapter XXVII

*Indian trail—Rough mountain travelling—Sufferings from
hunger and thirst—Powder River—Game in abundance—A
hunter's paradise—Mountain peak seen at a great distance
—One of the Big Horn chain—Rocky Mountains—Extent—
Appearance—Height—The Great American Desert—Various characteristics of the mountains—Indian superstitions
concerning them—Land of souls—Towns of the free and generous spirits—Happy hunting grounds.*

FOR THE TWO following days the travellers pursued a westerly course for thirty four miles, along a ridge of country
dividing the tributary waters of the Missouri and the Yellow
Stone. As landmarks they guided themselves by the summits
of the far distant mountains which they supposed to belong
to the Big Horn chain. They were gradually rising into a
higher temperature for the weather was cold for the season
with a sharp frost in the night and ice of an eighth of an inch
in thickness.

On the twenty second of August, early in the day they came
upon the trail of a numerous band. Rose and the other
hunters examined the foot prints with great attention, and determined it to be the trail of a party of Crows returning from
an annual trading visit to the Mandans. As this trail afforded
more commodious travelling they immediately struck into it,
and followed it for two days. It led them over rough hills and
through broken gullies, during which time they suffered great
fatigue from the ruggedness of the country. The weather, too,
which had recently been frosty was now oppressively warm
and there was a great scarcity of water, insomuch that a valuable dog belonging to Mr. M'Kenzie died of thirst.

At one time they had twenty five miles of painful travel without a drop of water, until they arrived at a small running
stream. Here they eagerly slaked their thirst, but, this being
allayed, the calls of hunger became equally importunate. Ever
since they had got among these barren and arid hills, where
there was a deficiency of grass, they had met with no buffaloes,
those animals keeping in the grassy meadows near the streams.

They were obliged, therefore, to have recourse to their corn meal, which they reserved for such emergencies. Some, however, were lucky enough to kill a wolf, which they cooked for supper, and pronounced excellent food.

The next morning they resumed their wayfaring, hungry and jaded, and had a dogged march of eighteen miles among the same kind of hills. At length they emerged upon a stream of clear water, one of the forks of the Powder River, and to their great joy, beheld once more wide grassy meadows stocked with herds of buffalo. For several days they kept along the banks of this river, ascending it about eighteen miles. It was a hunter's paradise; the buffaloes were in such abundance that they were enabled to kill as many as they pleased, and to jirk a sufficient supply of meat for several days' journeying. Here then they revelled and reposed after their hungry and weary travel, hunting and feasting, and reclining upon the grass. Their quiet, however, was a little marred, by coming upon traces of Indians who, they concluded, must be Crows; they were, therefore, obliged to keep a more vigilant watch than ever upon their horses.

For several days they had been directing their march towards the lofty mountain descried by Mr. Hunt and Mr. M'Kenzie on the 17th of August, the height of which rendered it a land mark over a vast extent of country. At first it had appeared to them solitary and detached; but as they advanced towards it, it proved to be the principal summit of a chain of mountains. Day by day it varied in form, or rather its lower peaks, and the summits of others of the chain emerged above the clear horizon, and finally the inferior line of hills which connected most of them rose to view. So far, however, are objects discernible in the pure atmosphere of these elevated plains, that from the place where they first descried the main mountain they had to travel a hundred and forty miles before they reached its base. Here they encamped on the thirtieth of August, having come nearly four hundred miles since leaving the Arickara village.

The mountain which now towered above them was one of the Big Horn chain, bordered by a river of the same name, and extending for a long distance rather east of north and west of south. It was a part of the great system of granite mountains which forms one of the most important and striking features of

North America, stretching parallel to the coast of the Pacific from the Isthmus of Panama almost to the Arctic Ocean; and presenting a corresponding chain to that of the Andes in the southern hemisphere. This vast range has acquired from its rugged and broken character and its summits of naked granite the appellation of The Rocky Mountains, a name by no means distinctive, as all elevated ranges are rocky. Among the early explorers it was known as the range of Chippewyan mountains, and this Indian name is the one it is likely to retain in poetic usage. Rising from the midst of vast plains and prairies, traversing several degrees of latitude, dividing the waters of the Atlantic and the Pacific, and seeming to bind with diverging ridges the level regions on its flanks, it has been figuratively termed the back bone of the northern continent.

The Rocky Mountains do not present a range of uniform elevation, but rather groups and occasionally detached peaks. Though some of these rise to the region of perpetual snows and are upwards of eleven thousand feet in real altitude yet their height from their immediate bases is not so great as might be imagined; as they swell up from elevated plains, several thousand feet above the level of the Ocean. These plains are often of a desolate sterility; mere sandy wastes, formed of the detritus of the granite heights, destitute of trees and herbage, scorched by the ardent and reflected rays of the summer's sun, and, in winter, swept by chilling blasts from the snow clad mountains. Such is a great part of that vast region extending north and south along the Mountains, several hundred miles in width, which has not improperly been termed The Great American desert. It is a region that almost discourages all hope of cultivation, and can only be traversed with safety by keeping near the streams which intersect it. Extensive plains likewise occur among the higher regions of the mountains, sometimes of considerable fertility. Indeed these lofty plats of table land seem to form a peculiar feature in the American continents. Some occur among the Cordilleras of the Andes, where cities and towns and cultivated farms are to be seen eight thousand feet above the level of the sea.

The Rocky Mountains, as we have already observed, occur sometimes singly or in groupes, and occasionally in collateral ridges. Between these are deep valleys with small streams winding through them, which find their way into the lower plains, augmenting as they proceed, and ultimately discharging themselves into those vast rivers, which traverse the prairies like great arteries and drain the continent.

While the granitic summits of the Rocky Mountains are bleak and bare, many of the interior ridges are scantily clothed with scrubbed pines, oaks, cedar and furze. Various parts of the mountains also bear traces of volcanic action. Some of the interior valleys are strewed with scoria and broken stones evidently of volcanic origin; the surrounding rocks bear the like character, and vestiges of extinguished craters are to be seen on the elevated heights.

We have already noticed the superstitious feelings with which the Indians regard the Black Hills; but this immense range of mountains, which divides all that they know of the world, and gives birth to such mighty rivers, is still more an object of awe and veneration. They call it "The crest of the world," and think that Wacondah, or the Master of life, as they designate the Supreme being, has his residence among these aerial heights. The tribes on the eastern prairies call them the Mountains of the Setting Sun. Some of them place the "Happy hunting grounds," their ideal paradise, among the recesses of these mountains; but say that they are invisible to living men. Here also is the "Land of Souls" in which are the "towns of the free and generous spirits," where those who have pleased the Master of life while living, enjoy after death all manner of delights.

Wonders are told of these mountains by the distant tribes whose warriors or hunters have ever wandered in their neighborhood. It is thought by some that, after death, they will have to travel to these mountains and ascend one of their highest and most rugged peaks, among rocks and snows and tumbling torrents. After many moons of painful toil they will reach the summit from whence they will have a view over the land of souls. There they will see the happy hunting grounds, with the souls of the brave and good living in tents in green meadows, by bright running streams, or hunting the herds of buffalo, and elks and deer which have been slain on earth. There too they will see the villages or towns of the free and generous spirits brightening in the midst of delicious prairies.

If they have acquitted themselves well while living, they will be permitted to descend and enjoy this happy country; if otherwise, they will but be tantalized with this prospect of it, and then hurled back from the mountain, to wander about the sandy plains and endure the eternal pangs of unsatisfied thirst and hunger.

Chapter XXVIII

THE TRAVELLERS had now arrived in the vicinity of the mountain regions infested by the Crow Indians. These restless marauders, as has already been observed, are apt to be continually on the prowl about the skirts of the mountains; and even when encamped in some deep and secluded glen, they keep scouts upon the cliffs and promontories, who, unseen themselves, can discern every living thing that moves over the subjacent plains and valleys. It was not to be expected that our travellers could pass unseen through a region thus vigilantly centinelled; accordingly, in the edge of the evening, not long after they had encamped at the foot of the Big Horn Sierra, a couple of wild looking beings, scantily clad in skins but well armed, and mounted on horses as wild looking as themselves, were seen approaching with great caution from among the rocks. They might have been mistaken for two of the evil spirits of the mountains so formidable in Indian fable.

Rose was immediately sent out to hold a parley with them and invite them to the camp. They proved to be two scouts from the same band that had been tracked for some days past, and which was now encamped at some distance in the folds of the mountain. They were easily prevailed upon to come to the camp, where they were well received, and, after remaining there until late in the evening, departed to make a report of all they had seen and experienced, to their companions.

The following day had scarce dawned when a troop of these wild mountain scamperers came galloping with whoops and yells into the camp, bringing an invitation from their chief for the white men to visit him. The tents were accordingly struck, the horses laden, and the party were soon on the march. The

Crow horsemen as they escorted them appeared to take pride in shewing off their equestrian skill and hardihood; careering at full speed on their half savage steeds, and dashing among rocks and crags and up and down the most rugged and dangerous places with perfect ease and unconcern.

A ride of sixteen miles brought them, in the afternoon, in sight of the Crow camp. It was composed of leathern tents pitched in a meadow on the border of a small clear stream at the foot of the mountain. A great number of horses were grazing in the vicinity, many of them doubtless captured in marauding excursions.

The Crow chieftain came forth to meet his guests with great professions of friendship and conducted them to his tents, pointing out, by the way, a convenient place where they might fix their camp. No sooner had they done so than Mr. Hunt opened some of the packages and made the chief a present of a scarlet blanket and a quantity of powder and ball; he gave him also some knives, trinkets and tobacco to be distributed among his warriors, with all which the grim potentate seemed, for the time, well pleased. As the Crows, however, were reputed to be perfidious in the extreme, and as errant freebooters as the bird after which they were so worthily named; and as their general feelings towards the whites were known to be by no means friendly, the intercourse with them was conducted with great circumspection.

The following day was passed in trading with the Crows for buffalo robes and skins and in bartering galled and jaded horses for others that were in good condition. Some of the men also purchased horses on their own account, so that the number now amounted to one hundred and twenty one, most of them sound and active, and fit for mountain service.

Their wants being supplied they ceased all further traffic, much to the dissatisfaction of the Crows, who became extremely urgent to continue the trade, and, finding their importunities of no avail, assumed an insolent and menacing tone. All this was attributed by Mr. Hunt and his associates, to the perfidious instigations of Rose the interpreter, whom they suspected of the desire to foment ill will between them and the savages, for the promotion of his nefarious plans. M'Lellan, with his usual *tranchant* mode of dealing out justice, resolved to shoot the desperado on the spot in case of any out break. Nothing of the kind, however, occurred. The Crows were probably daunted by the resolute, though quiet, demeanor of the white men, and the constant vigilance and armed preparation which they maintained; and Rose, if he really still harbored his knavish designs, must have perceived that they were suspected, and, if attempted to be carried into effect, might bring ruin on his own head.

The next morning, bright and early, Mr. Hunt prepared to resume his journeying. He took a ceremonious leave of the Crow chieftain and his vagabond warriors, and according to previous arrangements consigned to their cherishing friendship and fraternal adoption their worthy confederate Rose; who, having figured among the water pirates of the Mississippi, was well fitted to rise to distinction among the land pirates of the Rocky Mountains.

It is proper to add that the ruffian was well received among the tribe and appeared to be perfectly satisfied with the compromise he had made; feeling much more at his ease among savages than among white men. It is outcasts from civilization, fugitives from justice, and heartless desperadoes of this kind, who sow the seeds of enmity and bitterness among the unfortunate tribes of the frontier. There is no enemy so implacable against a country or a community as one of its own people who has rendered himself an alien by his crimes.

Right glad to be relieved from this treacherous companion, Mr. Hunt pursued his course along the skirts of the mountain in a southern direction; seeking for some practicable defile by which he might pass through it. None such presented, however, in the course of fifteen miles, and he encamped on a small stream, still on the outskirts. The green meadows which border these mountain streams are generally well stocked with game, and the hunters soon killed several fat elks, which supplied the camp with fresh meat. In the evening the travellers were surprized by an unwelcome visit from several Crows belonging to a different band from that which they had recently left, and who said their camp was among the mountains. The consciousness of being environed by such dangerous neighbors, and of being still within the range of Rose and his fellow ruffians, obliged the party to be continually on the alert and to maintain weary vigils throughout the night, lest they should be robbed of their horses.

On the third of September, finding that the mountain still stretched onwards, presenting a continued barrier, they endeavored to force a passage to the westward, but soon became entangled among rocks and precipices which set all their efforts at defiance. The mountain seemed for the most part rugged, bare and sterile; yet here and there it was clothed with pines, and with shrubs and flowering plants, some of which were in bloom. In toiling among these weary places their thirst became excessive, for no water was to be met with. Numbers of the men wandered off into rocky dells and ravines in hopes of finding some brook or fountain; some of whom lost their way and did not rejoin the main party.

After half a day of painful and fruitless scrambling, Mr. Hunt gave up the attempt to penetrate in this direction and, returning to the little stream on the skirts of the mountain, pitched his tents within six miles of his encampment of the preceding night. He now ordered that signals should be made for the stragglers in quest of water, but the night passed away without their return.

The next morning to their surprise Rose made his appearance at the camp, accompanied by some of his Crow associates. His unwelcome visit revived their suspicions, but he announced himself as a messenger of good will from the chief, who finding they had taken a wrong road, had sent Rose and his companions to guide them to a nearer and better one across the mountain.

Having no choice, being themselves utterly at fault, they set out under this questionable escort. They had not gone far before they fell in with the whole party of Crows, who, they now found, were going the same road with themselves. The two cavalcades of white and red men, therefore, pushed on together, and presented a wild and picturesque spectacle, as, equipped with various weapons and in various garbs, with trains of pack horses they wound in long lines through the rugged defiles and up and down the crags and steeps of the mountain.

The travellers had again an opportunity to see and admire the equestrian habitudes and address of this hard riding tribe.

They were all mounted, man, woman and child, for the Crows have horses in abundance so that no one goes on foot. The children are perfect imps on horseback. Among them was one so young that he could not yet speak. He was tied on a colt of two years old, but managed the reins as if by instinct, and plied the whip with true Indian prodigality. Mr. Hunt enquired the age of this infant jockey and was answered that "he had seen two winters!"

This is almost realizing the fable of the centaurs; nor can we wonder at the equestrian adroitness of these savages, who are thus in a manner cradled in the saddle, and become in infancy almost identified with the animal they bestride.

The mountain defiles were exceedingly rough and broken, and the travelling painful to the burthened horses. The party, therefore, proceeded but slowly, and were gradually left behind by the band of Crows, who had taken the lead. It is more than probable that Mr. Hunt loitered in his course, to get rid of such doubtful fellow travellers. Certain it is that he felt a sensation of relief as he saw the whole crew, the renegado Rose and all, disappear among the windings of the mountain, and heard the last yelp of the savages die away in the distance.

When they were fairly out of sight and out of hearing he encamped on the head waters of the little stream of the preceding day, having come about sixteen miles. Here he remained all the succeeding day, as well to give time for the Crows to get in the advance, as for the stragglers, who had wandered away in quest of water two days previously, to rejoin the camp. Indeed considerable uneasiness began to be felt concerning these men lest they should become utterly bewildered in the defiles of the mountains, or should fall into the hands of some marauding band of Savages. Some of the most experienced hunters were sent in search of them, others, in the mean time, employed themselves in hunting. The narrow valley in which they encamped, being watered by a running stream, yielded fresh pasturage, and, though in the heart of the Big Horn mountains, was well stocked with buffalo. Several of these were killed as also a grizly bear. In the evening, to the satisfaction of all parties, the stragglers made their appearance, and, provisions being in abundance there was hearty good cheer in the camp.

Chapter XXIX

RESUMING their course on the following morning, Mr. Hunt and his companions continued on westward through a rugged region of hills and rocks, but diversified in many places by grassy little glens; with springs of water, bright sparkling brooks, clumps of pine trees and a profusion of flowering plants which were in full bloom, although the weather was frosty. These beautiful and verdant recesses, running through and softening the rugged mountains, were cheering and refreshing to the way worn travellers.

In the course of the morning as they were entangled in a defile they beheld a small band of Savages, as wild looking as the surrounding scenery, who reconnoitered them warily from the rocks before they ventured to advance. Some of them were mounted on horses rudely caparisoned, with bridles or halters of buffalo hide, one end trailing after them on the ground. They proved to be a mixed party of Flatheads and Shoshonies or Snakes; and as these tribes will be frequently mentioned in the course of this work, we shall give a few introductory particulars concerning them.

The Flatheads in question are not to be confounded with those of the name who dwell about the lower waters of the Columbia; neither do they flatten their heads, as the others do. They inhabit the banks of a river on the west side of the mountains, and are described as simple, honest and hospitable. Like all people of similar character, whether civilized or savage, they are prone to be imposed upon; and are especially maltreated by the ruthless Blackfeet, who harass them in their villages, steal their horses by night, or openly carry them off in the face of day, without provoking pursuit or retaliation.

The Shoshonies are a branch of the once powerful and prosperous tribe of the Snakes, who possessed a glorious hunting country about the upper forks of the Missouri abounding in beaver and buffalo. Their hunting ground was occasionally invaded by the Blackfeet, but the Snakes battled bravely for their domains and a long and bloody feud existed, with variable success. At length the Hudson's Bay Company, extending their trade into the interior, had dealings with the Blackfeet, who were nearest to them, and supplied them with fire arms. The Snakes, who occasionally traded with the Spaniards, endeavored, but in vain, to obtain similar weapons; the Spanish traders wisely refused to arm them so formidably. The Blackfeet had now a vast advantage, and soon dispossessed the poor Snakes of their favorite hunting grounds, their land of plenty, and drove them from place to place, until they were fain to take refuge in the wildest and most desolate recesses of the Rocky Mountains. Even here they are subjected to occasional visits from their implacable foes, as long as they have horses, or any other property to tempt the plunderer. Thus by degrees the Snakes have become a scattered, broken spirited, impoverished people; keeping about lonely rivers and mountain streams and subsisting chiefly upon fish. Such of them as still possess horses and occasionally figure as hunters are called Shoshonies; but there is another class, the most abject and forlorn, who are called Shuckers, or more commonly Diggers and Root eaters. These are a shy, secret, solitary race, who keep in the most retired parts of the mountains, lurking like gnomes in caverns and clefts of the rocks, and subsisting in a great measure on the roots of the earth. Sometimes, in passing through a solitary mountain valley, the traveller comes perchance upon the bleeding carcass of a deer or buffalo that has just been slain. He looks round in vain for the hunter; the whole landscape is lifeless and deserted: At length he perceives a thread of smoke, curling up from among the crags and cliffs, and scrambling to the place, finds some forlorn and skulking brood of Diggers, terrified at being discovered.

The Shoshonies, however, who as has been observed, have still "horse to ride and weapon to wear," are somewhat bolder in their spirit, and more open and wide in their wanderings. In the autumn when salmon disappear from the rivers, and hunger begins to pinch, they even venture down into their ancient hunting grounds, to make a foray among the buffaloes.

In this perilous enterprize they are occasionally joined by the
Flatheads, the persecutions of the Blackfeet having produced a
close alliance and co-operation between these luckless and maltreated tribes. Still, notwithstanding their united force, every
step they take within the debatable ground, is taken in fear and
trembling, and with the utmost precaution: and an Indian
trader assures us that he has seen at least five hundred of them,
armed and equipped for action, and keeping watch upon the
hill tops while about fifty were hunting in the prairie. Their excursions are brief and hurried: as soon as they have collected
and jirked sufficient buffalo meat for winter provisions, they
pack their horses, abandon the dangerous hunting grounds
and hasten back to the mountains, happy if they have not the
terrible Blackfeet rattling after them.

Such a confederate band of Shoshonies and Flatheads, was
the one met by our travellers. It was bound on a visit to the
Arapahoes, a tribe inhabiting the banks of the Nebraska. They
were armed to the best of their scanty means, and some of the
Shoshonies had bucklers of buffalo hide, adorned with feathers
and leathern fringes, and which have a charmed virtue in their
eyes, from having been prepared, with mystic ceremonies by
their conjurors.

In company with this wandering band our travellers proceeded all day. In the evening they encamped near to each
other in a defile of the mountains, on the borders of a stream
running north and falling into Big Horn River. In the vicinity
of the camp they found gooseberries, strawberries and currants
in great abundance. The defile bore traces of having been a
thoroughfare for countless herds of buffaloes, though not one
was to be seen. The hunters succeeded in killing an elk and
several black tailed deer.

They were now in the bosom of the second Big Horn ridge,
with another lofty and snow crowned mountain full in view to
the west. Fifteen miles of western course brought them, on
the following day, down into an intervening plain, well stocked
with buffalo. Here the Snakes and Flatheads joined with the
white hunters in a successful hunt, that soon filled the
camp with provisions.

On the morning of the 9th of September the travellers
parted company with their Indian friends and continued on

their course to the west. A march of thirty miles brought them, in the evening, to the banks of a rapid and beautifully clear stream about a hundred yards wide. It is the north fork or branch of the Big Horn River, but bears its peculiar name of The Wind River, from being subject in the winter season to a continued blast which sweeps its banks and prevents the snow from lying on them. This blast is said to be caused by a narrow gap or funnel in the mountains through which the river forces its way between perpendicular precipices, resembling cut rocks.

This river gives its name to a whole range of mountains consisting of three parallel chains, eighty miles in length and about twenty or twenty five broad. One of its peaks is probably fifteen thousand feet above the level of the sea, being one of the highest of the Rocky Sierra. These mountains give rise, not merely to the Wind or Big Horn River, but to several branches of the Yellow Stone and the Missouri on the east, and of the Columbia and Colorado on the west; thus dividing the sources of these mighty streams.

For five succeeding days Mr. Hunt and his party continued up the course of the Wind River, to the distance of about eighty miles, crossing and recrossing it, according to its windings and the nature of its banks; sometimes passing through valleys, at other times scrambling over rocks and hills. The country in general was destitute of trees, but they passed through groves of wormwood, eight and ten feet in height, which they used occasionally for fuel, and they met with large quantities of wild flax.

The mountains were destitute of game; they came in sight of two grizly bears, but could not get near enough for a shot: provisions therefore began to be scanty. They saw large flights of the kind of thrush commonly called the Robin, and many smaller birds of migratory species; but the hills in general appeared lonely and with few signs of animal life. On the evening of the 14th of September, they encamped on the forks of the Wind or Big Horn River. The largest of these forks came from the range of Wind River Mountains.

The hunters who served as guides to the party in this part of their route, had assured Mr. Hunt that, by following up Wind River, and crossing a single mountain ridge, he would come upon the head waters of the Columbia. The scarcity of game, however, which already had been felt to a pinching degree, and which threatened them with famine among the sterile heights which lay before them, admonished them to change their course. It was determined, therefore, to make for a stream which, they were informed, passed through the neighboring mountains, to the south of west, on the grassy banks of which it was probable they would meet with buffalo. Accordingly, about three o'clock on the following day, meeting with a beaten Indian road which led in the proper direction, they struck into it turning their backs upon Wind River.

In the course of the day they came to a height that commanded an almost boundless prospect. Here one of the guides paused, and after considering the vast landscape attentively, pointed to three mountain peaks glistening with snow, which rose, he said, above a fork of Columbia River. They were hailed by the travellers with that joy with which a beacon on a sea shore is hailed by mariners after a long and dangerous voyage. It is true there was many a weary league to be traversed before they should reach these land marks, for, allowing for their evident height, and the extreme transparency of the atmosphere, they could not be much less than a hundred miles distant. Even after reaching them there would yet remain hundreds of miles of their journey to be accomplished. All these matters were forgotten in the joy at seeing the first land marks of the Columbia, that river which formed the bourne of the expedition. These remarkable peaks are known to some travellers as the Tetons; as they had been guiding points for many days, to Mr. Hunt, he gave them the name of the Pilot Knobs.

The travellers continued their course to the south of west for about forty miles, through a region so elevated that patches of snow lay on the highest summits, and on the northern declivities. At length they came to the desired stream, the object of their search, the waters of which flowed to the west. It was in fact a branch of the Colorado, which falls into the Gulf of California, and had received from the hunters the name of Spanish River, from information given by the Indians that Spaniards resided upon its lower waters.

The aspect of this river and its vicinity was cheering to the way worn and hungry travellers. Its banks were green, and there were grassy valleys running from it in various directions, into the heart of the rugged mountains, with herds of buffalo quietly grazing. The hunters sallied forth with keen alacrity, and soon returned laden with provisions.

In this part of the mountains Mr. Hunt met with three different kinds of gooseberries. The common purple, on a low and very thorny bush; a yellow kind, of an excellent flavor, growing on a stalk free from thorns; and a deep purple, of the size and taste of our winter grape, with a thorny stalk. There were also three kinds of currants, one very large and well tasted, of a purple colour, and growing on a bush eight or nine feet high. Another of a yellow colour, and of the size and taste of the large red currant, the bush four or five feet high; and the third a beautiful scarlet, resembling the strawberry in sweetness, though rather insipid, and growing on a low bush.

On the 17th they continued down the course of the river making fifteen miles to the south west. The river abounded with geese and ducks, and there were signs of its being inhabited by beaver and otters: indeed they were now approaching regions where these animals, the great objects of the Fur trade, are said to abound. They encamped for the night opposite the end of a mountain in the west, which was probably the last chain of the Rocky Mountains. On the following morning they abandoned the main course of Spanish River and taking a north west direction for eight miles came upon one of its little tributaries, issuing out of the bosom of the mountains, and running through green meadows, yielding pasturage to herds of buffalo. As these were probably the last of that animal they would meet with, they encamped on the grassy banks of the river, determining to spend several days in hunting, so as to be able to jerk sufficient meat to supply them until they should reach the waters of the Columbia, where they trusted to find fish enough for their support. A little repose, too, was necessary for both men and horses after their rugged and incessant marching, having in the course of the last seventeen days, traversed two hundred and sixty miles of rough, and, in many parts, sterile, mountain country.

Chapter XXX

A plentiful hunting camp—Shoshonie hunters—Hoback's
River—Mad River—Encampment near the Pilot Knobs—
A consultation—Preparations for a perilous voyage.

FIVE DAYS were passed by Mr. Hunt and his companions in
the fresh meadows watered by the bright little mountain
stream. The hunters made great havoc among the buffaloes,
and brought in quantities of meat; the voyageurs busied themselves about the fires, roasting and stewing for present purposes, or drying provisions for the journey; the pack horses,
eased of their burthens, rolled in the grass, or grazed at large
about the ample pastures; those of the party who had no call
upon their services, indulged in the luxury of perfect relaxation, and the camp presented a picture of rude feasting and
revelry, of mingled bustle and repose characteristic of a halt in
a fine hunting country.

In the course of one of their excursions some of the men
came in sight of a small party of Indians, who instantly fled in
great apparent consternation. They immediately returned to
camp with the intelligence: upon which Mr. Hunt and four
others flung themselves upon their horses and sallied forth to
reconnoiter. After riding for about eight miles they came upon
a wild mountain scene. A lonely green valley stretched before
them surrounded by rugged heights. A herd of buffalo were
careering madly through it, with a troop of Savage horsemen
in full chase, plying them with their bows and arrows. The appearance of Mr. Hunt and his companions put an abrupt end
to the hunt; the buffalo scuttled off in one direction while the
Indians plied their lashes and gallopped off in another, as fast
as their steeds could carry them. Mr. Hunt gave chase; there
was a sharp scamper, though of short continuance. Two young
Indians, who were indifferently mounted, were soon overtaken. They were terribly frightened and evidently gave themselves up for lost. By degrees their fears were allayed by kind
treatment, but they continued to regard the strangers with a
mixture of awe and wonder, for it was the first time in their
lives they had ever seen a white man.

They belonged to a party of Snakes who had come across the mountains on their autumnal hunting excursion to provide buffalo meat for the winter. Being persuaded of the peaceable intentions of Mr. Hunt and his companions they willingly conducted them to their camp. It was pitched in a narrow valley on the margin of a stream. The tents were of dressed skins; some of them fantastically painted; with horses grazing about them. The approach of the party caused a transient alarm in the camp, for these poor Indians were ever on the look out for cruel foes. No sooner, however, did they recognise the garb and complexion of their visitors than their apprehensions were changed into joy; for some of them had dealt with white men and knew them to be friendly and to abound with articles of singular value. They welcomed them, therefore, to their tents, set food before them; and entertained them to the best of their power.

They had been successful in their hunt, and their camp was full of jirked buffalo meat; all of the choicest kind and extremely fat. Mr. Hunt purchased enough of them, in addition to what had been killed and cured by his own hunters, to load all the horses excepting those reserved for the partners and the wife of Pierre Dorion. He found also a few beaver skins in their camp, for which he paid liberally as an inducement to them to hunt for more; informing them that some of his party intended to live among the mountains and trade with the native hunters for their peltries. The poor Snakes soon comprehended the advantages thus held out to them, and promised to exert themselves to procure a quantity of beaver skins for future traffic.

Being now well supplied with provisions Mr. Hunt broke up his encampment on the 24th of September and continued on to the west. A march of fifteen miles over a mountain ridge brought them to a stream about fifty feet in width, which Hoback, one of their guides, who had trapped about the neighborhood when in the service of Mr. Henry, recognized for one of the head waters of the Columbia. The travellers hailed it with delight, as the first stream they had encountered tending towards their point of destination. They kept along it for two days during which, from the contributions of many rills and brooks, it gradually swelled into a small river. As it

meandered among rocks and precipices they were frequently
obliged to ford it, and such was its rapidity that the men were
often in danger of being swept away. Sometimes the banks advanced so close upon the river, that they were obliged to
scramble up and down their rugged promontories, or to skirt
along their bases where there was scarce a foothold. Their
horses had dangerous falls in some of these passes. One of
them rolled, with his load, nearly two hundred feet down hill
into the river, but without receiving any injury. At length they
emerged from these stupendous defiles, and continued for several miles along the bank of Hoback's River, through one of
the stern mountain valleys. Here it was joined by a river of
greater magnitude and swifter current, and their united waters
swept off through the valley in one impetuous stream, which,
from its rapidity and turbulence, had received the name of Mad
River. At the confluence of these streams the travellers encamped. An important point in their arduous journey had been
attained, a few miles from their camp rose the three vast snowy
peaks called the Tetons, or the Pilot Knobs, the great landmarks of the Columbia, by which they had shaped their course
through this mountain wilderness. By their feet flowed the
rapid current of Mad River, a stream ample enough to admit of
the navigation of canoes, and down which they might possibly
be able to steer their course to the main body of the Columbia.
The Canadian voyageurs rejoiced at the idea of once more
launching themselves upon their favorite element; of exchanging their horses for canoes, and of gliding down the bosoms of
rivers, instead of scrambling over the backs of mountains. Others of the party, also, inexperienced in this kind of travelling,
considered their toils and troubles as drawing to a close. They
had conquered the chief difficulties of this great rocky barrier,
and now flattered themselves with the hope of an easy downward course for the rest of their journey. Little did they dream
of the hardships and perils by land and water, which were yet
to be encountered in the frightful wilderness that intervened
between them and the shores of the Pacific!

Chapter XXXI

ON THE BANKS of Mad River Mr. Hunt held a consultation with the other partners as to their future movements. The wild and impetuous current of the river rendered him doubtful whether it might not abound with impediments lower down, sufficient to render the navigation of it slow and perilous, if not impracticable. The hunters who had hitherto acted as guides, knew nothing of the character of the river below; what rocks, and shoals and rapids might obstruct it or through what mountains and deserts it might pass. Should they then abandon their horses, cast themselves loose in fragile barks upon this wild, doubtful and unknown river, or should they continue their more toilsome and tedious, but perhaps more certain wayfaring by land.

The vote, as might have been expected, was almost unanimous for embarcation, for when men are in difficulties every change seems to be for the better. The difficulty now was to find timber of sufficient size for the construction of canoes, the trees in these high mountain regions being chiefly a scrubbed growth of pines and cedars, aspens, haws and service berries, and a small kind of cotton tree with a leaf resembling that of the willow. There was a species of large fir, but so full of knots as to endanger the axe in hewing it. After searching for some time a growth of timber, of sufficient size, was found lower down the river, whereupon the encampment was moved to the vicinity.

The men were now set to work to fell trees, and the mountains echoed to the unwonted sound of their axes. While preparations were thus going on for a voyage down the river Mr. Hunt, who still entertained doubts of its practicability, despatched an exploring party, consisting of John Reed, the clerk, John Day the hunter and Pierre Dorion the interpreter, with orders to proceed for several days' march along the stream, and notice its course and character.

After their departure Mr. Hunt turned his thoughts to another object of importance. He had now arrived at the head waters of the Columbia, which were among the main points embraced by the enterprize of Mr. Astor. These upper streams were reputed to abound in beaver, and had as yet been unmolested by the white trapper. The numerous signs of beaver met with during the recent search for timber gave evidence that the neighborhood was a good "trapping ground." Here then it was proper to begin to cast loose those leashes of hardy trappers, that are detached from trading parties, in the very heart of the wilderness. The men detached in the present instance were Alexander Carson, Louis S' Michel, Pierre Detayé and Pierre Delaunay. Trappers generally go in pairs, that they may assist, protect and comfort each other in their lonely and perilous occupations. Thus Carson and S' Michel formed one couple and Detayé and Delaunay another. They were fitted out with traps, arms, ammunition, horses and every other requisite, and were to trap upon the upper part of Mad River, and upon the neighboring streams of the mountains. This would probably occupy them for some months; and, when they should have collected a sufficient quantity of peltries, they were to pack them upon their horses and make the best of their way to the mouth of Columbia River, or to any intermediate post which might be established by the Company. They took leave of their comrades and started off on their several courses with stout hearts and cheerful countenances; though these lonely cruisings into a wild and hostile wilderness seem to the uninitiated equivalent to being cast a drift in the ship's yawl in the midst of the ocean.

Of the perils that attend the lonely trapper the reader will have sufficient proof, when he comes, in the after part of this work, to learn the hard fortunes of these poor fellows in the course of their wild peregrinations.

The trappers had not long departed when two Snake Indians wandered into the camp. When they perceived that the strangers were fabricating canoes they shook their heads and gave them to understand that the river was not navigable. Their information, however, was scoffed at by some of the party, who were obstinately bent on embarcation, but was confirmed by the exploring party who returned after several days' absence. They had kept along the river with great difficulty for two days, and found it a narrow, crooked, turbulent stream, confined in a rocky channel, with many rapids, and occasionally over hung with precipices. From the summit of one of these they had caught a bird's eye view of its boisterous career, for a great distance, through the heart of the mountain, with impending rocks and cliffs. Satisfied, from this view, that it was useless to follow its course either by land or water, they had given up all further investigation.

These concurring reports determined Mr. Hunt to abandon Mad River and seek some more navigable stream. This determination was concurred in by all his associates excepting Mr. Miller, who had become impatient of the fatigue of land travel, and was for immediate embarcation at all hazards. This gentleman had been in a gloomy and irritated state of mind for some time past, being troubled with a bodily malady that rendered travelling on horseback extremely irksome to him, and being, moreover, discontented with having a smaller share in the expedition than his comrades. His unreasonable objections to a further march by land were over ruled, and the party prepared to decamp.

Robinson, Hoback and Rezner, the three hunters who had hitherto served as guides among the mountains, now stepped forward and advised Mr. Hunt to make for the post established during the preceding year by Mr. Henry of the Missouri Fur Company. They had been with Mr. Henry, and, as far as they could judge by the neighboring land marks, his post could not be very far off. They presumed there could be but one intervening ridge of mountains, which might be passed without any great difficulty. Henry's post, or fort, was on an upper branch of the Columbia, down which they made no doubt it would be easy to navigate in canoes.

The two Snake Indians being questioned in the matter, shewed a perfect knowledge of the situation of the post, and offered with great alacrity to guide them to the place. Their offer was accepted, greatly to the displeasure of Mr. Miller,

who seemed obstinately bent upon braving the perils of Mad
River.

The weather for a few days past had been stormy; with rain
and sleet. The Rocky Mountains are subject to tempestuous
winds from the west; these sometimes come in flaws or currents, making a path through the forests many yards in width,
and whirling off trunks and branches to a great distance. The
present storm subsided on the third of October; leaving all
the surrounding heights covered with snow: for, while rain
had fallen in the valley, it had snowed on the hill tops.

On the 4th they broke up their encampment, and crossed
the river, the water coming up to the girths of their horses. After travelling four miles they encamped at the foot of the
mountain, the last, as they hoped, which they should have to
traverse. Four days more took them across it, and over several plains, watered by beautiful little streams, tributaries of
Mad River. Near one of their encampments there was a hot
spring continually emitting a cloud of vapour. These elevated
plains, which give a peculiar character to the mountains, are
frequented by large gangs of antilopes fleet as the wind.

On the evening of the 8th of October, after a cold wintry
day, with gusts of westerly wind and flurries of snow, they arrived at the sought for post of Mr. Henry. Here he had fixed
himself, after being compelled by the hostilities of the Blackfeet, to abandon the upper waters of the Missouri. The post
however was deserted, for Mr. Henry had left it in the course
of the preceding spring, and, as it afterwards appeared, had
fallen in with Mr. Lisa at the Arickara village on the Missouri,
some time after the departure of Mr. Hunt and his party.

The weary travellers gladly took possession of the deserted
log huts which had formed the post, and which stood on the
bank of a stream upwards of a hundred yards wide, on which
they intended to embark. There being plenty of suitable timber in the neighborhood, Mr. Hunt immediately proceeded
to construct canoes. As he would have to leave his horses and
their accoutrements here, he determined to make this a trading post, where the trappers and hunters, to be distributed
about the country, might repair, and where the traders might
touch on their way through the mountains to and from the
establishment at the mouth of the Columbia. He informed

the two Snake Indians of this determination and engaged them
to remain in that neighborhood and take care of the horses
until the white men should return, promising them ample
rewards for their fidelity. It may seem a desperate chance to
trust to the faith and honesty of two such vagabonds; but, as
the horses would have, at all events, to be abandoned, and
would otherwise become the property of the first vagrant
horde that should encounter them, it was one chance in favor
of their being regained.

At this place another detachment of hunters prepared to separate from the party for the purpose of trapping beaver. Three
of these had already been in this neighborhood, being the veteran Robinson and his companions Hoback and Rezner, who
had accompanied Mr. Henry across the mountains, and who
had been picked up by Mr. Hunt on the Missouri, on their way
home to Kentucky. According to agreement they were fitted
out with horses, traps, ammunition and every thing requisite
for their undertaking, and were to bring in all the peltries they
should collect, either to this trading post, or to the establishment at the mouth of Columbia River. Another hunter, of the
name of Cass, was associated with them in their enterprize. It
is in this way that small knots of trappers and hunters are distributed about the wilderness by the fur companies, and like
cranes and bitterns, haunt its solitary streams. Robinson the
Kentuckian, the veteran of the "bloody ground," who, as has
already been noted, had been scalped by the Indians in his
younger days, was the leader of this little band. When they
were about to depart, Mr. Miller called the partners together,
and threw up his share in the company, declaring his intention
of joining the party of trappers.

This resolution struck every one with astonishment, Mr.
Miller being a man of education and of cultivated habits, and
little fitted for the rude life of a hunter. Beside, the precarious
and slender profits arising from such a life were beneath the
prospects of one who held a share in the general enterprize.
Mr. Hunt was especially concerned and mortified at his determination, as it was through his advice and influence he had
entered into the concern. He endeavored, therefore, to dissuade him from this sudden resolution; representing its rashness, and the hardships and perils to which it would expose

him. He earnestly advised him, however he might feel dissatisfied with the enterprize, still to continue on in company until they should reach the mouth of Columbia River. There they would meet the expedition that was to come by sea; when, should he still feel disposed to relinquish the undertaking, Mr. Hunt pledged himself to furnish him a passage home in one of the vessels belonging to the Company.

To all this, Miller replied abruptly, that it was useless to argue with him, as his mind was made up. They might furnish him, or not, as they pleased, with the necessary supplies, but he was determined to part company here, and set off with the trappers. So saying, he flung out of their presence without vouchsafing any further conversation.

Much as this wayward conduct gave them anxiety, the partners saw it was in vain to remonstrate. Every attention was paid to fit him out for his headstrong undertaking. He was provided with four horses, and all the articles he required. The two Snakes undertook to conduct him and his companions to an encampment of their tribe, lower down among the mountains, from whom they would receive information as to the best trapping grounds. After thus guiding them, the Snakes were to return to Fort Henry, as the new trading post was called, and take charge of the horses which the party would leave there, of which, after all the hunters were supplied, there remained seventy seven. These matters being all arranged, Mr. Miller set out with his companions, under guidance of the two Snakes, on the 10th of October; and much did it grieve the friends of that gentleman to see him thus wantonly casting himself loose upon savage life. How he and his comrades fared in the wilderness, and how the Snakes acquitted themselves of their trust, respecting the horses, will hereafter appear in the course of these rambling anecdotes.

Chapter XXXII

Scanty fare—A mendicant Snake—Embarcation on Henry River—Joy of the voyageurs—Arrival at Snake River—Rapids and breakers—Beginning of misfortunes—Snake encampments—Parley with a savage—A second disaster—Loss of a boatman—The Caldron Linn.

WHILE the canoes were in preparation, the hunters ranged about the neighborhood, but with little success. Tracks of buffaloes were to be seen in all directions, but none of a fresh date. There were some elk, but extremely wild; two only were killed. Antelopes were likewise seen, but too shy and fleet to be approached. A few beavers were taken every night, and salmon trout of a small size, so that the camp had principally to subsist upon dried buffalo meat.

On the 14th, a poor, half-naked Snake Indian, one of that forlorn caste called the Shuckers, or Diggers, made his appearance at the camp. He came from some lurking place among the rocks and cliffs, and presented a picture of that famishing wretchedness to which these lonely fugitives among the mountains are sometimes reduced. Having received wherewithal to allay his hunger, he disappeared, but in the course of a day or two returned to the camp bringing with him his son, a miserable boy, still more naked and forlorn than himself. Food was given to both; they skulked about the camp like hungry hounds, seeking what they might devour, and having gathered up the feet and entrails of some beavers that were lying about, slunk off with them to their den among the rocks.

By the 18th of October, fifteen canoes were completed, and on the following day the party embarked with their effects; leaving their horses grazing about the banks, and trusting to the honesty of the two Snakes and some special turn of good luck for their future recovery.

The current bore them along at a rapid rate; the light spirits of the Canadian voyageurs, which had occasionally flagged upon land, rose to their accustomed buoyancy on finding themselves again upon the water. They wielded their paddles with their wonted dexterity, and for the first time made the mountains echo with their favorite boat songs.

In the course of the day the little squadron arrived at the confluence of Henry and Mad rivers, which, thus united, swelled into a beautiful stream of a light pea green color, navigable for boats of any size, and which, from the place of junction, took the name of Snake River, a stream doomed to be the scene of much disaster to the travellers. The banks were here and there fringed with willow thickets and small cotton wood trees. The weather was cold, and it snowed all day, and great flocks of ducks and geese, sporting in the water or streaming through the air, gave token that winter was at hand; yet the hearts of the travellers were light, and, as they glided down the little river, they flattered themselves with the hope of soon reaching the Columbia. After making thirty miles in a southerly direction, they encamped for the night in a neighborhood which required some little vigilance, as there were recent traces of grizzly bears among the thickets.

On the following day the river increased in width and beauty; flowing parallel to a range of mountains on the left, which at times were finely reflected in its light green waters. The three snowy summits of the Pilot Knobs or Tetons, were still seen towering in the distance. After pursuing a swift but placid course for twenty miles, the current began to foam and brawl, and assume the wild and broken character common to the streams west of the Rocky Mountains. In fact the rivers which flow from those mountains to the Pacific, are essentially different from those which traverse the great prairies on their eastern declivities. The latter, though sometimes boisterous, are generally free from obstructions, and easily navigated; but the rivers to the west of the mountains descend more steeply and impetuously, and are continually liable to cascades and rapids. The latter abounded in the part of the river which the travellers were now descending. Two of the canoes filled among the breakers; the crews were saved, but much of the lading was lost or damaged, and one of the canoes drifted down the stream and was broken among the rocks.

On the following day, October 21st, they made but a short distance when they came to a dangerous strait, where the river was compressed for nearly half a mile between perpendicular rocks, reducing it to the width of twenty yards, and increasing its violence. Here they were obliged to pass the canoes down cautiously by a line from the impending banks. This consumed a great part of a day; and after they had re-embarked they were soon again impeded by rapids, when they had to unload their canoes and carry them and their cargoes for some distance by land. It is at these places, called "portages," that the Canadian voyageur exhibits his most valuable qualities; carrying heavy burdens, and toiling to and fro, on land and in the water, over rocks and precipices, among brakes and brambles, not only without a murmur, but with the greatest cheerfulness and alacrity, joking and laughing and singing scraps of old French ditties.

The spirits of the party, however, which had been elated on first varying their journeying from land to water, had now lost some of their buoyancy. Every thing ahead was wrapped in uncertainty. They knew nothing of the river on which they were floating. It had never before been navigated by a white man, nor could they meet with an Indian to give them any information concerning it. It kept on its course through a vast wilderness of silent and apparently uninhabited mountains, without a savage wigwam upon its banks, or bark upon its waters. The difficulties and perils they had already passed, made them apprehend others before them, that might effectually bar their progress. As they glided onward, however, they regained heart and hope. The current continued to be strong; but it was steady, and though they met with frequent rapids, none of them were bad. Mountains were constantly to be seen in different directions, but sometimes the swift river glided through prairies, and was bordered by small cotton wood trees and willows. These prairies at certain seasons are ranged by migratory herds of the wide-wandering buffalo, the tracks of which, though not of recent date, were frequently to be seen. Here, too, were to be found the prickly pear or Indian fig, a plant which loves a more southern climate. On the land were large flights of magpies, and American robins; whole fleets of ducks and geese navigated the river, or flew off in long streaming files at the approach of the canoes; while the frequent establishment of the pains-taking and quiet-loving beaver, showed that the solitude of these waters was rarely disturbed, even by the all-pervading savage.

They had now come near two hundred and eighty miles since leaving Fort Henry, yet without seeing a human being, or a human habitation; a wild and desert solitude extended on either side of the river, apparently almost destitute of animal life. At length, on the 24th of October, they were gladdened by the sight of some savage tents, and hastened to land, and visit them, for they were anxious to procure information to guide them on their route. On their approach, however, the savages fled in consternation. They proved to be a wandering band of Shoshonies. In their tents were great quantities of small fish about two inches long, together with roots and seeds, or grain, which they were drying for winter provisions. They appeared to be destitute of tools of any kind, yet there were bows and arrows very well made; the former were formed of pine, cedar or bone, strengthened by sinews, and the latter of the wood of rose bushes, and other crooked plants, but carefully straightened, and tipped with stone of a bottle-green color.

There were also vessels of willow and grass, so closely wrought as to hold water, and a seine neatly made with meshes, in the ordinary manner, of the fibres of wild flax or nettle. The humble effects of the poor savages remained unmolested by their visitors, and a few small articles, with a knife or two, were left in the camp, and were no doubt regarded as invaluable prizes.

Shortly after leaving this deserted camp and re embarking in the canoes, the travellers met with three of the Snakes on a triangular raft made of flags or reeds; such was their rude mode of navigating the river. They were entirely naked excepting small mantles of hare skins over their shoulders. The canoes approached near enough to gain a full view of them, but they were not to be brought to a parley.

All further progress for the day was barred by a fall in the river of about thirty feet perpendicular; at the head of which the party encamped for the night.

The next day was one of excessive toil and but little progress: the river winding through a wild rocky country and being interrupted by frequent rapids, among which the canoes were in great peril. On the succeeding day they again visited a camp of wandering Snakes, but the inhabitants fled with terror at the sight of a fleet of canoes, filled with white men coming down their solitary river.

As Mr. Hunt was extremely anxious to gain information concerning his route, he endeavored by all kinds of friendly signs to entice back the fugitives. At length one, who was on horseback, ventured back with fear and trembling. He was better clad, and in better condition than most of his vagrant tribe that Mr. Hunt had yet seen. The chief object of his return appeared to be to intercede for a quantity of dried meat and salmon trout which he had left behind; on which probably he depended for his winter's subsistence. The poor wretch approached with hesitation, the alternate dread of famine and of white men operating upon his mind. He made the most abject signs imploring Mr. Hunt not to carry off his food. The latter tried in every way to reassure him, and offered him knives in exchange for his provisions; great as was the temptation, the poor Snake could only prevail upon himself to spare a part; keeping a feverish watch over the rest, lest it should be taken away. It was in vain Mr. Hunt made enquiries of him concerning his route and the course of the river. The Indian was too much frightened and bewildered to comprehend him or to reply; he did nothing but alternately commend himself to the protection of the Good Spirit, and supplicate Mr. Hunt not to take away his fish and buffalo meat; and in this state they left him, trembling about his treasures.

In the course of that and the next day they made nearly eighty miles; the river inclining to the south of west, and being clear and beautiful, nearly half a mile in width with many populous communities of the beaver along its banks. The twenty eighth of October, however, was a day of disaster. The river again became rough and impetuous, and was chafed and broken by numerous rapids. These grew more and more dangerous and the utmost skill was required to steer among them. Mr. Crooks was seated in the second canoe of the squadron, and had an old experienced Canadian for steersman, named Antoine Clappine, one of the most valuable of the voyageurs. The leading canoe had glided safely among the turbulent and roaring surges, but in following it Mr. Crooks perceived that his canoe was bearing towards a rock. He called out to the steersman, but his warning voice was either unheard or unheeded. In the next moment they struck upon the rock. The canoe was split and overturned. There were five persons on board. Mr. Crooks and one of his companions were thrown amidst roaring breakers and a whirling current, but succeeded, by strong swimming, to reach the shore. Clappine and two others clung to the shattered bark and drifted with it to a rock. The wreck struck the rock with one end and swinging round flung poor Clappine off into the raging stream, which swept him away and he perished. His comrades succeeded in getting upon the rock, from whence they were afterwards taken off.

This disastrous event brought the whole squadron to a halt, and struck a chill into every bosom. Indeed they had arrived at a terrific strait that forbade all further progress in the canoes, and dismayed the most experienced voyageur. The whole body of the river was compressed into a space of less than thirty feet in width, between two ledges of rocks upwards of two hundred feet high, and formed a whirling and tumultuous vortex so frightfully agitated as to receive the name of "The Caldron Linn." Beyond this fearful abyss the river kept raging and roaring on, until lost to sight among impending precipices.

Chapter XXXIII

Gloomy council—Exploring parties—Discouraging reports—
Disastrous experiment—Detachments in quest of succour—
Caches, how made—Return of one of the detachments—
Unsuccessful—Further disappointments—The Devil's Scuttle
Hole.

M R. HUNT and his companions encamped upon the borders of the Caldron Linn, and held gloomy council as
to their future course. The recent wreck had dismayed even
the voyageurs, and the fate of their popular comrade Clappine,
one of the most adroit and experienced of their fraternity, had
struck sorrow to their hearts, for, with all their levity, these
thoughtless beings have great kindness towards each other.

The whole distance they had navigated since leaving
Henry's fort, was computed to be about three hundred and
forty miles; strong apprehensions were now entertained that
the tremendous impediments before them would oblige them
to abandon their canoes. It was determined to send exploring
parties on each side of the river to ascertain whether it was possible to navigate it further. Accordingly on the following
morning three men were despatched along the south bank,
while Mr. Hunt and three others proceeded along the north.
The two parties returned after a weary scramble among savage
rocks and precipices, and with very disheartening accounts.
For nearly forty miles that they had explored the river foamed
and roared along through a deep and narrow channel from
twenty to thirty yards wide, which it had worn, in the course
of ages, through the heart of a barren rocky country. The
precipices on each side were often two and three hundred feet
high, sometimes perpendicular and sometimes overhanging,
so that it was impossible, excepting in one or two places, to get
down to the margin of the stream. This dreary strait was rendered the more dangerous by frequent rapids, and occasionally
perpendicular falls from ten to forty feet in height: So that it
seemed almost hopeless to attempt to pass the canoes down it.

The party, however, who had explored the south side of the
river had found a place, about six miles from the camp, where

they thought it possible the canoes might be carried down the bank and launched upon the stream, and from whence they might make their way with the aid of occasional portages. Four of the best canoes were accordingly selected for the experiment and were transported to the place on the shoulders of sixteen of the men. At the same time Mr. Reed, the clerk, and three men were detached to explore the river still further down than the previous scouting parties had been, and at the same time to look out for Indians from whom provisions might be obtained, and a supply of horses, should it be found necessary to proceed by land.

The party who had been sent with the canoes returned on the following day weary and dejected. One of the canoes had been swept away with all the weapons and effects of four of the voyageurs, in attempting to pass it down a rapid by means of a line. The other three had stuck fast among the rocks, so that it was impossible to move them; the men returned, therefore, in despair, and declared the river unnavigable.

The situation of the unfortunate travellers was now gloomy in the extreme. They were in the heart of an unknown wilderness, untraversed as yet by a white man. They were at a loss what route to take, and how far they were from the ultimate place of their destination, nor could they meet, in these uninhabited wilds, with any human being to give them information. The repeated accidents to their canoes had reduced their stock of provisions to five days' allowance, and there was now every appearance of soon having famine added to their other sufferings.

This last circumstance rendered it more perilous to keep together than to separate. Accordingly, after a little anxious but bewildered council, it was determined that several small detachments should start off in different directions, headed by the several partners. Should any of them succeed in falling in with friendly Indians within a reasonable distance and obtaining a supply of provisions and horses, they were to return to the aid of the main body: otherwise they were to shift for themselves and shape their course according to circumstances; keeping the mouth of the Columbia River as the ultimate point of their wayfaring. Accordingly three several parties set off from the camp at Caldron Linn, in opposite directions.

Mr. M'Lellan with three men kept down along the bank of the river. Mr. Crooks, with five others, turned their steps up it; retracing by land the weary course they had made by water, intending, should they not find relief nearer at hand, to keep on until they should reach Henry's fort, where they hoped to find the horses they had left there, and to return with them to the main body.

The third party composed of four men was headed by Mr. M'Kenzie, who struck to the northward across the desert plains, in hopes of coming upon the main stream of the Columbia.

Having seen these three adventurous bands depart upon their forlorn expeditions, Mr. Hunt turned his thoughts to provide for the subsistence of the main body left to his charge, and to prepare for their future march. There remained with him thirty one men, beside the squaw and two children of Pierre Dorion. There was no game to be met with in the neighborhood, but beavers were occasionally trapped about the river banks, which afforded a scanty supply of food: in the mean time they comforted themselves that some one or other of the foraging detachments would be successful and return with relief.

Mr. Hunt now set to work, with all diligence, to prepare *caches* in which to deposite the baggage and merchandize, of which it would be necessary to disburthen themselves preparatory to their weary march by land; and here we shall give a brief description of those contrivances, so noted in the wilderness.

A cache is a term common among traders and hunters to designate a hiding place for provisions and effects. It is derived from the French word *cacher*, to conceal, and originated among the early colonists of Canada and Louisiana; but the secret depository which it designates was in use among the aboriginals long before the intrusion of the white men. It is, in fact, the only mode that migratory hordes have of preserving their valuables from robbery during their long absences from their villages or accustomed haunts, on hunting expeditions, or during the vicissitudes of war. The utmost skill and caution are required to render these places of concealment invisible to the lynx eye of an Indian. The first care is to seek out a proper situation, which is generally some dry low bank of clay on the margin of a water course. As soon as the precise spot is pitched upon, blankets, saddle cloths, and other coverings are spread over the surrounding grass and bushes, to prevent foot tracks, or any other derangement; and as few hands as possible are employed. A circle of about two feet in diameter is then nicely cut in the sod, which is carefully removed, with the loose soil immediately beneath it, and laid aside in a place where it will be safe from any thing that may change its appearance. The uncovered area is then digged perpendicularly to the depth of about three feet, and is then gradually widened so as to form a conical chamber six or seven feet deep. The whole of the earth displaced by this process, being of a different colour from that on the surface, is handed up in a vessel, and heaped into a skin or cloth, in which it is conveyed to the stream and thrown into the midst of the current, that it may be entirely carried off. Should the cache not be formed in the vicinity of a stream, the earth thus thrown up is carried to a distance and scattered in such manner as not to leave the minutest trace. The cave being formed, is well lined with dry grass, bark, sticks and poles, and occasionally a dried hide. The property intended to be hidden is then laid in, after having been well aired: a hide is spread over it, and dry grass, bark, brush and stones thrown in and trampled down until the pit is filled to the neck. The loose soil which had been put aside is then brought and rammed down firmly to prevent its caving in, and is frequently sprinkled with water to destroy the scent, lest the wolves and bears should be attracted to the place, and root up the concealed treasure. When the neck of the cache is nearly level with the surrounding surface, the sod is again fitted in with the utmost exactness and any bushes, stocks or stones that may have originally been about the spot, are restored to their former places. The blankets and other coverings are then removed from the surrounding herbage; all tracks are obliterated; the grass is gently raised by the hand to its natural position, and the minutest chip or straw is scrupulously gleaned up and thrown into the stream. After all is done the place is abandoned for the night, and, if all be right next morning, is not visited again, until there be a necessity for re opening the cache. Four men are sufficient in this way, to conceal the amount of three tons weight of merchandize in the course of two days. Nine caches were required to contain the goods and baggage which Mr. Hunt found it necessary to leave at this place.

Three days had been thus employed since the departure of the several detachments when that of Mr. Crooks unexpectedly made its appearance. A momentary joy was diffused through the camp, for they supposed succor to be at hand. It was soon dispelled. Mr. Crooks and his companions had become completely disheartened by their retrograde march through a bleak and barren country: and had found, computing from their progress and the accumulating difficulties besetting every step, that it would be impossible to reach Henry's fort and return to the main body in the course of the winter. They had determined, therefore, to rejoin their comrades, and share their lot.

One avenue of hope was thus closed upon the anxious sojourners at the Caldron Linn; their main expectation of relief was now from the two parties under Reed and M'Lellan, which had proceeded down the river; for, as to Mr. M'Kenzie's detachment, which had struck across the plains, they thought it would have sufficient difficulty in struggling forward through the trackless wilderness. For five days they continued to support themselves by trapping and fishing. Some fish of tolerable size were speared at night by the light of cedar torches; others that were very small, were caught in nets with fine meshes. The product of their fishing, however, was very scanty. Their trapping was also precarious; and the tails and bellies of the beavers were dried and put by for the journey.

At length two of the companions of Mr. Reed returned, and were hailed with the most anxious eagerness. Their report served but to encrease the general despondency. They had followed Mr. Reed for some distance below the point to which Mr. Hunt had explored, but had met with no Indians from whom to obtain information and relief. The river still presented the same furious aspect, brawling and boiling along a narrow and rugged channel, between rocks that rose like walls.

A lingering hope which had been indulged by some of the party, of proceeding by water, was now finally given up. The long and terrific strait of the river set all further progress at defiance, and in their disgust at the place and their vexation at the disasters sustained there, they gave it the indignant though not very decorous appellation of The Devil's Scuttle Hole.

Chapter XXXIV

Determination of the party to proceed on foot—Dreary deserts between Snake River and the Columbia—Distribution of effects preparatory to a march—Division of the party—Rugged march along the river—Wild and broken scenery—Shoshonies—Alarm of a Snake encampment—Intercourse with the Snakes—Horse dealing—Value of a tin kettle—Sufferings from thirst—A horse reclaimed—Fortitude of an Indian woman—Scarcity of food—Dog's flesh a dainty—News of Mr. Crooks and his party—Painful travelling among the mountains—Snow storms—A dreary mountain prospect—A bivouack during a wintry night—Return to the river bank.

THE RESOLUTION of Mr. Hunt and his companions was now taken to set out immediately on foot. As to the other detachments that had in a manner gone forth to seek their fortunes, there was little chance of their return; they would probably make their own way through the wilderness. At any rate, to linger in the vague hope of relief from them would be to run the risk of perishing with hunger. Beside, the winter was rapidly advancing and they had a long journey to make through an unknown country, where all kinds of perils might await them. They were yet, in fact, a thousand miles from Astoria, but the distance was unknown to them at the time: every thing before and around them was vague and conjectural and wore an aspect calculated to inspire despondency.

In abandoning the river they would have to launch forth upon vast trackless plains destitute of all means of subsistence, where they might perish of hunger and thirst. A dreary desert of sand and gravel extends from Snake River almost to the Columbia. Here and there is a thin and scanty herbage, insufficient for the pasturage of horse or buffalo. Indeed these treeless wastes between the Rocky Mountains and the Pacific, are even more desolate and barren than the naked, upper prairies on the Atlantic side; they present vast desert tracts that must ever defy cultivation, and interpose dreary and thirsty wilds between the habitations of man, in traversing which the wanderer will often be in danger of perishing.

Seeing the hopeless character of these wastes, Mr. Hunt and his companions determined to keep along the course of the river, where they would always have water at hand, and would be able occasionally to procure fish and beaver, and might perchance meet with Indians, from whom they could obtain provisions.

They now made their final preparations for the march. All their remaining stock of provisions consisted of forty pounds of Indian corn, twenty pounds of grease, about five pounds of portable soup, and a sufficient quantity of dried meat to allow each man a pittance of five pounds and a quarter, to be reserved for emergencies. This being properly distributed, they deposited all their goods and superfluous articles in the caches, taking nothing with them but what was indispensible to the journey. With all their management, each man had to carry twenty pounds weight beside his own articles and equipments.

That they might have the better chance of procuring subsistence in the scanty regions they were to traverse they divided their party into two bands, Mr. Hunt, with eighteen men, beside Pierre Dorion and his family, was to proceed down the north side of the river, while Mr. Crooks with eighteen men kept along the south side.

On the morning of the 9th of November the two parties separated and set forth on their several courses. Mr. Hunt and his companions followed along the right bank of the river, which made its way far below them, brawling at the foot of perpendicular precipices of solid rock two and three hundred feet high. For twenty eight miles that they travelled this day they found it impossible to get down to the margin of the stream. At the end of this distance they encamped for the night at a place which admitted a scrambling descent. It was with the greatest difficulty, however, that they succeeded in getting up a kettle of water from the river for the use of the camp. As some rain had fallen in the afternoon they passed the night under the shelter of the rocks.

The next day they continued thirty two miles to the north west, keeping along the river, which still ran in its deep cut channel. Here and there a sandy beach or a narrow strip of soil, fringed with dwarf willows, would extend for a little distance along the foot of the cliffs, and sometimes a reach of still water would intervene like a smooth mirror between the foaming rapids. As through the preceding day, they journeyed on without finding, except in one instance, any place where they could get down to the river's edge, and they were fain to allay the thirst caused by hard travelling, with the water collected in the hollows of the rocks.

In the course of their march on the following morning they fell into a beaten horse path leading along the river, which shewed that they were in the neighborhood of some Indian village or encampment. They had not proceeded far along it when they met with two Shoshonies, or Snakes. They approached with some appearance of uneasiness, and accosting Mr. Hunt held up a knife, which by signs they let him know they had received from some of the white men of the advance parties. It was with some difficulty that Mr. Hunt prevailed upon one of the savages to conduct him to the lodges of his people. Striking into a trail or path which led up from the river he guided them for some distance into the prairie, until they came in sight of a number of lodges made of straw and shaped like hay stacks.

Their approach, as on former occasions, caused the wildest affright among the inhabitants. The women hid such of their children as were too large to be carried and too small to take care of themselves, under straw, and, clasping their infants to their breasts, fled across the prairie. The men awaited the approach of the strangers, but evidently in great alarm.

Mr. Hunt entered the lodges and, as he was looking about, observed where the children were concealed; their black eyes glistening like those of snakes from beneath the straw. He lifted up the covering to look at them: the poor little beings were horribly frightened, and their fathers stood trembling as if a beast of prey were about to pounce upon the brood.

The friendly manner of Mr. Hunt soon dispelled these apprehensions: he succeeded in purchasing some excellent dried salmon and a dog, an animal much esteemed as food, by the natives, and when he returned to the river one of the Indians accompanied him. He now came to where lodges were frequent along the banks, and, after a day's journey of twenty six miles to the north west, encamped in a populous neighborhood. Forty or fifty of the natives soon visited the camp, conducting themselves in a very amicable manner. They were well clad, and all had buffalo robes, which they procured from some of the hunting tribes in exchange for salmon. Their habitations were very comfortable; each had its pile of worm wood at the door for fuel, and within was abundance of salmon, some fresh, but the greater part cured. When the white men visited the lodges, however, the women and children hid themselves through fear. Among the supplies obtained here were two dogs on which our travellers breakfasted and found them to be very excellent, well flavored and hearty food.

In the course of the three following days they made about sixty three miles, generally in a north west direction. They met with many of the natives in their straw built cabins, who received them without alarm. About their dwellings were immense quantities of the heads and skins of salmon, the best parts of which had been cured, and hidden in the ground. The women were badly clad; the children worse; their garments were buffalo robes, or the skins of foxes, wolves, hares and badgers, and sometimes the skins of ducks, sewed together, with the plumage on. Most of the skins must have been procured by traffic with other tribes, or in distant hunting excursions, for the naked prairies in the neighborhood afforded few animals except hares, which were abundant. There were signs of buffalos having been there, but a long time before.

On the 15th of November they made twenty eight miles along the river which was entirely free from rapids. The shores were lined with dead salmon, which tainted the whole atmosphere. The natives whom they met spoke of Mr. Reed's party having passed through that neighborhood. In the course of the day Mr. Hunt saw a few horses, but the owners of them took care to hurry them out of the way. All the provisions they were able to procure were two dogs and a salmon. On the following day they were still worse off, having to subsist on parched corn and the remains of their dried meat. The river this day had resumed its turbulent character, forcing its way through a narrow channel between steep rocks, and down violent rapids. They made twenty miles over a rugged road, gradually approaching a mountain in the north west, covered with snow, which had been in sight for three days past.

On the 17th they met with several Indians, one of whom had a horse. Mr. Hunt was extremely desirous of obtaining it as a pack horse, for the men, worn down by fatigue and hunger, found the loads of twenty pound weight which they had to carry, daily growing heavier and more galling. The Indians, however, along this river were never willing to part with their horses, having none to spare. The owner of the steed in question seemed proof against all temptation; article after article of great value in Indian eyes was offered and refused. The charms of an old tin kettle, however, were irresistible, and a bargain was concluded.

A great part of the following morning was consumed in lightening the packages of the men and arranging the load for the horse. At this encampment there was no wood for fuel, even the wormwood on which they had frequently depended, having disappeared. For the two last days they had made thirty miles to the north west.

On the 19th of November, Mr. Hunt was lucky enough to purchase another horse for his own use, giving in exchange a tomahawk, a knife, a fire steel, and some beads and gartering. In an evil hour, however, he took the advice of the Indians to abandon the river and follow a road or trail, leading into the prairie. He soon had cause to repent the change. The road led across a dreary waste, without verdure; and where there was neither fountain, nor pool, nor running stream. The men now began to experience the torments of thirst, aggravated by their usual diet of dried fish. The thirst of some of the Canadian voyageurs became so insupportable as to drive them to the most revolting means of allaying it. For twenty five miles did they toil on across this dismal desert, and laid themselves down at night, parched and disconsolate beside their worm wood fires; looking forward to still greater sufferings on the following day. Fortunately it began to rain in the night to their infinite relief; the water soon collected in puddles and afforded them delicious draughts.

Refreshed in this manner they resumed their wayfaring as soon as the first streak of dawn gave light enough for them to see their path. The rain continued all day so that they no longer suffered from thirst, but hunger took its place, for after travelling thirty three miles they had nothing to sup on but a little parched corn.

The next day brought them to the banks of a beautiful little stream, running to the west and fringed with groves of cotton wood and willow. On its borders was an Indian camp with a great many horses grazing around it. The inhabitants too appeared to be better clad than usual. The scene was altogether a cheering one to the poor half famished wanderers. They hastened to the lodges but on arriving at them, met with a check that at first dampened their cheerfulness. An Indian immediately laid claim to the horse of Mr. Hunt, saying that it had been stolen from him. There was no disproving a fact, supported by numerous bystanders, and which the horse stealing habits of the Indians rendered but too probable; so Mr. Hunt relinquished his steed to the claimant; not being able to retain him by a second purchase.

At this place they encamped for the night and made a sumptuous repast upon fish and a couple of dogs, procured from their Indian neighbors. The next day they kept along the river, but came to a halt after ten miles march, on account of the rain. Here they again got a supply of fish and dogs from the natives; and two of the men were fortunate enough each to get a horse in exchange for a buffalo robe. One of these men was Pierre Dorion, the half breed interpreter, to whose suffering family the horse was a most timely acquisition. And here we cannot but notice the wonderful patience, perseverance and hardihood of the Indian women, as exemplified in the conduct of the poor squaw of the interpreter. She was now far advanced in her pregnancy, and had two children to take care of; one four, and the other two years of age. The latter of course she had frequently to carry on her back, in addition to the burthen usually imposed upon the squaw, yet she had borne all her hardships without a murmur and throughout this weary and painful journey, had kept pace with the best of the pedestrians. Indeed on various occasions in the course of this enterprize, she displayed a force of character that won the respect and applause of the white men.

Mr. Hunt endeavored to gather some information from these Indians concerning the country, and the course of the rivers. His communications with them had to be by signs, and a few words which he had learnt, and of course were extremely vague. All that he could learn from them was, that the great river, the Columbia, was still far distant, but he could ascertain nothing as to the route he ought to take to arrive at it. For the two following days they continued westward upward of forty miles along the little stream, until they crossed it just before its junction with Snake River, which they found still running to the north. Before them was a wintry looking mountain covered with snow on all sides.

In three days more they made about seventy miles; fording two small rivers, the waters of which were very cold. Provisions were extremely scarce; their chief sustenance was portable soup; a meagre diet for weary pedestrians.

On the 27th of November the river led them into the mountains through a rocky defile where there was scarcely room to pass. They were frequently obliged to unload the horses to get them by the narrow places; and sometimes to wade through the water in getting round rocks and butting cliffs. All their food this day was a beaver which they had caught the night before; by evening, the cravings of hunger were so sharp, and the prospect of any supply among the mountains so faint, that they had to kill one of the horses. "The men," says Mr. Hunt, in his journal, "find the meat very good, and indeed, so should I, were it not for the attachment I have to the animal."

Early in the following day, after proceeding ten miles to the north, they came to two lodges of Shoshonies: who seemed in nearly as great an extremity as themselves, having just killed two horses for food. They had no other provisions excepting the seed of a weed which they gather in great quantities, and pound fine. It resembles hemp seed. Mr. Hunt purchased a bag of it and also some small pieces of horse flesh which he began to relish, pronouncing them "fat and tender."

From these Indians he received information that several white men had gone down the river, some one side, and a good many on the other; these last he concluded to be Mr. Crooks and his party. He was thus released from much anxiety about their safety, especially as the Indians spoke of Mr. Crooks having one of his dogs yet, which showed that he and his men had not been reduced to extremity of hunger.

As Mr. Hunt feared that he might be several days in passing through this mountain defile, and run the risk of famine, he encamped in the neighborhood of the Indians, for the purpose of bartering with them for a horse. The evening was expended in ineffectual trials. He offered a gun, a buffalo robe, and various other articles. The poor fellows had, probably, like himself, the fear of starvation before their eyes. At length the women, learning the object of his pressing solicitations, and tempting offers, set up such a terrible hue and cry, that he was fairly howled and scolded from the ground.

The next morning early, the Indians seemed very desirous to get rid of their visitors, fearing, probably, for the safety of their horses. In reply to Mr. Hunt's enquiries about the mountains, they told him that he would have to sleep but three nights more among them; and that six days' travelling would take him to the falls of the Columbia; information in which he put no faith, believing it was only given to induce him to set forward. These, he was told, were the last Snakes he would meet with, and that he would soon come to a nation called Sciatogas.

Forward then did he proceed on his tedious journey, which, at every step grew more painful. The road continued for two days, through narrow defiles, where they were repeatedly obliged to unload the horses. Sometimes the river passed through such rocky chasms and under such steep precipices that they had to leave it, and make their way, with excessive labor, over immense hills, almost impassable for horses. On some of these hills were a few pine trees, and their summits were covered with snow. On the second day of this scramble one of the hunters killed a black tailed deer, which afforded the half-starved travellers a sumptuous repast. Their progress these two days was twenty eight miles, a little to the northward of east.

The month of December set in drearily, with rain in the valleys, and snow upon the hills. They had to climb a mountain with snow to the midleg, which increased their painful toil. A small beaver supplied them with a scanty meal, which they eked out with frozen blackberries, haws, and chokecherries, which they found in the course of their scramble. Their journey this day, though excessively fatiguing, was but thirteen miles; and all the next day they had to remain encamped, not being able to see half a mile ahead, on account of a snow storm. Having nothing else to eat, they were compelled to kill

another of their horses. The next day they resumed their
march in snow and rain, but with all their efforts could only
get forward nine miles, having for a part of the distance to
unload the horses and carry the packs themselves. On the succeeding morning they were obliged to leave the river, and
scramble up the hills. From the summit of these, they got a
wide view of the surrounding country, and it was a prospect
almost sufficient to make them despair. In every direction
they beheld snowy mountains, partially sprinkled with pines
and other evergreens, and spreading a desert and toilsome
world around them. The wind howled over the bleak and
wintry landscape, and seemed to penetrate to the marrow of
their bones. They waded on through the snow which at every
step was more than knee deep.

After toiling in this way all day, they had the mortification
to find that they were but four miles distant from the encampment of the preceding night, such was the meandering
of the river among these dismal hills. Pinched with famine,
exhausted with fatigue, with evening approaching, and a wintry wild still lengthening as they advanced; they began to look
forward with sad forebodings to the night's exposure upon
this frightful waste. Fortunately they succeeded in reaching a
cluster of pines about sunset. Their axes were immediately at
work; they cut down trees, piled them up in great heaps, and
soon had huge fires "to cheer their cold and hungry hearts."

About three o'clock in the morning it again began to snow,
and at daybreak they found themselves, as it were, in a cloud;
scarcely being able to distinguish objects at the distance of a
hundred yards. Guiding themselves by the sound of running
water, they set out for the river, and by slipping and sliding
contrived to get down to its bank. One of the horses, missing
his footing, rolled down several hundred yards with his load,
but sustained no injury. The weather in the valley was less rigorous than on the hills. The snow lay but ankle deep, and
there was a quiet rain now falling. After creeping along for six
miles, they encamped on the border of the river. Being utterly
destitute of provisions, they were again compelled to kill one
of their horses to appease their famishing hunger.

Chapter XXXV

THE WANDERERS had now accomplished four hundred and seventy two miles of their dreary journey since leaving the Caldron Linn, how much further they had yet to travel, and what hardships to encounter, no one knew.

On the morning of the 6th of December, they left their dismal encampment, but had scarcely begun their march, when, to their surprise, they beheld a party of white men coming up along the opposite bank of the river. As they drew nearer, they were recognised for Mr. Crooks and his companions. When they came opposite, and could make themselves heard across the murmuring of the river, their first cry was for food; in fact, they were almost starved. Mr. Hunt immediately returned to the camp, and had a kind of canoe made out of the skin of the horse, killed on the preceding night. This was done after the Indian fashion, by drawing up the edges of the skin with thongs, and keeping them distended by sticks or thwarts pieces. In this frail bark, Gardepie, one of the Canadians, carried over a portion of the flesh of the horse to the famishing party on the opposite side of the river, and brought back with him Mr. Crooks, and the Canadian, Le Clerc. The forlorn and wasted looks, and starving condition of these two men, struck dismay to the hearts of Mr. Hunt's followers. They had been accustomed to each other's appearance, and to the gradual operation of hunger and hardship upon their frames, but the change in the looks of these men, since last they parted, was a type of the famine and desolation of the land; and they now began to indulge the horrible presentiment that they would all starve together, or be reduced to the direful alternative of casting lots!

When Mr. Crooks had appeased his hunger, he gave Mr.

Hunt some account of his wayfaring. On the side of the river, along which he had kept, he had met with but few Indians, and those were too miserably poor to yield much assistance. For the first eighteen days, after leaving the Caldron Linn, he and his men had been confined to half a meal in twenty four hours; for three days following, they had subsisted on a single beaver, a few wild cherries, and the soles of old moccasins, and for the last six days, their only animal food had been the carcass of a dog. They had been three days' journey further down the river than Mr. Hunt, always keeping as near to its banks as possible, and frequently climbing over sharp and rocky ridges that projected into the stream. At length they had arrived to where the mountains increased in height, and came closer to the river, with perpendicular precipices, which rendered it impossible to keep along the stream. The river here rushed with incredible velocity through a defile not more than thirty yards wide, where cascades and rapids succeeded each other almost without intermission. Even had the opposite banks, therefore, been such as to permit a continuance of their journey, it would have been madness to attempt to pass the tumultuous current, either on rafts or otherwise. Still bent, however, on pushing forward, they attempted to climb the opposing mountains; and struggled on through the snow for half a day until, coming to where they could command a prospect, they found that they were not half way to the summit, and that mountain upon mountain lay piled beyond them, in wintry desolation. Famished and emaciated as they were, to continue forward would be to perish; their only chance seemed to be to regain the river, and retrace their steps up its banks. It was in this forlorn and retrograde march that they had met Mr. Hunt and his party.

Mr. Crooks also gave information of some others of their fellow adventurers. He had spoken several days previously with Mr. Reed and Mr. M'Kenzie, who with their men were on the opposite side of the river, where it was impossible to get over to them. They informed him that Mr. M'Lellan had struck across from the little river above the mountains, in the hope of falling in with some of the tribe of Flatheads, who inhabit the western skirts of the Rocky range. As the companions of Reed and M'Kenzie were picked men, and had found provisions more abundant on their side of the river, they were in better condition, and more fitted to contend with the difficulties of the country, than those of Mr. Crooks, and when he lost sight of them, were pushing onward, down the course of the river.

Mr. Hunt took a night to revolve over his critical situation, and to determine what was to be done. No time was to be lost; he had twenty men and more, in his own party, to provide for, and Mr. Crooks and his men to relieve. To linger would be to starve. The idea of retracing his steps was intolerable, and, notwithstanding all the discouraging accounts of the ruggedness of the mountains lower down the river, he would have been disposed to attempt them, but the depth of the snow with which they were covered, deterred him; having already experienced the impossibility of forcing his way against such an impediment.

The only alternative, therefore, appeared to be, to return and seek the Indian bands scattered along the small rivers above the mountains. Perhaps, from some of these he might procure horses enough to support him until he could reach the Columbia; for he still cherished the hope of arriving at that river in the course of the winter, though he was apprehensive that few of Mr. Crooks' party would be sufficiently strong to follow him. Even in adopting this course, he had to make up his mind to the certainty of several days of famine at the outset, for it would take that time to reach the last Indian lodges from which he had parted, and until they should arrive there, his people would have nothing to subsist upon but haws and wild berries, excepting one miserable horse, which was little better than skin and bone.

After a night of sleepless cogitation, Mr. Hunt announced to his men the dreary alternative he had adopted, and preparations were made to take Mr. Crooks and Le Clerc accross the river, with the remainder of the meat, as the other party were to keep up along the opposite bank. The skin canoe had unfortunately been lost in the night; a raft was constructed, therefore, after the manner of the natives, of bundles of willows, but it could not be floated across the impetuous current. The men were directed, in consequence, to keep on along the river by themselves, while Mr. Crooks and Le Clerc would proceed with Mr. Hunt. They all, then, took up their retograde march with drooping spirits.

In a little while, it was found that Mr. Crooks and Le Clerc were so feeble as to walk with difficulty, so that Mr. Hunt was obliged to retard his pace, that they might keep up with him. His men grew impatient at the delay. They murmured that they had a long and desolate region to traverse, before they could arrive at the point where they might expect to find horses; that it was impossible for Crooks and Le Clerc, in their feeble condition, to get over it; that to remain with them would only be to starve in their company. They importuned Mr. Hunt, therefore, to leave these unfortunate men to their fate, and think only of the safety of himself and his party. Finding him not to be moved, either by entreaties or their clamors, they began to proceed without him, singly and in parties. Among those who thus went off was Pierre Dorion, the interpreter. Pierre owned the only remaining horse; which was now a mere skeleton. Mr. Hunt had suggested, in their present extremity, that it should be killed for food; to which the half breed flatly refused his assent, and cudgelling the miserable animal forward, pushed on sullenly, with the air of a man doggedly determined to quarrel for his right. In this way Mr. Hunt saw his men, one after another, break away, until but five remained to bear him company.

On the following morning, another raft was made, on which Mr. Crooks and Le Clerc again attempted to ferry themselves across the river, but after repeated trials, had to give up in despair. This caused additional delay: after which, they continued to crawl forward at a snail's pace. Some of the men who had remained with Mr. Hunt now became impatient of these incumbrances, and urged him, clamorously, to push forward, crying out that they should all starve. The night which succeeded was intensely cold, so that one of the men was severely frost-bitten. In the course of the night, Mr. Crooks was taken ill, and in the morning was still more incompetent to travel. Their situation was now desperate, for their stock of provisions was reduced to three beaver skins. Mr. Hunt, therefore, resolved to push on, overtake his people, and insist upon having the horse of Pierre Dorion sacrificed for the relief of all hands. Accordingly, he left two of his men to help Crooks and Le Clerc on their way, giving them two of the beaver skins for their support; the remaining skin he retained, as provision for himself and the three other men who struck forward with him.

Chapter XXXVI

ALL THAT DAY, Mr. Hunt and his three comrades travelled without eating. At night they made a tantalizing supper on their beaver skin, and were nearly exhausted by hunger and cold. The next day, December 10th, they overtook the advance party, who were all as much famished as themselves, some of them not having eaten since the morning of the seventh. Mr. Hunt now proposed the sacrifice of Pierre Dorion's skeleton horse. Here he again met with positive and vehement opposition from the half breed, who was too sullen and vindictive a fellow to be easily dealt with. What was singular, the men, though suffering such pinching hunger, interfered in favor of the horse. They represented, that it was better to keep on as long as possible without resorting to this last resource. Possibly the Indians, of whom they were in quest, might have shifted their encampment, in which case it would be time enough to kill the horse to escape starvation. Mr. Hunt, therefore, was prevailed upon to grant Pierre Dorion's horse a reprieve.

Fortunately they had not proceeded much further when, towards evening, they came in sight of a lodge of Shoshonies, with a number of horses grazing around it. The sight was as unexpected as it was joyous. Having seen no Indians in this neighborhood as they passed down the river, they must have subsequently come out from among the mountains.

Mr. Hunt, who first descried them, checked the eagerness of his companions, knowing the unwillingness of these Indians to part with their horses, and their aptness to hurry them off and conceal them in case of an alarm. This was no time to risk such a disappointment. Approaching, therefore, stealthily and silently, they came upon the savages by surprize, who fled in terror. Five of their horses were eagerly seized and one was despatched upon the spot. The carcass was immediately cut up and a part of it hastily cooked and ravenously devoured.

A man was now sent on horseback with a supply of the flesh to Mr. Crooks and his companions. He reached them in the night: they were so famished that the supply sent them seemed but to aggravate their hunger, and they were almost tempted to kill and eat the horse that had brought the messenger. Availing themselves of the assistance of the animal they reached the camp early in the morning.

On arriving there Mr. Crooks was shocked to find that, while the people on this side of the river were amply supplied with provisions, none had been sent to his own forlorn and famishing men on the opposite bank. He immediately caused a skin canoe to be constructed, and called out to his men to fill their camp kettles with water and hang them over the fire, that no time might be lost in cooking the meat the moment it should be received. The river was so narrow, though deep, that every thing could be distinctly heard and seen across it. The kettles were placed over the fire, and the water was boiling by the time the canoe was completed. When all was ready, however, no one would undertake to ferry the meat across. A vague and almost superstitious terror had infected the minds of Mr. Hunt's followers, enfeebled and rendered imaginative of horrors by the dismal scenes and sufferings through which they had passed. They regarded the haggard crew, hovering like spectres of famine on the opposite bank, with indefinite feelings of awe and apprehension, as if something desperate and dangerous was to be feared from them.

Mr. Crooks tried in vain to reason or shame them out of this singular state of mind. He then attempted to navigate the canoe himself, but found his strength incompetent to brave the impetuous current. The good feelings of Ben Jones the Kentuckian at length overcame his fears and he ventured over. The supply he brought was received with trembling avidity. A poor Canadian, however, named Jean Baptiste Prevost, whom famine had rendered wild and desperate, ran frantically about the bank, after Jones had returned, crying out to Mr. Hunt to send the canoe for him and take him from that horrible region of famine declaring that otherwise he would never march another step, but would lie down there and die.

The canoe was shortly sent over again under the management of Joseph Delaunay, with further supplies. Prevost immediately pressed forward to embark. Delaunay refused to admit him, telling him that there was now a sufficient supply of meat on his side of the river. He replied that it was not cooked and he should starve before it was ready; he implored therefore to be taken where he could get something to appease his hunger immediately. Finding the canoe putting off without him, he forced himself aboard. As he drew near the opposite shore and beheld meat roasting before the fires, he jumped up, shouted, clapped his hands and danced in a delirium of joy, until he upset the canoe. The poor wretch was swept away by the current and drowned, and it was with extreme difficulty that Delaunay reached the shore.

Mr. Hunt now sent all his men forward excepting two or three. In the evening he caused another horse to be killed and a canoe to be made out of the skin, in which he sent over a further supply of meat to the opposite party. The canoe brought back John Day, the Kentucky hunter, who came to join his former employer and commander, Mr. Crooks. Poor Day, once so active and vigorous, was now reduced to a condition even more feeble and emaciated than his companions. Mr. Crooks had such a value for the man, on account of his past services and faithful character, that he determined not to quit him; he exhorted Mr. Hunt, however, to proceed forward and join the party, as his presence was all important to the conduct of the expedition. One of the Canadians, Jean Baptiste Dubreuil, likewise remained with Mr. Crooks.

Mr. Hunt left two horses with them, and a part of the carcass of the last that had been killed. This, he hoped, would be sufficient to sustain them until they should reach the Indian encampment.

One of the chief dangers attending the enfeebled condition of Mr. Crooks and his companions was their being overtaken by the Indians whose horses had been seized: though

Mr. Hunt hoped that he had guarded against any resentment on the part of the savages, by leaving various articles in their lodge, more than sufficient to compensate for the outrage he had been compelled to commit.

Resuming his onward course Mr. Hunt came up with his people in the evening. The next day (December 13th) he beheld several Indians, with three horses, on the opposite side of the river, and after a time came to the two lodges which he had seen on going down. Here he endeavored in vain to barter a rifle for a horse, but again succeeded in effecting the purchase with an old tin kettle aided by a few beads.

The two succeeding days were cold and stormy; the snow was augmenting, and there was a good deal of ice running in the river. Their road, however, was becoming easier; they were getting out of the hills and finally emerged into the open country after twenty days of fatigue, famine, and hardship of every kind, in the ineffectual attempt to find a passage down the river.

They now encamped on a little willowed stream running from the east, which they had crossed on the 26th of November. Here they found a dozen lodges of Shoshonies, recently arrived, who informed them that had they persevered along the river they would have found their difficulties augment until they became absolutely insurmountable. This intelligence added to the anxiety of Mr. Hunt for the fate of Mr. M'Kenzie and his people who had kept on.

Mr. Hunt now followed up the little river and encamped at some lodges of Shoshonies from whom he procured a couple of horses, a dog, a few dried fish, and some roots and dried cherries. Two or three days were exhausted in obtaining information about the route, and what time it would take to get to the Sciatogas, a hospitable tribe, on the west side of the mountains, represented as having many horses. The replies were various, but concurred in saying that the distance was great, and would occupy from seventeen to twenty one nights. Mr. Hunt then tried to procure a guide; but though he sent to various lodges up and down the river, offering articles of great value in Indian estimation, no one would venture. The snow they said was waist deep in the mountains; and to all his offers they shook their heads, gave a shiver and replied "we shall freeze! we shall freeze!" At the same time they urged him to remain and pass the winter among them.

Mr. Hunt was in a dismal dilemma. To attempt the mountains without a guide would be certain death to him and all his people; to remain there, after having already been so long on the journey and at such great expense was worse to him he said than "two deaths." He now changed his tone with the Indians, charged them with deceiving him in respect to the mountains and talking with a "forked tongue," or, in other words, with lying. He upbraided them with their want of courage and told them they were women to shrink from the perils of such a journey. At length one of them, piqued by his taunts or tempted by his offers, agreed to be his guide; for which he was to receive a gun, a pistol, three knives, two horses, and a little of every article in possession of the party; a reward sufficient to make him one of the wealthiest of his vagabond nation.

Once more then, on the twenty first of December, they set out upon their wayfaring, with newly excited spirits. Two other Indians accompanied their guide who led them immediately back to Snake River, which they followed down for a short distance, in search of some Indian rafts made of reeds, on which they might cross. Finding none, Mr. Hunt caused a horse to be killed and a canoe to be made out of its skin. Here, on the opposite bank, they saw the thirteen men of Mr. Crooks' party; who had continued up along the river. They told Mr. Hunt, across the stream, that they had not seen Mr. Crooks and the two men who had remained with him since the day that he had separated from them.

The canoe proving too small another horse was killed, and the skin of it joined to that of the first. Night came on before the little bark had made more than two voyages. Being badly made it was taken apart and put together again by the light of the fire. The night was cold; the men were weary and disheartened with such varied and incessant toil and hardship. They crouched dull and drooping around their fires; many of them began to express a wish to remain where they were for the winter. The very necessity of crossing the river dismayed some of them in their present enfeebled and dejected state. It was rapid and turbulent and filled with floating ice, and they remembered that two of their comrades had already perished in its waters. Others looked forward with misgivings to the long and dismal journey through unknown regions that awaited them, when they should have passed this dreary flood.

At an early hour of the morning (December 23d) they began to cross the river. Much ice had formed during the night and they were obliged to break it for some distance on each shore. At length they all got over in safety to the west side; and their spirits rose on having achieved this perilous passage. Here they were rejoined by the people of Mr. Crooks, who had with them a horse and a dog which they had recently procured. The poor fellows were in the most squalid and emaciated state. Three of them were so completely prostrated in strength and spirits that they expressed a wish to remain among the Snakes. Mr. Hunt, therefore, gave them the canoe, that they might cross the river, and a few articles, with which to procure necessaries until they should meet with Mr. Crooks. There was another man, named Michel Carriere, who was almost equally reduced but he determined to proceed with his comrades, who were now incorporated with the party of Mr. Hunt. After the day's exertions they encamped together on the banks of the river. This was the last night they were to spend upon its borders. More than eight hundred miles of hard travelling and many weary days had it cost them; and the sufferings connected with it rendered it hateful in their remembrance so that the Canadian voyageurs always spoke of it as "La maudite riviere enragée"—the accursed Mad River: thus coupling a malediction with its name.

Chapter XXXVII

Departure from Snake River—Mountains to the north—
Wayworn travellers—An increase of the Dorion family—
A camp of Shoshonies—A New Year festival among the
Snakes—A wintry march through the mountains—A sunny
prospect, and milder climate—Indian horse tracks—Grassy
valleys—A camp of Sciatogas—Joy of the travellers—Dangers
of abundance—Habits of the Sciatogas—Fate of Carriere—
The Umatalla—Arrival at the banks of the Columbia—
Tidings of the scattered members of the expedition—Scenery
on the Columbia—Tidings of Astoria—Arrival at the falls.

O N THE 24TH of December, all things being arranged, Mr. Hunt turned his back upon the disastrous banks of Snake River, and struck his course westward for the mountains. His party, being augmented by the late followers of Mr. Crooks, amounted now to thirty two white men, three Indians, and the squaw and two children of Pierre Dorion. Five jaded, half starved horses were laden with their baggage, and, in case of need, were to furnish them with provisions. They travelled painfully about fourteen miles a day, over plains and among hills, rendered dreary by occasional falls of snow and rain. Their only sustenance was a scanty meal of horse flesh once in four and twenty hours.

On the third day the poor Canadian, Carriere, one of the famished party of Mr. Crooks, gave up in despair, and, lying down upon the ground declared he could go no further. Efforts were made to cheer him up, but it was found that the poor fellow was absolutely exhausted and could not keep on his legs. He was mounted, therefore, upon one of the horses, though the forlorn animal was in little better plight than himself.

On the 28th they came upon a small stream winding to the north, through a fine level valley; the mountains receding on each side. Here their Indian friends pointed out a chain of woody mountains to the left, running north and south and covered with snow; over which they would have to pass.

They kept along this valley for twenty one miles on the

438

29th, suffering much from a continual fall of snow and rain and being twice obliged to ford the icy stream.

Early in the following morning the squaw of Pierre Dorion, who had hitherto kept on without murmuring or flinching, was suddenly taken in labour, and enriched her husband with another child. As the fortitude and good conduct of the poor woman had gained for her the good will of the party, her situation caused concern and perplexity. Pierre, however, treated the matter as an occurrence that could soon be arranged and need cause no delay. He remained by his wife in the camp, with his other children and his horse, and promised soon to rejoin the main body, who proceeded on their march.

Finding that the little river entered the mountains, they abandoned it and turned off for a few miles among hills. Here another Canadian, named La Bonté, gave out, and had to be helped on horseback. As the horse was too weak to bear both him and his pack, Mr. Hunt took the latter upon his own shoulders. Thus, with difficulties augmenting at every step, they urged their toilsome way among the hills half famished, and faint at heart, when they came to where a fair valley spread out before them of great extent, and several leagues in width, with a beautiful stream meandering through it. A genial climate seemed to prevail here, for though the snow lay upon all the mountains within sight, there was none to be seen in the valley. The travellers gazed with delight upon this serene sunny landscape, but their joy was complete on beholding six lodges of Shoshonies pitched upon the borders of the stream, with a number of horses and dogs about them. They all pressed forward with eagerness and soon reached the camp. Here their first attention was to obtain provisions. A rifle, an old musket, a tomahawk, a tin kettle and a small quantity of ammunition soon procured them four horses, three dogs and some roots. Part of the live stock was immediately killed, cooked with all expedition and as promptly devoured. A hearty meal restored every one to good spirits.

In the course of the following morning the Dorion family made its re appearance. Pierre came trudging in the advance, followed by his valued, though skeleton steed, on which was mounted his squaw with the new born infant in her arms and her boy of two years old wrapped in a blanket and slung at her side. The mother looked as unconcerned as if nothing had happened to her; so easy is nature in her operations in the wilderness, when free from the enfeebling refinements of luxury and the tamperings and appliances of art.

The next morning ushered in the New Year. (1812) Mr. Hunt was about to resume his march when his men requested permission to celebrate the day. This was particularly urged by the Canadian voyageurs, with whom New Year's day is a favorite festival; and who never willingly give up a holyday, under any circumstances. There was no resisting such an application; so the day was passed in repose and revelry; the poor Canadians contrived to sing and dance in defiance of all their hardships; and there was a sumptuous New Year's banquet of dog's meat and horse flesh.

After two days of welcome rest, the travellers addressed themselves once more to their painful journey. The Indians of the lodges pointed out a distant gap through which they must pass in traversing the ridge of mountains. They assured them that they would be but little incommoded by snow, and in three days would arrive among the Sciatogas. Mr. Hunt, however, had been so frequently deceived by Indian accounts of routes and distances that he gave but little faith to this information.

The travellers continued their course due west for five days, crossing the valley and entering the mountains. Here the travelling became excessively toilsome across rough stony ridges, and amidst fallen trees. They were often knee deep in snow, and sometimes in the hollows between the ridges sank up to their waists. The weather was extremely cold; the sky covered with clouds so that for four days they had not a glimpse of the sun. In traversing the highest ridge they had a wide but chilling prospect over a wilderness of snowy mountains.

On the sixth of January, however, they had crossed the dividing summit of the chain and were evidently under the influence of a milder climate. The snow began to decrease; the sun once more emerged from the thick canopy of clouds, and shone cheeringly upon them, and they caught a sight of what appeared to be a plain stretching out in the west. They hailed it as the poor Israelites hailed the first glimpse of the promised land, for they flattered themselves that this might be the great plain of the Columbia, and that their painful pilgrimage might be drawing to a close.

It was now five days since they had left the lodges of the Shoshonies during which they had come about sixty miles, and their guide assured them that in the course of the next day they would see the Sciatogas.

On the following morning, therefore, they pushed forward, with eagerness, and soon fell upon a small stream which led them through a deep narrow defile, between stupendous ridges. Here among the rocks and precipices they saw gangs of that mountain loving animal the black tailed deer, and came to where great tracks of horses were to be seen in all directions, made by the Indian hunters.

The snow had entirely disappeared, and the hopes of soon coming upon some Indian encampment induced Mr. Hunt to press on. Many of the men, however, were so enfeebled that they could not keep up with the main body, but lagged at intervals behind; and some of them did not arrive at the night's encampment. In the course of this day's march the recently born child of Pierre Dorion died.

The march was resumed early the next morning, without waiting for the stragglers. The stream which they had followed throughout the preceding day was now swollen by the influx of another river; the declivities of the hills were green and the valleys were clothed with grass. At length the joyful cry was given of "an Indian camp!" It was yet in the distance, in the bosom of the green valley, but they could perceive that it consisted of numerous lodges, and that hundreds of horses were grazing the grassy meadows around it. The prospect of abundance of horse flesh diffused universal joy, for by this time the whole stock of travelling provisions was reduced to the skeleton steed of Pierre Dorion, and another wretched animal, equally emaciated, that had been repeatedly reprieved during the journey.

A forced march soon brought the weary and hungry travellers to the camp. It proved to be a strong party of Sciatogas and Tus-che-pas. There were thirty four lodges comfortably constructed of mats. The Indians too were better clothed than any of the wandering bands they had hitherto met on this side of the Rocky Mountains. Indeed they were as well clad as the generality of the wild hunter tribes. Each had a good buffalo or deer skin robe; and a deer skin hunting shirt and leggings. Upwards of two thousand horses were ranging the pastures around their encampment; but what delighted Mr. Hunt was, on entering the lodges, to behold brass kettles, axes, copper tea kettles, and various other articles of civilized manufacture, which shewed that these Indians had an indirect communication with the people of the sea coast who traded with the whites. He made eager enquiries of the Sciatogas and gathered from them that the Great River (the Columbia) was but two days' march distant, and that several white people had recently descended it; who he hoped might prove to be M'Lellan, M'Kenzie and their companions.

It was with the utmost joy and the most profound gratitude to heaven that Mr. Hunt found himself and his band of weary and famishing wanderers, thus safely extricated from the most perilous part of their long journey, and within the prospect of a termination of their toils. All the stragglers who had lagged behind arrived one after another, excepting the poor Canadian voyageur Carriere. He had been seen late in the preceding afternoon riding behind a Snake Indian, near some lodges of that nation a few miles distant from the last night's encampment; and it was expected that he would soon make his appearance.

The first object of Mr. Hunt was to obtain provisions for his men. A little venison of an indifferent quality and some roots were all that could be procured that evening; but the next day, he succeeded in purchasing a mare and colt, which were immediately killed, and the cravings of the half starved people in some degree appeased.

For several days they remained in the neighborhood of these Indians, reposing after all their hardships, and feasting upon horseflesh and roots, obtained in subsequent traffic. Many of the people ate to such excess as to render themselves sick, others were lame from their past journey; but all gradually recruited in the repose and abundance of the valley. Horses were obtained here much more readily, and at a cheaper rate, than among the Snakes. A blanket, a knife, or a half pound of blue beads, would purchase a steed, and at this rate many of the men bought horses for their individual use.

This tribe of Indians, who are represented as a proud spirited race and uncommonly cleanly, never eat horses or dogs, nor would they permit the raw flesh of either to be brought into their huts. They had a small quantity of venison in each lodge, but set so high a price upon it that the white men, in their impoverished state, could not afford to purchase it. They hunted the deer on horseback; "ringing" or surrounding them, and running them down in a circle. They were admirable horsemen, and their weapons were bows and arrows, which they managed with great dexterity. They were altogether primitive in their habits, and seemed to cling to the usages of savage life even when possessed of the aids of civilization. They had axes among them, yet they generally made use of a stone mallet wrought into the shape of a bottle, and wedges of elk horn, in splitting their wood. Though they might have two or three brass kettles hanging in their lodges yet they would frequently use vessels made of willow, for carrying water, and would even boil their meat in them, by means of hot stones. Their women wore caps of willow neatly worked and figured.

As Carriere, the Canadian straggler, did not make his appearance for two or three days after the encampment in the valley, two men were sent out on horseback in search of him. They returned, however, without success. The lodges of the Snake Indians near which he had been seen were removed, and they could find no trace of him. Several days more elapsed, yet nothing was seen or heard of him, or of the Snake horseman behind whom he had been last observed. It was feared, therefore, that he had either perished through hunger and fatigue; had been murdered by the Indians, or, being left to himself, had mistaken some hunting tracks for the trail of the party and been led astray and lost.

The river on the banks of which they were encamped emptied into the Columbia, was called by the natives the Eu-o-tal-la, or Umatalla, and abounded with beaver. In the course of their sojourn in the valley which it watered, they twice shifted their camp, proceeding about thirty miles down its course, which was to the west. A heavy fall of rain caused the river to overflow its banks, dislodged them from their encampment, and drowned three of their horses, which were tethered in the low ground.

Further conversation with the Indians satisfied them that they were in the neighborhood of the Columbia. The number of the white men who they said had passed down the river, agreed with that of M'Lellan, M'Kenzie and their companions, and encreased the hope of Mr. Hunt that they might have passed through the wilderness with safety.

These Indians had a vague story that white men were coming to trade among them; and they often spoke of two great men named Ke-koosh and Jacquean, who gave them tobacco and smoked with them. Jacquean they said had a house somewhere upon the Great River. Some of the Canadians supposed they were speaking of one Jacquean Finlay, a clerk of the North West Company, and inferred that the house must be some trading post on one of the tributary streams of the Columbia.

The Indians were overjoyed when they found this band of white men intended to return and trade with them. They promised to use all diligence in collecting quantities of beaver skins, and no doubt proceeded to make deadly war upon that sagacious, but ill fated animal, who, in general, lived in peaceful insignificance among his Indian neighbors, before the intrusion of the white trader. On the 20th of January Mr. Hunt took leave of these friendly Indians and of the river on which they were encamped and continued westward.

At length, on the following day, the way worn travellers lifted up their eyes and beheld before them the long sought waters of the Columbia. The sight was hailed with as much transport as if they had already reached the end of their pilgrimage: nor can we wonder at their joy. Two hundred and forty miles had they marched, through wintry wastes and rugged mountains, since leaving Snake River; and six months of perilous wayfaring had they experienced since their departure from the Arickara village on the Missouri. Their whole route by land and water from that point had been, according to their computation, seventeen hundred and fifty one miles, in the course of which they had endured all kinds of hardships. In fact the necessity of avoiding the dangerous country of the Blackfeet had obliged them to make a great bend to the south and to traverse a great additional extent of unknown wilderness.

The place where they struck the Columbia was some distance below the junction of its two great branches, Lewis, and Clarke rivers, and not far from the influx of the Wallah Wallah. It was here a beautiful stream, three quarters of a mile wide, totally free from trees; bordered in some places with steep rocks, in others with pebbled shores.

On the banks of the Columbia they found a miserable horde of Indians called Akai-chies, with no clothing but a scanty mantle of the skins of animals, and sometimes a pair of sleeves of wolf's skin. Their lodges were shaped like a tent and very light and warm, being covered with mats of rushes; beside which they had excavations on the ground, lined with mats, and occupied by the women, who were even more slightly clad than the men. These people subsisted chiefly by fishing; having canoes of a rude construction, being merely the trunks of pine trees split and hollowed out by fire. Their lodges were well stored with dried salmon and they had great quantities of fresh salmon trout of an excellent flavour, taken at the mouth of the Umatalla; of which the travellers obtained a most acceptable supply.

Finding that the road was on the north side of the river Mr. Hunt crossed and continued five or six days travelling rather slowly down along its banks, being much delayed by the straying of the horses and the attempts made by the Indians to steal them. They frequently passed lodges where they obtained fish and dogs. At one place the natives had just returned from hunting and had brought back a large quantity of elk and deer meat, but asked so high a price for it as to be beyond the funds of the travellers, so they had to content themselves with dog flesh. They had by this time, however, come to consider it very choice food, superior to horse flesh, and the minutes of the expedition speak rather exultingly now and then of their having made a "famous repast," where this viand happened to be unusually plenty.

They again learnt tidings of some of the scattered members of the expedition, supposed to be M'Kenzie, M'Lellan and their men, who had preceded them down the river, and had overturned one of their canoes, by which they lost many articles. All these floating pieces of intelligence of their fellow adventurers, who had separated from them in the heart of the wilderness, they received with eager interest.

The weather continued to be temperate, marking the superior softness of the climate on this side of the mountains. For a great part of the time the days were delightfully mild and clear, like the serene days of October, on the Atlantic borders. The country in general in the neighborhood of the river was a continual plain, low near the water, but rising gradually; destitute of trees, and almost without shrubs or plants of any kind excepting a few willow bushes. After travelling about sixty miles they came to where the country became very hilly and the river made its way between rocky banks and down numerous rapids. The Indians in this vicinity were better clad and altogether in more prosperous condition than those above, and, as Mr. Hunt thought, shewed their consciousness of ease by something like sauciness of manner. Thus prosperity is apt to produce arrogance in savage as well as in civilized life. In both conditions man is an animal that will not bear pampering.

From these people Mr. Hunt for the first time received vague, but deeply interesting intelligence of that part of the enterprize which had proceeded by sea to the mouth of the Columbia. The Indians spoke of a number of white men who had built a large house at the mouth of the Great River, and surrounded it with palisades. None of them had been down to Astoria themselves; but rumours spread widely and rapidly from mouth to mouth, among the Indian tribes, and are carried to the heart of the interior by hunting parties and migratory hordes.

The establishment of a trading emporium at such a point, also, was calculated to cause a sensation to the most remote parts of the vast wilderness beyond the mountains. It, in a manner, struck the pulse of the great vital river and vibrated up all its tributary streams.

It is surprising to notice how well this remote tribe of savages had learnt through intermediate gossips, the private feelings of the colonists at Astoria; it shews that Indians are not the incurious and indifferent observers that they have been represented. They told Mr. Hunt that the White people at the large house had been looking anxiously for many of their friends, whom they had expected to descend the Great River: and had been in much affliction, fearing that they were lost. Now, however, the arrival of him and his party would wipe away all their tears and they would dance and sing for joy.

On the thirty first day of January Mr. Hunt arrived at the falls of the Columbia and encamped at the Village of Wishram situated at the head of that dangerous pass of the river called "The Long Narrows."

Chapter XXXVIII

The village of Wish-ram—Roguery of the inhabitants—Their habitations—Tidings of Astoria—Of the Tonquin massacre —Thieves about the camp—A band of braggarts—Embarcation—Arrival at Astoria—A joyful reception—Old comrades —Adventures of Reed, M'Lellan and M'Kenzie among the Snake River Mountains—Rejoicing at Astoria.

OF THE VILLAGE of Wish-ram, the aborigines' fishing mart of the Columbia, we have given some account in an early chapter of this work.* The inhabitants held a traffic in the productions of the fisheries of the falls, and their village was the trading resort of the tribes from the coast and from the mountains. Mr. Hunt found the inhabitants shrewder and more intelligent than any Indians he had met with. Trade had sharpened their wits, though it had not improved their honesty; for they were a community of arrant rogues and freebooters. Their habitations comported with their circumstances, and were superior to any the travellers had yet seen west of the Rocky Mountains. In general the dwellings of the savages on the Pacific side of that great barrier, were mere tents and cabins of mats, or skins or straw, the country being destitute of timber. In Wish-ram, on the contrary, the houses were built of wood, with long sloping roofs. The floor was sunk about six feet below the surface of the ground, with a low door at the gable end, extremely narrow and partly sunk. Through this it was necessary to crawl and then to descend a short ladder. This inconvenient entrance was probably for the purpose of defence; there were loop holes also under the eaves, apparently for the discharge of arrows. The houses were large, generally containing two or three families. Immediately within the door were sleeping places ranged along the walls like berths in a ship; and furnished with pallets of matting. These extended along one half of the building; the remaining half was appropriated to the storing of dried fish.

*Chapter X, pp. 261–62.

The trading operations of the inhabitants of Wish-ram had given them a wider scope of information, and rendered their village a kind of head quarters of intelligence. Mr. Hunt was able, therefore, to collect more distinct tidings concerning the Settlement of Astoria and its affairs. One of the inhabitants had been at the trading post established by David Stuart on the Oakinagan, and had picked up a few words of English there. From him Mr. Hunt gleaned various particulars about that establishment, as well as about the general concerns of the enterprize. Others repeated the name of Mr. M'Kay, the partner who perished in the massacre on board of the Tonquin, and gave some account of that melancholy affair. They said Mr. M'Kay was a chief among the white men and had built a great house at the mouth of the river, but had left it, and sailed away in a large ship to the northward, where he had been attacked by bad Indians in canoes. Mr. Hunt was startled by this intelligence and made further enquiries. They informed him that the Indians had lashed their canoes to the ship and fought until they killed him and all his people. This is another instance of the clearness with which intelligence is transmitted from mouth to mouth among the Indian tribes. These tidings, though but partially credited by Mr. Hunt, filled his mind with anxious forebodings. He now endeavored to procure canoes in which to descend the Columbia, but none suitable for the purpose were to be obtained above the Narrows; he continued on, therefore, the distance of twelve miles and encamped on the bank of the river. The camp was soon surrounded by loitering savages, who went prowling about seeking what they might pilfer. Being baffled by the vigilance of the guard they endeavored to compass their ends by other means. Towards evening a number of warriors entered the camp in ruffling style; painted and dressed out as if for battle, and armed with lances, bows and arrows and scalping knives. They informed Mr. Hunt that a party of thirty or forty braves were coming up from a village below to attack the camp and carry off the horses, but that they were determined to stay with him and defend him. Mr. Hunt received them with great coldness, and, when they had finished their story, gave them a pipe to smoke. He then called up all hands, stationed centinels in different quarters, but told them to keep as vigilant an eye within the camp as without.

The warriors were evidently baffled by these precautions, and, having smoked their pipe and vapoured off their valor, took their departure. The farce, however, did not end here. After a little while the warriors returned ushering in another savage, still more heroically arrayed. This they announced as the chief of the belligerent village, but as a great pacificator. His people had been furiously bent upon the attack and would have doubtless carried it into effect, but this gallant chief had stood forth as the friend of white men, and had dispersed the throng by his own authority and prowess. Having vaunted this signal piece of service there was a significant pause; all evidently expecting some adequate reward. Mr. Hunt again produced the pipe, smoked with the chieftain and his worthy compeers; but made no further demonstrations of gratitude. They remained about the camp all night, but at day light returned baffled and crest fallen to their homes, with nothing but smoke for their pains.

Mr. Hunt now endeavored to procure canoes, of which he saw several about the neighborhood, extremely well made, with elevated stems and sterns, some of them capable of carrying three thousand pounds weight. He found it extremely difficult, however, to deal with these slippery people who seemed much more inclined to pilfer. Notwithstanding a strict guard maintained round the camp, various implements were stolen and several horses carried off. Among the latter we have to include the long cherished steed of Pierre Dorion. From some wilful caprice that worthy pitched his tent at some distance from the main body and tethered his invaluable steed beside it, from whence it was abstracted in the night to the infinite chagrin and mortification of the hybrid interpreter.

Having, after several days' negociation, procured the requisite number of canoes, Mr. Hunt would gladly have left this thievish neighborhood, but was detained until the 5th of February, by violent head winds accompanied by snow and rain. Even after he was enabled to get under way he had still to struggle against contrary winds and tempestuous weather. The current of the river, however, was in his favour; having made a portage at the grand rapid the canoes met with no further obstruction, and, on the afternoon of the 15th of February, swept round an intervening cape and came in sight of the infant settlement of Astoria. After eleven months' wandering in the wilderness, a great part of the time over trackless wastes where the sight of a savage wigwam was a rarity, we may imagine the delight of the poor weatherbeaten travellers at beholding the embryo establishment, with its magazines, habitations and picketed bulwarks, seated on a high point of land dominating a beautiful little bay, in which was a trim built shallop riding quietly at anchor. A shout of joy burst from each canoe at the long wished for sight. They urged their canoes across the bay and pulled with eagerness for shore, where all hands poured down from the settlement to receive and welcome them. Among the first to greet them on their landing were some of their old comrades and fellow sufferers, who, under the conduct of Reed, M'Lellan and M'Kenzie, had parted from them at the Caldron Linn. These had reached Astoria nearly a month previously, and, judging from their own narrow escape from starvation, had given up Mr. Hunt and his followers as lost. Their greeting was the more warm and cordial. As to the Canadian voyageurs, their mutual felicitations, as usual, were loud and vociferous, and it was almost ludicrous to behold these ancient "camerades" and "confreres" hugging and kissing each other on the river bank.

When the first greetings were over the different bands interchanged accounts of their several wanderings after separating at Snake River; we shall briefly notice a few of the leading particulars. It will be recollected by the reader that a small exploring detachment had proceeded down the river under the conduct of Mr. John Reed, a clerk of the Company: that another had set off under M'Lellan, and a third in a different direction, under M'Kenzie. After wandering for several days without meeting with Indians, or obtaining any supplies, they came together fortuitously among the Snake River Mountains, some distance below that disastrous pass or strait which had received the appellation of The Devil's Scuttle Hole. When thus united their party consisted of M'Kenzie, M'Lellan, Reed and eight men, chiefly Canadians.

Being all in the same predicament, without horses, provisions, or information of any kind, they all agreed that it would be worse than useless to return to Mr. Hunt and encumber him with so many starving men, and that their only course was to extricate themselves as soon as possible from this land of famine and misery, and make the best of their way for the

Columbia. They accordingly continued to follow the down-ward course of Snake River; clambering rocks and mountains and defying all the difficulties and dangers of that rugged de-file, which subsequently, when the snows had fallen, was found impassable by Messrs. Hunt and Crooks.

Though constantly near to the borders of the river, and for a great part of the time within sight of its current, one of their greatest sufferings was thirst. The river had worn its way in a deep channel through rocky mountains, destitute of brooks or springs. Its banks were so high and precipitous, that there was rarely any place where the travellers could get down to drink of its waters. Frequently they suffered for miles the torments of Tantalus; water continually within sight, yet fevered with the most parching thirst. Here and there they met with rain water collected in the hollows of the rocks, but more than once they were reduced to the utmost extremity; and some of the men had recourse to the last expedient to avoid perishing.

Their sufferings from hunger were equally severe. They could meet with no game, and subsisted for a time on strips of beaver skin broiled on the coals. These were doled out in scanty allowances, barely sufficient to keep up existence, and at length failed them altogether. Still they crept feebly on, scarce dragging one limb after another, until a severe snow storm brought them to a pause. To struggle against it, in their ex-hausted condition, was impossible, so cowering under an im-pending rock at the foot of a steep mountain, they prepared themselves for that wretched fate which seemed inevitable.

At this critical juncture, when famine stared them in the face, M'Lellan casting up his eyes, beheld an asahta, or Bighorn sheltering itself under a shelving rock on the side of the hill above them. Being in a more active plight than any of his com-rades, and an excellent marksman, he set off to get within shot of the animal. His companions watched his movements with breathless anxiety, for their lives depended upon his success. He made a cautious circuit; scrambled up the hill with the ut-most silence, and at length arrived, unperceived, within a proper distance. Here levelling his rifle he took so sure an aim that the Bighorn fell dead on the spot; a fortunate circum-stance, for, to pursue it, if merely wounded, would have been impossible in his emaciated state. The declivity of the hill enabled him to roll the carcass down to his companions, who were too feeble to climb the rocks. They fell to work to cut it up; yet exerted a remarkable self denial for men in their starving condition, for they contented themselves for the present with a soup made from the bones, reserving the flesh for future repasts. This providential relief gave them strength to pursue their journey, but they were frequently reduced to almost equal straits and it was only the smallness of their party, requiring a small supply of provisions, that enabled them to get through this desolate region with their lives.

At length, after twenty one days of toil and suffering, they got through these mountains and arrived at a tributary stream of that branch of the Columbia called Lewis River, of which Snake River forms the southern fork. In this neighborhood they met with wild horses, the first they had seen west of the Rocky Mountains. From hence they made their way to Lewis River where they fell in with a friendly tribe of Indians who freely administered to their necessities. On this river they procured two canoes in which they dropped down the stream to its confluence with the Columbia, and then down that river to Astoria where they arrived haggard and emaciated and perfectly in rags.

Thus all the leading persons of Mr. Hunt's expedition were once more gathered together excepting Mr. Crooks, of whose safety they entertained but little hope, considering the feeble condition in which they had been compelled to leave him in the heart of the wilderness.

A day was now given up to jubilee to celebrate the arrival of Mr. Hunt and his companions, and the joyful meeting of the various scattered bands of adventurers at Astoria. The colours were hoisted; the guns great and small were fired, there was a feast of fish, of beaver and venison, which relished well with men who had so long been glad to revel on horse flesh and dog's meat; a genial allowance of grog was issued to encrease the general animation, and the festivities wound up, as usual, with a grand dance at night, by the Canadian voyageurs.*

* The distance from S' Louis to Astoria, by the route travelled by Hunt and M'Kenzie, was upwards of 3500 miles, though in a direct line it does not exceed 1800.

Chapter XXXIX

*Scanty fare during the winter—A poor hunting ground—
The return of the fishing season—The uthlecan or smelt—
Its qualities—Vast shoals of it—Sturgeon—Indian modes of
taking it—The salmon—Different species—Nature of the
country about the coast—Forests and forest trees—A remarkable flowering vine—Animals—Birds—Reptiles—Climate
west of the Mountains—Mildness of the temperature—Soil
of the coast and the interior.*

THE WINTER had passed away tranquilly at Astoria. The apprehensions of hostility from the natives had subsided; indeed as the season advanced the Indians for the most part had disappeared from the neighborhood and abandoned the sea coast, so that, for want of their aid, the colonists had at times suffered considerably for want of provisions. The hunters belonging to the establishment made frequent and wide excursions but with very moderate success. There were some deer and a few bears to be found in the vicinity, and elk in great numbers; the country, however, was so rough and the woods so close and entangled, that it was almost impossible to beat up the game. The prevalent rains of winter, also, rendered it difficult for the hunter to keep his arms in order. The quantity of game, therefore, brought in by the hunters was extremely scanty, and it was frequently necessary to put all hands on very moderate allowance. Towards spring, however, the fishing season commenced, the season of plenty on the Columbia. About the beginning of February a small kind of fish, about six inches long, called by the natives the uthlecan, and resembling the smelt, made its appearance at the mouth of the river. It is said to be of delicious flavor, and so fat as to burn like a candle, for which it is often used by the natives. It enters the river in immense shoals, like solid columns, often extending to the depth of five or more feet, and is scooped up by the natives with small nets at the end of poles. In this way they will soon fill a canoe, or form a great heap upon the river banks. These fish constitute a principal article of their food, the women drying them and stringing them on cords.

As the uthlecan is only found in the lower part of the river, the arrival of it soon brought back the natives to the coast; who again resorted to the factory to trade, and from that time furnished plentiful supplies of fish.

The sturgeon makes its appearance in the river shortly after the uthlecan, and is taken in different ways, by the natives. Sometimes they spear it, but oftener they use the hook and line, and the net. Occasionally they sink a cord in the river by a heavy weight, with a buoy at the upper end to keep it floating. To this cord several hooks are attached by short lines, a few feet distant from each other, and baited with small fish. This apparatus is often set towards night, and by the next morning several sturgeon will be found hooked by it; for though a large and strong fish, it makes but little resistance when ensnared.

The salmon, which are the prime fish of the Columbia, and as important to the piscatory tribes as are the buffaloes to the hunters of the prairies, do not enter the river until towards the latter part of May, from which time, until the middle of August, they abound, and are taken in vast quantities, either with the spear or the seine and mostly in shallow water. An inferior species succeeds, and continues from August to December. It is remarkable for having a double row of teeth, half an inch long and extremely sharp, from whence it has received the name of the Dog toothed Salmon. It is generally killed with the spear in small rivulets and smoked for winter provision.

We have noticed in a former chapter the mode in which the salmon are taken and cured at the falls of the Columbia; and put up in parcels for exportation. From these different fisheries of the river tribes, the establishment at Astoria had to derive much of its precarious supplies of provisions.

A year's residence at the mouth of the Columbia, and various expeditions in the interior, had now given the Astorians some idea of the country. The whole coast is described as remarkably rugged and mountainous; with dense forests of hemlock, spruce, white and red cedar, cotton wood, white oak, white and swamp ash, willow and a few walnut. There is likewise an undergrowth of aromatic shrubs, creepers and clambering vines that render the forests almost impenetrable; together with berries of various kinds, such as gooseberries, strawberries, raspberries, both red and yellow, very large and finely flavored, whortleberries, cranberries, serviceberries, blackberries, currants, sloes and wild and choke cherries.

Among the flowering vines is one deserving of particular notice. Each flower is composed of six leaves or petals, about three inches in length, of a beautiful crimson, the inside spotted with white. Its leaves, of a fine green, are oval and disposed by threes. This plant climbs upon the trees without attaching itself to them; when it has reached the topmost branches, it descends perpendicularly, and as it continues to grow, extends from tree to tree, until its various stalks interlace the grove like the rigging of a ship. The stems or trunks of this vine are tougher and more flexible than willow, and are from fifty to one hundred fathoms in length. From the fibres, the Indians manufacture baskets of such close texture as to hold water.

The principal quadrupeds that had been seen by the colonists in their various expeditions were the elk, stag, fallow deer, hart, black and grizzly bear, antelope, Ahsahta or Big Horn, beaver, sea and river otter, muskrat, fox, wolf and panther, the latter extremely rare. The only domestic animals among the natives were horses and dogs.

The country abounded with aquatic and land birds, such as swans, wild geese, brant, ducks of almost every description, pelicans, herons, gulls, snipes, curlews, eagles, vultures, crows, ravens, magpies, woodpeckers, pigeons, partridges, pheasants, grouse, and a great variety of singing birds.

There were few reptiles, the only dangerous kinds were the rattlesnake and one striped with black, yellow and white, about four feet long. Among the lizard kind was one about nine or ten inches in length, exclusive of the tail, and three inches in circumference. The tail was round and of the same length as the body. The head was triangular covered with small square scales. The upper part of the body was likewise covered with small scales, green, yellow, black and blue. Each foot had five toes furnished with strong nails, probably to aid it in burrowing, as it usually lived under ground in the plains.

A remarkable fact characteristic of the country west of the Rocky Mountains is the mildness and equability of the climate. That great mountain barrier seems to divide the continent into different climates even in the same degrees of latitude. The rigorous winters and sultry summers, and all the capricious inequalities of temperature prevalent on the Atlantic side of the mountains, are but little felt on their western declivities. The countries between them and the Pacific are blest with milder and steadier temperature, resembling the climates of parallel latitudes in Europe. In the plains and valleys but little snow falls throughout the winter and usually melts while falling. It rarely lies on the ground more than two days at a time, except on the summits of the mountains. The winters are rainy rather than cold. The rains for five months, from the middle of October to the middle of March, are almost incessant and often accompanied by tremendous thunder and lightning. The winds prevalent at this season are from the south and south east, which usually bring rain. Those from the north to the south west are the harbingers of fair weather and a clear sky. The residue of the year, from the middle of March to the middle of October, an interval of seven months, is serene and delightful. There is scarcely any rain throughout this time, yet the face of the country is kept fresh and verdant by nightly dews, and occasionally by humid fogs in the mornings. These are not considered prejudicial to health, since both the natives and the whites sleep in the open air with perfect impunity.

While this equable and bland temperature prevails throughout the lower country, the peaks and ridges of the vast mountains by which it is dominated are covered with perpetual snow. This renders them discernible at a great distance, shining at times like bright summer clouds, at other times assuming the most aerial tints, and always forming brilliant and striking features in the vast landscape.

The mild temperature prevalent throughout the country is attributed by some to the succession of winds from the Pacific Ocean, extending from Latitude 20° to at least 50° North. These temper the heat of summer so that in the shade no one is incommoded by perspiration; they also soften the rigors of winter, and produce such a moderation in the climate that the inhabitants can wear the same dress throughout the year.

The soil in the neighborhood of the sea coast is of a brown colour inclining to red, and generally poor; being a mixture of clay and gravel. In the interior, and especially in the valleys of the Rocky Mountains, the soil is generally blackish; though sometimes yellow. It is frequently mixed with marl and with marine substances in a state of decomposition. This kind of soil extends to a considerable depth, as may be perceived in the deep cuts made by ravines, and by the beds of rivers. The vegetation in these valleys is much more abundant than near the coast; in fact, it is in these fertile intervals, locked up between rocky sierras, or scooped out from barren wastes, that population must extend itself as it were in veins and ramifications, if ever the regions beyond the mountains should become civilized.

Chapter XL

A BRIEF mention has already been made of the tribes or hordes existing about the lower part of the Columbia at the time of the settlement; a few more particulars concerning them may be acceptable. The four tribes nearest to Astoria, and with whom the traders had most intercourse, were, as has heretofore been observed, the Chinooks, the Clatsops, the Wahkiacums and the Cathlamets. The Chinooks resided chiefly along the banks of a river of the same name, running parallel to the sea coast, through a low country studded with stagnant pools, and emptying itself into Baker's bay, a few miles from Cape Disappointment. This was the tribe over which Comcomly, the one eyed chieftain, held sway: it boasted two hundred and fourteen fighting men. Their chief subsistence was on fish, with an occasional regale of the flesh of elk and deer, and of wild fowl from the neighboring ponds.

The Clatsops resided on both sides of Point Adams; they were the mere reliques of a tribe which had been nearly swept off by the small pox, and did not number more than one hundred and eighty fighting men.

The Wahkiacums, or Waak-i-cums, inhabited the north side of the Columbia and numbered sixty six warriors. They and the Chinooks were originally the same, but a dispute arising about two generations previous to the time of the settlement between the ruling chief and his brother, Wahkiacum, the latter seceded, and with his adherents, formed the present horde which continues to go by his name. In this way new tribes or clans are formed and lurking causes of hostility engendered.

459

The Cathlamets lived opposite to the lower village of the Wahkiacums, and numbered ninety four warriors.

These four tribes, or rather clans, have every appearance of springing from the same origin, resembling each other in person, dress, language and manners. They are rather a diminutive race, generally below five feet five inches, with crooked legs and thick ancles, a deformity caused by their passing so much of their time sitting or squatting upon the calves of their legs and their heels, in the bottom of their canoes; a favorite position, which they retain even when on shore. The women encrease this deformity by wearing tight bandages round the ancles, which prevent the circulation of the blood and cause a swelling of the muscles of the leg.

Neither sex can boast of personal beauty. Their faces are round with small but animated eyes. Their noses are broad and flat at top, and fleshy at the end with large nostrils. They have wide mouths, thick lips and short, irregular and dirty teeth. Indeed good teeth are seldom to be seen among the tribes west of the Rocky Mountains who live chiefly on fish.

In the early stages of their intercourse with white men these savages were but scantily clad. In summer time the men went entirely naked; in the winter and in bad weather, the men wore a small robe, reaching to the middle of the thigh, made of the skins of animals, or of the wool of the mountain sheep. Occasionally they wore a kind of mantle of matting, to keep off the rain; but, having thus protected the back and shoulders, they left the rest of the body naked.

The women wore similar robes, though shorter, not reaching below the waist: beside which they had a kind of petticoat, or fringe reaching from the waist to the knee, formed of the fibres of cedar bark, broken into strands, or a tissue of silk grass twisted and knotted at the ends. This was the usual dress of the women in summer, should the weather be inclement they added a vest of skins similar to the robe.

The men carefully eradicated every vestige of a beard, considering it a great deformity. They looked with disgust at the whiskers and well furnished chins of the white men, and in derision called them Long beards. Both sexes, on the other hand, cherished the hair of the head, which with them is generally black and rather coarse. They allowed it to grow to a great length, and were very proud and careful of it, some-times wearing it plaited, sometimes wound round the head in fanciful tresses. No greater affront could be offered to them than to cut off their treasured locks.

They had conical hats with narrow rims, neatly woven of bear grass or of the fibres of cedar bark, interwoven with de-signs of various shapes and colours; sometimes merely squares and triangles, at other times rude representations of canoes with men fishing and harpooning. These hats were nearly water proof and extremely durable.

The favorite ornaments of the men were collars of bears' claws, the proud trophies of hunting exploits; while the women and children wore similar decorations of elks' tusks. An inter-course with the white traders, however, soon effected a change in the toilettes of both sexes. They became fond of arraying themselves in any article of civilized dress which they could procure, and often made a most grotesque appearance. They adapted many articles of finery, also, to their own previous tastes. Both sexes were fond of adorning themselves with bracelets of iron, brass or copper. They were delighted also with blue and white beads, particularly the former, and wore broad tight bands of them round the waist and ancles; large rolls of them round the neck, and pendants of them in the ears. The men, especially, who, in savage life carry a passion for personal decoration farther than the females, did not think their gala equipments complete, unless they had a jewel of haïqua or wampum dangling at the nose. Thus arrayed, their hair besmeared with fish oil and their bodies bedaubed with red clay, they considered themselves irresistible.

When on warlike expeditions they painted their faces and bodies in the most hideous and grotesque manner, according to the universal practice of American Savages. Their arms were bows and arrows, spears and war clubs. Some wore a corslet formed of pieces of hard wood, laced together with bear's grass, so as to form a light coat of mail, pliant to the body; and a kind of casque of cedar bark, leather and bear's grass sufficient to protect the head from an arrow or a war club. A more complete article of defensive armour was a buff jerkin or shirt of great thickness, made of doublings of elk skin, and reaching to the feet, holes being left for the head and arms. This was perfectly arrow proof; add to which, it was often endowed with charmed virtues, by the spells and mystic ceremonials of the medicine man or conjurer.

Of the peculiar custom, prevalent among these people, of flattening the head, we have already spoken. It is one of those instances of human caprice, like the crippling of the feet of females in China, which are quite incomprehensible. This custom prevails principally among the tribes on the sea coast, and about the lower parts of the rivers. How far it extends along the coast we are not able to asertain. Some of the tribes, both north and south of the Columbia, practice it; but they all speak the Chinook language, and probably originated from the same stock. As far as we can learn the remoter tribes, which speak an entirely different language, do not flatten the head. This absurd custom declines, also, in receding from the shores of the Pacific; few traces of it are to be found among the tribes of the Rocky Mountains, and after crossing the mountains it disappears altogether. Those Indians, therefore, about the head waters of the Columbia, and in the solitary mountain regions, who are often called Flatheads, must not be supposed to be characterized by this deformity. It is an appellation often given by the hunters east of the mountain chain, to all the western Indians excepting the Snakes.

The religious belief of these people was extremely limited and confined; or rather, in all probability, their explanations were but little understood by their visitors. They had an idea of a benevolent and omnipotent Spirit, the creator of all things. They represent him as assuming various shapes at pleasure, but generally that of an immense bird. He usually inhabits the sun, but occasionally wings his way through the aerial regions, and sees all that is doing upon earth. Should any thing displease him he vents his wrath in terrific storms and tempests, the lightning being the flashes of his eyes, and the thunder the clapping of his wings. To propitiate his favor they offer to him annual sacrifices of salmon and venison, the first fruits of their fishing and hunting.

Beside this aerial spirit they believe in an inferior one who inhabits the fire, and of whom they are in perpetual dread, as, though he possesses equally the power of good and evil, the evil is apt to preponderate. They endeavor, therefore, to keep him in good humor by frequent offerings. He is supposed also to have great influence with the Winged Spirit, their sovereign protector and benefactor. They implore him, therefore, to act as their intercessor and procure them all desireable things, such as success in fishing and hunting, abundance of game, fleet horses, obedient wives and male children.

These Indians have likewise their priests, or conjurers, or medicine men, who pretend to be in the confidence of the deities, and the expounders and enforcers of their will. Each of these medicine men has his idols carved in wood representing the Spirits of the air and of the fire, under some rude and grotesque form of a horse, a bear, a beaver, or other quadruped, or that of a bird or fish. These idols are hung round with amulets and votive offerings, such as beavers' teeth, and bears' and eagles' claws.

When any chief personage is on his death bed, or dangerously ill, the medicine men are sent for. Each brings with him his idols with which he retires into a corner to hold a consultation. As doctors are prone to disagree, so these medicine men have now and then a violent altercation as to the malady of the patient, or the treatment of it. To settle this they beat their idols soundly against each other; which ever first loses a tooth or a claw is considered as confuted and his votary retires from the field.

Polygamy is not only allowed, but considered honorable, and the greater number of wives a man can maintain, the more important is he in the eyes of the tribe. The first wife, however, takes rank of all the others, and is considered mistress of the house. Still the domestic establishment is liable to jealousies and cabals, and the lord and master has much difficulty in maintaining harmony in his jangling household.

In the manuscript from which we draw many of these particulars, it is stated that he who exceeds his neighbors in the number of his wives, male children and slaves, is elected chief of the village; a title to office which we do not recollect ever before to have met with.

Feuds are frequent among these tribes, but are not very deadly. They have occasionally pitched battles, fought on appointed days, and at specified places, which are generally the banks of a rivulet. The adverse parties post themselves on the opposite sides of the stream, and at such distances that the battles often last a long while before any blood is shed. The number of killed and wounded seldom exceed half a dozen. Should the damage be equal on each side, the war is considered as honorably concluded; should one party lose more than the other, it is entitled to a compensation in slaves or other property, otherwise hostilities are liable to be renewed at a future day. They are much given also to predatory inroads into the territories of their enemies, and sometimes of their friendly neighbors. Should they fall upon a band of inferior force, or upon a village, weakly defended, they act with the ferocity of true poltroons, slaying all the men and carrying off the women and children as slaves. As to the property, it is packed upon horses which they bring with them for the purpose. They are mean and paltry as warriors, and altogether inferior in heroic qualities to the savages of the buffalo plains on the east side of the mountains.

A great portion of their time is passed in revelry, music, dancing and gambling. Their music scarcely deserves the name; the instruments being of the rudest kind. Their singing is harsh and discordant, the songs are chiefly extempore, relating to passing circumstances, the persons present, or any trifling object that strikes the attention of the singer. They have several kinds of dances, some of them lively and pleasing. The women are rarely permitted to dance with the men, but form groups apart, dancing to the same instrument and song.

They have a great passion for play, and a variety of games. To such a pitch of excitement are they sometimes roused, that they gamble away every thing they possess, even to their wives and children. They are notorious thieves, also, and proud of their dexterity. He who is frequently successful, gains much applause and popularity; but the clumsy thief, who is detected in some bungling attempt, is scoffed at and despised, and sometimes severely punished.

Such are a few leading characteristics of the natives in the neighborhood of Astoria. They appear to us inferior in many respects to the tribes east of the mountains, the bold rovers of the prairies; and to partake much of the Esquimaux character; elevated in some degree by a more genial climate and more varied style of living.

The habits of traffic engendered at the Cataracts of the Columbia have had their influence along the coast. The Chinooks and other Indians at the mouth of the river soon proved themselves keen traders, and in their early dealings with the Astorians never hesitated to ask three times what they considered the real value of an article. They were inquisitive, also, in the extreme, and impertinently intrusive; and were prone to indulge in scoffing and ridicule at the expence of the strangers.

In one thing, however, they shewed superior judgment and self command to most of their race; this was, in their abstinence from ardent spirits and the abhorrence and disgust with which they regarded a drunkard. On one occasion a son of Comcomly had been induced to drink freely at the factory, and went home in a state of intoxication, playing all kinds of mad pranks, until he sank into a stupor, in which he remained for two days. The old chieftain repaired to his friend M'Dougall with indignation flaming in his countenance and bitterly reproached him for having permitted his son to degrade himself into a beast and to render himself an object of scorn and laughter to his slaves.

Chapter XLI

As the spring opened the little settlement of Astoria was in agitation and prepared to send forth various expeditions. Several important things were to be done. It was necessary to send a supply of goods to the trading post of Mr. David Stuart, established in the preceding autumn on the Oakinagan. The cache, or secret deposit made by Mr. Hunt at the Caldron Linn was likewise to be visited, and the merchandize and other effects left there, to be brought to Astoria. A third object of moment was to send despatches overland to Mr. Astor at New York, informing him of the state of affairs at the settlement, and the fortunes of the several expeditions.

The task of carrying supplies to Oakinagan was assigned to Mr. Robert Stuart, a spirited and enterprizing young man, nephew to the one who had established the post. The cache was to be sought out by two of the clerks named Russell Farnham and Donald M'Gilles, conducted by a guide, and accompanied by eight men, to assist in bringing home the goods.

As to the despatches, they were confided to Mr. John Reed, the clerk, the same who had conducted one of the exploring detachments of Snake River. He was now to trace back his way across the mountains by the same route by which he had come, with no other companions or escort than Ben Jones the Kentucky hunter and two Canadians. As it was still hoped that Mr. Crooks might be in existence, and that Mr. Reed and his party might meet with him in the course of their route, they were charged with a small supply of goods and provisions, to aid that gentleman on his way to Astoria.

When the expedition of Reed was made known, Mr. M'Lellan announced his determination to accompany it. He had long been dissatisfied with the smallness of his interest in the copartnership, and had requested an additional number of shares; his request not being complied with, he resolved to abandon the Company. M'Lellan was a man of a singularly self willed and decided character, with whom persuasion was useless; he was permitted therefore to take his own course without opposition.

As to Reed he set about preparing for his hazardous journey with the zeal of a true Irishman. He had a tin case made, in which the letters and papers addressed to Mr. Astor were carefully soldered up. This case he intended to strap upon his shoulders, so as to bear it about with him, sleeping and waking, in all changes and chances, by land or by water, and never to part with it but with his life!

As the route of these several parties would be the same for nearly four hundred miles up the Columbia, and within that distance would lie through the piratical pass of the rapids and among the freebooting tribes of the river, it was thought adviseable to start about the same time, and to keep together. Accordingly on the 22d of March they all set off, to the number of seventeen men, in two canoes.

And here we cannot but pause to notice the hardihood of these several expeditions, so insignificant in point of force, and severally destined to traverse immense wildernesses, where larger parties had experienced so much danger and distress. When recruits were sought in the preceding year among experienced hunters and voyageurs at Montreal and S' Louis, it was considered dangerous to attempt to cross the Rocky Mountains with less than sixty men; and yet here we find Reed ready to push his way across those barriers with merely three companions. Such is the fearlessness, the insensibility to danger, which men acquire by the habitude of constant risk. The mind like the body becomes callous by exposure.

The little associated band proceeded up the river, under the command of Mr. Robert Stuart, and arrived early in the month of April at the Long Narrows, that notorious plundering place. Here it was necessary to unload the canoes, and to transport both them and their cargoes to the head of the Narrows by land. Their party was too few in number for the purpose. They were obliged, therefore, to seek the assistance of the Cathlasco

Indians, who undertook to carry the goods on their horses. Forward then they set, the Indians with their horses well freighted, and the first load convoyed by Reed and five men, well armed; the gallant Irishman striding along at the head, with his tin case of despatches glittering on his back. In passing, however, through a rocky and intricate defile, some of the freebooting vagabonds turned their horses up a narrow path and galloped off, carrying with them two bales of goods, and a number of smaller articles. To follow them was useless; indeed, it was with much ado that the convoy got into port with the residue of the cargoes; for some of the guards were pillaged of their knives and pocket handkerchiefs, and the lustrous tin case of Mr. John Reed was in imminent jeopardy.

Mr. Stuart heard of these depredations, and hastened forward to the relief of the convoy, but could not reach them before dusk, by which time they had arrived at the village of Wish-ram, already noted for its great fishery, and the knavish propensities of its inhabitants. Here they found themselves benighted in a strange place, and surrounded by savages bent on pilfering, if not upon open robbery. Not knowing what active course to take, they remained under arms all night, without closing an eye, and at the very first peep of dawn, when objects were yet scarce visible, every thing was hastily embarked, and, without seeking to recover the stolen effects, they pushed off from shore; "glad to bid adieu," as they said, "to this abominable nest of miscreants."

The worthies of Wish-ram, however, were not disposed to part so easily with their visitors. Their cupidity had been quickened by the plunder which they had already taken, and their confidence increased by the impunity with which their outrage had passed. They resolved, therefore, to take further toll of the travellers, and, if possible, to capture the tin case of despatches; which, shining conspicuously from afar, and being guarded by John Reed with such especial care, must, as they supposed, be "a great medicine."

Accordingly, Mr. Stuart and his comrades had not proceeded far in the canoes, when they beheld the whole rabble of Wish-ram stringing in groups along the bank, whooping and yelling, and gibbering in their wild jargon, and when they landed below the falls, they were surrounded by upwards of four hundred of these river ruffians, armed with bows and arrows, war clubs, and other savage weapons. These now pressed forward, with offers to carry the canoes and effects up the portage. Mr. Stuart declined forwarding the goods, alleging the lateness of the hour; but, to keep them in good humor, informed them that, if they conducted themselves well, their offered services might probably be accepted in the morning; in the meanwhile, he suggested that they might carry up the canoes. They accordingly set off with the two canoes on their shoulders, accompanied by a guard of eight men well armed.

When arrived at the head of the falls, the mischievous spirit of the savages broke out, and they were on the point of destroying the canoes, doubtless with a view to impede the white men from carrying forward their goods, and laying them open to further pilfering. They were with some difficulty prevented from committing this outrage by the interference of an old man, who appeared to have authority among them; and, in consequence of his harangue, the whole of the hostile band, with the exception of about fifty, crossed to the north side of the river, where they lay in wait, ready for further mischief.

In the meantime, Mr. Stuart, who had remained at the foot of the falls with the goods, and who knew that the proffered assistance of the savages was only for the purpose of having an opportunity to plunder, determined, if possible, to steal a march upon them, and defeat their machinations. In the dead of the night, therefore, about one o'clock, the moon shining brightly, he roused his party, and proposed that they should endeavor to transport the goods themselves, above the falls, before the sleeping savages could be aware of their operations. All hands sprang to the work with zeal, and hurried it on in the hope of getting all over before daylight. Mr. Stuart went forward with the first loads, and took his station at the head of the portage, while Mr. Reed and Mr. M'Lellan remained at the foot to forward the remainder.

The day dawned before the transportation was completed. Some of the fifty Indians who had remained on the south side of the river, perceived what was going on, and, feeling themselves too weak for an attack, gave the alarm to those on the opposite side, upwards of a hundred of whom embarked in several large canoes. Two loads of goods yet remained to be brought up. Mr. Stuart despatched some of the people for one of the loads, with a request to Mr. Reed to retain with him as many men as he thought necessary to guard the remaining load, as he suspected hostile intentions on the part of the Indians. Mr. Reed, however, refused to retain any of them, saying that M'Lellan and himself were sufficient to protect the small quantity that remained. The men accordingly departed with the load, while Reed and M'Lellan continued to mount guard over the residue. By this time, a number of the canoes had arrived from the opposite side. As they approached the shore, the unlucky tin box of John Reed, shining afar like the brilliant helmet of Euryalus, caught their eyes. No sooner did the canoes touch the shore, than they leaped forward on the rocks, set up a war whoop, and sprang forward to secure the glittering prize. Mr. M'Lellan, who was at the river bank, advanced to guard the goods, when one of the savages attempted to hoodwink him with his buffalo robe with one hand, and to stab him with the other. M'Lellan sprang back just far enough to avoid the blow, and raising his rifle, shot the ruffian through the heart.

In the meantime, Reed, who with the want of forethought of an Irishman, had neglected to remove the leathern cover from the lock of his rifle, was fumbling at the fastenings, when he received a blow on the head with a war club that laid him senseless on the ground. In a twinkling he was stripped of his rifle and pistols, and the tin box, the cause of all this onslaught, was borne off in triumph.

At this critical juncture, Mr. Stuart, who had heard the war whoop, hastened to the scene of action with Ben Jones, and seven others of the men. When he arrived, Reed was weltering in his blood, and an Indian standing over him and about to despatch him with a tomahawk. Stuart gave the word, when Ben Jones levelled his rifle, and shot the miscreant on the spot. The men then gave a cheer, and charged upon the main body of the savages, who took to instant flight. Reed was now raised from the ground, and borne senseless and bleeding to the upper end of the portage. Preparations were made to launch the canoes and embark in all haste, when it was found that they were too leaky to be put in the water, and that the oars had been left at the foot of the falls. A scene of confusion now ensued. The Indians were whooping and yelling, and running about like fiends. A panic seized upon the men, at being thus suddenly checked, the hearts of some of the Canadians died within them, and two young men actually fainted away. The moment they recovered their senses, Mr. Stuart ordered that they should be deprived of their arms, their under garments taken off, and that a piece of cloth should be tied round their waists, in imitation of a squaw; an Indian punishment for cowardice. Thus equipped, they were stowed away among the goods in one of the canoes. This ludicrous affair excited the mirth of the bolder spirits, even in the midst of their perils, and roused the pride of the wavering. The Indians having crossed back again to the north side, order was restored, some of the hands were sent back for the oars, others set to work to caulk and launch the canoes, and in a little while all were embarked and were continuing their voyage along the southern shore.

No sooner had they departed, than the Indians returned to the scene of action, bore off their two comrades, who had been shot, one of whom was still living, and returned to their village. Here they killed two horses; and drank the hot blood to give fierceness to their courage. They painted and arrayed themselves hideously for battle; performed the dead dance round the slain, and raised the war song of vengeance. Then mounting their horses, to the number of four hundred and fifty men, and brandishing their weapons, they set off along the northern bank of the river, to get ahead of the canoes, lie in wait for them, and take a terrible revenge on the white men.

They succeeded in getting some distance above the canoes without being discovered, and were crossing the river to post themselves on the side along which the white men were coasting, when they were fortunately descried. Mr. Stuart and his companions were immediately on the alert. As they drew near to the place where the savages had crossed, they observed them posted among steep and overhanging rocks, close along which the canoes would have to pass. Finding that the enemy had the advantage of the ground, the whites stopped short when within five hundred yards of them, and discharged and reloaded their pieces. They then made a fire, and dressed the wounds of Mr. Reed, who had received five severe gashes in the head. This being done, they lashed the canoes together, fastened them to a rock at a small distance from the shore, and there awaited the menaced attack.

They had not been long posted in this manner, when they saw a canoe approaching. It contained the war chief of the tribe, and three of his principal warriors. He drew near, and made a long harangue, in which he informed them that they had killed one and wounded another of his nation; that the relations of the slain cried out for vengeance, and he had been compelled to lead them to the fight. Still he wished to spare unnecessary bloodshed; he proposed, therefore, that Mr. Reed, who, he observed, was little better than a dead man, might be given up to be sacrificed to the manes of the deceased warrior. This would appease the fury of his friends; the hatchet would then be buried, and all thenceforward would be friends. The answer was a stern refusal and a defiance, and the war chief saw that the canoes were well prepared for a vigorous defence. He withdrew, therefore, and, returning to his warriors among the rocks held long deliberations. Blood for blood is a principle in Indian equity and Indian honor; but though the inhabitants of Wish-ram were men of war, they were likewise men of traffic, and it was suggested that honor for once might give way to profit. A negotiation was accordingly opened with the white men, and after some diplomacy, the matter was compromised for a blanket to cover the dead, and some tobacco to be smoked by the living. This being granted, the heroes of Wish-ram crossed the river once more, returned to their village to feast upon the horses whose blood they had so vaingloriously drunk, and the travellers pursued their voyage without further molestation.

The tin case, however, containing the important despatches for New York, was irretrievably lost; the very precaution taken by the worthy Hibernian to secure his missives, had, by rendering them conspicuous, produced their robbery. The object of his over-land journey, therefore, being defeated, he gave up the expedition. The whole party repaired with Mr. Robert Stuart to the establishment of Mr. David Stuart, on the Oakinagan River. After remaining here two or three days, they all set out on their return to Astoria, accompanied by Mr. David Stuart. This gentleman had a large quantity of beaver skins at his establishment, but did not think it prudent to take them with him, fearing the levy of "black mail" at the falls.

On their way down, when below the forks of the Columbia, they were hailed one day from the shore in English. Looking around, they descried two wretched men, entirely naked. They pulled to shore; the men came up and made themselves known. They proved to be Mr. Crooks and his faithful follower, John Day.

The reader will recollect, that Mr. Crooks, with Day and four Canadians, had been so reduced by famine and fatigue, that Mr. Hunt was obliged to leave them, in the month of December, on the banks of the Snake River. Their situation was the more critical, as they were in the neighborhood of a band of Shoshonies, whose horses had been forcibly seized by Mr. Hunt's party for provisions. Mr. Crooks remained here twenty days, detained by the extremely reduced state of John Day, who was utterly unable to travel, and whom he would not abandon, as Day had been in his employ on the Missouri, and had always proved himself most faithful. Fortunately the Shoshonies did not offer to molest them. They had never before seen white men, and seemed to entertain some superstitions with regard to them, for, though they would encamp near them in the day time, they would move off with their tents in the night; and finally disappeared, without taking leave.

When Day was sufficiently recovered to travel, they kept feebly on, sustaining themselves as well as they could, until in the month of February, when three of the Canadians, fearful of perishing with want, left Mr. Crooks on a small river, on the road by which Mr. Hunt had passed in quest of Indians. Mr. Crooks followed Mr. Hunt's track in the snow for several days, sleeping as usual in the open air, and suffering all kinds of hardships. At length, coming to a low prairie, he lost every appearance of the "trail," and wandered during the remainder of the winter in the mountains, subsisting sometimes on horse meat, sometimes on beavers and their skins, and a part of the time on roots.

About the last of March, the other Canadian gave out, and was left with a lodge of Shoshonies; but Mr. Crooks and John Day still kept on, and finding the snow sufficiently diminished, undertook, from Indian information, to cross the last mountain ridge. They happily succeeded, and afterwards fell in with the Wallah Wallahs, a tribe of Indians inhabiting the banks of a river of the same name, and reputed as being frank, hospitable and sincere. They proved worthy of the character, for they received the poor wanderers kindly, killed a horse for them to eat, and directed them on their way to the Columbia. They struck the river about the middle of April, and advanced down it one hundred miles, until they came within about twenty miles of the falls.

Here they met with some of the "chivalry" of that noted pass, who received them in a friendly way, and set food before them; but, while they were satisfying their hunger, perfidiously seized their rifles. They then stripped them naked, and drove them off, refusing the entreaties of Mr. Crooks for a flint and steel of which they had robbed him; and threatening his life if he did not instantly depart.

In this forlorn plight, still worse off than before, they renewed their wanderings. They now sought to find their way back to the hospitable Wallah Wallahs, and had advanced eighty miles along the river, when fortunately, on the very morning that they were going to leave the Columbia, and strike inland, the canoes of Mr. Stuart hove in sight.

It is needless to describe the joy of these poor men at once more finding themselves among countrymen and friends, or of the honest and hearty welcome with which they were received by their fellow adventurers. The whole party now continued down the river, passed all the dangerous places without interruption, and arrived safely at Astoria on the 11th of May.

Chapter XLII

HAVING TRACED the fortunes of the two expeditions by sea and land to the mouth of the Columbia, and presented a view of affairs at Astoria, we will return for a moment to the master spirit of the enterprize, who regulated the springs of Astoria, at his residence in New York.

It will be remembered, that a part of the plan of Mr. Astor was to furnish the Russian fur establishment on the north west coast with regular supplies, so as to render it independent of those casual vessels which cut up the trade and supplied the natives with arms. This plan had been countenanced by our own government, and likewise by Count Pahlen, the Russian minister at Washington. As its views, however, were important and extensive, and might eventually affect a wide course of commerce, Mr. Astor was desirous of establishing a complete arrangement on the subject with the Russian American Fur Company, under the sanction of the Russian government. For this purpose, in March, 1811, he despatched a confidential agent to S' Petersburgh, fully empowered to enter into the requisite negotiations. A passage was given to this gentleman by the government of the United States, in the John Adams, one of its armed vessels, bound to a European port.

The next step of Mr. Astor was, to despatch the annual ship contemplated on his general plan. He had as yet heard nothing of the success of the previous expeditions, and had to proceed upon the presumption that every thing had been effected according to his instructions. He accordingly fitted out a fine ship of four hundred and ninety tons, called the Beaver, and freighted her with a valuable cargo destined for the factory, at the mouth of the Columbia, the trade along the coast, and the supply of the Russian establishment. In this ship embarked a reinforcement, consisting of a partner, five clerks, fifteen American laborers, and six Canadian voyageurs. In choosing his agents for his first expedition, Mr. Astor had been obliged to have recourse to British subjects experienced in the Canadian fur trade; henceforth it was his intention, as much as possible, to select Americans, so as to secure an ascendancy of American influence in the management of the company, and to make it decidedly national.

Accordingly, Mr. John Clarke, the partner who took the lead in the present expedition, was a native of the United States, though he had passed much of his life in the north west, having been employed in the fur trade since the age of sixteen. Most of the clerks were young gentlemen of good connections in the American cities, some of whom embarked in the hope of gain, others through the mere spirit of adventure incident to youth.

The instructions given by Mr. Astor to Captain Sowle, the commander of the Beaver, were, in some respects, hypothetical, in consequence of the uncertainty resting upon the previous steps of the enterprize.

He was to touch at the Sandwich islands, enquire about the fortunes of the Tonquin, and whether an establishment had been formed at the mouth of the Columbia. If so, he was to take as many Sandwich islanders as his ship would accommodate, and proceed thither. On arriving at the river, he was to observe great caution, for even if an establishment should have been formed, it might have fallen into hostile hands. He was, therefore, to put in as if by casualty or distress, to give himself out as a coasting trader, and to say nothing about his ship being owned by Mr. Astor, until he had ascertained that every thing was right. In that case, he was to land such part of his cargo as was intended for the establishment, and to proceed to New Archangel with the supplies intended for the Russian post at that place, where he could receive peltries in payment. With these he was to return to Astoria; take in the furs collected there, and, having completed his cargo by trading along the coast, was to proceed to Canton. The captain received the same injunctions that had been given to Captain Thorn of the Tonquin, of great caution and circumspection in his intercourse with the natives, and that he should not permit more than one or two to be on board at a time.

The Beaver sailed from New York on the 10th of October, 1811, and reached the Sandwich islands without any occurrence of moment. Here a rumor was heard of the disastrous fate of the Tonquin. Deep solicitude was felt by every one on board for the fate of both expeditions, by sea and land. Doubts were entertained whether any establishment had been formed at the mouth of the Columbia, or whether any of the company would be found there. After much deliberation, the captain took twelve Sandwich islanders on board, for the service of the factory, should there be one in existence, and proceeded on his voyage.

On the 6th of May he arrived off the mouth of the Columbia, and running as near as possible, fired two signal guns. No answer was returned, nor was there any signal to be descried. Night coming on, the ship stood out to sea, and every heart drooped as the land faded away. On the following morning they again ran in within four miles of the shore, and fired other signal guns, but still without reply. A boat was then despatched, to sound the channel, and attempt an entrance; but returned without success, there being a tremendous swell, and breakers. Signal guns were fired again in the evening, but equally in vain, and once more the ship stood off to sea for the night. The captain now gave up all hope of finding any establishment at the place, and indulged in the most gloomy apprehensions. He feared his predecessors had been massacred before they had reached their place of destination; or if they should have erected a factory, that it had been surprised and destroyed by the natives.

In this moment of doubt and uncertainty, Mr. Clarke announced his determination, in case of the worst, to found an establishment with the present party, and all hands bravely engaged to stand by him in the undertaking. The next morning the ship stood in for the third time, and fired three signal guns, but with little hope of reply. To the great joy of the crew, three distinct guns were heard in answer. The apprehensions of all but Captain Sowle were now at rest. That cautious commander recollected the instructions given him by Mr. Astor, and determined to proceed with great circumspection. He was well aware of Indian treachery and cunning. It was not impossible, he observed, that these cannon might have been fired by the savages themselves. They might have surprised the fort, massacred its inmates; and these signal guns might only be decoys to lure him across the bar, that they might have a chance of cutting him off, and seizing his vessel.

At length a white flag was descried hoisted as a signal on Cape Disappointment. The passengers pointed to it in triumph, but the captain did not yet dismiss his doubts. A beacon fire blazed through the night on the same place, but the captain observed that all these signals might be treacherous.

On the following morning, May 9th, the vessel came to anchor off Cape Disappointment, outside of the bar. Towards noon an Indian canoe was seen making for the ship, and all hands were ordered to be on the alert. A few moments afterwards, a barge was perceived following the canoe. The hopes and fears of those on board of the ship were in tumultuous agitation, as the boat drew nigh that was to let them know the fortunes of the enterprize, and the fate of their predecessors. The captain, who was haunted with the idea of possible treachery, did not suffer his curiosity to get the better of his caution, but ordered a party of his men under arms, to receive the visitors. The canoe came first along side, in which were Comcomly and six Indians; in the barge were M'Dougall, M'Lellan, and eight Canadians. A little conversation with these gentlemen dispelled all the captain's fears, and the Beaver crossing the bar under their pilotage, anchored safely in Baker's bay.

Chapter XLIII

Active operations at Astoria—Various expeditions fitted out—Robert Stuart and a party destined for New York—Singular conduct of John Day—His fate—Piratical pass and hazardous portage—Rattlesnakes—Their abhorrence of tobacco—Arrival among the Wallah Wallahs—Purchase of horses—Departure of Stuart and his band for the mountains.

THE ARRIVAL of the Beaver with a reinforcement and supplies, gave new life and vigor to affairs at Astoria. These were means for extending the operations of the establishment, and founding interior trading posts. Two parties were immediately set on foot to proceed severally under the command of Messrs. M'Kenzie and Clarke, and establish posts above the forks of the Columbia, at points where most rivalry and opposition were apprehended from the North West Company.

A third party, headed by Mr. David Stuart, was to repair with supplies to the post of that gentleman on the Oakinagan. In addition to these expeditions, a fourth was necessary to convey despatches to Mr. Astor, at New York, in place of those unfortunately lost by John Reed. The safe conveyance of these despatches was highly important, as by them Mr. Astor would receive an account of the state of the factory, and regulate his reinforcements and supplies accordingly. The mission was one of peril and hardship, and required a man of nerve and vigor. It was confided to Robert Stuart, who, though he had never been across the mountains, and a very young man, had given proofs of his competency to the task. Four trusty and well-tried men, who had come over land in Mr. Hunt's expedition, were given as his guides and hunters. These were Ben Jones and John Day, the Kentuckians, and André Vallar and Francis Le Clerc, Canadians. Mr. M'Lellan again expressed his determination to take this opportunity of returning to the Atlantic states. In this he was joined by Mr. Crooks, who, notwithstanding all that he had suffered in the dismal journey of the preceding winter, was ready to retrace his steps and brave every danger and hardship, rather than remain at Astoria. This little handful of adventurous men we propose to accompany in its long and perilous peregrinations.

The several parties we have mentioned all set off in company on the 29th of June, under a salute of cannon from the fort. They were to keep together, for mutual protection, through the piratical passes of the river, and to separate, on their different destinations, at the forks of the Columbia. Their number, collectively, was nearly sixty, consisting of partners and clerks, Canadian voyageurs, Sandwich islanders, and American hunters; and they embarked in two barges and ten canoes.

They had scarcely got under way, when John Day, the Kentucky hunter, became restless, and uneasy, and extremely wayward in his deportment. This caused surprise, for in general he was remarked for his cheerful, manly deportment. It was supposed that the recollection of past sufferings might harass his mind in undertaking to retrace the scenes where they had been experienced. As the expedition advanced, however, his agitation increased. He began to talk wildly and incoherently, and to show manifest symptoms of derangement.

Mr. Crooks now informed his companions that in his desolate wanderings through the Snake River country during the preceding winter, in which he had been accompanied by John Day, the poor fellow's wits had been partially unsettled by the sufferings and horrors through which they had passed, and he doubted whether they had ever been restored to perfect sanity. It was still hoped that this agitation of spirit might pass away as they proceeded; but, on the contrary, it grew more and more violent. His comrades endeavored to divert his mind and to draw him into rational conversation, but he only became the more exasperated, uttering wild and incoherent ravings. The sight of any of the natives put him in an absolute fury, and he would heap on them the most opprobrious epithets; recollecting, no doubt, what he had suffered from Indian robbers.

On the evening of the 2d of July he became absolutely frantic, and attempted to destroy himself. Being disarmed, he sank into quietude, and professed the greatest remorse for the crime he had meditated. He then pretended to sleep, and having thus lulled suspicion, suddenly sprang up, just before daylight, seized a pair of loaded pistols, and endeavored to blow out his brains. In his hurry he fired too high, and the balls passed over his head. He was instantly secured, and placed under a guard in one of the boats. How to dispose of him was now the question, as it was impossible to keep him with the expedition. Fortunately Mr. Stuart met with some Indians accustomed to trade with Astoria. These undertook to conduct John Day back to the factory, and deliver him there in safety. It was with the utmost concern that his comrades saw the poor fellow depart; for, independent of his invaluable services as a first rate hunter, his frank and loyal qualities had made him a universal favorite. It may be as well to add that the Indians executed their task faithfully, and landed John Day among his friends at Astoria; but his constitution was completely broken by the hardships he had undergone, and he died within a year.

On the evening of the 6th of July the party arrived at the piratical pass of the river, and encamped at the foot of the first rapid. The next day, before the commencement of the portage, the greatest precautions were taken to guard against lurking treachery, or open attack. The weapons of every man were put in order, and his cartridge box replenished. Each one wore a kind of surcoat made of the skin of the elk, reaching from his neck to his knees, and answering the purpose of a shirt of mail, for it was arrow proof, and could even resist a musket ball at the distance of ninety yards. Thus armed and equipped, they posted their forces in military style. Five of the officers took their stations at each end of the portage, which was between three and four miles in length; a number of men mounted guard at short distances along the heights immediately overlooking the river, while the residue thus protected from surprise, employed themselves below in dragging up the barges and canoes, and carrying up the goods along the narrow margin of the rapids. With these precautions they all passed unmolested. The only accident that happened was the upsetting of one of the canoes, by which some of the goods sunk, and others floated down the stream. The alertness and rapacity of the hordes which infest these rapids, were immediately apparent. They pounced upon the floating merchandize with the keenness of regular wreckers. A bale of goods which landed upon one of the islands was immediately ripped open, one half of its contents divided among the captors, and the other half secreted in a lonely hut in a deep

ravine. Mr. Robert Stuart, however, set out in a canoe with five
men and an interpreter, ferreted out the wreckers in their
retreat, and succeeded in wresting from them their booty.

Similar precautions to those already mentioned, and to a still
greater extent, were observed in passing the long narrows, and
the falls, where they would be exposed to the depredations of
the chivalry of Wish-ram, and its freebooting neighborhood.
In fact, they had scarcely set their first watch one night, when
an alarm of "Indians!" was given. "To arms!" was the cry, and
every man was at his post in an instant. The alarm was explained; a war party of Shoshonies had surprised a canoe of the
natives just below the encampment, had murdered four men
and two women, and it was apprehended they would attack
the camp. The boats and canoes were immediately hauled up,
a breastwork was made of them, and the packages, forming
three sides of a square, with the river in the rear, and thus the
party remained fortified throughout the night.

The dawn, however, dispelled the alarm; the portage was
conducted in peace; the vagabond warriors of the vicinity
hovered about them while at work, but were kept at a wary
distance. They regarded the loads of merchandize with wistful eyes, but seeing the "long beards" so formidable in number, and so well prepared for action, they made no attempt
either by open force or sly pilfering to collect their usual toll,
but maintained a peaceful demeanor, and were afterwards rewarded for their good conduct with presents of tobacco.

Fifteen days were consumed in ascending from the foot of
the first rapid, to the head of the falls, a distance of about
eighty miles, but full of all kinds of obstructions. Having happily accomplished these difficult portages, the party, on the
19th of July, arrived at a smoother part of the river, and pursued their way up the stream with greater speed and facility.

They were now in the neighborhood where Mr. Crooks and
John Day had been so perfidiously robbed and stripped a few
months previously, when confiding in the proffered hospitality
of a ruffian band. On landing at night, therefore, a vigilant
guard was maintained about the camp. On the following
morning a number of Indians made their appearance, and
came prowling round the party while at breakfast. To his great
delight, Mr. Crooks recognized among them two of the mis-

creants by whom he had been robbed. They were instantly seized, bound hand and foot, and thrown into one of the canoes. Here they lay in doleful fright, expecting summary execution. Mr. Crooks, however, was not of a revengeful disposition, and agreed to release the culprits as soon as the pillaged property should be restored. Several savages immediately started off in different directions, and before night the rifles of Crooks and Day were produced; several of the smaller articles pilfered from them, however, could not be recovered.

The bands of the culprits were then removed, and they lost no time in taking their departure, still under the influence of abject terror, and scarcely crediting their senses that they had escaped the merited punishment of their offences.

The country on each side of the river now began to assume a different character. The hills, and cliffs, and forests, disappeared; vast sandy plains, scantily clothed here and there with short tufts of grass, parched by the summer sun, stretched far away to the north and south. The river was occasionally obstructed with rocks and rapids, but often there were smooth placid intervals, where the current was gentle, and the boatmen were enabled to lighten their labors with the assistance of the sail.

The natives in this part of the river resided entirely on the northern side. They were hunters, as well as fishermen, and had horses in plenty. Some of these were purchased by the party, as provisions, and killed on the spot, though they occasionally found a difficulty in procuring fuel wherewith to cook them. One of the greatest dangers that beset the travellers in this part of their expedition, was the vast number of rattlesnakes which infested the rocks about the rapids and portages, and on which the men were in danger of treading. They were often found, too, in quantities about the encampments. In one place, a nest of them lay coiled together, basking in the sun. Several guns loaded with shot were discharged at them, and thirty seven killed and wounded. To prevent any unwelcome visits from them in the night, tobacco was occasionally strewed around the tents, a weed for which they have a very proper abhorrence.

On the 28th of July the travellers arrived at the mouth of the Wallah Wallah, a bright, clear stream, about six feet deep, and fifty five yards wide, which flows rapidly over a bed of sand and gravel, and throws itself into the Columbia, a few miles below Lewis River. Here the combined parties that had thus far voyaged together, were to separate, each for its particular destination.

On the banks of the Wallah Wallah lived the hospitable tribe of the same name who had succored Mr. Crooks and John Day in the time of their extremity. No sooner did they hear of the arrival of the party, than they hastened to greet them. They built a great bonfire on the bank of the river, before the camp, and men and women danced round it to the cadence of their songs, in which they sang the praises of the white men, and welcomed them to their country.

On the following day a traffic was commenced, to procure horses for such of the party as intended to proceed by land. The Wallah Wallahs are an equestrian tribe. The equipments of their horses were rude and inconvenient. High saddles, roughly made of deer skin, stuffed with hair, which chafe the horse's back, and leave it raw; wooden stirrups, with a thong of raw hide wrapped round them; and for bridles they have cords of twisted horse hair, which they tie round the under jaw. They are like most Indians, bold, but hard riders, and when on horseback gallop about the most dangerous places, without fear for themselves, or pity for their steeds.

From these people Mr. Stuart purchased twenty horses for his party; some for the saddle, and others to transport the baggage. He was fortunate in procuring a noble animal for his own use, which was praised by the Indians for its great speed and bottom, and a high price set upon it. No people understand better the value of a horse, than these equestrian tribes; and no where is speed a greater requisite, as they frequently engage in the chase of the antelope, one of the fleetest of animals. Even after the Indian who sold this boasted horse to Mr. Stuart had concluded his bargain, he lingered about the animal, seeming loth to part from him, and to be sorry for what he had done.

A day or two were employed by Mr. Stuart in arranging packages and pack saddles, and making other preparations for his long and arduous journey. His party, by the loss of John Day, was now reduced to six, a small number for such an expedition. They were young men, however, full of courage, health, and good spirits, and stimulated, rather than appalled by danger.

On the morning of the 31st of July, all preparations being concluded, Mr. Stuart and his little band mounted their steeds and took a farewell of their fellow travellers, who gave them three hearty cheers as they set out on their dangerous journey. The course they took was to the southeast, towards the fated region of the Snake River. At an immense distance rose a chain of craggy mountains, which they would have to traverse; they were the same among which the travellers had experienced such sufferings from cold during the preceding winter, and from their azure tints, when seen at a distance, had received the name of the Blue Mountains.

Chapter XLIV

Route of Mr. Stuart—Dreary wilds—Thirsty travelling—A grove and streamlet—The Blue Mountains—A fertile plain with rivulets—Sulphur spring—Route along Snake River— Rumors of white men—The Snake and his horse—A Snake guide—A midnight decampment—Unexpected meeting with old comrades—Story of trappers' hardships—Salmon falls—A great fishery—Mode of spearing salmon—Arrival at the Caldron Linn—State of the caches—New resolution of the three Kentucky trappers.

IN RETRACING the route which had proved so disastrous to Mr. Hunt's party during the preceding winter, Mr. Stuart had trusted, in the present more favorable season, to find easy travelling and abundant supplies. On these great wastes and wilds, however, each season has its peculiar hardships. The travellers had not proceeded far, before they found themselves among naked and arid hills, with a soil composed of sand and clay, baked and brittle, that to all appearance had never been visited by the dews of heaven.

Not a spring, or pool, or running stream was to be seen; the sunburnt country was seamed and cut up by dry ravines, the beds of winter torrents, serving only to balk the hopes of man and beast, with the sight of dusty channels where water had once poured along in floods.

For a long summer day they continued onward without halting; a burning sky above their heads, a parched desert beneath their feet, with just wind enough to raise the light sand from the knolls, and envelope them in stifling clouds. The sufferings from thirst became intense; a fine young dog, their only companion of the kind, gave out, and expired. Evening drew on without any prospect of relief, and they were almost reduced to despair, when they descried something that looked like a fringe of forest, along the horizon. All were inspired with new hope, for they knew that on these arid wastes, in the neighborhood of trees, there is always water.

They now quickened their pace; the horses seemed to understand their motives, and to partake of their anticipations, for, though before, almost ready to give out, they now required neither whip nor spur. With all their exertions, it was late in the night before they drew near to the trees. As they approached, they heard, with transport, the rippling of a shallow stream. No sooner did the refreshing sound reach the ears of the horses, than the poor animals snuffed the air, rushed forward with ungovernable eagerness, and, plunging their muzzles into the water, drank until they seemed in danger of bursting. Their riders had but little more discretion, and required repeated draughts to quench their excessive thirst. Their weary march that day had been forty five miles, over a tract that might rival the deserts of Africa for aridity. Indeed, the sufferings of the traveller on these American deserts, is frequently more severe than in the wastes of Africa or Asia, from being less habituated and prepared to cope with them.

On the banks of this blessed stream the travellers encamped for the night; and so great had been their fatigue, and so sound and sweet was their sleep, that it was a late hour the next morning before they awoke. They now recognized the little river to be the Umatalla, the same on the banks of which Mr. Hunt and his followers had arrived after their painful struggle through the Blue Mountains, and experienced such a kind relief in the friendly camp of the Sciatogas.

That range of Blue Mountains now extended in the distance before them; they were the same among which poor Michel Carriere had perished. They form the southeast boundary of the great plains along the Columbia, dividing the waters of its main stream from those of Lewis River. They are, in fact, a part of a long chain, which stretches over a great extent of country, and includes in its links the Snake River Mountains.

The day was somewhat advanced before the travellers left the shady banks of the Umatalla. Their route gradually took them among the Blue Mountains, which assumed the most rugged aspect on a near approach. They were shagged with dense and gloomy forests, and cut up by deep and precipitous ravines, extremely toilsome to the horses. Sometimes the travellers had to follow the course of some brawling stream, with a broken, rocky bed, which the shouldering cliffs and promontories on either side, obliged them frequently to cross and recross. For some miles they struggled forward through these savage and darkly wooded defiles, when all at once the whole landscape changed, as if by magic. The rude mountains and rugged ravines softened into beautiful hills, and intervening meadows, with rivulets winding through fresh herbage, and sparkling and murmuring over gravelly beds, the whole forming a verdant and pastoral scene, which derived additional charms from being locked up in the bosom of such a hard-hearted region.

Emerging from the chain of Blue Mountains, they descended upon a vast plain, almost a dead level, sixty miles in circumference, of excellent soil, with fine streams meandering through it in every direction, their courses marked out in the wide landscape, by serpentine lines of cotton wood trees, and willows, which fringed their banks, and afforded sustenance to great numbers of beavers and otters.

In traversing this plain, they passed, close to the skirts of the hills, a great pool of water, three hundred yards in circumference, fed by a sulphur spring, about ten feet in diameter, boiling up in one corner. The vapor from this pool was extremely noisome, and tainted the air for a considerable distance. The place was much frequented by elk, which were found in considerable numbers in the adjacent mountains, and their horns, shed in the spring time, were strewed in every direction around the pond.

On the 10th of August, they reached the main body of Woodpile creek, the same stream which Mr. Hunt had ascended in the preceding year, shortly after his separation from Mr. Crooks.

On the banks of this stream they saw a herd of nineteen antelopes; a sight so unusual in that part of the country, that at first they doubted the evidence of their senses. They tried by every means to get within shot of them, but they were too shy and fleet, and after alternately bounding to a distance and then stopping to gaze with capricious curiosity at the hunter, they at length scampered out of sight.

On the 12th of August, the travellers arrived on the banks of Snake River, the scene of so many trials and mishaps to all of the present party excepting Mr. Stuart. They struck the river just above the place where it entered the mountains through which Messrs. Hunt and Crooks had vainly endeavored to find a passage. The river was here a rapid stream four hundred yards in width, with high sandy banks and here and there a scanty growth of willow. Up the southern side of the river they now bent their course, intending to visit the caches made by Mr. Hunt at the Caldron Linn.

On the second evening a solitary Snake Indian visited their camp at a late hour and informed them that there was a white man residing at one of the cantonments of his tribe about a day's journey higher up the river. It was immediately concluded that he must be one of the poor fellows, of Mr. Hunt's party, who had given out, exhausted by hunger and fatigue, in the wretched journey of the preceding winter. All present, who had borne a part in the sufferings of that journey, were eager now to press forward and bring relief to a lost comrade. Early the next morning, therefore, they pushed forward with unusual alacrity. For two days, however, did they travel without being able to find any trace of such a straggler.

On the evening of the second day they arrived at a place where a large river came in from the east, which was renowned among all the wandering hordes of the Snake nation for its salmon fishery, that fish being taken in incredible quantities in this neighborhood. Here, therefore, during the fishing season, the Snake Indians resort from far and near, to lay in their stock of salmon, which, with esculent roots, forms the principal food of the inhabitants of these barren regions.

On the bank of a small stream emptying into Snake River at this place, Mr. Stuart found an encampment of Shoshonies. He made the usual inquiry of them concerning the white man of whom he had received intelligence. No such person was dwelling among them, but they said there were white men residing with some of their nation on the opposite side of the river. This was still more animating information. Mr. Crooks now hoped that these might be the men of his party who, disheartened by perils and hardships, had preferred to remain among the Indians. Others thought they might be Mr. Miller and the hunters who had left the main body at Henry's fort, to trap among the mountain streams. Mr. Stuart halted, therefore, in the neighborhood of the Shoshonie lodges and sent an Indian across the river to seek out the white men in question and bring them to his camp.

The travellers passed a restless, miserable night. The place swarmed with myriads of musquitoes, which, with their stings and their music set all sleep at defiance. The morning dawn found them in a feverish irritable mood, and their spleen was completely aroused by the return of the Indian without any intelligence of the white men. They now considered themselves the dupes of Indian falsehoods and resolved to put no more confidence in Snakes. They soon, however, forgot this resolution. In the course of the morning an Indian came gallopping after them. Mr. Stuart waited to receive him. No sooner had he come up than, dismounting and throwing his arms round the neck of Mr. Stuart's horse, he began to kiss and caress the animal, who, on his part, seemed by no means surprized or displeased with his salutation. Mr. Stuart, who valued his horse highly, was somewhat annoyed by these transports: the cause of them was soon explained. The Snake said the horse had belonged to him and been the best in his possession, and that it had been stolen by the Wallah Wallahs. Mr. Stuart was by no means pleased with this recognition of his steed, nor disposed to admit any claim on the part of its ancient owner. In fact it was a noble animal, admirably shaped, of free and generous spirit, graceful in movement and fleet as an antelope. It was his intention if possible, to take the horse to New York, and present him to Mr. Astor.

In the mean time some of the party came up and immediately recognized in the Snake an old friend and ally. He was, in fact, one of the two guides who had conducted Mr. Hunt's party, in the preceding autumn, across Mad River Mountain to Fort Henry, and who subsequently departed with Mr. Miller and his fellow trappers to conduct them to a good trapping ground. The reader may recollect that these two trusty Snakes were engaged by Mr. Hunt to return and take charge of the horses which the party intended to leave at Fort Henry, when they should embark in canoes.

The party now crowded round the Snake and began to question him with eagerness. His replies were somewhat vague, and but partially understood. He told a long story about the horses, from which it appeared that they had been stolen by various wandering bands, and scattered in different directions. The cache too had been plundered, and the saddles

and other equipments carried off. His information concerning
Mr. Miller and his comrades was not more satisfactory. They
had trapped for some time about the upper streams, but had
fallen into the hands of a marauding party of Crows, who had
robbed them of horses, weapons and every thing.

Further questioning brought forth further intelligence, but
all of a disastrous kind. About ten days previously he had met
with three other white men, in very miserable plight, having
one horse each, and but one rifle among them. They also had
been plundered and maltreated by the Crows, those universal
freebooters. The Snake endeavored to pronounce the names
of these three men, and as far as his imperfect sounds could be
understood they were supposed to be three of the party of
four hunters, viz. Carson, S' Michel, Detayé and Delaunay,
who were detached from Mr. Hunt's party on the 28th of September to trap beaver on the head waters of the Columbia.

In the course of conversation the Indian informed them
that the route by which Mr. Hunt had crossed the Rocky
Mountains, was very bad and circuitous, and that he knew
one much shorter and easier. Mr. Stuart urged him to accompany them as guide, promising to reward him with a pistol
with powder and ball, a knife, an awl, some blue beads, a
blanket and a looking glass. Such a catalogue of riches was too
tempting to be resisted; beside, the poor Snake languished after the prairies; he was tired, he said, of salmon, and longed
for buffalo meat, and to have a grand buffalo hunt beyond the
mountains. He departed, therefore, with all speed to get his
arms and equipments for the journey, promising to rejoin
the party the next day. He kept his word, and, as he no
longer said any thing to Mr. Stuart on the subject of the pet
horse they journeyed very harmoniously together; though
now and then the Snake would regard his quondam steed with
a wistful eye.

They had not travelled many miles when they came to a
great bend of the river. Here the Snake informed them that,
by cutting across the hills they would save many miles of distance. The route across however would be a good day's journey. He advised them, therefore, to encamp here for the night
and set off early in the morning. They took his advice, though
they had come but nine miles that day.

On the following morning they rose bright and early, to
ascend the hills. On mustering their little party the guide was
missing. They supposed him to be somewhere in the neighborhood and proceeded to collect the horses. The vaunted
steed of Mr. Stuart was not to be found. A suspicion flashed
upon his mind. Search for the horse of the Snake!—He likewise was gone—the tracks of two horses, one after the other
were found, making off from the camp. They appeared as if
one horse had been mounted and the other led. They were
traced for a few miles above the camp until they both crossed
the river. It was plain, the Snake had taken an Indian mode of
recovering his horse, having quietly decamped with him in
the night.

New vows were made never more to trust in Snakes or any
other Indians. It was determined also to maintain hereafter the
strictest vigilance over their horses, dividing the night into
three watches and one person mounting guard at a time. They
resolved also to keep along the river instead of taking the short
cut recommended by the fugitive Snake, whom they now set
down for a thorough deceiver. The heat of the weather was
oppressive, and their horses were at times rendered almost
frantic by the stings of the prairie flies. The nights were suffo-
cating, and it was almost impossible to sleep from the swarms
of musquitoes.

On the 20th of August they resumed their march, keeping along the prairie parallel to Snake River. The day was sultry and some of the party, being parched with thirst, left the
line of march and scrambled down the bank of the river to
drink. The bank was overhung with willows, beneath which,
to their surprize, they beheld a man fishing. No sooner did
he see them than he uttered an exclamation of joy. It proved
to be John Hoback, one of their lost comrades. They had
scarcely exchanged greetings when three other men came
out from among the willows. They were Mr. Joseph Miller,
Jacob Rezner, and Robinson, the scalped Kentuckian, the
veteran of the Bloody ground.

The reader will perhaps recollect the abrupt and wilful
manner in which Mr. Miller threw up his interest as a partner
of the Company, and departed from Fort Henry in company
with these three trappers and a fourth named Cass. He may

likewise recognize in Robinson, Rezner and Hoback, the trio of Kentucky hunters, who had originally been in the service of Mr. Henry, and whom Mr. Hunt found floating down the Missouri, on their way homeward; and prevailed upon, once more to cross the mountains.

The haggard looks and naked condition of these men proved how much they had suffered. After leaving Mr. Hunt's party they had made their way about two hundred miles to the south ward, where they trapped beaver on a river which, according to their account discharged itself into the Ocean to the south of the Columbia, but which we apprehend to be Bear River, a stream emptying itself into Lake Bonneville, an immense body of salt water, west of the Rocky Mountains.

Having collected a considerable quantity of beaver skins, they made them into packs, loaded their horses and steered two hundred miles due east. Here they came upon an encampment of sixty lodges of Arapahayas, an outlawed band of the Arapahoes, and notorious robbers. These fell upon the poor trappers; robbed them of their peltries, most of their clothing, and several of their horses. They were glad to escape with their lives, and without being entirely stripped, and after proceeding about fifty miles further, made their halt for the winter.

Early in the spring they resumed their wayfaring but were unluckily overtaken by the same ruffian horde, who levied still further contributions, and carried off the remainder of their horses excepting two. With these they continued on, suffering the greatest hardships. They still retained rifles and ammunition, but were in a desert country where neither bird nor beast was to be found. Their only chance was to keep along the rivers and subsist by fishing, but at times no fish were to be taken, and then their sufferings were horrible. One of their horses was stolen among the mountains by the Snake Indians; the other, they said, was carried off by Cass who, according to their account, "villanously left them in their extremities." Certain dark doubts and surmises were afterwards circulated concerning the fate of that poor fellow, which, if true, shewed to what a desperate state of famine his comrades had been reduced.

Being now completely unhorsed, Mr. Miller and his three companions wandered on foot for several hundred miles, enduring hunger, thirst and fatigue while traversing the barren wastes which abound beyond the Rocky Mountains. At the time they were discovered by Mr. Stuart's party they were almost famished, and were fishing for a precarious meal.

Had Mr. Stuart made the short cut across the hills, avoiding this bend of the river, or had not some of his party accidentally gone down to the margin of the stream to drink, these poor wanderers might have remained undiscovered, and have perished in the wilderness.

Nothing could exceed their joy in thus meeting with their old comrades, or the heartiness with which they were welcomed. All hands immediately encamped; and the slender stores of the party were ransacked to furnish out a suitable regale.

The next morning they all set out together; Mr. Miller and his comrades being resolved to give up the life of a trapper and accompany Mr. Stuart back to S' Louis.

For several days they kept along the course of Snake River, occasionally making short cuts across hills and promontories where there were bends in the stream. In their way they passed several camps of Shoshonies, from some of whom they procured salmon, but in general they were too wretchedly poor to furnish any thing. It was the wish of Mr. Stuart to purchase horses for the recent recruits to his party but the Indians could not be prevailed upon to part with any, alleging that they had not enough for their own use.

On the 25th of August they reached a great fishing place to which they gave the name of The Salmon falls. Here there is a perpendicular fall of twenty feet on the north side of the river, while on the south side there is a succession of rapids. The salmon are taken here in incredible quantities, as they attempt to shoot the falls. It was now a favorable season, and there were about one hundred lodges of Shoshonies busily engaged killing and drying fish. The salmon begin to leap shortly after sunrise. At this time the Indians swim to the center of the falls where some station themselves on rocks and others stand to their waists in the water, all armed with spears, with which they assail the salmon as they attempt to leap or fall back exhausted. It is an incessant slaughter so great is the throng of the fish.

The construction of the spears thus used is peculiar. The head is a straight piece of elk horn about seven inches long; on the point of which an artificial barb is made fast with twine well gummed. The head is stuck on the end of the shaft; a very long pole of willow to which it is likewise connected by a strong cord a few inches in length. When the spearsman makes a sure blow he often strikes the head of the spear through the body of the fish. It comes off readily, and leaves the salmon struggling with the string through its body, while the pole is still held by the spearsman. Were it not for the precaution of the string, the willow shaft would be snapped by the struggles and the weight of the fish.

Mr. Miller, in the course of his wanderings, had been at these falls, and had seen several thousand salmon taken in the course of one afternoon. He declared that he had seen a salmon leap a distance of about thirty feet from the commencement of the foam at the foot of the fall completely to the top.

Having purchased a good supply of salmon from the fishermen the party resumed their journey and on the twenty ninth arrived at the Caldron Linn; the eventful scene of the preceding autumn. Here the first thing that met their eyes was a memento of the perplexities of that period: the wreck of a canoe lodged between two ledges of rocks. They endeavored to get down to it, but the river banks were too high and precipitous.

They now proceeded to that part of the neighborhood where Mr. Hunt and his party had made the caches, intending to take from them such articles as belonged to Mr. Crooks, M'Lellan and the Canadians. On reaching the spot they found, to their astonishment, six of the caches open and rifled of their contents, excepting a few books which lay scattered about the vicinity. They had the appearance of having been plundered in the course of the summer. There were tracks of wolves in every direction to and from the holes, from which Mr. Stuart concluded that these animals had first been attracted to the place by the smell of the skins contained in the caches, which they had probably torn up, and that their tracks had betrayed the secret to the Indians.

The three remaining caches had not been molested: they contained a few dry goods, some ammunition and a number of beaver traps. From these Mr. Stuart took whatever was requisite for his party; he then deposited within them all his superfluous baggage, and all the books and papers scattered around; the holes were then carefully closed up and all traces of them effaced.

And here we have to record another instance of the indomitable spirit of the western trappers. No sooner had the trio of Kentucky hunters, Robinson, Rezner and Hoback, found that they could once more be fitted out for a campaign of beaver trapping, than they forgot all that they had suffered and determined upon another trial of their fortunes; preferring to take their chance in the wilderness rather than return home ragged and penniless. As to Mr. Miller he declared his curiosity and his desire of travelling through the Indian countries fully satisfied; he adhered to his determination therefore to keep on with the party to S' Louis and to return to the bosom of civilized society.

The three hunters, therefore, Robinson, Rezner and Hoback were furnished, as far as the caches and the means of Mr. Stuart's party afforded, with the requisite munitions and equipments for a "two years' hunt;" but as their fitting out was yet incomplete, they resolved to wait in this neighborhood until Mr. Reed should arrive; whose arrival might soon be expected; as he was to set out for the caches about twenty days after Mr. Stuart parted with him at the Wallah Wallah River.

Mr. Stuart gave in charge to Robinson a letter to Mr. Reed reporting his safe journey thus far, and the state in which he had found the caches. A duplicate of this letter he elevated on a pole and set it up near the place of deposit.

All things being thus arranged Mr. Stuart and his little band, now seven in number, took leave of the three hardy trappers, wishing them all possible success in their lonely and perilous sojourn in the wilderness; and we, in like manner, shall leave them to their fortunes, promising to take them up again at some future page, and to close the story of their persevering and illfated enterprize.

Chapter XLV

*The Snake River deserts—Scanty fare—Bewildered travellers
—Prowling Indians—A giant Crow chief—A bully rebuked
—Indian signals—Smoke on the mountains—Mad River—
An alarm—An Indian foray—A scamper—A rude Indian
joke—A sharp shooter balked of his shot.*

O N THE 1ST of September Mr. Stuart and his companions
resumed their journey, bending their course eastward,
along the course of Snake River. As they advanced the country
opened. The hills which had hemmed in the river receded on
either hand, and great sandy and dusty plains extended before
them. Occasionally there were intervals of pasturage and the
banks of the river were fringed with willows and cotton
wood, so that its course might be traced from the hill tops,
winding under an umbrageous covert through a wide sun
burnt landscape. The soil, however, was generally poor; there
was in some places a miserable growth of wormwood, and a
plant called salt weed, resembling penny royal; but the summer
heat had parched the plains, and left but little pasturage. The
game too had disappeared. The hunter looked in vain over the
lifeless landscape; now and then a few antelope might be seen,
but not within reach of the rifle. We forbear to follow the travellers in a week's wandering over these barren wastes, where
they suffered much from hunger; having to depend upon a few
fish from the streams, and now and then a little dried salmon,
or a dog, procured from some forlorn lodge of Shoshonies.

Tired of these cheerless wastes, they left the banks of Snake
River on the 7th of September, under guidance of Mr. Miller,
who, having acquired some knowledge of the country during
his trapping campaign, undertook to conduct them across the
mountains by a better route than that by Fort Henry, and
one more out of the range of the Blackfeet. He proved, however, but an indifferent guide, and they soon became bewildered among rugged hills and unknown streams and burnt and
barren prairies.

At length they came to a river on which Mr. Miller had
trapped and to which they gave his name; though, as before

497

observed, we presume it to be the same called Bear River, which empties itself into Lake Bonneville. Up this river and its branches they kept for two or three days, supporting themselves precariously upon fish.

They soon found that they were in a dangerous neighborhood. On the 12th of September, having encamped early, they sallied forth with their rods to angle for their supper. On returning they beheld a number of Indians prowling about their camp, whom, to their infinite disquiet, they soon perceived to be Upsarokas or Crows.

Their chief came forward with a confident air. He was a dark herculean fellow, full six feet four inches in height, with a mingled air of the ruffian and the rogue. He conducted himself peaceably, however, and despatched some of his people to their camp, which was somewhere in the neighborhood and from whence they returned with a most acceptable supply of buffalo meat. He now signified to Mr. Stuart that he was going to trade with the Snakes who reside on the west base of the mountains below Henry's fort. Here they cultivate a delicate kind of tobacco much esteemed and sought after by the mountain tribes. There was something sinister, however, in the look of this Indian that inspired distrust. By degrees the number of his people encreased, until by midnight, there were twenty one of them about the camp, who began to be impudent and troublesome. The greatest uneasiness was now felt for the safety of the horses and effects, and every one kept vigilant watch throughout the night.

The morning dawned, however, without any unpleasant occurrence, and Mr. Stuart, having purchased all the buffalo meat that the Crows had to spare, prepared to depart. His Indian acquaintance, however, were disposed for further dealings, and, above all, anxious for a supply of gunpowder, for which they offered horses in exchange. Mr. Stuart declined to furnish them with the dangerous commodity. They became more importunate in their solicitations, until they met with a flat refusal.

The gigantic chief now stepped forward, assumed a swelling air, and, slapping himself upon the breast, gave Mr. Stuart to understand that he was a chief of great power and importance. He signified, further, that it was customary for great chiefs when they met, to make each other presents. He requested, therefore, that Mr. Stuart would alight and give him the horse upon which he was mounted. This was a noble animal, of one of the wild races of the prairies, on which Mr. Stuart set great value; he, of course, shook his head at the request of the Crow dignitary. Upon this the latter strode up to him and taking hold of him, moved him backwards and forwards in his saddle as if to make him feel that he was a mere child within his grasp. Mr. Stuart preserved his calmness, and still shook his head. The chief then seized the bridle and gave it a jerk that startled the horse, and nearly brought the rider to the ground. Mr. Stuart instantly drew forth a pistol and presented it at the head of the bully ruffian. In a twinkling his swaggering was at an end, and he dodged behind his horse to escape the expected shot. As his subject Crows gazed on the affray from a little distance, Mr. Stuart ordered his men to level their rifles at them, but not to fire. The whole crew scampered among the bushes, and, throwing themselves upon the ground, vanished from sight.

The chieftain thus left alone, was confounded for an instant, but recovering himself, with true Indian shrewdness burst into a loud laugh, and affected to turn off the whole matter as a piece of pleasantry. Mr. Stuart by no means relished such equivocal joking, but it was not his policy to get into a quarrel; so he joined, with the best grace he could assume, in the merriment of the jocular giant and to console the latter for the refusal of the horse, made him a present of twenty charges of powder. They parted, according to all outward professions, the best friends in the world; it was evident, however, that nothing but the smallness of his own force, and the martial array and alertness of the white men, had prevented the Crow chief from proceeding to open outrage. As it was, his worthy followers, in the course of their brief interview, had contrived to purloin a bag containing almost all the culinary utensils of the party.

The travellers now kept on their way due east, over a chain of hills. The recent rencontre shewed them that they were now in a land of danger, subject to the wide roamings of a predacious tribe; nor in fact had they gone many miles, before they beheld sights calculated to inspire anxiety and alarm. From the summits of some of the loftiest mountains, in different directions, columns of smoke began to rise. These they concluded to be signals made by the runners of the Crow chieftain, to summon the stragglers of his band, so as to pursue them with greater force. Signals of this kind, made by outrunners from one central point, will rouse a wide circuit of the mountains in a wonderfully short space of time; and bring the straggling hunters and warriors to the standard of their chieftain.

To keep as much as possible out of the way of these freebooters Mr. Stuart altered his course to the north, and, quitting the main stream of Miller's River, kept up a large branch that came in from the mountains. Here they encamped after a fatiguing march of twenty five miles. As the night drew on the horses were hobbled, or fettered, and tethered close to the camp; a vigilant watch was maintained until morning, and every one slept with his rifle on his arm.

At sunrise they were again on the march, still keeping to the north. They soon began to ascend the mountains and occasionally had wide prospects over the surrounding country. Not a sign of a Crow was to be seen; but this did not assure them of their security, well knowing the perseverance of these savages in dogging any party they intend to rob, and the stealthy way in which they can conceal their movements, keeping along ravines and defiles. After a mountain scramble of twenty one miles they encamped on the margin of a stream running to the north.

In the evening there was an alarm of Indians, and every one was instantly on the alert. They proved to be three miserable Snakes, who were no sooner informed that a band of Crows was prowling in the neighborhood than they made off with great signs of consternation.

A couple more of weary days and watchful nights brought them to a strong and rapid stream, running due north, which they concluded to be one of the upper branches of Snake River. It was probably the same since called Salt River. They determined to bend their course down this river, as it would take them still further out of the dangerous neighborhood of the Crows. They then would strike upon Mr. Hunt's track of the preceding autumn, and retrace it across the mountains. The attempt to find a better route under guidance of Mr. Miller had cost them a large bend to the south; in resuming Mr. Hunt's track they would at least be sure of their road. They accordingly turned down along the course of this stream, and at the end of three days' journey, came to where it was joined by a larger river, and assumed a more impetuous character, raging and roaring among rocks and precipices. It proved, in fact, to be Mad River, already noted in the expedition of Mr. Hunt. On the banks of this river they encamped on the 18th of September, at an early hour.

Six days had now elapsed since their interview with the Crows; during that time they had come nearly a hundred and fifty miles to the north and west, without seeing any signs of those marauders. They considered themselves therefore beyond the reach of molestation and began to relax in their vigilance, lingering occasionally for part of a day where there was good pasturage. The poor horses needed repose. They had been urged on, by forced marches, over rugged heights, among rocks and fallen timber, or over low swampy valleys, inundated by the labors of the beaver. These industrious animals abounded in all the mountain streams and water courses wherever there were willows for their subsistence. Many of these they had so completely dammed up as to inundate the low grounds, making shallow pools or lakes and extensive quagmires: by which the route of the travellers was often impeded.

On the 19th of September they rose at early dawn; some began to prepare breakfast, and others to arrange the packs preparatory to a march. The horses had been hobbled, but left at large to graze upon the adjacent pastures. Mr. Stuart was on the bank of the river at a short distance from the camp when he heard the alarm cry—"Indians! Indians!—to arms! to arms!"

A mounted Crow galloped past the camp bearing a red flag. He reined his steed on the summit of a neighboring knoll and waved his flaring banner. A diabolical yell now broke forth on the opposite side of the camp beyond where the horses were grazing, and a small troop of savages came galloping up whooping and making a terrific clamor. The horses took fright and dashed across the camp in the direction of the standard bearer, attracted by his waving flag. He instantly put spurs to his steed and scoured off, followed by the panic stricken herd, their fright being encreased by the yells of the savages in their rear.

At the first alarm Mr. Stuart and his comrades had seized their rifles and attempted to cut off the Indians who were pursuing the horses. Their attention was instantly distracted by whoops and yells in an opposite direction. They now apprehended that a reserve party was about to carry off their baggage. They ran to secure it. The reserve party, however, galloped by, whooping and yelling in triumph and derision. The last of them proved to be their commander, the identical giant joker already mentioned. He was not cast in the stern poetical mould of fashionable Indian heroism, but on the contrary, was grievously given to vulgar jocularity. As he passed Mr. Stuart and his companions he checked his horse, raised himself in the saddle, and clapping his hand on the most insulting part of his body, uttered some jeering words, which, fortunately for their delicacy they could not understand. The rifle of Ben Jones was levelled in an instant, and he was on the point of whizzing a bullet into the target so tauntingly displayed. "Not for your life! not for your life!," exclaimed Mr. Stuart, "you will bring destruction on us all!"

It was hard to restrain honest Ben when the mark was so fair and the insult so foul. "Oh Mr. Stuart," exclaimed he, "only let me have one crack at the infernal rascal and you may keep all the pay that is due to me."

"By heaven, if you fire," cried Mr. Stuart, "I'll blow your brains out."

By this time the Indian was far out of reach and had rejoined his men, and the whole dare devil band, with the captured horses, scuttled off along the defiles, their red flag flaunting over head and the rocks echoing to their whoops and yells and demoniac laughter.

The unhorsed travellers gazed after them in silent mortification and despair; yet Mr. Stuart could not but admire the style and spirit with which the whole exploit had been managed, and pronounced it one of the most daring and intrepid actions he had ever heard of among Indians. The whole number of the Crows did not exceed twenty. In this way a small gang of lurkers will hurry off the cavalry of a large war party, for when once a drove of horses are seized with a panic they become frantic and nothing short of broken necks can stop them.

No one was more annoyed by this unfortunate occurrence than Ben Jones. He declared he would actually have given his whole arrears of pay, amounting to upwards of a year's wages, rather than be balked of such a capital shot. Mr. Stuart, however, represented what might have been the consequence of so rash an act. Life for life is the Indian maxim. The whole tribe would have made common cause in avenging the death of a warrior. The party were but seven dismounted men, with a wide mountain region to traverse, infested by these people, and which might all be roused by signal fires. In fact the conduct of the band of marauders in question shewed the perseverance of savages when once they have fixed their minds upon a project. These fellows had evidently been silently and secretly dogging the party for a week past, and a distance of a hundred and fifty miles, keeping out of sight by day, lurking about the encampments at night, watching all their movements, and waiting for a favorable moment when they should be off their guard. The menace of Mr. Stuart, in their first interview, to shoot the giant chief with his pistol, and the fright caused among the warriors by presenting the rifles, had probably added the stimulus of pique to their usual horse stealing propensities, and in this mood of mind they would doubtless have followed the party throughout their whole course over the Rocky Mountains rather than be disappointed in their scheme.

Chapter XLVI

Travellers unhorsed—Pedestrian preparations—Prying spies —Bonfire of baggage—A march on foot—Rafting a river— The wounded elk—Indian trails—Wilful conduct of Mr. M'Lellan—Grand prospect from a mountain—Distant craters of volcanos—Illness of Mr. Crooks.

F EW REVERSES in this changeful world are more complete and disheartening than that of a traveller, suddenly unhorsed, in the midst of the wilderness. Our unfortunate travellers contemplated their situation for a time in perfect dismay. A long long journey over rugged mountains and immeasureable plains, lay before them, which they must painfully perform on foot, and every thing necessary for subsistence or defence, must be carried on their shoulders. Their dismay, however, was but transient, and they immediately set to work, with that prompt expediency produced by the exigencies of the wilderness, to fit themselves for the change in their condition.

Their first attention was to select from their baggage such articles as were indispensable to their journey; to make them up into convenient packs, and to deposit the residue in caches. The whole day was consumed in these occupations: At night they made a scanty meal of their remaining provisions and lay down to sleep with heavy hearts. In the morning they were up and alert at an early hour, and began to prepare their knapsacks for a march, while Ben Jones repaired to an old beaver trap which he had set in the river bank at some little distance from the camp. He was rejoiced to find a middle sized beaver there, sufficient for a morning's meal to his hungry comrades. On his way back with his prize, he observed two heads peering over the edge of an impending cliff several hundred feet high which he supposed to be a couple of wolves. As he continued on he now and then cast his eye up; the heads were still there, looking down with fixed and watchful gaze. A suspicion now flashed across his mind that they might be Indian scouts; and, had they not been far above the reach of his rifle, he would undoubtedly have regaled them with a shot.

On arriving at the camp he directed the attention of his comrades to these aerial observers. The same idea was at first entertained that they were wolves; but their immoveable watchfulness soon satisfied every one that they were Indians. It was concluded that they were watching the movements of the party to discover their place of concealment of such articles as they would be compelled to leave behind. There was no likelihood that the caches would escape the search of such keen eyes and experienced rummagers, and the idea was intolerable that any more booty should fall into their hands. To disappoint them, therefore, the travellers stripped the caches of the articles deposited there, and collecting together every thing that they could not carry away with them, made a bonfire of all that would burn, and threw the rest into the river. There was a forlorn satisfaction in thus balking the Crows by the destruction of their own property; and, having thus gratified their pique they shouldered their packs, about ten o'clock in the morning, and set out on their pedestrian wayfaring.

The route they took was down along the banks of Mad River. This stream makes its way through the defiles of the mountains into the plain below Fort Henry, where it terminates in Snake River. Mr. Stuart was in hopes of meeting with Snake encampments in the plain, where he might procure a couple of horses to transport the baggage. In such case he intended to resume his eastern course across the mountains and endeavor to reach the Cheyenne River before winter. Should he fail, however, of obtaining horses, he would probably be compelled to winter on the Pacific side of the mountains, somewhere on the head waters of the Spanish or Colorado river.

With all the care that had been observed in taking nothing with them that was not absolutely necessary, the poor pedestrians were heavily laden, and their burthens added to the fatigues of their rugged road. They suffered much too from hunger. The trout they caught were too poor to yield much nourishment; their main dependence, therefore, was upon an old beaver trap which they had providentially retained. Whenever they were fortunate enough to entrap a beaver it was cut up immediately and distributed, that each man might carry his share.

After two days of toilsome travel, during which they made but eighteen miles, they stopped on the 21st to build two rafts on which to cross to the north side of the river. On these they embarked, on the following morning, four on one raft, and three on the other, and pushed boldly from shore. Finding the rafts sufficiently firm and steady to withstand the rough and rapid water, they changed their minds and, instead of crossing, ventured to float down with the current. The river was in general very rapid, and from one to two hundred yards in width, winding in every direction through mountains of hard black rock, covered with pines and cedars. The mountains to the east of the river were spurs of the Rocky range, and of great magnitude; those on the west were little better than hills, bleak and barren, or scantily clothed with stunted grass.

Mad River though deserving its name from the impetuosity of its current, was free from rapids and cascades, and flowed on in a single channel between gravel banks, often fringed with cotton wood and dwarf willows in abundance. These gave sustenance to immense quantities of beaver, so that the voyagers found no difficulty in procuring food. Ben Jones, also, killed a fallow deer and a wolverine, and as they were enabled to carry the carcasses on their rafts, their larder was well supplied. Indeed they might have occasionally shot beavers that were swimming in the river as they floated by, but they humanely spared their lives, being in no want of meat at the time.

In this way they kept down the river for three days, drifting with the current and encamping on land at night, when they drew up their rafts on shore. Towards the evening of the third day they came to a little island on which they descried a gang of elk. Ben Jones landed and was fortunate enough to wound one which immediately took to the water, but, being unable to stem the current, drifted above a mile when it was over taken and drawn to shore. As a storm was gathering they now encamped on the margin of the river, where they remained all the next day sheltering themselves as well as they could from the rain and hail and snow, a sharp foretaste of the impending winter. During their encampment they employed themselves in jerking a part of the elk for future supply. In cutting up the carcass they found that the animal had been wounded by hunters, about a week previously, an arrow head and a musket ball remaining in the wounds. In the wilderness every trivial circumstance is a matter of anxious speculation. The Snake Indians have no guns; the elk, therefore, could not have been wounded by one of them. They were on the borders of the country infested by the Blackfeet, who carry fire arms. It was concluded, therefore, that the elk had been hunted by some of that wandering and hostile tribe who, of course, must be in the neighborhood. The idea put an end to the transient solace they had enjoyed in the comparative repose and abundance of the river.

For three days longer they continued to navigate with their rafts. The recent storm had rendered the weather extremely cold. They had now floated down the river about ninety one miles, when finding the mountains on the right diminished to moderate sized hills, they landed and prepared to resume their journey on foot. Accordingly, having spent a day in preparations, making moccasins, and parcelling out their jerked meat, in packs of twenty pounds to each man, they turned their backs upon the river on the 29th of September, and struck off to the north east; keeping along the southern skirt of the mountain on which Henry's fort was situated.

Their march was slow and toilsome; part of the time through an alluvial bottom thickly grown with cotton wood, hawthorn and willows, and part of the time over rough hills. Three antelopes came within shot but they dared not fire at them, lest the report of their rifles should betray them to the Blackfeet. In the course of the day they came upon a large horse track apparently about three weeks old, and in the evening encamped on the banks of a small stream, on a spot which had been the camping place of this same band.

On the following morning they still observed the Indian track, but after a time they came to where it separated in every direction and was lost. This shewed that the band had dispersed in various hunting parties and was, in all probability, still in the neighborhood; it was necessary, therefore, to proceed with the utmost caution. They kept a vigilant eye as they marched, upon every height where a scout might be posted, and scanned the solitary landscape and the distant ravines, to observe any column of smoke; but nothing of the kind was to be seen; all was indescribably stern and lifeless.

Towards evening they came to where there were several hot springs, strongly impregnated with iron and sulphur, and sending up a volume of vapour that tainted the surrounding atmosphere and might be seen at the distance of a couple of miles.

Near to these they encamped in a deep gulley, which afforded some concealment. To their great concern, Mr. Crooks, who had been indisposed for the two preceding days, had a violent fever in the night.

Shortly after day break they resumed their march. On emerging from the glen a consultation was held as to their course. Should they continue round the skirt of the mountain they would be in danger of falling in with the scattered parties of Blackfeet who were probably hunting in the plain. It was thought most adviseable, therefore, to strike directly across the mountain, since the route, though rugged and difficult would be most secure. This council was indignantly derided by M'Lellan as pusillanimous. Hot headed and impatient at all times, he had been rendered irascible by the fatigues of the journey and the condition of his feet, which were chafed and sore. He could not endure the idea of encountering the difficulties of the mountain and swore he would rather face all the Blackfeet in the country. He was over ruled, however, and the party began to ascend the mountain, striving, with the ardour and emulation of young men, who should be first up. M'Lellan who was double the age of some of his companions, soon began to lose breath and fall in the rear. In the distribution of burthens it was his turn to carry the old beaver trap. Piqued and irritated he suddenly came to a halt, swore he would carry it no further, and jerked it half way down the hill. He was offered in place of it a package of dried meat but this he scornfully threw upon the ground. They might carry it, he said, who needed it; for his part, he could provide his daily food with his rifle. He concluded by flinging off from the party and keeping along the skirts of the mountain, leaving those, he said, to climb rocks who were afraid to face Indians. It was in vain that Mr. Stuart represented to him the rashness of his conduct and the dangers to which he exposed himself: he rejected such counsel as craven. It was equally useless to represent the dangers to which he subjected his companions;

as he could be discovered at a great distance on these naked plains, and the Indians, seeing him, would know that there must be other white men within reach. M'Lellan turned a deaf ear to every remonstrance and kept on his wilful way.

It seems a strange instance of perverseness in this man thus to fling himself off alone, in a savage region, where solitude itself was dismal, but every encounter with his fellow man full of peril. Such however is the hardness of spirit, and the insensibility to danger that grow upon men in the wilderness. M'Lellan, moreover, was a man of peculiar temperament, ungovernable in his will, of a courage that absolutely knew no fear, and somewhat of a braggart spirit, that took a pride in doing desperate and harebrained things.

Mr. Stuart and his party found the passage of the mountain somewhat difficult on account of the snow, which in many places was of considerable depth though it was now but the 1st of October. They crossed the summit early in the afternoon, and beheld below them a plain about twenty miles wide, bounded on the opposite side by their old acquaintances the Pilot Knobs, those towering mountains which had served Mr. Hunt as land marks in part of his route of the preceding year. Through the intermediate plain wandered a river about fifty yards wide, sometimes gleaming in open day, but oftener running through willowed banks, which marked its serpentine course.

Those of the party who had been across these mountains pointed out much of the bearings of the country to Mr. Stuart. They shewed him in what direction must lie the deserted post called Henry's fort, where they had abandoned their horses and embarked in canoes, and they informed him that the stream which wandered through the plain below them, fell into Henry River, half way between the Fort and the mouth of Mad or Snake River. The character of all this mountain region was decidedly volcanic, and to the north west, between Henry's Fort and the source of the Missouri Mr. Stuart observed several very high peaks covered with snow, from two of which smoke ascended in considerable volumes, apparently from craters in a state of eruption.

On their way down the mountain when they had reached the skirts they descried M'Lellan at a distance in the advance traversing the plain. Whether he saw them or not, he shewed no disposition to rejoin them, but pursued his sullen and solitary way.

After descending into the plain they kept on about six miles until they reached the little river, which was here about knee deep, and richly fringed with willow. Here they encamped for the night.

At this encampment the fever of Mr. Crooks increased to such a degree that it was impossible for him to travel. Some of the men were strenuous for Mr. Stuart to proceed without him, urging the imminent danger they were exposed to by delay in that unknown and barren region, infested by the most treacherous and inveterate of foes. They represented that the season was rapidly advancing; the weather for some days had been extremely cold; the mountains were already almost impassable from snow, and would soon present effectual barriers. Their provisions were exhausted; there was no game to be seen, and they did not dare to use their rifles, through fear of drawing upon them the Blackfeet.

The picture thus presented, was too true to be contradicted, and made a deep impression on the mind of Mr. Stuart; but the idea of abandoning a fellow being, and a comrade, in such a forlorn situation, was too repugnant to his feelings to be admitted for an instant. He represented to the men that the malady of Mr. Crooks could not be of long duration, and that in all probability, he would be able to travel in the course of a few days. It was with great difficulty, however, that he prevailed upon them to abide the event.

Chapter XLVII

As the travellers were now in a dangerous neighbor-hood, where the report of a rifle might bring the savages upon them, they had to depend upon their old beaver trap for subsistence. The little river on which they were encamped gave many "beaver signs," and Ben Jones set off at day break, along the willowed banks, to find a proper trapping place. As he was making his way among the thickets with his trap on his shoulder and his rifle in his hand, he heard a crashing sound, and turning beheld a huge grizzly bear advancing upon him with a terrific growl. The sturdy Kentuckian was not to be intimidated by man or monster. Levelling his rifle he pulled the trigger. The bear was wounded, but not mortally: instead, however, of rushing upon his assailant, as is generally the case with this kind of bear, he retreated into the bushes. Jones followed him for some distance, but with suitable caution, and bruin effected his escape.

As there was every prospect of a detention of some days in this place, and as the supplies of the beaver trap were too precarious to be depended upon, it became absolutely necessary to run some risk of discovery by hunting in the neighborhood. Ben Jones, therefore, obtained permission to range with his rifle some distance from the camp, and set off to beat up the river banks in defiance of bear or Blackfeet.

He returned in great spirits in the course of a few hours, having come upon a gang of elk about six miles off, and killed five. This was joyful news, and the party immediately moved forward to the place where he had left the carcasses. They were obliged to support Mr. Crooks the whole distance, for he was unable to walk. Here they remained for two or three days, feasting heartily on elk meat, and drying as much as they would be able to carry away with them.

By the 5th of October some simple prescriptions, together with an "Indian sweat" had so far benefited Mr. Crooks that he was enabled to move about; they, therefore, set forward slowly, dividing his pack and accoutrements among them, and made a creeping day's progress of eight miles south. Their route for the most part lay through swamps caused by the industrious labours of the beaver. For this little animal had dammed up numerous small streams issuing from the Pilot Knob Mountains, so that the low grounds on their borders were completely inundated. In the course of their march they killed a grizzly bear, with fat on its flanks upwards of three inches in thickness. This was an acceptable addition to their stock of elk meat.

The next day Mr. Crooks was sufficiently recruited in strength to be able to carry his rifle and pistols, and they made a march of seventeen miles, along the borders of the plain.

Their journey daily became more toilsome and their sufferings more severe as they advanced. Keeping up the channel of a river they traversed the rugged summit of the Pilot Knob Mountain, covered with snow nine inches deep. For several days they continued, bending their course as much as possible to the east, over a succession of rocky heights, deep valleys and rapid streams. Sometimes their dizzy path lay along the margin of perpendicular precipices several hundred feet in height, where a single false step might precipitate them into the rocky bed of a torrent which roared below. Not the least part of their weary task was the fording of the numerous windings and branchings of the mountain rivers, all boisterous in their currents and icy cold.

Hunger was added to their other sufferings, and soon became the keenest. The small supply of bear and elk meat which they had been able to carry in addition to their previous burthens, served but for a very short time. In their anxiety to struggle forward they had but little time to hunt, and scarce any game came in their path. For three days they had nothing to eat but a small duck and a few poor trout. They occasionally saw numbers of antelopes and tried every art to get within shot; but the timid animals were more than commonly wild, and after tantalizing the hungry hunters for a time, bounded away beyond all chance of pursuit. At length they were fortunate enough to kill one; it was extremely meagre and yielded but a scanty supply, but on this they subsisted for several days.

On the 11th they encamped on a small stream near the foot of the Spanish River Mountain. Here they met with traces of that wayward and solitary being, M'Lellan, who was still keeping on a head of them through these lonely mountains. He had encamped the night before on this stream; they found the embers of the fire by which he had slept, and the remains of a miserable wolf on which he had supped. It was evident he had suffered, like themselves, the pangs of hunger, though he had fared better at this encampment; for they had not a mouthful to eat.

The next day they rose hungry and alert, and set out with the dawn to climb the mountain, which was steep and difficult. Traces of volcanic operations were to be seen in various directions. There was a species of clay also to be met with out of which the Indians manufacture pots and jars and dishes. It is very fine and light, of an agreeable smell and of a brown colour spotted with yellow, and dissolves readily in the mouth. Vessels manufactured of it are said to impart a pleasant smell and flavour to any liquids. These mountains abound also with mineral earths or chalks of various colours; especially two kinds of ochre, one a pale, the other a bright red, like vermillion; much used by the Indians, in painting their bodies.

About noon the travellers reached the "drains" and brooks that formed the head waters of the river, and later in the day descended to where the main body, a shallow stream about a hundred and sixty yards wide, poured through its mountain valley.

Here the poor famishing wanderers had expected to find buffalo in abundance, and had fed their hungry hopes during their scrambling toil, with the thoughts of roasted ribs, juicy humps, and broiled marrow bones. To their great disappointment the river banks were deserted; a few old tracks shewed where a herd of bulls had some time before passed along, but not a horn nor hump was to be seen in the sterile landscape. A few antelopes looked down upon them from the brow of

a crag, but flitted away out of sight at the least approach of
the hunter.

In the most starving mood they kept for several miles further along the bank of the river, seeking for "beaver signs."
Finding some, they encamped in the vicinity and Ben Jones
immediately proceeded to set the trap. They had scarce come
to a halt when they perceived a large smoke at some distance
to the south west. The sight was hailed with joy for they
trusted it might rise from some Indian camp where they could
procure something to eat, and the dread of starvation had
now overcome even the terror of the Blackfeet. Le Clerc, one
of the Canadians, was instantly despatched by Mr. Stuart to
reconnoiter; and the travellers sat up till a late hour, watching
and listening for his return, hoping he might bring them
food. Midnight arrived, but Le Clerc did not make his appearance, and they laid down once more supperless to sleep,
comforting themselves with the hopes that their old beaver
trap might furnish them with a breakfast.

At day break they hastened with famished eagerness to the
trap—they found in it the fore paw of a beaver; the sight of
which tantalized their hunger and added to their dejection.
They resumed their journey with flagging spirits, but had not
gone far when they perceived Le Clerc approaching at a distance. They hastened to meet him in hopes of tidings of good
cheer. He had none such to give them; but news of that
strange wanderer M'Lellan. The smoke had risen from his encampment, which took fire while he was at a little distance
from it fishing. Le Clerc found him in forlorn condition. His
fishing had been unsuccessful. During twelve days that he had
been wandering alone through these savage mountains he
had found scarce any thing to eat. He had been ill, way worn,
sick at heart, still he had kept forward, but now his strength
and his stubbornness were exhausted. He expressed his satisfaction at hearing that Mr. Stuart and his party were near,
and said he would wait at his camp for their arrival in hopes
they would give him something to eat, for without food he
declared he should not be able to proceed much further.

When the party reached the place they found the poor fellow lying on a parcel of withered grass, wasted to a perfect
skeleton and so feeble that he could scarce raise his head or

speak. The presence of his old comrades seemed to revive him; but they had no food to give him, for they themselves were almost starving. They urged him to rise and accompany them, but he shook his head. It was all in vain, he said, there was no prospect of their getting speedy relief, and without it he should perish by the way. He might as well, therefore, stay and die where he was. At length, after much persuasion, they got him upon his legs; his rifle and other effects were shared among them, and he was cheered and aided forward.

In this way they proceeded for seventeen miles over a level plain of sand, until, seeing a few antelopes in the distance, they encamped on the margin of a small stream. All now that were capable of the exertion turned out to hunt for a meal. Their efforts were fruitless and after dark they returned to their camp famished almost to desperation.

As they were preparing for the third time to lay down to sleep without a mouthful to eat, Le Clerc, one of the Canadians, gaunt and wild with hunger, approached Mr. Stuart with his gun in his hand. "It was all in vain," he said, "to attempt to proceed any further without food. They had a barren plain before them three or four days' journey in extent, on which nothing was to be procured. They must all perish before they could get to the end of it. It was better, therefore, that one should die to save the rest." He proposed, therefore, that they should cast lots; adding, as an inducement for Mr. Stuart to assent to the proposition, that he, as leader of the party, should be exempted.

Mr. Stuart shuddered at the horrible proposition, and endeavored to reason with the man, but his words were unavailing. At length, snatching up his rifle he threatened to shoot him on the spot if he persisted. The famished wretch dropped on his knees, begged pardon in the most abject terms, and promised never again to offend him with such a suggestion.

Quiet being restored to the forlorn encampment, each one sought repose. Mr. Stuart, however, was so exhausted by the agitation of the past scene, acting upon his emaciated frame, that he could scarce crawl to his miserable couch; where notwithstanding his fatigues he passed a sleepless night, revolving upon their dreary situation, and the desperate prospect before them.

Before daylight the next morning they were up and on their way; they had nothing to detain them; no breakfast to prepare and to linger was to perish. They proceeded, however, but slowly, for all were faint and weak. Here and there they passed the sculls and bones of buffaloes, which shewed that those animals must have been hunted here during the past season; the sight of these bones served only to mock their misery. After travelling about nine miles along the plain, they ascended a range of hills, and had scarcely gone two miles further when, to their great joy, they discovered "an old run-down buffalo bull," the laggard probably of some herd that had been hunted and harassed through the mountains. They now all stretched themselves out to encompass and make sure of this solitary animal, for their lives depended upon their success. After considerable trouble and infinite anxiety they at length succeeded in killing him. He was instantly flayed and cut up, and so ravenous was their hunger that they devoured some of the flesh raw. The residue they carried to a brook near by where they encamped, lit a fire, and began to cook.

Mr. Stuart was fearful that in their famished state they would eat to excess and injure themselves. He caused a soup to be made of some of the meat, and that each should take a quantity of it as a prelude to his supper. This may have had a beneficial effect, for though they sat up the greater part of the night, cooking and cramming, no one suffered any inconvenience.

The next morning the feasting was resumed, and about mid day, feeling somewhat recruited and refreshed, they set out on their journey with renovated spirits, shaping their course towards a mountain, the summit of which they saw towering in the east, and near to which they expected to find the head waters of the Missouri.

As they proceeded, they continued to see the skeletons of buffalos scattered about the plain in every direction, which shewed that there had been much hunting here by the Indians in the recent season. Further on they crossed a large Indian trail forming a deep path, about fifteen days old, which went in a north direction. They concluded it to have been made by some numerous band of Crows, who had hunted in this country for the greater part of the summer.

On the following day they forded a stream of considerable magnitude, with banks clothed with pine trees. Among these they found the traces of a large Indian camp which had evidently been the head quarters of a hunting expedition from the great quantities of buffalo bones strewed about the neighborhood. The camp had apparently been abandoned about a month.

In the centre was a singular lodge one hundred and fifty feet in circumference, supported by the trunks of twenty trees about twelve inches in diameter and forty four feet long. Across these were laid branches of pine and willow trees, so as to yield a tolerable shade. At the west end immediately opposite to the door, three bodies lay interred with their feet towards the east. At the head of each grave was a branch of red cedar firmly planted in the ground, at the foot was a large buffalo's scull, painted black. Savage ornaments were suspended in various parts of the edifice and a great number of children's moccasins. From the magnitude of this building, and the time and labour that must have been expended in erecting it, the bodies which it contained were probably those of noted warriors and hunters.

The next day (October 17th) they passed two large tributary streams of the Spanish River. They took their rise in the Wind River Mountains, which ranged along to the east, stupendously high and rugged, composed of vast masses of black rock, almost destitute of wood and covered in many places with snow. This day they saw a few buffalo bulls and some antelopes, but could not kill any; and their stock of provisions began to grow scanty as well as poor.

On the 18th, after crossing a mountain ridge, and traversing a plain, they waded one of the branches of Spanish River, and on ascending its bank, met with about a hundred and thirty Snake Indians. They were friendly in their demeanor, and conducted them to their encampment, which was about three miles distant. It consisted of about forty wigwams, constructed principally of pine branches. The Snakes, like most of their nation, were very poor; the marauding Crows, in their late excursion through the country, had picked this unlucky band to the very bone, carrying off their horses, several of their squaws, and most of their effects. In spite of their poverty, they were hospitable in the extreme, and made the hungry strangers welcome to their cabins. A few trinkets procured from them a supply of buffalo meat, and of leather for moccasins of which the party were greatly in need. The most valuable prize obtained from them, however, was a horse: it was a sorry old animal in truth, but it was the only one that remained to the poor fellows, after the fell swoop of the Crows; yet this they were prevailed upon to part with to their guests for a pistol, an axe, a knife, and a few other trifling articles.

They had doleful stories to tell of the Crows, who were encamped on a river at no great distance to the east, and were in such force that they dared not venture to seek any satisfaction for their outrages or to get back a horse or squaw. They endeavoured to excite the indignation of their visitors by accounts of robberies and murders committed on lonely white hunters and trappers by Crows and Blackfeet. Some of these were exaggerations of the outrages, already mentioned, sustained by some of the scattered members of Mr. Hunt's expedition; others were in all probability sheer fabrications, to which the Snakes seem to have been a little prone. Mr. Stuart assured them that the day was not far distant when the whites would make their power felt throughout that country, and take signal vengeance on the perpetrators of these misdeeds. The Snakes expressed great joy at the intelligence and offered their services to aid the righteous cause, brightening at the thoughts of taking the field with such potent allies, and doubtless anticipating their turn at stealing horses and abducting squaws. Their offers of course were accepted; the calumet of peace was produced, and the two forlorn powers smoked eternal friendship between themselves and vengeance upon their common spoilers the Crows.

Chapter XLVIII

B Y SUNRISE on the following morning (October 19th) the travellers had loaded their old horse with buffalo meat, sufficient for five days' provisions, and, taking leave of their new allies, the poor but hospitable Snakes, set forth, in somewhat better spirits; though the increasing cold of the weather, and the sight of the snowy mountains, which they had yet to traverse, were enough to chill their very hearts. The country along this branch of the Spanish River, as far as they could see, was perfectly level, bounded by ranges of lofty mountains both to the east and west. They proceeded about three miles to the south where they came again upon the large trace of Crow Indians which they had crossed four days previously; made no doubt by the same marauding band that had plundered the Snakes; and which, according to the account of the latter, was now encamped on a stream to the eastward. The trail kept on to the south east, and was so well beaten by horse and foot, that they supposed at least a hundred lodges had passed along it. As it formed, therefore, a convenient high way, and ran in a proper direction, they turned into it and determined to keep along it as far as safety would permit; as the Crow encampment must be some distance off, and it was not likely those savages would return upon their steps. They travelled forward, therefore, all that day in the track of their dangerous predecessors, which led them across mountain streams, and along ridges, and through narrow valleys, tending generally towards the south east. The wind blew coldly from the north east, with occasional flurries of snow which made them encamp early, on the sheltered banks of a brook. The two Canadians Vallér and Le Clerc killed a young buffalo bull in the evening which was in good condition and afforded them a plentiful supply of fresh beef. They loaded their spits, therefore, and crammed their camp kettle with meat, and while the wind whistled and the snow whirled around them, huddled around a rousing fire, basked in its warmth and comforted both soul and body with a hearty and invigorating meal. No enjoyments have greater zest than these snatched in the very midst of difficulty and danger; and it is probable the poor way worn and weather-beaten travellers relished these creature comforts the more highly, from the surrounding desolation and the dangerous proximity of the Crows.

The snow which had fallen in the night made it late in the morning before the party loaded their solitary pack horse and resumed their march. They had not gone far before the Crow trace which they were following changed its direction and bore to the north of east. They had already begun to feel themselves on dangerous ground in keeping along it, as they might be described by some scouts and spies of that race of Ishmaelites, whose predatory life required them to be constantly on the alert. On seeing the trace turn so much to the north, therefore, they abandoned it, and kept on their course to the south east for eighteen miles, through a beautifully undulating country, having the main chain of mountains on the left, and a considerably elevated ridge on the right. Here the mountain ridge which divides Wind River from the head waters of the Columbia and Spanish rivers ends abruptly and, winding to the north of east, becomes the dividing barrier between a branch of the Big Horn and Cheyenne rivers, and those head waters which flow into the Missouri below the Sioux country.

The ridge which lay on the right of the travellers having now become very low, they passed over it and came into a level plain about ten miles in circumference, and encrusted to the depth of a foot or eighteen inches with salt as white as snow. This is furnished by numerous salt springs of limpid water, which are continually welling up, overflowing their borders, and forming beautiful chrystalizations. The Indian tribes of the interior are excessively fond of this salt, and repair to the valley to collect it, but it is held in distaste by the tribes of the sea coast, who will eat nothing that has been cured or seasoned by it.

This evening they encamped on the banks of a small stream in the open prairie. The north east wind was keen and cutting, they had nothing wherewith to make a fire but a scanty growth of sage or wormwood, and were fain to wrap themselves up in their blankets and huddle themselves in their "nests" at an early hour. In the course of the evening Mr. M'Lellan who had now regained his strength, killed a buffalo, but it was some distance from the camp and they postponed supplying themselves from the carcass until the following morning.

The next day (October 21st) the cold continued accompanied by snow. They set forward on their bleak and toilsome way, keeping to the east north east, towards the lofty summit of a mountain which it was necessary for them to cross. Before they reached its base they passed another large trail steering a little to the right of the point of the mountain. This they presumed to have been made by another band of Crows, who had probably been hunting lower down on the Spanish River.

The severity of the weather compelled them to encamp at the end of fifteen miles, on the skirts of the mountain, where they found sufficient dry aspen trees to supply them with fire, but they sought in vain about the neighborhood for a spring or run of water.

At day break they were up and on the march, scrambling up the mountain side for the distance of eight painful miles. From the casual hints given in the travelling memoranda of Mr. Stuart, this mountain would seem to offer a rich field of speculation for the geologist. Here was a plain three miles in diameter, strewed with pumice stones and other volcanic reliques, with a lake in the center, occupying what had probably been the crater. Here were also, in some places, deposits of marine shells, indicating that this mountain crest had at some remote period been below the waves.

After pausing to repose, and to enjoy these grand but savage and awful scenes, they began to descend the eastern side of the mountain. The descent was rugged and romantic, along deep ravines and defiles, over hung with crags and cliffs, among which they beheld numbers of the Ahsahta or Big horn skipping fearlessly from rock to rock. Two of them they succeeded in bringing down with their rifles, as they peered fearlessly from the brow of their airy precipices.

Arrived at the foot of the mountain, the travellers found a rill of water oozing out of the earth, and resembling in

look and taste the water of the Missouri. Here they encamped
for the night and supped sumptuously upon their mountain
mutton, which they found in good condition and extremely
well tasted.

The morning was bright and intensely cold. Early in the day
they came upon a stream running to the east, between low
hills of bluish earth strongly impregnated with copperas.
Mr. Stuart supposed this to be one of the head waters of the
Missouri, and determined to follow its banks. After a march of
twenty six miles, however, he arrived at the summit of a hill,
the prospect of which induced him to alter his intention. He
beheld in every direction south of east a vast plain bounded
only by the horizon through which wandered the stream in
question in a south, south east direction. It could not therefore be a branch of the Missouri. He now gave up all idea of
taking this stream for his guide, and shaped his course towards
a range of mountains in the east about sixty miles distant, near
which he hoped to find another stream.

The weather was now so severe, and the hardships of travelling so great, that he resolved to halt for the winter at the first
eligible place. That night they had to encamp on the open
prairie, near a scanty pool of water, and without any wood to
make a fire. The north east wind blew keenly across the naked
waste, and they were fain to decamp from their inhospitable
bivouac before the dawn.

For two days they kept on in an eastward direction against
wintry blasts and occasional snow storms. They suffered also
from scarcity of water, having occasionally to use melted snow;
this, with the want of pasturage, reduced their old pack horse
sadly. They saw many tracks of buffalo, and some few bulls,
which however got the wind of them, and scampered off.

On the 26th of October they steered east north east for
a wooded ravine in a mountain at a small distance from the
base of which, to their great joy, they discovered an abundant
stream running between willowed banks. Here they halted for
the night, and Ben Jones having luckily trapped a beaver
and killed two buffalo bulls, they remained all the next day
encamped, feasting and reposing and allowing their jaded
horse to rest from his labours.

The little stream on which they were encamped was one
of the head waters of the Platte River which flows into the

Missouri; it was in fact the northern fork or branch of that river, though this the travellers did not discover until long afterwards. Pursuing the course of this stream for about twenty miles they came to where it forced a passage through a range of high hills, covered with cedars, into an extensive low country affording excellent pasture to numerous herds of buffalo. Here they killed three cows, which were the first they had been able to get, having hitherto had to content themselves with bull beef, which at this season of the year is very poor. The hump meat afforded them a repast fit for an epicure.

Late on the afternoon of the 30th they came to where the stream, now encreased to a considerable size, poured along in a ravine between precipices of red stone two hundred feet in height. For some distance it dashed along over huge masses of rock, with foaming violence as if exasperated by being compressed into so narrow a channel, and at length leaped down a chasm that looked dark and frightful in the gathering twilight.

For a part of the next day the wild river, in its capricious wanderings, led them through a variety of striking scenes. At one time they were upon high plains, like platforms among the mountains, with herds of buffaloes roaming about them; at another among rude rocky defiles, broken into cliffs and precipices, where the black tailed deer bounded off among the crags and the big horn basked on the sunny brow of the precipice.

In the after part of the day they came to another scene surpassing in savage grandeur those already described. They had been travelling for some distance through a pass of the mountains keeping parallel with the river as it roared along, out of sight, through a deep ravine. Sometimes their devious path approached the margin of cliffs below which the river foamed, and boiled and whirled among the masses of rock that had fallen into its channel. As they crept cautiously on, leading their solitary pack horse along these giddy heights, they all at once came to where the river thundered down a succession of precipices, throwing up clouds of spray, and making a prodigious din and uproar. The travellers remained for a time gazing with mingled awe and delight at this furious cataract, to which Mr. Stuart gave, from the colour of the impending rocks, the name of "The fiery narrows."

Chapter XLIX

T HE TRAVELLERS encamped for the night on the banks of the river below the cataract. The night was cold, with par- tial showers of rain and sleet. The morning dawned gloomily, the skies were sullen and overcast, and threatened further storms; but the little band resumed their journey in defiance of the weather. The encreasing rigour of the season, however, which makes itself felt early in these mountainous regions and on these naked and elevated plains, brought them to a pause, and a serious deliberation, after they had descended about thirty miles further along the course of the river.

All were convinced that it was vain to attempt to accom- plish their journey on foot at this inclement season. They had still many hundred miles to traverse before they should reach the main course of the Missouri, and their route would lay over immense prairies, naked and bleak and destitute of fuel. The question then was where to choose their wintering place, and whether or not to proceed further down the river. They had at first imagined it to be one of the head waters, or trib- utary streams, of the Missouri. Afterwards they had believed it to be the Rapid or Quicourt River, in which opinion they had not come nearer to the truth; they now, however, were persuaded, with equal fallacy, by its inclining somewhat to the north of east, that it was the Cheyenne. If so, by continuing down it much further they must arrive among the Indians from whom the river takes its name. Among these they would be sure to meet some of the Sioux tribe. These would apprize their relatives, the piratical Sioux of the Missouri, of the ap- proach of a band of white traders; so that, in the spring time, they would be likely to be way laid and robbed on their way down the river by some party in ambush upon its banks.

Even should this prove to be the Quicourt, or Rapid, River, it would not be prudent to winter much further down upon its banks, as though they might be out of the range of the Sioux, they would be in the neighborhood of the Poncas, a tribe nearly as dangerous. It was resolved, therefore, since they must winter somewhere on this side of the Missouri, to descend no lower, but to keep up in these solitary regions, where they would be in no danger of molestation.

They were brought the more promptly and unanimously to this decision by coming upon an excellent wintering place, that promised every thing requisite for their comfort. It was on a fine bend of the river, just below where it issued out from among a ridge of mountains, and bent towards the north east. Here was a beautiful low point of land, covered by cotton wood and surrounded by a thick growth of willow; so as to yield both shelter and fuel, as well as materials for building. The river swept by in a strong current, about a hundred and fifty yards wide. To the south east were mountains of moderate height, the nearest about two miles off, but the whole chain ranging to the east, south and south west as far as the eye could reach. Their summits were crowned with extensive tracts of pitch pine chequered with small patches of the quivering aspen. Lower down were thick forests of firs and red cedars, growing out in many places from the very fissures of the rocks. The mountains were broken and precipitous, with huge bluffs protruding from among the forests. Their rocky recesses and beetling cliffs afforded retreats to innumerable flocks of the big horn, while their woody summits and ravines abounded with bears and black tailed deer. These, with the numerous herds of buffalo that ranged the lower grounds along the river, promised the travellers abundant cheer in their winter quarters.

On the second of November, therefore, they pitched their camp for the winter on the woody point, and their first thought was to obtain a supply of provisions. Ben Jones and the two Canadians accordingly sallied forth, accompanied by two others of the party, leaving but one to watch the camp. Their hunting was uncommonly successful. In the course of two days they killed thirty two buffalos, and collected their meat on the margin of a small brook about a mile distant. Fortunately a severe frost froze the river, so that the meat was easily transported to the encampment. On a succeeding day a herd of buffalo came trampling through the woody bottom on the river banks and fifteen more were killed.

It was soon discovered, however, that there was game of a more dangerous nature in the neighborhood. On one occasion Mr. Crooks had wandered about a mile from the camp, and had ascended a small hill commanding a view of the river. He was without his rifle, a rare circumstance, for in these wild regions where one may put up a wild animal or a wild Indian at every turn, it is customary never to stir from the camp fire unarmed. The hill where he stood overlooked the place where the massacre of the buffalo had taken place. As he was looking around on the prospect his eye was caught by an object below moving directly towards him. To his dismay he discovered it to be a grizzly bear with two cubs. There was no tree at hand into which he could climb; to run would only be to provoke pursuit, and he should soon be overtaken. He threw himself on the ground, therefore, and lay motionless watching the movements of the animal with intense anxiety. It continued to advance until at the foot of the hill, when it turned and made into the woods, having probably gorged itself with buffalo flesh. Mr. Crooks made all haste back to the camp, rejoicing at his escape, and determining never to stir out again without his rifle. A few days after this circumstance a grizzly bear was shot in the neighborhood by Mr. Miller.

As the slaughter of so many buffaloes had provided the party with beef for the winter, in case they met with no further supply, they now set to work heart and hand to build a comfortable wigwam. In a little while the woody promontory rang with the unwonted sound of the axe. Some of its lofty trees were laid low, and by the second evening the cabin was complete. It was eight feet wide and eighteen feet long. The walls were six feet high and the whole was covered with buffalo skins. The fire place was in the centre and the smoke found its way out by a hole in the roof.

The hunters were next sent out to procure deer skins for garments, moccasins and other purposes. They made the mountains echo with their rifles and, in the course of two days' hunting, killed twenty eight Big horns and black tailed deer.

The party now revelled in abundance. After all that they had suffered from hunger, cold, fatigue and watchfulness; after all their perils from treacherous and savage men, they exulted in the snugness and security of their isolated cabin, hidden as they thought even from the prying eyes of Indian scouts, and stored with creature comforts; and they looked forward to a winter of peace and quietness; of roasting and boiling, and broiling, and feasting upon venison, and mountain mutton, and bear's meat, and marrow bones and buffalo humps and other hunters' dainties, and of dosing and reposing round their fire, and gossipping over past dangers and adventures, and telling long hunting stories, until spring should return; when they would make canoes of buffalo skins, and float themselves down the river.

From such halcyon dreams they were startled one morning at day break by a savage yelp. They started up and seized their rifles. The yelp was repeated by two or three voices. Cautiously peeping out they beheld, to their dismay, several Indian warriors among the trees, all armed and painted in warlike style; being evidently bent on some hostile purpose.

Miller changed countenance as he regarded them. "We are in trouble," said he, "these are some of the rascally Arapahays that robbed me last year." Not a word was uttered by the rest of the party, but they silently slung their powder horns and ball pouches and prepared for battle. M'Lellan who had taken his gun to pieces the evening before, put it together in all haste. He proposed that they should break out the clay from between the logs, so as to be able to fire upon the enemy.

"Not yet," replied Stuart—"it will not do to shew fear or distrust—we must first hold a parley. Some one must go out and meet them as a friend."

Who was to undertake the task—it was full of peril, as the envoy might be shot down at the threshold.

"The leader of a party," said Miller, "always takes the advance."

"Good!" replied Stuart. "I am ready." He immediately went forth: one of the Canadians followed him; the rest of the party remained in garrison, to keep the savages in check.

Stuart advanced holding his rifle in one hand, and extending the other to the savage that appeared to be the chief. The latter stepped forward and took it: his men followed his example, and all shook hands with Stuart in token of friendship.

They now explained their errand. They were a war party of Arapahay braves. Their village lay on a stream several days' journey to the eastward. It had been attacked and ravaged, during their absence, by a band of Crows who had carried off several of their women and most of their horses. They were in quest of vengeance. For sixteen days they had been tracking the Crows about the mountains, but had not yet come upon them. In the mean time they had met with scarcely any game and were half famished. About two days previously they had heard the report of fire arms among the mountains, and on searching in the direction of the sound, had come to a place where a deer had been killed. They had immediately put themselves upon the track of the hunters and by following it up had arrived at the cabin.

Mr. Stuart now invited the chief and another who appeared to be his lieutenant, into the hut, but made signs that no one else was to enter. The rest halted at the door; others came straggling up, until the whole party, to the number of twenty three, were gathered before the hut. They were armed with bows and arrows, tomahawks and scalping knives and some few with guns. All were painted and dressed for war, and had a wild and fierce appearance. Mr. Miller recognized among them some of the very fellows who had robbed him in the preceding year; and put his comrades upon their guard. Every man stood ready to resist the first act of hostility; the savages however conducted themselves peaceably, and shewed none of that swaggering arrogance which a war party is apt to assume.

On entering the hut the chief and his lieutenant cast a wistful look at the rafters, laden with venison and buffalo meat. Mr. Stuart made a merit of necessity and invited them to help themselves. They did not wait to be pressed. The rafters were soon eased of their burthen: venison and beef were passed out to the crew before the door, and a scene of gormandizing commenced, of which few can have an idea, who have not witnessed the gastronomic powers of an Indian, after an interval of fasting. This was kept up throughout the day; they paused now and then, it is true, for a brief interval, but only to return to the charge with renewed ardor. The chief and the lieutenant surpassed all the rest in the vigor and perseverance of their attacks; as if, from their station they were bound to signalize themselves in all onslaughts. Mr. Stuart kept them well supplied with choice bits, for it was his policy to over feed them and keep them from leaving the hut, where they served as hostages for the good conduct of their followers. Once only, in the course of the day, did the chief sally forth. Mr. Stuart and one of his men accompanied him, armed with their rifles, but without betraying any distrust. The chieftain soon returned and renewed his attack upon the larder. In a word, he and his worthy coadjutor the lieutenant ate until they were both stupified.

Towards evening the Indians made their preparations for the night according to the practice of war parties. Those outside of the hut threw up two breast works, into which they retired at a tolerably early hour and slept like over fed hounds. As to the chief and his lieutenant, they passed the night in the hut; in the course of which they two or three times, got up to eat. The travellers took turns, one at a time, to mount guard until the morning.

Scarce had the day dawned when the gormandizing was renewed by the whole band, and carried on with surprizing vigour until ten o'clock, when all prepared to depart. They had six days' journey yet to make, they said, before they should come up with the Crows, who they understood were encamped on a river to the northward. Their way lay through a hungry country where there was no game; they would, moreover, have but little time to hunt; they, therefore, craved a small supply of provisions for the journey. Mr. Stuart again invited them to help themselves. They did so with keen fore thought, loading themselves with the choicest parts of the meat and leaving the late plenteous larder far gone in a consumption. Their next request was for a supply of ammunition, having guns but no powder and ball. They promised to pay magnificently out of the spoils of their foray. "We are poor now," said they, "and are obliged to go on foot, but we shall soon come back laden with booty, and all mounted on horseback, with scalps hanging at our bridles. We will then give each of you a horse to keep you from being tired on your journey."

"Well," said Mr. Stuart, "when you bring the horses you shall have the ammunition, but not before." The Indians saw by his determined tone that all further entreaty would be unavailing, so they desisted, with a good-humoured laugh, and went off exceedingly well freighted both within and without, promising to be back again in the course of a fortnight.

No sooner were they out of hearing than the luckless travellers held another council. The security of their cabin was at an end, and with it all their dreams of a quiet and cosey winter. They were between two fires. On one side were their old enemies the Crows; on the other side the Arapahays—no less dangerous freebooters. As to the moderation of this war party, they considered it assumed to put them off their guard against some more favorable opportunity for a surprizal. It was determined, therefore, not to await their return, but to abandon, with all speed, this dangerous neighborhood. From the accounts of their recent visitors they were led to believe, though erroneously, that they were upon the Quicourt, or Rapid River. They proposed now to keep along it to its confluence with the Missouri; but, should they be prevented by the rigours of the season from proceeding so far, at least to reach a part of the river where they might be able to construct canoes of greater strength and durability than those of buffalo skins.

Accordingly, on the thirteenth of December they bade adieu, with many a regret, to their comfortable quarters, where, for five weeks, they had been indulging the sweets of repose, of plenty and of fancied security. They were still accompanied by their veteran pack horse; which the Arapahays had omitted to steal, either because they intended to steal him on their return, or because they thought him not worth stealing.

Chapter L

THE INTERVAL of comfort and repose which the party had enjoyed in their wigwam, rendered the renewal of their fatigues intolerable for the first two or three days. The snow lay deep and was slightly frozen on the surface, but not sufficiently to bear their weight. Their feet became sore by breaking through the crust, and their limbs weary by floundering on without firm foothold. So exhausted and dispirited were they, that they began to think it would be better to remain and run the risk of being killed by the Indians, than to drag on thus painfully with the probability of perishing by the way. Their miserable horse fared no better than themselves, having for the first day or two no other fodder than the ends of willow twigs and the bark of the cotton wood tree.

They all, however, appeared to gain patience and hardihood as they proceeded, and for fourteen days kept steadily on, making a distance of about three hundred and thirty miles. For some days the range of mountains which had been near to their wigwam, kept parallel to the river at no great distance, but at length subsided into hills. Sometimes they found the river bordered with alluvial bottoms and groves with cotton wood and willows; sometimes the adjacent country was naked and barren. In one place it ran for a considerable distance between rocky hills and promontories covered with cedars and pitch pines, and peopled with the big horn and the mountain deer; at other places it wandered through prairies well stocked with buffalos and antelopes. As they descended the course of the river they began to perceive the ash and white oak here and there among the cotton woods and willows; and at length caught a sight of some wild horses on the distant prairies.

The weather was various; at one time the snow lay deep, then they had a genial day or two, with the mildness and serenity of autumn; then again the frost was so severe that the river was sufficiently frozen to bear them upon the ice.

During the last three days of their fortnight's travel, however, the face of the country changed. The timber gradually diminished, until they could scarcely find fuel sufficient for culinary purposes. The game grew more and more scanty, and finally none were to be seen but a few miserable broken down buffalo bulls, not worth killing. The snow lay fifteen inches deep, and made the travelling grievously painful and toilsome. At length they came to an immense plain, where no vestige of timber was to be seen; nor a single quadruped to enliven the desolate landscape. Here then their hearts failed them and they held another consultation. The width of the river, which was upwards of a mile, its extreme shallowness, the frequency of quick sands, and various other characteristics had at length made them sensible of their errors with respect to it, and they now came to the correct conclusion that they were on the banks of the Platte or Shallow River. What were they to do? Pursue its course to the Missouri? To go on at this season of the year seemed dangerous in the extreme. There was no prospect of obtaining either food or firing. The country was destitute of trees, and though there might be drift wood along the river, it lay too deep beneath the snow for them to find it.

The weather was threatening a change, and a snow storm on these boundless wastes might prove as fatal as a whirlwind of sand on an Arabian desert. After much dreary deliberation, it was at length determined to retrace their three last days' journey, of seventy seven miles, to a place which they had remarked; where there was a sheltering growth of forest trees and a country abundant in game. Here they would once more set up their winter quarters, and await the opening of the navigation to launch themselves in canoes.

Accordingly, on the twenty seventh of December they faced about, retraced their steps and on the thirtieth regained the part of the river in question. Here the alluvial bottom was from one to two miles wide, and thickly covered with a forest of cotton wood trees; while herds of buffalo were scattered about the neighboring prairie, several of which soon fell beneath their rifles.

They encamped on the margin of the river, in a grove where there were trees large enough for canoes. Here they put up a shed for immediate shelter and immediately proceeded to erect a hut. New Year's day dawned when, as yet, but one wall of their cabin was completed; the genial and jovial day, however, was not permitted to pass uncelebrated even by this weather beaten crew of wanderers. All work was suspended except that of roasting and boiling. The choicest parts of the buffalo meat, with tongues and humps and marrow bones, were devoured in quantities that would astonish any one that has not lived among hunters or Indians; and as an extra regale, having no tobacco left, they cut up an old tobacco pouch, still redolent with the potent herb, and smoked it in honour of the day. Thus for a time in present revelry, however uncouth, they forgot all past troubles and all anxieties about the future, and their forlorn wigwam echoed to the sound of gaiety.

The next day they resumed their labors and by the sixth of the month it was complete. They soon killed abundance of buffalo, and again laid in a stock of winter provisions.

The party were more fortunate in this their second cantonment. The winter passed away without any Indian visitors; and the game continued to be plenty in the neighborhood. They felled two large trees and shaped them into canoes; and, as the spring opened, and a thaw of several days' continuance melted the ice in the river, they made every preparation for embarking. On the eighth of March they launched forth in their canoes, but soon found that the river had not depth sufficient even for such slender barks. It expanded into a wide but extremely shallow stream, with many sand bars, and occasionally various channels. They got one of their canoes a few miles down it, with extreme difficulty, sometimes wading, and dragging it over the shoals; at length they had to abandon the attempt and to resume their journey on foot, aided by their faithful old pack horse, who had recruited strength during the repose of the winter.

The weather delayed them for a few days, having suddenly become more rigorous than it had been at any time during the winter; but on the twentieth of March they were again on their journey.

In two days they arrived at the vast naked prairie, the wintry aspect of which had caused them, in December, to pause and turn back. It was now clothed in the early verdure of spring, and plentifully stocked with game. Still, when obliged to bivouac on its bare surface, without any shelter, and by a scanty fire of dry buffalo dung, they found the night blasts piercing cold. On one occasion a herd of buffalo, straying near their evening camp, they killed three of them merely for their hides, wherewith to make a shelter for the night.

They continued on for upwards of a hundred miles; with vast prairies extending before them as they advanced; sometimes diversified by undulating hills, but destitute of trees. In one place they saw a gang of sixty five wild horses, but as to the buffalos they seemed absolutely to cover the country. Wild geese abounded, and they passed extensive swamps that were alive with innumerable flocks of water fowl, among which were a few swans, but an endless variety of ducks.

The river continued a winding course to the east northeast, nearly a mile in width, but too shallow to float even an empty canoe.

The country spread out into a vast level plain, bounded by the horizon alone, excepting to the north, where a line of hills seemed like a long promontory stretching into the bosom of the ocean. The dreary sameness of the prairie wastes began to grow extremely irksome. The travellers longed for the sight of a forest, or grove, or single tree to break the level uniformity and began to notice every object that gave reason to hope they were drawing towards the end of this weary wilderness. Thus the occurrence of a particular kind of grass was hailed as a proof that they could not be far from the bottoms of the Missouri; and they were rejoiced at putting up several prairie hens, a kind of grouse seldom found far in the interior. In picking up drift wood for fuel, also, they found on some pieces the mark of an axe, which caused much speculation as to the time when and the persons by whom the trees had been felled. Thus they went on, like sailors at sea, who perceive in every floating weed and wandering bird, harbingers of the wished for land.

By the close of the month the weather became very mild, and, heavily burthened as they were, they found the noon tide temperature uncomfortably warm. On the thirtieth they came to three deserted hunting camps, either of Pawnees or Otoes, about which were buffalo sculls in all directions; and the frames on which the hides had been stretched and cured. They had apparently been occupied the preceding autumn.

For several days they kept patiently on, watching every sign that might give them an idea as to where they were, and how near to the banks of the Missouri. Though there were numerous traces of hunting parties and encampments, they were not of recent date. The country seemed deserted. The only human beings they met with were three Pawnee squaws, in a hut in the midst of a deserted camp. Their people had all gone to the south, in pursuit of the buffalo, and had left these poor women behind, being too sick and infirm to travel.

It is a common practice with the Pawnees and probably with other roving tribes, when departing on a distant expedition, which will not admit of incumbrance or delay, to leave their aged and infirm with a supply of provisions sufficient for a temporary subsistence. When this is exhausted they must perish, though sometimes their sufferings are abridged by hostile prowlers who may visit the deserted camp.

The poor squaws in question expected some such fate at the hands of the white strangers, and though the latter accosted them in the kindest manner, and made them presents of dried buffalo meat, it was impossible to soothe their alarm or get any information from them.

The first land mark by which the travellers were enabled to conjecture their position with any degree of confidence was an island about seventy miles in length, which they presumed to be Grand isle. If so they were within one hundred and forty miles of the Missouri. They kept on, therefore, with renewed spirit, and at the end of three days met with an Otoe Indian, by whom they were confirmed in their conjecture. They learnt at the same time another piece of information, of an uncomfortable nature. According to his account there was war between the United States and England, and in fact it had existed for a whole year, during which time they had been beyond the reach of all knowledge of the affairs of the civilized world.

The Otto conducted the travellers to his village, situated a short distance from the banks of the Platte. Here they were delighted to meet with two white men, Messrs. Doruin and Roi, Indian traders recently from S' Louis. Of these they had a thousand enquiries to make concerning all affairs foreign and domestic, during their year of sepulture in the wilderness; and especially about the events of the existing war.

They now prepared to abandon their weary travel by land, and to embark upon the water. A bargain was made with Mr. Doruin who engaged to furnish them with a canoe and provisions for the voyage in exchange for their venerable and well tried fellow traveller the old Snake horse.

Accordingly in a couple of days, the Indians employed by that gentleman, constructed for them a canoe twenty feet long, four feet wide, and eighteen inches deep. The frame was of poles and willow twigs, on which were stretched five elk and buffalo hides, sewed together with sinews, and the seams payed with unctuous mud. In this they embarked at an early hour of the 16th of April and drifted down ten miles with the stream when the wind being high they encamped and set to work to make oars, which they had not been able to procure at the Indian village.

Once more afloat, they went merrily down the stream and after making thirty five miles emerged into the broad turbid current of the Missouri. Here they were borne along briskly by the rapid stream, though, by the time their fragile bark had floated a couple of hundred miles, its frame began to shew the effects of the voyage. Luckily they came to the deserted wintering place of some hunting party, where they found two old wooden canoes. Taking possession of the largest, they again committed themselves to the current and after dropping down fifty five miles further, arrived safely at Fort Osage.

Here they found Lieutenant Brownson still in command; the officer who had given the expedition a hospitable reception on its way up the river, eighteen months previously. He received this remnant of the party with a cordial welcome, and endeavored in every way to promote their comfort and

enjoyment during their sojourn at the fort. The greatest luxury they met with on their return to the abode of civilized
man was bread, not having tasted any for nearly a year.

Their stay at Fort Osage was but short; on reembarking they
were furnished with an ample supply of provisions by the kindness of Lieutenant Brownson, and performed the rest of their
voyage without adverse circumstance. On the 30th of April
they arrived in perfect health and fine spirits at S' Louis, having
been ten months in performing this perilous expedition from
Astoria. Their return caused quite a sensation at the place,
bringing the first intelligence of the fortune of Mr. Hunt and
his party in their adventurous route across the Rocky Mountains, and of the new establishment on the shores of the Pacific.

Chapter LI

IT IS NOW necessary, in linking together the parts of this excursive narrative, that we notice the proceedings of Mr. Astor in support of his great undertaking. His project with respect to the Russian establishments along the north west coast, had been diligently prosecuted. The agent sent by him to St. Petersburgh, to negotiate in his name as president of the American Fur Company, had, under sanction of the Russian government, made a provisional agreement with the Russian Company.

By this agreement, which was ratified by Mr. Astor in 1813, the two companies bound themselves not to interfere with each other's trading and hunting grounds nor to furnish arms and ammunition to the Indians. They were to act in concert, also, against all interlopers, and to succor each other in case of danger. The American company was to have the exclusive right of supplying the Russian posts with goods and necessaries, receiving peltries in payment at stated prices. They were, also, if so requested by the Russian governor, to convey the furs of the Russian Company to Canton, sell them on commission and bring back the proceeds, at such freight as might be agreed on at the time.

This agreement was to continue in operation four years, and to be renewable for a similar term unless some unforeseen contingency should render a modification necessary. It was calculated to be of great service to the infant establishment at Astoria: dispelling the fears of hostile rivalry on the part of the foreign companies in its neighborhood and giving a formidable blow to the irregular trade along the coast. It was also the intention of Mr. Astor to have coasting vessels of his own, at Astoria, of small tonnage and draft of water, fitted for coasting service. These, having a place of shelter and deposit, could ply about the coast in short voyages in favorable weather, and would have vast advantage over chance ships, which must make long voyages, maintain numerous crews, and could only approach the coast at certain seasons of the year. He hoped, therefore, gradually to make Astoria the great emporium of the American fur trade in the Pacific and the nucleus of a powerful American state.

Unfortunately for these sanguine anticipations, before Mr. Astor had ratified the agreement, as above stated, war broke out between the United States and Great Britain. He perceived at once the peril of the case. The harbor of New York would, doubtless, be blockaded and the departure of the annual supply ship in the autumn prevented: or, if she should succeed in getting out to sea, she might be captured on her voyage.

In this emergency he wrote to Captain Sowle, Commander of the Beaver. The letter, which was addressed to him at Canton, directed him to proceed to the Factory at the mouth of the Columbia, with such articles as the establishment might need; and to remain there, subject to the orders of Mr. Hunt, should that gentleman be in command there.

The war continued. No tidings had yet been received from Astoria; the despatches having been delayed by the misadventure of Mr. Reed at the falls of the Columbia, and the unhorsing of Mr. Stuart by the Crows among the mountains. A painful uncertainty, also, prevailed about Mr. Hunt and his party. Nothing had been heard of them since their departure from the Arickara village; Lisa who parted from them there had predicted their destruction; and some of the traders of the North West Company had actually spread a rumor of their having been cut off by the Indians.

It was a hard trial of the courage and the means of an individual, to have to fit out another costly expedition where so much had already been expended, so much uncertainty prevailed, and where the risk of loss was so greatly enhanced that no insurance could be effected.

In spite of all these discouragements, Mr. Astor determined to send another ship to the relief of the settlement. He selected for this purpose a vessel called the Lark, remarkable for her fast sailing. The disordered state of the times, however, caused such delay that February arrived while the vessel was yet lingering in port.

At this juncture Mr. Astor learnt that the North West Company were preparing to send out an armed ship of twenty guns, called the Isaac Todd, to form an establishment at the mouth of the Columbia. These tidings gave him great uneasiness. A considerable proportion of the persons in his employ were Scotchmen and Canadians, and several of them had been in the service of the North West Company. Should Mr. Hunt have failed to arrive at Astoria the whole establishment would be under the control of Mr. M'Dougall, of whose fidelity he had received very disparaging accounts from Captain Thorn. The British government, also, might deem it worth while to send a force against the establishment, having been urged to do so some time previously, by the North West Company.

Under all these circumstances Mr. Astor wrote to Mr. Monroe, then Secretary of State, requesting protection from the government of the United States. He represented the importance of his settlement in a commercial point of view, and the shelter it might afford to the American vessels in those seas. All he asked was that the American government would throw forty or fifty men into the fort at his establishment, which would be sufficient for its defence until he could send reinforcements over land.

He waited in vain for a reply to this letter, the government, no doubt, being engrossed at the time by an overwhelming crowd of affairs. The month of March arrived and the Lark was ordered by Mr. Astor to put to sea. The officer who was to command her shrunk from his engagement, and in the exigency of the moment she was given in charge to Mr. Northrop the Mate. Mr. Nicholas G. Ogden, a gentleman on whose talents and integrity the highest reliance could be placed, sailed as supercargo. The Lark put to sea in the beginning of March 1813.

By this opportunity Mr. Astor wrote to Mr. Hunt, as head of the establishment at the mouth of the Columbia, for he would not allow himself to doubt of his welfare. "I always think you are well," said he, "and that I shall see you again, which heaven, I hope, will grant."

He warned him to be on his guard against any attempt to surprize the post; suggesting the probability of armed hostility on the part of the North West Company: and expressing his indignation at the ungrateful returns made by that association for his frank and open conduct and advantageous overtures. "Were I on the spot," said he, "and had the management of affairs, I would defy them all; but as it is, every thing depends upon you and your friends about you. *Our enterprize is grand and deserves success, and I hope in God it will meet it.* If my object was merely gain of money I should say think whether it is best to save what we can and abandon the place, *but the very idea is like a dagger to my heart.*" This extract is sufficient to shew the spirit and the views which actuated Mr. Astor in this great undertaking.

Week after week, and month after month elapsed, without any thing to dispel the painful incertitude that hung over every part of this enterprize. Though a man of resolute spirit and not easily cast down, the dangers impending over this darling scheme of his ambition had a gradual effect upon the spirits of Mr. Astor. He was sitting one gloomy evening by his window revolving over the loss of the Tonquin, and the fate of her unfortunate crew, and fearing that some equally tragical calamity might have befallen the adventurers across the Mountains, when the evening newspaper was brought to him. The first paragraph that caught his eye announced the arrival of Mr. Stuart and his party at S' Louis, with intelligence that Mr. Hunt and his companions had effected their perilous expedition to the mouth of the Columbia. This was a gleam of sunshine that for a time dispelled every cloud, and he now looked forward with sanguine hope to the accomplishment of all his plans.

Chapter LII

THE COURSE of our narrative now takes us back to the regions beyond the mountains, to dispose of the parties that set out from Astoria in company with Mr. Robert Stuart, and whom he left on the banks of the Wallah Wallah. Those parties likewise separated from each other shortly after his departure, proceeding to their respective destinations, but agreeing to meet at the mouth of the Wallah Wallah about the beginning of June in the following year, with such peltries as they should have collected in the interim, so as to convoy each other through the dangerous passes of the Columbia.

Mr. David Stuart, one of the partners, proceeded with his men to the post already established by him at the mouth of the Oakinagan; having furnished this with goods and ammunition he proceeded three hundred miles up that river, where he established another post in a good trading neighborhood.

Mr. Clarke, another partner, conducted his little band up Lewis River to the mouth of a small stream coming in from the north, to which the Canadians gave the name of the Pavion. Here he found a village or encampment of forty huts or tents covered with mats and inhabited by *Nez percés* or Pierced nose Indians as they are called by the traders; but Chopunnish, as they are called by themselves. They are a hardy, laborious and somewhat knavish race, who lead a precarious life, fishing and digging roots during the summer and autumn, hunting the deer on snow shoes during the winter, and traversing the Rocky Mountains in the spring to trade for buffalo skins with the hunting tribes of the Missouri. In these migrations they are liable to be way laid and attacked by the Blackfeet and other warlike and predatory tribes, and driven back across the mountains with the loss of their horses, and of many of their comrades.

A life of this unsettled and precarious kind is apt to render men selfish, and such Mr. Clarke found the inhabitants of this village, who were deficient in the usual hospitality of Indians; parting with every thing with extreme reluctance, and shewing no sensibility to any act of kindness. At the time of his arrival they were all occupied in catching and curing salmon. The men were stout, robust, active and good looking, and the women handsomer than those of the tribes nearer to the coast.

It was the plan of Mr. Clarke to lay up his boats here and proceed by land to his place of destination, which was among the Spokan tribe of Indians about a hundred and fifty miles distant. He accordingly endeavored to purchase horses for the journey, but in this he had to contend with the sordid disposition of these people. They asked high prices for their horses, and were so difficult to deal with that Mr. Clarke was detained seven days among them before he could procure a sufficient number. During that time he was annoyed by repeated pilferings, for which he could get no redress. The chief promised to recover the stolen articles; but failed to do so, alleging that the thieves belonged to a distant tribe and had made off with their booty. With this excuse Mr. Clarke was fain to content himself, though he laid up in his heart a bitter grudge against the whole Pierced nose race, which it will be found he took occasion subsequently to gratify in a signal manner.

Having made arrangements for his departure Mr. Clarke laid up his barge and canoes in a sheltered place on the banks of a small bay overgrown with shrubs and willows, confiding them to the care of the Nez percé chief, who on being promised an ample compensation, engaged to have a guardian eye upon them. Then mounting his steed and putting himself at the head of his little caravan, he shook the dust off his feet as he turned his back upon this village of rogues and hard dealers.

We shall not follow him minutely in his journey; which lay at times over steep and rocky hills, and among crags and precipices; at other times over vast naked and sun burnt plains, abounding with rattlesnakes, in traversing which both men and horses suffered intolerably from heat and thirst. The place on which he fixed for a trading post was a fine point of land at the junction of the Pointed heart and Spokan rivers. His establishment was intended to compete with a trading post of the North West Company situated at no great distance, and to rival it in the trade with the Spokan Indians; as well as with the Cootonais and Flatheads. In this neighborhood we shall leave him for the present.

Mr. M'Kenzie, who conducted the third party from the Wallah Wallah, navigated for several days up the south branch of the Columbia, named the Camöenum by the natives, but commonly called Lewis River, in honor of the first explorer. Wandering bands of various tribes were seen along this river, travelling in various directions: for the Indians generally are restless roving beings, continually intent on enterprizes of war, traffic and hunting. Some of these people were driving large gangs of horses, as if to a distant market. Having arrived at the mouth of the Shahaptan he ascended some distance up that river and established his trading post upon its banks. This appeared to be a great thoroughfare for the tribes from the neighborhood of the falls of the Columbia, in their expeditions to make war upon the tribes of the Rocky Mountains; to hunt buffalo on the plains beyond, or to traffic for roots and buffalo robes. It was the season of migration, and the Indians from various distant parts were passing and repassing in great numbers.

Mr. M'Kenzie now detached a small band, under the conduct of Mr. John Reed, to visit the caches made by Mr. Hunt at the Caldron Linn, and to bring the contents to his post; as he depended, in some measure, on them for his supplies of goods and ammunition. They had not been gone a week when two Indians arrived of the Pallatapalla tribe, who live upon a river of the same name. These communicated the unwelcome intelligence that the caches had been robbed. They said that some of their tribe had, in the course of the preceding spring, been across the mountains which separated them from Snake River, and had traded horses with the Snakes in exchange for blankets, robes and goods of various descriptions. These articles the Snakes had procured from caches to which they were guided by some white men who resided among them, and who afterwards accompanied them across the Rocky Mountains. This intelligence was extremely perplexing to Mr. M'Kenzie, but the truth of part of it was confirmed by the two Indians, who brought them an English saddle and bridle, which was recognized as having belonged to Mr. Crooks. The perfidy of the white men who revealed the secret of the caches was however perfectly inexplicable. We shall presently account for it, in narrating the expedition of Mr. Reed.

That worthy Hibernian proceeded on his mission with his usual alacrity. His forlorn travels of the preceding winter had made him acquainted with the topography of the country and he reached Snake River without any material difficulty. Here, in an encampment of the natives, he met with six white men, wanderers from the main expedition of Mr. Hunt, who, after having had their respective shares of adventures and mishaps, had fortunately come together at this place.

Three of these men were Turcotte, La Chapelle and Francis Landry; the three Canadian voyageurs who, it may be recollected, had left Mr. Crooks in February in the neighborhood of Snake River, being dismayed by the encreasing hardships of the journey, and fearful of perishing of hunger. They had returned to a Snake encampment, where they passed the residue of the winter.

Early in the spring, being utterly destitute and in great extremity, and having worn out the hospitality of the Snakes, they determined to avail themselves of the buried treasures within their knowledge. They accordingly informed the Snake chieftains that they knew where a great quantity of goods had been left in caches, enough to enrich the whole tribe; and offered to conduct them to the place, on condition of being rewarded with horses and provisions. The chieftains pledged their faith and honor as great men and Snakes, and the three Canadians conducted them to the place of deposit at the Caldron Linn. This is the way that the savages got knowledge of the caches, and not by following the tracks of wolves, as Mr. Stuart had supposed. Never did money diggers turn up a miser's hoard with more eager delight than did the savages lay open the treasures of the caches. Blankets and robes, brass trinkets and blue beads were drawn forth with chuckling exultation, and long strips of scarlet cloth produced yells of extacy.

The rifling of the caches effected a change in the fortunes and deportment of the whole party. The Snakes were better clad and equipped than ever were Snakes before, and the three Canadians, suddenly finding themselves with horse to ride and weapon to wear, were, like beggars on horseback, ready to ride on any wild scamper. An opportunity soon presented. The Snakes determined on a hunting match on the buffalo prairies, to lay in a supply of beef, that they might live in plenty as became men of their improved condition. The three newly mounted cavaliers must fain accompany them. They all traversed the Rocky Mountains in safety, descended to the head waters of the Missouri and made great havoc among the buffalos.

Their hunting camp was full of meat; they were gorging themselves, like true Indians, with present plenty, and drying and jirking great quantities for a winter's supply. In the midst of their revelry and good cheer the camp was surprized by the Blackfeet. Several of the Snakes were slain on the spot; the residue, with their three Canadian allies, fled to the Mountains, stripped of horses, buffalo meat, every thing; and made their way back to the old encampment on Snake River, poorer than ever, but esteeming themselves fortunate in having escaped with their lives. They had not been long there when the Canadians were cheered by the sight of a companion in misfortune, Dubreuil, the poor voyageur who had left Mr. Crooks in March, being too much exhausted to keep on with him.

Not long afterwards three other straggling members of the main expedition made their appearance. These were Carson, St. Michel and Pierre Delaunay, three of the trappers who, in company with Pierre Detayé, had been left among the mountains by Mr. Hunt, to trap beaver, in the preceding month of September. They had departed from the main body well armed and provided, with horses to ride, and horses to carry the peltries they were to collect. They came wandering into the Snake camp as ragged and destitute as their predecessors. It appears that they had finished their trapping and were making their way in the spring to the Missouri when they were met and attacked by a powerful band of the all pervading Crows. They made a desperate resistance and killed seven of the savages, but were overpowered by numbers. Pierre Detayé was slain; the rest were robbed of horses and effects and obliged to turn back, when they fell in with their old companions as already mentioned.

We should observe that at the heels of Pierre Delaunay came draggling an Indian wife whom he had picked up in his wanderings, having grown weary of celibacy among the savages.

The whole seven of this forlorn fraternity of adventurers, thus accidentally congregated on the banks of Snake River, were making arrangements once more to cross the Mountains, when some Indian scouts brought word of the approach of the little band headed by John Reed.

The latter, having heard the several stories of these wanderers, took them all into his party, and set out for the Caldron Linn, to clear out two or three of the caches which had not been revealed to the Indians. At that place he met with Robinson, the Kentucky veteran who, with his two comrades Rezner and Hoback, had remained there when Mr. Stuart went on. This adventurous trio had been trapping higher up the river, but Robinson had come down in a canoe, to await the expected arrival of the party, and obtain horses and equipments. He told Reed the story of the robbery of his party by the Arapahays, but it differed, in some particulars, from the account given by him to Mr. Stuart. In that he had represented Cass as having shamefully deserted his companions in their extremity, carrying off with him a horse: in the one now given he spoke of him as having been killed in the affray with the Arapahays. This discrepancy, of which of course Reed could have had no knowledge at the time, concurred with other circumstances, to occasion afterwards some mysterious speculations and dark surmises as to the real fate of Cass; but as no substantial grounds were ever adduced for them, we forbear to throw any deeper shades into this story of sufferings in the wilderness.

Mr. Reed having gathered the remainder of the goods from the caches, put himself at the head of his party, now augmented by the seven men thus casually picked up and the squaw of Pierre Delaunay, and made his way successfully to M'Kenzie's post on the waters of the Shahaptan.

Chapter LIII

AFTER the departure of the different detachments, or *brigades*, as they are called by the fur traders, the Beaver prepared for her voyage along the coast and her visit to the Russian establishment at New Archangel, where she was to carry supplies. It had been determined in the council of partners at Astoria, that Mr. Hunt should embark in this vessel, for the purpose of acquainting himself with the coasting trade and of making arrangements with the commander of the Russian post, and that he should be relanded in October, at Astoria, by the Beaver, on her way to the Sandwich islands and Canton.

The Beaver put to sea in the month of August. Her departure, and that of the various brigades, left the fortress of Astoria but slightly garrisoned. This was soon perceived by some of the Indian tribes, and the consequence was increased insolence of deportment and a disposition to hostility. It was now the fishing season, when the tribes from the northern coast drew into the neighborhood of the Columbia. These were warlike and perfidious in their dispositions; and noted for their attempts to surprize trading ships. Among them were numbers of the Neweetees, the ferocious tribe that massacred the crew of the Tonquin.

Great precautions, therefore, were taken at the factory to guard against surprize while these dangerous intruders were in the vicinity. Galleries were constructed inside of the palisades; the bastions were heightened and centinels were posted day and night. Fortunately the Chinooks and other tribes resident in the vicinity manifested the most pacific disposition. Old Comcomly who held sway over them was a shrewd calculator. He was aware of the advantages of having the whites as neighbors and allies, and of the consequence derived to himself and his people from acting as intermediate traders between them and the distant tribes. He had, therefore, by this time become a firm friend of the Astorians, and formed a kind of barrier between them and the hostile intruders from the north.

The summer of 1812 passed away without any of the hostilities that had been apprehended; the Neweetees and other dangerous visitors to the neighborhood finished their fishing and returned home, and the inmates of the factory once more felt secure from attack.

It now became necessary to guard against other evils. The season of scarcity arrived, which commences in October and lasts until the end of January. To provide for the support of the garrison the shallop was employed to forage about the shores of the river. A number of the men, also, under the command of some of the clerks, were sent to quarter themselves on the banks of the Wollamut, (the Multnomah of Lewis and Clark) a fine river which disembogues itself into the Columbia about sixty miles above Astoria. The country bordering on this river is finely diversified with prairies and hills and forests of oak, ash, maple and cedar. It abounded at that time with elk and deer, and the streams were well stocked with beaver. Here the party after supplying their own wants, were enabled to pack up quantities of dried meat and send it by canoes to Astoria.

The month of October elapsed without the return of the Beaver: November, December, January passed away, and still nothing was seen or heard of her. Gloomy apprehensions now began to be entertained: she might have been wrecked in the course of her coasting voyage, or surprized, like the Tonquin, by some of the treacherous tribes of the north.

No one indulged more in these apprehensions than M'Dougall, who had now the charge of the establishment. He no longer evinced the bustling confidence and buoyancy which once characterized him. Command seemed to have lost its charms for him; or rather, he gave way to the most abject despondency, decrying the whole enterprize, magnifying every untoward circumstance, and foreboding nothing but evil.

While in this moody state he was surprized, on the 16th of January, by the sudden appearance of M'Kenzie, way worn and weather beaten by a long wintry journey from his post on the Shahaptan, and with a face the very frontispiece for a volume of misfortune. M'Kenzie had been heartily disgusted and disappointed at his post. It was in the midst of the Tushepaws, a powerful and warlike nation, divided into many tribes under different chiefs, who possessed innumerable horses, but, not having turned their attention to beaver trapping had no furs to offer. According to M'Kenzie they were but a "'rascally tribe;" from which we may infer that they were prone to consult their own interests more than comported with the interests of a greedy Indian trader.

Game being scarce, he was obliged to rely for the most part, on horse flesh for subsistence, and the Indians, discovering his necessities, adopted a policy usual in civilized trade, and raised the price of horses to an exorbitant rate, knowing that he and his men must eat or die. In this way the goods he had brought to trade for beaver skins were likely to be bartered for horse flesh, and all the proceeds devoured upon the spot.

He had despatched trappers in various directions, but the country around did not offer more beaver than his own station. In this emergency he began to think of abandoning his unprofitable post; sending his goods to the posts of Clarke and David Stuart who could make a better use of them as they were in a good beaver country, and returning with his party to Astoria, to seek some better destination. With this view he repaired to the post of Mr. Clarke to hold a consultation. While the two partners were in conference in Mr. Clarke's wigwam an unexpected visitor came bustling in upon them. This was Mr. John George M'Tavish, a partner of the North West Company who had charge of the rival trading posts established in that neighborhood. Mr. M'Tavish was the delighted messenger of bad news. He had been to Lake Winnipeg, where he received an express from Canada containing the declaration of war and President Madison's proclamation, which he handed with the most officious complaisance to Messrs. Clarke and

M'Kenzie. He moreover told them that he had received a fresh supply of goods from the North West posts on the other side of the Rocky Mountains, and was prepared for vigorous opposition to the establishments of the American company. He capped the climax of this obliging, but belligerent, intelligence by informing them that the armed ship Isaac Todd, was to be at the mouth of the Columbia about the beginning of March, to get possession of the trade of the river, and that he was ordered to join her there at that time.

The receipt of this news determined M'Kenzie. He immediately returned to the Shahaptan; broke up his establishment; deposited his goods in *cache*, and hastened with all his people to Astoria.

The intelligence thus brought completed the dismay of M'Dougall and seemed to produce a complete confusion of mind. He held Council of War with M'Kenzie, at which some of the clerks were present, but of course had no votes. They gave up all hope of maintaining their post at Astoria. The Beaver had probably been lost; they could receive no aid from the United States, as all the ports would be blockaded. From England nothing could be expected but hostility. It was determined, therefore, to abandon the establishment in the course of the following spring and return across the Rocky Mountains.

In pursuance of this resolution they suspended all trade with the natives except for provisions, having already more peltries than they could carry away, and having need of all the goods for the clothing and subsistence of their people during the remainder of their sojourn and on their journey across the Mountains. Their intention of abandoning Astoria was, however, kept secret from the men lest they should at once give up all labour and become restless and insubordinate.

In the mean time M'Kenzie set off for his post at the Shahaptan, to get his goods from the caches and buy horses and provisions with them for the caravan across the mountains. He was charged with despatches from M'Dougall to Messrs. Stuart and Clarke, apprising them of the intended migration, that they might make timely preparations.

M'Kenzie was accompanied by two of the clerks, Mr. John Reed, the Irishman, and Mr. Alfred Seton of New York. They embarked in two canoes manned by seventeen men and ascended the river without any incident of importance until they arrived in the eventful neighborhood of the rapids. They made the portage of the narrows and the falls early in the afternoon and, having partaken of a scanty meal, had now a long evening on their hands.

On the opposite side of the river lay the village of Wish-ram of freebooting renown. Here lived the savages who had robbed and maltreated Reed when bearing his tin box of despatches. It was known that the rifle of which he was despoiled was retained as a trophy at the village. M'Kenzie offered to cross the river and demand the rifle if any one would accompany him. It was a hare brained project, for these villages were noted for the ruffian character of their inhabitants; yet two volunteers promptly stepped forward,—Alfred Seton the clerk, and Joe de la Pierre the cook. The trio soon reached the opposite side of the river. On landing they freshly primed their rifles and pistols. A path winding for about a hundred yards among rocks and crags led to the village. No notice seemed to be taken of their approach. Not a solitary being, man, woman or child greeted them. The very dogs, those noisy pests of an Indian town, kept silence. On entering the village a boy made his appearance and pointed to a house of larger dimensions than the rest. They had to stoop to enter it; as soon as they had passed the threshold, the narrow passage behind them was filled up by a sudden rush of Indians who had before kept out of sight.

M'Kenzie and his companions found themselves in a rude chamber about twenty five feet long and twenty wide. A bright fire was blazing at one end, near which sat the chief, about sixty years old. A large number of Indians wrapped in buffalo robes were squatted in rows, three deep, forming a semi circle round three sides of the room. A single glance around sufficed to shew them the grim and dangerous assemblage into which they had intruded, and that all retreat was cut off by the mass which blocked up the entrance.

The chief pointed to the vacant side of the room opposite to the door, and motioned for them to take their seats. They complied. A dead pause ensued. The grim warriors around sat like statues; each muffled in his robe with his fierce eyes bent on the intruders. The latter felt they were in a perilous predicament.

"Keep your eyes on the chief while I am addressing him," said M'Kenzie to his companions. "Should he give any sign to his band shoot him and make for the door."

M'Kenzie advanced and offered the pipe of peace to the chief, but it was refused. He then made a regular speech, explaining the object of their visit, and proposing to give in exchange for the rifle two blankets, an axe, some beads and tobacco.

When he had done the chief rose; began to address him in a low voice but soon became loud and violent and ended by working himself up into a furious passion. He upbraided the white men for their sordid conduct in passing and repassing through their neighborhood without giving them a blanket or any other article of goods, merely because they had no furs to barter in exchange, and he alluded with menaces of vengeance, to the death of the Indian killed by the whites in the skirmish at the Falls.

Matters were verging to a crisis. It was evident the surrounding savages were only waiting a signal from the chief to spring upon their prey. M'Kenzie and his companions had gradually risen on their feet during the speech and had brought their rifles to a horizontal position, the barrels resting in their left hands; the muzzle of M'Kenzie's piece was within three feet of the speaker's heart. They cocked their rifles; the click of the locks for a moment suffused the dark cheek of the savage and there was a pause. They coolly but promptly advanced to the door; the Indians fell back in awe and suffered them to pass. The sun was just setting as they emerged from this dangerous den. They took the precaution to keep along the tops of the rocks as much as possible on their way back to the canoe, and reached their camp in safety, congratulating themselves on their escape, and feeling no desire to make a second visit to the grim warriors of Wish-ram.

M'Kenzie and his party resumed their journey the next morning. At some distance above the Falls of the Columbia they observed two bark canoes filled with white men coming down the river, to the full chant of a set of Canadian voyageurs. A parley ensued. It was a detachment of North Westers, under the command of Mr. John George M'Tavish, bound, full of song and spirit, to the mouth of the Columbia to await the arrival of the Isaac Todd.

M'Kenzie and M'Tavish came to a halt and landing encamped together for the night. The voyageurs of either party hailed each other as brothers and old "camerades," and they mingled together as if united by one common interest, instead of belonging to rival companies and trading under hostile flags.

In the morning they proceeded on their different ways, in style correspondent to their different fortunes, the one toiling painfully against the stream, the other sweeping down gaily with the current.

M'Kenzie arrived safely at his deserted post on the Shahaptan, but found to his chagrin that his caches had been discovered and rifled by the Indians. Here was a dilemma, for, on the stolen goods he had depended to purchase horses of the Indians. He sent out men in all directions to endeavor to discover the thieves, and despatched Mr. Reed to the posts of Messrs. Clarke and David Stuart with the letters of Mr. M'Dougall.

The resolution announced in these letters, to break up and depart from Astoria, was condemned by both Clarke and Stuart. These two gentlemen had been very successful at their posts and considered it rash and pusillanimous to abandon, on the first difficulty, an enterprize of such great cost and ample promise. They made no arrangements, therefore, for leaving the country but acted with a view to the maintenance of their new and prosperous establishments.

The regular time approached, when the partners of the interior posts were to rendezvous at the mouth of the Wallah Wallah, on their way to Astoria with the peltries they had collected. Mr. Clarke accordingly packed all his furs on twenty eight horses, and leaving a clerk and four men to take charge of the post, departed on the 25th of May with the residue of his force.

On the 30th he arrived at the confluence of the Pavion and Lewis rivers, where he had left his barge and canoes in the guardianship of the old Pierced nose chieftain. That dignitary had acquitted himself more faithfully of his charge than

Mr. Clarke had expected, and the canoes were found in very tolerable order. Some repairs were necessary, and, while they were making them, the party encamped close by the village. Having had repeated and vexatious proofs of the pilfering propensities of this tribe during his former visit, Mr. Clarke ordered that a wary eye should be kept upon them.

He was a tall, good looking man, and somewhat given to pomp and circumstance, which made him an object of note in the eyes of the wondering savages. He was stately too in his appointments, and had a silver goblet or drinking cup, out of which he would drink with a magnificent air and then lock it up in a large *garde vin*, which accompanied him in his travels and stood in his tent. This goblet had originally been sent as a present from Mr. Astor to Mr. M'Kay, the partner who had unfortunately been blown up in the Tonquin. As it reached Astoria after the departure of that gentleman it had remained in the possession of Mr. Clarke.

A silver goblet was too glittering a prize not to catch the eye of a Pierced nose. It was like the shining tin case of John Reed. Such a wonder had never been seen in the land before. The Indians talked about it to one another. They marked the care with which it was deposited in the *garde vin*, like a relique in its shrine and concluded that it must be a "Great Medicine." That night Mr. Clarke neglected to lock up his treasure; in the morning the sacred casket was open—the precious relique gone!

Clarke was now outrageous. All the past vexations that he had suffered from this pilfering community rose to mind, and he threatened that unless the goblet was promptly returned, he would hang the thief should he eventually discover him. The day passed away, however, without the restoration of the cup. At night sentinels were secretly posted about the camp. With all their vigilance a Pierced nose contrived to get into the camp unperceived and to load himself with booty; it was only on his retreat that he was discovered and taken.

At daybreak the culprit was brought to trial and promptly convicted. He stood responsible for all the spoliations of the camp; the precious goblet among the number, and Mr. Clarke passed sentence of death upon him.

A gibbet was accordingly constructed of oars: the chief of the village and his people were assembled and the culprit was produced, with his legs and arms pinioned. Clarke then made a harangue. He reminded the tribe of the benefits he had bestowed upon them during his former visit, and the many thefts and other misdeeds which he had overlooked. The prisoner, especially, had always been peculiarly well treated by the white men, but had repeatedly been guilty of pilfering. He was to be punished for his own misdeeds and as a warning to his tribe.

The Indians now gathered round Mr. Clarke and interceded for the culprit. They were willing he should be punished severely but implored that his life might be spared. The companions too of Mr. Clarke considered the sentence too severe and advised him to mitigate it; but he was inexorable. He was not naturally a stern or cruel man; but from his boyhood he had lived in the Indian country among Indian traders, and held the life of a savage extremely cheap. He was, moreover, a firm believer in the doctrine of intimidation.

Farnham, a clerk, a tall "Green mountain boy" from Vermont, who had been robbed of a pistol, acted as executioner. The signal was given and the poor Pierced nose, resisting, struggling and screaming in the most frightful manner, was launched into eternity. The Indians stood round gazing in silence and mute awe, but made no attempt to oppose the execution, nor testified any emotion when it was over. They locked up their feelings within their bosoms until an opportunity should arrive to gratify them with a bloody act of vengeance.

To say nothing of the needless severity of this act, its impolicy was glaringly obvious. Mr. M'Lennon and three men were to return to the post with the horses, their loads having been transferred to the canoes. They would have to pass through a tract of country infested by this tribe, who were all horsemen and hard riders and might pursue them to take vengeance for the death of their comrade. M'Lennon, however, was a resolute fellow and made light of all dangers. He and his three men were present at the execution, and set off as soon as life was extinct in the victim; but, to use the words of one of their comrades, "they did not let the grass grow under the heels of their horses as they clattered out of the Pierced nose country," and were glad to find themselves in safety at the post.

Mr. Clarke and his party embarked about the same time in their canoes and early on the following day reached the mouth of the Wallah Wallah, where they found Messrs. Stuart and M'Kenzie awaiting them; the latter having recovered part of the goods stolen from his cache. Clarke informed them of the signal punishment he had inflicted on the Pierced nose, evidently expecting to excite their admiration by such a hardy act of justice, performed in the very midst of the Indian country, but was mortified at finding it strongly censured as inhuman, unnecessary and likely to provoke hostilities.

The parties thus united formed a squadron of two boats and six canoes with which they performed their voyage in safety down the river, and arrived at Astoria on the 12th of June, bringing with them a valuable stock of peltries.

About ten days previously the brigade which had been quartered on the banks of the Wallamut, had arrived with numerous packs of beaver, the result of a few months' sojourn on that river. These were the first fruits of the enterprize, gathered by men as yet mere strangers in the land; but they were such as to give substantial grounds for sanguine anticipations of profit, when the country should be more completely explored, and the trade established.

Chapter LIV

THE PARTNERS found Mr. M'Dougall in all the bustle of preparation; having about nine days previously announced at the factory his intention of breaking up the establishment, and fixed upon the 1st of July for the time of departure. Messrs. Stuart and Clarke felt highly displeased at his taking so precipitate a step, without waiting for their concurrence, when he must have known that their arrival could not be far distant.

Indeed the whole conduct of Mr. M'Dougall was such as to awaken strong doubts as to his loyal devotion to the cause. His old sympathies with the North West Company seemed to have revived. He had received M'Tavish and his party with uncalled for hospitality, as though they were friends and allies; instead of being a party of observation: come to reconnoiter the state of affairs at Astoria, and to await the arrival of a hostile ship. Had they been left to themselves they would have been starved off for want of provisions, or driven away by the Chinooks, who only wanted a signal from the factory to treat them as intruders and enemies. M'Dougall, on the contrary, had supplied them from the stores of the garrison, and had gained them the favor of the Indians by treating them as friends.

Having set his mind fixedly on the project of breaking up the establishment at Astoria in the current year, M'Dougall was sorely disappointed at finding that Messrs. Stuart and Clarke had omitted to comply with his request to purchase horses and provisions for the caravan across the Mountains. It was now too late to make the necessary preparations in time for traversing the mountains before winter, and the project had to be postponed.

In the mean time the non arrival of the annual ship, and the apprehensions entertained of the loss of the Beaver and of

Mr. Hunt, had their effect upon the minds of Messrs. Stuart and Clarke: and they began to listen to the desponding representations of M'Dougall, seconded by M'Kenzie, who inveighed against their situation as desperate and forlorn; left to shift for themselves or perish upon a barbarous coast; neglected by those who sent them there, and threatened with dangers of every kind. In this way they were brought to consent to the plan of abandoning the country in the ensuing year.

About this time M'Tavish applied at the factory to purchase a small supply of goods wherewith to trade his way back to his post on the upper waters of the Columbia, having waited in vain for the arrival of the Isaac Todd. His request brought on a consultation among the partners. M'Dougall urged that it should be complied with. He furthermore proposed that they should give up to M'Tavish, for a proper consideration, the post on the Spokan and all its dependencies, as they had not sufficient goods on hand to supply that fort themselves, and to keep up a competition with the North West Company in the trade with the neighboring Indians. This last representation has since been proved incorrect. By inventories it appears that their stock in hand for the supply of the interior posts, was superior to that of the North West Company; so that they had nothing to fear from competition.

Through the influence of Messrs. M'Dougall and M'Kenzie this proposition was adopted; and was promptly accepted by M'Tavish. The merchandize sold to him amounted to eight hundred and fifty eight dollars, to be paid for, in the following spring, in horses, or in any other manner most acceptable to the partners at that period.

This agreement being concluded, the partners formed their plans for the year that they would yet have to pass in the country. Their objects were chiefly present subsistence and the purchase of horses for the contemplated journey, though they were likewise to collect as much peltries as their diminished means would command. Accordingly, it was arranged that David Stuart should return to his former post on the Oakinagan, and Mr. Clarke should make his sojourn among the Flatheads; John Reed the sturdy Hibernian was to undertake the Snake River country, accompanied by Pierre Dorion and Pierre Delaunay as hunters, and Francis Landry,

Jean Baptiste Turcotte, André La Chapelle and Giles Le Clerc, Canadian voyageurs.

Astoria, however, was the post about which they felt the greatest solicitude, and on which they all more or less depended. The maintenance of this in safety throughout the coming year was, therefore, their grand consideration. Mr. M'Dougall was to continue in command at it, with a party of forty men. They would have to depend chiefly upon the neighboring savages for their subsistence. These, at present, were friendly, but it was to be feared that, when they should discover the exigencies of the post, and its real weakness, they might proceed to hostilities; or at any rate might cease to furnish their usual supplies. It was important therefore to render the place as independent as possible of the surrounding tribes for its support; and it was accordingly resolved that M'Kenzie with four hunters and eight common men should winter in the abundant country of the Wollamut, from whence they might be enabled to furnish a constant supply of provisions to Astoria.

As there was too great a proportion of clerks for the number of privates in the service, the engagements of three of them, Cox, Ross and M'Lennon were surrendered to them, and they immediately enrolled themselves in the service of the North West Company, glad no doubt to escape from what they considered a sinking ship.

Having made all these arrangements the four partners on the first of July signed a formal manifesto, stating the alarming state of their affairs from the non arrival of the annual ship; and the absence and apprehended loss of the Beaver; their want of goods, their despair of receiving any further supply, their ignorance of the coast, and their disappointment as to the interior trade, which they pronounced unequal to the expenses incurred and incompetent to stand against the powerful opposition of the North West Company. And as by the 16th article of the Company's agreement they were authorized to abandon this undertaking and dissolve the concern, if before the period of five years, it should be found unprofitable; they now formally announced their intention to do so on the 1st day of June of the ensuing year, unless, in the interim, they should receive the necessary support and supplies from Mr. Astor or the stockholders, with orders to continue.

This instrument, accompanied by private letters of similar import, was delivered to Mr. M'Tavish who departed on the 5th of July. He engaged to forward the despatches to Mr. Astor by the usual winter express, sent overland by the North West Company.

The manifesto was signed with great reluctance by Messrs. Clarke and D. Stuart, whose experience by no means justified the discouraging account given in it of the internal trade, and who considered the main difficulties of exploring an unknown and savage country, and of ascertaining the best trading and trapping grounds, in a great measure overcome. They were over ruled, however, by the urgent instances of M'Dougall and M'Kenzie, who, having resolved upon abandoning the enterprize, were desirous of making as strong a case as possible to excuse their conduct to Mr. Astor and to the world.

Chapter LV

W HILE difficulties and disasters had been gathering about the infant settlement of Astoria the mind of its projector at New York was a prey to great anxiety. The Ship Lark despatched by him with supplies for the establishment sailed on the 6th of March 1813. Within a fortnight afterwards he received intelligence which justified all his apprehensions of hostility on the part of the British. The North West Company had made a second memorial to that government, representing Astoria as an American establishment, stating the vast scope of its contemplated operations, magnifying the strength of its fortifications, and expressing their fears that, unless crushed in the bud, it would effect the downfall of their trade.

Influenced by these representations the British government ordered the Frigate Phoebe to be detached as a convoy for the armed ship Isaac Todd, which was ready to sail with men and munitions for forming a new establishment. They were to proceed together to the mouth of the Columbia, capture or destroy whatever American fortress they should find there, and plant the British flag on its ruins.

Informed of these movements, Mr. Astor lost no time in addressing a second letter to the Secretary of State communicating this intelligence and requesting that it might be laid before the president; as no notice, however, had been taken of his previous letter he contented himself with this simple communication, and made no further application for aid.

Awakened now to the danger that menaced the establishment at Astoria, and aware of the importance of protecting this foothold of American commerce and empire on the shores of the Pacific, the government determined to send the frigate Adams, Captain Crane, upon this service. On hearing of this determination Mr. Astor immediately proceeded to fit out a ship called the Enterprize, to sail in company with the Adams, freighted with additional supplies and reinforcements for Astoria.

About the middle of June, while in the midst of these preparations, Mr. Astor received a letter from Mr. R. Stuart dated S' Louis, May 1st, confirming the intelligence already received through the public newspapers, of his safe return, and of the arrival of Mr. Hunt and his party at Astoria and giving the most flattering accounts of the prosperity of the enterprize. So deep had been the anxiety of Mr. Astor, for the success of this great object of his ambition, that this gleam of good news was almost overpowering. "I felt ready," said he, "to fall upon my knees in a transport of gratitude."

At the same time he heard that the Beaver had made good her voyage from New York to the Columbia. This was additional ground of hope for the welfare of the little colony. The post being thus relieved and strengthened with an American at its head, and a ship of war about to sail for its protection, the prospect for the future seemed full of encouragement, and Mr. Astor proceeded with fresh vigour to fit out his merchant ship.

Unfortunately for Astoria, this bright gleam of sunshine was soon overclouded. Just as the Adams had received her complement of men and the two vessels were ready for sea, news came from Commodore Chauncey, commanding on Lake Ontario, that a reinforcement of seamen was wanted in that quarter. The demand was urgent, the crew of the Adams were immediately transferred to that service and the ship was laid up.

This was a most ill timed and discouraging blow, but Mr. Astor would not yet allow himself to pause in his undertaking. He determined to send the Enterprize to sea alone, and let her take the chance of making her unprotected way across the Ocean. Just at this time, however, a British force made its appearance off the Hook; and the port of New York was effectually blockaded. To send a ship to sea under these circumstances would be to expose her to almost certain capture. The Enterprize was therefore unloaded and dismantled, and Mr. Astor was obliged to comfort himself with the hope that the Lark might reach Astoria in safety, and that aided by her supplies, and by the good management of Mr. Hunt and his associates, the little colony might be able to maintain itself until the return of peace.

Chapter LVI

W E HAVE hitherto had so much to relate of a gloomy and disastrous nature, that it is with a feeling of momentary relief we turn to something of a more pleasing complexion, and record the first, and indeed only nuptials in high life that took place in the infant settlement of Astoria.

M'Dougall, who appears to have been a man of a thousand projects, and of great, though somewhat irregular ambition, suddenly conceived the idea of seeking the hand of one of the native princesses, a daughter of the one eyed potentate Comcomly, who held sway over the fishing tribe of the Chinooks and had long supplied the factory with smelts and sturgeons.

Some accounts give rather a romantic origin to this affair, tracing it to the stormy night, when M'Dougall, in the course of an exploring expedition, was driven by stress of weather, to seek shelter in the royal abode of Comcomly. Then and there he was first struck with the charms of this piscatory princess, as she exerted herself to entertain her father's guest.

The "journal of Astoria," however, which was kept under his own eye, records this union as a high state alliance and great stroke of policy. The factory had to depend, in a great measure, on the Chinooks for provisions. They were at present friendly, but it was to be feared they would prove otherwise should they discover the weakness and the exigencies of the post, and the intention to leave the country. This alliance, therefore, would infallibly rivet Comcomly to the interests of the Astorians and with him the powerful tribe of the Chinooks. Be this as it may, and it is hard to fathom the real policy of governors and princes, M'Dougall despatched two of the clerks as ambassadors extraordinary to wait upon the one eyed chieftain and make overtures for the hand of his daughter.

The Chinooks, though not a very refined nation, have notions of matrimonial arrangements that would not disgrace the most refined sticklers for settlements and pin money. The suitor repairs not to the bower of his mistress, but to her father's lodge and throws down a present at his feet. His wishes are then disclosed by some discreet friend employed by him for the purpose. If the suitor and his present find favor in the eyes of the father, he breaks the matter to his daughter and enquires into the state of her inclinations. Should her answer be favorable the suit is accepted; and the lover has to make further presents to the father of horses, canoes and other valuables, according to the beauty and merits of the bride; looking forward to a return in kind whenever they shall go to house keeping.

We have more than once had occasion to speak of the shrewdness of Comcomly, but never was it exerted more adroitly than on this occasion. He was a great friend of M'Dougall and pleased with the idea of having so distinguished a son in law; but so favorable an opportunity of benefiting his own fortune was not likely to occur a second time, and he determined to make the most of it. Accordingly the negotiation was protracted with true diplomatic skill. Conference after conference was held with the two ambassadors: Comcomly was extravagant in his terms; rating the charms of his daughter at the highest price, and indeed she is represented as having one of the flattest and most aristocratical heads in the tribe. At length the preliminaries were all happily adjusted. On the 20th of July, early in the afternoon, a squadron of canoes crossed over from the village of the Chinooks, bearing the royal family of Comcomly and all his court.

That worthy Sachem landed in princely state arrayed in a bright blue blanket and red breech clout, with an extra quantity of paint and feathers, attended by a train of half naked warriors and nobles. A horse was in waiting to receive the princess, who was mounted behind one of the clerks, and thus conveyed, coy but complaint to the fortress. Here she was received with devout, though decent joy by her expecting bridegroom.

Her bridal adornments, it is true, at first caused some little dismay, having painted and anointed herself for the occasion according to the Chinook toilette; by dint, however, of copious ablutions, she was freed from all adventitious tint and fragrance, and entered into the nuptial state, the cleanest princess that had ever been known of the somewhat unctuous tribe of the Chinooks.

From that time forward Comcomly was a daily visitor at the fort, and was admitted into the most intimate counsels of his son in law. He took an interest in every thing that was going forward, but was particularly frequent in his visits to the blacksmith's shop; tasking the labors of the artificer in iron for every kind of weapon and implement suited to the savage state, insomuch that the necessary business of the factory was often postponed to attend to his requisitions.

The honey moon had scarce passed away, and M'Dougall was seated with his bride in the fortress of Astoria when, about noon of the 20th of August, Gassacop, the son of Comcomly, hurried into his presence with great agitation and announced a ship at the mouth of the river. The news produced a vast sensation. Was it a ship of peace or war? Was it American or British? Was it the Beaver or the Isaac Todd? M'Dougall hurried to the water side, threw himself into a boat, and ordered the hands to pull with all speed for the mouth of the harbor.

Those in the fort remained watching the entrance of the river, anxious to know whether they were to prepare for greeting a friend or fighting an enemy. At length the ship was descried crossing the bar, and bending her course towards Astoria. Every gaze was fixed upon her in silent scrutiny until the American flag was recognized. A general shout was the first expression of joy, and next a salutation was thundered from the cannon of the fort.

The vessel came to anchor on the opposite side of the river and returned the salute. The boat of Mr. M'Dougall went on board, and was seen returning late in the afternoon. The Astorians watched her with straining eyes to discover who were on board, but the sun went down and the evening closed in before she was sufficiently near. At length she reached the land and Mr. Hunt stepped on shore. He was hailed as one risen from the dead, and his return was a signal for merriment almost equal to that which prevailed at the nuptials of M'Dougall.

We must now explain the cause of this gentleman's long absence, which had given rise to such gloomy and dispiriting surmises.

Chapter LVII

IT WILL be recollected that the destination of the Beaver when she sailed from Astoria on the 4th of August in 1812, was to proceed northwardly along the Coast to Sheetka or New Archangel, there to dispose of that part of her cargo intended for the supply of the Russian establishment at that place, and then to return to Astoria, where it was expected she would arrive in October.

New Archangel is situated in Norfolk Sound, Lat. 57° 2' N. Long. 135° 50' W. It was the head quarters of the different colonies of the Russian Fur Company, and the common rendezvous of the American vessels trading along the Coast.

The Beaver met with nothing worthy of particular mention in her voyage and arrived at New Archangel on the nineteenth of August. The place at that time was the residence of Count Baranoff, the governor of the different colonies: a rough, rugged, hospitable, hard drinking old Russian, somewhat of a soldier, somewhat of a trader; above all a boon companion of the old roystering school, with a strong cross of the bear.

Mr. Hunt found this hyperborean veteran ensconced in a fort which crested the whole of a high rocky promontory. It mounted one hundred guns large and small and was impregnable to Indian attack unaided by artillery. Here the old governor lorded it over sixty Russians, who formed the corps of the trading establishment, beside an indefinite number of Indian hunters of the Kodiak tribe, who were continually coming and going, or lounging and loitering about the fort like so many hounds round a sportsman's hunting quarters. Though a loose liver among his guests the governor was a strict disciplinarian among his men; keeping them in perfect subjection and having seven on guard night and day.

Beside the immediate serfs and dependants just mentioned, the old Russian potentate exerted a considerable sway over a numerous and irregular class of maritime traders, who looked to him for aid and munitions, and through whom he may be said to have, in some degree, extended his power along the whole north west coast. These were American captains of vessels engaged in a particular department of trade. One of these captains would come in a manner empty handed to New Archangel. Here his ship would be furnished with about fifty canoes and a hundred Kodiak hunters and fitted out with provisions and every thing necessary for hunting the sea otter on the Coast of California, where the Russians have another establishment. The ship would ply along the California coast from place to place, dropping parties of otter hunters in their canoes, furnishing them only with water, and leaving them to depend upon their own dexterity for a maintenance. When a sufficient cargo was collected, she would gather up her canoes and hunters, and return with them to Archangel; where the Captain would render in the returns of his voyage and received one half of the skins for his share.

Over these coasting captains, as we have hinted, the veteran governor exerted some sort of sway, but it was of a peculiar and characteristic kind; it was the tyranny of the table. They were obliged to join him in his "prosnics" or carousals and to drink "potations pottle deep." His carousals too were not of the most quiet kind, nor were his potations as mild as nectar. "He is continually," said Mr. Hunt, "giving entertainments by way of parade, and if you do not drink raw rum and boiling punch as strong as sulphur, he will insult you as soon as he gets drunk, which is very shortly after sitting down to table."

As to any "temperance captain" who stood fast to his faith and refused to give up his sobriety he might go elsewhere for a market, for he stood no chance with the governor. Rarely, however, did any cold water caitiff of the kind darken the door of old Baranhoff; the coasting captains knew too well his humour and their own interests; they joined in his revels, they drank, and sang, and whooped and hiccuped until they all got "half seas over," and then affairs went on swimmingly.

An awful warning to all "flinchers" occurred shortly before Mr. Hunt's arrival. A young naval officer had recently been sent out by the Emperor to take command of one of the Company's vessels. The Governor, as usual, had him at his "prosnics" and plied him with fiery potations. The young man stood on the defensive until the old count's ire was completely kindled; he carried his point and made the green horn tipsey, willy nilly. In proportion as they grew fuddled they grew noisy, they quarrelled in their cups; the youngster paid old Baranhoff in his own coin by rating him soundly; in reward for which, when sober, he was taken the rounds of four pickets, and received seventy nine lashes, taled out with Russian punctuality of punishment.

Such was the old grizzled bear with whom Mr. Hunt had to do his business. How he managed to cope with his humours; whether he pledged him in raw rum and blazing punch and "clinked the can" with him as they made their bargains, does not appear upon record: we must infer, however, from his general observations on the absolute sway of this hard drinking potentate, that he had to conform to the customs of his court, and that their business transactions presented a maudlin mixture of punch and peltry.

The greatest annoyance to Mr. Hunt, however, was the delay to which he was subjected, in disposing of the cargo of the ship and getting the requisite returns. With all the Governor's devotion to the bottle he never obfuscated his faculties sufficiently to lose sight of his interest, and is represented by Mr. Hunt as keen, not to say crafty, at a bargain, as the most arrant water drinker. A long time was expended in negotiating with him, and by the time the bargain was concluded the month of October had arrived. To add to the delay he was to be paid for his cargo in seal skins. Now it so happened that there was none of this kind of peltry at the fort of old Baranhoff. It was necessary, therefore, for Mr. Hunt to proceed to a seal catching establishment which the Russian company had at the island of S' Paul, in the Sea of Kamschatka. He accordingly set sail on the 4th of October, after having spent forty five days at New Archangel boosing and bargaining with its roystering commander, and right glad was he to escape from the clutches of this "old man of the sea."

The Beaver arrived at S' Paul's on the 31st of October, by which time, according to arrangement, he ought to have been back at Astoria. The Island of S' Paul's is in Latitude 57° N. longitude 170° or 171° W. Its shores in certain places and at certain seasons are covered with seals, while others are playing about in the water. Of these the Russians take only the small ones, from seven to ten months old, and carefully select the males, giving the females their freedom, that the breed may not be diminished. The islanders, however, kill the large ones for provisions, and for skins wherewith to cover their canoes. They drive them from the shore over the rocks until within a short distance of their habitations, where they kill them. By this means they save themselves the trouble of carrying the skins, and have the flesh at hand. This is thrown in heaps, and when the season for skinning is over, they take out the entrails and make one heap of the blubber. This with drift wood serves for fuel, for the island is entirely destitute of trees. They make another heap of the flesh; which, with the eggs of sea fowls preserved in oil, an occasional sea lion, a few ducks in winter and some wild roots, composes their food.

Mr. Hunt found seven Russians at the island, and one hundred hunters, natives of Oonalaska, with their families. They lived in cabins that looked like caves; being for the most part formed of the jaw bone of a whale, put up as rafters, across which were laid pieces of drift wood covered over with long grass, the skins of large sea animals, and earth; so as to be quite comfortable in despite of the rigours of the climate though we are told they had as ancient and fish like an odour "as had the quarters of Jonah, when lodged within the whale."

In one of these odoriferous mansions Mr. Hunt occasionally took up his abode that he might be at hand to hasten the loading of the ship. The operation, however, was somewhat slow, for it was necessary to overhaul and inspect every pack to prevent imposition, and the peltries had then to be conveyed in large boats, made of skins, to the ship, which was some little distance from the shore, standing off and on.

One night while Mr. Hunt was on shore, with some others of the crew, there rose a terrible gale. When the day broke the ship was not to be seen. He watched for her with anxious eyes until night but in vain. Day after day of boisterous storms, and howling wintry weather, were passed in watchfulness and solicitude. Nothing was to be seen but a dark and angry sea and a scowling northern sky, and at night he retired within the jaws of the whale and nestled disconsolately among seal skins.

At length on the 13th of November the Beaver made her appearance; much the worse for the stormy conflicts she had sustained in those hyperborean seas. She had been obliged to carry a press of sail in heavy gales, to be able to hold her ground, and had consequently sustained great damage in her canvass and rigging. Mr. Hunt lost no time in hurrying the residue of the cargo on board of her; then bidding adieu to his seal fishing friends and his whale bone habitation, he put forth once more to sea.

He was now for making the best of his way to Astoria, and fortunate would it have been for the interests of that place and the interests of Mr. Astor had he done so; but unluckily a perplexing question rose in his mind. The sails and rigging of the Beaver had been much rent and shattered in the late storm; would she be able to stand the hard gales to be expected in making Columbia River at this season? Was it prudent, also, at this boisterous time of the year to risk the valuable cargo which she now had on board, by crossing and recrossing the dangerous bar of that river? These doubts were probably suggested or enforced by Captain Sowles, who, it has already been seen, was an over cautious, or rather a timid seaman, and they may have had some weight with Mr. Hunt; but there were other considerations which more strongly swayed his mind. The lateness of the season and the unforeseen delays the ship had encountered at New Archangel, and by being obliged to proceed to S' Paul's, had put her so much back in her calculated time, that there was a risk of her arriving so late at Canton, as to come to a bad market, both for the sale of her peltries and the purchase of a return cargo. He considered it to the interest of the Company, therefore, that he should proceed at once to the Sandwich islands; there wait the arrival of the annual vessel from New York, take passage in her to Astoria, and suffer the Beaver to continue on to Canton.

On the other hand, he was urged to the other course by his engagements; by the plan of the voyage marked out for the Beaver by Mr. Astor, by his inclination, and the possibility that the establishment might need his presence, and by the recollection that there must already be a large amount of peltries collected at Astoria, and waiting for the return of the Beaver, to convey them to market.

These conflicting questions perplexed and agitated his mind, and gave rise to much anxious reflection, for he was a conscientious man that seems ever to have aimed at a faithful discharge of his duties, and to have had the interests of his employers earnestly at heart. His decision in the present instance was injudicious and proved unfortunate. It was, to bear away for the Sandwich islands. He persuaded himself that it was matter of necessity and that the distressed condition of the ship left him no other alternative; but we rather suspect he was so persuaded by the representations of the timid Captain. They accordingly stood for the Sandwich islands; arrived at Woahoo, where the ship underwent the necessary repairs and again put to sea on the first of January 1813: leaving Mr. Hunt on the island.

We will follow the Beaver to Canton, as her fortunes in some measure exemplify the evil of commanders of ships acting contrary to orders; and as they form a part of the tissue of cross purposes that marred the great commercial enterprize we have undertaken to record.

The Beaver arrived safe at Canton, where Captain Sowle found the letter of Mr. Astor, giving him information of the war, and directing him to convey the intelligence to Astoria. He wrote a reply dictated either by timidity or obstinacy, in which he declined complying with the orders of Mr. Astor, but said he would wait for the return of peace, and then come home. The other proceedings of Captain Sowles were equally wrong headed and unlucky. He was offered one hundred and fifty thousand dollars for the fur he had taken on board at S' Paul's. The goods for which it had been procured, cost but twenty five thousand dollars in New York. Had he accepted this offer and re-invested the amount in Nankeens, which at that time, in consequence of the interruption to commerce by the war, were at two thirds of their usual price, the whole would have brought three hundred thousand dollars in New York. It is true, the war would have rendered it unsafe to attempt the homeward voyage; but he might have put the goods in store at Canton until after the peace, and have sailed without risk of capture to Astoria; bringing to the partners at that place tidings of the great profits realized on the outward cargo, and the still greater to be expected from the returns. The news of such a brilliant commencement to their undertaking would have counter balanced the gloomy tidings of the war; it would have infused new spirits into them all, and given them courage and constancy to persevere in the enterprize. Captain Sowle, however, refused the offer of one hundred and fifty thousand dollars and stood wavering and chaffering for higher terms. The furs began to fall in value; this only encreased his irresolution; they sunk so much that he feared to sell at all; he borrowed money on Mr. Astor's account at an interest of eighteen per cent, and laid up his ship to await the return of peace.

In the mean while Mr. Hunt soon saw reason to repent the resolution he had adopted in altering the destination of the ship. His stay at the Sandwich islands was prolonged far beyond all expectation. He looked in vain for the annual ship in the spring. Month after month passed by, and still she did not make her appearance. He too proved the danger of departing from orders. Had he returned from S' Paul's to Astoria, all the anxiety and despondency about his fate and about the whole course of the undertaking would have been obviated. The Beaver would have received the furs collected at the factory and taken them to Canton, and great gains instead of great losses would have been the result. The greatest blunder, however, was that committed by Captain Sowles.

At length about the 20th of June, the ship Albatross, Captain Smith, arrived from China, and brought the first tidings of the War to the Sandwich Islands. Mr. Hunt was no longer in doubt and perplexity as to the reason of the non appearance of the annual ship. His first thoughts were for the welfare of Astoria, and, concluding that the inhabitants would probably be in want of provisions, he chartered the Albatross for two thousand dollars, to land him with some supplies at the mouth of the Columbia: where he arrived, as we have seen, on the twentieth of August; after a year's seafaring that might have furnished a chapter in the wanderings of Sindbad.

Chapter LVIII

Arrangements among the partners—Mr. Hunt sails in the Albatross—Arrives at the Marquesas—News of the Frigate Phoebe—Mr. Hunt proceeds to the Sandwich Islands—Voyage of the Lark—Her shipwreck—Transactions with the natives of the Sandwich Islands—Conduct of Tamaahmaah.

MR. HUNT was overwhelmed with surprize when he learnt the resolution taken by the partners to abandon Astoria. He soon found, however, that matters had gone too far, and the minds of his colleagues had become too firmly bent upon the measure to render any opposition of avail. He was beset, too, with the same disparaging accounts of the interior trade, and of the whole concerns and prospects of the Company that had been rendered to Mr. Astor. His own experience had been full of perplexities and discouragements. He had a conscientious anxiety for the interests of Mr. Astor, and, not comprehending the extended views of that gentleman and his habit of operating with great amounts, he had from the first been daunted by the enormous expenses required and had become disheartened by the subsequent losses sustained, which appeared to him to be ruinous in their magnitude. By degrees, therefore, he was brought to acquiesce in the step taken by his colleagues as perhaps adviseable in the exigencies of the case; his only care was to wind up the business with as little further loss as possible to Mr. Astor.

A large stock of valuable furs was collected at the Factory, which it was necessary to get to a market. There were twenty five Sandwich islanders also in the employ of the Company, whom they were bound by express agreement, to restore to their native country. For these purposes a ship was necessary.

The Albatross was bound to the Marquesas and thence to the Sandwich islands. It was resolved that Mr. Hunt should sail in her in quest of a vessel, and should return if possible by the 1st of January, bringing with him a supply of provisions. Should any thing occur, however, to prevent his return, an arrangement was to be proposed to Mr. M'Tavish to transfer such of the men as were so disposed, from the service of the

American Fur Company into that of the North West, the latter becoming responsible for the wages due them, on receiving an equivalent in goods from the store house of the Factory. As a means of facilitating the despatch of business Mr. M'Dougall proposed that, in case Mr. Hunt should not return, the whole arrangement with Mr. M'Tavish should be left solely to him. This was assented to; the contingency being considered possible but not probable.

It is proper to note, that, on the first announcement by Mr. M'Dougall of his intention to break up the establishment, three of the clerks, British subjects, had, with his consent, passed into the service of the North West Company, and departed with Mr. M'Tavish for his post in the interior.

Having arranged all these matters during a sojourn of six days at Astoria, Mr. Hunt set sail in the Albatross on the 26th of August, and arrived, without accident at the Marquesas. He had not been there long when Commodore Porter arrived in the Frigate Essex, bringing in a number of stout London whalers as prizes, having made a sweeping cruize in the Pacific. From Commodore Porter he received the alarming intelligence that the British Frigate Phoebe, with a store ship mounted with battering pieces, calculated to attack forts, had arrived at Rio Janeiro, where she had been joined by the Sloops of War Cherub and Racoon, and they had all sailed in company on the 6th of July for the Pacific, bound, as it was supposed, to Columbia River.

Here then was the death warrant of unfortunate Astoria! The anxious mind of Mr. Hunt was in greater perplexity than ever. He had been eager to extricate the property of Mr. Astor from a failing concern with as little loss as possible; there was now danger that the whole would be swallowed up. How was it to be snatched from the gulph? It was impossible to charter a ship for the purpose now that a British squadron was on its way to the River. He applied to purchase one of the whale ships brought in by Commodore Porter. The Commodore demanded twenty five thousand Dollars for her. The price appeared exorbitant, and no bargain could be made. Mr. Hunt then urged the Commodore to fit out one of his prizes and send her to Astoria, to bring off the property and part of the people, but he declined, "from want of authority." He assured

Mr. Hunt, however, that he would endeavor to fall in with the enemy, or, should he hear of their having certainly gone to the Columbia, he would either follow or anticipate them, should his circumstances warrant such a step.

In this tantalizing state of suspense Mr. Hunt was detained at the Marquesas until November 23d when he proceeded in the Albatross to the Sandwich islands. He still cherished a faint hope that, notwithstanding the war, and all other discouraging circumstances, the annual ship might have been sent by Mr. Astor, and might have touched at the islands and proceeded to the Columbia. He knew the pride and interest taken by that gentleman in his great enterprize, and that he would not be deterred by dangers and difficulties from prosecuting it; much less would he leave the infant establishment without succour and support in the time of trouble. In this, we have seen, he did but justice to Mr. Astor, and we must now turn to notice the cause of the non arrival of the vessel which he had despatched with reinforcements and supplies. Her voyage forms another chapter of accidents in this eventful story.

The Lark sailed from New York on the 6th of March 1813, and proceeded prosperously on her voyage until within a few degrees of the Sandwich Islands. Here a gale sprang up that soon blew with tremendous violence. The Lark was a stanch and noble ship and for a time buffetted bravely with the storm. Unluckily, however, she "broached to" and was struck by a heavy sea that hove her on her beam ends. The helm too was knocked to leeward, all command of the vessel was lost, and another mountain wave completely overset her.

Orders were given to cut away the masts. In the hurry and confusion the boats also were unfortunately cut adrift. The wreck then righted, but was a mere hulk, full of water with a heavy sea washing over it and all the hatches off. On mustering the crew one man was missing, who was discovered below in the forecastle, drowned.

In cutting away the masts it had been utterly impossible to observe the necessary precaution of commencing with the lee rigging that being, from the position of the ship, completely under water. The masts and spars, therefore, being linked to the wreck by the shrouds and rigging, remained along side for four days. During all this time, the ship lay rolling in the trough of the sea, the heavy surges breaking over her, and the spars heaving and banging to and fro, bruizing the half drowned sailors that clung to the bow sprit and the stumps of the masts. The sufferings of these poor fellows were intolerable. They stood to their waists in water, in imminent peril of being washed off by every surge. In this position they dared not sleep lest they should let go their holds and be swept away. The only dry place on the wreck was the bow sprit. Here they took turns to be tied on, for half an hour at a time, and in this way gained short snatches of sleep.

On the 14th the first mate died at his post and was swept off by the surges. On the 17th two seamen, faint and exhausted, were washed overboard. The next wave threw their bodies back upon the deck, where they remained swashing backward and forward, ghastly objects to the almost perishing survivors. Mr. Ogden the supercargo, who was at the bow sprit, called to the men nearest to the bodies, to fasten them to the wreck; as a last horrible resource in case of being driven to extremity by famine!

On the 17th the gale gradually subsided and the sea became calm. The sailors now crawled feebly about the wreck and began to relieve it from the main incumbrances. The spars were cleared away, the anchors and guns heaved overboard; the spritsail yard was rigged for a jury mast and a mizen topsail set upon it. A sort of stage was made of a few broken spars, on which the crew were raised above the surface of the water, so as to be enabled to keep themselves dry and to sleep comfortably. Still their sufferings from hunger and thirst were great; but there was a Sandwich islander on board, an expert swimmer, who found his way into the cabin and occasionally brought up a few bottles of wine and porter, and at length got into the run and secured a quarter cask of wine. A little raw pork was likewise procured, and dealt out with a sparing hand. The horrors of their situation were increased by the sight of numerous sharks prowling about the wreck, as if waiting for their prey. On the 24th the cook, a black man, died and was cast into the sea, where he was instantly seized on by these ravenous monsters.

They had been several days making slow head way under their scanty sail when, on the 25th, they came in sight of land.

It was about fifteen leagues distant and they remained two or three days drifting along in sight of it. On the 28th they descried, to their great transport, a canoe approaching managed by natives. They came along side, and brought a most welcome supply of potatoes. They informed them that the land they had made was one of the Sandwich islands. The second mate and one of the seamen went on shore in the canoe for water and provisions, and to procure aid from the islanders in towing the wreck into a harbour.

Neither of the men returned, nor was any assistance sent from shore. The next day ten or twelve canoes came along side, but roamed round the wreck like so many sharks, and would render no aid in towing her to land.

The sea continued to break over the vessel with such violence that it was impossible to stand at the helm without the assistance of lashings. The crew were now so worn down by famine and thirst that the Captain saw it would be impossible for them to withstand the breaking of the sea when the ship should ground; he deemed the only chance for their lives, therefore, was to get to land in the canoes, and stand ready to receive and protect the wreck when she should drift to shore. Accordingly they all got safe to land, but had scarcely touched the beach when they were surrounded by the natives, who stripped them almost naked. The name of this inhospitable island was Tahoorowa.

In the course of the night the wreck came drifting to the strand, with the surf thundering around her, and shortly afterwards bilged. On the following morning numerous casks of provisions floated on shore. The natives staved them for the sake of the iron hoops but would not allow the crew to help themselves to the contents, nor to go on board of the wreck.

As the crew were in want of every thing, and as it might be a long time before any opportunity occurred for them to get away from these islands: Mr. Ogden, as soon as he could get a chance, made his way to the island of Owyhee, and endeavored to make some arrangement with the King for the relief of his companions in misfortune.

The illustrious Tamaahmaah, as we have shewn on a former occasion, was a shrewd bargainer, and in the present instance proved himself an experienced wrecker. His negotiations with

M'Dougall and the other "Eris of the great American Fur Company" had but little effect on present circumstances, and he proceeded to avail himself of their misfortunes. He agreed to furnish the crew with provisions during their stay in his territories, and to return to them all their clothing that could be found, but he stipulated that the wreck should be abandoned to him as a waif cast by fortune on his shores. With these conditions Mr. Ogden was fain to comply. Upon this the great Tamaahmaah deputed his favorite John Young, the tarpawlin governor of Owyhee, to proceed with a number of the royal guards and take possession of the wreck on behalf of the crown. This was done accordingly, and the property and crew were removed to Owyhee. The royal bounty appears to have been but scanty in its dispensations. The crew fared but meagerly, though, on reading the journal of the voyage it is singular to find them, after all the hardships they had suffered, so sensitive about petty inconveniences as to exclaim against the King as a "savage monster" for refusing them a "pot to cook in" and denying Mr. Ogden the use of a knife and fork which had been saved from the wreck.

Such was the unfortunate catastrophe of the Lark; had she reached her destination in safety, affairs at Astoria might have taken a different course. A strange fatality seems to have attended all the expeditions by sea, nor were those by land much less disastrous.

Captain Northrop was still at the Sandwich islands on December 20th when Mr. Hunt arrived. The latter immediately purchased, for ten thousand dollars, a brig called the Pedlar and put Captain Northrop in command of her. They set sail for Astoria on the 22d of January, intending to remove the property from thence as speedily as possible to the Russian settlements on the north west coast, to prevent it from falling into the hands of the British. Such were the orders of Mr. Astor, sent out by the Lark. We will now leave Mr. Hunt on his voyage and return to see what has taken place at Astoria during his absence.

Chapter LIX

O N THE SECOND of October, about five weeks after
Mr. Hunt had sailed in the Albatross from Astoria,
Mr. M'Kenzie set off with two canoes and twelve men for the
posts of Messrs. Stuart and Clarke, to apprize them of the
new arrangements determined upon in the recent conference
of the partners at the factory.

He had not ascended the river a hundred miles when he
met a squadron of ten canoes sweeping merrily down under British colours, the Canadian oarsmen as usual in full
song.

It was an armament fitted out by M'Tavish, who had with
him Mr. J. Stuart, another partner of the North West Company, together with seven clerks and sixty eight men, seventy
five souls in all. They had heard of the Frigate Phoebe and the
Isaac Todd being on the high seas and were on their way
down to await their arrival. In one of the canoes Mr. Clarke
came passenger, the alarming intelligence having brought
him down from his post on the Spokan. Mr. M'Kenzie immediately determined to return with him to Astoria and veer-
ing about, the two parties encamped together for the night.
The leaders, of course, observed a due decorum, but some
of the subalterns could not restrain their chuckling exultation, boasting that they would soon plant the British standard
on the walls of Astoria and drive the Americans out of the
country.

In the course of the evening Mr. M'Kenzie had a secret conference with Mr. Clarke in which they agreed to set off privately before day light and get down in time to apprize
M'Dougall of the approach of these North Westers. The latter, however, were completely on the alert. Just as M'Kenzie's

canoes were about to push off, they were joined by a couple from the North West squadron, in which were M'Tavish
with two clerks and eleven men. With these he intended to
push forward and make arrangements, leaving the rest of the
convoy, in which was a large quantity of furs, to await his
orders.

The two parties arrived at Astoria on the 7th of October.
The North Westers encamped under the guns of the fort, and
displayed the British colours. The young men in the fort,
natives of the United States, were on the point of hoisting the
American flag, but were forbidden by Mr. M'Dougall. They
were astonished at such a prohibition, and were exceedingly
galled by the tone and manner assumed by the clerks and retainers of the North West Company, who ruffled about in
that swelling and braggart style which grows up among these
heroes of the wilderness; they, in fact, considered themselves lords of the ascendant, and regarded the hampered and
harassed Astorians as a conquered people.

On the following day M'Dougall convened the clerks and
read to them an extract of a letter from his uncle Mr. Angus
Shaw, one of the principal partners of the North West Company, announcing the coming of the Phoebe and Isaac Todd
"to take and destroy every thing American on the North West
Coast."

This intelligence was received without dismay by such of
the clerks as were natives of the United States. They had felt
indignant at seeing their national flag struck by a Canadian
commander, and the British flag flouted as it were in their
faces. They had been stung to the quick, also, by the vaunting airs assumed by the North Westers. In this mood of mind
they would willingly have nailed their colours to the staff and
defied the frigate. She could not come within many miles of
the fort, they observed, and any boats she might send could
be destroyed by their cannon.

There were cooler and more calculating spirits, however,
who had the control of affairs and felt nothing of the patri-
otic pride and indignation of these youths. The extract of
the letter had, apparently, been read by M'Dougall merely to
prepare the way for a preconcerted stroke of management.

On that same day Mr. M'Tavish proposed to purchase the whole stock of goods and furs belonging to the Company, both at Astoria and in the interior, at cost and charges. Mr. M'Dougall undertook to comply; assuming the whole management of the negotiation in virtue of the power vested in him in case of the nonarrival of Mr. Hunt. That power, however, was limited and specific and did not extend to an operation of this nature and extent; no objection, however, was made to his assumption, and he and M'Tavish soon made a preliminary arrangement, perfectly satisfactory to the latter.

Mr. Stuart and the reserve party of North Westers arrived shortly afterwards and encamped with M'Tavish. The former exclaimed loudly against the terms of the arrangement, and insisted upon a reduction of the prices. New negotiations had now to be entered into. The demands of the North Westers were made in a peremptory tone, and they seemed disposed to dictate like conquerors. The Americans looked on with indignation and impatience. They considered M'Dougall as acting if not a perfidious, certainly a craven part. He was continually repairing to the camp to negotiate, instead of keeping within his walls and receiving overtures in his fortress. His case, they observed, was not so desperate as to excuse such crouching. He might in fact hold out for his own terms. The North West party had lost their ammunition; they had no goods to trade with the natives for provisions, and they were so destitute that M'Dougall had absolutely to feed them while he negotiated with them. He, on the contrary, was well lodged and victualed, had sixty men, with arms, ammunition, boats and every thing requisite either for defence or retreat. The party beneath the guns of his fort were at his mercy. Should an enemy appear in the offing, he could pack up the most valuable part of the property and retire to some place of concealment, or make off for the interior.

These considerations, however, had no weight with Mr. M'Dougall, or were overruled by other motives. The terms of sale were lowered by him to the standard fixed by Mr. Stuart, and an agreement executed on the 16th of October, by which the furs and merchandize of all kinds in the country, belonging to Mr. Astor, passed into the possession of the North

West Company at about a third of their real value.* A safe passage through the North West posts was guaranteed to such as did not choose to enter into the service of that Company, and the amount of wages due to them was to be deducted from the price paid for Astoria.

The conduct and motives of Mr. M'Dougall throughout the whole of this proceeding have been strongly questioned by the other partners. He has been accused of availing himself of a wrong construction of powers vested in him at his own request, and of sacrificing the interests of Mr. Astor to the North West Company, under the promise or hope of advantage to himself.

He always insisted, however, that he made the best bargain for Mr. Astor that circumstances would permit: the frigate being hourly expected, in which case the whole property of that gentleman would be liable to capture; that the return of Mr. Hunt was problematical, the frigate intending to cruise along the coast for two years and clear it of all American vessels. He moreover averred, and M'Tavish corroborated his averment by certificate, that he proposed an arrangement to that gentleman, by which the furs were to be sent to Canton and sold there at Mr. Astor's risk and for his account, but the proposition was not acceded to.

Notwithstanding all his representations, several of the per-

---

* Not quite $40,000 were allowed for furs worth upwards of $100,000. Beaver was valued at $2 per skin though worth $5. Land otter at 50 cents though worth $5. Sea otter at $12 worth from $45 to $60 and for several kinds of furs nothing was allowed. Moreover the goods and merchandize for the Indian trade ought to have brought three times the amount for which they were sold.

The following estimate has been made of the articles on hand and the prices:

17,705 lbs. beaver parchment	valued at	$2.00	worth	$5.00
465 old coat beaver	" "	1.66	"	3.50
907 Land otter	" "	.50	"	5.00
68 Sea otter	" "	12.00	"45 to	60.00
30 " "	" "	5.00	"	25.00

Nothing was allowed for

179 Mink skins	worth each	.40
22 Raccoon	" "	.40
38 Lynx	" "	2.00
18 Fox	" "	1.00
106 "	" "	1.50
71 Black bear	" "	4.00
16 Grizly "	" "	10.00

sons present at the transaction, and acquainted with the whole course of the affair, and among the number Mr. M'Kenzie himself, his occasional coadjutor, remained firm in the belief that he had acted a hollow part. Neither did he succeed in exculpating himself to Mr. Astor; that gentleman declaring, in a letter written some time afterwards to Mr. Hunt, that he considered the property virtually given away. "Had our place and our property," he adds, "been fairly captured, I should have preferred it. I should not feel as if I were disgraced."

All these may be unmerited suspicions; but it certainly is a circumstance strongly corroborative of them that Mr. M'Dougall shortly after concluding this agreement, became a member of the North West Company and received a share productive of a handsome income.

Chapter LX

*Arrival of a strange sail—Agitation at Astoria—Warlike of-
fer of Comcomly—Astoria taken possession of by the British—
Indignation of Comcomly at the conduct of his son in law.*

ON THE MORNING of the 30th of November a sail was descried doubling Cape Disappointment. It came to anchor in Baker's bay, and proved to be a ship of war. Of what
nation? was now the anxious enquiry. If English, why did it
come alone?—Where was the merchant vessel that was to
have accompanied it? If American, what was to become of the
newly acquired possessions of the North West Company?

In this dilemma M'Tavish, in all haste, loaded two barges
with all the packages of furs bearing the mark of the North
West Company, and made off for Tongue point, three miles up
the river. There he was to await a preconcerted signal from
M'Dougall on ascertaining the character of the ship. If it
should prove American, M'Tavish would have a fair start and
could bear off his rich cargo to the interior. It is singular that
this prompt mode of conveying valuable but easily trans-
portable effects beyond the reach of a hostile ship, should not
have suggested itself while the property belonged to Mr. Astor.

In the mean time M'Dougall, who still remained nominal
chief at the fort, launched a canoe manned by men recently in
the employ of the American Fur Company, and steered for
the ship. On the way he instructed his men to pass themselves
for Americans or Englishmen, according to the exigencies of
the case.

The vessel proved to be the British Sloop of War Racoon,
of twenty six guns and one hundred and twenty men, commanded by Captain Black. According to the account of that
officer the Frigate Phoebe and the two sloops of war Cherub
and Racoon had sailed in convoy of the Isaac Todd from Rio
Janeiro. On board of the Phoebe was Mr. John M'Donald, a
partner of the North West Company, embarked as passenger;
to profit by the anticipated catastrophe at Astoria. The convoy
was separated by stress of weather off Cape Horn. The three

ships of war came together again at the island of Juan Fernandez, their appointed rendezvous, but waited in vain for the Isaac Todd.

In the mean time intelligence was received of the mischief that Commodore Porter was doing among the British whale ships. Commodore Hillyer immediately set sail in quest of him with the Phoebe and the Cherub, transferring Mr. M'Donald to the Racoon, and ordering that vessel to proceed to the Columbia.

The officers of the Racoon were in high spirits. The agents of the North West Company, in instigating this expedition, had talked of immense booty to be made by the fortunate captors of Astoria. Mr. M'Donald had kept up the excitement during the voyage, so that not a midshipman but revelled in dreams of ample prize money, nor a lieutenant that would have sold his chance for a thousand pounds. Their disappointment, therefore, may easily be conceived when they learnt that their warlike attack upon Astoria had been forestalled by a snug commercial arrangement; that their anticipated booty had become British property in the regular course of traffic, and that all this had been effected by the very company which had been instrumental in getting them sent on what they now stigmatized as a fool's errand. They felt as if they had been duped and made tools of by a set of shrewd men of traffic, who had employed them to crack the nut, while they carried off the kernel. In a word, M'Dougall found himself so ungraciously received by his countrymen on board of the ship, that he was glad to cut short his visit and return to shore. He was busy at the fort, making preparations for the reception of the captain of the Racoon, when his one eyed Indian father in law made his appearance with a train of Chinook warriors, all painted and equipped in warlike style.

Old Comcomly had beheld with dismay the arrival of a "big war canoe" displaying the British flag. The shrewd old savage had become something of a politician in the course of his daily visits at the fort. He knew of the war existing between the nations, but knew nothing of the arrangement between M'Dougall and M'Tavish. He trembled, therefore, for the power of his white son in law, and the new fledged grandeur of his daughter, and assembled his warriors in all haste. "King George," said he, "has sent this great canoe to destroy the fort and make slaves of all the inhabitants. Shall we suffer it? The Americans are the first white men that have fixed themselves in the land. They have treated us like brothers. Their great chief has taken my daughter to be his squaw; we are therefore as one people."

His warriors all determined to stand by the Americans to the last, and to this effect they came painted and armed for battle. Comcomly made a spirited war speech to his son in law. He offered to kill every one of King George's men that should attempt to land. It was an easy matter. The ship could not approach within six miles of the fort; the crew could only land in boats. The woods reached to the water's edge; in these he and his warriors would conceal themselves and shoot down the enemy as fast as they put foot on shore.

M'Dougall was, doubtless, properly sensible of this parental devotion on the part of his Savage father in law, and perhaps a little rebuked by the game spirit so opposite to his own. He assured Comcomly, however, that his solicitude for the safety of himself and the princess was superfluous; as, though the ship belonged to King George, her crew would not injure the Americans or their Indian allies. He advised him and his warriors, therefore, to lay aside their weapons and war shirts, wash off the paint from their faces and bodies, and appear like clean and civil savages to receive the strangers courteously.

Comcomly was sorely puzzled at this advice, which accorded so little with his Indian notions of receiving a hostile nation; and it was only after repeated and positive assurances of the amicable intentions of the strangers that he was induced to lower his fighting tone. He said something to his warriors explanatory of this singular posture of affairs, and in vindication, perhaps, of the pacific temper of his son in law. They all gave a shrug and an Indian grunt of acquiescence and went off sulkily to their village to lay aside their weapons for the present.

The proper arrangements being made for the reception of Captain Black, that officer caused his ship's boats to be manned, and landed with befitting state at Astoria. From the talk that had been made by the North West Company of the strength of the place, and the armament they had required to assist in its reduction, he expected to find a fortress of some importance. When he beheld nothing but stockades and bastions calculated for defence against naked savages, he felt an emotion of indignant surprize, mingled with something of the ludicrous. "Is this the fort," cried he, "about which I have heard so much talking?—D——n me but I'd batter it down in two hours with a four pounder!"

When he learnt, however, the amount of rich furs that had been passed into the hands of the North Westers, he was outrageous, and insisted that an inventory should be taken of all the property purchased of the Americans "with a view to ulterior measures in England for the recovery of the value from the North West Company."

As he grew cool however he gave over all idea of preferring such a claim, and reconciled himself, as well as he could, to the idea of having been forestalled by his bargaining coadjutors.

On the 12th of December the fate of Astoria was consummated by a regular ceremonial. Captain Black attended by his officers entered the fort: caused the British standard to be erected, broke a bottle of wine and declared in a loud voice that he took possession of the establishment and of the country in the name of his Britannic majesty, changing the name of Astoria to that of Fort George.

The Indian warriors who had offered their services to repel the strangers, were present on this occasion. It was explained to them as being a friendly arrangement and transfer, but they shook their heads grimly and considered it an act of subjugation of their ancient allies. They regretted that they had complied with M'Dougall's wishes in laying aside their arms, and remarked that, however the Americans might conceal the fact they were undoubtedly all slaves: nor could they be persuaded of the contrary until they beheld the Racoon depart without taking away any prisoners.

As to Comcomly he no longer prided himself upon his White son in law, but, whenever he was asked about him shook his head and replied that his daughter had made a mistake, and, instead of getting a great warrior for a husband, had married herself to a squaw.

Chapter LXI

HAVING given the catastrophe at the Fort of Astoria, it remains now but to gather up a few loose ends of this widely excursive narrative and conclude. On the 28th of February the Brig Pedlar anchored in Columbia River. It will be recollected that Mr. Hunt had purchased this vessel at the Sandwich Islands, to take off the furs collected at the factory, and to restore the Sandwich islanders to their homes. When that gentleman learnt, however, the precipitate and summary manner in which the property had been bargained away by Mr. M'Dougall, he expressed his indignation in the strongest terms, and determined to make an effort to get back the furs. As soon as his wishes were known in this respect M'Dougall came to sound him on behalf of the North West Company, intimating that he had no doubt the peltries might be repurchased at an advance of 50 per Cent. This overture was not calculated to soothe the angry feelings of Mr. Hunt, and his indignation was complete when he discovered that M'Dougall had become a partner of the North West Company, and had actually been so since the 23d of December. He had kept his partnership a secret, however; had retained the papers of the Pacific Fur Company in his possession; and had continued to act as Mr. Astor's agent, though two of the partners of the other company, Mr. M'Kenzie and Mr. Clarke, were present. He had moreover divulged to his new associates all that he knew as to Mr. Astor's plans and affairs, and had made copies of his business letters for their perusal.

Mr. Hunt now considered the whole conduct of M'Dougall hollow and collusive. His only thought was, therefore, to get all the papers of the concern out of his hands and bring the business to a close; for the interests of Mr. Astor were yet completely at stake, the drafts of the North West Company in his favor for the purchase money not having yet been obtained. With some difficulty he succeeded in getting possession of the papers. The bills or drafts were delivered without hesitation. The latter he remitted to Mr. Astor by some of his associates who were about to cross the continent to New York. This done he embarked on board the Pedlar, on the third of April, accompanied by two of the clerks, Mr. Seton and Mr. Halsey, and bade a final adieu to Astoria.

The next day, April 4th, Messrs. Clarke, M'Kenzie, David Stuart, and such of the Astorians as had not entered into the service of the North West Company, set out to cross the Rocky Mountains. It is not our intention to take the reader another journey across those rugged barriers; but we will step forward with the travellers to a distance on their way, merely to relate their interview with a character already noted in this work.

As the party were proceeding up the Columbia, near the mouth of the Wallah Wallah River, several Indian canoes put off from the shore to overtake them, and a voice called upon them in French, and requested them to stop. They accordingly put to shore, and were joined by those in the canoes. To their surprize they recognized in the person who had hailed them the Indian wife of Pierre Dorion, accompanied by her two children. She had a story to tell involving the fate of several of our unfortunate adventurers.

Mr. John Reed, the Hibernian, it will be remembered, had been detached during the summer to the Snake River. His party consisted of four Canadians, Gilles Le Clerc, Francois Landry, Jean Baptiste Turcot and Andre La Chapelle together with two hunters, Pierre Dorion and Pierre Delaunay; Dorion as usual being accompanied by his wife and children. The objects of this expedition were two fold: to trap beaver, and to search for the three hunters, Robinson, Hoback and Rezner.

In the course of the autumn Reed lost one man, Landry, by death; another one, Pierre Delaunay, who was of a sullen, perverse disposition, left him in a moody fit, and was never heard of afterwards. The number of his party was not, however, reduced by these losses, as the three hunters, Robinson, Hoback and Rezner had joined it.

Reed now built a house on the Snake River, for their winter quarters, which being completed the party set about trapping. Rezner, Le Clerc and Pierre Dorion went about five days' journey from the wintering house, to a part of the country well stocked with beaver. Here they put up a hut and proceeded to trap with great success. While the men were out hunting, Pierre Dorion's wife remained at home to dress the skins and prepare the meals. She was thus employed one evening about the beginning of January, cooking the supper of the hunters, when she heard footsteps, and Le Clerc staggered, pale and bleeding, into the hut. He informed her that a party of savages had surprized them, while at their traps, and had killed Rezner and her husband. He had barely strength left to give this information, when he sank upon the ground.

The poor woman saw that the only chance for life was instant flight, but in this exigency, shewed that presence of mind and force of character for which she had frequently been noted. With great difficulty she caught two of the horses belonging to the party. Then collecting her clothes and a small quantity of beaver meat and dried salmon, she packed them upon one of the horses, and helped the wounded man to mount upon it. On the other horse she mounted with her two children, and hurried away from this dangerous neighborhood, directing her flight to Mr. Reed's establishment. On the third day she descried a number of Indians on horseback proceeding in an easterly direction. She immediately dismounted with her children, and helped Le Clerc likewise to dismount, and all concealed themselves. Fortunately they escaped the sharp eyes of the savages, but had to proceed with the utmost caution. That night they slept without fire or water; she managed to keep her children warm in her arms; but before morning poor Le Clerc died.

With the dawn of day the resolute woman resumed her course, and, on the fourth day reached the house of Mr. Reed. It was deserted, and all around were marks of blood and signs of a ferocious massacre. Not doubting that Mr. Reed and his party had all fallen victims, she turned, in fresh horror, from the spot. For two days she continued hurrying forward, ready to sink for want of food, but more solicitous about her children than herself. At length she reached a range of rocky mountains near the upper part of the Wallah Wallah River. Here she chose a wild lonely ravine, as her place of winter refuge. She had fortunately a buffalo robe and three deer skins; of these and of pine bark and cedar branches she constructed a rude wig wam which she pitched beside a mountain spring. Having no other food she killed the two horses and smoked their flesh. The skins aided to cover her hut. Here she dragged out the winter with no other company than her two children. Towards the middle of March her provisions were nearly exhausted. She therefore packed up the remainder, slung it on her back, and with her helpless little ones set out again on her wanderings. Crossing the ridge of mountains she descended to the banks of the Wallah Wallah and kept along them until she arrived where that river throws itself into the Columbia. She was hospitably received and entertained by the Wallah Wallahs and had been nearly two weeks among them when the two canoes passed.

On being interrogated she could assign no reason for this murderous attack of the savages; it appeared to be perfectly wanton and unprovoked. Some of the Astorians supposed it an act of butchery by a roving band of Blackfeet. Others, however, and with greater probability of correctness, have ascribed it to the tribe of Pierced nose Indians, in revenge for the death of their comrade hanged by order of Mr. Clarke. If so, it shows that these sudden and apparently wanton outbreakings of sanguinary violence on the part of savages, have often some previous, though perhaps remote, provocation.

The narrative of the Indian woman closes the checquered adventures of some of the personages of this motley story; such as the honest Hibernian Reed, and Dorion the hybred interpreter. Turcot and La Chapelle were two of the men who fell off from Mr. Crooks in the course of his wintry journey, and had subsequently such disastrous times among the Indians. We cannot but feel some sympathy with that persevering trio of Kentuckians, Robinson, Rezner, and Hoback; who twice turned back when on their way homeward, and lingered in the wilderness to perish by the hands of savages.

The return parties from Astoria, both by sea and land, experienced on the way as many adventures, vicissitudes and mishaps as the far famed heroes of the Odyssey: they reached their destination at different times, bearing tidings to Mr. Astor of the unfortunate termination of his enterprize. That gentleman, however, was not disposed even yet to give the matter up as lost. On the contrary, his spirit was roused by what he considered ungenerous and unmerited conduct on the part of the North West Company. "After their treatment of me," said he in a letter to Mr. Hunt, "I have no idea of remaining quiet and idle." He determined, therefore, as soon as circumstances would permit, to resume his enterprize.

At the return of peace Astoria with the adjacent country, reverted to the United States by the treaty of Ghent, on the principle of *status ante bellum*, and Captain Biddle was despatched in the Sloop of War Ontario, to take formal repossession. In the winter of 1815 a law was passed by Congress prohibiting all traffic of British traders within the territories of the United States.

The favorable moment seemed now to Mr. Astor to have arrived for the revival of his favorite enterprize, but new difficulties had grown up to impede it. The North West Company were now in complete occupation of the Columbia River and its chief tributary streams, holding the posts which he had established and carrying on a trade throughout the neighboring region in defiance of the prohibitory law of Congress, which in effect was a dead letter beyond the Mountains.

To dispossess them would be an undertaking of almost a belligerent nature; for their agents and retainers were well armed and skilled in the use of weapons, as is usual with Indian traders. The ferocious and bloody contests which had taken place between the rival trading parties of the North West and Hudson's Bay companies, had shewn what might be expected from commercial feuds in the lawless depths of the wilderness. Mr. Astor did not think it adviseable, therefore, to attempt the matter without the protection of the American flag, under which his people might rally in case of need. He accordingly made an informal overture to the President of the United States, Mr. Madison, through Mr. Gallatin, offering to renew his enterprize and to re establish Astoria, provided it would be protected by the American flag and made a military post; stating that the whole force required would not exceed

a lieutenant's command. The application, approved and recommended by Mr. Gallatin, one of the most enlightened
statesmen of our country, was favorably received, but no step
was taken in consequence, the President not being disposed,
in all probability, to commit himself by any direct countenance or overt act. Discouraged by this supineness on the part
of Government, Mr. Astor did not think fit to renew his overtures in a more formal manner, and the favorable moment for
the reoccupation of Astoria was suffered to pass unimproved.

The British trading establishments were thus enabled without molestation to strike deep their roots and extend their
ramifications, in despite of the prohibition of Congress, until
they had spread themselves over the rich field of enterprize
opened by Mr. Astor. The British government soon began to
perceive the importance of this region, and to desire to include it within their territorial domains. A question has consequently risen as to the right to the soil, and has become one
of the most perplexing now open between the United States
and Great Britain. In the first treaty relative to it, under date
of October 20th 1818, the question was left unsettled, and it
was agreed that the Country on the North West Coast of
America, westward of the Rocky Mountains, claimed by either
nation, should be open to the inhabitants of both for ten
years, for the purposes of trade, with the equal right of navigating all its rivers. When these ten years had expired a subsequent treaty in 1828 extended the arrangement to ten
additional years. So the matter stands at present.

On casting back our eyes over the series of events we have
recorded, we see no reason to attribute the failure of this
great commercial undertaking, to any fault in the scheme, or
omission in the execution of it, on the part of the projector.
It was a magnificent enterprize; well concerted and carried on
without regard to difficulties or expense. A succession of adverse circumstances and cross purposes, however, beset it
almost from the outset; some of them in fact arising from neglect of the orders and instructions of Mr. Astor. The first
crippling blow was the loss of the Tonquin, which clearly
would not have happened, had Mr. Astor's earnest injunctions with regard to the natives been attended to. Had this
ship performed her voyage prosperously and revisited Astoria

in due time, the trade of the establishment would have taken its pre concerted course, and the spirits of all concerned, been kept up by a confident prospect of success. Her dismal catastrophe struck a chill into every heart, and prepared the way for subsequent despondency.

Another cause of embarrassment and loss was the departure from the plan of Mr. Astor as to the voyage of the Beaver, subsequent to her visiting Astoria. The variation from this plan produced a series of cross purposes disastrous to the establishment, and detained Mr. Hunt absent from his post when his presence there was of vital importance to the enterprize. So essential is it for an agent in any great and complicated undertaking to execute faithfully and to the letter, the part marked out for him by the master mind which has concerted the whole.

The breaking out of the War between the United States and Great Britain multiplied the hazards and embarrassments of the enterprize. The disappointment as to convoy, rendered it difficult to keep up reinforcements and supplies; and the loss of the Lark added to the tissue of misadventures.

That Mr. Astor battled resolutely against every difficulty and pursued his course in defiance of every loss, has been sufficiently shewn. Had he been seconded by suitable agents and properly protected by government, the ultimate failure of his plan might yet have been averted. It was his great misfortune that his agents were not imbued with his own spirit. Some had not capacity sufficient to comprehend the real nature and extent of his scheme; others were alien in feeling and interest, and had been brought up in the service of a rival company. Whatever sympathies they might originally have had with him were impaired if not destroyed by the war. They looked upon his cause as desperate, and only considered how they might make interest to regain a situation under their former employers. The absence of Mr. Hunt, the only real representative of Mr. Astor, at the time of the capitulation with the North West Company, completed the series of cross purposes. Had that gentleman been present, the transfer in all probability would not have taken place.

It is painful at all times to see a grand and beneficial stroke of genius fail of its aim: but we regret the failure of this enterprize in a national point of view; for, had it been crowned with success it would have redounded greatly to the advantage and extension of our commerce. The profits drawn from the country in question by the British Fur Company, though of ample amount, form no criterion by which to judge of the advantages that would have arisen had it been entirely in the hands of citizens of the United States. That company, as has been shown, is limited in the nature and scope of its operations, and can make but little use of the maritime facilities held out by an emporium and a harbor on that coast. In our hands, beside the roving bands of trappers and traders, the country would have been explored and settled by industrious husbandmen; and the fertile valleys bordering its rivers, and shut up among its mountains, would have been made to pour forth their agricultural treasures to contribute to the general wealth.

In respect to commerce, we should have had a line of trading posts from the Mississippi and the Missouri across the Rocky Mountains, forming a high road from the great regions of the west to the shores of the Pacific. We should have had a fortified post and port at the mouth of the Columbia, commanding the trade of that river and its tributaries, and of a wide extent of country and sea coast; carrying on an active and profitable commerce with the Sandwich islands, and a direct and frequent communication with China. In a word, Astoria might have realized the anticipations of Mr. Astor, so well understood and appreciated by Mr. Jefferson, in gradually becoming a commercial empire beyond the Mountains, peopled by "free and independent Americans, and linked with us by ties of blood and interest."

We repeat, therefore, our sincere regret that our government should have neglected the overture of Mr. Astor and suffered the moment to pass by when full possession of this region might have been taken quietly as a matter of course, and a military post established without disputes at Astoria. Our statesmen have become sensible when too late, of the importance of this measure. Bills have repeatedly been brought into Congress for the purpose, but without success, and our rightful possessions on that coast, as well as our trade on the Pacific, have no rallying point protected by the national flag and by a military force.

In the mean time the second period of ten years is fast elapsing. In 1838, the question of title will again come up, and most probably, in the present amicable state of our relations with Great Britain, will be again postponed. Every year, however, the litigated claim is growing in importance. There is no pride so jealous and irritable as the pride of territory. As one wave of emigration after another rolls into the vast regions of the west, and our settlements stretch towards the Rocky Mountains, the eager eyes of our pioneers will pry beyond, and they will become impatient of any barrier or impediment in the way of what they consider a grand outlet of our empire. Should any circumstance, therefore, unfortunately occur to disturb the present harmony of the two nations, this ill-adjusted question, which now lies dormant, may suddenly start up into one of belligerent import, and Astoria become the watchword in a contest for dominion on the shores of the Pacific.

Since the above was written, the question of dominion over the vast territory beyond the Rocky Mountains, which for a time threatened to disturb the peaceful relations with our transatlantic kindred, has been finally settled in a spirit of mutual concession, and the venerable projector whose early enterprise forms the subject of this work had the satisfaction of knowing, ere his eyes closed upon the world, that the flag of his country again waved over "ASTORIA."

APPENDIX

Draught of a petition to Congress, sent by Mr. Astor in 1812.

To the honorable the Senate and House of Representatives of
    the United States, in Congress assembled,

The petition of the American Fur Company respectfully
    sheweth:

That the trade with the several Indian tribes of North
America, has, for many years past, been almost exclusively carried on by the merchants of Canada; who, having formed
powerful and extensive associations for that purpose, being
aided by British capital, and being encouraged by the favor
and protection of the British government, could not be opposed, with any prospect of success by individuals of the
United States.

That by means of the above trade, thus systematically pursued, not only the inhabitants of the United States have been
deprived of commercial profits and advantages, to which they
appear to have just and natural pretensions, but a great and
dangerous influence has been established over the Indian
tribes, difficult to be counteracted, and capable of being exerted at critical periods, to the great injury and annoyance of
our frontier settlements.

That in order to obtain at least a part of the above trade,
and more particularly that which is within the boundaries of
the United States, your petitioners, in the year 1808, obtained an act of incorporation from the state of New York,
whereby they are enabled, with a competent capital, to carry
on the said trade with the Indians in such manner as may be
conformable to the laws and regulations of the United States,
in relation to such commerce.

That the capital mentioned in the said act, amounting to
one million of dollars, having been duly formed, your petitioners entered with zeal and alacrity into those large and important arrangements, which were necessary for, or conducive
to, the object of their incorporation; and, among other things,
purchased a great part of the stock in trade, and trading estab-

lishments, of the Michilimackinac Company of Canada.—
Your petitioners also, with the expectation of great public and
private advantage from the use of the said establishments, ordered, during the spring and summer of 1810, an assortment
of goods from England, suitable for the Indian trade; which,
in consequence of the President's proclamation of November
of that year, were shipped to Canada instead of New York,
and have been transported, under a very heavy expense, into
the interior of the country. But as they could not legally be
brought into the Indian country within the boundaries of the
United States, they have been stored on the island of St.
Joseph, in Lake Huron, where they now remain.

Your petitioners, with great deference and implicit submission to the wisdom of the national legislature, beg leave to
suggest for consideration, whether they have not some claim
to national attention and encouragement, from the nature
and importance of their undertaking; which, though hazardous and uncertain as it concerns their private emolument,
must, at any rate, redound to the public security and advantage. If their undertaking shall appear to be of the description
given, they would further suggest to your honorable bodies,
that unless they can procure a regular supply for the trade in
which they are engaged, it may languish, and be finally abandoned by American citizens; when it will revert to its former
channel, with additional, and perhaps with irresistible, power.

Under these circumstances, and upon all those considerations of public policy which will present themselves to your
honorable bodies, in connexion with those already mentioned,
your petitioners respectfully pray that a law may be passed
to enable the President, or any of the heads of departments
acting under his authority, to grant permits for the introduction of goods necessary for the supply of the Indians, into the
Indian country that is within the boundaries of the United
States, under such regulations, and with such restrictions, as
may secure the public revenue and promote the public welfare.

And your petitioners shall ever pray, &c.

In witness whereof, the common seal of the American Fur
    Company is hereunto affixed, the   day of March, 1812.

By order of the Corporation.

AN ACT to enable the American Fur Company, and other citizens, to introduce goods necessary for the Indian trade
into the territories within the boundaries of the United
States.

WHEREAS, the public peace and welfare require that the native
Indian tribes, residing within the boundaries of the United
States, should receive their necessary supplies under the authority and from the citizens of the United States: Therefore,
be it enacted by the Senate and House of Representatives of
the United States, in Congress assembled, that it shall be lawful for the President of the United States, or any of the heads
of departments, thereunto by him duly authorized, from time
to time to grant permits to the American Fur Company, their
agents or factors, or any other citizens of the United States engaged in the Indian trade, to introduce into the Indian country, within the boundaries of the United States, such goods,
wares, and merchandise, as may be necessary for the said trade,
under such regulations and restrictions as the said President or
heads of departments may judge proper; any law or regulation
to the contrary, in anywise, notwithstanding.

Letter from Mr. Gallatin to Mr. Astor, dated

NEW YORK, *August 5, 1835.*

Dear Sir,—
    In compliance with your request, I will state such facts as I
recollect, touching the subjects mentioned in your letter of
28th ult. I may be mistaken respecting dates and details, and
will only relate general facts, which I well remember.
    In conformity with the treaty of 1794 with Great Britain,
the citizens and subjects of each country were permitted to
trade with the Indians residing in the territories of the other
party. The reciprocity was altogether nominal. Since the conquest of Canada, the British had inherited from the French

the whole fur trade, through the great lakes and their communications, with all the western Indians, whether residing in the British dominions or the United States. They kept the important western posts on those lakes till about the year 1797. And the defensive Indian war, which the United States had to sustain from 1776 to 1795, had still more alienated the Indians, and secured to the British their exclusive trade, carried through the lakes, wherever the Indians in that quarter lived. No American could, without imminent danger of property and life, carry on that trade, even within the United States, by the way of either Michilimackinac or St. Mary's. And independent of the loss of commerce, Great Britain was enabled to preserve a most dangerous influence over our Indians.

It was under these circumstances that you communicated to our government the prospect you had to be able, and your intention, to purchase one half of the interest of the Canadian Fur Company, engaged in trade by the way of Michilimackinac with our own Indians. You wished to know whether the plan met with the approbation of government, and how far you could rely on its protection and encouragement. This overture was received with great satisfaction by the administration, and Mr. Jefferson, then President, wrote you to that effect. I was also directed, as Secretary of the Treasury, to write to you an official letter to the same purpose. On investigating the subject, it was found that the Executive had no authority to give you any direct aid; and I believe that you received nothing more than an entire approbation of your plan, and general assurances of the protection due to every citizen engaged in lawful and useful pursuits.

You did effect the contemplated purchase, but in what year I do not recollect. Immediately before the war, you represented that a large quantity of merchandise, intended for the Indian trade, and including arms and munitions of war, belonging to that concern of which you owned one half, was deposited at a post on Lake Huron, within the British dominions; that, in order to prevent their ultimately falling into the hands of Indians who might prove hostile, you were desirous to try to have them conveyed into the United States; but that you were prevented by the then existing law of nonintercourse with the British dominions.

The Executive could not annul the provisions of that law. But I was directed to instruct the collectors on the lakes, in case you or your agents should voluntarily bring in and deliver to them any parts of the goods above mentioned, to receive and keep them in their guard, and not to commence prosecutions until further instructions: the intention being then to apply to Congress for an act remitting the forfeiture and penalties. I wrote accordingly, to that effect, to the collectors of Detroit and Michilimackinac.

The attempt to obtain the goods did not, however, succeed; and I cannot say how far the failure injured you. But the war proved fatal to another much more extensive and important enterprise.

Previous to that time, but I also forget the year, you had undertaken to carry on a trade on your own account, though I believe under the New York charter of the American Fur Company, with the Indians west of the Rocky Mountains. This project was also communicated to government, and met, of course, with its full approbation, and best wishes for your success. You carried it on, on the most extensive scale, sending several ships to the mouth of the Columbia River, and a large party by land across the mountains, and finally founding the establishment of Astoria.

This unfortunately fell into the hands of the enemy during the war, from circumstances with which I am but imperfectly acquainted—being then absent on a foreign mission. I returned in September, 1815, and sailed again on a mission to France in June, 1816. During that period I visited Washington twice—in October or November, 1815, and in March, 1816. On one of those two occasions, and I believe on the last, you mentioned to me that you were disposed once more to renew the attempt, and to re-establish Astoria, provided you had the protection of the American flag; for which purpose, a lieutenant's command would be sufficient to you. You requested me to mention this to the President, which I did. Mr. Madison said he would consider the subject, and, although he did not commit himself, I thought that he received the proposal favorably. The message was verbal, and I do not know whether the application was ever renewed in a more formal manner. I sailed soon after for Europe, and was seven years absent. I never had the pleasure, since 1816, to see Mr. Madison, and never heard again any thing concerning the subject in question.

I remain, dear sir, very respectfully,

Your obedient servant,

ALBERT GALLATIN

JOHN JACOB ASTOR, ESQ.,
New York.

Notices of the present state of the Fur Trade, chiefly extracted from an article published in Silliman's Journal for January, 1834.

The North West Company did not long enjoy the sway they had acquired over the trading regions of the Columbia. A competition, ruinous in its expenses, which had long existed between them and the Hudson's Bay Company, ended in their downfall and the ruin of most of the partners. The relics of the company became merged in the rival association, and the whole business was conducted under the name of the Hudson's Bay Company.

This coalition took place in 1821. They then abandoned Astoria, and built a large establishment sixty miles up the river, on the right bank, which they called Fort Vancouver. This was in a neighborhood where provisions could be more readily procured, and where there was less danger from molestation by any naval force. The company are said to carry on an active and prosperous trade, and to give great encouragement to settlers. They are extremely jealous, however, of any interference or participation in their trade, and monopolize it from the coast of the Pacific to the mountains, and for a considerable extent north and south. The American traders and trappers who venture across the mountains, instead of enjoying the participation in the trade of the river and its tributaries, that had been stipulated by treaty, are obliged to keep to the south, out of the track of the Hudson's Bay parties.

Mr. Astor has withdrawn entirely from the American Fur Company, as he has, in fact, from active business of every kind. That company is now headed by Mr. Ramsay Crooks; its principal establishment is at Michilimackinac, and it receives its furs from the posts depending on that station, and from those on the Mississippi, Missouri, and Yellow Stone rivers, and the great range of country extending thence to the Rocky Mountains. This company has steamboats in its employ, with which it ascends the rivers, and penetrates to a vast distance into the bosom of those regions formerly so painfully explored in keel-boats and barges, or by weary parties on horseback and on foot. The first irruption of steamboats into the heart of these vast wildernesses is said to have caused the utmost astonishment and affright among their savage inhabitants.

In addition to the main companies already mentioned, minor associations have been formed, which push their way in the most intrepid manner to the remote parts of the far west, and beyond the mountain barriers. One of the most noted of these is Ashley's company, from St. Louis, who trap for themselves, and drive an extensive trade with the Indians. The spirit, enterprize, and hardihood of Ashley, are themes of the highest eulogy in the far west, and his adventures and exploits furnish abundance of frontier stories.

Another company of one hundred and fifty persons from New York, formed in 1831, and headed by Captain Bonneville of the United States army, has pushed its enterprizes into tracts before but little known, and has brought considerable quantities of furs from the region between the Rocky Mountains and the coasts of Monterey and Upper California, on the Buenaventura and Timpanogos rivers.

The fur countries from the Pacific east to the Rocky Mountains, are now occupied (exclusive of private combinations and individual trappers and traders) by the Russians, on the north west from Bhering's Strait to Queen Charlotte's Island in N. Lat. 53°, and by the Hudson's Bay Company thence, south of the Columbia river; while Ashley's company, and that under Captain Bonneville, take the remainder of the region to California. Indeed, the whole compass from the Mississippi to the Pacific Ocean is traversed in every direction. The mountains and forests, from the Arctic Sea to the Gulf of Mexico, are threaded, through every maze, by the hunter. Every river and tributary stream, from the Columbia to the mouth of the Rio del Norte, and from the M'Kenzie to the Colorado of the West, from their head springs to their junction, are searched and trapped for beaver. Almost all the American furs, which do not belong to the Hudson's Bay Company, find their way to New York, and are either distributed thence for home consumption, or sent to foreign markets.

The Hudson's Bay Company ship their furs from their factories of York fort and from Moose river, on Hudson's Bay; their collection from Grand river, &c., they ship from Canada; and the collection from Columbia river goes to London. None of their furs come to the United States, except through the London market.

The export trade of furs from the United States is chiefly to London. Some quantities have been sent to Canton, and some few to Hamburgh; and an increasing export trade in beaver, otter, nutria, and vicunia wool, prepared for the hatter's use, is carried on with Mexico. Some furs are exported from Baltimore, Philadelphia, and Boston; but the principal shipments from the United States are from New York to London, from whence they are sent to Leipsic, a well-known mart for furs, where they are disposed of during the great fair in that city, and distributed to every part of the continent.

The United States import from South America, nutria, vicunia, chinchilla, and a few deer skins; also fur seals from the Lobos islands, off the river Plate. A quantity of beaver, otter, &c., are brought annually from Santa Fé. Dressed furs for edgings, linings, caps, muffs, &c., such as squirrel, genet, fitch skins, and blue rabbit, are received from the north of Europe; also coney and hare's fur; but the largest importations are from London, where is concentrated nearly the whole of the North American fur trade.

Such is the present state of the fur trade, by which it will appear that the extended sway of the Hudson's Bay Company, and its monopoly of the region of which Astoria was the key, has operated to turn the main current of this opulent trade into the coffers of Great Britain, and to render London the emporium instead of New York, as Mr. Astor had intended.

We will subjoin a few observations on the animals sought after in this traffic, extracted from the same intelligent source with the preceding remarks.

Of the fur-bearing animals, "the precious ermine," so called by way of pre-eminence, is found, of the best quality, only in the cold regions of Europe and Asia.* Its fur is of the most perfect whiteness, except the tip of its tail, which is of a brilliant shining black. With these black tips tacked on the skins, they are beautifully spotted, producing an effect often imitated, but never equalled in other furs. The ermine is of the genus Mustela, (weasel,) and resembles the common weasel in its form; is from fourteen to sixteen inches from the tip of the nose to the end of the tail. The body is from ten to twelve inches long. It lives in hollow trees, river banks, and especially in beech forests; preys on small birds, is very shy, sleeping during the day, and employing the night in search of food. The fur of the older animals is preferred to the younger. It is taken by snares and traps, and sometimes shot with blunt arrows. Attempts have been made to domesticate it; but it is extremely wild, and has been found untameable.

The sable can scarcely be called second to the ermine. It is a native of northern Europe and Siberia, and is also of the genus Mustela. In Samoieda, Yakutsk, Kamschatka, and Russian Lapland, it is found of the richest quality, and darkest color. In its habits, it resembles the ermine. It preys on small squirrels and birds, sleeps by day, and prowls for food during the night. It is so like the marten in every particular except its size, and the dark shade of its color, that naturalists have not decided whether it is the richest and finest of the marten tribe, or a variety of that species.† It varies in dimensions from eighteen to twenty inches.

The rich dark shades of the sable, and the snowy whiteness of the ermine, the great depth, and the peculiar, almost flowing softness of their skins and fur, have combined to gain them a preference in all countries, and in all ages of the world. In this age, they maintain the same relative estimate in regard to other furs, as when they marked the rank of the proud crusader, and were emblazoned in heraldry: but in most European nations, they are now worn promiscuously by the opulent.

* An animal called the stoat, a kind of ermine, is said to be found in North America, but very inferior to the European and Asiatic.

† The finest fur and the darkest color are most esteemed; and whether the difference arises from the age of the animal, or from some peculiarity of location, is not known. They do not vary more from the common marten, than the Arabian horse from the shaggy Canadian.

The martens from Northern Asia and the mountains of Kamschatka are much superior to the American, though in every pack of American marten skins there are a certain number which are beautifully shaded, and of a dark brown olive color, of great depth and richness.

Next these in value, for ornament and utility, are the sea otter, the mink, and the fiery fox.

The fiery fox is the bright red of Asia; is more brilliantly colored and of finer fur than any other of the genus. It is highly valued for the splendor of its red color and the fineness of its fur. It is the standard of value on the north eastern coast of Asia.

The sea otter, which was first introduced into commerce in 1725, from the Aleutian and Kurile islands, is an exceedingly fine, soft, close fur, jet black in winter with a silken gloss. The fur of the young animal is of a beautiful brown color. It is met with in great abundance in Bhering's island, Kamschatka, Aleutian and Fox islands, and is also taken on the opposite coasts of North America. It is sometimes taken with nets, but more frequently with clubs and spears. Their food is principally lobster and other shell fish.

In 1780 furs had become so scarce in Siberia, that the supply was insufficient for the demand in the Asiatic countries. It was at this time that the sea otter was introduced into the markets for China. The skins brought such incredible prices, as to originate immediately several American and British expeditions to the northern islands of the Pacific, to Nootka Sound, and the north west coast of America; but the Russians already had possession of the tract which they now hold, and had arranged a trade for the sea otter with the Koudek tribes. They do not engross the trade, however; the American north west trading ships procure them, all along the coast, from the Indians.

At one period, the fur seals formed no inconsiderable item in the trade. South Georgia, in south latitude 55°, discovered in 1675, was explored by Captain Cook in 1771. The Americans immediately commenced carrying seal skins thence to China, where they obtained the most exorbitant prices. One million two hundred thousand skins have been taken from that island alone, and nearly an equal number from the island of Desolation, since they were first restored for the purposes of commerce.

The discovery of the South Shetlands, 63° south latitude, in 1818, added surprisingly to the trade in fur seals. The number taken from the South Shetlands in 1821 and 1822 amounted to three hundred and twenty thousand. This valuable animal is now almost extinct in all these islands, owing to the exterminating system adopted by the hunters. They are still taken on the Lobos islands, where the provident government of Montevideo restrict the fishery, or hunting, within certain limits, which insures an annual return of the seals. At certain seasons these amphibia, for the purpose of renewing their coat, come up on the dark frowning rocks and precipices, where there is not a trace of vegetation. In the middle of January, the islands are partially cleared of snow, where a few patches of short straggling grass spring up in favorable situations; but the seals do not resort to it for food. They remain on the rocks not less than two months, without any sustenance, when they return much emaciated to the sea.

Bears of various species and colors, many varieties of the fox, the wolf, the beaver, the otter, the marten, the raccoon, the badger, the wolverine, the mink, the lynx, the muskrat, the woodchuck, the rabbit, the hare, and the squirrel, are natives of North America.

The beaver, otter, lynx, fisher, hare, and raccoon, are used principally for hats; while the bears of several varieties furnish an excellent material for sleigh linings, for cavalry caps, and other military equipments. The fur of the black fox is the most valuable of any of the American varieties; and next to that the red, which is exported to China and Smyrna. In China, the red is employed for trimmings, linings, and robes; the latter being variegated, by adding the black fur of the paws, in spots or waves. There are many other varieties of American fox, such as the gray, the white, the cross, the silver, and the dun-colored. The silver fox is a rare animal, a native of the woody country below the falls of the Columbia river. It has a long, thick, deep lead-colored fur, intermingled with long hairs, invariably white at the top, forming a bright lustrous silver gray, esteemed by some more beautiful than any other kind of fox.

The skins of the buffalo, of the Rocky mountain sheep, of various deer, and of the antelope, are included in the fur trade with the Indians and trappers of the north and west.

Fox and seal skins are sent from Greenland to Denmark. The white fur of the arctic fox and polar bear is sometimes found in the packs brought to the traders by the most northern tribes of Indians, but is not particularly valuable. The silver-tipped rabbit is peculiar to England, and is sent thence to Russia and China.

Other furs are employed and valued according to the caprices of fashion, as well in those countries where they are needed for defences against the severity of the seasons, as among the inhabitants of milder climates, who, being of Tartar or Sclavonian descent, are said to inherit an attachment to furred clothing. Such are the inhabitants of Poland, of Southern Russia, of China, of Persia, of Turkey, and all the nations of Gothic origin in the middle and western parts of Europe. Under the burning suns of Syria and Egypt, and the mild climes of Bucharia and Independent Tartary, there is also a constant demand, and a great consumption, where there exists no physical necessity. In our own temperate latitudes, besides their use in the arts, they are in request for ornament and warmth during the winter, and large quantities are annually consumed for both purposes in the United States.

From the foregoing statements, it appears that the fur trade must henceforward decline. The advanced state of geographical science shows that no new countries remain to be explored. In North America, the animals are slowly decreasing, from the persevering efforts and the indiscriminate slaughter practised by the hunters, and by the appropriation to the uses of man of those forests and rivers which have afforded them food and protection. They recede with the aborigines, before the tide of civilization; but a diminished supply will remain in the mountains and uncultivated tracts of this and other countries, if the avidity of the hunter can be restrained within proper limitations.

Height of the Rocky Mountains.

Various estimates have been made of the height of the Rocky Mountains, but it is doubtful whether any have, as yet, done justice to their real altitude, which promises to place them only

second to the highest mountains of the known world. Their
height has been diminished to the eye by the great elevation of
the plains from which they rise. They consist, according to
Long, of ridges, knobs, and peaks, variously disposed. The
more elevated parts are covered with perpetual snows, which
contribute to give them a luminous, and, at a great distance,
even a brilliant appearance; whence they derived, among some
of the first discoverers, the name of the Shining Mountains.

James's Peak has generally been cited as the highest of the
chain; and its elevation above the common level has been ascertained, by a trigonometrical measurement, to be about
eight thousand five hundred feet. Mr. Long, however, judged,
from the position of the snow near the summits of other
peaks and ridges at no great distance from it, that they were
much higher. Having heard Professor Renwick, of New York,
express an opinion of the altitude of these mountains far beyond what had usually been ascribed to them, we applied to
him for the authority on which he grounded his observation,
and here subjoin his reply:—

COLUMBIA COLLEGE, NEW YORK, *February 23, 1836.*
Dear Sir,—

In compliance with your request, I have to communicate
some facts in relation to the heights of the Rocky Mountains,
and the sources whence I obtained the information.

In conversation with Simon M'Gillivray, Esq., a partner of
the North West Company, he stated to me his impression,
that the mountains in the vicinity of the route pursued by the
traders of that company were nearly as high as the Himalayas.
He had himself crossed by this route, seen the snowy summits
of the peaks, and experienced a degree of cold which required
a spirit thermometer to indicate it. His authority for the estimate of the heights was a gentleman who had been employed
for several years as surveyor of that company. This conversation occurred about sixteen years since.

A year or two afterwards, I had the pleasure of dining,
at Major Delafield's, with Mr. Thompson, the gentleman
referred to by Mr. M'Gillivray. I inquired of him in relation
to the circumstances mentioned by Mr. M'Gillivray, and he
stated, that, by the joint means of the barometer and trigono-

metric measurement, he had ascertained the height of one of the peaks to be about twenty-five thousand feet, and there were others of nearly the same height in the vicinity.

I am, dear Sir,

Yours truly,

JAMES RENWICK.

To W. IRVING, Esq.

Suggestions with respect to the Indian tribes, and the protection of our Trade.

In the course of this work, a few general remarks have been hazarded respecting the Indian tribes of the prairies, and the dangers to be apprehended from them in future times to our trade beyond the Rocky Mountains and with the Spanish frontiers. Since writing those remarks, we have met with some excellent observations and suggestions, in manuscript, on the same subject, written by Captain Bonneville, of the United States army, who has lately returned from a long residence among the tribes of the Rocky Mountains. Captain B. approves highly of the plan recently adopted by the United States government for the organization of a regiment of dragoons for the protection of our western frontier, and the trade across the prairies. "No other species of military force," he observes, "is at all competent to cope with these restless and wandering hordes, who require to be opposed with swiftness quite as much as with strength; and the consciousness that a troop, uniting these qualifications, is always on the alert to avenge their outrages upon the settlers and traders, will go very far towards restraining them from the perpetration of those thefts and murders which they have heretofore committed with impunity, whenever stratagem or superiority of force has given them the advantage. Their interest already has done something towards their pacification with our countrymen. From the traders among them, they receive their supplies in the greatest abundance, and upon very equitable terms; and when it is remembered that a very considerable amount of property is yearly distributed among them by the govern-

ment, as presents, it will readily be perceived that they are
greatly dependant upon us for their most valued resources. If,
superadded to this inducement, a frequent display of military
power be made in their territories, there can be little doubt
that the desired security and peace will be speedily afforded to
our own people. But the idea of establishing a permanent
amity and concord amongst the various east and west tribes
themselves, seems to me, if not wholly impracticable, at least
infinitely more difficult than many excellent philanthropists
have hoped and believed. Those nations which have so lately
emigrated from the midst of our settlements to live upon our
western borders, and have made some progress in agriculture
and the arts of civilization, have, in the property they have acquired, and the protection and aid extended to them, too
many advantages to be induced readily to take up arms
against us, particularly if they can be brought to the full conviction that their new homes will be permanent and undisturbed; and there is every reason and motive, in policy as well
as humanity, for our ameliorating their condition by every
means in our power. But the case is far different with regard
to the Osages, the Kanzas, the Pawnees, and other roving
hordes beyond the frontiers of the settlements. Wild and restless in their character and habits, they are by no means so susceptible of control or civilization; and they are urged by
strong, and, to them, irresistible causes in their situation and
necessities, to the daily perpetration of violence and fraud.
Their permanent subsistence, for example, is derived from the
buffalo hunting grounds, which lie a great distance from their
towns. Twice a year they are obliged to make long and dangerous expeditions, to procure the necessary provisions for
themselves and their families. For this purpose, horses are absolutely requisite, for their own comfort and safety, as well as
for the transportation of their food, and their little stock of
valuables; and without them they would be reduced, during a
great portion of the year, to a state of abject misery and privation. They have no brood mares, nor any trade sufficiently
valuable to supply their yearly losses, and endeavor to keep up
their stock by stealing horses from the other tribes to the west
and south-west. Our own people, and the tribes immediately
upon our borders, may indeed be protected from their depre-

dations; and the Kanzas, Osages, Pawnees, and others, may be induced to remain at peace among themselves, so long as they are permitted to pursue the old custom of levying upon the Camanches and other remote nations for their complement of steeds for the warriors, and pack-horses for their transportations to and from the hunting ground. But the instant they are forced to maintain a peaceful and inoffensive demeanor towards the tribes along the Mexican border, and find that every violation of their rights is followed by the avenging arm of our government, the result must be, that, reduced to a wretchedness and want which they can ill brook, and feeling the certainty of punishment for every attempt to ameliorate their condition in the only way they as yet comprehend, they will abandon their unfruitful territory, and remove to the neighborhood of the Mexican lands, and there carry on a vigorous predatory warfare indiscriminately upon the Mexicans and our own people trading or travelling in that quarter.

"The Indians of the prairies are almost innumerable. Their superior horsemanship, which, in my opinion, far exceeds that of any other people on the face of the earth, their daring bravery, their cunning and skill in the warfare of the wilderness, and the astonishing rapidity and secrecy with which they are accustomed to move in their martial expeditions, will always render them most dangerous and vexatious neighbors, when their necessities or their discontents may drive them to hostility with our frontiers. Their mode and principles of warfare will always protect them from final and irretrievable defeat, and secure their families from participating in any blow, however severe, which our retribution might deal out to them.

"The Camanches lay the Mexicans under contribution for horses and mules, which they are always engaged in stealing from them in incredible numbers; and from the Camanches, all the roving tribes of the far west, by a similar exertion of skill and daring, supply themselves in turn. It seems to me, therefore, under all these circumstances, that the apparent futility of any philanthropic schemes for the benefit of these nations, and a regard for our own protection, concur in recommending that we remain satisfied with maintaining peace upon our own immediate borders, and leave the Mexicans and the Camanches, and all the tribes hostile to these last, to settle their differences and difficulties in their own way.

"In order to give full security and protection to our trading parties circulating in all directions through the great prairies, I am under the impression, that a few judicious measures on the part of the government, involving a very limited expense, would be sufficient. And, in attaining this end, which of itself has already become an object of public interest and import, another, of much greater consequence, might be brought about, viz., the securing to the states a most valuable and increasing trade, now carried on by caravans directly to Santa Fé.

"As to the first desideratum: the Indians can only be made to respect the lives and property of the American parties, by rendering them dependant upon us for their supplies; which can alone be done with complete effect by the establishment of a trading post, with resident traders, at some point which will unite a sufficient number of advantages to attract the several tribes to itself, in preference to their present places of resort for that purpose; for it is a well known fact, that the Indians will always protect their trader, and those in whom he is interested, so long as they derive benefits from him. The alternative presented to those at the north, by the residence of the agents of the Hudson's Bay Company amongst them, renders the condition of our people in that quarter less secure; but I think it will appear, at once, upon the most cursory examination, that no such opposition further south could be maintained, so as to weaken the benefits of such an establishment as is here suggested.

"In considering this matter, the first question which presents itself is, where do these tribes now make their exchanges, and obtain their necessary supplies? They resort almost exclusively to the Mexicans, who, themselves, purchase from us whatever the Indians most seek for. In this point of view, therefore, *cæteris paribus*, it would be an easy matter for us to monopolize the whole traffic. All that is wanting is some location more convenient for the natives than that offered by the Mexicans, to give us the undisputed superiority; and the selection of such a point requires but a knowledge of the single fact, that these nations invariably winter upon the head waters of the Arkansas, and there prepare all their buffalo robes for trade. These robes are heavy, and, to the Indian, very difficult of transportation. Nothing but necessity induces them to travel any great distance with such inconvenient baggage. A post, therefore, established upon the head waters of the Arkansas, must infallibly secure an uncontested preference over that of the Mexicans, even at their prices and rates of barter. Then let the dragoons occasionally move about among these people in large parties, impressing them with the proper estimate of our power to protect and to punish, and at once we have complete and assured security for all citizens whose enterprise may lead them beyond the border, and an end to the outrages and depredations which now dog the footsteps of the traveller in the prairies, and arrest and repress the most advantageous commerce. Such a post need not be stronger than fifty men; twenty-five to be employed as hunters, to supply the garrison, and the residue as a defence against any hostility. Situated here upon the good lands of the Arkansas, in the midst of abundance of timber, while it might be kept up at a most inconsiderable expense, such an establishment within ninety miles of Santa Fé or Tous would be more than justified by the other and more important advantage before alluded to, leaving the protection of the traders with the Indian tribes entirely out of the question.

"This great trade, carried on by caravans to Santa Fé, annually loads one hundred wagons with merchandise, which is bartered in the northern provinces of Mexico for cash and for beaver furs. The numerous articles excluded as contraband, and the exorbitant duties laid upon all those that are admitted by the Mexican government, present so many obstacles to commerce, that I am well persuaded, that if a post, such as is here suggested, should be established on the Arkansas, it would become the place of deposite, not only for the present trade, but for one infinitely more extended. Here the Mexicans might purchase their supplies, and might well afford to sell them at prices which would silence all competition from any other quarter.

"These two trades, with the Mexicans and the Indians, centring at this post, would give rise to a large village of traders and laborers, and would undoubtedly be hailed, by all that section of country, as a permanent and invaluable advantage. A few pack-horses would carry all the clothing and ammunition necessary for the post during the first year, and two light field-pieces would be all the artillery required for its defence. Afterwards, all the horses required for the use of the establishment might be purchased from the Mexicans at the low price of ten dollars each; and, at the same time, whatever animals might be needed to supply the losses among the dragoons traversing the neighborhood, could be readily procured. The Upper Missouri Indians can furnish horses, at very cheap rates, to any number of the same troops who might be detailed for the defence of the northern frontier; and, in other respects, a very limited outlay of money would suffice to maintain a post in that section of the country.

"From these considerations, and my own personal observation, I am, therefore, disposed to believe, that two posts established by the government, one at the mouth of the Yellow Stone river, and one on the Arkansas, would completely protect all our people in every section of the great wilderness of the west; while other advantages, at least with regard to one of them, confirm and urge the suggestion. A fort at the mouth of Yellow Stone, garrisoned by fifty men, would be perfectly safe. The establishment might be constructed simply with a view to the stores, stables for the dragoons' horses, and quarters for the regular garrison; the rest being provided with sheds or lodges, erected in the vicinity, for their residence during the winter months."

THE ADVENTURES OF
CAPTAIN BONNEVILLE

Contents

INTRODUCTORY NOTICE

While engaged in writing an account of the grand enterprise of ASTORIA, it was my practice to seek all kinds of oral information connected with the subject. Nowhere did I pick up more interesting particulars than at the table of Mr. John Jacob Astor; who, being the patriarch of the Fur Trade in the United States, was accustomed to have at his board various persons of adventurous turn, some of whom had been engaged in his own great undertaking; others, on their own account, had made expeditions to the Rocky Mountains and the waters of the Columbia.

Among these personages, one who peculiarly took my fancy, was Captain BONNEVILLE, of the United States' army; who, in a rambling kind of enterprise, had strangely engrafted the trapper and hunter upon the soldier. As his expeditions and adventures will form the leading theme of the following pages, a few biographical particulars concerning him may not be unacceptable.

Captain Bonneville is of French parentage. His father was a worthy old emigrant, who came to this country many years since, and took up his abode in New York. He is represented as a man not much calculated for the sordid struggle of a money-making world, but possessed of a happy temperament, a festivity of imagination, and a simplicity of heart, that made him proof against its rubs and trials. He was an excellent scholar: well acquainted with Latin and Greek, and fond of the modern classics. His book was his elysium; once immersed in the pages of Voltaire, Corneille, or Racine, or of his favorite English author, Shakspeare, he forgot the world and all its concerns. Often would he be seen in summer weather, seated under one of the trees on the Battery, or the portico of St. Paul's church in Broadway, his bald head uncovered, his hat lying by his side, his eyes riveted to the page of his book, and his whole soul so engaged, as to lose all consciousness of the passing throng or the passing hour.

Captain Bonneville, it will be found, inherited something of his father's *bonhommie*, and his excitable imagination; though

629

the latter was somewhat disciplined in early years, by mathematical studies. He was educated at our national Military Academy at West Point, where he acquitted himself very creditably; thence, he entered the army, in which he has ever since continued.

The nature of our military service took him to the frontier, where, for a number of years, he was stationed at various posts in the Far West. Here he was brought into frequent intercourse with Indian traders, mountain trappers, and other pioneers of the wilderness; and became so excited by their tales of wild scenes and wild adventures, and their accounts of vast and magnificent regions as yet unexplored, that an expedition to the Rocky Mountains became the ardent desire of his heart, and an enterprise to explore untrodden tracts, the leading object of his ambition.

By degrees he shaped this vague day-dream into a practical reality. Having made himself acquainted with all the requisites for a trading enterprise beyond the mountains, he determined to undertake it. A leave of absence, and a sanction of his expedition, was obtained from the major general in chief, on his offering to combine public utility with his private projects, and to collect statistical information for the War Department, concerning the wild countries and wild tribes he might visit in the course of his journeyings.

Nothing now was wanting to the darling project of the captain, but the ways and means. The expedition would require an outfit of many thousand dollars; a staggering obstacle to a soldier, whose capital is seldom any thing more than his sword. Full of that buoyant hope, however, which belongs to the sanguine temperament, he repaired to New York, the great focus of American enterprise, where there are always funds ready for any scheme, however chimerical or romantic. Here he had the good fortune to meet with a gentleman of high respectability and influence, who had been his associate in boyhood, and who cherished a schoolfellow friendship for him. He took a generous interest in the scheme of the captain; introduced him to commercial men of his acquaintance, and in a little while an association was formed, and the necessary funds were raised to carry the proposed measure into effect. One of the most efficient persons in this association was

Mr. Alfred Seton, who, when quite a youth, had accompanied one of the expeditions sent out by Mr. Astor to his commercial establishments on the Columbia, and had distinguished himself by his activity and courage at one of the interior posts. Mr. Seton was one of the American youths who were at Astoria at the time of its surrender to the British, and who manifested such grief and indignation at seeing the flag of their country hauled down. The hope of seeing that flag once more planted on the shores of the Columbia, may have entered into his motives for engaging in the present enterprise.

Thus backed and provided, Captain Bonneville undertook his expedition into the Far West, and was soon beyond the Rocky Mountains. Year after year elapsed without his return. The term of his leave of absence expired, yet no report was made of him at head quarters at Washington. He was considered virtually dead or lost, and his name was stricken from the army list.

It was in the autumn of 1835, at the country seat of Mr. John Jacob Astor, at Hellgate, that I first met with Captain Bonneville. He was then just returned from a residence of upwards of three years among the mountains, and was on his way to report himself at head quarters, in the hopes of being reinstated in the service. From all that I could learn, his wanderings in the wilderness, though they had gratified his curiosity and his love of adventure, had not much benefited his fortunes. Like Corporal Trim in his campaigns, he had "satisfied the sentiment," and that was all. In fact, he was too much of the frank, freehearted soldier, and had inherited too much of his father's temperament, to make a scheming trapper, or a thrifty bargainer. There was something in the whole appearance of the captain that prepossessed me in his favor. He was of the middle size, well made and well set; and a military frock of foreign cut, that had seen service, gave him a look of compactness. His countenance was frank, open, and engaging; well browned by the sun, and had something of a French expression. He had a pleasant black eye, a high forehead, and, while he kept his hat on, the look of a man in the jocund prime of his days; but the moment his head was uncovered, a bald crown gained him credit for a few more years than he was really entitled to.

Being extremely curious, at the time, about every thing connected with the Far West, I addressed numerous questions to him. They drew from him a number of extremely striking details, which were given with mingled modesty and frankness; and in a gentleness of manner, and a soft tone of voice, contrasting singularly with the wild and often startling nature of his themes. It was difficult to conceive the mild, quiet-looking personage before you, the actual hero of the stirring scenes related.

In the course of three or four months, happening to be at the city of Washington, I again came upon the captain, who was attending the slow adjustment of his affairs with the War Department. I found him quartered with a worthy brother in arms, a major in the army. Here he was writing at a table, covered with maps and papers, in the centre of a large barrack room, fancifully decorated with Indian arms, and trophies, and war dresses, and the skins of various wild animals, and hung round with pictures of Indian games and ceremonies, and scenes of war and hunting. In a word, the captain was beguiling the tediousness of attendance at court, by an attempt at authorship; and was rewriting and extending his travelling notes, and making maps of the regions he had explored. As he sat at the table, in this curious apartment, with his high bald head of somewhat foreign cast, he reminded me of some of those antique pictures of authors that I have seen in old Spanish volumes.

The result of his labors was a mass of manuscript, which he subsequently put at my disposal, to fit it for publication and bring it before the world. I found it full of interesting details of life among the mountains, and of the singular castes and races, both white men and red men, among whom he had sojourned. It bore, too, throughout, the impress of his character, his *bon-hommie*, his kindliness of spirit, and his susceptibility to the grand and beautiful.

That manuscript has formed the staple of the following work. I have occasionally interwoven facts and details, gathered from various sources, especially from the conversations and journals of some of the captain's contemporaries, who were actors in the scenes he describes. I have also given it a tone and coloring drawn from my own observation, during an excursion into the Indian country beyond the bounds of civilization; as I before observed, however, the work is substantially the narrative of the worthy captain, and many of its most graphic passages are but little varied from his own language.

I shall conclude this notice by a dedication which he had made of his manuscript to his hospitable brother in arms, in whose quarters I found him occupied in his literary labors; it is a dedication which, I believe, possesses the qualities, not always found in complimentary documents of the kind, of being sincere, and being merited.

TO

JAMES HARVEY HOOK,
MAJOR, U.S.A.

WHOSE JEALOUSY OF ITS HONOR,
WHOSE ANXIETY FOR ITS INTERESTS,
AND
WHOSE SENSIBILITY FOR ITS WANTS,
HAVE ENDEARED HIM TO THE SERVICE AS

THE SOLDIER'S FRIEND;

AND WHOSE GENERAL AMENITY, CONSTANT CHEERFULNESS,
DISINTERESTED HOSPITALITY, AND UNWEARIED
BENEVOLENCE, ENTITLE HIM TO THE
STILL LOFTIER TITLE OF

THE FRIEND OF MAN,

THIS WORK IS INSCRIBED,
ETC.

Chapter I

State of the fur trade of the Rocky Mountains—American en-
terprises—General Ashley and his associates—Sublette, a fa-
mous leader—Yearly rendezvous among the mountains—
Stratagems and dangers of the trade—Bands of trappers—
Indian banditti—Crows and Blackfeet—Mountaineers—
Traders of the Far West—Character and habits of the trapper

IN a recent work we have given an account of the grand enterprise of Mr. John Jacob Astor, to establish an American
emporium for the fur trade at the mouth of the Columbia, or
Oregon River; of the failure of that enterprise through the capture of Astoria by the British, in 1814; and of the way in which
the control of the trade of the Columbia and its dependancies
fell into the hands of the Northwest Company. We have stated,
likewise, the unfortunate supineness of the American government, in neglecting the application of Mr. Astor for the protection of the American flag, and a small military force, to
enable him to reinstate himself in the possession of Astoria at
the return of peace; when the post was formally given up by
the British government, though still occupied by the Northwest Company. By that supineness the sovereignty in the country has been virtually lost to the United States; and it will cost
both governments much trouble and difficulty to settle matters on that just and rightful footing, on which they would
readily have been placed, had the proposition of Mr. Astor
been attended to. We shall now state a few particulars of subsequent events, so as to lead the reader up to the period of
which we are about to treat, and to prepare him for the circumstances of our narrative.

In consequence of the apathy and neglect of the American
government, Mr. Astor abandoned all thoughts of regaining
Astoria, and made no further attempt to extend his enterprises
beyond the Rocky Mountains; and the Northwest Company
considered themselves the lords of the country. They did not
long enjoy unmolested the sway which they had somewhat
surreptitiously attained. A fierce competition ensued between

them and their old rivals, the Hudson's Bay Company; which was carried on at great cost and sacrifice, and occasionally with the loss of life. It ended in the ruin of most of the partners of the Northwest Company; and the merging of the relics of that establishment, in 1821, in the rival association. From that time, the Hudson's Bay Company enjoyed a monopoly of the Indian trade from the coast of the Pacific to the Rocky Mountains, and for a considerable extent north and south. They removed their emporium from Astoria to Fort Vancouver, a strong post on the left bank of the Columbia River, about sixty miles from its mouth; whence they furnished their interior posts, and sent forth their brigades of trappers.

The Rocky Mountains formed a vast barrier between them and the United States, and their stern and awful defiles, their rugged valleys, and the great western plains watered by their rivers, remained almost a terra incognita to the American trapper. The difficulties experienced in 1808, by Mr. Henry of the Missouri Company, the first American who trapped upon the head waters of the Columbia; and the frightful hardships sustained by Wilson P. Hunt, Ramsay Crooks, Robert Stuart, and other intrepid Astorians, in their ill-fated expeditions across the mountains, appeared for a time to check all further enterprise in that direction. The American traders contented themselves with following up the head branches of the Missouri, the Yellowstone, and other rivers and streams on the Atlantic side of the mountains, but forbore to attempt those great snow-crowned sierras.

One of the first to revive these tramontane expeditions was General Ashley, of Missouri, a man whose courage and achievements in the prosecution of his enterprises, have rendered him famous in the Far West. In conjunction with Mr. Henry, already mentioned, he established a post on the banks of the Yellowstone River, in 1822, and in the following year pushed a resolute band of trappers across the mountains to the banks of the Green River or Colorado of the West, often known by the Indian name of the Seeds-ke-dee Agie.* This attempt was followed up and sustained by others, until in 1825 a footing was

---

*i.e. The Prairie Hen River. Agie in the Crow language signifies river.

secured, and a complete system of trapping organized beyond the mountains.

It is difficult to do justice to the courage, fortitude, and perseverance of the pioneers of the fur trade, who conducted these early expeditions, and first broke their way through a wilderness where every thing was calculated to deter and dismay them. They had to traverse the most dreary and desolate mountains, and barren and trackless wastes, uninhabited by man, or occasionally infested by predatory and cruel savages. They knew nothing of the country beyond the verge of their horizon, and had to gather information as they wandered. They beheld volcanic plains stretching around them, and ranges of mountains piled up to the clouds, and glistening with eternal frost: but knew nothing of their defiles, nor how they were to be penetrated or traversed. They launched themselves in frail canoes on rivers, without knowing whither their swift current would carry them, or what rocks, and shoals, and rapids, they might encounter in their course. They had to be continually on the alert, too, against the mountain tribes, who beset every defile, laid ambuscades in their path, or attacked them in their night encampments; so that, of the hardy bands of trappers that first entered into these regions, three-fifths are said to have fallen by the hands of savage foes.

In this wild and warlike school a number of leaders have sprung up, originally in the employ, subsequently partners of Ashley; among these we may mention Smith, Fitzpatrick, Bridger, Robert Campbell, and William Sublette; whose adventures and exploits partake of the wildest spirit of romance. The association commenced by General Ashley underwent various modifications. That gentleman having acquired sufficient fortune, sold out his interest and retired; and the leading spirit that succeeded him was Captain William Sublette: a man worthy of note, as his name has become renowned in frontier story. He is a native of Kentucky, and of game descent; his maternal grandfather, Colonel Whitley, a companion of Boone, having been one of the pioneers of the West, celebrated in Indian warfare, and killed in one of the contests of the "Bloody Ground." We shall frequently have occasion to speak of this Sublette, and always to the credit of his game qualities. In 1830, the association took the name of the

Rocky Mountain Fur Company, of which Captain Sublette and Robert Campbell were prominent members.

In the meantime, the success of this company attracted the attention and excited the emulation of the American Fur Company, and brought them once more into the field of their ancient enterprise. Mr. Astor, the founder of the association, had retired from busy life, and the concerns of the company were ably managed by Mr. Ramsay Crooks, of Snake River renown, who still officiates as its president. A competition immediately ensued between the two companies, for the trade with the mountain tribes, and the trapping of the head waters of the Columbia, and the other great tributaries of the Pacific. Beside the regular operations of these formidable rivals, there have been from time to time desultory enterprises, or rather experiments, of minor associations, or of adventurous individuals, beside roving bands of independent trappers, who either hunt for themselves, or engage for a single season, in the service of one or other of the main companies.

The consequence is, that the Rocky Mountains and the ulterior regions, from the Russian possessions in the north, down to the Spanish settlements of California, have been traversed and ransacked in every direction by bands of hunters and Indian traders; so that there is scarcely a mountain pass, or defile, that is not known and threaded in their restless migrations, nor a nameless stream that is not haunted by the lonely trapper.

The American fur companies keep no established posts beyond the mountains. Every thing there is regulated by resident partners; that is to say, partners who reside in the tramontane country, but who move about from place to place, either with Indian tribes, whose traffic they wish to monopolize, or with main bodies of their own men, whom they employ in trading and trapping. In the meantime, they detach bands, or "brigades" as they are termed, of trappers in various directions, assigning to each a portion of country as a hunting, or trapping ground. In the months of June and July, when there is an interval between the hunting seasons, a general rendezvous is held, at some designated place in the mountains, where the affairs of the past year are settled by the resident partners, and the plans for the following year arranged.

To this rendezvous repair the various brigades of trappers from their widely separated hunting grounds, bringing in the products of their year's campaign. Hither also repair the Indian tribes accustomed to traffic their peltries with the company. Bands of free trappers resort hither also, to sell the furs they have collected; or to engage their services for the next hunting season.

To this rendezvous the company sends annually a convoy of supplies from its establishment on the Atlantic frontier, under the guidance of some experienced partner or officer. On the arrival of this convoy, the resident partner at the rendezvous depends, to set all his next year's machinery in motion.

Now as the rival companies keep a vigilant eye upon each other, and are anxious to discover each other's plans and movements, they generally contrive to hold their annual assemblages at no great distance apart. An eager competition exists also between their respective convoys of supplies, which shall first reach its place of rendezvous. For this purpose, they set off with the first appearance of grass on the Atlantic frontier, and push with all diligence for the mountains. The company that can first open its tempting supplies of coffee, tobacco, ammunition, scarlet cloth, blankets, bright shawls and glittering trinkets, has the greatest chance to get all the peltries and furs of the Indians and free trappers, and to engage their services for the next season. It is able, also, to fit out and despatch its own trappers the soonest, so as to get the start of its competitors, and to have the first dash into the hunting and trapping grounds.

A new species of strategy has sprung out of this hunting and trapping competition. The constant study of the rival bands is to forestall and outwit each other; to supplant each other in the good will and custom of the Indian tribes; to cross each other's plans; to mislead each other as to routes; in a word, next to his own advantage, the study of the Indian trader is the disadvantage of his competitor.

The influx of this wandering trade has had its effects on the habits of the mountain tribes. They have found the trapping of the beaver their most profitable species of hunting; and the traffic with the white man has opened to them sources of luxury of which they previously had no idea. The introduction of fire-arms has rendered them more successful hunters, but at the same time, more formidable foes; some of them, incorrigibly savage and warlike in their nature, have found the expeditions of the fur traders, grand objects of profitable adventure. To waylay and harass a band of trappers with their pack-horses, when embarrassed in the rugged defiles of the mountains, has become as favorite an exploit with these Indians as the plunder of a caravan to the Arab of the desert. The Crows and Blackfeet, who were such terrors in the path of the early adventurers to Astoria, still continue their predatory habits, but seem to have brought them to greater system. They know the routes and resorts of the trappers; where to waylay them on their journeys; where to find them in the hunting seasons, and where to hover about them in winter quarters. The life of a trapper, therefore, is a perpetual state militant, and he must sleep with his weapons in his hands.

A new order of trappers and traders, also, have grown out of this system of things. In the old times of the great Northwest Company, when the trade in furs was pursued chiefly about the lakes and rivers, the expeditions were carried on in batteaux and canoes. The voyageurs or boatmen were the rank and file in the service of the trader, and even the hardy "men of the north," those great rufflers and game birds, were fain to be paddled from point to point of their migrations.

A totally different class has now sprung up, "the Mountaineers," the traders and trappers that scale the vast mountain chains, and pursue their hazardous vocations amidst their wild recesses. They move from place to place on horseback. The equestrian exercises, therefore, in which they are engaged; the nature of the countries they traverse; vast plains and mountains, pure and exhilarating in atmospheric qualities; seem to make them physically and mentally a more lively and mercurial race than the fur traders and trappers of former days, the self-vaunting "men of the north." A man who bestrides a horse, must be essentially different from a man who cowers in a canoe. We find them, accordingly, hardy, lithe, vigorous and active; extravagant in word, and thought, and deed; heedless of hardship; daring of danger; prodigal of the present, and thoughtless of the future.

A difference is to be perceived even between these mountain hunters and those of the lower regions along the waters of the Missouri. The latter, generally French creoles, live comfortably in cabins and log huts, well sheltered from the inclemencies of the seasons. They are within the reach of frequent supplies from the settlements; their life is comparatively free from danger, and from most of the vicissitudes of the upper wilderness. The consequence is, that they are less hardy, self-dependant and game-spirited, than the mountaineer. If the latter by chance comes among them on his way to and from the settlements, he is like a game-cock among the common roosters of the poultry-yard. Accustomed to live in tents, or to bivouac in the open air, he despises the comforts and is impatient of the confinement of the log house. If his meal is not ready in season, he takes his rifle, hies to the forest or prairie, shoots his own game, lights his fire, and cooks his repast. With his horse and his rifle, he is independent of the world, and spurns at all its restraints. The very superintendents at the lower posts will not put him to mess with the common men, the hirelings of the establishment, but treat him as something superior.

There is, perhaps, no class of men on the face of the earth, says Captain Bonneville, who lead a life of more continued exertion, peril, and excitement, and who are more enamoured of their occupations, than the free trappers of the West. No toil, no danger, no privation can turn the trapper from his pursuit. His passionate excitement at times resembles a mania. In vain may the most vigilant and cruel savages beset his path; in vain may rocks, and precipices, and wintry torrents oppose his progress; let but a single track of a beaver meet his eye, and he forgets all dangers and defies all difficulties. At times, he may be seen with his traps on his shoulder, buffeting his way across rapid streams, amidst floating blocks of ice: at other times, he is to be found with his traps swung on his back clambering the most rugged mountains, scaling or descending the most frightful precipices, searching, by routes inaccessible to the horse, and never before trodden by white man, for springs and lakes unknown to his comrades, and where he may meet with his favorite game. Such is the mountaineer, the hardy trapper of the West; and such, as we have slightly sketched it, is the wild, Robin Hood kind of life, with all its strange and motley populace, now existing in full vigor among the Rocky Mountains.

Having thus given the reader some idea of the actual state of the fur trade in the interior of our vast continent, and made him acquainted with the wild chivalry of the mountains, we will no longer delay the introduction of Captain Bonneville and his band into this field of their enterprise, but launch them at once upon the perilous plains of the Far West.

Chapter II

IT WAS on the first of May, 1832, that Captain Bonneville took
his departure from the frontier post of Fort Osage, on the
Missouri. He had enlisted a party of one hundred and ten
men, most of whom had been in the Indian country, and some
of whom were experienced hunters and trappers. Fort Osage,
and other places on the borders of the western wilderness,
abound with characters of the kind, ready for any expedition.

The ordinary mode of transportation in these great inland
expeditions of the fur traders is on mules and pack-horses; but
Captain Bonneville substituted waggons. Though he was to
travel through a trackless wilderness, yet the greater part of
his route would lie across open plains, destitute of forests, and
where wheel carriages can pass in every direction. The chief
difficulty occurs in passing the deep ravines cut through the
prairies by streams and winter torrents. Here it is often necessary to dig a road down the banks, and to make bridges for
the waggons.

In transporting his baggage in vehicles of this kind, Captain
Bonneville thought he would save the great delay caused every
morning by packing the horses, and the labor of unpacking in
the evening. Fewer horses also would be required, and less risk
incurred of their wandering away, or being frightened or carried off by the Indians. The waggons, also, would be more easily defended, and might form a kind of fortification in case of
attack in the open prairies. A train of twenty waggons, drawn
by oxen, or by four mules or horses each, and laden with mer-

chandise, ammunition, and provisions, were disposed in two columns in the centre of the party, which was equally divided into a van and a rear guard. As sub-leaders or lieutenants in his expedition, Captain Bonneville had made choice of Mr. J. R. Walker and Mr. M. S. Cerré. The former was a native of Tennessee, about six feet high, strong built, dark complexioned, brave in spirit, though mild in manners. He had resided for many years in Missouri, on the frontier; had been among the earliest adventurers to Santa Fe, where he went to trap beaver, and was taken by the Spaniards. Being liberated, he engaged with the Spaniards and Sioux Indians in a war against the Pawnees; then returned to Missouri, and had acted by turns as sheriff, trader, trapper, until he was enlisted as a leader by Captain Bonneville.

Cerré, his other leader, had likewise been in expeditions to Santa Fe, in which he had endured much hardship. He was of the middle size, light complexioned, and though but about twenty-five years of age, was considered an experienced Indian trader. It was a great object with Captain Bonneville to get to the mountains before the summer heats and summer flies should render the travelling across the prairies distressing; and before the annual assemblages of people connected with the fur trade, should have broken up, and dispersed to the hunting grounds.

The two rival associations already mentioned, the American Fur Company and the Rocky Mountain Fur Company, had their several places of rendezvous for the present year at no great distance apart, in Pierre's Hole, a deep valley in the heart of the mountains, and thither Captain Bonneville intended to shape his course.

It is not easy to do justice to the exulting feelings of the worthy captain, at finding himself at the head of a stout band of hunters, trappers, and woodmen; fairly launched on the broad prairies, with his face to the boundless West. The tamest inhabitant of cities, the veriest spoiled child of civilization, feels his heart dilate and his pulse beat high, on finding himself on horseback in the glorious wilderness; what then must be the excitement of one whose imagination had been stimulated by a residence on the frontier, and to whom the wilderness was a region of romance!

His hardy followers partook of his excitement. Most of them had already experienced the wild freedom of savage life, and looked forward to a renewal of past scenes of adventure and exploit. Their very appearance and equipment exhibited a piebald mixture, half civilized and half savage. Many of them looked more like Indians than white men, in their garbs and accoutrements, and their very horses were caparisoned in barbaric style, with fantastic trappings. The outset of a band of adventurers on one of these expeditions is always animated and joyous. The welkin rang with their shouts and yelps, after the manner of the savages; and with boisterous jokes and light-hearted laughter. As they passed the straggling hamlets and solitary cabins that fringe the skirts of the frontier, they would startle their inmates by Indian yells and war-whoops, or regale them with grotesque feats of horsemanship, well suited to their half savage appearance. Most of these abodes were inhabited by men who had themselves been in similar expeditions; they welcomed the travellers, therefore, as brother trappers, treated them with a hunter's hospitality, and cheered them with an honest God speed, at parting.

And here we would remark a great difference, in point of character and quality, between the two classes of trappers, the "American" and "French," as they are called in contradistinction. The latter is meant to designate the French Creole of Canada or Louisiana; the former, the trapper of the old American stock, from Kentucky, Tennessee, and others of the western states. The French trapper is represented as a lighter, softer, more self-indulgent kind of man. He must have his Indian wife, his lodge, and his petty conveniences. He is gay and thoughtless, takes little heed of landmarks, depends upon his leaders and companions to think for the common weal, and, if left to himself, is easily perplexed and lost.

The American trapper stands by himself, and is peerless for the service of the wilderness. Drop him in the midst of a prairie, or in the heart of the mountains, and he is never at a loss. He notices every landmark; can retrace his route through the most monotonous plains, or the most perplexed labyrinths of the mountains; no danger nor difficulty can appal him, and he scorns to complain under any privation. In equipping the two kinds of trappers, the Creole and Canadian are apt to prefer the light fusee; the American always grasps his rifle: he despises what he calls the "shot-gun." We give these estimates on the authority of a trader of long experience, and a foreigner by birth. "I consider one American," said he, "equal to three Canadians in point of sagacity, aptness at resources, self-dependence, and fearlessness of spirit. In fact, no one can cope with him as a stark tramper of the wilderness."

Beside the two classes of trappers just mentioned, Captain Bonneville had enlisted several Delaware Indians in his employ, on whose hunting qualifications he placed great reliance.

On the 6th of May the travellers passed the last border habitation, and bade a long farewell to the ease and security of civilization. The buoyant and clamorous spirits with which they had commenced their march, gradually subsided as they entered upon its difficulties. They found the prairies saturated with the heavy cold rains, prevalent in certain seasons of the year in this part of the country. The waggon wheels sank deep in the mire, the horses were often to the fetlock, and both steed and rider were completely jaded by the evening of the 12th, when they reached the Kansas River; a fine stream about three hundred yards wide, entering the Missouri from the south. Though fordable in almost every part at the end of summer and during the autumn, yet it was necessary to construct a raft for the transportation of the waggons and effects. All this was done in the course of the following day, and by evening, the whole party arrived at the agency of the Kansas tribe. This was under the superintendence of General Clark, brother of the celebrated traveller of the same name, who, with Lewis, made the first expedition down the waters of the Columbia. He was living like a patriarch, surrounded by laborers and interpreters, all snugly housed, and provided with excellent farms. The functionary next in consequence to the agent, was the blacksmith, a most important, and indeed, indispensable personage in a frontier community. The Kansas resemble the Osages in features, dress, and language: they raise corn and hunt the buffalo, ranging the Kansas River, and its tributary streams; at the time of the captain's visit, they were at war with the Pawnees of the Nebraska, or Platte River.

The unusual sight of a train of waggons, caused quite a sensation among these savages; who thronged about the caravan, examining every thing minutely, and asking a thousand questions: exhibiting a degree of excitability, and a lively curiosity, totally opposite to that apathy with which their race is so often reproached.

The personage who most attracted the captain's attention at this place, was "White Plume," the Kansas chief, and they soon became good friends. White Plume (we are pleased with his chivalrous *soubriquet*) inhabited a large stone house, built for him by order of the American government: but the establishment had not been carried out in corresponding style. It might be palace without, but it was wigwam within; so that, between the stateliness of his mansion, and the squalidness of his furniture, the gallant White Plume presented some such whimsical incongruity as we see in the gala equipments of an Indian chief, on a treaty-making embassy at Washington, who has been generously decked out in cocked hat and military coat, in contrast to his breech-clout and leathern leggings; being grand officer at top, and ragged Indian at bottom.

White Plume was so taken with the courtesy of the captain, and pleased with one or two presents received from him, that he accompanied him a day's journey on his march, and passed a night in his camp, on the margin of a small stream. The method of encamping generally observed by the captain, was as follows: The twenty waggons were disposed in a square, at the distance of thirty-three feet from each other. In every interval there was a mess stationed; and each mess had its fire, where the men cooked, ate, gossiped, and slept. The horses were placed in the centre of the square, with a guard stationed over them at night.

The horses were "side lined," as it is termed: that is to say, the fore and hind foot on the same side of the animal were tied together, so as to be within eighteen inches of each other. A horse thus fettered is for a time sadly embarrassed, but soon becomes sufficiently accustomed to the restraint to move about slowly. It prevents his wandering; and his being easily carried off at night by lurking Indians. When a horse that is "foot free," is tied to one thus secured, the latter forms, as it were, a pivot, round which the other runs and curvets, in case of alarm.

The encampment of which we are speaking, presented a striking scene. The various mess-fires were surrounded by picturesque groups, standing, sitting, and reclining; some busied in cooking, others in cleaning their weapons: while the frequent laugh told that the rough joke, or merry story was going on. In the middle of the camp, before the principal lodge, sat the two chieftains, Captain Bonneville and White Plume, in soldier-like communion, the captain delighted with the opportunity of meeting, on social terms, with one of the red warriors of the wilderness, the unsophisticated children of nature. The latter was squatted on his buffalo robe, his strong features and red skin glaring in the broad light of a blazing fire, while he recounted astounding tales of the bloody exploits of his tribe and himself, in their wars with the Pawnees; for there are no old soldiers more given to long campaigning stories, than Indian "braves."

The feuds of White Plume, however, had not been confined to the red men; he had much to say of brushes with bee hunters, a class of offenders for whom he seemed to cherish a particular abhorrence. As the species of hunting prosecuted by these worthies is not laid down in any of the ancient books of venerie, and is, in fact, peculiar to our western frontier, a word or two on the subject may not be unacceptable to the reader.

The bee hunter is generally some settler on the verge of the prairies; a long, lank fellow, of fever and ague complexion, acquired from living on new soil, and in a hut built of green logs. In the autumn, when the harvest is over, these frontier settlers form parties of two or three, and prepare for a bee hunt. Having provided themselves with a waggon, and a number of empty casks, they sally off, armed with their rifles, into the wilderness, directing their course east, west, north, or south, without any regard to the ordinance of the American government, which strictly forbids all trespass upon the lands belonging to the Indian tribes.

The belts of woodland that traverse the lower prairies, and border the rivers, are peopled by innumerable swarms of wild bees, which make their hives in hollow trees, and fill them with honey tolled from the rich flowers of the prairies. The bees, according to popular assertion, are migrating like the settlers, to the West. An Indian trader, well experienced in the country, informs us that within ten years that he has passed in the Far West, the bee has advanced westward above a hundred miles. It is said on the Missouri, that the wild turkey and the

wild bee go up the river together: neither are found in the upper regions. It is but recently that the wild turkey has been
killed on the Nebraska, or Platte; and his travelling competitor, the wild bee, appeared there about the same time.

Be all this as it may: the course of our party of bee hunters,
is to make a wide circuit through the woody river bottoms, and
the patches of forest on the prairies, marking, as they go out,
every tree in which they have detected a hive. These marks are
generally respected by any other bee hunter that should come
upon their track. When they have marked sufficient to fill all
their casks, they turn their faces homeward, cut down the trees
as they proceed, and having loaded their waggon with honey
and wax, return well pleased to the settlements.

Now it so happens that the Indians relish wild honey as
highly as do the white men, and are the more delighted with
this natural luxury from its having, in many instances, but recently made its appearance in their lands. The consequence is,
numberless disputes and conflicts between them and the bee
hunters: and often a party of the latter, returning, laden with
rich spoil, from one of their forays, are apt to be waylaid by
the native lords of the soil; their honey to be seized, their harness cut to pieces, and themselves left to find their way home
the best way they can, happy to escape with no greater personal harm than a sound rib-roasting.

Such were the marauders of whose offences the gallant
White Plume made the most bitter complaint. They were
chiefly the settlers of the western part of Missouri, who are the
most famous bee hunters on the frontier, and whose favorite
hunting ground lies within the lands of the Kansas tribe. According to the account of White Plume, however, matters
were pretty fairly balanced between him and the offenders; he
having as often treated them to a taste of the bitter, as they
had robbed him of the sweets.

It is but justice to this gallant chief to say, that he gave
proofs of having acquired some of the lights of civilization
from his proximity to the whites, as was evinced in his knowledge of driving a bargain. He required hard cash in return for
some corn with which he supplied the worthy captain, and left
the latter at a loss which most to admire, his native chivalry as
a brave, or his acquired adroitness as a trader.

Chapter III

Wide prairies—Vegetable productions—Tabular hills—Slabs of sandstone—Nebraska or Platte River—Scanty fare—Buffalo sculls—Waggons turned into boats—Herds of Buffalo—Cliffs resembling castles—The Chimney—Scott's Bluffs —Story connected with them—The bighorn or ahsahta—Its nature and habits—Difference between that and the "woolly sheep," or goat of the mountains

FROM the middle to the end of May, Captain Bonneville pursued a western course over vast undulating plains, destitute of tree or shrub, rendered miry by occasional rain, and cut up by deep water courses, where they had to dig roads for their waggons down the soft crumbling banks, and to throw bridges across the streams. The weather had attained the summer heat; the thermometer standing about fifty-seven degrees in the morning, early, but rising to about ninety degrees at noon. The incessant breezes, however, which sweep these vast plains, render the heats endurable. Game was scanty, and they had to eke out their scanty fare with wild roots and vegetables, such as the Indian potato, the wild onion, and the prairie tomato, and they met with quantities of "red root," from which the hunters make a very palatable beverage. The only human being that crossed their path was a Kansas warrior, returning from some solitary expedition of bravado or revenge, bearing a Pawnee scalp as a trophy.

The country gradually rose as they proceeded westward, and their route took them over high ridges, commanding wide and beautiful prospects. The vast plain was studded on the west with innumerable hills of conical shape, such as are seen north of the Arkansas River. These hills have their summits apparently cut off about the same elevation, so as to leave flat surfaces at top. It is conjectured by some, that the whole country may originally have been of the altitude of these tabular hills; but through some process of nature may have sunk to its present level; these insulated eminences being protected by broad foundations of solid rock.

Captain Bonneville mentions another geological phenomenon north of Red River, where the surface of the earth, in considerable tracts of country, is covered with broad slabs of sandstone, having the form and position of grave-stones, and looking as if they had been forced up by some subterranean agitation. "The resemblance," says he, "which these very remarkable spots have in many places to old churchyards is curious in the extreme. One might almost fancy himself among the tombs of the pre-Adamites."

On the 2d of June, they arrived on the main stream of the Nebraska or Platte River; twenty-five miles below the head of the Great Island. The low banks of this river give it an appearance of great width. Captain Bonneville measured it in one place, and found it twenty-two hundred yards from bank to bank. Its depth was from three to six feet, the bottom full of quicksands. The Nebraska is studded with islands covered with that species of poplar called the cotton-wood tree. Keeping up along the course of this river for several days, they were obliged, from the scarcity of game, to put themselves upon short allowance, and, occasionally, to kill a steer. They bore their daily labors and privations, however, with great good humor, taking their tone, in all probability, from the bouyant spirit of their leader. "If the weather was inclement," says the captain, "we watched the clouds, and hoped for a sight of the blue sky and the merry sun. If food was scanty, we regaled ourselves with the hope of soon falling in with herds of buffalo, and having nothing to do but slay and eat." We doubt whether the genial captain is not describing the cheeriness of his own breast, which gave a cheery aspect to every thing around him.

There certainly were evidences, however, that the country was not always equally destitute of game. At one place, they observed a field decorated with buffalo sculls, arranged in circles, curves, and other mathematical figures, as if for some mystic rite or ceremony. They were almost innumerable, and seemed to have been a vast hecatomb offered up in thanksgiving to the Great Spirit for some signal success in the chase.

On the 11th of June, they came to the fork of the Nebraska, where it divides itself into two equal and beautiful streams. One of these branches rises in the west southwest, near the head waters of the Arkansas. Up the course of this branch, as Captain Bonneville was well aware, lay the route to the Camanche and Kioway Indians, and to the northern Mexican settlements; of the other branch he knew nothing. Its sources might lie among wild and inaccessible cliffs, and tumble and foam down rugged defiles and over craggy precipices; but its direction was in the true course, and up this stream he determined to prosecute his route to the Rocky Mountains. Finding it impossible, from quicksands and other dangerous impediments, to cross the river in this neighborhood, he kept up along the south fork for two days, merely seeking a safe fording place. At length he encamped, caused the bodies of the waggons to be dislodged from the wheels, covered with buffalo hides, and besmeared with a compound of tallow and ashes; thus forming rude boats. In these, they ferried their effects across the stream, which was six hundred yards wide, with a swift and strong current. Three men were in each boat, to manage it; others waded across, pushing the barks before them. Thus all crossed in safety. A march of nine miles took them over high rolling prairies to the north fork; their eyes being regaled with the welcome sight of herds of buffalo at a distance, some careering the plain, others grazing and reposing in the natural meadows.

Skirting along the north fork for a day or two, excessively annoyed by musquitoes and buffalo gnats, they reached, in the evening of the 17th, a small but beautiful grove, from which issued the confused notes of singing birds, the first they had heard since crossing the boundary of Missouri. After so many days of weary travelling, through a naked, monotonous and silent country, it was delightful once more to hear the song of the bird, and to behold the verdure of the grove. It was a beautiful sunset, and a sight of the glowing rays, mantling the tree tops and rustling branches, gladdened every heart. They pitched their camp in the grove, kindled their fires, partook merrily of their rude fare, and resigned themselves to the sweetest sleep they had enjoyed since their outset upon the prairies.

The country now became rugged and broken. High bluffs advanced upon the river, and forced the travellers occasionally to leave its banks and wind their course into the interior. In one of the wild and solitary passes, they were startled by the trail of four or five pedestrians, whom they supposed to be spies from some predatory camp of either Arickara or Crow Indians. This obliged them to redouble their vigilance at night, and to keep especial watch upon their horses. In these rugged and elevated regions they began to see the black-tailed deer, a species larger than the ordinary kind, and chiefly found in rocky and mountainous countries. They had reached also a great buffalo range; Captain Bonneville ascended a high bluff, commanding an extensive view of the surrounding plains. As far as his eye could reach, the country seemed absolutely blackened by innumerable herds. No language, he says, could convey an adequate idea of the vast living mass thus presented to his eye. He remarked that the bulls and cows generally congregated in separate herds.

Opposite to the camp at this place, was a singular phenomenon, which is among the curiosities of the country. It is called the chimney. The lower part is a conical mound, rising out of the naked plain; from the summit shoots up a shaft or column, about one hundred and twenty feet in height, from which it derives its name. The height of the whole, according to Captain Bonneville, is a hundred and seventy-five yards. It is composed of indurated clay, with alternate layers of red and white sandstone, and may be seen at the distance of upwards of thirty miles.

On the 21st, they encamped amidst high and beetling cliffs of indurated clay and sandstone, bearing the semblance of towers, castles, churches, and fortified cities. At a distance, it was scarcely possible to persuade oneself that the works of art were not mingled with these fantastic freaks of nature. They have received the name of Scott's Bluffs, from a melancholy circumstance. A number of years since, a party were descending the upper part of the river in canoes, when their frail barks were overturned and all their powder spoiled. Their rifles being thus rendered useless, they were unable to procure food by hunting, and had to depend upon roots and wild fruits for subsistence. After suffering extremely from hunger, they arrived at Laramie's Fork, a small tributary of the north branch of the Nebraska, about sixty miles above the cliffs just mentioned. Here one of the party, by the name of Scott, was taken ill; and his companions came to a halt, until he should recover health and strength sufficient to proceed. While they were searching round in quest of edible roots, they discovered a fresh trail of white men, who had evidently but recently preceded them. What was to be done? By a forced march they might overtake this party, and thus be able to reach the settlements in safety. Should they linger, they might all perish of famine and exhaustion. Scott, however, was incapable of moving; they were too feeble to aid him forward, and dreaded that such a clog would prevent their coming up with the advance party. They determined, therefore, to abandon him to his fate. Accordingly, under pretence of seeking food, and such simples as might be efficacious in his malady, they deserted him and hastened forward upon the trail. They succeeded in overtaking the party of which they were in quest, but concealed their faithless desertion of Scott; alleging that he had died of disease.

On the ensuing summer, these very individuals visiting these parts in company with others, came suddenly upon the bleached bones and grinning scull of a human skeleton, which, by certain signs they recognised for the remains of Scott. This was sixty long miles from the place where they had abandoned him; and it appeared that the wretched man had crawled that immense distance before death put an end to his miseries. The wild and picturesque bluffs in the neighborhood of his lonely grave have ever since borne his name.

Amidst this wild and striking scenery, Captain Bonneville, for the first time, beheld flocks of the ahsahta or bighorn, an animal which frequents these cliffs in great numbers. They accord with the nature of such scenery, and add much to its romantic effect; bounding like goats from crag to crag, often trooping along the lofty shelves of the mountains, under the guidance of some venerable patriarch, with horns twisted lower than his muzzle, and sometimes peering over the edge of a precipice, so high that they appear scarce bigger than crows; indeed, it seems a pleasure to them to seek the most rugged and frightful situations, doubtless from a feeling of security.

This animal is commonly called the mountain sheep, and is often confounded with another animal, the "woolly sheep," found more to the northward, about the country of the Flatheads. The latter likewise inhabits cliffs in summer, but descends into the valleys in the winter. It has white wool, like a sheep, mingled with a thin growth of long hair; but it has short legs, a deep belly, and a beard like a goat. Its horns are about five inches long, slightly curved backwards, black as jet, and beautifully polished. Its hoofs are of the same color. This animal is by no means so active as the bighorn; it does not bound much, but sits a good deal upon its haunches. It is not so plentiful either; rarely more than two or three are seen at a time. Its wool alone gives it a resemblance to the sheep; it is more properly of the goat genus. The flesh is said to have a musty flavor; some have thought the fleece might be valuable, as it is said to be as fine as that of the goat of Cashmere, but it is not to be procured in sufficient quantities.

The ahsahta, argali, or bighorn, on the contrary, has short hair like a deer, and resembles it in shape, but has the head and horns of a sheep, and its flesh is said to be delicious mutton. The Indians consider it more sweet and delicate than any other kind of venison. It abounds in the Rocky Mountains, from the fiftieth degree of north latitude, quite down to California; generally in the highest regions capable of vegetation; sometimes it ventures into the valleys, but on the least alarm, regains its favorite cliffs and precipices, where it is perilous, if not impossible for the hunter to follow.*

*Dimensions of a male of this species, from the nose to the base of the tail, five feet; length of the tail, four inches; girth of the body, four feet; height, three feet eight inches; the horn, three feet six inches long; one foot three inches in circumference at base.

Chapter IV

WHEN on the march, Captain Bonneville always sent some of his best hunters in the advance to reconnoitre the country, as well as to look out for game. On the 24th of June, as the caravan was slowly journeying up the banks of the Nebraska, the hunters came galloping back, waving their caps, and giving the alarm cry, Indians! Indians!

The captain immediately ordered a halt: the hunters now came up and announced that a large war party of Crow Indians were just above, on the river. The captain knew the character of these savages; one of the most roving, warlike, crafty, and predatory tribes of the mountains; horse-stealers of the first order, and easily provoked to acts of sanguinary violence. Orders were accordingly given to prepare for action, and every one promptly took the post that had been assigned him, in the general order of the march, in all cases of warlike emergency.

Every thing being put in battle array, the captain took the lead of his little band, and moved on slowly and warily. In a little while he beheld the Crow warriors emerging from among the bluffs. There were about sixty of them; fine martial looking fellows, painted and arrayed for war, and mounted on horses decked out with all kinds of wild trappings. They came prancing along in gallant style, with many wild and dextrous evolutions, for none can surpass them in horsemanship; and their bright colors, and flaunting and fantastic embellishments, glaring and sparkling in the morning sunshine, gave them really a striking appearance.

Their mode of approach, to one not acquainted with the tactics and ceremonies of this rude chivalry of the wilderness, had an air of direct hostility. They came galloping forward in a body as if about to make a furious charge, but, when close at hand, opened to the right and left, and wheeled in wide circles round the travellers, whooping and yelling like maniacs.

This done, their mock fury sank into a calm, and the chief approaching the captain, who had remained warily drawn up, though informed of the pacific nature of the manœuvre, extended to him the hand of friendship. The pipe of peace was smoked, and now all was good fellowship.

The Crows were in pursuit of a band of Cheyennes, who had attacked their village in the night, and killed one of their people. They had already been five and twenty days on the track of the marauders, and were determined not to return home until they had sated their revenge.

A few days previously, some of their scouts, who were ranging the country at a distance from the main body, had discovered the party of Captain Bonneville. They had dogged it for a time in secret, astonished at the long train of waggons and oxen, and especially struck with the sight of a cow and calf, quietly following the caravan; supposing them to be some kind of tame buffalo. Having satisfied their curiosity, they carried back to their chief intelligence of all that they had seen. He had, in consequence, diverged from his pursuit of vengeance to behold the wonders described to him. "Now that we have met you," said he to Captain Bonneville, "and have seen these marvels with our own eyes, our hearts are glad." In fact, nothing could exceed the curiosity evinced by these people as to the objects before them. Waggons had never been seen by them before, and they examined them with the greatest minuteness; but the calf was the peculiar object of their admiration. They watched it with intense interest as it licked the hands accustomed to feed it, and were struck with the mild expression of its countenance, and its perfect docility.

After much sage consultation, they at length determined that it must be the "great medicine" of the white party: an appellation given by the Indians to any thing of supernatural and mysterious power, that is guarded as a talisman. They were completely thrown out in their conjecture, however, by an offer of the white men to exchange the calf for a horse; their estimation of the great medicine sank in an instant, and they declined the bargain.

At the request of the Crow chieftain the two parties encamped together, and passed the residue of the day in company. The captain was well pleased with every opportunity to gain a knowledge of the "unsophisticated sons of nature," who had so long been objects of his poetic speculations; and indeed this wild, horse-stealing tribe, is one of the most notorious of the mountains. The chief, of course, had his scalps to show and his battles to recount. The Blackfoot is the hereditary enemy of the Crow, towards whom hostility is like a cherished principle of religion; for every tribe, beside its casual antagonists, has some enduring foe with whom there can be no permanent reconciliation. The Crows and Blackfeet, upon the whole, are enemies worthy of each other, being rogues and ruffians of the first water. As their predatory excursions extend over the same regions, they often come in contact with each other, and these casual conflicts serve to keep their wits awake and their passions alive.

The present party of Crows, however, evinced nothing of the invidious character for which they are renowned. During the day and night that they were encamped in company with the travellers, their conduct was friendly in the extreme. They were, in fact, quite irksome in their attentions, and had a caressing manner at times quite importunate. It was not until after separation on the following morning, that the captain and his men ascertained the secret of all this loving kindness. In the course of their fraternal caresses, the Crows had contrived to empty the pockets of their white brothers; to abstract the very buttons from their coats, and, above all, to make free with their hunting knives.

By equal altitudes of the sun, taken at this last encampment, Captain Bonneville ascertained his latitude to be 41° 47′ north. The thermometer, at six o'clock in the morning, stood at fifty-nine degrees; at two o'clock, P.M., at ninety-two degrees; and at six o'clock in the evening, at seventy degrees.

The Black Hills, or Mountains, now began to be seen at a distance, printing the horizon with their rugged and broken outlines; and threatening to oppose a difficult barrier in the way of the travellers.

On the 26th of June, the travellers encamped at Laramie's Fork, a clear and beautiful stream, rising in the west-southwest, maintaining an average width of twenty yards, and winding through broad meadows abounding in currants and gooseberries, and adorned with groves and clumps of trees.

By an observation of Jupiter's satellites, with a Dolland reflecting telescope, Captain Bonneville ascertained the longitude to be 102° 57' west of Greenwich.

We will here step ahead of our narrative to observe, that about three years after the time of which we are treating, Mr. Robert Campbell, formerly of the Rocky Mountain Fur Company, descended the Platte from this fork, in skin canoes, thus proving, what had always been discredited, that the river was navigable. About the same time, he built a fort or trading post at Laramie's Fork, which he named Fort William, after his friend and partner, Mr. William Sublette. Since that time, the Platte has become a highway for the fur traders.

For some days past, Captain Bonneville had been made sensible of the great elevation of country into which he was gradually ascending, by the effect of the dryness and rarefaction of the atmosphere upon his waggons. The wood-work shrunk; the paint boxes of the wheels were continually working out, and it was necessary to support the spokes by stout props to prevent their falling asunder. The travellers were now entering one of those great steppes of the Far West, where the prevalent aridity of the atmosphere renders the country unfit for cultivation. In these regions, there is a fresh sweet growth of grass in the spring, but it is scanty and short, and parches up in the course of the summer, so that there is none for the hunters to set fire to in the autumn. It is a common observation, that "above the forks of the Platte the grass does not burn." All attempts at agriculture and gardening in the neighborhood of Fort William, have been attended with very little success. The grain and vegetables raised there have been scanty in quantity and poor in quality. The great elevation of these plains, and the dryness of the atmosphere, will tend to retain these immense regions in a state of pristine wildness.

In the course of a day or two more, the travellers entered that wild and broken tract of the Crow country called the Black Hills, and here their journey became toilsome in the extreme.

Rugged steeps and deep ravines incessantly obstructed their progress, so that a great part of the day was spent in the painful toil of digging through banks, filling up ravines, forcing the waggons up the most forbidding ascents, or swinging them with ropes down the face of dangerous precipices. The shoes of their horses were worn out, and their feet injured by the rugged and stony roads. The travellers were annoyed also by frequent but brief storms, which would come hurrying over the hills, or through the mountain defiles, rage with great fury for a short time, and then pass off, leaving every thing calm and serene again.

For several nights the camp had been infested by vagabond Indian dogs, prowling about in quest of food. They were about the size of a large pointer; with ears short and erect, and a long bushy tail—altogether, they bore a striking resemblance to a wolf. These skulking visiters would keep about the purlieus of the camp until daylight; when, on the first stir of life among the sleepers, they would scamper off until they reached some rising ground, where they would take their seats, and keep a sharp and hungry watch upon every movement. The moment the travellers were fairly on the march, and the camp was abandoned, these starveling hangers-on would hasten to the deserted fires, to seize upon the half-picked bones, the offals and garbage that lay about; and, having made a hasty meal, with many a snap and snarl and growl, would follow leisurely on the trail of the caravan. Many attempts were made to coax or catch them, but in vain. Their quick and suspicious eyes caught the slightest sinister movement, and they turned and scampered off. At length one was taken. He was terribly alarmed, and crouched and trembled as if expecting instant death. Soothed, however, by caresses, he began after a time to gather confidence and wag his tail, and at length was brought to follow close at the heels of his captors, still, however, darting around furtive and suspicious glances, and evincing a disposition to scamper off upon the least alarm.

On the first of July, the band of Crow warriors again crossed their path. They came in vaunting and vainglorious style; displaying five Cheyenne scalps, the trophies of their vengeance. They were now bound homewards to appease the manes of their comrade by these proofs that his death had been revenged, and intended to have scalp-dances and other triumphant rejoicings. Captain Bonneville and his men, however, were by no means disposed to renew their confiding intimacy with these crafty savages, and above all, took care to avoid their pilfering caresses. They remarked one precaution of the Crows with respect to their horses; to protect their hoofs from the sharp and jagged rocks among which they had to pass, they had covered them with shoes of buffalo hide.

The route of the travellers lay generally along the course of the Nebraska or Platte, but occasionally, where steep promontories advanced to the margin of the stream, they were obliged to make inland circuits. One of these took them through a bold and stern country, bordered by a range of low mountains, running east and west. Every thing around bore traces of some fearful convulsion of nature in times long past. Hitherto the various strata of rock had exhibited a gentle elevation towards the southwest, but here, every thing appeared to have been subverted, and thrown out of place. In many places there were heavy beds of white sandstone resting upon red. Immense strata of rocks jutted up into crags and cliffs; and sometimes formed perpendicular walls and overhanging precipices. An air of sterility prevailed over these savage wastes. The valleys were destitute of herbage, and scantily clothed with a stunted species of wormwood, generally known among traders and trappers by the name of sage. From an elevated point of their march through this region, the travellers caught a beautiful view of the Powder River Mountains away to the north, stretching along the very verge of the horizon, and seeming, from the snow with which they were mantled, to be a chain of small white clouds, connecting sky and earth.

Though the thermometer at mid-day ranged from eighty to ninety, and even sometimes rose to ninety-three degrees, yet occasional spots of snow were to be seen on the tops of the low mountains, among which the travellers were journeying; proofs of the great elevation of the whole region.

The Nebraska, in its passage through the Black Hills, is confined to a much narrower channel than that through which it flows in the plains below; but it is deeper and clearer, and rushes with a stronger current. The scenery, also, is more varied and beautiful. Sometimes it glides rapidly, but smoothly, through a picturesque valley, between wooded banks; then, forcing its way into the bosom of rugged mountains, it rushes impetuously through narrow defiles, roaring and foaming down rocks and rapids, until it is again soothed to rest in some peaceful valley.

On the 12th of July, Captain Bonneville abandoned the main stream of the Nebraska, which was continually shouldered by rugged promontories, and making a bend to the southwest, for a couple of days, part of the time over plains of loose sand, encamped on the 14th, on the banks of the Sweet Water, a stream about twenty yards in breadth, and four or five feet deep, flowing between low banks over a sandy soil, and forming one of the forks or upper branches of the Nebraska. Up this stream they now shaped their course for several successive days, tending, generally, to the west. The soil was light and sandy; the country much diversified. Frequently the plains were studded with isolated blocks of rock, sometimes in the shape of a half globe, and from three to four hundred feet high. These singular masses had occasionally a very imposing, and even sublime appearance, rising from the midst of a savage and lonely landscape.

As the travellers continued to advance, they became more and more sensible of the elevation of the country. The hills around were more generally capped with snow. The men complained of cramps and colics, sore lips and mouths, and violent headaches. The wood-work of the waggons also shrank so much, that it was with difficulty the wheels were kept from falling to pieces. The country bordering upon the river was frequently gashed with deep ravines, or traversed by high bluffs, to avoid which, the travellers were obliged to make wide circuits through the plains. In the course of these, they came upon immense herds of buffalo, which kept scouring off in the van, like a retreating army.

Among the motley retainers of the camp was Tom Cain, a raw Irishman, who officiated as cook, whose various blunders and expedients in his novel situation, and in the wild scenes and wild kind of life into which he had suddenly been thrown, had made him a kind of butt or droll of the camp. Tom, however, began to discover an ambition superior to his station; and the conversation of the hunters, and their stories of their exploits, inspired him with a desire to elevate himself to the dignity of their order. The buffalo in such immense droves presented a tempting opportunity for making his first essay. He rode, in the line of march, all prepared for action: his powder flask and shot pouch knowingly slung at the pommel of his saddle, to be at hand; his rifle balanced on his shoulder. While in this plight, a troop of buffalo came trotting by in great alarm. In an instant, Tom sprang from his horse and gave chase on foot. Finding they were leaving him behind, he levelled his rifle and pulled trigger. His shot produced no other effect than to increase the speed of the buffalo, and to frighten his own horse, who took to his heels, and scampered off with all the ammunition. Tom scampered after him, hallooing with might and main, and the wild horse and wild Irishman soon disappeared among the ravines of the prairie. Captain Bonneville, who was at the head of the line, and had seen the transaction at a distance, detached a party in pursuit of Tom. After a long interval they returned, leading the frightened horse; but though they had scoured the country, and looked out and shouted from every height, they had seen nothing of his rider.

As Captain Bonneville knew Tom's utter awkwardness and inexperience, and the dangers of a bewildered Irishman in the midst of a prairie, he halted and encamped at an early hour, that there might be a regular hunt for him in the morning.

At early dawn on the following day scouts were sent off in every direction, while the main body, after breakfast, proceeded slowly on its course. It was not until the middle of the afternoon, that the hunters returned with honest Tom mounted behind one of them. They had found him in a complete state of perplexity and amazement. His appearance caused shouts of merriment in the camp,—but Tom for once could not join in the mirth raised at his expense: he was completely chapfallen, and apparently cured of the hunting mania for the rest of his life.

Chapter V

IT WAS on the 20th of July, that Captain Bonneville first came in sight of the grand region of his hopes and anticipations, the Rocky Mountains. He had been making a bend to the south, to avoid some obstacles along the river, and had attained a high, rocky ridge, when a magnificent prospect burst upon his sight. To the west, rose the Wind River Mountains, with their bleached and snowy summits towering into the clouds. These stretched far to the north-northwest, until they melted away into what appeared to be faint clouds, but which the experienced eyes of the veteran hunters of the party recognised for the rugged mountains of the Yellowstone; at the feet of which, extended the wild Crow country: a perilous, though profitable region for the trapper.

To the southwest, the eye ranged over an immense extent of wilderness, with what appeared to be a snowy vapor resting upon its horizon. This, however, was pointed out as another branch of the Great Chippewyan, or Rocky chain; being the Eutaw Mountains, at whose basis, the wandering tribe of hunters of the same name pitch their tents.

We can imagine the enthusiasm of the worthy captain, when he beheld the vast and mountainous scene of his adventurous enterprise thus suddenly unveiled before him. We can imagine with what feelings of awe and admiration he must have contemplated the Wind River Sierra, or bed of mountains; that great fountain head, from whose springs, and lakes, and melted snows, some of those mighty rivers take their rise, which wander over hundreds of miles of varied country and clime, and find their way to the opposite waves of the Atlantic and the Pacific.

The Wind River Mountains are, in fact, among the most remarkable of the whole Rocky chain; and would appear to be among the loftiest. They form, as it were, a great bed of mountains, about eighty miles in length, and from twenty to thirty in breadth; with rugged peaks, covered with eternal snows, and deep, narrow valleys, full of springs, and brooks, and rock-bound lakes. From this great treasury of waters, issue forth limpid streams, which augmenting as they descend, become main tributaries of the Missouri, on the one side, and the Columbia, on the other; and give rise to the Seeds-ke-dee Agie, or Green River, the great Colorado of the West, that empties its current into the Gulf of California.

The Wind River Mountains are notorious in hunters' and trappers' stories: their rugged defiles, and the rough tracts about their neighborhood, having been lurking places for the predatory hordes of the mountains, and scenes of rough encounter with Crows and Blackfeet. It was to the west of these mountains, in the valley of the Seeds-ke-dee Agie, or Green River, that Captain Bonneville intended to make a halt, for the purpose of giving repose to his people and his horses, after their weary journeying; and of collecting information as to his future course. This Green River valley, and its immediate neighborhood, as we have already observed, formed the main point of rendezvous, for the present year, of the rival fur companies, and the motley populace, civilized and savage, connected with them. Several days of rugged travel, however, yet remained for the captain and his men, before they should encamp in this desired resting place.

On the 21st of July, as they were pursuing their course through one of the meadows of the Sweet Water, they beheld a horse grazing at a little distance. He showed no alarm at their approach, but suffered himself quietly to be taken, evincing a perfect state of tameness. The scouts of the party were instantly on the look out for the owners of this animal; lest some dangerous band of savages might be lurking in the vicinity. After a narrow search, they discovered the trail of an Indian party, which had evidently passed through that neighborhood but recently. The horse was accordingly taken possession of, as an estray; but a more vigilant watch than usual was kept round the camp at nights, lest his former owners should be upon the prowl.

The travellers had now attained so high an elevation, that on the 23d of July, at daybreak, there was considerable ice in the water-buckets, and the thermometer stood at twenty-two degrees. The rarity of the atmosphere continued to affect the wood-work of the waggons, and the wheels were incessantly falling to pieces. A remedy was at length devised. The tire of each wheel was taken off; a band of wood was nailed round the exterior of the felloes, the tire was then made red hot, replaced round the wheel, and suddenly cooled with water. By this means, the whole was bound together with great compactness.

The extreme elevation of these great steppes, which range along the feet of the Rocky Mountains, take away from the seeming height of their peaks, which yield to few in the known world in point of altitude above the level of the sea.

On the 24th, the travellers took final leave of the Sweet Water, and, keeping westwardly, over a low and very rocky ridge, one of the most southern spurs of the Wind River Mountains, they encamped, after a march of seven hours and a half, on the banks of a small clear stream, running to the south, in which they caught a number of fine trout.

The sight of these fish was hailed with pleasure, as a sign that they had reached the waters which flow into the Pacific; for it is only on the western streams of the Rocky Mountains that trout are to be taken. The stream on which they had thus encamped, proved, in effect, to be tributary to the Seeds-ke-dee Agie, or Green River, into which it flowed, at some distance to the south.

Captain Bonneville now considered himself as having fairly passed the crest of the Rocky Mountains; and felt some degree of exultation in being the first individual that had crossed, north of the settled provinces of Mexico, from the waters of the Atlantic to those of the Pacific, with waggons. Mr. William Sublette, the enterprising leader of the Rocky Mountain Fur Company, had, two or three years previously, reached the valley of the Wind River, which lies on the northeast of the mountains; but had proceeded with them no further.

A vast valley now spread itself before the travellers, bounded on one side, by the Wind River Mountains, and to the west, by a long range of high hills. This, Captain Bonneville was assured by a veteran hunter in his company, was the great valley of the Seeds-ke-dee; and the same informant would fain have persuaded him, that a small stream, three feet deep, which he came to on the 25th, was that river. The captain was convinced, however, that the stream was too insignificant to drain so wide a valley, and the adjacent mountains: he encamped, therefore, at an early hour, on its borders, that he might take the whole of the next day to reach the main river; which he presumed to flow between him and the distant range of western hills.

On the 26th of July, he commenced his march at an early hour, making directly across the valley, towards the hills in the west; proceeding at as brisk a rate as the jaded condition of his horses would permit. About eleven o'clock in the morning, a great cloud of dust was descried in the rear, advancing directly on the trail of the party. The alarm was given; they all came to a halt, and held a council of war. Some conjectured that the band of Indians, whose trail they had discovered in the neighborhood of the stray horse, had been lying in wait for them, in some secret fastness of the mountains; and were about to attack them on the open plain, where they would have no shelter. Preparations were immediately made for defence; and a scouting party sent off to reconnoitre. They soon came galloping back, making signals that all was well. The cloud of dust was made by a band of fifty or sixty mounted trappers, belonging to the American Fur Company, who soon came up, leading their pack-horses. They were headed by Mr. Fontenelle, an experienced leader, or "partisan," as a chief of a party is called, in the technical language of the trappers.

Mr. Fontenelle informed Captain Bonneville, that he was on his way from the company's trading post, on the Yellowstone, to the yearly rendezvous, with reinforcements and supplies for their hunting and trading parties beyond the mountains; and that he expected to meet, by appointment, with a band of free trappers in that very neighborhood. He had fallen upon the trail of Captain Bonneville's party, just after leaving the Nebraska; and, finding that they had frightened off all the game, had been obliged to push on, by forced marches, to avoid famine: both men and horses were, therefore, much travel-worn; but this was no place to halt; the plain before them, he said, was destitute of grass and water, neither of which would be met with short of the Green River, which was yet at a considerable distance. He hoped, he added, as his party were all on horseback, to reach the river, with hard travelling, by night fall: but he doubted the possibility of Captain Bonneville's arrival there with his waggons, before the day following. Having imparted this information, he pushed forward with all speed.

Captain Bonneville followed on as fast as circumstances would permit. The ground was firm and gravelly; but the horses were too much fatigued to move rapidly. After a long and harassing day's march, without pausing for a noontide meal, they were compelled, at nine o'clock at night, to encamp in an open plain, destitute of water or pasturage. On the following morning, the horses were turned loose at the peep of day; to slake their thirst, if possible, from the dew collected on the sparse grass, here and there springing up among dry sand banks. The soil of a great part of this Green River valley, is a whitish clay, into which the rain cannot penetrate, but which dries and cracks with the sun. In some places it produces a salt weed, and grass along the margins of the streams; but the wider expanses of it, are desolate and barren. It was not until noon, that Captain Bonneville reached the banks of the Seeds-ke-dee, or Colorado of the West; in the meantime, the sufferings of both men and horses had been excessive, and it was with almost frantic eagerness that they hurried to allay their burning thirst, in the limpid current of the river.

Fontenelle and his party had not fared much better: the chief part had managed to reach the river by nightfall, but were nearly knocked up by the exertion; the horses of others sank under them, and they were obliged to pass the night upon the road.

On the following morning, July 28th, Fontenelle moved his camp across the river; while Captain Bonneville proceeded some little distance below, where there was a small but fresh meadow, yielding abundant pasturage. Here the poor jaded horses were turned out to graze, and take their rest: the weary journey up the mountains had worn them down in flesh and spirit; but this last march across the thirsty plain, had nearly finished them.

The captain had here the first taste of the boasted strategy of the fur trade. During his brief, but social encampment, in company with Fontenelle, that experienced trapper had managed to win over a number of Delaware Indians, whom the captain had brought with him, by offering them four hundred dollars each, for the ensuing autumnal hunt. The captain was somewhat astonished, when he saw these hunters, on whose services he had calculated securely, suddenly pack up their traps, and go over to the rival camp. That he might in some measure, however, be even with his competitor, he despatched two scouts to look out for the band of free trappers, who were to meet Fontenelle in this neighborhood, and to endeavor to bring them to his camp.

As it would be necessary to remain some time in this neighborhood, that both men and horses might repose, and recruit their strength; and as it was a region full of danger, Captain Bonneville proceeded to fortify his camp with breastworks of logs and pickets.

These precautions were, at that time, peculiarly necessary, from the bands of Blackfeet Indians which were roving about the neighborhood. These savages are the most dangerous banditti of the mountains, and the inveterate foe of the trappers. They are Ishmaelites of the first order; always with weapon in hand, ready for action. The young braves of the tribe, who are destitute of property, go to war for booty; to gain horses, and acquire the means of setting up a lodge, supporting a family, and entitling themselves to a seat in the public councils. The veteran warriors fight merely for the love of the thing, and the consequence which success gives them among their people.

They are capital horsemen, and are generally well mounted on short, stout horses, similar to the prairie ponies, to be met with at St. Louis. When on a war party, however, they go on foot, to enable them to skulk through the country with greater secrecy; to keep in thickets and ravines, and use more adroit subterfuges and stratagems. Their mode of warfare is entirely by ambush, surprise, and sudden assaults in the night time. If they succeed in causing a panic, they dash forward with headlong fury: if the enemy is on the alert and shows no signs of fear, they become wary and deliberate in their movements.

Some of them are armed in the primitive style, with bows and arrows; the greater part have American fusees, made after the fashion of those of the Hudson's Bay Company. These they procure at the trading post of the American Fur Company, on Marias River, where they traffic their peltries for arms, ammunition, clothing, and trinkets. They are extremely fond of spirituous liquors and tobacco; for which nuisances they are ready to exchange, not merely their guns and horses, but even their wives and daughters. As they are a treacherous race, and have cherished a lurking hostility to the whites, ever since one of their tribe was killed by Mr. Lewis, the associate of General Clark, in his exploring expedition across the Rocky Mountains, the American Fur Company is obliged constantly to keep at that post a garrison of sixty or seventy men.

Under the general name of Blackfeet, are comprehended several tribes: such as the Surcies, the Peagans, the Blood Indians, and the Gros Ventres of the Prairies: who roam about the southern branches of the Yellowstone and Missouri Rivers, together with some other tribes further north.

The bands infesting the Wind River Mountains, and the country adjacent, at the time of which we are treating, were Gros Ventres *of the Prairies,* which are not to be confounded with Gros Ventres *of the Missouri,* who keep about the *lower* part of that river, and are friendly to the white man.

This hostile band keeps about the head waters of the Missouri, and numbers about nine hundred fighting men. Once in the course of two or three years they abandon their usual abodes, and make a visit to the Arapahoes of the Arkansas. Their route lies either through the Crow country, and the Black Hills, or through the lands of the Nez Percés, Flatheads, Bannacks, and Shoshonies. As they enjoy their favorite state of hostility with all these tribes, their expeditions are prone to be conducted in the most lawless and predatory style; nor do they hesitate to extend their maraudings to any party of white men they meet with; following their trails; hovering about their camps; waylaying and dogging the caravans of the free traders, and murdering the solitary trapper. The consequences are, frequent and desperate fights between them and the "mountaineers," in the wild defiles and fastnesses of the Rocky Mountains.

The band in question was, at this time, on their way home-ward from one of their customary visits to the Arapahoes; and in the ensuing chapter, we shall treat of some bloody encoun-ters between them and the trappers, which had taken place just before the arrival of Captain Bonneville among the mountains.

Chapter VI

LEAVING Captain Bonneville and his band ensconced within their fortified camp in the Green River valley, we shall step back and accompany a party of the Rocky Mountain Fur Company in its progress, with supplies from St. Louis, to the annual rendezvous at Pierre's Hole. This party consisted of sixty men, well mounted, and conducting a line of pack-horses. They were commanded by Captain William Sublette, a partner in the company, and one of the most active, intrepid, and renowned leaders in this half military kind of service. He was accompanied by his associate in business, and tried companion in danger, Mr. Robert Campbell, one of the pioneers of the trade beyond the mountains, who had commanded trapping parties there in times of the greatest peril.

As these worthy compeers were on their route to the frontier, they fell in with another expedition, likewise on its way to the mountains. This was a party of regular "down-easters," that is to say, people of New England, who, with the all penetrating, and all pervading spirit of their race, were now pushing their way into a new field of enterprise, with which they were totally unacquainted. The party had been fitted out, and was maintained and commanded by Mr. Nathaniel J. Wyeth, of Boston.* This gentleman had conceived an idea, that a profitable fishery for salmon might be established on the Columbia River, and connected with the fur trade. He had, accordingly, invested capital in goods, calculated, as he supposed, for the Indian trade, and had enlisted a number of eastern men in his employ, who had never been in the Far West, nor knew any thing of the wilderness. With these, he was bravely steering his

---

* In the former editions of this work we have erroneously given this enterprising individual the title of captain.

way across the continent, undismayed by danger, difficulty, or distance, in the same way that a New England coaster and his neighbors will coolly launch forth on a voyage to the Black Sea, or a whaling cruise to the Pacific.

With all their national aptitude at expedient and resource, Wyeth and his men felt themselves completely at a loss when they reached the frontier, and found that the wilderness required experience and habitudes, of which they were totally deficient. Not one of the party, except the leader, had ever seen an Indian or handled a rifle; they were without guide or interpreter, and totally unacquainted with "wood craft," and the modes of making their way among savage hordes, and subsisting themselves, during long marches over wild mountains and barren plains.

In this predicament, Captain Sublette found them, in a manner becalmed, or rather run aground, at the little frontier town of Independence, in Missouri, and kindly took them in tow. The two parties travelled amicably together; the frontier men of Sublette's party gave their Yankee comrades some lessons in hunting, and some insight into the art and mystery of dealing with the Indians, and they all arrived without accident at the upper branches of the Nebraska or Platte River.

In the course of their march, Mr. Fitzpatrick, the partner of the company who was resident at that time beyond the mountains, came down from the rendezvous at Pierre's Hole to meet them, and hurry them forward. He travelled in company with them until they reached the Sweet Water; then taking a couple of horses, one for the saddle, and the other as a packhorse, he started off express for Pierre's Hole, to make arrangements against their arrival, that he might commence his hunting campaign before the rival company.

Fitzpatrick was a hardy and experienced mountaineer, and knew all the passes and defiles. As he was pursuing his lonely course up the Green River valley, he descried several horsemen at a distance, and came to a halt to reconnoitre. He supposed them to be some detachment from the rendezvous, or a party of friendly Indians. They perceived him, and setting up the war-whoop, dashed forward at full speed: he saw at once his mistake and his peril—they were Blackfeet. Springing upon his fleetest horse, and abandoning the other to the enemy, he made for the mountains, and succeeded in escaping up one of the most dangerous defiles. Here he concealed himself until he thought the Indians had gone off, when he returned into the valley. He was again pursued, lost his remaining horse, and only escaped by scrambling up among the cliffs. For several days he remained lurking among rocks and precipices, and almost famished, having but one remaining charge in his rifle, which he kept for self-defence.

In the meantime, Sublette and Campbell, with their fellow traveller, Wyeth, had pursued their march unmolested, and arrived in the Green River valley, totally unconscious that there was any lurking enemy at hand. They had encamped one night on the banks of a small stream, which came down from the Wind River Mountains, when about midnight, a band of Indians burst upon their camp, with horrible yells and whoops, and a discharge of guns and arrows. Happily no other harm was done than wounding one mule, and causing several horses to break loose from their pickets. The camp was instantly in arms; but the Indians retreated with yells of exultation, carrying off several of the horses, under covert of the night.

This was somewhat of a disagreeable foretaste of mountain life to some of Wyeth's band, accustomed only to the regular and peaceful life of New England; nor was it altogether to the taste of Captain Sublette's men, who were chiefly creoles and townsmen from St. Louis. They continued their march the next morning, keeping scouts ahead and upon their flanks, and arrived without further molestation at Pierre's Hole.

The first inquiry of Captain Sublette, on reaching the rendezvous, was for Fitzpatrick. He had not arrived, nor had any intelligence been received concerning him. Great uneasiness was now entertained, lest he should have fallen into the hands of the Blackfeet, who had made the midnight attack upon the camp. It was a matter of general joy, therefore, when he made his appearance, conducted by two half-breed Iroquois hunters. He had lurked for several days among the mountains, until almost starved; at length he escaped the vigilance of his enemies in the night, and was so fortunate as to meet the two Iroquois hunters, who, being on horseback, conveyed him without further difficulty to the rendezvous. He arrived there so emaciated, that he could scarcely be recognised.

The valley called Pierre's Hole, is about thirty miles in length and fifteen in width, bounded to the west and south by low and broken ridges, and overlooked to the east by three lofty mountains, called the Three Tetons, which domineer as landmarks over a vast extent of country.

A fine stream, fed by rivulets and mountain springs, pours through the valley towards the north, dividing it into nearly equal parts. The meadows on its borders are broad and extensive, covered with willow and cotton-wood trees, so closely interlocked and matted together, as to be nearly impassable.

In this valley was congregated the motley populace connected with the fur trade. Here the two rival companies had their encampments, with their retainers of all kinds: traders, trappers, hunters, and half-breeds, assembled from all quarters, awaiting their yearly supplies, and their orders to start off in new directions. Here, also, the savage tribes connected with the trade, the Nez Percés or Chopunnish Indians, and Flatheads, had pitched their lodges beside the streams, and with their squaws, awaited the distribution of goods and finery. There was, moreover, a band of fifteen free trappers, commanded by a gallant leader from Arkansas, named Sinclair, who held their encampment a little apart from the rest. Such was the wild and heterogeneous assemblage, amounting to several hundred men, civilized and savage, distributed in tents and lodges in the several camps.

The arrival of Captain Sublette with supplies, put the Rocky Mountain Fur Company in full activity. The wares and merchandise were quickly opened, and as quickly disposed of to trappers and Indians; the usual excitement and revelry took place, after which, all hands began to disperse to their several destinations.

On the 17th of July, a small brigade of fourteen trappers, led by Milton Sublette, brother of the captain, set out with the intention of proceeding to the southwest. They were accompanied by Sinclair and his fifteen free trappers; Wyeth, also, and his New-England band of beaver hunters and salmon fishers, now dwindled down to eleven, took this opportunity to prosecute their cruise in the wilderness, in company with such experienced pilots. On the first day, they proceeded about eight miles to the southeast, and encamped for the night, still in the valley of Pierre's Hole. On the following morning, just as they were raising their camp, they observed a long line of people pouring down a defile of the mountains. They at first supposed them to be Fontenelle and his party, whose arrival had been daily expected. Wyeth, however, reconnoitered them with a spyglass, and soon perceived they were Indians. They were divided into two parties, forming, in the whole, about one hundred and fifty persons, men, women, and children. Some were on horseback, fantastically painted and arrayed, with scarlet blankets fluttering in the wind. The greater part, however, were on foot. They had perceived the trappers before they were themselves discovered, and came down yelling and whooping into the plain. On nearer approach, they were ascertained to be Blackfeet.

One of the trappers of Sublette's brigade, a half-breed, named Antoine Godin, now mounted his horse, and rode forth as if to hold a conference. He was the son of an Iroquois hunter, who had been cruelly murdered by the Blackfeet at a small stream below the mountains, which still bears his name. In company with Antoine rode forth a Flathead Indian, whose once powerful tribe had been completely broken down in their wars with the Blackfeet. Both of them, therefore, cherished the most vengeful hostility against these marauders of the mountains. The Blackfeet came to a halt. One of the chiefs advanced singly and unarmed, bearing the pipe of peace. This overture was certainly pacific; but Antoine and the Flathead were predisposed to hostility, and pretended to consider it a treacherous movement.

"Is your piece charged?" said Antoine to his red companion.

"It is."

"Then cock it, and follow me."

They met the Blackfoot chief half way, who extended his hand in friendship. Antoine grasped it.

"Fire!" cried he.

The Flathead levelled his piece, and brought the Blackfoot to the ground. Antoine snatched off his scarlet blanket, which was richly ornamented, and galloped off with it as a trophy to the camp, the bullets of the enemy whistling after him. The Indians immediately threw themselves into the edge of a swamp, among willows and cotton-wood trees, interwoven with vines. Here they began to fortify themselves; the women digging a trench, and throwing up a breastwork of logs and branches, deep hid in the bosom of the wood, while the warriors skirmished at the edge to keep the trappers at bay.

The latter took their station in a ravine in front, whence they kept up a scattering fire. As to Wyeth and his little band of "down-easters," they were perfectly astounded by this second specimen of life in the wilderness; the men being, especially, unused to bush-fighting and the use of the rifle, were at a loss how to proceed. Wyeth, however, acted as a skilful commander. He got all his horses into camp and secured them; then, making a breastwork of his packs of goods, he charged his men to remain in garrison, and not to stir out of their fort. For himself, he mingled with the other leaders, determined to take his share in the conflict.

In the meantime, an express had been sent off to the rendezvous for reinforcements. Captain Sublette, and his associate, Campbell, were at their camp when the express came galloping across the plain, waving his cap, and giving the alarm; "Blackfeet! Blackfeet! a fight in the upper part of the valley!—to arms! to arms!"

The alarm was passed from camp to camp. It was a common cause. Every one turned out with horse and rifle. The Nez Percés and Flatheads joined. As fast as horseman could arm and mount he galloped off; the valley was soon alive with white men and red men scouring at full speed.

Sublette ordered his men to keep to the camp, being recruits from St. Louis, and unused to Indian warfare. He and his friend Campbell prepared for action. Throwing off their coats, rolling up their sleeves, and arming themselves with pistols and rifles, they mounted their horses and dashed forward among the first. As they rode along, they made their wills in soldierlike style; each stating how his effects should be disposed of in case of his death, and appointing the other his executor.

The Blackfeet warriors had supposed the brigade of Milton Sublette all the foe they had to deal with, and were astonished to behold the whole valley suddenly swarming with horsemen, galloping to the field of action. They withdrew into their fort, which was completely hid from sight in the dark and tangled wood. Most of their women and children had retreated to the mountains. The trappers now sallied forth and approached the swamp, firing into the thickets at random; the Blackfeet had a better sight at their adversaries, who were in the open field, and a half-breed was wounded in the shoulder.

When Captain Sublette arrived, he urged to penetrate the swamp and storm the fort, but all hung back in awe of the dismal horrors of the place, and the danger of attacking such desperadoes in their savage den. The very Indian allies, though accustomed to bush-fighting, regarded it as almost impenetrable, and full of frightful danger. Sublette was not to be turned from his purpose, but offered to lead the way into the swamp. Campbell stepped forward to accompany him. Before entering the perilous wood, Sublette took his brothers aside, and told them that in case he fell, Campbell, who knew his will, was to be his executor. This done, he grasped his rifle and pushed into the thickets, followed by Campbell. Sinclair, the partisan from Arkansas, was at the edge of the wood with his brother and a few of his men. Excited by the gallant example of the two friends, he pressed forward to share their dangers.

The swamp was produced by the labors of the beaver, which, by damming up a stream, had inundated a portion of the valley. The place was all overgrown with woods and thickets, so closely matted and entangled, that it was impossible to see ten paces ahead, and the three associates in peril had to crawl along, one after another, making their way by putting the branches and vines aside; but doing it with caution, lest they should attract the eye of some lurking marksman. They took the lead by turns, each advancing about twenty yards at a time, and now and then hallooing to their men to follow. Some of the latter gradually entered the swamp, and followed a little distance in their rear.

They had now reached a more open part of the wood, and had glimpses of the rude fortress from between the trees. It was a mere breastwork, as we have said, of logs and branches, with blankets, buffalo robes, and the leathern covers of lodges, extended round the top as a screen. The movements of the leaders, as they groped their way, had been descried by the sharp-sighted enemy. As Sinclair, who was in the advance, was putting some branches aside, he was shot through the body.

He fell on the spot. "Take me to my brother," said he to Campbell. The latter gave him in charge to some of the men, who conveyed him out of the swamp.

Sublette now took the advance. As he was reconnoitring the fort, he perceived an Indian peeping through an aperture. In an instant his rifle was levelled and discharged, and the ball struck the savage in the eye. While he was reloading, he called to Campbell, and pointed out to him the hole; "Watch that place," said he, "and you will soon have a fair chance for a shot." Scarce had he uttered the words, when a ball struck him in the shoulder, and almost wheeled him round. His first thought was to take hold of his arm with his other hand, and move it up and down. He ascertained to his satisfaction, that the bone was not broken. The next moment he was so faint that he could not stand. Campbell took him in his arms and carried him out of the thicket. The same shot that struck Sublette, wounded another man in the head.

A brisk fire was now opened by the mountaineers from the wood, answered occasionally from the fort. Unluckily, the trappers and their allies, in searching for the fort, had got scattered, so that Wyeth, and a number of Nez Percés, approached the fort on the northwest side, while others did the same on the opposite quarter. A cross fire thus took place, which occasionally did mischief to friends as well as foes. An Indian was shot down, close to Wyeth, by a ball which, he was convinced, had been sped from the rifle of a trapper on the other side of the fort.

The number of whites and their Indian allies, had by this time so much increased by arrivals from the rendezvous, that the Blackfeet were completely overmatched. They kept doggedly in their fort, however, making no offer of surrender. An occasional firing into the breastwork was kept up during the day. Now and then, one of the Indian allies, in bravado, would rush up to the fort, fire over the ramparts, tear off a buffalo robe or a scarlet blanket, and return with it in triumph to his comrades. Most of the savage garrison that fell, however, were killed in the first part of the attack.

At one time it was resolved to set fire to the fort; and the squaws belonging to the allies, were employed to collect combustibles. This, however, was abandoned; the Nez Percés being unwilling to destroy the robes and blankets, and other spoils of the enemy, which they felt sure would fall into their hands.

The Indians, when fighting, are prone to taunt and revile each other. During one of the pauses of the battle, the voice of the Blackfeet chief was heard.

"So long," said he, "as we had powder and ball, we fought you in the open field: when those were spent, we retreated here to die with our women and children. You may burn us in our fort; but, stay by our ashes, and you who are so hungry for fighting, will soon have enough. There are four hundred lodges of our brethren at hand. They will soon be here—their arms are strong—their hearts are big—they will avenge us!"

This speech was translated two or three times by Nez Percé and creole interpreters. By the time it was rendered into English, the chief was made to say, that four hundred lodges of his tribe were attacking the encampment at the other end of the valley. Every one now was for hurrying to the defence of the rendezvous. A party was left to keep watch upon the fort; the rest galloped off to the camp. As night came on, the trappers drew out of the swamp, and remained about the skirts of the wood. By morning, their companions returned from the rendezvous, with the report that all was safe. As the day opened, they ventured within the swamp and approached the fort. All was silent. They advanced up to it without opposition. They entered: it had been abandoned in the night, and the Blackfeet had effected their retreat, carrying off their wounded on litters made of branches, leaving bloody traces on the herbage. The bodies of ten Indians were found within the fort; among them the one shot in the eye by Sublette. The Blackfeet afterwards reported that they had lost twenty-six warriors in this battle. Thirty-two horses were likewise found killed; among them were some of those recently carried off from Sublette's party, in the night; which showed that these were the very savages that had attacked him. They proved to be an advance party of the main body of Blackfeet; which had been upon the trail of Sublette's party. Five white men and one half-breed were killed, and several wounded. Seven of the Nez Percés were also killed, and six wounded. They had an old chief, who was reputed as invulnerable. In the course of the action he was hit by a spent ball, and threw up blood; but his skin was unbroken. His people were now fully convinced that he was proof against powder and ball.

A striking circumstance is related as having occurred, the morning after the battle. As some of the trappers and their Indian allies were approaching the fort, through the woods, they beheld an Indian woman, of noble form and features, leaning against a tree. Their surprise at her lingering here alone, to fall into the hands of her enemies, was dispelled, when they saw the corpse of a warrior at her feet. Either she was so lost in grief, as not to perceive their approach; or a proud spirit kept her silent and motionless. The Indians set up a yell, on discovering her, and before the trappers could interfere, her mangled body fell upon the corpse which she had refused to abandon. We have heard this anecdote discredited by one of the leaders who had been in the battle: but the fact may have taken place without his seeing it, and been concealed from him. It is an instance of female devotion, even to the death, which we are well disposed to believe and to record.

After the battle, the brigade of Milton Sublette, together with the free trappers, and Wyeth's New-England band, remained some days at the rendezvous, to see if the main body of Blackfeet intended to make an attack; nothing of the kind occurring, they once more put themselves in motion, and proceeded on their route towards the southwest.

Captain Sublette having distributed his supplies, had intended to set off on his return to St. Louis, taking with him the peltries collected from the trappers and Indians. His wound, however, obliged him to postpone his departure. Several who were to have accompanied him, became impatient of this delay. Among these was a young Bostonian, Mr. Joseph More, one of the followers of Mr. Wyeth, who had seen enough of mountain life and savage warfare, and was eager to return to the abodes of civilization. He and six others, among whom were a Mr. Foy, of Mississippi, Mr. Alfred K. Stephens, of St. Louis, and two grandsons of the celebrated Daniel Boone, set out together, in advance of Sublette's party, thinking they would make their own way through the mountains.

It was just five days after the battle of the swamp, that these seven companions were making their way through Jackson's Hole, a valley not far from the Three Tetons, when, as they were descending a hill, a party of Blackfeet that lay in ambush, started up with terrific yells. The horse of the young Bostonian, who was in front, wheeled round with affright, and threw his unskilful rider. The young man scrambled up the side of the hill, but, unaccustomed to such wild scenes, lost his presence of mind, and stood, as if paralyzed, on the edge of a bank, until the Blackfeet came up, and slew him on the spot. His comrades had fled on the first alarm; but two of them, Foy and Stephens, seeing his danger, paused when they had got half way up the hill, turned back, dismounted, and hastened to his assistance. Foy was instantly killed. Stephens was severely wounded, but escaped, to die five days afterwards. The survivors returned to the camp of Captain Sublette, bringing tidings of this new disaster. That hardy leader, as soon as he could bear the journey, set out on his return to St. Louis, accompanied by Campbell. As they had a number of pack horses richly laden with peltries to convoy, they chose a different route through the mountains, out of the way, as they hoped, of the lurking bands of Blackfeet. They succeeded in making the frontier in safety. We remember to have seen them with their band, about two or three months afterwards, passing through a skirt of woodland in the upper part of Missouri. Their long cavalcade stretched in single file for nearly half a mile. Sublette still wore his arm in a sling. The mountaineers in their rude hunting dresses, armed with rifles, and roughly mounted, and leading their pack horses down a hill of the forest, looked like banditti returning with plunder. On the top of some of the packs were perched several half-breed children, perfect little imps, with wild black eyes glaring from among elf locks. These, I was told, were children of the trappers: pledges of love from their squaw spouses in the wilderness.

Chapter VII

Retreat of the Blackfeet—Fontenelle's camp in danger—Captain Bonneville and the Blackfeet—Free trappers—Their character, habits, dress, equipments, horses—Game fellows of the mountains—Their visit to the camp—Good fellowship and good cheer—A carouse—A swagger, a brawl, and a reconciliation

THE BLACKFEET WARRIORS, when they effected their midnight retreat from their wild fastness in Pierre's Hole, fell back into the valley of the Seeds-ke-dee, or Green River, where they joined the main body of their band. The whole force amounted to several hundred fighting men, gloomy and exasperated by their late disaster. They had with them their wives and children, which incapacitated them for any bold and extensive enterprise of a warlike nature; but when, in the course of their wanderings, they came in sight of the encampment of Fontenelle, who had moved some distance up Green River valley, in search of the free trappers, they put up tremendous war-cries and advanced fiercely, as if to attack it. Second thoughts caused them to moderate their fury. They recollected the severe lesson just received, and could not but remark the strength of Fontenelle's position; which had been chosen with great judgment.

A formal talk ensued. The Blackfeet said nothing of the late battle, of which Fontenelle had as yet received no accounts; the latter, however, knew the hostile and perfidious nature of these savages, and took care to inform them of the encampment of Captain Bonneville, that they might know there were more white men in the neighborhood.

The conference ended, Fontenelle sent a Delaware Indian of his party to conduct fifteen of the Blackfeet to the camp of Captain Bonneville. There was at that time two Crow Indians in the captain's camp, who had recently arrived there. They looked with dismay at this deputation from their implacable enemies, and gave the captain a terrible character of them, assuring him that the best thing he could possibly do, was to put those Blackfeet deputies to death on the spot. The captain, however, who had heard nothing of the conflict at Pierre's Hole, declined all compliance with this sage counsel. He treated the grim warriors with his usual urbanity. They passed some little time at the camp; saw, no doubt, that every thing was conducted with military skill and vigilance; and that such an enemy was not to be easily surprised, nor to be molested with impunity, and then departed, to report all they had seen to their comrades.

The two scouts, which Captain Bonneville had sent out to seek for the band of free trappers, expected by Fontenelle, and to invite them to his camp, had been successful in their search, and on the 12th of August, those worthies made their appearance.

To explain the meaning of the appellation, free trapper, it is necessary to state the terms on which the men enlist in the service of the fur companies. Some have regular wages, and are furnished with weapons, horses, traps, and other requisites. These are under command, and bound to do every duty required of them connected with the service; such as hunting, trapping, loading and unloading the horses, mounting guard; and, in short, all the drudgery of the camp. These are the hired trappers.

The free trappers are a more independent class; and in describing them, we shall do little more than transcribe the graphic description of them by Captain Bonneville. "They come and go," says he, "when and where they please; provide their own horses, arms, and other equipments; trap and trade on their own account, and dispose of their skins and peltries to the highest bidder. Sometimes in a dangerous hunting ground, they attach themselves to the camp of some trader for protection. Here they come under some restrictions; they have to conform to the ordinary rules for trapping, and to submit to such restraints, and to take part in such general duties, as are established for the good order and safety of the camp. In return for this protection, and for their camp keeping, they are bound to dispose of all the beaver they take, to the trader who commands the camp, at a certain rate per skin; or, should they prefer seeking a market elsewhere, they are to make him an allowance, of from thirty to forty dollars for the whole hunt."

There is an inferior order, who, either from prudence or poverty, come to these dangerous hunting grounds without horses or accoutrements, and are furnished by the traders. These, like the hired trappers, are bound to exert themselves to the utmost in taking beavers, which, without skinning, they render in at the trader's lodge, where a stipulated price for each is placed to their credit. These, though generally included in the generic name of free trappers, have the more specific title of skin trappers.

The wandering whites who mingle for any length of time with the savages, have invariably a proneness to adopt savage habitudes; but none more so than the free trappers. It is a matter of vanity and ambition with them to discard every thing that may bear the stamp of civilized life, and to adopt the manners, habits, dress, gesture, and even walk of the Indian. You cannot pay a free trapper a greater compliment, than to persuade him you have mistaken him for an Indian brave; and, in truth, the counterfeit is complete. His hair, suffered to attain to a great length, is carefully combed out, and either left to fall carelessly over his shoulders, or plaited neatly and tied up in otter skins, or parti-colored ribands. A hunting shirt of ruffled calico of bright dyes, or of ornamented leather, falls to his knee; below which, curiously fashioned leggins, ornamented with strings, fringes, and a profusion of hawks' bells, reach to a costly pair of moccasins of the finest Indian fabric, richly embroidered with beads. A blanket of scarlet, or some other bright color, hangs from his shoulders, and is girt round his waist with a red sash, in which he bestows his pistols, knife, and the stem of his Indian pipe; preparations either for peace or war. His gun is lavishly decorated with brass tacks and vermilion, and provided with a fringed cover, occasionally of buckskin, ornamented here and there with a feather. His horse, the noble minister to the pride, pleasure, and profit of the mountaineer, is selected for his speed and spirit, and prancing gait, and holds a place in his estimation second only to himself. He shares largely of his bounty, and of his pride and pomp of trapping. He is caparisoned in the most dashing and fantastic style; the bridles and crupper are weightily embossed with beads and cockades; and head, mane, and tail, are interwoven with abundance of eagles' plumes, which flutter in the wind. To complete this grotesque equipment, the proud animal is bestreaked and bespotted with vermilion, or with white clay, whichever presents the most glaring contrast to his real color.

Such is the account given by Captain Bonneville of these rangers of the wilderness, and their appearance at the camp was strikingly characteristic. They came dashing forward at full speed, firing their fusees, and yelling in Indian style. Their dark sunburnt faces, and long flowing hair, their leggins, flaps, moccasins, and richly dyed blankets, and their painted horses gaudily caparisoned, gave them so much the air and appearance of Indians, that it was difficult to persuade oneself that they were white men, and had been brought up in civilized life.

Captain Bonneville, who was delighted with the game look of these cavaliers of the mountains, welcomed them heartily to his camp, and ordered a free allowance of grog to regale them, which soon put them in the most braggart spirits. They pronounced the captain the finest fellow in the world, and his men all *bons garçons*, jovial lads, and swore they would pass the day with them. They did so; and a day it was, of boast, and swagger, and rodomontado. The prime bullies and braves among the free trappers had each his circle of novices, from among the captain's band; mere greenhorns, men unused to Indian life; *mangeurs de lard*, or pork eaters; as such new comers are superciliously called by the veterans of the wilderness. These he would astonish and delight by the hour, with prodigious tales of his doings among the Indians; and of the wonders he had seen, and the wonders he had performed, in his adventurous peregrinations among the mountains.

In the evening, the free trappers drew off, and returned to the camp of Fontenelle, highly delighted with their visit and with their new acquaintances, and promising to return the following day. They kept their word: day after day their visits were repeated; they became "hail fellow well met" with Captain Bonneville's men; treat after treat succeeded, until both parties got most potently convinced, or rather confounded by liquor. Now came on confusion and uproar. The free trappers were no longer suffered to have all the swagger to themselves. The camp bullies and prime trappers of the party began to ruffle up, and to brag, in turn, of their perils and achievements. Each now tried to out-boast and out-talk the other; a quarrel ensued as a matter of course, and a general fight, according to frontier usage. The two factions drew out their forces for a pitched battle. They fell to work and belabored each other with might and main; kicks and cuffs and dry blows were as well bestowed as they were well merited, until, having fought to their hearts' content, and been drubbed into a familiar acquaintance with each other's prowess and good qualities, they ended the fight by becoming firmer friends than they could have been rendered by a year's peaceable companionship.

While Captain Bonneville amused himself by observing the habits and characteristics of this singular class of men; and indulged them, for the time, in all their vagaries, he profited by the opportunity to collect from them information concerning the different parts of the country, about which they had been accustomed to range: the characters of the tribes, and, in short, every thing important to his enterprise. He also succeeded in securing the services of several to guide and aid him in his peregrinations among the mountains, and to trap for him during the ensuing season. Having strengthened his party with such valuable recruits, he felt in some measure consoled for the loss of the Delaware Indians, decoyed from him by Mr. Fontenelle.

Chapter VIII

Plans for the winter—Salmon River—Abundance of salmon west of the mountains—New arrangements—Caches —Cerré's detachment—Movements in Fontenelle's camp— Departure of the Blackfeet—Their fortunes—Wind Mountain streams—Buckeye, the Delaware hunter, and the grizzly bear—Bones of murdered travellers—Visit to Pierre's Hole— Traces of the battle—Nez Percé Indians—Arrival at Salmon River

THE INFORMATION derived from the free trappers, deter mined Captain Bonneville as to his further movements. He learnt that in the Green River valley the winters were severe, the snow frequently falling to the depth of several feet; and that there was no good wintering ground in the neighborhood. The upper part of the Salmon River was represented as far more eligible, beside being in an excellent beaver country; and thither the captain resolved to bend his course.

The Salmon River is one of the upper branches of the Oregon or Columbia; and takes its rise from various sources, among a group of mountains to the northwest of the Wind River chain. It owes its name to the immense shoals of salmon which ascend it in the months of September and October. The salmon on the west side of the Rocky Mountains, are, like the buffalo on the eastern plains, vast migratory supplies for the wants of man, that come and go with the seasons. As the buffalo in countless throngs find their certain way in the transient pasturage on the prairies, along the fresh banks of the rivers, and up every valley and green defile of the mountains, so the salmon at their allotted seasons, regulated by a sublime and all-seeing Providence, swarm in myriads up the great rivers, and find their way up their main branches, and into the minutest tributary streams; so as to pervade the great arid plains, and to penetrate even among barren mountains. Thus wandering tribes are fed in the desert places of the wilderness, where there is no herbage for the animals of the chase, and where, but for these periodical supplies, it would be impossible for man to subsist.

The rapid currents of the rivers which run into the Pacific, render the ascent of them very exhausting to the salmon. When the fish first run up the rivers, they are fat and in fine order. The struggle against impetuous streams and frequent rapids, gradually renders them thin and weak, and great numbers are seen floating down the rivers on their backs. As the season advances and the water becomes chilled, they are flung in myriads on the shores, where the wolves and bears assemble to banquet on them. Often they rot in such quantities along the river banks, as to taint the atmosphere. They are commonly from two to three feet long.

Captain Bonneville now made his arrangements for the autumn and the winter. The nature of the country through which he was about to travel, rendered it impossible to proceed with waggons. He had more goods and supplies of various kinds, also, than were required for present purposes, or than could be conveniently transported on horseback; aided, therefore, by a few confidential men, he made *caches*, or secret pits, during the night, when all the rest of the camp were asleep, and in these deposited the superfluous effects, together with the waggons. All traces of the caches were then carefully obliterated. This is a common expedient with the traders and trappers of the mountains. Having no established posts and magazines, they make these caches or deposits at certain points, whither they repair, occasionally, for supplies. It is an expedient derived from the wandering tribes of Indians.

Many of the horses were still so weak and lame, as to be unfit for a long scramble through the mountains. These were collected into one cavalcade, and given in charge to an experienced trapper, of the name of Matthieu. He was to proceed westward, with a brigade of trappers, to Bear River; a stream to the west of the Green River or Colorado, where there was good pasturage for the horses. In this neighborhood it was expected he would meet the Shoshonie villages or bands,* on their yearly migrations, with whom he was to trade for peltries

* A *village* of Indians, in trappers' language, does not always imply a fixed community; but often a wandering horde or band. The Shoshonies, like most of the mountain tribes, have no settled residences; but are a nomadic people, dwelling in tents or lodges, and shifting their encampments from place to place, according as fish and game abound.

and provisions. After he had traded with these people, finished his trapping, and recruited the strength of the horses, he was to proceed to Salmon River and rejoin Captain Bonneville, who intended to fix his quarters there for the winter.

While these arrangements were in progress in the camp of Captain Bonneville, there was a sudden bustle and stir in the camp of Fontenelle. One of the partners of the American Fur Company had arrived, in all haste, from the rendezvous at Pierre's Hole, in quest of the supplies. The competition between the two rival companies was just now at its height, and prosecuted with unusual zeal. The tramontane concerns of the Rocky Mountain Fur Company were managed by two resident partners, Fitzpatrick and Bridger; those of the American Fur Company, by Vanderburgh and Dripps. The latter were ignorant of the mountain regions, but trusted to make up by vigilance and activity for their want of knowledge of the country.

Fitzpatrick, an experienced trader and trapper, knew the evils of competition in the same hunting grounds, and had proposed that the two companies should divide the country, so as to hunt in different directions: this proposition being rejected, he had exerted himself to get first into the field. His exertions, as has already been shown, were effectual. The early arrival of Sublette, with supplies, had enabled the various brigades of the Rocky Mountain Company to start off to their respective hunting grounds. Fitzpatrick himself, with his associate, Bridger, had pushed off with a strong party of trappers, for a prime beaver country to the north-northwest.

This had put Vanderburgh upon his mettle. He had hastened on to meet Fontenelle. Finding him at his camp in Green River valley, he immediately furnished himself with the supplies; put himself at the head of the free trappers and Delawares, and set off with all speed, determined to follow hard upon the heels of Fitzpatrick and Bridger. Of the adventures of these parties among the mountains, and the disastrous effects of their competition, we shall have occasion to treat in a future chapter.

Fontenelle, having now delivered his supplies and accomplished his errand, struck his tents and set off on his return to the Yellowstone. Captain Bonneville and his band, therefore, remained alone in the Green River valley; and their situation might have been perilous, had the Blackfeet band still lingered in the vicinity. Those marauders, however, had been dismayed at finding so many resolute and well-appointed parties of white men in this neighborhood. They had, therefore, abandoned this part of the country, passing over the head waters of the Green River, and bending their course toward the Yellowstone. Misfortune pursued them. Their route lay through the country of their deadly enemies, the Crows. In the Wind River valley, which lies east of the mountains, they were encountered by a powerful war party of that tribe, and completely put to rout. Forty of them were killed, many of their women and children captured, and the scattered fugitives hunted like wild beasts, until they were completely chased out of the Crow country.

On the 22d of August Captain Bonneville broke up his camp, and set out on his route for Salmon River. His baggage was arranged in packs, three to a mule, or packhorse; one being disposed on each side of the animal, and one on the top; the three forming a load of from one hundred and eighty to two hundred and twenty pounds. This is the trappers' style of loading their packhorses; his men, however, were inexpert at adjusting the packs; which were prone to get loose and slip off; so that it was necessary to keep a rear guard, to assist in reloading. A few days' experience, however, brought them into proper training.

Their march lay up the valley of the Seeds-ke-dee, overlooked to the right by the lofty peaks of the Wind River Mountains. From bright little lakes and fountain heads of this remarkable bed of mountains, poured forth the tributary streams of the Seeds-ke-dee. Some came rushing down gullies and ravines; others tumbling in crystal cascades from inaccessible clefts and rocks, winding their way in rapid and pellucid currents across the valley, to throw themselves into the main river. So transparent were these waters, that the trout, with which they abounded, could be seen gliding about as if in the air; and their pebbly beds were distinctly visible at the depth of many feet. This beautiful and diaphanous quality of the Rocky Mountain streams, prevails for a long time after they have mingled their waters and swollen into important rivers.

Issuing from the upper part of the valley, Captain Bonneville continued to the east-northeast, across rough and lofty ridges, and deep rocky defiles, extremely fatiguing both to man and horse. Among his hunters was a Delaware Indian who had remained faithful to him. His name was Buckeye. He had often prided himself on his skill and success in coping with the grizzly bear, that terror of the hunters. Though crippled in the left arm, he declared he had no hesitation to close with a wounded bear, and attack him with a sword. If armed with a rifle, he was willing to brave the animal when in full force and fury. He had twice an opportunity of proving his prowess, in the course of this mountain journey, and was each time successful. His mode was to seat himself upon the ground, with his rifle cocked and resting on his lame arm. Thus prepared, he would await the approach of the bear with perfect coolness, nor pull trigger until he was close at hand. In each instance, he laid the monster dead upon the spot.

A march of three or four days, through savage and lonely scenes, brought Captain Bonneville to the fatal defile of Jackson's Hole, where poor More and Foy had been surprised and murdered by the Blackfeet. The feelings of the Captain were shocked at beholding the bones of these unfortunate young men bleaching among the rocks; and he caused them to be decently interred.

On the 3d of September he arrived on the summit of a mountain which commanded a full view of the eventful valley of Pierre's Hole; whence he could trace the winding of its streams through green meadows, and forests of willow and cotton-wood: and have a prospect, between distant mountains, of the lava plains of Snake River, dimly spread forth like a sleeping ocean below.

After enjoying this magnificent prospect, he descended into the valley, and visited the scenes of the late desperate conflict. There were the remains of the rude fortress in the swamp, shattered by rifle shot, and strewed with the mingled bones of savages and horses. There was the late populous and noisy rendezvous, with the traces of trappers' camps and Indian lodges; but their fires were extinguished, the motley assemblage of trappers and hunters, white traders and Indian braves, had all dispersed to different points of the wilderness, and the valley had relapsed into its pristine solitude and silence.

That night the captain encamped upon the battle ground; the next day, he resumed his toilsome peregrinations through the mountains. For upwards of two weeks he continued his painful march; both men and horses suffering excessively at times from hunger and thirst. At length, on the 19th of September, he reached the upper waters of Salmon River.

The weather was cold, and there were symptoms of an impending storm. The night set in, but Buckeye, the Delaware Indian, was missing. He had left the party early in the morning, to hunt by himself, according to his custom. Fears were entertained, lest he should lose his way, and become bewildered in tempestuous weather. These fears increased on the following morning, when a violent snow storm came on, which soon covered the earth to the depth of several inches. Captain Bonneville immediately encamped, and sent out scouts in every direction. After some search, Buckeye was discovered, quietly seated, at a considerable distance in the rear, waiting the expected approach of the party, not knowing that they had passed, the snow having covered their trail.

On the ensuing morning, they resumed their march at an early hour, but had not proceeded far, when the hunters, who were beating up the country in the advance, came galloping back, making signals to encamp, and crying Indians! Indians!

Captain Bonneville immediately struck into a skirt of wood and prepared for action. The savages were now seen trooping over the hills in great numbers. One of them left the main body and came forward singly, making signals of peace. He announced them as a band of Nez Percés* or Pierced-nose Indians, friendly to the whites, whereupon an invitation was returned by Captain Bonneville, for them to come and encamp with him. They halted for a short time to make their toilette, an operation as important with an Indian warrior, as with a fashionable beauty. This done, they arranged themselves in martial style, the chiefs leading the van, the braves following in a long line, painted and decorated, and topped off with flut-

---

* We should observe that this tribe is universally called by its French name, which is pronounced by the trappers, *Nepercy*. There are two main branches of this tribe, the upper Nepercys and the lower Nepercys, as we shall show hereafter.

tering plumes. In this way they advanced, shouting and singing, firing off their fusees, and clashing their shields. The two parties encamped hard by each other. The Nez Percés were on a hunting expedition, but had been almost famished on their march. They had no provisions left but a few dried salmon, yet finding the white men equally in want, they generously offered to share even this meagre pittance, and frequently repeated the offer, with an earnestness that left no doubt of their sincerity. Their generosity won the heart of Captain Bonneville, and produced the most cordial good will on the part of his men. For the two days that the parties remained in company, the most amicable intercourse prevailed, and they parted the best of friends. Captain Bonneville detached a few men, under Mr. Cerré, an able leader, to accompany the Nez Percés on their hunting expedition, and to trade with them for meat for the winter's supply. After this, he proceeded down the river, about five miles below the forks, when he came to a halt on the 26th of September, to establish his winter quarters.

Chapter IX

I T WAS gratifying to Captain Bonneville, after so long and toilsome a course of travel, to relieve his poor jaded horses of the burdens under which they were almost ready to give out, and to behold them rolling upon the grass, and taking a long repose after all their sufferings. Indeed, so exhausted were they, that those employed under the saddle were no longer capable of hunting for the daily subsistence of the camp.

All hands now set to work to prepare a winter cantonment. A temporary fortification was thrown up for the protection of the party; a secure and comfortable pen, into which the horses could be driven at night; and huts were built for the reception of the merchandise.

This done, Captain Bonneville made a distribution of his forces: twenty men were to remain with him in garrison to protect the property; the rest were organized into three brigades, and sent off in different directions, to subsist themselves by hunting the buffalo, until the snow should become too deep.

Indeed, it would have been impossible to provide for the whole party in this neighborhood. It was at the extreme western limit of the buffalo range, and these animals had recently been completely hunted out of the neighborhood by the Nez Percés, so that, although the hunters of the garrison were continually on the alert, ranging the country round, they brought in scarce game sufficient to keep famine from the door. Now and then there was a scanty meal of fish or wild fowl, occasionally an antelope; but frequently the cravings of hunger had to be appeased with roots, or the flesh of wolves and muskrats. Rarely could the inmates of the cantonment boast of having made a full meal, and never of having wherewithal for the morrow. In this way they starved along until the 8th of October, when they were joined by a party of five families of Nez Percés, who in some measure reconciled them to the hardships of their situation, by exhibiting a lot still more destitute. A more forlorn set they had never encountered: they had not a morsel of meat or fish; nor any thing to subsist on, excepting roots, wild rosebuds, the barks of certain plants, and other vegetable productions; neither had they any weapon for hunting or defence, excepting an old spear: yet the poor fellows made no murmur nor complaint; but seemed accustomed to their hard fare. If they could not teach the white man their practical stoicism, they at least made them acquainted with the edible properties of roots and wild rosebuds, and furnished them a supply from their own store. The necessities of the camp at length became so urgent, that Captain Bonneville determined to despatch a party to the Horse Prairie, a plain to the north of his cantonment, to procure a supply of provisions. When the men were about to depart, he proposed to the Nez Percés that they, or some of them, should join the hunting party. To his surprise, they promptly declined. He inquired the reason for their refusal, seeing that they were in nearly as starving a situation as his own people. They replied that it was a sacred day with them, and the Great Spirit would be angry should they devote it to hunting. They offered, however, to accompany the party if it would delay its departure until the following day; but this the pinching demands of hunger would not permit, and the detachment proceeded.

A few days afterwards, four of them signified to Captain Bonneville that they were about to hunt. "What!" exclaimed he, "without guns or arrows; and with only one old spear? What do you expect to kill?" They smiled among themselves, but made no answer. Preparatory to the chase, they performed some religious rites, and offered up to the Great Spirit a few short prayers for safety and success; then, having received the blessings of their wives, they leaped upon their horses and departed, leaving the whole party of Christian spectators amazed and rebuked by this lesson of faith and dependence on a supreme and benevolent Being. "Accustomed," adds Captain Bonneville, "as I had heretofore been, to find the wretched Indian revelling in blood, and stained by every vice which can degrade human nature, I could scarcely realize the scene which I had witnessed. Wonder at such unaffected tenderness and piety, where it was least to have been sought, contended in all our bosoms with shame and confusion, at receiving such pure and wholesome instructions from creatures so far below us in all the arts and comforts of life." The simple prayers of the poor Indians were not unheard. In the course of four or five days they returned, laden with meat. Captain Bonneville was curious to know how they had attained such success with such scanty means. They gave him to understand that they had chased the herds of buffalo at full speed, until they tired them down, when they easily despatched them with the spear, and made use of the same weapon to flay the carcasses. To carry through their lesson to their Christian friends, the poor savages were as charitable as they had been pious, and generously shared with them the spoils of their hunting: giving them food enough to last for several days.

A further and more intimate intercourse with this tribe, gave Captain Bonneville still greater cause to admire their strong devotional feeling. "Simply to call these people religious," says he, "would convey but a faint idea of the deep hue of piety and devotion which pervades their whole conduct. Their honesty is immaculate, and their purity of purpose, and their observance of the rites of their religion, are most uniform and remarkable. They are, certainly, more like a nation of saints than a horde of savages."

In fact, the antibelligerant policy of this tribe, may have sprung from the doctrines of Christian charity, for it would appear that they had imbibed some notions of the Christian faith from Catholic missionaries and traders who had been among them. They even had a rude calendar of the fasts and festivals of the Romish Church, and some traces of its ceremonials. These have become blended with their own wild rites, and present a strange medley; civilized and barbarous. On the Sabbath, men, women and children array themselves in their best style, and assemble round a pole erected at the head of the camp. Here they go through a wild fantastic ceremonial; strongly resembling the religious dance of the Shaking Quakers; but from its enthusiasm, much more striking and impressive. During the intervals of the ceremony, the principal chiefs, who officiate as priests, instruct them in their duties, and exhort them to virtue and good deeds.

"There is something antique and patriarchal," observes Captain Bonneville, "in this union of the offices of leader and priest; as there is in many of their customs and manners, which are all strongly imbued with religion."

The worthy captain, indeed, appears to have been strongly interested by this gleam of unlooked for light amidst the darkness of the wilderness. He exerted himself, during his sojourn among this simple and well-disposed people, to inculcate, as far as he was able, the gentle and humanizing precepts of the Christian faith, and to make them acquainted with the leading points of its history; and it speaks highly for the purity and benignity of his heart, that he derived unmixed happiness from the task.

"Many a time," says he, "was my little lodge thronged, or rather piled with hearers, for they lay on the ground, one leaning over the other, until there was no further room, all listening with greedy ears to the wonders which the Great Spirit had revealed to the white man. No other subject gave them half the satisfaction, or commanded half the attention; and but few scenes in my life remain so freshly on my memory, or are so pleasurably recalled to my contemplation, as these hours of intercourse with a distant and benighted race in the midst of the desert."

The only excesses indulged in by this temperate and exemplary people, appear to be gambling and horseracing. In these they engage with an eagerness that amounts to infatuation. Knots of gamblers will assemble before one of their lodge fires, early in the evening, and remain absorbed in the chances and changes of the game until long after dawn of the following day. As the night advances, they wax warmer and warmer. Bets increase in amount, one loss only serves to lead to a greater, until in the course of a single night's gambling, the richest chief may become the poorest varlet in the camp.

Chapter X

ON THE 12TH of October, two young Indians of the Nez
Percé tribe arrived at Captain Bonneville's encampment.
They were on their way homeward, but had been obliged to
swerve from their ordinary route through the mountains, by
deep snows. Their new route took them through the Horse
Prairie. In traversing it, they had been attracted by the distant
smoke of a camp fire, and, on stealing near to reconnoitre,
had discovered a war party of Blackfeet. They had several
horses with them; and, as they generally go on foot on warlike excursions, it was concluded that these horses had been
captured in the course of their maraudings.

This intelligence awakened solicitude in the mind of Captain
Bonneville, for the party of hunters whom he had sent to that
neighborhood; and the Nez Percés, when informed of the circumstance, shook their heads, and declared their belief that the
horses they had seen had been stolen from that very party.

Anxious for information on the subject, Captain Bonneville
despatched two hunters to beat up the country in that direction. They searched in vain; not a trace of the men could be
found; but they got into a region destitute of game, where
they were wellnigh famished. At one time, they were three entire days without a mouthful of food; at length they beheld a
buffalo grazing at the foot of a mountain. After manœuvring
so as to get within shot, they fired, but merely wounded him.
He took to flight, and they followed him over hill and dale,
with the eagerness and perseverance of starving men. A more
lucky shot brought him to the ground. Stanfield sprang upon
him, plunged his knife into his throat, and allayed his raging
hunger by drinking his blood. A fire was instantly kindled beside the carcass, when the two hunters cooked, and ate again
and again, until, perfectly gorged, they sank to sleep before

their hunting fire. On the following morning they rose early, made another hearty meal, then loading themselves with buffalo meat, set out on their return to the camp, to report the fruitlessness of their mission.

At length, after six weeks' absence, the hunters made their appearance, and were received with joy, proportioned to the anxiety that had been felt on their account. They had hunted with success on the prairie, but, while busy drying buffalo meat, were joined by a few panic-stricken Flatheads, who informed them that a powerful band of Blackfeet were at hand. The hunters immediately abandoned the dangerous hunting ground, and accompanied the Flatheads to their village. Here they found Mr. Cerré, and the detachment of hunters sent with him to accompany the hunting party of the Nez Percés.

After remaining some time at the village, until they supposed the Blackfeet to have left the neighborhood, they set off with some of Mr. Cerré's men, for the cantonment at Salmon River, where they arrived without accident. They informed Captain Bonneville, however, that not far from his quarters, they had found a wallet of fresh meat and a cord, which they supposed had been left by some prowling Blackfeet. A few days afterwards, Mr. Cerré, with the remainder of his men, likewise arrived at the cantonment.

Mr. Walker, one of the subleaders, who had gone with a band of twenty hunters, to range the country just beyond the Horse Prairie, had, likewise, his share of adventures with the all pervading Blackfeet. At one of his encampments, the guard stationed to keep watch round the camp, grew weary of their duty, and feeling a little too secure, and too much at home on these prairies, retired to a small grove of willows, to amuse themselves with a social game of cards, called "old sledge," which is as popular among these trampers of the prairies, as whist or ecarté among the polite circles of the cities. From the midst of their sport, they were suddenly roused by a discharge of fire-arms, and a shrill war-whoop. Starting on their feet, and snatching up their rifles, they beheld in dismay their horses and mules already in possession of the enemy, who had stolen upon the camp unperceived, while they were spell-bound by the magic of old sledge. The Indians sprang upon the animals barebacked, and endeavored to urge them off, under a galling

fire, that did some execution. The mules, however, confounded by the hurly-burly, and disliking their new riders,
kicked up their heels and dismounted half of them, in spite of
their horsemanship. This threw the rest into confusion, they
endeavored to protect their unhorsed comrades from the furious assaults of the whites; but, after a scene of "confusion
worse confounded," horses and mules were abandoned, and
the Indians betook themselves to the bushes. Here, they
quickly scratched holes in the earth, about two feet deep, in
which they prostrated themselves, and while thus screened
from the shots of the white men, were enabled to make such
use of their bows and arrows, and fusees, as to repulse their assailants, and to effect their retreat. This adventure threw a temporary stigma upon the game of "old sledge."

In the course of the autumn, four Iroquois hunters, driven
by the snow from their hunting grounds, made their appearance at the cantonment. They were kindly welcomed, and
during their sojourn, made themselves useful in a variety of
ways, being excellent trappers, and first-rate woodsmen. They
were of the remnants of a party of Iroquois hunters, that
came from Canada into these mountain regions many years
previously, in the employ of the Hudson's Bay Company.
They were led by a brave chieftain, named Pierre, who fell by
the hands of the Blackfeet, and gave his name to the fated valley of Pierre's Hole. This branch of the Iroquois tribe has ever
since remained among these mountains, at mortal enmity
with the Blackfeet, and have lost many of their prime hunters
in their feuds with that ferocious race. Some of them fell in
with General Ashley, in the course of one of his gallant excursions into the wilderness, and have continued ever since in
the employ of the company.

Among the motley visiters to the winter quarters of Captain
Bonneville, was a party of Pends Oreilles, (or Hanging-ears)
and their chief. These Indians have a strong resemblance, in
character and customs, to the Nez Percés. They amount to
about three hundred lodges, and are well armed, and possess
great numbers of horses. During the spring, summer, and autumn, they hunt the buffalo about the head waters of the
Missouri, Henry's Fork of the Snake River, and the northern
branches of Salmon River. Their winter quarters are upon the

Racine Amère, where they subsist upon roots and dried buffalo meat. Upon this river the Hudson's Bay Company have established a trading post, where the Pends Oreilles and the Flatheads bring their peltries to exchange for arms, clothing, and trinkets.

This tribe, like the Nez Percés, evince strong and peculiar feelings of natural piety. Their religion is not a mere superstitious fear, like that of most savages; they evince abstract notions of morality; a deep reverence for an overruling Spirit, and a respect for the rights of their fellow-men. In one respect, their religion partakes of the pacific doctrines of the Quakers. They hold that the Great Spirit is displeased with all nations who wantonly engage in war; they abstain, therefore, from all aggressive hostilities. But though thus unoffending in their policy, they are called upon continually to wage defensive warfare; especially with the Blackfeet; with whom, in the course of their hunting expeditions, they come in frequent collision, and have desperate battles. Their conduct as warriors, is without fear or reproach, and they can never be driven to abandon their hunting grounds.

Like most savages, they are firm believers in dreams, and in the power and efficacy of charms and amulets, or medicines, as they term them. Some of their braves, also, who have had numerous hairbreadth 'scapes, like the old Nez Percé chief, in the battle of Pierre's Hole, are believed to wear a charmed life, and to be bullet proof. Of these gifted beings, marvellous anecdotes are related, which are most potently believed by their fellow-savages, and sometimes almost credited by the white hunters.

Chapter XI

WHILE Captain Bonneville and his men are sojourning among the Nez Percés, on Salmon River, we will inquire after the fortunes of those doughty rivals of the Rocky Mountain and American Fur Companies, who started off for the trapping grounds to the north-northwest.

Fitzpatrick and Bridger, of the former company, as we have already shown, having received their supplies, had taken the lead, and hoped to have the first sweep of the hunting ground. Vanderburgh and Dripps, however, the two resident partners of the opposite company, by extraordinary exertions, were enabled soon to put themselves upon their traces, and pressed forward with such speed as to overtake them just as they had reached the heart of the beaver country. In fact, being ignorant of the best trapping grounds, it was their object to follow on, and profit by the superior knowledge of the other party.

Nothing could equal the chagrin of Fitzpatrick and Bridger, at being dogged by their inexperienced rivals; especially after their offer to divide the country with them. They tried in every way to blind and baffle them; to steal a march upon them, or lead them on a wrong scent; but all in vain. Vanderburgh made up by activity and intelligence, for his ignorance of the country: was always wary, always on the alert; discovered every movement of his rivals, however secret, and was not to be eluded or misled.

Fitzpatrick, and his colleague, now lost all patience: since the others persisted in following them, they determined to give them an unprofitable chase, and to sacrifice the hunting season, rather than share the products with their rivals. They accordingly took up their line of march down the course of the Missouri, keeping the main Blackfoot trail, and tramping doggedly forward, without stopping to set a single trap. The others beat the hoof after them for some time, but by degrees began to perceive that they were on a wild-goose chase, and getting into a country perfectly barren to the trapper. They now came to a halt, and bethought themselves how to make up for lost time, and improve the remainder of the season. It was thought best to divide their forces and try different trapping grounds. While Dripps went in one direction, Vanderburgh, with about fifty men, proceeded in another. The latter, in his headlong march, had got into the very heart of the Blackfoot country, yet seems to have been unconscious of his danger. As his scouts were out one day, they came upon the traces of a recent band of savages. There were the deserted fires still smoking, surrounded by the carcasses of buffaloes just killed. It was evident a party of Blackfeet had been frightened from their hunting camp, and had retreated, probably to seek reinforcements. The scouts hastened back to the camp, and told Vanderburgh what they had seen. He made light of the alarm, and, taking nine men with him, galloped off to reconnoitre for himself. He found the deserted hunting camp just as they had represented it; there lay the carcasses of buffaloes, partly dismembered; there were the smouldering fires, still sending up their wreaths of smoke: every thing bore traces of recent and hasty retreat; and gave reason to believe that the savages were still lurking in the neighborhood. With heedless daring, Vanderburgh put himself upon their trail, to trace them to their place of concealment. It led him over prairies, and through skirts of woodland, until it entered a dark and dangerous ravine. Vanderburgh pushed in, without hesitation, followed by his little band. They soon found themselves in a gloomy dell, between steep banks overhung with trees; where the profound silence was only broken by the tramp of their own horses.

Suddenly the horrid war-whoop burst on their ears, mingled with the sharp report of rifles, and a legion of savages sprang from their concealments, yelling, and shaking their buffalo robes, to frighten the horses. Vanderburgh's horse fell, mortally wounded by the first discharge. In his fall, he pinned his rider to the ground; who called in vain upon his men to assist in extricating him. One was shot down and scalped at a few paces distance: most of the others were severely wounded, and sought their safety in flight. The savages approached to despatch the unfortunate leader, as he lay struggling beneath his horse. He had still his rifle in his hand, and his pistols in his belt. The first savage that advanced received the contents of the rifle in his breast, and fell dead upon the spot; but before Vanderburgh could draw a pistol, a blow from a tomahawk laid him prostrate, and he was despatched by repeated wounds.

Such was the fate of Major Henry Vanderburgh: one of the best and worthiest leaders of the American Fur Company; who, by his manly bearing and dauntless courage, is said to have made himself universally popular among the bold-hearted rovers of the wilderness.

Those of the little band who escaped, fled in consternation to the camp, and spread direful reports of the force and ferocity of the enemy. The party, being without a head, were in complete confusion and dismay, and made a precipitate retreat, without attempting to recover the remains of their butchered leader. They made no halt until they reached the encampment of the Pends Oreilles, or Hanging-ears, where they offered a reward for the recovery of the body, but without success; it never could be found.

In the meantime Fitzpatrick and Bridger, of the Rocky Mountain Company, fared but little better than their rivals. In their eagerness to mislead them, they had betrayed themselves into danger, and got into a region infested with the Blackfeet. They soon found that foes were on the watch for them; but they were experienced in Indian warfare, and not to be surprised at night, nor drawn into an ambush in the daytime. As the evening advanced, the horses were all brought in and picketed, and a guard was stationed round the camp. At the earliest streak of day one of the leaders would mount his horse, and gallop off full speed for about half a mile; then look round for Indian trails, to ascertain whether there had been any lurkers round the camp: returning slowly, he would reconnoitre every ravine and thicket, where there might be an ambush. This done, he would gallop off in an opposite direction and repeat the same scrutiny. Finding all things safe, the horses would be turned loose to graze; but always under the eye of a guard.

A caution equally vigilant was observed in the march, on approaching any defile or place where an enemy might lie in wait; and scouts were always kept in the advance, or along the ridges and rising grounds on the flanks.

At length, one day, a large band of Blackfeet appeared in the open field, but in the vicinity of rocks and cliffs. They kept at a wary distance, but made friendly signs. The trappers replied in the same way, but likewise kept aloof. A small party of Indians now advanced, bearing the pipe of peace: they were met by an equal number of white men, and they formed a group, midway between the two bands, where the pipe was circulated from hand to hand, and smoked with all due ceremony. An instance of natural affection took place at this pacific meeting. Among the free trappers, in the Rocky Mountain band, was a spirited young Mexican, named Loretto; who, in the course of his wanderings, had ransomed a beautiful Blackfoot girl from a band of Crows, by whom she had been captured. He made her his wife, after the Indian style, and she had followed his fortunes ever since, with the most devoted affection.

Among the Blackfeet warriors who advanced with the calumet of peace, she recognised a brother. Leaving her infant with Loretto, she rushed forward and threw herself upon her brother's neck; who clasped his long lost sister to his heart, with a warmth of affection but little compatible with the reputed stoicism of the savage.

While this scene was taking place, Bridger left the main body of trappers, and rode slowly towards the group of smokers, with his rifle resting across the pommel of his saddle. The chief of the Blackfeet stepped forward to meet him. From some unfortunate feeling of distrust, Bridger cocked his rifle just as the chief was extending his hand in friendship. The quick ear of the savage caught the click of the lock; in a twinkling, he grasped the barrel, forced the muzzle downward, and the contents were discharged into the earth at his feet. His next movement was to wrest the weapon from the hand of Bridger, and fell him with it to the earth. He might have found this no easy task, had not the unfortunate leader received two arrows in his back during the struggle.

The chief now sprang into the vacant saddle and galloped off to his band. A wild hurry-scurry scene ensued; each party took to the banks, the rocks, and trees, to gain favorable positions, and an irregular firing was kept up on either side, without much effect. The Indian girl had been hurried off by her people, at the outbreak of the affray. She would have returned, through the dangers of the fight, to her husband and her child, but was prevented by her brother. The young Mexican saw her struggles and her agony, and heard her piercing cries. With a generous impulse, he caught up the child in his arms, rushed forward, regardless of Indian shaft or rifle, and placed it in safety upon her bosom. Even the savage heart of the Blackfoot chief was reached by this noble deed. He pronounced Loretto a madman for his temerity, but bade him depart in peace. The young Mexican hesitated: he urged to have his wife restored to him, but her brother interfered, and the countenance of the chief grew dark. The girl, he said, belonged to his tribe—she must remain with her people. Loretto would still have lingered, but his wife implored him to depart, lest his life should be endangered. It was with the greatest reluctance that he returned to his companions.

The approach of night put an end to the skirmishing fire of the adverse parties, and the savages drew off without renewing their hostilities. We cannot but remark, that both in this affair, and in that at Pierre's Hole, the affray commenced by a hostile act on the part of white men, at the moment when the Indian warrior was extending the hand of amity. In neither instance, as far as circumstances have been stated to us by different persons, do we see any reason to suspect the savage chiefs of perfidy in their overtures of friendship. They advanced in the confiding way, usual among Indians, when they bear the pipe of peace, and consider themselves sacred from attack. If we violate the sanctity of this ceremonial, by any hostile movement on our part, it is we who incur the charge of faithlessness; and we doubt not, that in both these instances, the white men have been considered by the Blackfeet as the aggressors, and have, in consequence, been held up as men not to be trusted.

A word to conclude the romantic incident of Loretto and his Indian bride. A few months subsequent to the event just related, the young Mexican settled his accounts with the Rocky Mountain Company, and obtained his discharge. He then left his comrades and set off to rejoin his wife and child among her people; and we understand that, at the time we are writing these pages, he resides at a trading-house established of late by the American Fur Company, in the Blackfoot country, where he acts as an interpreter, and has his Indian girl with him.

Chapter XII

A winter camp in the wilderness—Medley of trappers, hunters, and Indians—Scarcity of game—New arrangements in the camp—Detachments sent to a distance—Carelessness of the Indians when encamped—Sickness among the Indians—Excellent character of the Nez Percés—The captain's effort as a pacificator—A Nez Percé's argument in favor of war—Robberies by the Blackfeet—Long suffering of the Nez Percés—A hunter's elysium among the mountains —More robberies—The captain preaches up a crusade—The effect upon his hearers

FOR the greater part of the month of November, Captain Bonneville remained in his temporary post on Salmon River. He was now in the full enjoyment of his wishes; leading a hunter's life in the heart of the wilderness, with all its wild populace around him. Beside his own people, motley in character and costume: Creole, Kentuckian, Indian, half-breed, hired trapper, and free trapper: he was surrounded by encampments of Nez Percés and Flatheads, with their droves of horses covering the hills and plains. It was, he declares, a wild and bustling scene. The hunting parties of white men and red men, continually sallying forth and returning; the groups at the various encampments, some cooking, some working, some amusing themselves at different games; the neighing of horses, the braying of asses, the resounding strokes of the axe, the sharp report of the rifle, the whoop, the halloo, and the frequent burst of laughter, all in the midst of a region suddenly roused from perfect silence and loneliness by this transient hunters' sojourn, realized, he says, the idea of a "populous solitude."

The kind and genial character of the captain had, evidently, its influence on the opposite races thus fortuitously congregated together. The most perfect harmony prevailed between them. The Indians, he says, were friendly in their dispositions, and honest to the most scrupulous degree, in their intercourse with the white men. It is true, they were somewhat importunate in their curiosity, and apt to be continually in the way, examining every thing with keen and prying eye, and

709

watching every movement of the white men. All this, however, was borne with great good-humor by the captain, and through his example, by his men. Indeed, throughout all his transactions, he shows himself the friend of the poor Indians, and his conduct towards them is above all praise.

The Nez Percés, the Flatheads, and the Hanging-ears, pride themselves upon the number of their horses, of which they possess more in proportion, than any other of the mountain tribes within the buffalo range. Many of the Indian warriors and hunters, encamped around Captain Bonneville, possess from thirty to forty horses each. Their horses are stout, well built ponies, of great wind, and capable of enduring the severest hardship and fatigue. The swiftest of them, however, are those obtained from the whites, while sufficiently young to become acclimated and inured to the rough service of the mountains.

By degrees, the populousness of this encampment began to produce its inconveniences. The immense droves of horses, owned by the Indians, consumed the herbage of the surrounding hills; while, to drive them to any distant pasturage, in a neighborhood abounding with lurking and deadly enemies, would be to endanger the loss, both of man and beast. Game, too, began to grow scarce. It was soon hunted and frightened out of the vicinity, and though the Indians made a wide circuit through the mountains, in the hope of driving the buffalo towards the cantonment, their expedition was unsuccessful. It was plain that so large a party could not subsist themselves there, nor in any one place, throughout the winter. Captain Bonneville, therefore, altered his whole arrangements. He detached fifty men towards the south, to winter upon Snake River, and to trap about its waters in the spring, with orders to rejoin him in the month of July, at Horse Creek, in Green River valley, which he had fixed upon as the general rendezvous of his company for the ensuing year.

Of all his late party, he now retained with him merely a small number of free trappers, with whom he intended to sojourn among the Nez Percés and Flatheads, and adopt the Indian mode of moving with the game and grass. Those bands, in effect, shortly afterwards broke up their encampments and set off for a less beaten neighborhood. Captain

Bonneville remained behind for a few days, that he might se-cretly prepare *caches*, in which to deposit every thing not re-quired for current use. Thus lightened of all superfluous incumbrance, he set off on the 20th of November to rejoin his Indian allies. He found them encamped in a secluded part of the country, at the head of a small stream. Considering them-selves out of all danger in this sequestered spot, from their old enemies, the Blackfeet, their encampment manifested the most negligent security. Their lodges were scattered in every direction, and their horses covered every hill for a great dis-tance round, grazing upon the upland bunch grass, which grew in great abundance, and though dry, retained its nutri-tious properties, instead of losing them, like other grasses, in the autumn.

When the Nez Percés, Flatheads, and Pends Oreilles are en-camped in a dangerous neighborhood, says Captain Bon-neville, the greatest care is taken of their horses, those prime articles of Indian wealth, and objects of Indian depredation. Each warrior has his horse tied by one foot at night, to a stake planted before his lodge. Here they remain until broad day-light; by that time, the young men of the camp are already ranging over the surrounding hills. Each family then drives its horses to some eligible spot, where they are left to graze un-attended. A young Indian repairs occasionally to the pasture, to give them water, and to see that all is well. So accustomed are the horses to this management, that they keep together in the pasture where they have been left. As the sun sinks behind the hills, they may be seen moving from all points towards the camp, where they surrender themselves, to be tied up for the night. Even in situations of danger, the Indians rarely set guards over their camp at night, intrusting that office entirely to their vigilant and well trained dogs.

In an encampment, however, of such fancied security as that in which Captain Bonneville found his Indian friends, much of these precautions with respect to their horses are omitted. They merely drive them, at nightfall, to some sequestered little dell, and leave them there, at perfect liberty, until the morning.

One object of Captain Bonneville in wintering among these Indians, was to procure a supply of horses against the spring.

They were, however, extremely unwilling to part with any, and it was with great difficulty that he purchased, at the rate of twenty dollars each, a few for the use of some of his free trappers, who were on foot, and dependant on him for their equipment.

In this encampment, Captain Bonneville remained from the 21st of November to the 9th of December. During this period, the thermometer ranged from thirteen to forty-two degrees. There were occasional falls of snow; but it generally melted away almost immediately, and the tender blades of new grass began to shoot up among the old. On the 7th of December, however, the thermometer fell to seven degrees.

The reader will recollect that, on distributing his forces, when in Green River valley, Captain Bonneville had detached a party, headed by a leader of the name of Matthieu, with all the weak and disabled horses, to sojourn about Bear River, meet the Shoshonie bands, and afterwards to rejoin him at his winter camp on Salmon River.

More than sufficient time had elapsed, yet Matthieu failed to make his appearance, and uneasiness began to be felt on his account. Captain Bonneville sent out four men, to range the country through which he would have to pass, and endeavor to get some information concerning him; for his route lay across the great Snake River plain, which spreads itself out like an Arabian desert, and on which a cavalcade could be descried at a great distance. The scouts soon returned, having proceeded no further than the edge of the plain; pretending that their horses were lame, but it was evident they had feared to venture, with so small a force, into these exposed and dangerous regions.

A disease, which Captain Bonneville supposed to be pneumonia, now appeared among the Indians, carrying off numbers of them, after an illness of three or four days. The worthy captain acted as physician, prescribing profuse sweatings and copious breedings, and uniformly with success, if the patient was subsequently treated with proper care. In extraordinary cases, the poor savages called in the aid of their own doctors or conjurors, who officiated with great noise and mummery, but with little benefit. Those who died during this epidemic, were buried in graves, after the manner of the whites, but without any regard to the direction of the head. It is a fact worthy of notice, that, while this malady made such ravages among the natives, not a single white man had the slightest symptom of it.

A familiar intercourse of some standing with the Pierced-nose and Flathead Indians, had now convinced Captain Bonneville of their amicable and inoffensive character; he began to take a strong interest in them, and conceived the idea of becoming a pacificator, and healing the deadly feud between them and the Blackfeet, in which they were so deplorably the sufferers. He proposed the matter to some of the leaders, and urged that they should meet the Blackfeet chiefs in a grand pacific conference, offering to send two of his men to the enemy's camp with pipe, tobacco, and flag of truce, to negotiate the proposed meeting.

The Nez Percés and Flathead sages, upon this, held a council of war of two days duration, in which there was abundance of hard smoking and long talking, and both eloquence and tobacco were nearly exhausted. At length they came to a decision to reject the worthy captain's proposition, and upon pretty substantial grounds, as the reader may judge.

"War," said the chiefs, "is a bloody business, and full of evil; but it keeps the eyes of the chiefs always open, and makes the limbs of the young men strong and supple. In war, every one is on the alert. If we see a trail, we know it must be an enemy; if the Blackfeet come to us, we know it is for war, and we are ready. Peace, on the other hand, sounds no alarm; the eyes of the chiefs are closed in sleep, and the young men are sleek and lazy. The horses stray into the mountains; the women and their little babes go about alone. But the heart of a Blackfoot is a lie, and his tongue is a trap. If he says peace, it is to deceive; he comes to us as a brother: he smokes his pipe with us; but when he sees us weak, and off of our guard, he will slay and steal. We will have no such peace; let there be war!"

With this reasoning, Captain Bonneville was fain to acquiesce; but, since the sagacious Flatheads and their allies were content to remain in a state of warfare, he wished them, at least, to exercise the boasted vigilance which war was to produce, and to keep their eyes open. He represented to them the impossibility, that two such considerable clans could move about the country without leaving trails by which they might be traced. Besides, among the Blackfeet braves were several Nez Percés, who had been taken prisoners in early youth, adopted by their captors, and trained up and imbued with warlike and predatory notions; these had lost all sympathies with their native tribe, and would be prone to lead the enemy to their secret haunts. He exhorted them, therefore, to keep upon the alert, and never to remit their vigilance, while within the range of so crafty and cruel a foe. All these counsels were lost upon his easy and simple minded hearers. A careless indifference reigned throughout their encampments, and their horses were permitted to range the hills at night in perfect freedom. Captain Bonneville had his own horses brought in at night, and properly picketed and guarded. The evil he apprehended soon took place. In a single night, a swoop was made through the neighboring pastures by the Blackfeet, and eighty-six of the finest horses carried off. A whip and a rope were left in a conspicuous situation by the robbers, as a taunt to the simpletons they had unhorsed.

Long before sunrise, the news of this calamity spread like wildfire through the different encampments. Captain Bonneville, whose own horses remained safe at their pickets, watched in momentary expectation of an outbreak of warriors, Pierced-nose and Flathead, in furious pursuit of the marauders; but no such thing—they contented themselves with searching diligently over hill and dale, to glean up such horses as had escaped the hands of the marauders, and then resigned themselves to their loss with the most exemplary quiescence.

Some, it is true, who were entirely unhorsed, set out on a begging visit to their cousins, as they call them, the Lower Nez Percés, who inhabit the lower country about the Columbia, and possess horses in abundance. To these they repair when in difficulty, and seldom fail, by dint of begging and bartering, to get themselves once more mounted on horseback.

Game had now become scarce in the neighborhood of the camp, and it was necessary, according to Indian custom, to move off to a less beaten ground. Captain Bonneville proposed the Horse Prairie; but his Indian friends objected, that many of the Nez Percés had gone to visit their cousins, and that the whites were few in number, so that their united force was not sufficient to venture upon the buffalo grounds, which were infested by bands of Blackfeet.

They now spoke of a place at no great distance, which they represented as a perfect hunter's elysium. It was on the right branch, or head stream of the river, locked up among cliffs and precipices, where there was no danger from roving bands, and where the Blackfeet dare not enter. Here, they said, the elk abounded, and the mountain sheep were to be seen trooping upon the rocks and hills. A little distance beyond it, also, herds of buffalo were to be met with, out of the range of danger. Thither they proposed to move their camp.

The proposition pleased the captain, who was desirous, through the Indians, of becoming acquainted with all the secret places of the land. Accordingly, on the 9th of December, they struck their tents, and moved forward by short stages, as many of the Indians were yet feeble from the late malady.

Following up the right fork of the river, they came to where it entered a deep gorge of the mountains, up which, lay the secluded region so much vaunted by the Indians. Captain Bonneville halted, and encamped for three days, before entering the gorge. In the meantime, he detached five of his free trappers to scour the hills and kill as many elk as possible, before the main body should enter, as they would then be soon frightened away by the various Indian hunting parties.

While thus encamped, they were still liable to the marauds of the Blackfeet, and Captain Bonneville admonished his Indian friends to be upon their guard. The Nez Percés, however, notwithstanding their recent loss, were still careless of their horses; merely driving them to some secluded spot, and leaving them there for the night, without setting any guard upon them. The consequence was a second swoop, in which forty-one were carried off. This was borne with equal philosophy with the first, and no effort was made either to recover the horses, or to take vengeance on the thieves.

The Nez Percáes, however, grew more cautious with respect to their remaining horses, driving them regularly to the camp every evening, and fastening them to pickets. Captain Bonneville, however, told them that this was not enough. It was evident they were dogged by a daring and persevering enemy, who was encouraged by past impunity; they should, therefore, take more than usual precautions, and post a guard at night over their cavalry. They could not, however, be persuaded to depart from their usual custom. The horse once picketed, the care of the owner was over for the night, and he slept profoundly. None waked in the camp but the gamblers, who, absorbed in their play, were more difficult to be roused to external circumstances than even the sleepers.

The Blackfeet are bold enemies, and fond of hazardous exploits. The band that were hovering about the neighborhood, finding they had such pacific people to deal with, redoubled their daring. The horses being now picketed before the lodges, a number of Blackfeet scouts penetrated in the early part of the night, into the very centre of the camp. Here they went about among the lodges, as calmly and deliberately as if at home, quietly cutting loose the horses that stood picketed by the lodges of their sleeping owners. One of these prowlers, more adventurous than the rest, approached a fire, round which a group of Nez Percés were gambling with the most intense eagerness. Here he stood for some time, muffled up in his robe, peering over the shoulders of the players, watching the changes of their countenances and the fluctuations of the game. So completely engrossed were they, that the presence of this muffled eavesdropper was unnoticed, and having executed his bravado, he retired undiscovered.

Having cut loose as many horses as they could conveniently carry off, the Blackfeet scouts rejoined their comrades, and all remained patiently round the camp. By degrees, the horses, finding themselves at liberty, took their route towards their customary grazing ground. As they emerged from the camp, they were silently taken possession of, until, having secured about thirty, the Blackfeet sprang on their backs and scampered off. The clatter of hoofs startled the gamblers from their game. They gave the alarm, which soon roused the sleepers from every lodge. Still all was quiescent; no marshalling of forces, no saddling of steed and dashing off in pursuit, no talk of retribution for their repeated outrages. The patience of Captain Bonneville was at length exhausted. He had played the part of a pacificator without success; he now altered his tone, and resolved, if possible, to rouse their war spirit.

Accordingly, convoking their chiefs, he inveighed against their craven policy, and urged the necessity of vigorous and retributive measures, that would check the confidence and presumption of their enemies, if not inspire them with awe. For this purpose, he advised that a war party should be immediately sent off on the trail of the marauders, to follow them, if necessary, into the very heart of the Blackfoot country, and not to leave them until they had taken signal vengeance. Beside this, he recommended the organization of minor war parties, to make reprisals to the extent of the losses sustained. "Unless you rouse yourselves from your apathy," said he, "and strike some bold and decisive blow, you will cease to be considered men, or objects of manly warfare. The very squaws and children of the Blackfeet will be sent against you, while their warriors reserve themselves for nobler antagonists."

This harangue had evidently a momentary effect upon the pride of the hearers. After a short pause, however, one of the orators arose. It was bad, he said, to go to war for mere revenge. The Great Spirit had given them a heart for peace, not for war. They had lost horses, it was true, but they could easily get others from their cousins, the Lower Nez Percés, without incurring any risk; whereas, in war they should lose men, who were not so readily replaced. As to their late losses, an increased watchfulness would prevent any more misfortunes of the kind. He disapproved, therefore, of all hostile measures; and all the other chiefs concurred in his opinion.

Captain Bonneville again took up the point. "It is true," said he, "the Great Spirit has given you a heart to love your friends; but he has also given you an arm to strike your enemies. Unless you do something speedily to put an end to this continual plundering, I must say farewell. As yet, I have sustained no loss; thanks to the precautions which you have slighted: but my property is too unsafe here; my turn will come next; I and my people will share the contempt you are bringing upon yourselves, and will be thought, like you, poor-spirited beings, who may at any time be plundered with impunity."

The conference broke up with some signs of excitement on the part of the Indians. Early the next morning, a party of thirty men set off in pursuit of the foe, and Captain Bonneville hoped to hear a good account of the Blackfeet marauders. To his disappointment, the war party came lagging back on the following day, leading a few old, sorry, broken-down horses, which the freebooters had not been able to urge to sufficient speed. This effort exhausted the martial spirit, and satisfied the wounded pride of the Nez Percés, and they relapsed into their usual state of passive indifference.

Chapter XIII

Story of Kosato, the Renegade Blackfoot

IF THE MEEKNESS and longsuffering of the Pierced-noses grieved the spirit of Captain Bonneville, there was another individual in the camp, to whom they were still more annoying. This was a Blackfoot renegado, named Kosato, a fiery, hot-blooded youth, who, with a beautiful girl of the same tribe, had taken refuge among the Nez Percés. Though adopted into the tribe, he still retained the warlike spirit of his race, and loathed the peaceful, inoffensive habits of those around him. The hunting of the deer, the elk, and the buffalo, which was the height of their ambition, was too tame to satisfy his wild and restless nature. His heart burned for the foray, the ambush, the skirmish, the scamper, and all the haps and hazards of roving and predatory warfare.

The recent hoverings of the Blackfeet about the camp, their nightly prowls, and daring and successful marauds, had kept him in a fever and a flutter; like a hawk in a cage, who hears his late companions swooping and screaming in wild liberty above him. The attempt of Captain Bonneville to rouse the war spirit of the Nez Percés, and prompt them to retaliation, was ardently seconded by Kosato. For several days he was incessantly devising schemes of vengeance, and endeavoring to set on foot an expedition that should carry dismay and desolation into the Blackfeet towns. All his art was exerted to touch upon those springs of human action with which he was most familiar. He drew the listening savages around him by his nervous eloquence; taunted them with recitals of past wrongs and insults; drew glowing pictures of triumphs and trophies within their reach; recounted tales of daring and romantic enterprise; of secret marchings; covert lurkings; midnight surprisals; sackings, burnings, plunderings, scalpings: together with the triumphant return, and the feasting and rejoicing of the victors. These wild tales were intermingled with the beating of the drum; the yell, the war-whoop and the war-dance, so inspiring to Indian valor. All, however, were lost upon the peaceful spirits of his hearers: not a Nez Percé was to be roused to vengeance, or stimulated to glorious war. In the bitterness of his heart, the Blackfoot renegado repined at the mishap which had severed him from a race of congenial spirits, and driven him to take refuge among beings so destitute of martial fire.

The character and conduct of this man attracted the attention of Captain Bonneville, and he was anxious to hear the reason why he had deserted his tribe, and why he looked back upon them with such deadly hostility. Kosato told him his own story briefly:—it gives a picture of the deep, strong passions that work in the bosoms of these miscalled stoics.

"You see my wife," said he: "she is good; she is beautiful— I love her.—Yet, she has been the cause of all my troubles. She was the wife of my chief. I loved her more than he did; and she knew it. We talked together; we laughed together: we were always seeking each other's society; but we were as innocent as children. The chief grew jealous, and commanded her to speak with me no more. His heart became hard toward her; his jealousy grew more furious. He beat her without cause and without mercy; and threatened to kill her outright if she even looked at me. Do you want traces of his fury? Look at that scar! His rage against me was no less persecuting. War parties of the Crows were hovering round us; our young men had seen their trail. All hearts were roused for action; my horses were before my lodge. Suddenly the chief came, took them to his own pickets, and called them his own. What could I do?—he was a chief. I durst not speak, but my heart was burning. I joined no longer in the council, the hunt, or the war-feast. What had I to do there? an unhorsed, degraded warrior. I kept by myself, and thought of nothing but these wrongs and outrages.

"I was sitting one evening upon a knoll that overlooked the meadow where the horses were pastured. I saw the horses that were once mine grazing among those of the chief. This maddened me, and I sat brooding for a time over the injuries I had suffered, and the cruelties which she I loved had endured for my sake, until my heart swelled and grew sore, and my teeth were clenched. As I looked down upon the meadow, I saw the chief walking among his horses. I fastened my eyes on him as a hawk's; my blood boiled; I drew my breath hard.

He went among the willows. In an instant I was on my feet; my hand was on my knife—I flew rather than ran—before he was aware, I sprang upon him, and with two blows laid him dead at my feet. I covered his body with earth, and strewed bushes over the place; then hastened to her I loved, told her what I had done, and urged her to fly with me. She only answered me with tears. I reminded her of the wrongs I had suffered, and of the blows and stripes she had endured from the deceased; I had done nothing but an act of justice. I again urged her to fly; but she only wept the more, and bade me go. My heart was heavy, but my eyes were dry. I folded my arms. ' 'Tis well,' said I; 'Kosato will go alone to the desert. None will be with him but the wild beasts of the desert. The seekers of blood may follow on his trail. They may come upon him when he sleeps, and glut their revenge; but you will be safe. Kosato will go alone.'

"I turned away. She sprang after me, and strained me in her arms. 'No,' cried she, 'Kosato shall not go alone! Wherever he goes, I will go—he shall never part from me.'

"We hastily took in our hands such things as we most needed, and stealing quietly from the village, mounted the first horses we encountered. Speeding day and night, we soon reached this tribe. They received us with welcome, and we have dwelt with them in peace. They are good and kind; they are honest; but their hearts are the hearts of women."

Such was the story of Kosato, as related by him to Captain Bonneville. It is of a kind that often occurs in Indian life; where love elopements from tribe to tribe are as frequent as among the novel-read heroes and heroines of sentimental civilization, and often give rise to bloody and lasting feuds.

Chapter XIV

O N THE 19TH of December, Captain Bonneville and his confederate Indians, raised their camp, and entered the narrow gorge made by the north fork of Salmon River. Up this lay the secure and plenteous hunting region so temptingly described by the Indians.

Since leaving Green River, the plains had invariably been of loose sand or coarse gravel, and the rocky formation of the mountains of primitive limestone. The rivers, in general, were skirted with willows and bitter cotton-wood trees, and the prairies covered with wormwood. In the hollow breast of the mountains which they were now penetrating, the surrounding heights were clothed with pine; while the declivities of the lower hills afforded abundance of bunch grass for the horses.

As the Indians had represented, they were now in a natural fastness of the mountains, the ingress and egress of which was by a deep gorge, so narrow, rugged, and difficult, as to prevent secret approach or rapid retreat, and to admit of easy defence. The Blackfeet, therefore, refrained from venturing in after the Nez Percés, awaiting a better chance, when they should once more emerge into the open country.

Captain Bonneville soon found that the Indians had not exaggerated the advantages of this region. Beside numerous gangs of elk, large flocks of the ahsahta or bighorn, the mountain sheep, were to be seen bounding among the precipices. These simple animals were easily circumvented and destroyed. A few hunters may surround a flock and kill as many as they please. Numbers were daily brought into camp, and the flesh of those which were young and fat, was extolled as superior to the finest mutton.

Here, then, there was a cessation from toil, from hunger, and alarm. Past ills and dangers were forgotten. The hunt, the game, the song, the story, the rough though good-humored joke, made time pass joyously away, and plenty and security reigned throughout the camp.

Idleness and ease, it is said, lead to love, and love to matrimony, in civilized life, and the same process takes place in the wilderness. Filled with good cheer and mountain mutton, one of the free trappers began to repine at the solitude of his lodge, and to experience the force of that great law of nature, "it is not meet for man to live alone."

After a night of grave cogitation, he repaired to Kowsoter, the Pierced-nose chief; and unfolded to him the secret workings of his bosom.

"I want," said he, "a wife. Give me one from among your tribe. Not a young, giddy-pated girl, that will think of nothing but flaunting and finery, but a sober, discreet, hard-working squaw; one that will share my lot without flinching, however hard it may be; that can take care of my lodge, and be a companion and a helpmate to me in the wilderness." Kowsoter promised to look round among the females of his tribe, and procure such a one as he desired. Two days were requisite for the search. At the expiration of these, Kowsoter called at his lodge, and informed him that he would bring his bride to him in the course of the afternoon. He kept his word. At the appointed time he approached, leading the bride, a comely copper-colored dame, attired in her Indian finery. Her father, mother, brothers by the half dozen, and cousins by the score, all followed on to grace the ceremony, and greet the new and important relative.

The trapper received his new and numerous family connexion with proper solemnity; he placed his bride beside him, and, filling the pipe, the great symbol of peace, with his best tobacco, took two or three whiffs, then handed it to the chief, who transferred it to the father of the bride, from whom it was passed on from hand to hand and mouth to mouth of the whole circle of kinsmen round the fire; all maintaining the most profound and becoming silence.

After several pipes had been filled and emptied in this solemn ceremonial, the chief addressed the bride; detailing, at considerable length, the duties of a wife; which, among Indians, are little less onerous than those of the packhorse; this done, he turned to her friends, and congratulated them upon the great alliance she had made. They showed a due sense of their good fortune, especially when the nuptial presents came to be distributed among the chiefs and relatives, amounting to about one hundred and eighty dollars. The company soon retired, and now the worthy trapper found, indeed, that he had no green girl to deal with; for the knowing dame at once assumed the style and dignity of a trapper's wife, taking possession of the lodge as her undisputed empire; arranging every thing according to her own taste and habitudes; and appearing as much at home, and on as easy terms with the trapper, as if they had been man and wife for years.

We have already given a picture of a free trapper and his horse, as furnished by Captain Bonneville: we shall here subjoin, as a companion picture, his description of a free trapper's wife, that the reader may have a correct idea of the kind of blessing the worthy hunter in question had invoked to solace him in the wilderness.

"The free trapper, while a bachelor, has no greater pet than his horse; but the moment he takes a wife, (a sort of brevet rank in matrimony occasionally bestowed upon some Indian fair one, like the heroes of ancient chivalry, in the open field,) he discovers that he has a still more fanciful and capricious animal on which to lavish his expenses.

"No sooner does an Indian belle experience this promotion, than all her notions at once rise and expand to the dignity of her situation; and the purse of her lover, and his credit into the bargain, are tasked to the utmost to fit her out in becoming style. The wife of a free trapper to be equipped and arrayed like any ordinary and undistinguished squaw? Perish the grovelling thought! In the first place, she must have a horse for her own riding; but no jaded, sorry, earth-spirited hack; such as is sometimes assigned by an Indian husband for the transportation of his squaw and her papooses: the wife of a free trapper must have the most beautiful animal she can lay her eyes on. And then, as to his decoration: headstall, breastbands, saddle and crupper, are lavishly embroidered with beads, and hung with thimbles, hawks' bells, and bunches of ribands. From each side of the saddle hangs an *esquimoot*, a sort of pocket, in which she bestows the residue of her trinkets and nicknacks, which cannot be crowded on the decoration of her horse or herself. Over this she folds with great care, a drapery of scarlet and bright-colored calicoes, and now considers the caparison of her steed complete.

"As to her own person, she is even still more extravagant. Her hair, esteemed beautiful in proportion to its length, is carefully plaited, and made to fall with seeming negligence over either breast. Her riding hat is stuck full of party-colored feathers; her robe, fashioned somewhat after that of the whites, is of red, green, and sometimes gray cloth, but always of the finest texture that can be procured. Her leggins and moccasins are of the most beautiful and expensive workmanship, and, fitting neatly to the foot and ankle, which, with the Indian women are generally well formed and delicate, look extremely pretty. Then as to jewelry: in the way of finger-rings, ear-rings, necklaces, and other female glories, nothing within reach of the trapper's means is omitted, that can tend to impress the beholder with an idea of the lady's high estate. To finish the whole, she selects from among her blankets of various dyes, one of some glowing color, and throwing it over her shoulders with a native grace, vaults into the saddle of her gay prancing steed, and is ready to follow her mountaineer 'to the last gasp with love and loyalty.'"

Such is the general picture of the free trapper's wife, given by Captain Bonneville; how far it applied in its details to the one in question, does not altogether appear, though it would seem from the outset of her connubial career, that she was ready to avail herself of all the pomp and circumstance of her new condition. It is worthy of mention, that wherever there are several wives of free trappers in a camp, the keenest rivalry exists between them, to the sore detriment of their husbands' purses. Their whole time is expended, and their ingenuity tasked by endeavors to eclipse each other in dress and decoration. The jealousies and heartburnings thus occasioned among these, so styled, children of nature, are equally intense with those of the rival leaders of style and fashion in the luxurious abodes of civilized life.

The genial festival of Christmas, which throughout all Christendom lights up the fireside of home with mirth and jollity, followed hard upon the wedding just described. Though far from kindred and friends, Captain Bonneville and his hand-ful of free trappers were not disposed to suffer the festival to pass unenjoyed; they were in a region of good cheer, and were disposed to be joyous; so it was determined to "light up the yule clog," and celebrate a merry Christmas in the heart of the wilderness.

On Christmas-eve, accordingly, they began their rude fêtes and rejoicings. In the course of the night, the free trappers surrounded the lodge of the Pierced-nose chief, and in lieu of Christmas carols, saluted him with a *feu de joie*.

Kowsoter received it in a truly Christian spirit, and after a speech, in which he expressed his high gratification at the honor done him, invited the whole company to a feast on the following day. His invitation was glady accepted. A Christmas dinner in the wigwam of an Indian chief! There was novelty in the idea. Not one failed to be present. The banquet was served up in primitive style: skins of various kinds, nicely dressed for the occasion, were spread upon the ground; upon these were heaped up abundance of venison, elk meat, and mountain mutton; with various bitter roots, which the Indians use as condiments.

After a short prayer, the company all seated themselves crosslegged, in Turkish fashion, to the banquet, which passed off with great hilarity. After which, various games of strength and agility, by both white men and Indians, closed the Christmas festivities.

Chapter XV

A hunt after hunters—Hungry times—A voracious repast—
Wintry weather—Godin's River—Splendid winter scene on
the great lava plain of Snake River—Severe travelling and
tramping in the snow—Manœuvres of a solitary Indian
horseman—Encampment on Snake River—Banneck In-
dians—The Horse chief—His charmed life

THE CONTINUED absence of Matthieu and his party had, by this time, caused great uneasiness in the mind of Captain Bonneville; and, finding there was no dependance to be placed upon the perseverance and courage of scouting parties, in so perilous a quest, he determined to set out himself on the search, and to keep on until he should ascertain something of the object of his solicitude.

Accordingly, on the 26th December he left the camp, accompanied by thirteen stark trappers and hunters, all well mounted and armed for dangerous enterprise. On the following morning they passed out at the head of the mountain gorge, and sallied forth into the open plain. As they confidently expected a brush with the Blackfeet, or some other predatory horde, they moved with great circumspection, and kept vigilant watch in their encampments.

In the course of another day they left the main branch of Salmon River, and proceeded south towards a pass called John Day's Defile. It was severe and arduous travelling. The plains were swept by keen and bitter blasts of wintry wind; the ground was generally covered with snow, game was scarce, so that hunger generally prevailed in the camp, while the want of pasturage soon began to manifest itself in the declining vigor of the horses.

The party had scarcely encamped on the afternoon of the 28th, when two of the hunters who had sallied forth in quest of game came galloping back in great alarm. While hunting they had perceived a party of savages, evidently manœuvring to cut them off from the camp; and nothing had saved them from being entrapped but the speed of their horses.

These tidings struck dismay into the camp. Captain Bonneville endeavored to reassure his men by representing the position of their encampment, and its capability of defence. He then ordered the horses to be driven in and picketed, and threw up a rough breastwork of fallen trunks of trees, and the vegetable rubbish of the wilderness. Within this barrier was maintained a vigilant watch throughout the night, which passed away without alarm. At early dawn they scrutinized the surrounding plain, to discover whether any enemies had been lurking about during the night: not a foot print, however, was to be discovered in the coarse gravel with which the plain was covered.

Hunger now began to cause more uneasiness than the apprehensions of surrounding enemies. After marching a few miles they encamped at the foot of a mountain, in hopes of finding buffalo. It was not until the next day that they discovered a pair of fine bulls on the edge of the plain, among rocks and ravines. Having now been two days and a half without a mouthful of food, they took especial care that these animals should not escape them. While some of the surest marksmen advanced cautiously with their rifles into the rough ground, four of the best mounted horsemen took their stations in the plain, to run the bulls down should they only be maimed.

The buffalo were wounded, and set off in headlong flight. The half-famished horses were too weak to overtake them on the frozen ground, but succeeded in driving them on the ice, where they slipped and fell, and were easily despatched. The hunters loaded themselves with beef for present and future supply, and then returned and encamped at the last night's fire. Here they passed the remainder of the day, cooking and eating with a voracity proportioned to previous starvation; forgetting in the hearty revel of the moment, the certain dangers with which they were environed.

The cravings of hunger being satisfied, they now began to debate about their further progress. The men were much disheartened by the hardships they had already endured. Indeed, two who had been in the rear guard, taking advantage of their position, had deserted and returned to the lodges of the Nez Percés. The prospect ahead was enough to stagger the stoutest heart. They were in the dead of winter. As far as the eye could reach the wild landscape was wrapped in snow; which was evidently deepening as they advanced. Over this they would have to toil, with the icy wind blowing in their faces: their horses might give out through want of pasturage; and they themselves must expect intervals of horrible famine like that they had already experienced.

With Captain Bonneville, however, perseverance was a matter of pride; and having undertaken this enterprise, nothing could turn him back until it was accomplished: though he declares that, had he anticipated the difficulties and sufferings which attended it, he should have flinched from the undertaking.

Onward, therefore, the little band urged their way, keeping along the course of a stream called John Day's Creek. The cold was so intense that they had frequently to dismount and travel on foot, lest they should freeze in their saddles. The days, which, at this season, are short enough even in the open prairies, were narrowed to a few hours by the high mountains, which allowed the travellers but a brief enjoyment of the cheering rays of the sun. The snow was, generally, at least twenty inches in depth, and in many places much more: those who dismounted had to beat their way with toilsome steps. Eight miles were considered a good day's journey. The horses were almost famished; for the herbage was covered by the deep snow, so that they had nothing to subsist upon but scanty whisps of the dry bunch grass which peered above the surface, and the small branches and twigs of frozen willows and wormwood.

In this way they urged their slow and painful course to the south, down John Day's Creek, until it lost itself in a swamp. Here they encamped upon the ice among stiffened willows, where they were obliged to beat down and clear away the snow to procure pasturage for their horses.

Hence, they toiled on to Godin's River; so called after an Iroquois hunter in the service of Sublette; who was murdered there by the Blackfeet. Many of the features of this remote wilderness are thus named after scenes of violence and bloodshed that occurred to the early pioneers. It was an act of filial vengeance on the part of Godin's son, Antoine, that, as the reader may recollect, brought on the recent battle at Pierre's Hole.

From Godin's River Captain Bonneville and his followers came out upon the plain of the Three Butes; so called from three singular and isolated hills that rise from the midst. It is a part of the great desert of Snake River, one of the most remarkable tracts beyond the mountains. Could they have experienced a respite from their sufferings and anxieties, the immense landscape spread out before them was calculated to inspire admiration. Winter has its beauties and glories, as well as summer; and Captain Bonneville had the soul to appreciate them.

Far away, says he, over the vast plains, and up the steep sides of the lofty mountains, the snow lay spread in dazzling whiteness: and whenever the sun emerged in the morning above the giant peaks, or burst forth from among clouds in his mid-day course, mountain and dell, glazed rock and frosted tree, glowed and sparkled with surpassing lustre. The tall pines seemed sprinkled with a silver dust, and the willows, studded with minute icicles reflecting the prismatic rays, brought to mind the fairy trees conjured up by the caliph's story-teller, to adorn his vale of diamonds.

The poor wanderers, however, nearly starved with hunger and cold, were in no mood to enjoy the glories of these brilliant scenes; though they stamped pictures on their memory, which have been recalled with delight in more genial situations.

Encamping at the west Bute, they found a place swept by the winds, so that it was bare of snow, and there was abundance of bunch grass. Here the horses were turned loose to graze throughout the night. Though for once they had ample pasturage, yet the keen winds were so intense, that, in the morning, a mule was found frozen to death. The trappers gathered round and mourned over him as over a cherished friend. They feared their half-famished horses would soon share his fate, for there seemed scarce blood enough left in their veins to withstand the freezing cold. To beat the way further through the snow with these enfeebled animals, seemed next to impossible; and despondency began to creep over their hearts, when, fortunately, they discovered a trail made by some hunting party.

Into this they immediately entered, and proceeded with less difficulty. Shortly afterward, a fine buffalo bull came bounding across the snow, and was instantly brought down by the hunters. A fire was soon blazing and crackling, and an ample repast soon cooked, and sooner despatched, after which, they made some further progress and then encamped. One of the men reached the camp nearly frozen to death; but good cheer and a blazing fire gradually restored life, and put his blood in circulation.

Having now a beaten path, they proceeded the next morning with more facility; indeed, the snow decreased in depth as they receded from the mountains, and the temperature became more mild. In the course of the day, they discovered a solitary horseman hovering at a distance before them on the plain. They spurred on to overtake him; but he was better mounted on a fresher steed, and kept at a wary distance, reconnoitring them with evident distrust: for the wild dress of the free trappers, their leggins, blankets, and cloth caps garnished with fur and topped off with feathers; even their very elflocks and weather-bronzed complexions, gave them the look of Indians rather than white men, and made him mistake them for a war party of some hostile tribe.

After much manoeuvring, the wild horseman was at length brought to a parley; but even then he conducted himself with the caution of a knowing prowler of the prairies. Dismounting from his horse, and using him as a breastwork, he levelled his gun across his back, and, thus prepared for defence, like a wary cruiser upon the high seas, he permitted himself to be approached within speaking distance.

He proved to be an Indian of the Banneck tribe, belonging to a band at no great distance. It was some time before he could be persuaded that he was conversing with a party of white men, and induced to lay aside his reserve and join them. He then gave them the interesting intelligence, that there were two companies of white men encamped in the neighborhood. This was cheering news to Captain Bonneville; who hoped to find in one of them the long sought party of Matthieu. Pushing forward, therefore, with renovated spirits, he reached Snake River by nightfall and there fixed his encampment.

Early the next morning (13th January, 1833), diligent search was made about the neighborhood for traces of the reported parties of white men. An encampment was soon discovered, about four miles further up the river; in which Captain Bonneville, to his great joy, found two of Matthieu's men, from whom he learnt that the rest of his party would be there in the course of a few days. It was a matter of great pride and self-gratulation to Captain Bonneville, that he had thus accomplished his dreary and doubtful enterprise; and he determined to pass some time in this encampment, both to await the return of Matthieu, and to give needful repose to men and horses.

It was, in fact, one of the most eligible and delightful wintering grounds in that whole range of country. The Snake River here wound its devious way between low banks through the great plain of the Three Butes; and was bordered by wide and fertile meadows. It was studded with islands, which, like the alluvial bottoms, were covered with groves of cotton-wood, thickets of willow, tracts of good lowland grass, and abundance of green rushes. The adjacent plains, were so vast in extent, that no single band of Indians could drive the buffalo out of them; nor was the snow of sufficient depth to give any serious inconvenience. Indeed, during the sojourn of Captain Bonneville in this neighborhood, which was in the heart of winter, he found the weather, with the exception of a few cold and stormy days, generally mild and pleasant; freezing a little at night, but invariably thawing with the morning's sun—resembling the spring weather in the middle part of the United States.

The lofty range of the Three Tetons, those great landmarks of the Rocky Mountains, rising in the east, and circling away to the north and west of the great plain of Snake River; and the mountains of Salt River and Portneuf towards the south, catch the earliest falls of snow. Their white robes lengthen as the winter advances, and spread themselves far into the plain, driving the buffalo in herds to the banks of the river in quest of food; where they are easily slain in great numbers.

Such were the palpable advantages of this winter encampment; added to which, it was secure from the prowlings and plunderings of any petty band of roving Blackfeet: the difficulties of retreat rendering it unwise for those crafty depredators to venture an attack, unless with an overpowering force.

About ten miles below the encampment lay the Banneck Indians; numbering about one hundred and twenty lodges. They are brave and cunning warriors, and deadly foes of the Blackfeet; whom they easily overcome in battles where their forces are equal. They are not vengeful and enterprising in warfare, however; seldom sending war parties to attack the Blackfeet towns, but contenting themselves with defending their own territories and homes. About one-third of their warriors are armed with fusees; the rest with bows and arrows.

As soon as the spring opens, they move down the right bank of Snake River, and encamp at the heads of the Boisée and Payette. Here their horses wax fat on good pasturage, while the tribe revels in plenty upon the flesh of deer, elk, bear, and beaver. They then descend a little further, and are met by the Lower Nez Percés, with whom they trade for horses; giving in exchange beaver, buffalo, and buffalo robes. Hence they strike upon the tributary streams on the left bank of Snake River, and encamp at the rise of the Portneuf and Blackfoot streams, in the buffalo range. Their horses, although of the Nez Percé breed, are inferior to the parent stock, from being ridden at too early an age; being often bought when but two years old, and immediately put to hard work. They have fewer horses, also, than most of these migratory tribes.

At the time that Captain Bonneville came into the neighborhood of these Indians, they were all in mourning for their chief, surnamed The Horse. This chief was said to possess a charmed life, or rather, to be invulnerable to lead; no bullet having ever hit him, though he had been in repeated battles, and often shot at by the surest marksmen. He had shown great magnanimity in his intercourse with the white men. One of the great men of his family had been slain in an attack upon a band of trappers passing through the territories of his tribe. Vengeance had been sworn by the Bannecks; but The Horse interfered, declaring himself the friend of white men, and, having great influence and authority among his people, he compelled them to forego all vindictive plans, and to conduct themselves amicably whenever they came in contact with the traders.

This chief had bravely fallen in resisting an attack made by the Blackfeet upon his tribe, while encamped at the head of Godin's River. His fall in nowise lessened the faith of his people in his charmed life; for they declared that it was not a bullet which laid him low, but a bit of horn which had been shot into him by some Blackfoot marksman; aware, no doubt, of the inefficacy of lead. Since his death, there was no one with sufficient influence over the tribe to restrain the wild and predatory propensities of the young men. The consequence was, they had become troublesome and dangerous neighbors; openly friendly, for the sake of traffic, but disposed to commit secret depredations, and to molest any small party that might fall within their reach.

Chapter XVI

Misadventures of Matthieu and his party—Return to the caches at Salmon River—Battle between Nez Percés and Blackfeet—Heroism of a Nez Percé woman—Enrolled among the braves

O N THE 3D of February, Matthieu, with the residue of his band, arrived in camp. He had a disastrous story to relate. After parting with Captain Bonneville in Green River valley, he had proceeded to the westward, keeping to the north of the Eutaw Mountains, a spur of the great Rocky chain. Here he experienced the most rugged travelling for his horses, and soon discovered that there was but little chance of meeting the Shoshonie bands. He now proceeded along Bear River, a stream much frequented by trappers; intending to shape his course to Salmon River, to rejoin Captain Bonneville.

He was misled, however, either through the ignorance or treachery of an Indian guide, and conducted into a wild valley, where he lay encamped during the autumn and the early part of the winter, nearly buried in snow, and almost starved. Early in the season he detached five men, with nine horses, to proceed to the neighborhood of the Sheep Rock, on Bear River, where game was plenty, and there to procure a supply for the camp. They had not proceeded far on their expedition, when their trail was discovered by a party of nine or ten Indians, who immediately commenced a lurking pursuit, dogging them secretly for five or six days. So long as their encampments were well chosen, and a proper watch maintained, the wary savages kept aloof; at length, observing that they were badly encamped, in a situation where they might be approached with secrecy, the enemy crept stealthily along under cover of the river bank, preparing to burst suddenly upon their prey.

They had not advanced within striking distance, however, before they were discovered by one of the trappers. He immediately, but silently, gave the alarm to his companions. They all sprang upon their horses, and prepared to retreat to a safe position. One of the party, however, named Jennings, doubted the correctness of the alarm, and, before he mounted his horse, wanted to ascertain the fact. His companions urged him to mount, but in vain; he was incredulous and obstinate. A volley of fire-arms by the savages dispelled his doubts; but so overpowered his nerves, that he was unable to get into his saddle. His comrades, seeing his peril and confusion, generously leapt from their horses to protect him. A shot from a rifle brought him to the earth; in his agony, he called upon the others not to desert him. Two of them, Le Roy and Ross, after fighting desperately, were captured by the savages; the remaining two vaulted into their saddles, and saved themselves by headlong flight, being pursued for nearly thirty miles. They got safe back to Matthieu's camp, where their story inspired such dread of lurking Indians, that the hunters could not be prevailed upon to undertake another foray in quest of provisions. They remained, therefore, almost starving in their camp; now and then killing an old or disabled horse for food, while the elk and the mountain sheep roamed unmolested among the surrounding mountains.

The disastrous surprisal of this hunting party, is cited by Captain Bonneville to show the importance of vigilant watching and judicious encampments in the Indian country. Most of these kind of disasters to traders and trappers arise from some careless inattention to the state of their arms and ammunition, the placing of their horses at night, the position of their camping ground, and the posting of their night watches. The Indian is a vigilant and crafty foe; by no means given to harebrained assaults; he seldom attacks when he finds his foe well prepared and on the alert. Caution is at least as efficacious a protection against him as courage.

The Indians who made this attack were at first supposed to be Blackfeet; until Captain Bonneville found, subsequently, in the camp of the Bannecks a horse, saddle, and bridle, which he recognised as having belonged to one of the hunters. The Bannecks, however, stoutly denied having taken these spoils in fight, and persisted in affirming that the outrage had been perpetrated by a Blackfoot band.

Captain Bonneville remained on Snake River nearly three weeks after the arrival of Matthieu and his party. At length, his horses having recovered strength sufficient for a journey, he prepared to return to the Nez Percés, or rather to visit his *caches* on Salmon River; that he might take thence goods and equipments for the opening season. Accordingly, leaving sixteen men at Snake River, he set out, on the 19th of February, with sixteen others, on his journey to the caches.

Fording the river, he proceeded to the borders of the deep snow, when he encamped under the lee of immense piles of burnt rock. On the 21st, he was again floundering through the snow, on the great Snake River plain, where it lay to the depth of thirty inches. It was sufficiently encrusted to bear a pedestrian; but the poor horses broke through the crust, and plunged and strained at every step. So lacerated were they by the ice, that it was necessary to change the front every hundred yards, and put a different one in the advance, to break the way. The open prairies were swept by a piercing and biting wind from the northwest. At night, they had to task their ingenuity to provide shelter and keep from freezing. In the first place, they dug deep holes in the snow, piling it up in ramparts to windward, as a protection against the blast. Beneath these, they spread buffalo skins; upon which they stretched themselves in full dress, with caps, cloaks, and moccasins, and covered themselves with numerous blankets; notwithstanding all which, they were often severely pinched with the cold.

On the 28th of February, they arrived on the banks of Godin's River. This stream emerges from the mountains opposite an eastern branch of the Malade River, running southeast, forms a deep and swift current about twenty yards wide, passing rapidly through a defile to which it gives its name, and then enters the great plain, where, after meandering about forty miles, it is finally lost in the region of the Burnt Rocks.

On the banks of this river, Captain Bonneville was so fortunate as to come upon a buffalo trail. Following it up, he entered the defile, where he remained encamped for two days, to allow the hunters time to kill and dry a supply of buffalo beef. In this sheltered defile, the weather was moderate, and grass was already sprouting more than an inch in height. There was abundance, too, of the salt weed; which grows most plentiful in clayey and gravelly barrens. It resembles penny-royal, and derives its name from a partial saltness. It is a nourishing food for the horses in the winter, but they reject it the moment the young grass affords sufficient pasturage.

On the 6th of March, having cured sufficient meat, the party resumed their march, and moved on with comparative ease, excepting where they had to make their way through snow drifts which had been piled up by the wind.

On the 11th, a small cloud of smoke was observed rising in a deep part of the defile. An encampment was instantly formed, and scouts were sent out to reconnoitre. They returned with intelligence that it was a hunting party of Flatheads, returning from the buffalo range laden with meat. Captain Bonneville joined them the next day, and persuaded them to proceed with his party a few miles below, to the caches, whither he proposed also to invite the Nez Percés, whom he hoped to find somewhere in this neighborhood. In fact, on the 13th, he was rejoined by that friendly tribe, who, since he separated from them on Salmon River, had likewise been out to hunt the buffalo, but had continued to be haunted and harassed by their old enemies the Blackfeet, who, as usual, had contrived to carry off many of their horses.

In the course of this hunting expedition, a small band of ten lodges separated from the main body, in search of better pasturage for their horses. About the 1st of March, the scattered parties of Blackfoot banditti united to the number of three hundred fighting men, and determined upon some signal blow. Proceeding to the former camping ground of the Nez Percés, they found the lodges deserted; upon which, they hid themselves among the willows and thickets, watching for some straggler, who might guide them to the present "whereabout" of their intended victims. As fortune would have it, Kosato, the Blackfoot renegado, was the first to pass along, accompanied by his blood-bought bride. He was on his way from the main body of hunters to the little band of ten lodges. The Blackfeet knew and marked him as he passed; he was within bowshot of their ambuscade; yet, much as they thirsted for his blood, they forebore to launch a shaft; sparing him for the moment, that he might lead them to their prey. Secretly following his trail, they discovered the lodges of the unfortunate Nez Percés, and assailed them with shouts and yellings. The Nez Percés numbered only twenty men, and but nine were armed with fusees. They showed themselves, however, as brave and skilful in war as they had been mild and longsuffering in peace.

Their first care was to dig holes inside of their lodges; thus ensconced, they fought desperately, laying several of the enemy dead upon the ground; while they, though some of them were wounded, lost not a single warrior.

During the heat of the battle, a woman of the Nez Percés, seeing her warrior badly wounded and unable to fight, seized his bow and arrows, and bravely and successfully defended his person, contributing to the safety of the whole party.

In another part of the field of action, a Nez Percé had crouched behind the trunk of a fallen tree, and kept up a galling fire from his covert. A Blackfoot seeing this, procured a round log, and placing it before him as he lay prostrate, rolled it forward towards the trunk of the tree behind which his enemy lay crouched. It was a moment of breathless interest: whoever first showed himself would be in danger of a shot. The Nez Percé put an end to the suspense. The moment the logs touched, he sprang upon his feet, and discharged the contents of his fusee into the back of his antagonist. By this time, the Blackfeet had got possession of the horses; several of their warriors lay dead on the field, and the Nez Percés, ensconced in their lodges, seemed resolved to defend themselves to the last gasp. It so happened that the chief of the Blackfeet party was a renegade from the Nez Percés; unlike Kosato, however, he had no vindictive rage against his native tribe, but was rather disposed, now he had got the booty, to spare all unnecessary effusion of blood. He held a long parley, therefore, with the besieged, and finally drew off his warriors, taking with him seventy horses. It appeared, afterwards, that the bullets of the Blackfeet had been entirely expended in the course of the battle, so that they were obliged to make use of stones as substitutes.

At the outset of the fight, Kosato, the renegade, fought with fury rather than valor: animating the others by word as well as deed. A wound in the head from a rifle-ball laid him senseless on the earth. There his body remained when the battle was over, and the victors were leading off the horses. His wife hung over him with frantic lamentations. The conquerors paused and urged her to leave the lifeless renegado, and return with them to her kindred. She refused to listen to their solicitations, and they passed on. As she sat watching the features of Kosato, and giving way to passionate grief, she thought she perceived him to breathe. She was not mistaken. The ball, which had been nearly spent before it struck him, had stunned instead of killing him. By the ministry of his faithful wife, he gradually recovered; reviving to a redoubled love for her, and hatred of his tribe.

As to the female who had so bravely defended her husband, she was elevated by the tribe to a rank far above her sex, and, beside other honorable distinctions, was thenceforward permitted to take a part in the war dances of the braves!

Chapter XVII

CAPTAIN BONNEVILLE found his caches perfectly secure, and having secretly opened them, he selected such articles as were necessary to equip the free trappers, and to supply the inconsiderable trade with the Indians, after which he closed them again. The free trappers being newly rigged out and supplied, were in high spirits, and swaggered gayly about the camp. To compensate all hands for past sufferings, and to give a cheerful spur to further operations, Captain Bonneville now gave the men what, in frontier phrase, is termed "a regular blow out." It was a day of uncouth gambols, and frolics, and rude feasting. The Indians joined in the sports and games, and all was mirth and good fellowship.

It was now the middle of March, and Captain Bonneville made preparations to open the spring campaign. He had pitched upon Malade River for his main trapping ground for the season. This is a stream which rises among the great bed of mountains north of the Lava Plain, and after a winding course, falls into Snake River. Previous to his departure, the captain despatched Mr. Cerré with a few men, to visit the Indian villages and purchase horses; he furnished his clerk, Mr. Hodgkiss, also, with a small stock of goods, to keep up a trade with the Indians during the spring, for such peltries as they might collect, appointing the caches on Salmon River as the point of rendezvous, where they were to rejoin him on the 15th of June following.

This done, he set out for Malade River with a band of twenty-eight men, composed of hired and free trappers, and Indian hunters, together with eight squaws. Their route lay up along the right fork of Salmon River, as it passes through the deep defile of the mountains. They travelled very slowly, not above five miles a day, for many of the horses were so weak that they faltered and staggered as they walked. Pasturage, however, was now growing plentiful. There was abundance of fresh grass, which in some places had attained such height as to wave in the wind. The native flocks of the wilderness, the mountain sheep, as they are called by the trappers, were continually to be seen upon the hills between which they passed, and a good supply of mutton was provided by the hunters, as they were advancing towards a region of scarcity.

In the course of his journey, Captain Bonneville had occasion to remark an instance of the many notions, and almost superstitions, which prevail among the Indians, and among some of the white men, with respect to the sagacity of the beaver. The Indian hunters of his party were in the habit of exploring all the streams along which they passed, in search of "beaver lodges," and occasionally set their traps with some success. One of them, however, though an experienced and skilful trapper, was invariably unsuccessful. Astonished and mortified at such unusual bad luck, he at length conceived the idea, that there was some odor about his person, of which the beaver got scent, and retreated at his approach. He immediately set about a thorough purification. Making a rude sweating house on the banks of the river, he would shut himself up until in a reeking perspiration, and then suddenly emerging, would plunge into the river. A number of these sweatings and plungings having, as he supposed, rendered his person perfectly "inodorous," he resumed his trapping with renovated hope.

About the beginning of April, they encamped upon Godin's River, where they found the swamp full of "muskrat houses." Here, therefore, Captain Bonneville determined to remain a few days and make his first regular attempt at trapping. That his maiden campaign might open with spirit, he promised the Indians and free trappers an extra price for every muskrat they should take. All now set to work for the next day's sport. The utmost animation and gayety prevailed throughout the camp. Every thing looked auspicious for their spring campaign. The abundance of muskrats in the swamp, was but an earnest of the nobler game they were to find when they should reach the Malade River, and have a capital beaver country all to themselves, where they might trap at their leisure, without molestation.

In the midst of their gayety, a hunter came galloping into the camp, shouting, or rather yelling, "A trail! a trail!—lodge poles! lodge poles!"

These were words full of meaning to a trapper's ear. They intimated that there was some band in the neighborhood, and probably a hunting party, as they had lodge poles for an encampment. The hunter came up and told his story. He had discovered a fresh trail, in which the traces made by the dragging of lodge poles were distinctly visible. The buffalo, too, had just been driven out of the neighborhood, which showed that the hunters had already been on the range.

The gayety of the camp was at an end; all preparations for muskrat trapping were suspended, and all hands sallied forth to examine the trail. Their worst fears were soon confirmed. Infallible signs showed the unknown party, in the advance, to be white men; doubtless, some rival band of trappers! Here was competition when least expected; and that, too, by a party already in the advance, who were driving the game before them. Captain Bonneville had now a taste of the sudden transitions to which a trapper's life is subject. The buoyant confidence in an uninterrupted hunt was at an end; every countenance lowered with gloom and disappointment.

Captain Bonneville immediately despatched two spies to overtake the rival party, and endeavor to learn their plans; in the meantime, he turned his back upon the swamp and its muskrat houses, and followed on at "long camps," which, in trapper's language, is equivalent to long stages. On the 6th of April, he met his spies returning. They had kept on the trail like hounds, until they overtook the party at the south end of Godin's Defile. Here they found them comfortably encamped, twenty-two prime trappers, all well appointed, with excellent horses in capital condition, led by Milton Sublette, and an able coadjutor, named Gervais, and in full march for the Malade hunting ground.

This was stunning news. The Malade River was the only trapping ground within reach; but to have to compete there with veteran trappers, perfectly at home among the mountains, and admirably mounted, while they were so poorly provided with horses and trappers, and had but one man in their party acquainted with the country—it was out of the question!

The only hope that now remained, was that the snow, which still lay deep among the mountains of Godin's River, and blocked up the usual pass to the Malade country, might detain the other party, until Captain Bonneville's horses should get once more into good condition in their present ample pasturage.

The rival parties now encamped together; not out of companionship, but to keep an eye upon each other. Day after day passed by, without any possibility of getting to the Malade country. Sublette and Gervais endeavored to force their way across the mountain; but the snows lay so deep as to oblige them to turn back. In the meantime, the captain's horses were daily gaining strength, and their hoofs improving, which had been worn and battered by mountain service. The captain, also, was increasing his stock of provisions, so that the delay was all in his favor.

To any one who merely contemplates a map of the country, this difficulty of getting from Godin's to Malade River will appear inexplicable, as the intervening mountains terminate in the great Snake River plain, so that, apparently, it would be perfectly easy to proceed round their bases.

Here, however, occur some of the striking phenomena of this wild and sublime region. The great lower plain which extends to the feet of these mountains, is broken up near their bases into crests and ridges, resembling the surges of the ocean breaking on a rocky shore.

In a line with the mountains, the plain is gashed with numerous and dangerous chasms, from four to ten feet wide, and of great depth. Captain Bonneville attempted to sound some of these openings, but without any satisfactory result. A stone dropped into one of them reverberated against the sides for apparently a very great depth, and, by its sound, indicated the same kind of substance with the surface, as long as the strokes could be heard. The horse, instinctively sagacious in avoiding danger, shrinks back in alarm from the least of these chasms; pricking up his ears, snorting and pawing, until permitted to turn away.

We have been told by a person well acquainted with the country, that it is sometimes necessary to travel fifty and sixty miles, to get round one of these tremendous ravines. Considerable streams, like that of Godin's River, that run with a bold, free current, lose themselves in this plain; some of them end in swamps, others suddenly disappear; finding, no doubt, subterranean outlets.

Opposite to these chasms, Snake River makes two desperate leaps over precipices, at a short distance from each other; one twenty, the other forty feet in height.

The volcanic plain in question, forms an area of about sixty miles in diameter, where nothing meets the eye but a desolate and awful waste; where no grass grows nor water runs, and where nothing is to be seen but lava. Ranges of mountains skirt this plain, and, in Captain Bonneville's opinion, were formerly connected, until rent asunder by some convulsion of nature. Far to the east, the Three Tetons lift their heads sublimely, and dominate this wide sea of lava;—one of the most striking features of a wilderness where every thing seems on a scale of stern and simple grandeur.

We look forward with impatience for some able geologist to explore this sublime, but almost unknown region.

It was not until the 25th of April, that the two parties of trappers broke up their encampments, and undertook to cross over the southwest end of the mountain by a pass explored by their scouts. From various points of the mountain, they commanded boundless prospects of the lava plain, stretching away in cold and gloomy barrenness as far as the eye could reach. On the evening of the 26th, they reached the plain west of the mountain, watered by the Malade, the Boisée, and other streams, which comprised the contemplated trapping ground.

The country around the Boisée (or Woody) River, is extolled by Captain Bonneville as the most enchanting he had seen in the Far West: presenting the mingled grandeur and beauty of mountain and plain; of bright running streams and vast grassy meadows, waving to the breeze.

We shall not follow the captain throughout his trapping campaign, which lasted until the beginning of June; nor detail all the manœuvres of the rival trapping parties, and their various schemes to outwit and out-trap each other. Suffice it to say, that after having visited and camped about various streams with various success, Captain Bonneville set forward early in June for the appointed rendezvous at the caches. On the way, he treated his party to a grand buffalo hunt. The scouts had reported numerous herds in a plain beyond an intervening height. There was an immediate halt; the fleetest horses were forthwith mounted, and the party advanced to the summit of the hill. Hence, they beheld the great plain below absolutely swarming with buffalo. Captain Bonneville now appointed the place where he would encamp; and towards which the hunters were to drive the game. He cautioned the latter to advance slowly, reserving the strength and speed of the horses, until within a moderate distance of the herds. Twenty-two horsemen descended cautiously into the plain, conformably to these directions. "It was a beautiful sight," says the captain, "to see the runners, as they are called, advancing in column, at a slow trot, until within two hundred and fifty yards of the outskirts of the herd, then dashing on at full speed, until lost in the immense multitude of buffaloes scouring the plain in every direction." All was now tumult and wild confusion. In the meantime, Captain Bonneville and the residue of the party moved on to the appointed camping ground; thither the most expert runners succeeded in driving numbers of buffalo, which were killed hard by the camp, and the flesh transported thither without difficulty. In a little while the whole camp looked like one great slaughter-house; the carcasses were skilfully cut up, great fires were made, scaffolds erected for drying and jerking beef, and an ample provision was made for future subsistence. On the 15th of June, the precise day appointed for the rendezvous, Captain Bonneville and his party arrived safely at the caches.

Here he was joined by the other detachments of his main party, all in good health and spirits. The *caches* were again opened, supplies of various kinds taken out, and a liberal allowance of *aquavitæ* distributed throughout the camp, to celebrate with proper conviviality this merry meeting.

Chapter XVIII

HAVING NOW a pretty strong party, well armed and
equipped, Captain Bonneville no longer felt the necessity of fortifying himself in the secret places and fastnesses of
the mountains; but sallied forth boldly into the Snake River
plain, in search of his clerk, Hodgkiss, who had remained with
the Nez Percés. He found him on the 24th of June, and
learnt from him another chapter of misfortunes which had recently befallen that ill-fated race.

After the departure of Captain Bonneville, in March,
Kosato, the renegade Blackfoot, had recovered from the
wound received in battle; and with his strength revived all his
deadly hostility to his native tribe. He now resumed his efforts to stir up the Nez Percés to reprisals upon their old
enemies; reminding them incessantly of all the outrages and
robberies they had recently experienced, and assuring them
that such would continue to be their lot, until they proved
themselves men by some signal retaliation.

The impassioned eloquence of the desperado, at length
produced an effect; and a band of braves enlisted under
his guidance, to penetrate into the Blackfoot country, harass
their villages, carry off their horses, and commit all kinds of
depredations.

Kosato pushed forward on his foray, as far as the Horse
Prairie; where he came upon a strong party of Blackfeet. Without waiting to estimate their force, he attacked them with
characteristic fury, and was bravely seconded by his followers.
The contest, for a time, was hot and bloody: at length, as is
customary with these two tribes, they paused, and held a long
parley, or rather a war of words.

"What need," said the Blackfoot chief, tauntingly, "have the Nez Percés to leave their homes, and sally forth on war parties, when they have danger enough at their own doors? If you want fighting, return to your villages; you will have plenty of it there. The Blackfeet warriors have hitherto made war upon you as children. They are now coming as men. A great force is at hand; they are on their way to your towns, and are determined to rub out the very name of the Nez Percés from the mountains. Return, I say, to your towns, and fight there, if you wish to live any longer as a people."

Kosato took him at his word; for he knew the character of his native tribe. Hastening back with his band to the Nez Percés village, he told all that he had seen and heard; and urged the most prompt and strenuous measures for defence. The Nez Percés, however, heard him with their accustomed phlegm: the threat of the Blackfeet had been often made, and as often had proved a mere bravado; such they pronounced it to be at present, and, of course, took no precautions.

They were soon convinced that it was no empty menace. In a few days, a band of three hundred Blackfeet warriors appeared upon the hills. All now was consternation in the village. The force of the Nez Percés was too small to cope with the enemy in open fight; many of the young men having gone to their relatives on the Columbia to procure horses. The sages met in hurried council. What was to be done to ward off a blow which threatened annihilation? In this moment of imminent peril, a Pierced-nose chief, named Blue John by the whites, offered to approach secretly with a small, but chosen band, through a defile which led to the encampment of the enemy, and, by a sudden onset, to drive off the horses. Should this blow be successful, the spirit and strength of the invaders would be broken, and the Nez Percés, having horses, would be more than a match for them. Should it fail, the village would not be worse off than at present, when destruction appeared inevitable.

Twenty-nine of the choicest warriors instantly volunteered to follow Blue John in this hazardous enterprise. They prepared for it with the solemnity and devotion peculiar to the tribe. Blue John consulted his medicine, or talismanic charm, such as every chief keeps in his lodge as a supernatural protection. The oracle assured him that his enterprise would be completely successful, provided no rain should fall before he had passed through the defile; but should it rain, his band would be utterly cut off.

The day was clear and bright; and Blue John anticipated that the skies would be propitious. He departed in high game spirit with his forlorn hope; and never did band of braves make a more gallant display: horsemen and horses being decorated and equipped in the fiercest and most glaring style; glittering with arms and ornaments, and fluttering with feathers.

The weather continued serene, until they reached the defile; but just as they were entering it, a black cloud rose over the mountain crest, and there was a sudden shower. The warriors turned to their leader as if to read his opinion of this unlucky omen; but the countenance of Blue John remained un-changed, and they all continued to press forward. It was their hope to make their way, undiscovered, to the very vicinity of the Blackfoot camp: but they had not proceeded far in the defile, when they met a scouting party of the enemy. They attacked and drove them among the hills, and were pursu-ing them with great eagerness, when they heard shouts and yells behind them, and beheld the main body of the Blackfeet advancing.

The second chief wavered a little at the sight, and proposed an instant retreat. "We came to fight!" replied Blue John, sternly. Then giving his war-whoop, he sprang forward to the conflict. His braves followed him. They made a headlong charge upon the enemy; not with the hope of victory, but the determination to sell their lives dearly. A frightful carnage, rather than a regular battle, succeeded. The forlorn band laid heaps of their enemies dead at their feet, but were over-whelmed with numbers, and pressed into a gorge of the mountain, where they continued to fight until they were cut to pieces. One, only, of the thirty survived. He sprang on the horse of a Blackfoot warrior whom he had slain, and escaping at full speed, brought home the baleful tidings to his village.

Who can paint the horror and desolation of the inhabitants? The flower of their warriors laid low, and a ferocious enemy at their doors. The air was rent by the shrieks and lamentations of the women, who, casting off their ornaments, and tearing their

hair, wandered about, frantically bewailing the dead, and pre-
dicting destruction to the living. The remaining warriors
armed themselves for obstinate defence; but showed by their
gloomy looks and sullen silence, that they considered defence
hopeless. To their surprise, the Blackfeet refrained from pursuing their advantage: perhaps satisfied with the blood already
shed, or disheartened by the loss they had themselves sustained. At any rate, they disappeared from the hills, and it was
soon ascertained that they had returned to the Horse Prairie.

The unfortunate Nez Percés now began once more to
breathe. A few of their warriors, taking packhorses, repaired to
the defile to bring away the bodies of their slaughtered
brethren. They found them mere headless trunks; and the
wounds with which they were covered, showed how bravely
they had fought. Their hearts, too, had been torn out and carried off; a proof of their signal valor: for in devouring the heart
of a foe renowned for bravery, or who has distinguished himself in battle, the Indian victor thinks he appropriates to himself the courage of the deceased.

Gathering the mangled bodies of the slain, and strapping
them across their packhorses, the warriors returned, in dismal
procession, to the village. The tribe came forth to meet them;
the women with piercing cries and wailings; the men with
downcast countenances, in which gloom and sorrow seemed
fixed as if in marble. The mutilated and almost undistinguish-
able bodies were placed in rows upon the ground, in the
midst of the assemblage; and the scene of heart-rending anguish and lamentation that ensued, would have confounded
those who insist on Indian stoicism.

Such was the disastrous event that had overwhelmed the
Nez Percés tribe, during the absence of Captain Bonneville:
and he was informed that Kosato, the renegade, who, being
stationed in the village, had been prevented from going on
the forlorn hope, was again striving to rouse the vindictive
feelings of his adopted brethren, and to prompt them to
revenge the slaughter of their devoted braves.

During his sojourn on the Snake River plain, Captain
Bonneville made one of his first essays at the strategy of the fur
trade. There was at this time an assemblage of Nez Percés,
Flatheads, and Cottonois Indians, encamped together upon

the plain; well provided with beaver, which they had collected during the spring. These they were waiting to traffic with a resident trader of the Hudson's Bay Company, who was stationed among them, and with whom they were accustomed to deal. As it happened, the trader was almost entirely destitute of Indian goods; his spring supply not having yet reached him. Captain Bonneville had secret intelligence that the supplies were on their way, and would soon arrive; he hoped, however, by a prompt move, to anticipate their arrival and secure the market to himself. Throwing himself, therefore, among the Indians, he opened his packs of merchandise, and displayed the most tempting wares; bright cloths, and scarlet blankets, and glittering ornaments, and every thing gay and glorious in the eyes of warrior or squaw: all, however, was in vain. The Hudson's Bay trader was a perfect master of his business; thoroughly acquainted with the Indians he had to deal with, and held such control over them, that none dared to act openly in opposition to his wishes: nay, more—he came nigh turning the tables upon the captain, and shaking the allegiance of some of his free trappers, by distributing liquors among them. The latter, therefore, was glad to give up a competition, where the war was likely to be carried into his own camp.

In fact, the traders of the Hudson's Bay Company have advantages over all competitors in the trade beyond the Rocky Mountains. That huge monopoly centres within itself not merely its own hereditary and long established power and influence; but also those of its ancient rival, but now integral part, the famous Northwest Company. It has thus its races of traders, trappers, hunters, and voyageurs, born and brought up in its service, and inheriting from preceding generations a knowledge and aptitude in every thing connected with Indian life, and Indian traffic. In the process of years, this company has been enabled to spread its ramifications in every direction; its system of intercourse is founded upon a long and intimate knowledge of the character and necessities of the various tribes; and of all the fastnesses, defiles, and favorable hunting grounds of the country. Their capital, also, and the manner in which their supplies are distributed at various posts, or forwarded by regular caravans, keep their traders well supplied, and enable them to furnish their goods to the

Indians at a cheap rate. Their men, too, being chiefly drawn from the Canadas, where they enjoy great influence and control, are engaged at the most trifling wages, and supported at little cost: the provisions which they take with them being little more than Indian corn and grease. They are brought, also, into the most perfect discipline and subordination, especially when their leaders have once got them to their scene of action in the heart of the wilderness.

These circumstances combine to give the leaders of the Hudson's Bay Company a decided advantage over all the American companies that come within their range; so that any close competition with them is almost hopeless.

Shortly after Captain Bonneville's ineffectual attempt to participate in the trade of the associated camp, the supplies of the Hudson's Bay Company arrived; and the resident trader was enabled to monopolize the market.

It was now the beginning of July; in the latter part of which month, Captain Bonneville had appointed a rendezvous at Horse Creek, in Green River valley, with some of the parties which he had detached in the preceding year. He now turned his thoughts in that direction, and prepared for the journey.

The Cottonois were anxious for him to proceed at once to their country; which, they assured him, abounded in beaver. The lands of this tribe lie immediately north of those of the Flatheads, and are open to the inroads of the Blackfeet. It is true, the latter professed to be their allies; but they had been guilty of so many acts of perfidy, that the Cottonois had, latterly, renounced their hollow friendship, and attached themselves to the Flatheads and Nez Percés. These they had accompanied in their migrations, rather than remain alone at home, exposed to the outrages of the Blackfeet. They were now apprehensive that these marauders would range their country during their absence, and destroy the beaver: this was their reason for urging Captain Bonneville to make it his autumnal hunting ground. The latter, however, was not to be tempted: his engagements required his presence at the rendezvous in Green River valley; and he had already formed his ulterior plans.

An unexpected difficulty now arose. The free trappers suddenly made a stand, and declined to accompany him. It was a long and a weary journey: the route lay through Pierre's Hole, and other mountain passes infested by the Blackfeet, and recently the scenes of sanguinary conflicts. They were not disposed to undertake such unnecessary toils and dangers, when they had good and secure trapping grounds nearer at hand, on the head waters of Salmon River.

As these were free and independent fellows, whose will and whim were apt to be law—who had the whole wilderness before them, "where to choose," and the trader of a rival company at hand, ready to pay for their services—it was necessary to bend to their wishes. Captain Bonneville fitted them out, therefore, for the hunting ground in question; appointing Mr. Hodgkiss to act as their partisan, or leader, and fixing a rendezvous where he should meet them in the course of the ensuing winter. The brigade consisted of twenty-one free trappers, and four or five hired men as camp-keepers. This was not the exact arrangement of a trapping party; which, when accurately organized, is composed of two-thirds trappers, whose duty leads them continually abroad in pursuit of game, and one-third camp-keepers; who cook, pack, and unpack; set up the tents, take care of the horses, and do all other duties usually consigned by the Indians to their women. This part of the service is apt to be fulfilled by French creoles from Canada and the valley of the Mississippi.

In the meantime, the associated Indians having completed their trade, and received their supplies, were all ready to disperse in various directions. As there was a formidable band of Blackfeet just over a mountain to the northeast, by which Hodgkiss and his free trappers would have to pass; and as it was known that those sharp-sighted marauders had their scouts out, watching every movement of the encampments, so as to cut off stragglers, or weak detachments, Captain Bonneville prevailed upon the Nez Percés to accompany Hodgkiss and his party, until they should be beyond the range of the enemy.

The Cottonois, and the Pends Oreilles, determined to move together at the same time; and to pass close under the mountain infested by the Blackfeet; while Captain Bonneville, with his party, was to strike in an opposite direction to the south-southeast, bending his course for Pierre's Hole, on his way to Green River.

Accordingly, on the 6th of July, all the camps were raised at the same moment; each party taking its separate route. The scene was wild and picturesque: the long lines of traders, trappers, and Indians, with their rugged, and fantastic dresses and accoutrements; their varied weapons, their innumerable horses, some under the saddle, some burthened with packages, others following in droves; all stretching in lengthening cavalcades across the vast landscape, and making for different points of the plains and mountains.

Chapter XIX

*Precautions in dangerous defiles—Trappers' mode of defence
on a prairie—A mysterious visiter—Arrival in Green River
valley—Adventures of the detachments—The forlorn partisan
—His tale of disasters*

As the route of Captain Bonneville lay through what was
considered the most perilous part of this region of dangers, he took all his measures with military skill, and observed
the strictest circumspection. When on the march, a small
scouting party was thrown in the advance, to reconnoitre the
country through which they were to pass. The encampments
were selected with great care, and a watch was kept up night
and day. The horses were brought in and picketed at night,
and at daybreak a party was sent out to scour the neighborhood for half a mile round, beating up every grove and thicket
that could give shelter to a lurking foe. When all was reported
safe, the horses were cast loose and turned out to graze. Were
such precautions generally observed by traders and hunters,
we should not so often hear of parties being surprised by the
Indians.

Having stated the military arrangements of the captain, we
may here mention a mode of defence on the open prairie,
which we have heard from a veteran in the Indian trade.
When a party of trappers is on a journey with a convoy of
goods or peltries, every man has three packhorses under his
care; each horse laden with three packs. Every man is provided with a picket with an iron head, a mallet, and hobbles,
or leathern fetters for the horses. The trappers proceed across
the prairie in a long line; or sometimes three parallel lines,
sufficiently distant from each other to prevent the packs from
interfering. At an alarm, when there is no covert at hand, the
line wheels so as to bring the front to the rear and form a circle. All then dismount, drive their pickets into the ground in
the centre, fasten the horses to them, and hobble their fore
legs, so that, in case of alarm, they cannot break away. They
then unload them, and dispose of their packs as breastworks
on the periphery of the circle; each man having nine packs

behind which to shelter himself. In this promptly formed fortress, they await the assault of the enemy, and are enabled to set large bands of Indians at defiance.

The first night of his march, Captain Bonneville encamped upon Henry's Fork, an upper branch of Snake River, called after the first American trader that erected a fort beyond the mountains. About an hour after all hands had come to a halt, the clatter of hoofs was heard, and a solitary female, of the Nez Percé tribe, came galloping up. She was mounted on a mestang or half wild horse, which she managed with a long rope hitched round the under jaw by way of bridle. Dismounting, she walked silently into the midst of the camp, and there seated herself on the ground, still holding her horse by the long halter.

The sudden and lonely apparition of this woman, and her calm, yet resolute demeanor, awakened universal curiosity. The hunters and trappers gathered round, and gazed on her as something mysterious. She remained silent, but maintained her air of calmness and self-possession. Captain Bonneville approached and interrogated her as to the object of her mysterious visit. Her answer was brief but earnest—"I love the whites—I will go with them." She was forthwith invited to a lodge, of which she readily took possession, and from that time forward was considered one of the camp.

In consequence, very probably, of the military precautions of Captain Bonneville, he conducted his party in safety through this hazardous region. No accident of a disastrous kind occurred, excepting the loss of a horse, which, in passing along the giddy edge of the precipice, called the Cornice, a dangerous pass between Jackson's and Pierre's Hole, fell over the brink and was dashed to pieces.

On the 13th of July, (1833,) Captain Bonneville arrived at Green River. As he entered the valley, he beheld it strewed in every direction with the carcasses of buffaloes. It was evident that Indians had recently been there, and in great numbers. Alarmed at this sight, he came to a halt, and as soon as it was dark, sent out spies to his place of rendezvous on Horse Creek, where he had expected to meet with his detached parties of trappers on the following day. Early in the morning, the spies made their appearance in the camp, and with them came three trappers of one of his bands, from the rendezvous, who told him his people were all there expecting him. As to the slaughter among the buffaloes, it had been made by a friendly band of Shoshonies, who had fallen in with his trapping parties, and accompanied them to the rendezvous. Having imparted this intelligence, the three worthies from the rendezvous broached a small keg of "alcohol" which they had brought with them, to enliven this merry meeting. The liquor went briskly round; all absent friends were toasted, and the party moved forward to the rendezvous in high spirits.

The meeting of associated bands, who have been separated from each other on these hazardous enterprises, is always interesting; each having its tale of perils and adventures to relate. Such was the case with the various detachments of Captain Bonneville's company, thus brought together on Horse Creek. Here was the detachment of fifty men which he had sent from Salmon River, in the preceding month of November, to winter on Snake River. They had met with many crosses and losses in the course of their spring hunt, not so much from Indians as from white men. They had come in competition with rival trapping parties, particularly one belonging to the Rocky Mountain Fur Company; and they had long stories to relate of their manœuvres to forestall or distress each other. In fact, in these virulent and sordid competitions, the trappers of each party were more intent upon injuring their rivals, than benefiting themselves; breaking each other's traps, trampling and tearing to pieces the beaver lodges, and doing every thing in their power to mar the success of the hunt. We forbear to detail these pitiful contentions.

The most lamentable tale of disasters, however, that Captain Bonneville had to hear, was from a partisan, whom he had detached in the preceding year, with twenty men, to hunt through the outskirts of the Crow country, and on the tributary streams of the Yellowstone; whence he was to proceed and join him in his winter quarters on Salmon River. This partisan appeared at the rendezvous without his party, and a sorrowful tale of disasters had he to relate. In hunting the Crow country, he fell in with a village of that tribe; notorious rogues, jockeys, and horse stealers, and errant scamperers of the mountains. These decoyed most of his men to desert, and carry off horses, traps, and accoutrements. When he attempted to retake the deserters, the Crow warriors ruffled up to him and declared the deserters were their good friends, had determined to remain among them, and should not be molested. The poor partisan, therefore, was fain to leave his vagabonds among these birds of their own feather, and, being too weak in numbers to attempt the dangerous pass across the mountains to meet Captain Bonneville on Salmon River, he made, with the few that remained faithful to him, for the neighborhood of Tullock's Fort, on the Yellowstone, under the protection of which he went into winter quarters.

He soon found out that the neighborhood of the fort was nearly as bad as the neighborhood of the Crows. His men were continually stealing away thither, with whatever beaver skins they could secrete or lay their hands on. These they would exchange with the hangers-on of the fort for whiskey, and then revel in drunkenness and debauchery.

The unlucky partisan made another move. Associating with his party a few free trappers, whom he met with in this neighborhood, he started off early in the spring to trap on the head waters of Powder River. In the course of the journey, his horses were so much jaded in traversing a steep mountain, that he was induced to turn them loose to graze during the night. The place was lonely; the pass was rugged; there was not the sign of an Indian in the neighborhood; not a blade of grass that had been turned by a footstep. But who can calculate on security in the midst of the Indian country, where the foe lurks in silence and secrecy, and seems to come and go on the wings of the wind? The horses had scarce been turned loose, when a couple of Arickara (or Rickaree) warriors entered the camp. They affected a frank and friendly demeanor; but their appearance and movements awakened the suspicions of some of the veteran trappers, well versed in Indian wiles. Convinced that they were spies sent on some sinister errand, they took them into custody, and set to work to drive in the horses. It was too late—the horses were already gone. In fact, a war party of Arickaras had been hovering on their trail for several days, watching with the patience and perseverance of Indians, for some moment of negligence and fancied security, to make a successful swoop. The two spies had evidently been

sent into the camp to create a diversion, while their confeder-
ates carried off the spoil.

The unlucky partisan, thus robbed of his horses, turned furiously on his prisoners, ordered them to be bound hand and
foot, and swore to put them to death unless his property were
restored. The robbers, who soon found that their spies were
in captivity, now made their appearance on horseback, and
held a parley. The sight of them, mounted on the very horses
they had stolen, set the blood of the mountaineers in a fer-
ment; but it was useless to attack them, as they would have
but to turn their steeds and scamper out of the reach of
pedestrians. A negotiation was now attempted. The Arickaras
offered what they considered fair terms; to barter one horse,
or even two horses, for a prisoner. The mountaineers spurned
at their offer, and declared that, unless all the horses were relinquished, the prisoners should be burnt to death. To give
force to their threat, a pyre of logs and fagots was heaped up
and kindled into a blaze.

The parley continued; the Arickaras released one horse and
then another, in earnest of their proposition; finding, however,
that nothing short of the relinquishment of all their spoils
would purchase the lives of the captives, they abandoned them
to their fate, moving off with many parting words and lamentable howlings. The prisoners seeing them depart, and knowing the horrible fate that awaited them, made a desperate
effort to escape. They partially succeeded, but were severely
wounded and retaken; then dragged to the blazing pyre, and
burnt to death in the sight of their retreating comrades.

Such are the savage cruelties that white men learn to practise, who mingle in savage life; and such are the acts that lead
to terrible recrimination on the part of the Indians. Should we
hear of any atrocities committed by the Arickaras upon captive
white men, let this signal and recent provocation be borne in
mind. Individual cases of the kind dwell in the recollections
of whole tribes; and it is a point of honor and conscience to
revenge them.

The loss of his horses completed the ruin of the unlucky
partisan. It was out of his power to prosecute his hunting, or
to maintain his party; the only thought now was how to get
back to civilized life. At the first water course, his men built

canoes and committed themselves to the stream. Some engaged themselves at various trading establishments at which they touched, others got back to the settlements. As to the partisan, he found an opportunity to make his way to the rendezvous at Green River valley; which he reached in time to render to Captain Bonneville this forlorn account of his misadventures.

Chapter XX

THE Green River valley was at this time the scene of one of those general gatherings of traders, trappers, and Indians, that we have already mentioned. The three rival companies, which, for a year past had been endeavoring to out-trade, out-trap, and outwit each other, were here encamped in close proximity, awaiting their annual supplies. About four miles from the rendezvous of Captain Bonneville was that of the American Fur Company, hard by which, was that also of the Rocky Mountain Fur Company.

After the eager rivalry and almost hostility displayed by these companies in their late campaigns, it might be expected that, when thus brought in juxtaposition, they would hold themselves warily and sternly aloof from each other, and, should they happen to come in contact, brawl and bloodshed would ensue.

No such thing! Never did rival lawyers, after a wrangle at the bar, meet with more social good-humor at a circuit dinner. The hunting season over, all past tricks and manœuvres are forgotten, all feuds and bickerings buried in oblivion. From the middle of June to the middle of September, all trapping is suspended; for the beavers are then shedding their furs, and their skins are of little value. This, then, is the trapper's holiday, when he is all for fun and frolic, and ready for a saturnalia among the mountains.

At the present season, too, all parties were in good-humor. The year had been productive. Competition, by threatening to lessen their profits, had quickened their wits, roused their energies, and made them turn every favorable chance to the best advantage; so that, on assembling at their respective places of rendezvous, each company found itself in possession of a rich stock of peltries.

The leaders of the different companies, therefore, mingled on terms of perfect good fellowship; interchanging visits, and regaling each other in the best style their respective camps afforded. But the rich treat for the worthy captain was to see the "chivalry" of the various encampments, engaged in contests of skill at running, jumping, wrestling, shooting with the rifle, and running horses. And then their rough hunters' feastings and carousals. They drank together, they sang, they laughed, they whooped; they tried to outbrag and outlie each other in stories of their adventures and achievements. Here the free trappers were in all their glory; they considered themselves the "cocks of the walk," and always carried the highest crests. Now and then familiarity was pushed too far, and would effervesce into a brawl, and a "rough and tumble" fight; but it all ended in cordial reconciliation and maudlin endearment.

The presence of the Shoshonie tribe contributed occasionally to cause temporary jealousies and feuds. The Shoshonie beauties became objects of rivalry among some of the amorous mountaineers. Happy was the trapper who could muster up a red blanket, a string of gay beads, or a paper of precious vermilion, with which to win the smiles of a Shoshonie fair one.

The caravans of supplies arrived at the valley just at this period of gallantry and good fellowship. Now commenced a scene of eager competition and wild prodigality at the different encampments. Bales were hastily ripped open, and all their motley contents poured forth. A mania for purchasing spread itself throughout the several bands,—munitions for war, for hunting, for gallantry, were seized upon with equal avidity—rifles, hunting knives, traps, scarlet cloth, red blankets, garish beads, and glittering trinkets, were bought at any price, and scores run up without any thought how they were ever to be rubbed off. The free trappers, especially, were extravagant in their purchases. For a free mountaineer to pause at a paltry consideration of dollars and cents, in the attainment of any object that might strike his fancy, would stamp him with the mark of the beast in the estimation of his comrades. For a trader to refuse one of these free and flourishing blades a credit, whatever unpaid scores might stare him in the face, would be a flagrant affront scarcely to be forgiven.

Now succeeded another outbreak of revelry and extravagance. The trappers were newly fitted out and arrayed; and dashed about with their horses caparisoned in Indian style. The Shoshonie beauties also flaunted about in all the colors of the rainbow. Every freak of prodigality was indulged to its full extent, and in a little while most of the trappers, having squandered away all their wages, and perhaps run knee deep in debt, were ready for another hard campaign in the wilderness.

During this season of folly and frolic, there was an alarm of mad wolves in the two lower camps. One or more of these animals entered the camps for three nights successively, and bit several of the people.

Captain Bonneville relates the case of an Indian, who was a universal favorite in the lower camp. He had been bitten by one of these animals. Being out with a party shortly afterwards, he grew silent and gloomy, and lagged behind the rest as if he wished to leave them. They halted and urged him to move faster, but he entreated them not to approach him, and, leaping from his horse, began to roll frantically on the earth, gnashing his teeth and foaming at the mouth. Still he retained his senses, and warned his companions not to come near him, as he should not be able to restrain himself from biting them. They hurried off to obtain relief; but on their return he was nowhere to be found. His horse and his accoutrements remained upon the spot. Three or four days afterwards, a solitary Indian, believed to be the same, was observed crossing a valley, and pursued; but he darted away into the fastnesses of the mountains, and was seen no more.

Another instance we have from a different person who was present in the encampment. One of the men of the Rocky Mountain Fur Company had been bitten. He set out shortly afterwards, in company with two white men, on his return to the settlements. In the course of a few days he shewed symptoms of hydrophobia, and became raving towards night. At length, breaking away from his companions he rushed into a thicket of willows, where they left him to his fate!

Chapter XXI

CAPTAIN BONNEVILLE now found himself at the head of a
hardy, well seasoned, and well appointed company of
trappers, all benefited by at least one year's experience among
the mountains, and capable of protecting themselves from Indian wiles and stratagems, and of providing for their subsistence wherever game was to be found. He had, also, an
excellent troop of horses, in prime condition and fit for hard
service. He determined, therefore, to strike out into some of
the bolder parts of his scheme. One of these was to carry his expeditions into some of the unknown tracts of the Far West, beyond what is generally termed the buffalo range. This would
have something of the merit and charm of discovery, so dear to
every brave and adventurous spirit. Another favorite project
was to establish a trading post on the lower part of the Columbia River, near the Multnomah valley, and to endeavor to retrieve for his country some of the lost trade of Astoria.

The first of the above mentioned views was, at present, up-
permost in his mind—the exploring of unknown regions.
Among the grand features of the wilderness about which he
was roaming, one had made a vivid impression on his mind,
and been clothed by his imagination with vague and ideal
charms. This is a great lake of salt water, laving the feet of the
mountains, but extending far to the west-southwest, into one
of those vast and elevated plateaus of land, which range high
above the level of the Pacific.

Captain Bonneville gives a striking account of the lake
when seen from the land. As you ascend the mountains about
its shores, says he, you behold this immense body of water
spreading itself before you, and stretching further and further,
in one wide and far reaching expanse, until the eye, wearied
with continued and strained attention, rests in the blue dim-
ness of distance, upon lofty ranges of mountains, confidently
asserted to rise from the bosom of the waters. Nearer to you,

the smooth and unruffled surface is studded with little islands, where the mountain sheep roam in considerable numbers. What extent of lowland may be encompassed by the high peaks beyond, must remain for the present matter of mere conjecture; though from the form of the summits, and the breaks which may be discovered among them, there can be little doubt that they are the sources of streams calculated to water large tracts, which are probably concealed from view by the rotundity of the lake's surface. At some future day, in all probability, the rich harvest of beaver fur, which may be reasonably anticipated in such a spot, will tempt adventurers to reduce all this doubtful region to the palpable certainty of a beaten track. At present, however, destitute of the means of making boats, the trapper stands upon the shore, and gazes upon a promised land which his feet are never to tread.

Such is the somewhat fanciful view which Captain Bonneville gives of this great body of water. He has evidently taken part of his ideas concerning it from the representations of others, who have somewhat exaggerated its features. It is reported to be about one hundred and fifty miles long, and fifty miles broad. The ranges of mountain peaks which Captain Bonneville speaks of, as rising from its bosom, are probably the summits of mountains beyond it, which may be visible at a vast distance, when viewed from an eminence, in the transparent atmosphere of these lofty regions. Several large islands certainly exist in the lake; one of which is said to be mountainous, but not by any means to the extent required to furnish the series of peaks above mentioned.

Captain Sublette, in one of his early expeditions across the mountains, is said to have sent four men in a skin canoe, to explore the lake, who professed to have navigated all around it; but to have suffered excessively from thirst, the water of the lake being extremely salt, and there being no fresh streams running into it.

Captain Bonneville doubts this report, or that the men accomplished the circumnavigation, because, he says, the lake receives several large streams from the mountains which bound it to the east. In the spring, when these streams are swollen by rain and by the melting of the snows, the lake rises several feet above its ordinary level; during the summer, it gradually subsides again, leaving a sparkling zone of the finest salt upon its shores.

The elevation of the vast plateau on which this lake is situated, is estimated by Captain Bonneville at one and three-fourths of a mile above the level of the ocean. The admirable purity and transparency of the atmosphere in this region, allowing objects to be seen, and the report of fire-arms to be heard, at an astonishing distance; and its extreme dryness, causing the wheels of waggons to fall to pieces, as instanced in former passages of this work, are proofs of the great altitude of the Rocky Mountain plains. That a body of salt water should exist at such a height, is cited as a singular phenomenon by Captain Bonneville, though the salt lake of Mexico is not much inferior in elevation.*

To have this lake properly explored, and all its secrets revealed, was the grand scheme of the captain for the present year; and while it was one in which his imagination evidently took a leading part, he believed it would be attended with great profit, from the numerous beaver streams with which the lake must be fringed.

This momentous undertaking he confided to his lieutenant, Mr. Walker, in whose experience and ability he had great confidence. He instructed him to keep along the shores of the lake, and trap in all the streams on his route; also to keep a journal, and minutely to record the events of his journey, and every thing curious or interesting, making maps or charts of his route, and of the surrounding country.

No pains nor expense were spared in fitting out the party, of forty men, which he was to command. They had complete supplies for a year, and were to meet Captain Bonneville in the ensuing summer, in the valley of Bear River, the largest tributary of the Salt Lake, which was to be his point of general rendezvous.

The next care of Captain Bonneville, was to arrange for the safe transportation of the peltries which he had collected, to the Atlantic states. Mr. Robert Campbell, the partner of

* The lake of Tezcuco which surrounds the city of Mexico, the largest and lowest of the five lakes on the Mexican plateau, and one of the most impregnated with saline particles, is seven thousand four hundred and sixty-eight feet, or nearly one mile and a half above the level of the sea.

Sublette, was at this time in the rendezvous of the Rocky Mountain Fur Company, having brought up their supplies. He was about to set off on his return, with the peltries collected during the year, and intended to proceed through the Crow country, to the head of navigation on the Bighorn River, and to descend in boats down that river, the Missouri, and the Yellowstone, to St. Louis.

Captain Bonneville determined to forward his peltries by the same route, under the especial care of Mr. Cerré. By way of escort, he would accompany Cerré to the point of embarcation, and then to make an autumnal hunt in the Crow country.

Chapter XXII

The Crow country—A Crow paradise—Habits of the Crows
—Anecdotes of Rose, the renegade white man—His fights
with the Blackfeet—His elevation—His death—Arapooish,
the Crow chief—His eagle—Adventure of Robert Campbell
—Honor among Crows

BEFORE we accompany Captain Bonneville into the Crow country, we will impart a few facts about this wild region, and the wild people who inhabit it. We are not aware of the precise boundaries, if there are any, of the country claimed by the Crows; it appears to extend from the Black Hills to the Rocky Mountains, including a part of their lofty ranges, and embracing many of the plains and valleys watered by the Wind River, the Yellowstone, the Powder River, the Little Missouri, and the Nebraska. The country varies in soil and climate; there are vast plains of sand and clay, studded with large red sand hills: other parts are mountainous and picturesque: it possesses warm springs, and coal mines, and abounds with game.

But let us give the account of the country as rendered by Arapooish, a Crow chief, to Mr. Robert Campbell, of the Rocky Mountain Fur Company.

"The Crow country," said he, "is a good country. The Great Spirit has put it exactly in the right place; while you are in it you fare well; whenever you go out of it, which ever way you travel, you fare worse.

"If you go to the south, you have to wander over great barren plains; the water is warm and bad, and you meet the fever and ague.

"To the north it is cold; the winters are long and bitter, with no grass; you cannot keep horses there, but must travel with dogs. What is a country without horses!

"On the Columbia they are poor and dirty, paddle about in canoes, and eat fish. Their teeth are worn out; they are always taking fishbones out of their mouths. Fish is poor food.

"To the east, they dwell in villages; they live well; but they drink the muddy water of the Missouri—that is bad. A Crow's dog would not drink such water.

"About the forks of the Missouri is a fine country; good water; good grass; plenty of buffalo. In summer, it is almost as good as the Crow country; but in winter it is cold; the grass is gone; and there is no salt weed for the horses.

"The Crow country is exactly in the right place. It has snowy mountains and sunny plains; all kinds of climates and good things for every season. When the summer heats scorch the prairies, you can draw up under the mountains, where the air is sweet and cool, the grass fresh, and the bright streams come tumbling out of the snow banks. There you can hunt the elk, the deer, and the antelope, when their skins are fit for dressing; there you will find plenty of white bears and mountain sheep.

"In the autumn, when your horses are fat and strong from the mountain pastures, you can go down into the plains and hunt the buffalo, or trap beaver on the streams. And when winter comes on, you can take shelter in the woody bottoms along the river; there you will find buffalo meat for yourselves, and cotton-wood bark for your horses: or you may winter in the Wind River valley, where there is salt weed in abundance.

"The Crow country is exactly in the right place. Every thing good is to be found there. There is no country like the Crow country."

Such is the eulogium on his country by Arapooish.

We have had repeated occasions to speak of the restless and predatory habits of the Crows. They can muster fifteen hundred fighting men; but their incessant wars with the Blackfeet, and their vagabond, predatory habits, are gradually wearing them out.

In a recent work, we related the circumstance of a white man named Rose, an outlaw, and a designing vagabond, who acted as guide and interpreter to Mr. Hunt and his party, on their journey across the mountains to Astoria; who came near betraying them into the hands of the Crows, and who remained among the tribe, marrying one of their women, and adopting their congenial habits.* A few anecdotes of the subsequent fortunes of that renegado may not be uninteresting, especially as they are connected with the fortunes of the tribe.

* See Astoria.

Rose was powerful in frame and fearless in spirit: and soon by his daring deeds took his rank among the first braves of the tribe. He aspired to command, and knew it was only to be attained by desperate exploits. He distinguished himself in repeated actions with the Blackfeet. On one occasion, a band of those savages had fortified themselves within a breastwork, and could not be harmed. Rose proposed to storm the work. "Who will take the lead?" was the demand. "I!" cried he; and putting himself at their head, rushed forward. The first Blackfoot that opposed him, he shot down with his rifle, and, snatching up the war-club of his victim, killed four others within the fort. The victory was complete, and Rose returned to the Crow village covered with glory, and bearing five Blackfoot scalps, to be erected as a trophy before his lodge. From this time, he was known among the Crows by the name of Che-ku-kaats, or, "the man who killed five." He became chief of the village, or rather band, and for a time was the popular idol. His popularity soon awakened envy among the native braves; he was a stranger, an intruder, a white man. A party seceded from his command. Feuds and civil wars succeeded that lasted for two or three years, until Rose, having contrived to set his adopted brethren by the ears, left them, and went down the Missouri in 1823. Here he fell in with one of the earliest trapping expeditions sent by General Ashley across the mountains. It was conducted by Smith, Fitzpatrick, and Sublette. Rose enlisted with them as guide and interpreter. When he got them among the Crows, he was exceedingly generous with their goods; making presents to the braves of his adopted tribe, as became a high-minded chief.

This, doubtless, helped to revive his popularity. In that expedition, Smith and Fitzpatrick were robbed of their horses in Green River valley; the place where the robbery took place still bears the name of Horse Creek. We are not informed whether the horses were stolen through the instigation and management of Rose; it is not improbable, for such was the perfidy he had intended to practise on a former occasion towards Mr. Hunt and his party.

The last anecdote we have of Rose is from an Indian trader. When General Atkinson made his military expedition up the Missouri, in 1825, to protect the fur trade, he held a conference with the Crow nation, at which Rose figured as Indian dignitary and Crow interpreter. The military were stationed at some little distance from the scene of the "big talk"; while the general and the chiefs were smoking pipes and making speeches, the officers, supposing all was friendly, left the troops, and drew near the scene of ceremonial. Some of the more knowing Crows, perceiving this, stole quietly to the camp, and, unobserved, contrived to stop the touch-holes of the fieldpieces with dirt. Shortly after, a misunderstanding occurred in the conference: some of the Indians, knowing the cannon to be useless, became insolent. A tumult arose. In the confusion, Colonel Fallon snapped a pistol in the face of a brave, and knocked him down with the butt end. The Crows were all in a fury. A chance medley fight was on the point of taking place, when Rose, his natural sympathies as a white man suddenly recurring, broke the stock of his fusee over the head of a Crow warrior, and laid so vigorously about him with the barrel, that he soon put the whole throng to flight. Luckily, as no lives had been lost, this sturdy ribroasting calmed the fury of the Crows, and the tumult ended without serious consequences.

What was the ultimate fate of this vagabond hero is not distinctly known. Some report him to have fallen a victim to disease, brought on by his licentious life; others assert that he was murdered in a feud among the Crows. After all, his residence among these savages, and the influence he acquired over them, had, for a time, some beneficial effects. He is said, not merely to have rendered them more formidable to the Blackfeet, but to have opened their eyes to the policy of cultivating the friendship of the white men.

After Rose's death, his policy continued to be cultivated, with indifferent success, by Arapooish, the chief already mentioned, who had been his great friend, and whose character he had contributed to develope. This sagacious chief endeavored on every occasion, to restrain the predatory propensities of his tribe when directed against the white men. "If we keep friends with them," said he, "we have nothing to fear from the Blackfeet, and can rule the mountains." Arapooish pretended to be a great "medicine man;" a character among the Indians which is a compound of priest, doctor, prophet, and conjuror.

He carried about with him a tame eagle, as his "medicine" or familiar. With the white men, he acknowledged that this was all charlatanism; but said it was necessary, to give him weight and influence among his people.

Mr. Robert Campbell, from whom we have most of these facts, in the course of one of his trapping expeditions, was quartered in the village of Arapooish, and a guest in the lodge of the chieftain. He had collected a large quantity of furs, and, fearful of being plundered, deposited but a part in the lodge of the chief; the rest he buried in a cache. One night, Arapooish came into the lodge with a cloudy brow, and seated himself for a time without saying a word. At length, turning to Campbell, "You have more furs with you," said he, "than you have brought into my lodge?"

"I have," replied Campbell.

"Where are they?"

Campbell knew the uselessness of any prevarication with an Indian; and the importance of complete frankness. He described the exact place where he had concealed his peltries.

" 'Tis well," replied Arapooish; "you speak straight. It is just as you say. But your cache has been robbed. Go and see how many skins have been taken from it."

Campbell examined the cache, and estimated his loss to be about one hundred and fifty beaver skins.

Arapooish now summoned a meeting of the village. He bitterly reproached his people for robbing a stranger who had confided to their honor; and commanded that whoever had taken the skins, should bring them back: declaring that, as Campbell was his guest and an inmate of his lodge, he would not eat nor drink until every skin was restored to him.

The meeting broke up, and every one dispersed. Arapooish now charged Campbell to give neither reward nor thanks to any one who should bring in the beaver skins, but to keep count as they were delivered.

In a little while, the skins began to make their appearance, a few at a time; they were laid down in the lodge, and those who brought them departed without saying a word. The day passed away. Arapooish sat in one corner of his lodge, wrapped up in his robe, scarcely moving a muscle of his countenance. When night arrived, he demanded if all the skins had been brought in. Above a hundred had been given up, and Campbell expressed himself contented. Not so the Crow chieftain. He fasted all that night, nor tasted a drop of water. In the morning, some more skins were brought in, and continued to come, one and two at a time, throughout the day: until but a few were wanting to make the number complete. Campbell was now anxious to put an end to this fasting of the old chief, and again declared that he was perfectly satisfied. Arapooish demanded what number of skins were yet wanting. On being told, he whispered to some of his people, who disappeared. After a time the number were brought in, though it was evident they were not any of the skins that had been stolen, but others gleaned in the village.

"Is all right now?" demanded Arapooish.

"All is right," replied Campbell.

"Good! Now bring me meat and drink!"

When they were alone together, Arapooish had a conversation with his guest.

"When you come another time among the Crows," said he, "don't hide your goods: trust to them and they will not wrong you. Put your goods in the lodge of a chief, and they are sacred; hide them in a cache, and any one who finds will steal them. My people have now given up your goods for my sake; but there are some foolish young men in the village, who may be disposed to be troublesome. Don't linger therefore, but pack your horses and be off."

Campbell took his advice, and made his way safely out of the Crow country. He has ever since maintained, that the Crows are not so black as they are painted. "Trust to their honor," says he, "and you are safe: trust to their honesty, and they will steal the hair off of your head."

Having given these few preliminary particulars, we will resume the course of our narrative.

Chapter XXIII

O N THE 25TH of July, Captain Bonneville struck his tents, and set out on his route for the Bighorn: at the head of a party of fifty-six men, including those who were to embark with Cerré. Crossing the Green River valley, he proceeded along the south point of the Wind River range of mountains, and soon fell upon the track of Mr. Robert Campbell's party, which had preceded him by a day. This he pursued, until he perceived that it led down the banks of the Sweet Water to the southeast. As this was different from his proposed direction, he left it; and turning to the northeast, soon came upon the waters of the Popo Agie. This stream takes it rise in the Wind River Mountains. Its name, like most Indian names, is charac-teristic. *Popo*, in the Crow language, signifying head; and *Agie*, river. It is the head of a long river, extending from the south end of the Wind River Mountains in a northeast direction, un-til it falls into the Yellowstone. Its course is generally through plains, but is twice crossed by chains of mountains; the first called the Littlehorn; the second, the Bighorn. After it has forced its way through the first chain, it is called the Horn River; after the second chain, it is called the Bighorn River. Its passage through this last chain is rough and violent; making repeated falls, and rushing down long and furious rapids, which threaten destruction to the navigator; though a hardy trapper is said to have shot down them in a canoe. At the foot of these rapids, is the head of navigation; where it was the intention of the parties to construct boats, and embark.

Proceeding down along the Popo Agie, Captain Bonneville came again in full view of the "Bluffs," as they are called, extending from the base of the Wind River Mountains far away to the east, and presenting to the eye a confusion of hills and cliffs of red sandstone; some peaked and angular; some round; some broken into crags and precipices, and piled up in fantastic masses; but all naked and sterile. There appeared to be no soil favorable to vegetation; nothing but coarse gravel: yet, over all this isolated, barren landscape, were diffused such atmospherical tints and hues, as to blend the whole into harmony and beauty.

In this neighborhood, the captain made search for "the great Tar Spring," one of the wonders of the mountains; the medicinal properties of which, he had heard extravagantly lauded by the trappers. After a toilsome search, he found it at the foot of a sandbluff, a little to the east of the Wind River Mountains; where it exuded in a small stream of the color and consistency of tar. The men immediately hastened to collect a quantity of it, to use as an ointment for the galled backs of their horses, and as a balsam for their own pains and aches. From the description given of it, it is evidently the bituminous oil, called petrolium, or naptha, which forms a principal ingredient in the potent medicine called British Oil. It is found in various parts of Europe and Asia, in several of the West India Islands, and in some places of the United States. In the state of New York, it is called Seneca Oil, from being found near the Seneca Lake.

The Crow country has other natural curiosities, which are held in superstitious awe by the Indians, and considered great marvels by the trappers. Such is the Burning Mountain, on Powder River, abounding with anthracite coal. Here the earth is hot and cracked; in many places emitting smoke and sulphurous vapors, as if covering concealed fires. A volcanic tract of similar character is found on Stinking River, one of the tributaries of the Bighorn, which takes its unhappy name from the odor derived from sulphurous springs and streams. This last mentioned place was first discovered by Colter, a hunter belonging to Lewis and Clark's exploring party, who came upon it in the course of his lonely wanderings, and gave such an account of its gloomy terrors; its hidden fires, smoking pits, noxious steams, and the all-pervading "smell of brimstone," that it received, and has ever since retained among trappers, the name of "Colter's Hell!"

Resuming his descent along the left bank of the Popo Agie, Captain Bonneville soon reached the plains; where he found several large streams entering from the west. Among these was Wind River, which gives its name to the mountains among which it takes its rise. This is one of the most important streams of the Crow country. The river being much swollen, Captain Bonneville halted at its mouth, and sent out scouts to look for a fording place. While thus encamped, he beheld, in the course of the afternoon, a long line of horsemen descending the slope of the hills on the opposite side of the Popo Agie. His first idea was, that they were Indians: he soon discovered, however, that they were white men; and, by the long line of packhorses, ascertained them to be the convoy of Campbell, which, having descended the Sweet Water, was now on its way to the Horn River.

The two parties came together two or three days afterwards, on the 4th of August, after having passed through the gap of the Littlehorn Mountain. In company with Campbell's convoy, was a trapping party of the Rocky Mountain Company, headed by Fitzpatrick; who, after Campbell's embarcation on the Bighorn, was to take charge of all the horses, and proceed on a trapping campaign. There were, moreover, two chance companions in the rival camp. One was Captain Stewart, of the British army, a gentleman of noble connexions, who was amusing himself by a wandering tour in the Far West; in the course of which, he had lived in hunter's style: accompanying various bands of traders, trappers, and Indians; and manifesting that relish for the wilderness that belongs to men of game spirit.

The other casual inmate of Mr. Campbell's camp was Mr. Nathaniel Wyeth; the self-same leader of the band of New-England salmon fishers, with whom we parted company in the valley of Pierre's Hole, after the battle with the Blackfeet. A few days after that affair, he again set out from the rendezvous in company with Milton Sublette and his brigade of trappers. On his march, he visited the battle ground, and penetrated to the deserted fort of the Blackfeet in the midst of the wood. It was a dismal scene. The fort was strewed with the mouldering bodies of the slain; while vultures soared aloft, or sat brooding on the trees around; and Indian dogs howled about the place, as if bewailing the death of their masters. Wyeth travelled for a considerable distance to the southwest, in company with Milton Sublette, when they separated; and the former, with eleven men, the remnant of his band, pushed on for Snake River; kept down the course of that eventful stream; traversed the Blue Mountains, trapping beaver occasionally by the way, and finally, after hardships of all kinds, arrived on the 29th of October, at Vancouver, on the Columbia, the main factory of the Hudson's Bay Company.

He experienced hospitable treatment at the hands of the agents of that company; but his men, heartily tired of wandering in the wilderness, or tempted by other prospects, refused, for the most part, to continue any longer in his service. Some set off for the Sandwich Islands; some entered into other employ. Wyeth found, too, that a great part of the goods he had brought with him were unfitted for the Indian trade: in a word, his expedition, undertaken entirely on his own resources, proved a failure. He lost every thing invested in it, but his hopes. These were as strong as ever. He took note of every thing, therefore, that could be of service to him in the further prosecution of his project; collected all the information within his reach, and then set off, accompanied by merely two men, on his return journey across the continent. He had got thus far "by hook and by crook," a mode in which a New-England man can make his way all over the world, and through all kinds of difficulties, and was now bound for Boston; in full confidence of being able to form a company for the salmon fishery and fur trade of the Columbia.

The party of Mr. Campbell had met with a disaster in the course of their route from the Sweet Water. Three or four of the men who were reconnoitring the country in the advance of the main body, were visited one night in their camp, by fifteen or twenty Shoshonies. Considering this tribe as perfectly friendly, they received them in the most cordial and confiding manner. In the course of the night, the man on guard near the horses fell sound asleep; upon which a Shoshonie shot him in the head, and nearly killed him. The savages then made off with the horses, leaving the rest of the party to find their way to the main body on foot.

The rival companies of Captain Bonneville and Mr. Campbell, thus fortuitously brought together, now prosecuted their journey in great good fellowship; forming a joint camp of about a hundred men. The captain, however, began to entertain doubts that Fitzpatrick and his trappers, who kept profound silence as to their future movements, intended to hunt the same grounds which he had selected for his autumnal campaign; which lay to the west of the Horn River, on its tributary streams. In the course of his march, therefore, he secretly detached a small party of trappers, to make their way to those hunting grounds, while he continued on with the main body; appointing a rendezvous, at the next full moon, about the 28th of August, at a place called the Medicine Lodge.

On reaching the second chain, called the Bighorn Mountains, where the river forced its impetuous way through a precipitous defile, with cascades and rapids, the travellers were obliged to leave its banks, and traverse the mountains by a rugged and frightful route, emphatically called the "Bad Pass." Descending the opposite side, they again made for the river banks; and about the middle of August, reached the point below the rapids, where the river becomes navigable for boats. Here Captain Bonneville detached a second party of trappers, consisting of ten men, to seek and join those whom he had detached while on the route; appointing for them the same rendezvous, (at the Medicine Lodge,) on the 28th of August.

All hands now set to work to construct "bull boats," as they are technically called; a light, fragile kind of bark, characteristic of the expedients and inventions of the wilderness; being formed of buffalo skins, stretched on frames. They are sometimes, also, called skin boats. Wyeth was the first ready; and with his usual promptness and hardihood, launched his frail bark, singly, on this wild and hazardous voyage, down an almost interminable succession of rivers, winding through countries teeming with savage hordes. Milton Sublette, his former fellow traveller, and his companion in the battle scenes of Pierre's Hole, took passage in his boat. His crew consisted of two white men, and two Indians. We shall hear further of Wyeth, and his wild voyage, in the course of our wanderings about the Far West.

The remaining parties soon completed their several armaments. That of Captain Bonneville was composed of three bull boats, in which he embarked all his peltries, giving them in charge of Mr. Cerré, with a party of thirty-six men. Mr. Campbell took command of his own boats, and the little squadrons were soon gliding down the bright current of the Bighorn.

The secret precautions which Captain Bonneville had taken, to throw his men first into the trapping ground west of the Bighorn, were, probably, superfluous. It did not appear that Fitzpatrick had intended to hunt in that direction. The moment Mr. Campbell and his men embarked with the peltries, Fitzpatrick took charge of all the horses, amounting to above a hundred, and struck off to the east, to trap upon Littlehorn, Powder, and Tongue Rivers. He was accompanied by Captain Stewart, who was desirous of having a range about the Crow country. Of the adventures they met with in that region of vagabonds and horse stealers, we shall have something to relate hereafter.

Captain Bonneville being now left to prosecute his trapping campaign without rivalry, set out, on the 17th of August, for the rendezvous at Medicine Lodge. He had but four men remaining with him, and forty-six horses to take care of: with these he had to make his way over mountain and plain, through a marauding, horse stealing region, full of peril for a numerous cavalcade so slightly manned. He addressed himself to his difficult journey, however, with his usual alacrity of spirit.

In the afternoon of his first day's journey, on drawing near to the Bighorn Mountain, on the summit of which he intended to encamp for the night, he observed, to his disquiet, a cloud of smoke rising from its base. He came to a halt, and watched it anxiously. It was very irregular; sometimes it would almost die away; and then would mount up in heavy volumes. There was, apparently, a large party encamped there; probably, some ruffian horde of Blackfeet. At any rate, it would not do for so small a number of men, with so numerous a cavalcade, to venture within sight of any wandering tribe. Captain Bonneville and his companions, therefore, avoided this dangerous neighborhood; and, proceeding with extreme caution, reached the summit of the mountain, apparently without being discovered. Here they found a deserted Blackfoot fort, in which they ensconced themselves; disposed of every thing as securely as possible, and passed the night without molestation. Early the next morning, they descended the south side of the mountain into the great plain extending between it and the Littlehorn range. Here they soon came upon numerous footprints, and the carcasses of buffaloes; by which they knew there must be Indians not far off. Captain Bonneville now began to feel solicitude about the two small parties of trappers which he had detached; lest the Indians should have come upon them before they had united their forces. But he felt still more solicitude about his own party: for it was hardly to be expected he could traverse these naked plains undiscovered, when Indians were abroad; and should he be discovered, his chance would be a desperate one. Every thing now depended upon the greatest circumspection. It was dangerous to discharge a gun, or light a fire, or make the least noise, where such quick-eared and quick-sighted enemies were at hand. In the course of the day, they saw indubitable signs that the buffalo had been roaming there in great numbers, and had recently been frightened away. That night they encamped with the greatest care; and threw up a strong breastwork for their protection.

For the two succeeding days, they pressed forward rapidly, but cautiously, across the great plain; fording the tributary streams of the Horn River: encamping one night among thickets; the next, on an island; meeting, repeatedly, with traces of Indians; and now and then, in passing through a defile, experiencing alarms that induced them to cock their rifles.

On the last day of their march, hunger got the better of their caution, and they shot a fine buffalo bull; at the risk of being betrayed by the report. They did not halt to make a meal, but carried the meat on with them to the place of rendezvous, the Medicine Lodge, where they arrived safely, in the evening, and celebrated their arrival by a hearty supper.

The next morning, they erected a strong pen for the horses, and a fortress of logs for themselves; and continued to observe the greatest caution. Their cooking was all done at mid-day, when the fire makes no glare, and a moderate smoke cannot be perceived at any great distance. In the morning and the evening, when the wind is lulled, the smoke rises perpendicularly in a blue column, or floats in light clouds above the tree tops, and can be discovered from afar.

In this way, the little party remained for several days, cautiously encamped, until, on the 29th of August, the two detachments they had been expecting, arrived together at the rendezvous. They, as usual, had their several tales of adventures to relate to the captain, which we will furnish to the reader in the next chapter.

Chapter XXIV

THE ADVENTURES of the detachment of ten are the first in order. These trappers, when they separated from Captain Bonneville at the place where the furs were embarked, proceeded to the foot of the Bighorn Mountain, and having encamped, one of them mounted his mule and went out to set his trap in a neighboring stream. He had not proceeded far when his steed came to a full stop. The trapper kicked and cudgelled, but to every blow and kick, the mule snorted and kicked up, but still refused to budge an inch. The rider now cast his eyes warily around in search of some cause for this demur, when, to his dismay, he discovered an Indian fort within gunshot distance, lowering through the twilight. In a twinkling, he wheeled about; his mule now seemed as eager to get on as himself, and in a few moments brought him, clattering with his traps, among his comrades. He was jeered at for his alacrity in retreating; his report was treated as a false alarm; his brother trappers contented themselves with reconnoitring the fort at a distance, and pronounced that it was deserted.

As night set in, the usual precaution, enjoined by Captain Bonneville on his men, was observed. The horses were brought in and tied, and a guard stationed over them. This done, the men wrapped themselves in their blankets, stretched themselves before the fire, and being fatigued with a long day's march, and gorged with a hearty supper, were soon in a profound sleep.

The camp fires gradually died away; all was dark and silent; the sentinel stationed to watch the horses had marched as far, and supped as heartily as any of his companions, and while they snored, he began to nod at his post. After a time, a low trampling noise reached his ear. He half opened his closing eyes, and beheld two or three elks moving about the lodges, picking, and smelling, and grazing here and there. The sight of elk within the purlieus of the camp caused some little surprise; but, having had his supper, he cared not for elk meat, and, suffering them to graze about unmolested, soon relapsed into a doze.

Suddenly, before daybreak, a discharge of fire-arms, and a struggle and tramp of horses, made every one start to his feet. The first move was to secure the horses. Some were gone; others were struggling, and kicking, and trembling, for there was a horrible uproar of whoops, and yells, and fire-arms. Several trappers stole quietly from the camp, and succeeded in driving in the horses which had broken away; the rest were tethered still more strongly. A breastwork was thrown up of saddles, baggage, and camp furniture, and all hands waited anxiously for daylight. The Indians, in the meantime, collected on a neighboring height, kept up the most horrible clamor, in hopes of striking a panic into the camp, or frightening off the horses. When the day dawned. the trappers attacked them briskly and drove them to some distance. A desultory firing was kept up for an hour, when the Indians, seeing nothing was to be gained, gave up the contest and retired. They proved to be a war party of Blackfeet, who, while in search of the Crow tribe, had fallen upon the trail of Captain Bonneville on the Popo Agie, and dogged him to the Bighorn; but had been completely baffled by his vigilance. They had then waylaid the present detachment, and were actually housed in perfect silence within their fort, when the mule of the trapper made such a dead point.

The savages went off uttering the wildest denunciations of hostility, mingled with opprobrious terms in broken English, and gesticulations of the most insulting kind.

In this melée, one white man was wounded, and two horses were killed. On preparing the morning's meal, however, a number of cups, knives, and other articles were missing, which had doubtless been carried off by the fictitious elk, during the slumber of the very sagacious sentinel.

As the Indians had gone off in the direction which the trappers had intended to travel, the latter changed their route, and pushed forward rapidly through the "Bad Pass," nor halted until night; when, supposing themselves out of the reach of the enemy, they contented themselves with tying up their horses and posting a guard. They had scarce laid down to sleep, when a dog strayed into the camp with a small pack of moccasins tied upon his back; for dogs are made to carry burthens among the Indians. The sentinel, more knowing than he of the preceding night, awoke his companions and reported the circumstance. It was evident that Indians were at hand. All were instantly at work; a strong pen was soon constructed for the horses, after completing which, they resumed their slumbers with the composure of men long inured to dangers.

In the next night, the prowling of dogs about the camp, and various suspicious noises, showed that Indians were still hovering about them. Hurrying on by long marches, they at length fell upon a trail, which, with the experienced eye of veteran woodmen, they soon discovered to be that of the party of trappers detached by Captain Bonneville when on his march, and which they were sent to join. They likewise ascertained from various signs, that this party had suffered some maltreatment from the Indians. They now pursued the trail with intense anxiety; it carried them to the banks of the stream called the Gray Bull, and down along its course, until they came to where it empties into the Horn River. Here, to their great joy, they discovered the comrades of whom they were in search, all strongly fortified, and in a state of great watchfulness and anxiety.

We now take up the adventures of this first detachment of trappers. These men, after parting with the main body under Captain Bonneville, had proceeded slowly for several days up the course of the river, trapping beaver as they went. One morning, as they were about to visit their traps, one of the camp-keepers pointed to a fine elk, grazing at a distance, and requested them to shoot it. Three of the trappers started off for the purpose. In passing a thicket, they were fired upon by some savages in ambush, and at the same time, the pretended elk, throwing off his hide and his horns, started forth an Indian warrior.

One of the three trappers had been brought down by the volley; the others fled to the camp, and all hands, seizing up whatever they could carry off, retreated to a small island in

the river, and took refuge among the willows. Here they were
soon joined by their comrade who had fallen, but who had
merely been wounded in the neck.

In the meantime, the Indians took possession of the deserted camp, with all the traps, accoutrements, and horses.
While they were busy among the spoils, a solitary trapper,
who had been absent at his work, came sauntering to the
camp with his traps on his back. He had approached near by,
when an Indian came forward and motioned him to keep
away; at the same moment, he was perceived by his comrades
on the island, and warned of his danger with loud cries. The
poor fellow stood for a moment, bewildered and aghast, then
dropping his traps, wheeled and made off at full speed, quickened by a sportive volley which the Indians rattled after him.

In high good-humor with their easy triumph, the savages
now formed a circle round the fire and performed a war
dance, with the unlucky trappers for rueful spectators. This
done, emboldened by what they considered cowardice on the
part of the white men, they neglected their usual mode of
bush fighting, and advanced openly within twenty paces of
the willows. A sharp volley from the trappers brought them to
a sudden halt, and laid three of them breathless. The chief,
who had stationed himself on an eminence to direct all the
movements of his people, seeing three of his warriors laid low,
ordered the rest to retire. They immediately did so, and the
whole band soon disappeared behind a point of woods, carrying off with them the horses, traps, and the greater part of
the baggage.

It was just after this misfortune, that the party of ten men
discovered this forlorn band of trappers in a fortress, which
they had thrown up after their disaster. They were so perfectly
dismayed, that they could not be induced even to go in quest
of their traps, which they had set in a neighboring stream.
The two parties now joined their forces, and made their way,
without further misfortune, to the rendezvous.

Captain Bonneville perceived from the reports of these parties, as well as from what he had observed himself in his recent
march, that he was in a neighborhood teeming with danger.
Two wandering Snake Indians, also, who visited the camp, assured him that there were two large bands of Crows marching

rapidly upon him. He broke up his encampment, therefore, on the 1st of September, made his way to the south, across the Littlehorn Mountain, until he reached Wind River, and then turning westward, moved slowly up the banks of that stream, giving time for his men to trap as he proceeded. As it was not in the plan of the present hunting campaign to go near the caches on Green River, and as the trappers were in want of traps to replace those they had lost, Captain Bonneville undertook to visit the caches, and procure a supply. To accompany him in this hazardous expedition, which would take him through the defiles of the Wind River Mountains, and up the Green River valley, he took but three men; the main party were to continue on trapping up towards the head of Wind River, near which he was to rejoin them, just about the place where that stream issues from the mountains. We shall accompany the captain on his adventurous errand.

Chapter XXV

*Captain Bonneville sets out for Green River valley—Journey
up the Popo Agie—Buffaloes—The staring white bears—The
smoke—The warm springs—Attempt to traverse the Wind
River Mountains—The Great Slope—Mountain dells and
chasms—Crystal lakes—Ascent of a snowy peak—Sublime
prospect—A panorama—"Les dignes de pitie," or wild men
of the mountains*

HAVING forded Wind River a little above its mouth,
Captain Bonneville and his three companions proceeded across a gravelly plain, until they fell upon the Popo
Agie, up the left bank of which they held their course, nearly
in a southerly direction. Here they came upon numerous
droves of buffalo, and halted for the purpose of procuring a
supply of beef. As the hunters were stealing cautiously to get
within shot of the game, two small white bears suddenly presented themselves in their path, and, rising upon their hind
legs, contemplated them for some time, with a whimsically
solemn gaze. The hunters remained motionless; whereupon
the bears, having apparently satisfied their curiosity, lowered
themselves upon all fours, and began to withdraw. The hunters
now advanced, upon which the bears turned, rose again upon
their haunches, and repeated their serio-comic examination.
This was repeated several times, until the hunters, piqued
at their unmannerly staring, rebuked it with a discharge of
their rifles. The bears made an awkward bound or two, as if
wounded, and then walked off with great gravity, seeming to
commune together, and every now and then turning to take
another look at the hunters. It was well for the latter that
the bears were but half grown, and had not yet acquired the
ferocity of their kind.

The buffalo were somewhat startled at the report of the
fire-arms; but the hunters succeeded in killing a couple of fine
cows, and, having secured the best of the meat, continued
forward until some time after dark, when, encamping in a
large thicket of willows, they made a great fire, roasted buffalo beef enough for half a score, disposed of the whole of it

with keen relish and high glee, and then "turned in" for the night and slept soundly, like weary and well fed hunters.

At daylight they were in the saddle again, and skirted along the river, passing through fresh grassy meadows, and a succession of beautiful groves of willows and cotton-wood. Towards evening, Captain Bonneville observed a smoke at a distance rising from among hills, directly in the route he was pursuing. Apprehensive of some hostile band, he concealed the horses in a thicket, and, accompanied by one of his men, crawled cautiously up a height, from which he could overlook the scene of danger. Here, with a spyglass, he reconnoitered the surrounding country, but not a lodge nor fire, not a man, horse, nor dog, was to be discovered: in short, the smoke which had caused such alarm proved to be the vapor from several warm, or rather hot springs of considerable magnitude, pouring forth streams in every direction over a bottom of white clay. One of the springs was about twenty-five yards in diameter, and so deep, that the water was of a bright green color.

They were now advancing diagonally upon the chain of Wind River Mountains, which lay between them and Green River valley. To coast round their southern points would be a wide circuit; whereas, could they force a way through them, they might proceed in a straight line. The mountains were lofty, with snowy peaks and cragged sides; it was hoped, however, that some practicable defile might be found. They attempted, accordingly, to penetrate the mountains by following up one of the branches of the Popo Agie, but soon found themselves in the midst of stupendous crags and precipices, that barred all progress. Retracing their steps, and falling back upon the river, they consulted where to make another attempt. They were too close beneath the mountains to scan them generally, but they now recollected having noticed, from the plain, a beautiful slope, rising, at an angle of about thirty degrees, and apparently without any break, until it reached the snowy region. Seeking this gentle acclivity, they began to ascend it with alacrity, trusting to find at the top one of those elevated plains which prevail among the Rocky Mountains. The slope was covered with coarse gravel, interspersed with plates of freestone. They attained the summit with some toil, but found, instead of a level, or rather undulating plain, that they were on the brink of a deep and precipitous ravine, from the bottom of which, rose a second slope, similar to the one they had just ascended. Down into this profound ravine they made their way by a rugged path, or rather fissure of the rocks, and then labored up the second slope. They gained the summit only to find themselves on another ravine, and now perceived that this vast mountain which had presented such a sloping and even side to the distant beholder on the plain, was shagged by frightful precipices, and seamed with longitudinal chasms, deep and dangerous.

In one of these wild dells they passed the night, and slept soundly and sweetly after their fatigues. Two days more of arduous climbing and scrambling only served to admit them into the heart of this mountainous and awful solitude: where difficulties increased as they proceeded. Sometimes they scrambled from rock to rock, up the bed of some mountain stream, dashing its bright way down to the plains; sometimes they availed themselves of the paths made by the deer and the mountain sheep, which, however, often took them to the brink of fearful precipices, or led to rugged defiles, impassable for their horses. At one place, they were obliged to slide their horses down the face of a rock, in which attempt some of the poor animals lost their footing, rolled to the bottom, and came near being dashed to pieces.

In the afternoon of the second day, the travellers attained one of the elevated valleys locked up in this singular bed of mountains. Here were two bright and beautiful little lakes, set like mirrors in the midst of stern and rocky heights, and surrounded by grassy meadows, inexpressibly refreshing to the eye. These probably were among the sources of those mighty streams which take their rise among these mountains, and wander hundreds of miles through the plains.

In the green pastures bordering upon these lakes, the travellers halted to repose, and to give their weary horses time to crop the sweet and tender herbage. They had now ascended to a great height above the level of the plains, yet they beheld huge crags of granite piled one upon another, and beetling like battlements far above them. While two of the men remained in the camp with the horses, Captain Bonneville, accompanied by the other men, set out to climb a neighboring height, hoping to gain a commanding prospect, and discern some practicable route through this stupendous labyrinth. After much toil, he reached the summit of a lofty cliff, but it was only to behold gigantic peaks rising all around, and towering far into the snowy regions of the atmosphere. Selecting one which appeared to be the highest, he crossed a narrow intervening valley, and began to scale it. He soon found that he had undertaken a tremendous task; but the pride of man is never more obstinate than when climbing mountains. The ascent was so steep and rugged that he and his companions were frequently obliged to clamber on hands and knees, with their guns slung upon their backs. Frequently exhausted with fatigue, and dripping with perspiration, they threw themselves upon the snow, and took handfulls of it to allay their parching thirst. At one place, they even stripped off their coats and hung them upon the bushes, and thus lightly clad, proceeded to scramble over these eternal snows. As they ascended still higher, there were cool breezes that refreshed and braced them, and springing with new ardor to their task, they at length attained the summit.

Here a scene burst upon the view of Captain Bonneville, that for a time astonished and overwhelmed him with its immensity. He stood, in fact, upon that dividing ridge which Indians regard as the crest of the world; and on each side of which, the landscape may be said to decline to the two cardinal oceans of the globe. Whichever way he turned his eye, it was confounded by the vastness and variety of objects. Beneath him, the Rocky Mountains seemed to open all their secret recesses: deep solemn valleys; treasured lakes; dreary passes; rugged defiles, and foaming torrents; while beyond their savage precincts, the eye was lost in an almost immeasurable landscape; stretching on every side into dim and hazy distance, like the expanse of a summer's sea. Whichever way he looked, he beheld vast plains glimmering with reflected sunshine; mighty streams wandering on their shining course toward either ocean, and snowy mountains, chain beyond chain, and peak beyond peak, till they melted like clouds into the horizon. For a time, the Indian fable seemed realized: he had attained that height from which the Blackfoot warrior, after death, first catches a view of the land of souls, and beholds the happy hunting grounds spread out below him, brightening with the

abodes of the free and generous spirits. The captain stood for
a long while gazing upon this scene, lost in a crowd of vague
and indefinite ideas and sensations. A long drawn inspiration at
length relieved him from this enthralment of the mind, and he
began to analyze the parts of this vast panorama. A simple enu-
meration of a few of its features, may give some idea of its col-
lective grandeur and magnificence.

The peak on which the captain had taken his stand, commanded the whole Wind River chain; which, in fact, may
rather be considered one immense mountain, broken into
snowy peaks and lateral spurs, and seamed with narrow valleys.
Some of these valleys glittered with silver lakes and gushing
streams; the fountain heads, as it were, of the mighty tributaries to the Atlantic and Pacific Oceans. Beyond the snowy
peaks, to the south, and far, far below the mountain range, the
gentle river, called the Sweet Water, was seen pursuing its tranquil way through the rugged region of the Black Hills. In the
east, the head waters of Wind River wandered through a plain,
until, mingling in one powerful current, they forced their way
through the range of Horn Mountains, and were lost to view.
To the north, were caught glimpses of the upper streams of the
Yellowstone, that great tributary of the Missouri. In another
direction were to be seen some of the sources of the Oregon
or Columbia, flowing to the northwest, past those towering
landmarks the Three Tetons, and pouring down into the great
lava plain; while almost at the captain's feet, the Green River,
or Colorado of the West, set forth on its wandering pilgrimage
to the Gulf of California; at first a mere mountain torrent,
dashing northward over crag and precipice, in a succession of
cascades, and tumbling into the plain, where, expanding into
an ample river, it circled away to the south, and after alternately shining out and disappearing in the mazes of the vast
landscape, was finally lost in a horizon of mountains. The day
was calm and cloudless, and the atmosphere so pure that objects were discernable at an astonishing distance. The whole of
this immense area was enclosed by an outer range of shadowy
peaks, some of them faintly marked on the horizon, which
seemed to wall it in from the rest of the earth.

It is to be regretted that Captain Bonneville had no instruments with him with which to ascertain the altitude of this

peak. He gives it as his opinion, that it is the loftiest point of the North American continent; but of this we have no satisfactory proof. It is certain that the Rocky Mountains are of an altitude vastly superior to what was formerly supposed. We rather incline to the opinion that the highest peak is further to the northward, and is the same measured by Mr. Thompson, surveyor to the Northwest Company; who, by the joint means of the barometer and trigonometric measurement, ascertained it to be twenty-five thousand feet above the level of the sea; an elevation only inferior to that of the Himalayas.*

For a long time, Captain Bonneville remained gazing around him with wonder and enthusiasm; at length the chill and wintry winds, whirling about the snow-clad height, admonished him to descend. He soon regained the spot where he and his companions had thrown off their coats, which were now gladly resumed, and, retracing their course down the peak, they safely rejoined their companions on the border of the lake.

Notwithstanding the savage, and almost inaccessible nature of these mountains, they have their inhabitants. As one of the party was out hunting, he came upon the solitary track of a man, in a lonely valley. Following it up, he reached the brow of a cliff, whence he beheld three savages running across the valley below him. He fired his gun to call their attention, hoping to induce them to turn back. They only fled the faster, and disappeared among the rocks. The hunter returned and reported what he had seen. Captain Bonneville at once concluded that these belonged to a kind of hermit race, scanty in number, that inhabit the highest and most inaccessible fastnesses. They speak the Shoshonie language, and probably are offsets from that tribe, though they have peculiarities of their own, which distinguish them from all other Indians. They are miserably poor; own no horses, and are destitute of every convenience to be derived from an intercourse with the whites. Their weapons are bows and stone-pointed arrows, with which they hunt the deer, the elk, and the mountain sheep. They are to be found scattered about the countries of the Shoshonie, Flathead, Crow, and Blackfeet tribes; but their

* See the letter of Professor Renwick, in the Appendix to Astoria.

residences are always in lonely places, and the clefts of the rocks.

Their footsteps are often seen by the trappers in the high and solitary valleys among the mountains, and the smokes of their fires descried among the precipices, but they themselves are rarely met with, and still more rarely brought to a parley, so great is their shyness, and their dread of strangers.

As their poverty offers no temptation to the marauder, and as they are inoffensive in their habits, they are never the objects of warfare: should one of them, however, fall into the hands of a war party, he is sure to be made a sacrifice, for the sake of that savage trophy, a scalp, and that barbarous ceremony, a scalp dance. These forlorn beings, forming a mere link between human nature and the brute, have been looked down upon with pity and contempt by the Creole trappers, who have given them the appellation of "les dignes de pitie," or "the objects of pity." They appear more worthy to be called, the wild men of the mountains.

Chapter XXVI

A retrograde move—Channel of a mountain torrent—Alpine scenery—Cascades—Beaver valleys—Beavers at work—Their architecture—Their modes of felling trees—Mode of trapping beaver—Contests of skill—A beaver "up to trap"—Arrival at the Green River caches

THE VIEW from the snowy peak of the Wind River Mountains, while it had excited Captain Bonneville's enthusiasm, had satisfied him that it would be useless to force a passage westward, through multiplying barriers of cliffs and precipices. Turning his face eastward, therefore, he endeavored to regain the plains, intending to make the circuit round the southern point of the mountain. To descend, and to extricate himself from the heart of this rock-piled wilderness, was almost as difficult as to penetrate it. Taking his course down the ravine of a tumbling stream, the commencement of some future river, he descended from rock to rock, and shelf to shelf, between stupendous cliffs and beetling crags, that sprang up to the sky. Often he had to cross and recross the rushing torrent, as it wound foaming and roaring down its broken channel, or was walled by perpendicular precipices; and imminent was the hazard of breaking the legs of the horses in the clefts and fissures of slippery rocks. The whole scenery of this deep ravine was of Alpine wildness and sublimity. Sometimes the travellers passed beneath cascades which pitched from such lofty heights, that the water fell into the stream like heavy rain. In other places, torrents came tumbling from crag to crag, dashing into foam and spray, and making tremendous din and uproar.

On the second day of their descent, the travellers having got beyond the steepest pitch of the mountains, came to where the deep and rugged ravine began occasionally to expand into small levels or valleys, and the stream to assume for short intervals a more peaceful character. Here, not merely the river itself, but every rivulet flowing into it, was dammed up by communities of industrious beavers, so as to inundate the neighborhood, and make continual swamps.

During a mid-day halt in one of these beaver valleys, Captain Bonneville left his companions, and strolled down the course of the stream to reconnoitre. He had not proceeded far, when he came to a beaver pond, and caught a glimpse of one of its painstaking inhabitants busily at work upon the dam. The curiosity of the captain was aroused, to behold the mode of operating of this far-famed architect; he moved forward, therefore, with the utmost caution, parting the branches of the water willows without making any noise, until having attained a position commanding a view of the whole pond, he stretched himself flat on the ground, and watched the solitary workman. In a little while, three others appeared at the head of the dam, bringing sticks and bushes. With these they proceeded directly to the barrier, which Captain Bonneville perceived was in need of repair. Having deposited their loads upon the broken part, they dived into the water, and shortly reappeared at the surface. Each now brought a quantity of mud, with which he would plaster the sticks and bushes just deposited. This kind of masonry was continued for some time, repeated supplies of wood and mud being brought, and treated in the same manner. This done, the industrious beavers indulged in a little recreation, chasing each other about the pond, dodging and whisking about on the surface, or diving to the bottom; and in their frolic, often slapping their tails on the water with a loud clacking sound. While they were thus amusing themselves, another of the fraternity made his appearance, and looked gravely on their sports for some time, without offering to join in them. He then climbed the bank close to where the captain was concealed, and, rearing himself on his hind quarters, in a sitting position, put his fore paws against a young pine tree, and began to cut the bark with his teeth. At times he would tear off a small piece, and holding it between his paws, and retaining his sedentary position, would feed himself with it, after the fashion of a monkey. The object of the beaver, however, was evidently to cut down the tree; and he was proceeding with his work, when he was alarmed by the approach of Captain Bonneville's men, who, feeling anxious at the protracted absence of their leader, were coming in search of him. At the sound of their voices, all the beavers, busy as well as idle, dived at once beneath the surface, and were no more to be seen. Captain

Bonneville regretted this interruption. He had heard much of the sagacity of the beaver in cutting down trees, in which it is said, they manage to make them fall into the water, and in such a position and direction as may be most favorable for conveyance to the desired point. In the present instance, the tree was a tall straight pine, and as it grew perpendicularly, and there was not a breath of air stirring, the beaver could have felled it in any direction he pleased, if really capable of exercising a discretion in the matter. He was evidently engaged in "belting" the tree, and his first incision had been on the side nearest to the water.

Captain Bonneville, however, discredits on the whole, the alleged sagacity of the beaver in this particular, and thinks the animal has no other aim than to get the tree down, without any of the subtle calculation as to its mode or direction of falling. This attribute, he thinks, has been ascribed to them from the circumstance, that most trees growing near water courses, either lean bodily towards the stream, or stretch their largest limbs in that direction, to benefit by the space, the light, and the air to be found there. The beaver, of course, attacks those trees which are nearest at hand, and on the banks of the stream or pond. He makes incisions round them, or, in technical phrase, belts them with his teeth, and when they fall, they naturally take the direction in which their trunks or branches preponderate.

"I have often," says Captain Bonneville, "seen trees measuring eighteen inches in diameter, at the places where they had been cut through by the beaver, but they lay in all directions, and often very inconveniently for the after purposes of the animal. In fact, so little ingenuity do they at times display in this particular, that at one of our camps on Snake River, a beaver was found with his head wedged into the cut which he had made, the tree having fallen upon him and held him prisoner until he died."

Great choice, according to the captain, is certainly displayed by the beaver in selecting the wood which is to furnish bark for winter provision. The whole beaver household, old and young, set out upon this business, and will often make long journeys before they are suited. Sometimes they cut down trees of the largest size, and then cull the branches, the bark of which is most to their taste. These they cut into lengths of about three feet, convey them to the water, and float them to their lodges, where they are stored away for winter. They are studious of cleanliness and comfort in their lodges, and after their repasts, will carry out the sticks from which they have eaten the bark, and throw them into the current beyond the barrier. They are jealous, too, of their territories, and extremely pugnacious, never permitting a strange beaver to enter their premises, and often fighting with such virulence as almost to tear each other to pieces. In the spring, which is the breeding season, the male leaves the female at home, and sets off on a tour of pleasure, rambling often to a great distance, recreating himself in every clear and quiet expanse of water on his way, and climbing the banks occasionally to feast upon the tender sprouts of the young willows. As summer advances, he gives up his bachelor rambles, and bethinking himself of housekeeping duties, returns home to his mate and his new progeny, and marshals them all for the foraging expedition in quest of winter provisions.

After having shown the public spirit of this praiseworthy little animal as a member of a community, and his amiable and exemplary conduct as the father of a family, we grieve to record the perils with which he is environed, and the snares set for him and his painstaking household.

Practice, says Captain Bonneville, has given such a quickness of eye to the experienced trapper in all that relates to his pursuit, that he can detect the slightest sign of beaver, however wild; and although the lodge may be concealed by close thickets and overhanging willows, he can generally, at a single glance, make an accurate guess at the number of its inmates. He now goes to work to set his trap; planting it upon the shore, in some chosen place, two or three inches below the surface of the water, and secures it by a chain to a pole set deep in the mud. A small twig is then stripped of its bark, and one end is dipped in the "medicine," as the trappers term the peculiar bait which they employ. This end of the stick rises about four inches above the surface of the water, the other end is planted between the jaws of the trap. The beaver, possessing an acute sense of smell, is soon attracted by the odor of the bait. As he raises his nose towards it, his foot is caught in the trap. In his fright he throws a somerest into the deep water. The trap, being fastened to the pole, resists all his efforts to drag it to the shore; the chain by which it is fastened defies his teeth; he struggles for a time, and at length sinks to the bottom and is drowned.

Upon rocky bottoms, where it is not possible to plant the pole, it is thrown into the stream. The beaver, when entrapped, often gets fastened by the chain to sunken logs or floating timber; if he gets to shore, he is entangled in the thickets of brook willows. In such cases, however, it costs the trapper a diligent search, and sometimes a bout at swimming, before he finds his game.

Occasionally it happens that several members of a beaver family are trapped in succession. The survivors then become extremely shy, and can scarcely be "brought to medicine," to use the trapper's phrase for "taking the bait." In such case, the trapper gives up the use of the bait, and conceals his traps in the usual paths and crossing places of the household. The beaver now being completely "up to trap," approaches them cautiously, and springs them ingeniously with a stick. At other times, he turns the traps bottom upwards, by the same means, and occasionally even drags them to the barrier and conceals them in the mud. The trapper now gives up the contest of ingenuity, and shouldering his traps, marches off, admitting that he is not yet "up to beaver."

On the day following Captain Bonneville's supervision of the industrious and frolicsome community of beavers, of which he has given so edifying an account, he succeeded in extricating himself from the Wind River Mountains, and regaining the plain to the eastward, made a great bend to the south, so as to go round the bases of the mountains, and arrived without further incident of importance, at the old place of rendezvous in Green River valley, on the 17th of September.

He found the caches, in which he had deposited his superfluous goods and equipments, all safe, and having opened and taken from them the necessary supplies, he closed them again; taking care to obliterate all traces that might betray them to the keen eyes of Indian marauders.

Chapter XXVII

ON THE 18TH of September, Captain Bonneville and his three companions set out, bright and early, to rejoin the main party, from which they had parted on Wind River. Their route lay up the Green River valley, with that stream on their right hand, and beyond it, the range of Wind River Mountains. At the head of the valley, they were to pass through a defile which would bring them out beyond the northern end of these mountains, to the head of Wind River; where they expected to meet the main party, according to arrangement.

We have already adverted to the dangerous nature of this neighborhood, infested by roving bands of Crows and Blackfeet; to whom the numerous defiles and passes of the country afford capital places for ambush and surprise. The travellers, therefore, kept a vigilant eye upon every thing that might give intimation of lurking danger.

About two hours after mid-day, as they reached the summit of a hill, they discovered buffalo on the plain below, running in every direction. One of the men, too, fancied he heard the report of a gun. It was concluded, therefore, that there was some party of Indians below, hunting the buffalo.

The horses were immediately concealed in a narrow ravine; and the captain, mounting an eminence, but concealing himself from view, reconnoitred the whole neighborhood with a telescope. Not an Indian was to be seen: so, after halting about an hour, he resumed his journey. Convinced, however, that he was in a dangerous neighborhood, he advanced with the utmost caution; winding his way through hollows and ravines,

799

and avoiding, as much as possible, any open tract, or rising ground, that might betray his little party to the watchful eye of an Indian scout.

Arriving, at length, at the edge of the open meadow-land bordering on the river, he again observed the buffalo, as far as he could see, scampering in great alarm. Once more concealing the horses, he and his companions remained for a long time watching the various groups of the animals, as each caught the panic and started off: but they sought in vain to discover the cause.

They were now about to enter the mountain defile, at the head of Green River valley, where they might be waylaid and attacked: they, therefore, arranged the packs on their horses, in the manner most secure and convenient for sudden flight, should such be necessary. This done, they again set forward, keeping the most anxious look out in every direction.

It was now drawing towards evening; but they could not think of encamping for the night, in a place so full of danger. Captain Bonneville, therefore, determined to halt about sunset, kindle a fire, as if for encampment, cook and eat supper; but, as soon as it was sufficiently dark, to make a rapid move for the summit of the mountain, and seek some secluded spot for their night's lodgings.

Accordingly, as the sun went down, the little party came to a halt, made a large fire, spitted their buffalo meat on wooden sticks, and, when sufficiently roasted, planted the savory viands before them; cutting off huge slices with their hunting knives, and supping with a hunter's appetite. The light of their fire would not fail, as they knew, to attract the attention of any Indian horde in the neighborhood: but they trusted to be off and away, before any prowlers could reach the place. While they were supping thus hastily, however, one of their party suddenly started up, and shouted "Indians!" All were instantly on their feet, with their rifles in their hands; but could see no enemy. The man, however, declared that he had seen an Indian advancing, cautiously, along the trail which they had made in coming to the encampment; who, the moment he was perceived, had thrown himself on the ground, and disappeared. He urged Captain Bonneville instantly to decamp. The captain, however, took the matter more coolly. The single fact, that the Indian had endeavored to hide himself, convinced him that he was not one of a party, on the advance to make an attack. He was, probably, some scout, who had followed up their trail, until he came in sight of their fire. He would, in such case, return, and report what he had seen to his companions. These, supposing the white men had encamped for the night, would keep aloof until very late; when all should be asleep. They would then, according to Indian tactics, make their stealthy approaches, and place themselves in ambush around, preparatory to their attack, at the usual hour of daylight.

Such was Captain Bonneville's conclusion; in consequence of which, he counselled his men to keep perfectly quiet, and act as if free from all alarm, until the proper time arrived for a move. They, accordingly, continued their repast with pretended appetite and jollity; and then trimmed and replenished their fire, as if for a bivouac. As soon, however, as the night had completely set in, they left their fire blazing; walked quietly among the willows, and then leaping into their saddles, made off as noiselessly as possible. In proportion as they left the point of danger behind them, they relaxed in their rigid and anxious taciturnity, and began to joke at the expense of their enemy: whom they pictured to themselves, mousing in the neighborhood of their deserted fire, waiting for the proper time of attack, and preparing for a grand disappointment.

About midnight, feeling satisfied that they had gained a secure distance, they posted one of their number to keep watch; in case the enemy should follow on their trail: and then, turning abruptly into a dense and matted thicket of willows, halted for the night at the foot of the mountain, instead of making for the summit, as they had originally intended.

A trapper in the wilderness, like a sailor on the ocean, snatches morsels of enjoyment in the midst of trouble, and sleeps soundly when surrounded by danger. The little party now made their arrangements for sleep with perfect calmness: they did not venture to make a fire and cook, it is true; though generally done by hunters whenever they come to a halt, and have provisions. They comforted themselves, however, by smoking a tranquil pipe; and then calling in the watch, and turning loose the horses, stretched themselves on their pallets, agreed that whoever should first awake, should rouse the rest;

and in a little while were all in as sound sleep as though in the midst of a fortress.

A little before day, they were all on the alert; it was the hour for Indian maraud. A sentinel was immediately detached, to post himself at a little distance on their trail, and give the alarm, should he see or hear an enemy.

With the first blink of dawn, the rest sought the horses; brought them to the camp, and tied them up, until an hour after sunrise: when, the sentinel having reported that all was well, they sprang once more into their saddles, and pursued the most covert and secret paths up the mountain, avoiding the direct route.

At noon, they halted and made a hasty repast; and then bent their course so as to regain the route from which they had diverged. They were now made sensible of the danger from which they had just escaped. There were tracks of Indians who had evidently been in pursuit of them; but had recently returned, baffled in their search.

Trusting that they had now got a fair start, and could not be overtaken before night, even in case the Indians should renew the chase, they pushed briskly forward, and did not encamp until late; when they cautiously concealed themselves in a secure nook of the mountains.

Without any further alarm, they made their way to the head waters of Wind River; and reached the neighborhood in which they had appointed the rendezvous with their companions. It was within the precincts of the Crow country; the Wind River valley being one of the favorite haunts of that restless tribe. After much searching, Captain Bonneville came upon a trail which had evidently been made by his main party. It was so old, however, that he feared his people might have left the neighborhood; driven off, perhaps, by some of those war parties which were on the prowl. He continued his search with great anxiety, and no little fatigue; for his horses were jaded, and almost crippled, by their forced marches and scramblings through rocky defiles.

On the following day, about noon, Captain Bonneville came upon a deserted camp of his people, from which they had, evidently, turned back; but he could find no signs to indicate why they had done so; whether they had met with misfortune, or molestation, or in what direction they had gone. He was now, more than ever, perplexed.

On the following day, he resumed his march with increasing anxiety. The feet of his horses had by this time become so worn and wounded by the rocks, that he had to make moccasins for them of buffalo hide. About noon, he came to another deserted camp of his men; but soon after lost their trail. After great search, he once more found it, turning in a southerly direction along the eastern bases of the Wind River Mountains, which towered to the right. He now pushed forward with all possible speed, in hopes of overtaking the party. At night, he slept at another of their camps, from which they had but recently departed. When the day dawned sufficiently to distinguish objects, he perceived the danger that must be dogging the heels of his main party. All about the camp were traces of Indians, who must have been prowling about it at the time his people had passed the night there; and who must still be hovering about them. Convinced, now, that the main party could not be at any great distance, he mounted a scout on the best horse, and sent him forward to overtake them, to warn them of their danger, and to order them to halt, until he should regain them.

In the afternoon, to his great joy, he met the scout returning, with six comrades from the main party, leading fresh horses for his accommodation: and on the following day (September 25th), all hands were once more reunited; after a separation of nearly three weeks. Their meeting was hearty and joyous; for they had both experienced dangers and perplexities.

The main party, in pursuing their course up the Wind River valley, had been dogged the whole way by a war party of Crows. In one place, they had been fired upon; but without injury: in another place, one of their horses had been cut loose, and carried off. At length, they were so closely beset, that they were obliged to make a retrograde move; lest they should be surprised and overcome. This was the movement which had caused such perplexity to Captain Bonneville.

The whole party now remained encamped for two or three days, to give repose to both men and horses. Some of the trappers, however, pursued their vocations about the neighboring streams. While one of them was setting his traps, he heard the tramp of horses; and looking up, beheld a party of Crow braves moving along at no great distance, with a considerable cavalcade. The trapper hastened to conceal himself, but was discerned by the quick eye of the savages. With whoops and yells, they dragged him from his hiding-place, flourished over his head their tomahawks and scalping-knives, and for a time, the poor trapper gave himself up for lost. Fortunately, the Crows were in a jocose, rather than a sanguinary mood. They amused themselves heartily, for a while, at the expense of his terrors; and after having played off divers Crow pranks and pleasantries, suffered him to depart unharmed. It is true, they stripped him completely; one taking his horse, another his gun, a third his traps, a fourth his blanket; and so on, through all his accoutrements, and even his clothing, until he was stark naked; but then they generously made him a present of an old tattered buffalo robe, and dismissed him, with many complimentary speeches, and much laughter. When the trapper returned to the camp, in such sorry plight, he was greeted with peals of laughter from his comrades; and seemed more mortified by the style in which he had been dismissed, than rejoiced at escaping with his life. A circumstance which he related to Captain Bonneville, gave some insight into the cause of this extreme jocularity on the part of the Crows. They had evidently had a run of luck, and, like winning gamblers, were in high good-humor. Among twenty-six fine horses, and some mules, which composed their cavalcade, the trapper recognised a number which had belonged to Fitzpatrick's brigade, when they parted company on the Bighorn. It was supposed, therefore, that these vagabonds had been on his trail, and robbed him of part of his cavalry.

On the day following this affair, three Crows came into Captain Bonneville's camp, with the most easy, innocent, if not impudent air, imaginable; walking about with that imperturbable coolness and unconcern, in which the Indian rivals the fine gentleman. As they had not been of the set which stripped the trapper, though evidently of the same band, they were not molested. Indeed, Captain Bonneville treated them with his usual kindness and hospitality; permitting them to remain all day in the camp, and even to pass the night there. At the same time, however, he caused a strict watch to be maintained on all their movements; and at night, stationed an armed sentinel near them. The Crows remonstrated against the latter being armed. This only made the captain suspect them to be spies, who meditated treachery: he redoubled, therefore, his precautions. At the same time, he assured his guests, that while they were perfectly welcome to the shelter and comfort of his camp, yet, should any of their tribe venture to approach during the night, they would certainly be shot; which would be a very unfortunate circumstance, and much to be deplored. To the latter remark, they fully assented; and shortly afterward commenced a wild song, or chant, which they kept up for a long time, and in which, they very probably gave their friends, who might be prowling around the camp, notice that the white men were on the alert. The night passed away without disturbance. In the morning, the three Crow guests were very pressing that Captain Bonneville and his party should accompany them to their camp, which they said was close by. Instead of accepting their invitation, Captain Bonneville took his departure with all possible despatch; eager to be out of the vicinity of such a piratical horde: nor did he relax the diligence of his march, until, on the second day, he reached the banks of the Sweet Water, beyond the limits of the Crow country, and a heavy fall of snow had obliterated all traces of his course.

He now continued on for some few days, at a slower pace, round the point of the mountain towards Green River, and arrived once more at the caches, on the 14th of October.

Here they found traces of the band of Indians who had hunted them in the defile towards the head waters of Wind River. Having lost all trace of them on their way over the mountains, they had turned and followed back their trail down Green River valley to the caches. One of these they had discovered and broken open, but it fortunately contained nothing but fragments of old iron, which they had scattered about in all directions, and then departed. In examining their deserted camp, Captain Bonneville discovered that it numbered thirty-nine fires, and had more reason than ever to congratulate himself on having escaped the clutches of such a formidable band of freebooters.

He now turned his course southward, under cover of the mountains, and on the 25th of October reached Liberge's

Ford, a tributary of the Colorado, where he came suddenly upon the trail of this same war party, which had crossed the stream so recently, that the banks were yet wet with the water that had been splashed upon them. To judge from their tracks, they could not be less than three hundred warriors, and apparently of the Crow nation.

Captain Bonneville was extremely uneasy lest this overpowering force should come upon him in some place where he would not have the means of fortifying himself promptly. He now moved towards Hane's Fork, another tributary of the Colorado, where he encamped, and remained during the 26th of October. Seeing a large cloud of smoke to the south, he supposed it to arise from some encampment of Shoshonies, and sent scouts to procure information, and to purchase a lodge. It was, in fact, a band of Shoshonies, but with them were encamped Fitzpatrick and his party of trappers. That active leader had an eventful story to relate of his fortunes in the country of the Crows. After parting with Captain Bonneville on the banks of the Bighorn, he made for the west, to trap upon Powder and Tongue Rivers. He had between twenty and thirty men with him, and about one hundred horses. So large a cavalcade could not pass through the Crow country without attracting the attention of its freebooting hordes. A large band of Crows were soon on their traces, and came up with them on the 5th of September, just as they had reached Tongue River. The Crow chief came forward with great appearance of friendship, and proposed to Fitzpatrick that they should encamp together. The latter, however, not having any faith in Crows, declined the invitation, and pitched his camp three miles off. He then rode over, with two or three men, to visit the Crow chief, by whom he was received with great apparent cordiality. In the meantime, however, a party of young braves, who considered them absolved by his distrust from all scruples of honor, made a circuit privately, and dashed into his encampment. Captain Stewart, who had remained there in the absence of Fitzpatrick, behaved with great spirit; but the Crows were too numerous and active. They had got possession of the camp, and soon made booty of every thing—carrying off all the horses. On their way back they met Fitzpatrick returning to his camp; and finished their exploit by rifling and nearly stripping him.

A negotiation now took place between the plundered white men and the triumphant Crows; what eloquence and management Fitzpatrick made use of, we do not know, but he succeeded in prevailing upon the Crow chieftain to return him his horses and many of his traps; together with his rifles and a few rounds of ammunition for each man. He then set out with all speed to abandon the Crow country, before he should meet with any fresh disasters.

After his departure, the consciences of some of the most orthodox Crows pricked them sorely for having suffered such a cavalcade to escape out of their hands. Anxious to wipe off so foul a stigma on the reputation of the Crow nation, they followed on his trail, nor quit hovering about him on his march until they had stolen a number of his best horses and mules. It was, doubtless, this same band which came upon the lonely trapper on the Popo Agie, and generously gave him an old buffalo robe in exchange for his rifle, his traps, and all his accoutrements. With these anecdotes, we shall, for the present, take our leave of the Crow country and its vagabond chivalry.

Chapter XXVIII

A region of natural curiosities—The plain of white clay—
Hot springs—The Beer Spring—Departure to seek the free
trappers—Plain of Portneuf—Lava—Chasms and gullies—
Banneck Indians—Their hunt of the buffalo—Hunters' feast
—Trencher heroes—Bullying of an absent foe—The damp
comrade—The Indian spy—Meeting with Hodgkiss—His ad-
ventures—Poordevil Indians—Triumph of the Bannecks—
Blackfeet policy in war

CROSSING an elevated ridge, Captain Bonneville now came
upon Bear River, which, from its source to its entrance
into the Great Salt Lake, describes the figure of a horseshoe.
One of the principal head waters of this river, although supposed to abound with beaver, has never been visited by the
trapper; rising among rugged mountains, and being barricadoed by fallen pine trees and tremendous precipices.

Proceeding down this river, the party encamped, on the 6th
of November, at the outlet of a lake about thirty miles long,
and from two to three miles in width, completely embedded
in low ranges of mountains, and connected with Bear River
by an impassable swamp. It is called the Little Lake, to distinguish it from the great one of salt water.

On the 10th of November, Captain Bonneville visited a
place in the neighborhood which is quite a region of natural
curiosities. An area of about half a mile square presents a level
surface of white clay, or fullers' earth, perfectly spotless, resembling a great slab of Parian marble, or a sheet of dazzling
snow. The effect is strikingly beautiful at all times: in summer,
when it is surrounded with verdure, or in autumn, when it
contrasts its bright immaculate surface with the withered
herbage. Seen from a distant eminence, it then shines like a
mirror, set in the brown landscape. Around this plain are clustered numerous springs of various sizes and temperatures. One
of them, of scalding heat, boils furiously and incessantly, rising
to the height of two or three feet. In another place, there is an
aperture in the earth, from which rushes a column of steam
that forms a perpetual cloud. The ground for some distance

around sounds hollow, and startles the solitary trapper, as he hears the tramp of his horse giving the sound of a muffled drum. He pictures to himself a mysterious gulf below, a place of hidden fires: and gazes round him with awe and uneasiness.

The most noted curiosity, however, of this singular region, is the *Beer Spring*, of which trappers give wonderful accounts. They are said to turn aside from their route through the country to drink of its waters, with as much eagerness as the Arab seeks some famous well of the desert. Captain Bonneville describes it as having the taste of beer. His men drank it with avidity, and in copious draughts. It did not appear to him to possess any medicinal properties, or to produce any peculiar effects. The Indians, however, refuse to taste it, and endeavor to persuade the white men from doing so.

We have heard this also called the Soda Spring; and described as containing iron and sulphur. It probably possesses some of the properties of the Ballston water.

The time had now arrived for Captain Bonneville to go in quest of the party of free trappers, detached in the beginning of July, under the command of Mr. Hodgkiss, to trap upon the head waters of Salmon River. His intention was to unite them with the party with which he was at present travelling, that all might go into quarters together for the winter. Accordingly, on the 11th of November, he took a temporary leave of his band, appointing a rendezvous on Snake River, and, accompanied by three men, set out upon his journey. His route lay across the plain of the Portneuf, a tributary stream of Snake River, called after an unfortunate Canadian trapper, murdered by the Indians. The whole country through which he passed, bore evidence of volcanic convulsions and conflagrations in the olden time. Great masses of lava lay scattered about in every direction; the crags and cliffs had apparently been under the action of fire; the rocks in some places seemed to have been in a state of fusion; the plain was rent and split with deep chasms and gullies, some of which were partly filled with lava.

They had not proceeded far, however, before they saw a party of horsemen, galloping full tilt towards them. They instantly turned, and made full speed for the covert of a woody stream, to fortify themselves among the trees. The Indians came to a halt, and one of them came forward alone. He reached Captain Bonneville and his men just as they were dismounting and about to post themselves. A few words dispelled all uneasiness. It was a party of twenty-five Banneck Indians, friendly to the whites, and they proposed, through their envoy, that both parties should encamp together, and hunt the buffalo, of which they had discovered several large herds hard by. Captain Bonneville cheerfully assented to their proposition, being curious to see their manner of hunting.

Both parties accordingly encamped together on a convenient spot, and prepared for the hunt. The Indians first posted a boy on a small hill near the camp, to keep a look out for enemies. The "runners," then, as they are called, mounted on fleet horses, and armed with bows and arrows, moved slowly and cautiously toward the buffalo, keeping as much as possible out of sight, in hollows and ravines. When within a proper distance, a signal was given, and they all opened at once like a pack of hounds, with a full chorus of yells, dashing into the midst of the herds, and launching their arrows to the right and left. The plain seemed absolutely to shake under the tramp of the buffalo, as they scoured off. The cows in headlong panic, the bulls furious with rage, uttering deep roars, and occasionally turning with a desperate rush upon their pursuers. Nothing could surpass the spirit, grace, and dexterity, with which the Indians managed their horses; wheeling and coursing among the affrighted herd, and launching their arrows with unerring aim. In the midst of the apparent confusion, they selected their victims with perfect judgment, generally aiming at the fattest of the cows, the flesh of the bull being nearly worthless, at this season of the year. In a few minutes, each of the hunters had crippled three or four cows. A single shot was sufficient for the purpose, and the animal, once maimed, was left to be completely despatched at the end of the chase. Frequently, a cow was killed on the spot by a single arrow. In one instance, Captain Bonneville saw an Indian shoot his arrow completely through the body of a cow, so that it struck in the ground beyond. The bulls, however, are not so easily killed as the cows, and always cost the hunters several arrows; sometimes making battle upon the horses, and chasing them furiously, though severely wounded, with the darts still sticking in their flesh.

The grand scamper of the hunt being over, the Indians proceeded to despatch the animals that had been disabled; then
cutting up the carcasses, they returned with loads of meat to
the camp, where the choicest pieces were soon roasting before
large fires, and a hunter's feast succeeded; at which Captain
Bonneville and his men were qualified, by previous fasting, to
perform their parts with great vigor.

Some men are said to wax valorous upon a full stomach, and
such seemed to be the case with the Banneck braves, who, in
proportion as they crammed themselves with buffalo beef,
grew stout of heart, until, the supper at an end, they began to
chant war songs, setting forth their mighty deeds, and the vic-
tories they had gained over the Blackfeet. Warming with the
theme, and inflating themselves with their own eulogies, these
magnanimous heroes of the trencher would start up, advance a
short distance beyond the light of the fire, and apostrophize
most vehemently their Blackfeet enemies, as though they had
been within hearing. Ruffling, and swelling, and snorting, and
slapping their breasts, and brandishing their arms, they would
vociferate all their exploits; reminding the Blackfeet how they
had drenched their towns in tears and blood; enumerate the
blows they had inflicted, the warriors they had slain, the scalps
they had brought off in triumph. Then, having said every thing
that could stir a man's spleen or pique his valor, they would
dare their imaginary hearers, now that the Bannecks were few
in number, to come and take their revenge—receiving no reply
to this valorous bravado, they would conclude by all kinds of
sneers and insults, deriding the Blackfeet for dastards and
poltroons, that dared not accept their challenge. Such is the
kind of swaggering and rodomontade in which the "red men"
are prone to indulge in their vainglorious moments; for, with
all their vaunted taciturnity, they are vehemently prone at times
to become eloquent about their exploits, and to sound their
own trumpet.

Having vented their valor in this fierce effervescence, the
Banneck braves gradually calmed down, lowered their crests,
smoothed their ruffled feathers, and betook themselves to
sleep, without placing a single guard over their camp; so that,
had the Blackfeet taken them at their word, but few of these
braggart heroes might have survived for any further boasting.

On the following morning, Captain Bonneville purchased a supply of buffalo meat from his braggadocio friends; who, with all their vaporing, were in fact a very forlorn horde, destitute of fire-arms, and of almost every thing that constitutes riches in savage life. The bargain concluded, the Bannecks set off for their village, which was situated, they said, at the mouth of the Portneuf, and Captain Bonneville and his companions shaped their course towards Snake River.

Arrived on the banks of that river, he found it rapid and boisterous, but not too deep to be forded. In traversing it, however, one of the horses was swept suddenly from his footing, and his rider was flung from the saddle into the midst of the stream. Both horse and horseman were extricated without any damage, excepting that the latter was completely drenched, so that it was necessary to kindle a fire to dry him. While they were thus occupied, one of the party looking up, perceived an Indian scout cautiously reconnoitring them from the summit of a neighboring hill. The moment he found himself discovered, he disappeared behind the hill. From his furtive movements, Captain Bonneville suspected him to be a scout from the Blackfeet camp, and that he had gone to report what he had seen to his companions. It would not do to loiter in such a neighborhood, so the kindling of the fire was abandoned, the drenched horseman mounted in dripping condition, and the little band pushed forward directly into the plain, going at a smart pace, until they had gained a considerable distance from the place of supposed danger. Here encamping for the night, in the midst of abundance of sage, or wormwood, which afforded fodder for their horses, they kindled a huge fire for the benefit of their damp comrade, and then proceeded to prepare a sumptuous supper of buffalo humps and ribs, and other choice bits, which they had brought with them. After a hearty repast, relished with an appetite unknown to city epicures, they stretched themselves upon their couches of skins, and under the starry canopy of heaven, enjoyed the sound and sweet sleep of hardy and well-fed mountaineers.

They continued on their journey for several days, without any incident worthy of notice, and on the 19th of November, came upon traces of the party of which they were in search; such as burnt patches of prairie, and deserted camping grounds. All these were carefully examined, to discover by their freshness or antiquity the probable time that the trappers had left them; at length, after much wandering and investigating, they came upon the regular trail of the hunting party, which led into the mountains, and following it up briskly, came about two o'clock in the afternoon of the 20th, upon the encampment of Hodgkiss and his band of free trappers, in the bosom of a mountain valley.

It will be recollected that these free trappers, who were masters of themselves and their movements, had refused to accompany Captain Bonneville back to Green River in the preceding month of July, preferring to trap about the upper waters of the Salmon River, where they expected to find plenty of beaver, and a less dangerous neighborhood. Their hunt had not been very successful. They had penetrated the great range of mountains among which some of the upper branches of Salmon River take their rise, but had become so entangled among immense and almost impassable barricades of fallen pines, and so impeded by tremendous precipices, that a great part of their season had been wasted among those mountains. At one time, they had made their way through them, and reached the Boisée River; but meeting with a band of Banneck Indians, from whom they apprehended hostilities, they had again taken shelter among the mountains, where they were found by Captain Bonneville. In the neighborhood of their encampment, the captain had the good fortune to meet with a family of those wanderers of the mountains, emphatically called "les dignes de pitie," or Poordevil Indians. These, however, appear to have forfeited the title, for they had with them a fine lot of skins of beaver, elk, deer, and mountain sheep. These, Captain Bonneville purchased from them at a fair valuation, and sent them off astonished at their own wealth, and no doubt objects of envy to all their pitiful tribe.

Being now reinforced by Hodgkiss and his band of free trappers, Captain Bonneville put himself at the head of the united parties, and set out to rejoin those he had recently left at the Beer Spring, that they might all go into winter quarters on Snake River. On his route, he encountered many heavy falls of snow, which melted almost immediately, so as not to impede his march, and on the 4th of December, he found his other party, encamped at the very place where he had partaken in the buffalo hunt with the Bannecks.

That braggart horde was encamped but about three miles off, and were just then in high glee and festivity, and more swaggering than ever, celebrating a prodigious victory. It appeared that a party of their braves being out on a hunting excursion, discovered a band of Blackfeet moving, as they thought, to surprise their hunting camp. The Bannecks immediately posted themselves on each side of a dark ravine, through which the enemy must pass, and, just as they were entangled in the midst of it, attacked them with great fury. The Blackfeet, struck with sudden panic, threw off their buffalo robes and fled, leaving one of their warriors dead on the spot. The victors eagerly gathered up the spoils; but their greatest prize was the scalp of the Blackfoot brave. This they bore off in triumph to their village, where it had ever since been an object of the greatest exultation and rejoicing. It had been elevated upon a pole in the centre of the village, where the warriors had celebrated the scalp dance round it, with war feasts, war songs, and warlike harangues. It had then been given up to the women and boys; who had paraded it up and down the village with shouts and chants, and antic dances; occasionally saluting it with all kinds of taunts, invectives and revilings.

The Blackfeet, in this affair, do not appear to have acted up to the character which has rendered them objects of such terror. Indeed, their conduct in war, to the inexperienced observer, is full of inconsistencies; at one time they are headlong in courage, and heedless of danger; at another time, cautious almost to cowardice. To understand these apparent incongruities, one must know their principles of warfare. A war party, however triumphant, if they lose a warrior in the fight, bring back a cause of mourning to their people, which casts a shade over the glory of their achievement. Hence, the Indian is often less fierce and reckless in general battle, than he is in a private brawl; and the chiefs are checked in their boldest undertakings by the fear of sacrificing their warriors.

This peculiarity is not confined to the Blackfeet. Among the Osages, says Captain Bonneville, when a warrior falls in battle, his comrades, though they may have fought with consummate valor, and won a glorious victory, will leave their arms upon the field of battle, and returning home with dejected countenances, will halt without the encampment, and wait until the relatives of the slain come forth and invite them to mingle again with their people.

Chapter XXIX

I N ESTABLISHING his winter camp near the Portneuf, Captain Bonneville had drawn off to some little distance from his Banneck friends, to avoid all annoyance from their intimacy or intrusions. In so doing, however, he had been obliged to take up his quarters on the extreme edge of the flat land, where he was encompassed with ice and snow, and had nothing better for his horses to subsist on, than wormwood. The Bannecks, on the contrary, were encamped among fine springs of water, where there was grass in abundance. Some of these springs gush out of the earth in sufficient quantity to turn a mill; and furnish beautiful streams, clear as crystal, and full of trout of a large size; which may be seen darting about the transparent water.

Winter now set in regularly. The snow had fallen frequently, and in large quantities, and covered the ground to the depth of a foot; and the continued coldness of the weather prevented any thaw.

By degrees, a distrust which at first subsisted between the Indians and the trappers, subsided, and gave way to mutual confidence and good-will. A few presents convinced the chiefs that the white men were their friends: nor were the white men wanting in proofs of the honesty and good faith of their savage neighbors. Occasionally, the deep snow and the want of fodder obliged them to turn their weakest horses out to roam in quest of sustenance. If they at any time strayed to the camp of the Bannecks, they were immediately brought back. It must be confessed, however, that if the stray horse happened, by any chance, to be in vigorous plight and good condition, though he was equally sure to be returned by the honest Bannecks, yet, it was always after the lapse of several days, and in a very gaunt and jaded state; and always with the remark, that they had found him a long way off. The uncharitable were apt to surmise that he had, in the interim, been well used up in a buffalo hunt: but those accustomed to Indian morality in the matter of horseflesh, considered it a singular evidence of honesty, that he should be brought back at all.

Being convinced, therefore, from these, and other circumstances, that his people were encamped in the neighborhood of a tribe as honest as they were valiant; and satisfied that they would pass their winter unmolested; Captain Bonneville prepared for a reconnoitring expedition of great extent and peril. This was, to penetrate to the Hudson's Bay establishments on the banks of the Columbia, and to make himself acquainted with the country and the Indian tribes; it being one part of his scheme to establish a trading post somewhere on the lower part of the river, so as to participate in the trade lost to the United States by the capture of Astoria. This expedition would, of course, take him through the Snake River country, and across the Blue Mountains; the scenes of so much hardship and disaster to Hunt and Crooks, and their Astorian bands, who first explored it: and he would have to pass through it in the same frightful season; the depth of winter.

The idea of risk and hardship, however, only served to stimulate the adventurous spirit of the captain. He chose three companions for his journey; put up a small stock of necessaries in the most portable form, and selected five horses and mules for themselves and their baggage. He proposed to rejoin his band in the early part of March, at the winter encampment near the Portneuf. All these arrangements being completed, he mounted his horse on Christmas morning, and set off with his three comrades. They halted a little beyond the Banneck camp, and made their Christmas dinner; which, if not a very merry, was a very hearty one; after which, they resumed their journey.

They were obliged to travel slowly, to spare their horses; for the snow had increased in depth to eighteen inches: and though somewhat packed and frozen, was not sufficiently so to yield firm footing. Their route lay to the west, down along the left side of Snake River; and they were several days in reaching the first, or American Falls. The banks of the river, for a considerable distance, both above and below the falls, have a volcanic character: masses of basaltic rock are piled one upon another; the water makes its way through their broken chasms, boiling through narrow channels, or pitching in beautiful cascades over ridges of basaltic columns.

Beyond these falls, they came to a picturesque, but inconsiderable stream, called the Cassié. It runs through a level valley, about four miles wide, where the soil is good; but the prevalent coldness and dryness of the climate is unfavorable to vegetation. Near to this stream there is a small mountain of mica slate, including garnets. Granite, in small blocks, is likewise seen in this neighborhood, and white sandstone. From this river, the travellers had a prospect of the snowy heights of the Salmon River Mountains to the north; the nearest, at least fifty miles distant.

In pursuing his course westward, Captain Bonneville generally kept several miles from Snake River, crossing the heads of its tributary streams; though he often found the open country so encumbered by volcanic rocks, as to render travelling extremely difficult. Whenever he approached Snake River, he found it running through a broad chasm, with steep, perpendicular sides of basaltic rock. After several days' travel across a level plain, he came to a part of the river which filled him with astonishment and admiration. As far as the eye could reach, the river was walled in by perpendicular cliffs two hundred and fifty feet high, beetling like dark and gloomy battlements, while blocks and fragments lay in masses at their feet, in the midst of the boiling and whirling current. Just above, the whole stream pitched in one cascade above forty feet in height, with a thundering sound, casting up a volume of spray that hung in the air like a silver mist. These are called by some the Fishing Falls; as the salmon are taken here in immense quantities. They cannot get by these falls.

After encamping at this place all night, Captain Bonneville, at sunrise, descended with his party through a narrow ravine, or rather crevice, in the vast wall of basaltic rock which bordered the river; this being the only mode, for many miles, of getting to the margin of the stream.

The snow lay in a thin crust along the banks of the river, so that their travelling was much more easy than it had been hitherto. There were foot tracks, also, made by the natives, which greatly facilitated their progress. Occasionally, they met the inhabitants of this wild region; a timid race, and but scantily provided with the necessaries of life. Their dress consisted of a mantle about four feet square, formed of strips of rabbit skins sewed together: this they hung over their shoulders, in the ordinary Indian mode of wearing the blanket. Their weapons were bows and arrows; the latter tipped with obsidian, which abounds in the neighborhood. Their huts were shaped like haystacks, and constructed of branches of willow covered with long grass, so as to be warm and comfortable. Occasionally, they were surrounded by small inclosures of wormwood, about three feet high, which gave them a cottage-like appearance. Three or four of these tenements were occasionally grouped together in some wild and striking situation, and had a picturesque effect. Sometimes they were in sufficient number to form a small hamlet. From these people, Captain Bonneville's party frequently purchased salmon, dried in an admirable manner, as were likewise the roes. This seemed to be their prime article of food; but they were extremely anxious to get buffalo meat in exchange.

The high walls and rocks, within which the travellers had been so long enclosed, now occasionally presented openings, through which they were enabled to ascend to the plain, and to cut off considerable bends of the river.

Throughout the whole extent of this vast and singular chasm, the scenery of the river is said to be of the most wild and romantic character. The rocks present every variety of masses and grouping. Numerous small streams come rushing and boiling through narrow clefts and ravines: one of a considerable size issued from the face of a precipice, within twenty-five feet of its summit; and after running in nearly a horizontal line for about one hundred feet, fell, by numerous small cascades, to the rocky bank of the river.

In its career through this vast and singular defile, Snake River is upwards of three hundred yards wide, and as clear as spring water. Sometimes it steals along with a tranquil and noiseless course; at other times, for miles and miles, it dashes on in a thousand rapids, wild and beautiful to the eye, and lulling the ear with the soft tumult of plashing waters.

Many of the tributary streams of Snake River, rival it in the wildness and picturesqueness of their scenery. That called the Bruneau is particularly cited. It runs through a tremendous chasm, rather than a valley, extending upwards of a hundred and fifty miles. You come upon it on a sudden, in traversing a level plain. It seems as if you could throw a stone across from cliff to cliff; yet, the valley is near two thousand feet deep: so that the river looks like an inconsiderable stream. Basaltic rocks rise perpendicularly, so that it is impossible to get from the plain to the water, or from the river margin to the plain. The current is bright and limpid. Hot springs are found on the borders of this river. One bursts out of the cliffs forty feet above the river, in a stream sufficient to turn a mill, and sends up a cloud of vapor.

We find a characteristic picture of this volcanic region of mountains and streams, furnished by the journal of Mr. Wyeth, which lies before us; who ascended a peak in the neighborhood we are describing. From this summit, the country, he says, appears an indescribable chaos; the tops of the hills exhibit the same strata as far as the eye can reach; and appear to have once formed the level of the country; and the valleys to be formed by the sinking of the earth, rather than the rising of the hills. Through the deep cracks and chasms thus formed, the rivers and brooks make their way, which renders it difficult to follow them. All these basaltic channels are called cut rocks by the trappers. Many of the mountain streams disappear in the plains; either absorbed by their thirsty soil, and by the porous surface of the lava, or swallowed up in gulfs and chasms.

On the 12th of January (1834), Captain Bonneville reached Powder River; much the largest stream that he had seen since leaving the Portneuf. He struck it about three miles above its entrance into Snake River. Here he found himself above the lower narrows and defiles of the latter river, and in an open and level country. The natives now made their appearance in considerable numbers, and evinced the most insatiable curiosity respecting the white men; sitting in groups for hours together, exposed to the bleakest winds, merely for the pleasure of gazing upon the strangers, and watching every movement. These are of that branch of the great Snake tribe called Shoshokoes, or Root Diggers, from their subsisting, in a great measure, on the roots of the earth; though they likewise take fish in great quantities, and hunt, in a small way. They are, in general, very poor; destitute of most of the comforts of life, and extremely indolent: but a mild, inoffensive race. They differ, in many respects, from the other branch of the Snake tribe, the Shoshonies; who possess horses, are more roving and adventurous, and hunt the buffalo.

On the following day, as Captain Bonneville approached the mouth of Powder River, he discovered at least a hundred families of these Diggers, as they are familiarly called, assembled in one place. The women and children kept at a distance, perched among the rocks and cliffs; their eager curiosity being somewhat dashed with fear. From their elevated posts, they scrutinized the strangers with the most intense earnestness; regarding them with almost as much awe as if they had been beings of a supernatural order.

The men, however, were by no means so shy and reserved; but importuned Captain Bonneville and his companions excessively by their curiosity. Nothing escaped their notice; and any thing they could lay their hands on, underwent the most minute examination. To get rid of such inquisitive neighbors, the travellers kept on for a considerable distance, before they encamped for the night.

The country, hereabout, was generally level and sandy; producing very little grass, but a considerable quantity of sage or wormwood. The plains were diversified by isolated hills, all cut off, as it were, about the same height, so as to have tabular summits. In this they resembled the isolated hills of the great prairies, east of the Rocky Mountains; especially those found on the plains of the Arkansas.

The high precipices which had hitherto walled in the channel of the Snake River, had now disappeared; and the banks were of the ordinary height. It should be observed, that the great valleys or plains, through which the Snake River wound its course, were generally of great breadth, extending on each side from thirty to forty miles; where the view was bounded by unbroken ridges of mountains.

The travellers found but little snow in the neighborhood of Powder River, though the weather continued intensely cold. They learnt a lesson, however, from their forlorn friends, the

Root Diggers, which they subsequently found of great service in their wintry wanderings. They frequently observed them to be furnished with long ropes, twisted from the bark of the wormwood. This they used as a slow match, carrying it always lighted. Whenever they wished to warm themselves, they would gather together a little dry wormwood, apply the match, and in an instant produce a cheering blaze.

Captain Bonneville gives a cheerless account of a village of these Diggers, which he saw in crossing the plain below Powder River. "They live," says he, "without any further protection from the inclemency of the season, than a sort of break-weather, about three feet high, composed of sage, (or wormwood,) and erected around them in the shape of a half moon." Whenever he met with them, however, they had always a large suite of half-starved dogs: for these animals, in savage, as well as in civilized life, seem to be the concomitants of beggary.

These dogs, it must be allowed, were of more use than the beggarly curs of cities. The Indian children used them in hunting the small game of the neighborhood, such as rabbits and prairie dogs; in which mongrel kind of chase they acquitted themselves with some credit.

Sometimes the Diggers aspire to nobler game, and succeed in entrapping the antelope, the fleetest animal of the prairies. The process by which this is effected is somewhat singular. When the snow has disappeared, says Captain Bonneville, and the ground become soft, the women go into the thickest fields of wormwood, and pulling it up in great quantities, construct with it a hedge, about three feet high, enclosing about a hundred acres. A single opening is left for the admission of the game. This done, the women conceal themselves behind the wormwood, and wait patiently for the coming of the antelopes; which sometimes enter this spacious trap in considerable numbers. As soon as they are in, the women give the signal, and the men hasten to play their part. But one of them enters the pen at a time; and, after chasing the terrified animals round the enclosure, is relieved by one of his companions. In this way, the hunters take their turns, relieving each other, and keeping up a continued pursuit by relays, without fatigue to themselves. The poor antelopes, in the end, are so wearied down, that the whole party of men enter and despatch them with clubs; not one escaping that has entered the enclosure. The most curious circumstance in this chase is, that an animal so fleet and agile as the antelope, and straining for its life, should range round and round this fated enclosure, without attempting to overleap the low barrier which surrounds it. Such, however, is said to be the fact; and such their only mode of hunting the antelope.

Notwithstanding the absence of all comfort and convenience in their habitations, and the general squalidness of their appearance, the Shoshokoes do not appear to be destitute of ingenuity. They manufacture good ropes, and even a tolerably fine thread, from a sort of weed found in their neighborhood: and construct bowls and jugs out of a kind of basket-work formed from small strips of wood plaited: these, by the aid of a little wax, they render perfectly water tight. Beside the roots on which they mainly depend for subsistence, they collect great quantities of seed, of various kinds, beaten with one hand out of the tops of the plants into wooden bowls held for that purpose. The seed thus collected is winnowed and parched, and ground between two stones into a kind of meal or flour; which, when mixed with water, forms a very palatable paste or gruel.

Some of these people, more provident and industrious than the rest, lay up a stock of dried salmon, and other fish, for winter: with these, they were ready to traffic with the travellers for any objects of utility in Indian life; giving a large quantity in exchange for an awl, a knife, or a fishhook. Others were in the most abject state of want and starvation; and would even gather up the fishbones which the travellers threw away after a repast, warm them over again at the fire, and pick them with the greatest avidity.

The further Captain Bonneville advanced into the country of these Root Diggers, the more evidence he perceived of their rude and forlorn condition. "They were destitute," says he, "of the necessary covering to protect them from the weather; and seemed to be in the most unsophisticated ignorance of any other propriety or advantage in the use of clothing. One old dame had absolutely nothing on her person but a thread round her neck, from which was pendant a solitary bead."

What stage of human destitution, however, is too destitute for vanity! Though these naked and forlorn-looking beings had neither toilet to arrange, nor beauty to contemplate, their greatest passion was for a mirror. It was a "great medicine," in their eyes. The sight of one was sufficient, at any time, to throw them into a paroxysm of eagerness and delight; and they were ready to give any thing they had, for the smallest fragment in which they might behold their squalid features. With this simple instance of vanity, in its primitive but vigorous state, we shall close our remarks on the Root Diggers.

Chapter XXX

THE TEMPERATURE of the regions west of the Rocky Mountains is much milder than in the same latitudes on the Atlantic side; the upper plains, however, which lie at a distance from the seacoast, are subject in winter to considerable vicissitude; being traversed by lofty "sierras," crowned with perpetual snow, which often produce flaws and streaks of intense cold. This was experienced by Captain Bonneville and his companions in their progress westward. At the time when they left the Bannecks, Snake River was frozen hard: as they proceeded, the ice became broken and floating; it gradually disappeared, and the weather became warm and pleasant, as they approached a tributary stream called the Little Wyer; and the soil, which was generally of a watery clay, with occasional intervals of sand, was soft to the tread of the horses. After a time, however, the mountains approached and flanked the river; the snow lay deep in the valleys, and the current was once more ice bound.

Here they were visited by a party of Root Diggers, who were apparently rising in the world, for they had "horse to ride and weapon to wear," and were altogether better clad and equipped than any of the tribe that Captain Bonneville had met with. They were just from the plain of Boisée River, where they had left a number of their tribe, all as well provided as themselves; having guns, horses, and comfortable clothing. All these they obtained from the Lower Nez Percés, with whom they were in habits of frequent traffic. They appeared to have imbibed from that tribe their noncombative principles, being mild and inoffensive in their manners. Like them, also, they had something of religious feelings; for Captain Bonneville observed that, before eating, they washed their hands, and made a short prayer; which he understood was their invariable custom. From these Indians, he obtained a considerable supply of fish, and an excellent and well-conditioned horse, to replace one which had become too weak for the journey.

The travellers now moved forward with renovated spirits; the snow, it is true, lay deeper and deeper as they advanced, but they trudged on merrily, considering themselves well provided for the journey, which could not be of much longer duration.

They had intended to proceed up the banks of Gun Creek, a stream which flows into Snake River from the west; but were assured by the natives that the route in that direction was impracticable. The latter advised them to keep along Snake River, where they would not be impeded by the snow. Taking one of the Diggers for a guide, they set off along the river, and to their joy soon found the country free from snow, as had been predicted, so that their horses once more had the benefit of tolerable pasturage. Their Digger proved an excellent guide; trudging cheerily in the advance. He made an unsuccessful shot or two at a deer and a beaver; but at night found a rabbit hole, whence he extracted the occupant, upon which, with the addition of a fish given him by the travellers, he made a hearty supper, and retired to rest, filled with good cheer and good-humor.

The next day the travellers came to where the hills closed upon the river, leaving here and there intervals of undulating meadow land. The river was sheeted with ice, broken into hills at long intervals. The Digger kept on ahead of the party, crossing and recrossing the river in pursuit of game, until, unluckily, encountering a brother Digger, he stole off with him, without the ceremony of leave-taking.

Being now left to themselves, they proceeded until they came to some Indian huts, the inhabitants of which spoke a language totally different from any they had yet heard. One, however, understood the Nez Percé language, and through him they made inquiries as to their route. These Indians were extremely kind and honest, and furnished them with a small quantity of meat; but none of them could be induced to act as guides.

Immediately in the route of the travellers lay a high mountain, which they ascended with some difficulty. The prospect from the summit was grand but disheartening. Directly before them towered the loftiest peaks of Immahah, rising far higher than the elevated ground on which they stood: on the other hand, they were enabled to scan the course of the river, dashing along through deep chasms, between rocks and precipices, until lost in a distant wilderness of mountains, which closed the savage landscape.

They remained for a long time, contemplating with perplexed and anxious eye, this wild congregation of mountain barriers, and seeking to discover some practicable passage. The approach of evening obliged them to give up the task, and to seek some camping ground for the night. Moving briskly forward, and plunging and tossing through a succession of deep snow drifts, they at length reached a valley known among trappers as the "Grand Rond," which they found entirely free from snow.

This is a beautiful and very fertile valley, about twenty miles long and five or six broad; a bright cold stream called the *Fourche de glace,* or Ice River, runs through it. Its sheltered situation, embosomed in mountains, renders it good pasturing ground in the winter time; when the elk come down to it in great numbers, driven out of the mountains by the snow. The Indians then resort to it to hunt. They likewise come to it in the summer time to dig the camash root, of which it produces immense quantities. When this plant is in blossom, the whole valley is tinted by its blue flowers, and looks like the ocean, when overcast by a cloud.

After passing a night in this valley, the travellers in the morning scaled the neighboring hills, to look out for a more eligible route than that upon which they had unluckily fallen; and, after much reconnoitring, determined to make their way once more to the river, and to travel upon the ice when the banks should prove impassable.

On the second day after this determination, they were again upon Snake River, but contrary to their expectations, it was nearly free from ice. A narrow riband ran along the shore, and sometimes there was a kind of bridge across the stream, formed of old ice and snow. For a short time, they jogged along the bank, with tolerable facility, but at length came to where the river forced its way into the heart of the mountains, winding between tremendous walls of basaltic rock, that rose perpendicularly from the water edge, frowning in bleak and gloomy grandeur. Here difficulties of all kinds beset their path. The snow was from two to three feet deep, but soft and yielding, so that the horses had no foothold, but kept plunging forward, straining themselves by perpetual efforts. Sometimes the crags and promontories forced them upon the narrow riband of ice that bordered the shore: sometimes they had to scramble over vast masses of rock which had tumbled from the impending precipices; sometimes they had to cross the stream upon the hazardous bridges of ice and snow, sinking to the knee at every step; sometimes they had to scale slippery acclivities, and to pass along narrow cornices, glazed with ice and sleet, a shouldering wall of rock on one side, a yawning precipice on the other; where a single false step would have been fatal. In a lower and less dangerous pass, two of their horses actually fell into the river; one was saved with much difficulty, but the boldness of the shore prevented their rescuing the other, and he was swept away by the rapid current.

In this way they struggled forward, manfully braving difficulties and dangers, until they came to where the bed of the river was narrowed to a mere chasm, with perpendicular walls of rock that defied all further progress. Turning their faces now to the mountain, they endeavored to cross directly over it; but, after clambering nearly to the summit, found their path closed by insurmountable barriers.

Nothing now remained but to retrace their steps. To descend a cragged mountain, however, was more difficult and dangerous than to ascend it. They had to lower themselves, cautiously and slowly, from steep to steep; and, while they managed with difficulty to maintain their own footing, to aid their horses by holding on firmly to the rope halters, as the poor animals stumbled among slippery rocks, or slid down icy declivities. Thus, after a day of intense cold, and severe and incessant toil, amidst the wildest of scenery, they managed, about nightfall, to reach the camping ground, from which they had started in the morning, and for the first time in the course of their rugged and perilous expedition, felt their hearts quailing under their multiplied hardships.

A hearty supper, a tranquillizing pipe, and a sound night's sleep, put them all in better mood, and in the morning they held a consultation as to their future movements. About four miles behind, they had remarked a small ridge of mountains approaching closely to the river. It was determined to scale this ridge, and seek a passage into the valley which must lie beyond. Should they fail in this, but one alternative remained. To kill their horses, dry the flesh for provisions, make boats of the hides, and, in these, commit themselves to the stream—a measure hazardous in the extreme.

A short march brought them to the foot of the mountain, but its steep and cragged sides almost discouraged hope. The only chance of scaling it was by broken masses of rock, piled one upon another, which formed a succession of crags, reaching nearly to the summit. Up these they wrought their way with indescribable difficulty and peril, in a zigzag course: climbing from rock to rock; and helping their horses up after them, which scrambled among the crags like mountain goats; now and then dislodging some huge stone, which, the moment they had left it, would roll down the mountain, crashing and rebounding with terrific din. It was some time after dark before they reached a kind of platform on the summit of the mountain, where they could venture to encamp. The winds, which swept this naked height, had whirled all the snow into the valley beneath, so that the horses found tolerable winter pasturage on the dry grass which remained exposed. The travellers, though hungry in the extreme, were fain to make a very frugal supper: for they saw their journey was likely to be prolonged much beyond the anticipated term.

In fact, on the following day they discerned that, although already at a great elevation, they were only as yet upon the shoulder of the mountain. It proved to be a great sierra, or ridge, of immense height, running parallel to the course of the river, swelling by degrees to lofty peaks, but the outline gashed by deep and precipitous ravines. This, in fact, was a part of the chain of Blue Mountains, in which the first adventurers to Astoria experienced such hardships.

We will not pretend to accompany the travellers step by step in this tremendous mountain scramble, into which they had unconsciously betrayed themselves. Day after day did their toil continue; peak after peak had they to traverse, struggling with difficulties and hardships known only to the mountain trapper. As their course lay north, they had to ascend the southern faces of the heights, where the sun had melted the snow, so as to render the ascent wet and slippery, and to keep both men and horses continually on the strain; while on the northern sides, the snow lay in such heavy masses, that it was necessary to beat a track, down which the horses might be led. Every now and then, also, their way was impeded by tall and numerous pines, some of which had fallen, and lay in every direction.

In the midst of these toils and hardships, their provisions gave out. For three days they were without food, and so reduced that they could scarcely drag themselves along. At length one of the mules, being about to give out from fatigue and famine, they hastened to despatch him. Husbanding this miserable supply, they dried the flesh, and for three days subsisted upon the nutriment extracted from the bones. As to the meat, it was packed and preserved as long as they could do without it, not knowing how long they might remain bewildered in these desolate regions.

One of the men was now despatched ahead, to reconnoitre the country, and to discover, if possible, some more practicable route. In the meantime, the rest of the party moved on slowly. After a lapse of three days, the scout rejoined them. He informed them that Snake River ran immediately below the sierra or mountainous ridge, upon which they were travelling; that it was free from precipices, and was at no great distance from them in a direct line; but that it would be impossible for them to reach it without making a weary circuit. Their only course would be to cross the mountain ridge to the left.

Up this mountain, therefore, the weary travellers directed their steps: and the ascent, in their present weak and exhausted state, was one of the severest parts of this most painful journey. For two days were they toiling slowly from cliff to cliff, beating at every step a path through the snow for their faltering horses. At length they reached the summit where the snow was blown off; but in descending on the opposite side, they were often plunging through deep drifts, piled in the hollows and ravines.

Their provisions were now exhausted, and they and their horses almost ready to give out with fatigue and hunger; when one afternoon, just as the sun was sinking behind a blue line of distant mountain, they came to the brow of a height from which they beheld the smooth valley of the Immahah stretched out in smiling verdure below them.

The sight inspired almost a frenzy of delight. Roused to new ardor, they forgot, for a time, their fatigues, and hurried down the mountain, dragging their jaded horses after them, and sometimes compelling them to slide a distance of thirty or forty feet at a time. At length they reached the banks of the Immahah. The young grass was just beginning to sprout, and the whole valley wore an aspect of softness, verdure, and repose, heightened by the contrast of the frightful region from which they had just descended. To add to their joy, they observed Indian trails along the margin of the stream, and other signs, which gave them reason to believe that there was an encampment of the Lower Nez Percés in the neighborhood, as it was within the accustomed range of that pacific and hospitable tribe.

The prospect of a supply of food stimulated them to new exertion, and they continued on as fast as the enfeebled state of themselves and their steeds would permit. At length, one of the men, more exhausted than the rest, threw himself upon the grass, and declared he could go no further. It was in vain to attempt to rouse him; his spirit had given out, and his replies only showed the dogged apathy of despair. His companions, therefore, encamped on the spot, kindled a blazing fire, and searched about for roots with which to strengthen and revive him. They all then made a starveling repast; but gathering round the fire, talked over past dangers and troubles, soothed themselves with the persuasion that all were now at an end, and went to sleep with the comforting hope that the morrow would bring them into plentiful quarters.

Chapter XXXI

*Progress in the valley—An Indian cavalier—The captain
falls into a lethargy—A Nez Percé patriarch—Hospitable
treatment—The Bald Head—Bargaining—Value of an old
plaid cloak—The family horse—The cost of an Indian present*

A TRANQUIL night's rest had sufficiently restored the broken-down traveller, to enable him to resume his wayfaring; and all hands set forward on the Indian trail. With all
their eagerness to arrive within reach of succor, such was their
feeble and emaciated condition, that they advanced but
slowly. Nor is it a matter of surprise that they should almost
have lost heart, as well as strength. It was now (the 16th of
February), fifty-three days that they had been travelling in the
midst of winter; exposed to all kinds of privations and hardships: and for the last twenty days, they had been entangled in
the wild and desolate labyrinths of the snowy mountains;
climbing and descending icy precipices; and nearly starved
with cold and hunger.

All the morning they continued following the Indian trail,
without seeing a human being; and were beginning to be discouraged, when, about noon, they discovered a horseman at a
distance. He was coming directly towards them; but on discovering them, suddenly reined up his steed, came to a halt,
and, after reconnoitring them for a time with great earnestness, seemed about to make a cautious retreat. They eagerly
made signs of peace, and endeavored, with the utmost anxiety,
to induce him to approach. He remained for some time in
doubt; but at length, having satisfied himself that they were
not enemies, came galloping up to them. He was a fine,
haughty looking savage, fancifully decorated, and mounted on
a high-mettled steed with gaudy trappings and equipments. It
was evident that he was a warrior of some consequence among
his tribe. His whole deportment had something in it of barbaric dignity: he felt, perhaps, his temporary superiority in
personal array, and in the spirit of his steed, to the poor,
ragged, travel-worn trappers, and their half-starved horses.
Approaching them with an air of protection, he gave them his

hand, and, in the Nez Percé language, invited them to his camp, which was only a few miles distant; where he had plenty to eat, and plenty of horses; and would cheerfully share his good things with them.

His hospitable invitation was joyfully accepted: he lingered but a moment, to give directions by which they might find his camp; and then, wheeling round, and giving the reins to his mettlesome steed, was soon out of sight. The travellers followed, with gladdened hearts, but at a snail's pace; for their poor horses could scarcely drag one leg after the other. Captain Bonneville, however, experienced a sudden and singular change of feeling. Hitherto, the necessity of conducting his party, and of providing against every emergency, had kept his mind upon the stretch, and his whole system braced and excited. In no one instance had he flagged in spirit, or felt disposed to succumb. Now, however, that all danger was over, and the march of a few miles would bring them to repose and abundance, his energies suddenly deserted him; and every faculty, mental and physical, was totally relaxed. He had not proceeded two miles from the point where he had had the interview with the Nez Percé chief, when he threw himself upon the earth, without the power or will to move a muscle, or exert a thought, and sank almost instantly into a profound and dreamless sleep. His companions again came to a halt, and encamped beside him: and there they passed the night.

The next morning, Captain Bonneville awakened from his long and heavy sleep, much refreshed; and they all resumed their creeping progress. They had not been long on the march, when eight or ten of the Nez Percé tribe came galloping to meet them, leading fresh horses to bear them to their camp. Thus gallantly mounted, they felt new life infused into their languid frames, and dashing forward, were soon at the lodges of the Nez Percés. Here they found about twelve families living together, under the patriarchal sway of an ancient and venerable chief. He received them with the hospitality of the golden age; and with something of the same kind of fare: for, while he opened his arms to make them welcome, the only repast he set before them consisted of roots. They could have wished for something more hearty and substantial; but, for want of better, made a voracious meal on these humble viands.

The repast being over, the best pipe was lighted and sent round: and this was a most welcome luxury, having lost their smoking apparatus twelve days before, among the mountains.

While they were thus enjoying themselves, their poor horses were led to the best pastures in the neighborhood; where they were turned loose to revel on the fresh sprouting grass: so that they had better fare than their masters.

Captain Bonneville soon felt himself quite at home, among these quiet, inoffensive people. His long residence among their cousins, the Upper Nez Percés, had made him conversant with their language, modes of expression, and all their habitudes. He soon found, too, that he was well known among them, by report at least, from the constant interchange of visits and messages between the two branches of the tribe. They at first addressed him by his name; giving him his title of captain, with a French accent: but they soon gave him a title of their own; which, as usual with Indian titles, had a peculiar signification. In the case of the captain, it had somewhat of a whimsical origin.

As he sat chatting and smoking in the midst of them, he would occasionally take off his cap. Whenever he did so, there was a sensation in the surrounding circle. The Indians would half rise from their recumbent posture, and gaze upon his uncovered head, with their usual exclamation of astonishment. The worthy captain was completely bald; a phenomenon very surprising in their eyes. They were at a loss to know whether he had been scalped in battle, or enjoyed a natural immunity from that belligerant infliction. In a little while, he became known among them by an Indian name, signifying "the bald chief." "A soubriquet," observes the captain, "for which I can find no parallel in history, since the days of 'Charles the Bald.' "

Although the travellers had banqueted on roots, and been regaled with tobacco smoke, yet, their stomachs craved more generous fare. In approaching the lodges of the Nez Percés, they had indulged in fond anticipations of venison and dried salmon: and dreams of the kind still haunted their imaginations, and could not be conjured down. The keen appetites of mountain trappers, quickened by a fortnight's fasting, at length got the better of all scruples of pride, and they fairly begged some fish or flesh from the hospitable savages.

The latter, however, were slow to break in upon their winter store, which was very limited: but were ready to furnish roots in abundance, which they pronounced excellent food. At length, Captain Bonneville thought of a means of attaining the much-coveted gratification.

He had about him, he says, a trusty plaid; an old and valued travelling companion and comforter; upon which the rains had descended, and the snows and winds beaten, without further effect than somewhat to tarnish its primitive lustre. This coat of many colors had excited the admiration, and inflamed the covetousness of both warriors and squaws, to an extravagant degree. An idea now occurred to Captain Bonneville, to convert this rainbow garment into the savory viands so much desired. There was a momentary struggle in his mind, between old associations and projected indulgence; and his decision in favor of the latter was made, he says, with a greater promptness, perhaps, than true taste and sentiment might have required. In a few moments, his plaid cloak was cut into numerous strips. "Of these," continues he, "with the newly developed talent of a man-milliner, I speedily constructed turbans *à la Turque*, and fanciful head-gears of divers conformations. These, judiciously distributed among such of the womenkind as seemed of most consequence and interest in the eyes of the *patres conscripti*, brought us, in a little while, abundance of dried salmon and deers' hearts; on which we made a sumptuous supper. Another, and a more satisfactory smoke, succeeded this repast; and sweet slumbers answering the peaceful invocation of our pipes, wrapped us in that delicious rest, which is only won by toil and travail."

As to Captain Bonneville, he slept in the lodge of the venerable patriarch, who had evidently conceived a most disinterested affection for him; as was shown on the following morning. The travellers, invigorated by a good supper, and "fresh from the bath of repose," were about to resume their journey, when this affectionate old chief took the captain aside, to let him know how much he loved him. As a proof of his regard, he had determined to give him a fine horse; which would go further than words, and put his good-will beyond all question. So saying, he made a signal, and forthwith a beautiful young horse, of a brown color, was led, prancing and snorting, to the place. Captain Bonneville was suitably affected by this mark of friendship; but his experience in what is proverbially called "Indian giving," made him aware that a parting pledge was necessary on his own part, to prove that this friendship was reciprocated. He accordingly placed a handsome rifle in the hands of the venerable chief; whose benevolent heart was evidently touched and gratified by this outward and visible sign of amity.

Having now, as he thought, balanced this little account of friendship, the captain was about to shift his saddle to this noble gift-horse, when the affectionate patriarch plucked him by the sleeve, and introduced to him a whimpering, whining, leathern-skinned old squaw, that might have passed for an Egyptian mummy, without drying. "This," said he, "is my wife; she is a good wife—I love her very much.—She loves the horse—she loves him a great deal—she will cry very much at losing him.—I do not know how I shall comfort her—and that makes my heart very sore."

What could the worthy captain do, to console the tender-hearted old squaw; and, peradventure, to save the venerable patriarch from a curtain lecture? He bethought himself of a pair of earbobs: it was true, the patriarch's better-half was of an age and appearance that seemed to put personal vanity out of the question: but when is personal vanity extinct? The moment he produced the glittering earbobs, the whimpering and whining of the sempiternal beldame was at an end. She eagerly placed the precious baubles in her ears, and, though as ugly as the Witch of Endor, went off with a sideling gait, and coquettish air, as though she had been a perfect Semiramis.

The captain had now saddled his newly acquired steed, and his foot was in the stirrup, when the affectionate patriarch again stepped forward, and presented to him a young Pierced-nose, who had a peculiarly sulky look. "This," said the venerable chief, "is my son: he is very good; a great horseman—he always took care of this very fine horse—he brought him up from a colt, and made him what he is.—He is very fond of this fine horse—he loves him like a brother—his heart will be very heavy when this fine horse leaves the camp."

What could the captain do, to reward the youthful hope of this venerable pair, and comfort him for the loss of his fosterbrother, the horse? He bethought him of a hatchet, which might be spared from his slender stores. No sooner did he place the implement in the hands of the young hopeful, than his countenance brightened up, and he went off rejoicing in his hatchet, to the full as much as did his respectable mother in her earbobs.

The captain was now in the saddle, and about to start, when the affectionate old patriarch stepped forward, for the third time, and, while he laid one hand gently on the mane of the horse, held up the rifle in the other. "This rifle," said he, "shall be my great medicine. I will hug it to my heart—I will always love it, for the sake of my good friend, the bald-headed chief.—But a rifle, by itself, is dumb—I cannot make it speak. If I had a little powder and ball, I would take it out with me, and would now and then shoot a deer: and when I brought the meat home to my hungry family, I would say—this was killed by the rifle of my friend, the bald-headed chief, to whom I gave that very fine horse."

There was no resisting this appeal: the captain, forthwith, furnished the coveted supply of powder and ball; but at the same time, put spurs to his very fine gift-horse, and the first trial of his speed was to get out of all further manifestation of friendship, on the part of the affectionate old patriarch and his insinuating family.

Chapter XXXII

Nez Percé camp—A chief with a hard name—The Big Hearts of the east—Hospitable treatment—The Indian guides—Mysterious councils—The loquacious chief—Indian tomb—Grand Indian reception—An Indian feast— Town-criers—Honesty of the Nez Percés—The captain's attempt at healing

FOLLOWING the course of the Immahah, Captain Bonneville and his three companions soon reached the vicinity of Snake River. Their route now lay over a succession of steep and isolated hills, with profound valleys. On the second day, after taking leave of the affectionate old patriarch, as they were descending into one of those deep and abrupt intervales, they descried a smoke, and shortly afterwards came in sight of a small encampment of Nez Percés.

The Indians, when they ascertained that it was a party of white men approaching, greeted them with a salute of fire-arms, and invited them to encamp. This band was likewise under the sway of a venerable chief named Yo-mus-ro-y-e-cut; a name which we shall be careful not to inflict oftener than is necessary upon the reader. This ancient and hard-named chieftain, welcomed Captain Bonneville to his camp with the same hospitality and loving kindness that he had experienced from his predecessor. He told the captain that he had often heard of the Americans and their generous deeds, and that his Buffalo brethren (the Upper Nez Percés,) had always spoken of them as the Big-hearted whites of the East, the very good friends of the Nez Percés.

Captain Bonneville felt somewhat uneasy under the responsibility of this magnanimous but costly appellation; and began to fear he might be involved in a second interchange of pledges of friendship. He hastened, therefore, to let the old chief know his poverty-stricken state, and how little there was to be expected from him.

He informed him that he and his comrades had long resided among the Upper Nez Percés, and loved them so much, that they had thrown their arms around them, and now held them close to their hearts. That he had received such good accounts from the Upper Nez Percés of their cousins, the Lower Nez Percés, that he had become desirous of knowing them as friends and brothers. That he and his companions had accordingly loaded a mule with presents and set off for the country of the Lower Nez Percés; but, unfortunately, had been entrapped for many days among the snowy mountains; and that the mule with all the presents had fallen into Snake River, and been swept away by the rapid current. That instead, therefore, of arriving among their friends, the Nez Percés, with light hearts and full hands, they came naked, hungry, and broken down; and instead of making them presents, must depend upon them even for food. "But," concluded he, "we are going to the white men's fort on the Wallah-Wallah, and will soon return; and then we will meet our Nez Percé friends like the true Big Hearts of the East."

Whether the hint thrown out in the latter part of the speech had any effect, or whether the old chief acted from the hospitable feelings which, according to the captain, are really inherent in the Nez Percé tribe, he certainly showed no disposition to relax his friendship on learning the destitute circumstances of his guests. On the contrary, he urged the captain to remain with them until the following day, when he would accompany him on his journey, and make him acquainted with all his people. In the meantime, he would have a colt killed, and cut up for travelling provisions. This, he carefully explained, was intended not as an article of traffic, but as a gift; for he saw that his guests were hungry and in need of food.

Captain Bonneville gladly assented to this hospitable arrangement. The carcass of the colt was forthcoming in due season, but the captain insisted that one half of it should be set apart for the use of the chieftain's family.

At an early hour of the following morning, the little party resumed their journey, accompanied by the old chief and an Indian guide. Their route was over a rugged and broken country; where the hills were slippery with ice and snow. Their horses, too, were so weak and jaded, that they could scarcely climb the steep ascents, or maintain their foothold on the frozen declivities. Throughout the whole of the journey, the old chief and the guide were unremitting in their good offices, and continually on the alert to select the best roads, and assist them through all difficulties. Indeed, the captain and his comrades had to be dependant on their Indian friends for almost every thing, for they had lost their tobacco and pipes, those great comforts of the trapper, and had but a few charges of powder left, which it was necessary to husband for the purpose of lighting their fires.

In the course of the day the old chief had several private consultations with the guide, and showed evident signs of being occupied with some mysterious matter of mighty import. What it was, Captain Bonneville could not fathom, nor did he make much effort to do so. From some casual sentences that he overheard, he perceived that it was something from which the old man promised himself much satisfaction, and to which he attached a little vainglory, but which he wished to keep a secret; so he suffered him to spin out his petty plans unmolested.

In the evening when they encamped, the old chief and his privy counsellor, the guide, had another mysterious colloquy, after which the guide mounted his horse and departed on some secret mission, while the chief resumed his seat at the fire, and sat humming to himself in a pleasing but mystic reverie.

The next morning, the travellers descended into the valley of the Way-lee-way, a considerable tributary of Snake River. Here they met the guide returning from his secret errand. Another private conference was held between him and the old managing chief, who now seemed more inflated than ever with mystery and self-importance. Numerous fresh trails, and various other signs, persuaded Captain Bonneville that there must be a considerable village of Nez Percés in the neighborhood; but as his worthy companion, the old chief, said nothing on the subject, and as it appeared to be in some way connected with his secret operations, he asked no questions, but patiently awaited the development of his mystery.

As they journeyed on, they came to where two or three Indians were bathing in a small stream. The good old chief immediately came to a halt, and had a long conversation with them, in the course of which, he repeated to them the whole history which Captain Bonneville had related to him. In fact, he seems to have been a very sociable, communicative old man; by no means afflicted with that taciturnity generally charged upon the Indians. On the contrary, he was fond of long talks and long smokings, and evidently was proud of his new friend, the bald-headed chief, and took a pleasure in sounding his praises, and setting forth the power and glory of the Big Hearts of the East.

Having disburthened himself of every thing he had to relate to his bathing friends, he left them to their aquatic disports, and proceeded onward with the captain and his companions. As they approached the Way-lee-way, however, the communicative old chief met with another and a very different occasion to exert his colloquial powers. On the banks of the river stood an isolated mound covered with grass. He pointed to it with some emotion. "The big heart and the strong arm," said he, "lie buried beneath that sod."

It was, in fact, the grave of one of his friends; a chosen warrior of the tribe; who had been slain on this spot when in pursuit of a war party of Shoshokoes, who had stolen the horses of the village. The enemy bore off his scalp as a trophy; but his friends found his body in this lonely place, and committed it to the earth with ceremonials characteristic of their pious and reverential feelings. They gathered round the grave and mourned; the warriors were silent in their grief; but the women and children bewailed their loss with loud lamentations. "For three days," said the old man, "we performed the solemn dances for the dead, and prayed the great spirit that our brother might be happy in the land of brave warriors and hunters. Then we killed at his grave fifteen of our best and strongest horses, to serve him when he should arrive at the happy hunting grounds; and having done all this, we returned sorrowfully to our homes."

While the chief was still talking, an Indian scout came galloping up, and, presenting him with a powder-horn, wheeled round, and was speedily out of sight. The eyes of the old chief now brightened; and all his self-importance returned. His petty mystery was about to explode. Turning to Captain Bonneville, he pointed to a hill hard by, and informed him, that behind it was a village governed by a little chief, whom he had notified of the approach of the bald-headed chief, and a party of the

Big Hearts of the East, and that he was prepared to receive them in becoming style. As, among other ceremonials, he intended to salute them with a discharge of fire-arms, he had sent the horn of gunpowder that they might return the salute in a manner correspondent to his dignity.

They now proceeded on until they doubled the point of the hill, when the whole population of the village broke upon their view, drawn out in the most imposing style, and arrayed in all their finery. The effect of the whole was wild and fantastic, yet singularly striking. In the front rank were the chiefs and principal warriors, glaringly painted and decorated; behind them were arranged the rest of the people, men, women, and children.

Captain Bonneville and his party advanced slowly, exchanging salutes of fire-arms. When arrived within a respectful distance they dismounted. The chiefs then came forward successively, according to their respective characters and consequence, to offer the hand of good-fellowship; each filing off when he had shaken hands, to make way for his successor. Those in the next rank followed in the same order, and so on, until all had given the pledge of friendship. During all this time, the chief, according to custom, took his stand beside the guests. If any of his people advanced whom he judged unworthy of the friendship or confidence of the white men, he motioned them off by a wave of the hand, and they would submissively walk away. When Captain Bonneville turned upon him an inquiring look, he would observe, "he is a bad man," or something quite as concise, and there was an end of the matter.

Mats, poles, and other materials were now brought, and a comfortable lodge was soon erected for the strangers, where they were kept constantly supplied with wood and water, and other necessaries; and all their effects were placed in safe keeping. Their horses, too, were unsaddled, and turned loose to graze, and a guard set to keep watch upon them.

All this being adjusted, they were conducted to the main building or council house of the village, where an ample repast, or rather banquet, was spread, which seemed to realize all the gastronomical dreams that had tantalized them during their long starvation; for here they beheld not merely fish and roots in abundance, but the flesh of deer and elk, and the choicest pieces of buffalo meat. It is needless to say how vigorously they acquitted themselves on this occasion, and how unnecessary it was for their hosts to practise the usual cramming principle of Indian hospitality.

When the repast was over, a long talk ensued. The chief showed the same curiosity evinced by his tribe generally, to obtain information concerning the United States, of which they knew little but what they derived through their cousins, the Upper Nez Percés; as their traffic is almost exclusively with the British traders of the Hudson's Bay Company. Captain Bonneville did his best to set forth the merits of his nation, and the importance of their friendship to the red men, in which he was ably seconded by his worthy friend, the old chief with the hard name, who did all that he could to glorify the Big Hearts of the East.

The chief, and all present, listened with profound attention, and evidently with great interest; nor were the important facts thus set forth, confined to the audience in the lodge; for sentence after sentence was loudly repeated by a crier for the benefit of the whole village.

This custom of promulgating every thing by criers, is not confined to the Nez Percés, but prevails among many other tribes. It has its advantage where there are no gazettes to publish the news of the day, or to report the proceedings of important meetings. And in fact, reports of this kind, viva voce, made in the hearing of all parties, and liable to be contradicted or corrected on the spot, are more likely to convey accurate information to the public mind, than those circulated through the press. The office of crier is generally filled by some old man, who is good for little else. A village has generally several of these walking newspapers, as they are termed by the whites, who go about proclaiming the news of the day, giving notice of public councils; expeditions, dances, feasts, and other ceremonials, and advertising any thing lost. While Captain Bonneville remained among the Nez Percés, if a glove, handkerchief, or any thing of similar value, was lost or mislaid, it was carried by the finder to the lodge of the chief, and proclamation was made by one of their criers, for the owner to come and claim his property.

How difficult it is to get at the true character of these wandering tribes of the wilderness! In a recent work, we have had to speak of this tribe of Indians from the experience of other traders who had casually been among them, and who represented them as selfish, inhospitable, exorbitant in their dealings, and much addicted to thieving.* Captain Bonneville, on the contrary, who resided much among them, and had repeated opportunities of ascertaining their real character, invariably speaks of them as kind and hospitable, scrupulously honest, and remarkable, above all other Indians that he had met with, for a strong feeling of religion. In fact, so enthusiastic is he in their praise, that he pronounces them, all ignorant and barbarous as they are by their condition, one of the purest-hearted people on the face of the earth.

Some cures which Captain Bonneville had effected in simple cases, among the Upper Nez Percés, had reached the ears of their cousins here, and gained for him the reputation of a great medicine man. He had not been long in the village, therefore, before his lodge began to be the resort of the sick and the infirm. The captain felt the value of the reputation thus accidentally and cheaply acquired, and endeavored to sustain it. As he had arrived at that age when every man is, experimentally, something of a physician, he was enabled to turn to advantage the little knowledge in the healing art which he had casually picked up; and was sufficiently successful in two or three cases, to convince the simple Indians that report had not exaggerated his medical talents. The only patient that effectually baffled his skill, or rather discouraged any attempt at relief, was an antiquated squaw with a churchyard cough, and one leg in the grave; it being shrunk and rendered useless by a rheumatic affection. This was a case beyond his mark; however, he comforted the old woman with a promise that he would endeavor to procure something to relieve her, at the fort on the Wallah-Wallah, and would bring it on his return; with which assurance her husband was so well satisfied, that he presented the captain with a colt, to be killed as provisions for the journey: a medical fee which was thankfully accepted.

* Vide Astoria, chap. lii.

While among these Indians, Captain Bonneville unexpectedly found an owner for the horse which he had purchased
from a Root Digger at the Big Wyer. The Indian satisfactorily
proved that the horse had been stolen from him some time
previous, by some unknown thief. "However," said the considerate savage, "you got him in fair trade—you are more in
want of horses than I am: keep him; he is yours—he is a good
horse; use him well."

Thus, in the continual experience of acts of kindness and
generosity, which his destitute condition did not allow him to
reciprocate, Captain Bonneville passed some short time
among these good people, more and more impressed with the
general excellence of their character.

Chapter XXXIII

Scenery of the Way-lee-way—A substitute for tobacco—Sublime scenery of Snake River—The garrulous old chief and his cousin—A Nez Percé meeting—A stolen skin—The scapegoat dog—Mysterious conferences—The little chief—His hospitality—The captain's account of the United States—His healing skill

---

IN RESUMING his journey, Captain Bonneville was conducted by the same Nez Percé guide, whose knowledge of the country was important in choosing the routes and resting places. He also continued to be accompanied by the worthy old chief with the hard name, who seemed bent upon doing the honors of the country, and introducing him to every branch of his tribe. The Way-lee-way, down the banks of which, Captain Bonneville and his companions were now travelling, is a considerable stream winding through a succession of bold and beautiful scenes. Sometimes the landscape towered into bold and mountainous heights that partook of sublimity; at other times, it stretched along the water side in fresh smiling meadows, and graceful undulating valleys.

Frequently in their route they encountered small parties of the Nez Percés, with whom they invariably stopped to shake hands; and who, generally, evinced great curiosity concerning them and their adventures; a curiosity which never failed to be thoroughly satisfied by the replies of the worthy Yo-mus-ro-y-e-cut, who kindly took upon himself to be spokesman of the party.

The incessant smoking of pipes incident to the long talks of this excellent, but somewhat garrulous old chief, at length exhausted all his stock of tobacco, so that he had no longer a whiff with which to regale his white companions. In this emergency, he cut up the stem of his pipe into fine shavings, which he mixed with certain herbs, and thus manufactured a temporary succedaneum, to enable him to accompany his long colloquies and harangues with the customary fragrant cloud.

If the scenery of the Way-lee-way had charmed the travellers with its mingled amenity and grandeur, that which broke upon them on once more reaching Snake River, filled them with admiration and astonishment. At times, the river was overhung by dark and stupendous rocks, rising like gigantic walls and battlements; these would be rent by wide and yawning chasms, that seemed to speak of past convulsions of nature. Sometimes the river was of a glassy smoothness and placidity; at other times it roared along in impetuous rapids and foaming cascades. Here, the rocks were piled in the most fantastic crags and precipices; and in another place, they were succeeded by delightful valleys carpeted with green sward. The whole of this wild and varied scenery was dominated by immense mountains rearing their distant peaks into the clouds. "The grandeur and originality of the views, presented on every side," says Captain Bonneville, "beggar both the pencil and the pen. Nothing we had ever gazed upon in any other region could for a moment compare in wild majesty and impressive sternness, with the series of scenes which here at every turn astonished our senses, and filled us with awe and delight."

Indeed, from all that we can gather from the journal before us, and the accounts of other travellers, who passed through these regions in the memorable enterprise of Astoria, we are inclined to think that Snake River must be one of the most remarkable for varied and striking scenery of all the rivers of this continent. From its head waters in the Rocky Mountains, to its junction with the Columbia, its windings are upwards of six hundred miles through every variety of landscape. Rising in a volcanic region, amidst extinguished craters, and mountains awful with the traces of ancient fires, it makes its way through great plains of lava and sandy deserts, penetrates vast sierras or mountainous chains, broken into romantic and often frightful precipices, and crowned with eternal snows; and at other times, careers through green and smiling meadows, and wide landscapes of Italian grace and beauty. Wildness and sublimity, however, appear to be its prevailing characteristics.

Captain Bonneville and his companions had pursued their journey a considerable distance down the course of Snake River, when the old chief halted on the bank, and dismounting, recommended that they should turn their horses loose to graze, while he summoned a cousin of his from a group of lodges on the opposite side of the stream. His summons was quickly answered. An Indian of an active, elastic form, leaped into a light canoe of cotton-wood, and vigorously plying the paddle, soon shot across the river. Bounding on shore, he advanced with a buoyant air and frank demeanor, and gave his right hand to each of the party in turn. The old chief, whose hard name we forbear to repeat, now presented Captain Bonneville, in form, to his cousin, whose name, we regret to say, was no less hard, being nothing less than Hay-she-in-cow-cow. The latter evinced the usual curiosity to know all about the strangers, whence they came, whither they were going, the object of their journey, and the adventures they had experienced. All these, of course, were amply and eloquently set forth by the communicative old chief. To all his grandiloquent account of the bald-headed chief and his countrymen, the Big Hearts of the East, his cousin listened with great attention, and replied in the customary style of Indian welcome. He then desired the party to await his return, and, springing into his canoe, darted across the river. In a little while he returned, bringing a most welcome supply of tobacco, and a small stock of provisions for the road, declaring his intention of accompanying the party. Having no horse, he mounted behind one of the men, observing that he should procure a steed for himself on the following day.

They all now jogged on very sociably and cheerily together. Not many miles beyond, they met others of the tribe, among whom was one, whom Captain Bonneville and his comrades had known during their residence among the Upper Nez Percés, and who welcomed them with open arms. In this neighborhood was the home of their guide, who took leave of them with a profusion of good wishes for their safety and happiness. That night they put up in the hut of a Nez Percé, where they were visited by several warriors from the other side of the river, friends of the old chief and his cousin, who came to have a talk and a smoke with the white men. The heart of the good old chief was overflowing with good-will at thus being surrounded by his new and old friends, and he talked with more spirit and vivacity than ever. The evening passed away in perfect harmony and good-humor, and it was not until a late hour that the visiters took their leave and recrossed the river.

After this constant picture of worth and virtue on the part of the Nez Percé tribe, we grieve to have to record a circumstance calculated to throw a temporary shade upon the name. In the course of the social and harmonious evening just mentioned, one of the captain's men, who happened to be something of a virtuoso in his way, and fond of collecting curiosities, produced a small skin, a great rarity in the eyes of men conversant in peltries. It attracted much attention among the visiters from beyond the river, who passed it from one to the other, examined it with looks of lively admiration, and pronounced it a great medicine.

In the morning, when the captain and his party were about to set off, the precious skin was missing. Search was made for it in the hut, but it was nowhere to be found; and it was strongly suspected that it had been purloined by some of the connoisseurs from the other side of the river.

The old chief and his cousin were indignant at the supposed delinquency of their friends across the water, and called out for them to come over and answer for their shameful conduct. The others answered to the call with all the promptitude of perfect innocence, and spurned at the idea of their being capable of such outrage upon any of the Big-hearted nation. All were at a loss on whom to fix the crime of abstracting the invaluable skin, when by chance the eyes of the worthies from beyond the water, fell upon an unhappy cur, belonging to the owner of the hut. He was a gallows-looking dog, but not more so than most Indian dogs, who, take them in the mass, are little better than a generation of vipers. Be that as it may, he was instantly accused of having devoured the skin in question. A dog accused is generally a dog condemned; and a dog condemned is generally a dog executed. So was it in the present instance. The unfortunate cur was arraigned; his thievish looks substantiated his guilt, and he was condemned by his judges from across the river to be hanged. In vain the Indians of the hut, with whom he was a great favorite, interceded in his behalf. In vain Captain Bonneville and his comrades petitioned that his life might be spared. His judges were inexorable. He was doubly guilty: first, in having robbed their good friends, the Big Hearts of the East; secondly, in having brought a doubt on the honor of the Nez Percé tribe. He was, accordingly, swung aloft, and pelted with stones to make his death more certain. The sentence of the judges being thus thoroughly executed, a post mortem examination of the body of the dog was held, to establish his delinquency beyond all doubt, and to leave the Nez Percés without a shadow of suspicion. Great interest, of course, was manifested by all present during this operation. The body of the dog was opened, the intestines rigorously scrutinized, but, to the horror of all concerned, not a particle of the skin was to be found—the dog had been unjustly executed!

A great clamor now ensued, but the most clamorous was the party from across the river, whose jealousy of their good name now prompted them to the most vociferous vindications of their innocence. It was with the utmost difficulty that the captain and his comrades could calm their lively sensibilities, by accounting for the disappearance of the skin in a dozen different ways, until all idea of its having been stolen was entirely out of the question.

The meeting now broke up. The warriors returned across the river, the captain and his comrades proceeded on their journey; but the spirits of the communicative old chief, Yo-mus-ro-y-e-cut, were for a time completely dampened, and he evinced great mortification at what had just occurred. He rode on in silence, except, that now and then he would give way to a burst of indignation, and exclaim, with a shake of the head and a toss of the hand toward the opposite shore—"bad men, very bad men across the river;" to each of which brief exclamations, his worthy cousin, Hay-she-in-cow-cow, would respond by a deep guttural sound of acquiescence, equivalent to an amen.

After some time, the countenance of the old chief again cleared up, and he fell into repeated conferences in an under tone, with his cousin, which ended in the departure of the latter, who, applying the lash to his horse, dashed forward and was soon out of sight. In fact, they were drawing near to the village of another chief, likewise distinguished by an appellation of some longitude, O-push-y-e-cut; but commonly known as the great chief. The cousin had been sent ahead to give notice of their approach; a herald appeared as before, bearing a powderhorn, to enable them to respond to the intended salute. A scene ensued, on their approach to the village, similar to that which had occurred at the village of the little chief. The whole population appeared in the field, drawn up in lines, arrayed with the customary regard to rank and dignity. Then came on the firing of salutes, and the shaking of hands, in which last ceremonial, every individual, man, woman, and child, participated; for the Indians have an idea that it is as indispensable an overture of friendship among the whites as smoking of the pipe is among the red men. The travellers were next ushered to the banquet, where all the choicest viands that the village could furnish, were served up in rich profusion. They were afterwards entertained by feats of agility and horse-races; indeed, their visit to the village seemed the signal for complete festivity. In the meantime, a skin lodge had been spread for their accommodation, their horses and baggage were taken care of, and wood and water supplied in abundance. At night, therefore, they retired to their quarters, to enjoy, as they supposed, the repose of which they stood in need. No such thing, however, was in store for them. A crowd of visiters awaited their appearance, all eager for a smoke and a talk. The pipe was immediately lighted, and constantly replenished and kept alive until the night was far advanced. As usual, the utmost eagerness was evinced by the guests to learn every thing within the scope of their comprehension respecting the Americans, for whom they professed the most fraternal regard. The captain, in his replies, made use of familiar illustrations, calculated to strike their minds, and impress them with such an idea of the might of his nation, as would induce them to treat with kindness and respect all stragglers that might fall in their path. To their inquiries as to the numbers of the people of the United States, he assured them that they were as countless as the blades of grass in the prairies, and that, great as Snake River was, if they were all encamped upon its banks, they would drink it dry in a single day. To these and similar statistics, they listened with profound attention, and apparently, implicit belief. It was, indeed, a striking scene: the captain, with his hunter's dress and bald head in the midst, holding forth, and his wild auditors seated around like so many statues, the fire lighting up their painted faces and muscular figures, all fixed and motionless, excepting when the pipe was passed, a question propounded, or a startling fact in statistics received with a movement of surprise and a half suppressed ejaculation of wonder and delight.

The fame of the captain as a healer of diseases, had accompanied him to this village, and the great chief, O-push-y-e-cut, now entreated him to exert his skill on his daughter, who had been for three days racked with pains, for which the Piercednose doctors could devise no alleviation. The captain found her extended on a pallet of mats in excruciating pain. Her father manifested the strongest paternal affection for her, and assured the captain that if he would but cure her, he would place the Americans near his heart. The worthy captain needed no such inducement. His kind heart was already touched by the sufferings of the poor girl, and his sympathies quickened by her appearance; for she was but about sixteen years of age, and uncommonly beautiful in form and feature. The only difficulty with the captain was, that he knew nothing of her malady, and that his medical science was of the most haphazard kind. After considering and cogitating for some time, as a man is apt to do when in a maze of vague ideas, he made a desperate dash at a remedy. By his directions, the girl was placed in a sort of rude vapor bath, much used by the Nez Percés, where she was kept until near fainting. He then gave her a dose of gunpowder dissolved in cold water, and ordered her to be wrapped in buffalo robes and put to sleep under a load of furs and blankets. The remedy succeeded: the next morning she was free from pain, though extremely languid; whereupon, the captain prescribed for her a bowl of colt's head broth, and that she should be kept for a time on simple diet.

The great chief was unbounded in his expressions of gratitude for the recovery of his daughter. He would fain have detained the captain a long time as his guest, but the time for departure had arrived. When the captain's horse was brought for him to mount, the chief declared that the steed was not worthy of him, and sent for one of his best horses, which he presented in its stead; declaring that it made his heart glad to see his friend so well mounted. He then appointed a young Nez Percé to accompany his guests to the next village, and "to carry his talk" concerning them; and the two parties separated with mutual expressions of kindness and feelings of good-will.

The vapor bath of which we have made mention is in frequent use among the Nez Percé tribe, chiefly for cleanliness. Their sweating houses, as they call them, are small and close lodges, and the vapor is produced by water poured slowly upon red hot stones.

On passing the limits of O-push-y-e-cut's domains, the travellers left the elevated table lands, and all the wild and romantic scenery which has just been described. They now traversed a gently undulating country, of such fertility that it excited the rapturous admiration of two of the captain's followers, a Kentuckian and a native of Ohio. They declared that it surpassed any land they had ever seen, and often exclaimed, what a delight it would be just to run a plough through such a rich and teeming soil, and see it open its bountiful promise before the share.

Another halt and sojourn of a night was made at the village of a chief named He-mim-el-pilp, where similar ceremonies were observed and hospitality experienced, as at the preceding villages. They now pursued a west-southwest course through a beautiful and fertile region, better wooded than most of the tracts through which they had passed. In their progress, they met with several bands of Nez Percés, by whom they were invariably treated with the utmost kindness. Within seven days after leaving the domain of He-mim-el-pilp, they struck the Columbia River at Fort Wallah-Wallah, where they arrived on the 4th of March, 1834.

Chapter XXXIV

FORT WALLAH-WALLAH is a trading post of the Hudson's Bay Company, situated just above the mouth of the river of the same name, and on the left bank of the Columbia. It is built of drift wood, and calculated merely for defence against any attack of the natives. At the time of Captain Bonneville's arrival, the whole garrison mustered but six or eight men; and the post was under the superintendence of Mr. Pambrun, an agent of the Hudson's Bay Company.

The great post and fort of the company, forming the emporium of its trade on the Pacific, is Fort Vancouver; situated on the right bank of the Columbia, about sixty miles from the sea, and just above the mouth of the Wallamut. To this point, the company removed its establishment from Astoria, in 1821, after its coalition with the Northwest Company.

Captain Bonneville and his comrades experienced a polite reception from Mr. Pambrun, the superintendent: for, however hostile the members of the British Company may be to the enterprises of American traders, they have always manifested great courtesy and hospitality to the traders themselves.

Fort Wallah-Wallah is surrounded by the tribe of the same name, as well as by the Skynses, and the Nez Percés; who bring to it the furs and peltries collected in their hunting expeditions. The Wallah-Wallahs are a degenerate, worn out tribe. The Nez Percés are the most numerous and tractable of the three tribes just mentioned. Mr. Pambrun informed Captain Bonneville, that he had been at some pains to introduce the Christian religion, in the Roman Catholic form, among them; where it had evidently taken root; but had become altered and modified, to suit their peculiar habits of thought, and motives of action: retaining, however, the principal points of faith and its entire precepts of morality. The same gentleman had given them a code of laws, to which they conformed with scrupulous fidelity. Polygamy, which once prevailed among them to a great extent, was now rarely indulged. All the crimes denounced by the Christian faith, met with severe punishment among them. Even theft, so venial a crime among the Indians, had recently been punished with hanging, by sentence of a chief.

There certainly appears to be a peculiar susceptibility of moral and religious improvement among this tribe: and they would seem to be one of the very, very few, that have benefited in morals and manners, by an intercourse with white men. The parties which visited them about twenty years previously, in the expedition fitted out by Mr. Astor, complained of their selfishness, their extortion, and their thievish propensities. The very reverse of those qualities prevailed among them during the prolonged sojourns of Captain Bonneville.

The Lower Nez Percés range upon the Way-lee-way, Immahah, Yenghies, and other of the streams west of the mountains. They hunt the beaver, elk, deer, white bear, and mountain sheep. Beside the flesh of these animals, they use a number of roots for food; some of which would be well worth transplanting and cultivating in the Atlantic states. Among these is the kamash; a sweet root, about the form and size of an onion; and said to be really delicious. The cowish, also, or biscuit root, about the size of a walnut; which they reduce to a very palatable flour: together with the jackap, aisish, quako, and others; which they cook by steaming them in the ground.

In August and September, these Indians keep along the rivers, where they catch and dry great quantities of salmon; which, while they last, are their principal food. In the winter, they congregate in villages formed of comfortable huts, or lodges, covered with mats. They are generally clad in deer skins, or woollens, and extremely well armed. Above all, they are celebrated for owning great numbers of horses; which they mark, and then suffer to range in droves in their most fertile plains. These horses are principally of the pony breed; but remarkably stout and long winded. They are brought in great numbers to the establishments of the Hudson's Bay Company, and sold for a mere trifle.

Such is the account given by Captain Bonneville, of the Nez Percés; who, if not viewed by him with too partial an eye, are certainly among the gentlest, and least barbarous people of these remote wildernesses. They invariably signified to him their earnest wish that an American post might be established among them; and repeatedly declared that they would trade with Americans, in preference to any other people.

Captain Bonneville had intended to remain some time in this neighborhood, to form an acquaintance with the natives, and to collect information, and establish connexions that might be advantageous in the way of trade. The delays, however, which he had experienced on his journey, obliged him to shorten his sojourn, and to set off as soon as possible; so as to reach the rendezvous at the Portneuf, at the appointed time. He had seen enough to convince him that an American trade might be carried on with advantage in this quarter; and he determined soon to return with a stronger party, more completely fitted for the purpose.

As he stood in need of some supplies for his journey, he applied to purchase them of Mr. Pambrun; but soon found the difference between being treated as a guest, or as a rival trader. The worthy superintendent, who had extended to him all the genial rites of hospitality, now suddenly assumed a withered-up aspect and demeanor, and observed that, however he might feel disposed to serve him, personally, he felt bound by his duty to the Hudson's Bay Company, to do nothing which should facilitate or encourage the visits of other traders among the Indians in that part of the country. He endeavored to dissuade Captain Bonneville from returning through the Blue Mountains; assuring him it would be extremely difficult and dangerous, if not impracticable, at this season of the year; and advised him to accompany Mr. Payette, a leader of the Hudson's Bay Company, who was about to depart with a number of men, by a more circuitous, but safe route: to carry supplies to the company's agent, resident among the Upper Nez Percés. Captain Bonneville, however, piqued at his having refused to furnish him with supplies, and doubting the sincerity of his advice, determined to return by the more direct route through the mountains; though varying his course, in some respects, from that by which he had come, in consequence of information gathered among the neighboring Indians.

Accordingly, on the 6th of March, he and his three companions, accompanied by their Nez Percé guides, set out on their return. In the early part of their course, they touched again at several of the Nez Percé villages, where they had experienced such kind treatment on their way down. They were always welcomed with cordiality; and every thing was done to cheer them on their journey.

On leaving the Way-lee-way village, they were joined by a Nez Percé, whose society was welcomed on account of the general gratitude and good-will they felt for his tribe. He soon proved a heavy clog upon the little party; being doltish and taciturn; lazy in the extreme, and a huge feeder. His only proof of intellect was in shrewdly avoiding all labor, and availing himself of the toil of others. When on the march, he always lagged behind the rest, leaving to them the task of breaking a way through all difficulties and impediments, and leisurely and lazily jogging along the track, which they had beaten through the snow. At the evening encampment, when others were busy gathering fuel, providing for the horses, and cooking the evening repast, this worthy Sancho of the wilderness would take his seat quietly and cozily by the fire, puffing away at his pipe, and eyeing in silence, but with wistful intensity of gaze, the savory morsels roasting for supper.

When mealtime arrived, however, then came his season of activity. He no longer hung back, and waited for others to take the lead, but distinguished himself by a brilliancy of onset, and a sustained vigor and duration of attack, that completely shamed the efforts of his competitors—albeit, experienced trencher-men of no mean prowess. Never had they witnessed such power of mastication, and such marvellous capacity of stomach, as in this native and uncultivated gastronome. Having, by repeated and prolonged assaults, at length completely gorged himself, he would wrap himself up, and lie with the torpor of an anaconda; slowly digesting his way on to the next repast.

The gormandizing powers of this worthy, were, at first, matters of surprise and merriment to the travellers: but they

soon became too serious for a joke; threatening devastation to
the fleshpots; and he was regarded askance, at his meals, as a
regular kill-crop, destined to waste the substance of the party.
Nothing but a sense of the obligations they were under to his
nation, induced them to bear with such a guest: but he proceeded, speedily, to relieve them from the weight of these
obligations, by eating a receipt in full.

Chapter XXXV

As Captain Bonneville and his men were encamped one evening among the hills near Snake River, seated before their fire, enjoying a hearty supper, they were suddenly surprised by the visit of an uninvited guest. He was a ragged, half-naked Indian hunter, armed with bow and arrows, and had the carcass of a fine buck thrown across his shoulder. Advancing with an alert step, and free and easy air, he threw the buck on the ground, and, without waiting for an invitation, seated himself at their mess, helped himself without ceremony, and chatted to the right and left in the liveliest and most unembarrassed manner. No adroit and veteran dinner hunter of a metropolis could have acquitted himself more knowingly. The travellers were at first completely taken by surprise, and could not but admire the facility with which this ragged cosmopolite had made himself at home among them. While they stared, he went on, making the most of the good cheer upon which he had so fortunately alighted; and was soon elbow deep in "pot luck," and greased from the tip of his nose to the back of his ears.

As the company recovered from their surprise, they began to feel annoyed at this intrusion. Their uninvited guest, unlike the generality of his tribe, was somewhat dirty as well as ragged, and they had no relish for such a messmate. Heaping up, therefore, an abundant portion of the "provant" upon a piece of bark, which served for a dish, they invited him to confine himself thereto, instead of foraging in the general mess.

He complied with the most accommodating spirit imaginable; and went on eating and chatting, and laughing and smearing himself, until his whole countenance shone with grease and good-humor. In the course of his repast, his attention was caught by the figure of the gastronome, who, as usual, was gorging himself in dogged silence. A droll cut of the eye showed either that he knew him of old, or perceived at once his characteristics. He immediately made him the butt of his pleasantries; and cracked off two or three good hits, that caused the sluggish dolt to prick up his ears, and delighted all the company. From this time, the uninvited guest was taken into favor: his jokes began to be relished; his careless, free and easy air, to be considered singularly amusing; and in the end, he was pronounced by the travellers one of the merriest companions and most entertaining vagabonds they had met with in the wilderness.

Supper being over, the redoubtable She-wee-she-ouaiter, for such was the simple name by which he announced himself, declared his intention of keeping company with the party for a day or two, if they had no objection; and by way of backing his self-invitation, presented the carcass of the buck as an earnest of his hunting abilities. By this time, he had so completely effaced the unfavorable impression made by his first appearance, that he was made welcome to the camp, and the Nez Percé guide undertook to give him lodging for the night. The next morning, at break of day, he borrowed a gun, and was off among the hills, nor was any thing more seen of him until a few minutes after the party had encamped for the evening, when he again made his appearance, in his usual frank, careless manner; and threw down the carcass of another noble deer, which he had borne on his back for a considerable distance.

This evening he was the life of the party, and his open, communicative disposition, free from all disguise, soon put them in possession of his history. He had been a kind of prodigal son in his native village; living a loose, heedless life, and disregarding the precepts and imperative commands of the chiefs. He had, in consequence, been expelled from the village, but, in nowise disheartened at this banishment, had betaken himself to the society of the border Indians, and had led a careless, haphazard, vagabond life, perfectly consonant to his humors; heedless of the future, so long as he had wherewithal for the present; and fearing no lack of food, so long as he had the implements of the chase, and a fair hunting ground.

Finding him very expert as a hunter, and being pleased with his eccentricities, and his strange and merry humor; Captain Bonneville fitted him out handsomely as the Nimrod of the party, who all soon became quite attached to him. One of the earliest and most signal services he performed, was to exorcise the insatiate kill-crop, that had hitherto oppressed the party. In fact, the doltish Nez Percé, who had seemed so perfectly insensible to rough treatment of every kind, by which the travellers had endeavored to elbow him out of their society, could not withstand the good-humored bantering, and occasionally, sharp wit of She-wee-she. He evidently quailed under his jokes, and sat blinking like an owl in daylight, when pestered by the flouts and peckings of mischievous birds. At length his place was found vacant at mealtime; no one knew when he went off, or whither he had gone, but he was seen no more, and the vast surplus that remained when the repast was over, showed what a mighty gormandizer had departed.

Relieved from this incubus, the little party now went on cheerily. She-wee-she kept them in fun as well as food. His hunting was always successful: he was ever ready to render any assistance in the camp or on the march; while his jokes, his antics, and the very cut of his countenance, so full of whim and comicality, kept every one in good-humor.

In this way they journeyed on until they arrived on the banks of the Immahah, and encamped near to the Nez Percé lodges. Here She-wee-she took a sudden notion to visit his people, and show off the state of worldly prosperity to which he had so suddenly attained. He accordingly departed in the morning, arrayed in hunter's style, and well appointed with every thing befitting his vocation. The buoyancy of his gait, the elasticity of his step, and the hilarity of his countenance, showed that he anticipated, with chuckling satisfaction, the surprise he was about to give those who had ejected him from their society in rags. But what a change was there in his whole appearance when he rejoined the party in the evening! He came skulking into camp like a beaten cur, with his tail between his legs. All his finery was gone; he was naked as when he was born, with the exception of a scanty flap that answered the purpose of a fig leaf. His fellow travellers at first did not know him, but supposed it to be some vagrant Root Digger sneaking into the camp; but when they recognised in this forlorn object their prime wag, She-wee-she, whom they had seen depart in the morning in such high glee and high feather, they could not contain their merriment, but hailed him with loud and repeated peals of laughter.

She-wee-she was not of a spirit to be easily cast down; he soon joined in the merriment as heartily as any one, and seemed to consider his reverse of fortune an excellent joke. Captain Bonneville, however, thought proper to check his good-humor, and demanded, with some degree of sternness, the cause of his altered condition. He replied in the most natural and self-complacent style imaginable, "that he had been among his cousins, who were very poor: they had been delighted to see him; still more delighted with his good fortune: they had taken him to their arms; admired his equipments: one had begged for this; another for that"—in fine, what with the poor devil's inherent heedlessness, and the real generosity of his disposition, his needy cousins had succeeded in stripping him of all his clothes and accoutrements, excepting the fig leaf with which he had returned to camp.

Seeing his total want of care and forethought, Captain Bonneville determined to let him suffer a little, in hopes it might prove a salutary lesson; and, at any rate, to make him no more presents while in the neighborhood of his needy cousins. He was left, therefore, to shift for himself in his naked condition; which, however, did not seem to give him any concern, or to abate one jot of his good-humor. In the course of his lounging about the camp, however, he got possession of a deer skin: whereupon, cutting a slit in the middle, he thrust his head through it, so that the two ends hung down before and behind, something like a South American poncho, or the tabard of a herald. These ends he tied together, under the armpits; and thus arrayed, presented himself once more before the captain, with an air of perfect self-satisfaction, as though he thought it impossible for any fault to be found with his toilet.

A little further journeying brought the travellers to the petty village of Nez Percés, governed by the worthy and affectionate old patriarch who had made Captain Bonneville the costly present of the very fine horse. The old man welcomed them once more to his village with his usual cordiality, and his respectable squaw and hopeful son, cherishing grateful recollections of the hatchet and earbobs, joined in a chorus of friendly gratulation.

As the much-vaunted steed, once the joy and pride of this interesting family, was now nearly knocked up by travelling, and totally inadequate to the mountain scramble that lay ahead, Captain Bonneville restored him to the venerable patriarch, with renewed acknowledgments for the invaluable gift. Somewhat to his surprise, he was immediately supplied with a fine two years old colt in his stead, a substitution which, he afterwards learnt, according to Indian custom in such cases, he might have claimed as a matter of right. We do not find that any after claims were made on account of this colt. This donation may be regarded, therefore, as a signal punctilio of Indian honor; but it will be found that the animal soon proved an unlucky acquisition to the party.

While at this village, the Nez Percé guide had held consultations with some of the inhabitants as to the mountain tract the party were about to traverse. He now began to wear an anxious aspect, and to indulge in gloomy forebodings. The snow, he had been told, lay to a great depth in the passes of the mountains; and difficulties would increase as he proceeded. He begged Captain Bonneville, therefore, to travel very slowly, so as to keep the horses in strength and spirit for the hard times they would have to encounter. The captain surrendered the regulation of the march entirely to his discretion, and pushed on in the advance, amusing himself with hunting, so as generally to kill a deer or two in the course of the day, and arriving, before the rest of the party, at the spot designated by the guide for the evening's encampment.

In the meantime, the others plodded on at the heels of the guide, accompanied by that merry vagabond, She-wee-she. The primitive garb worn by this droll, left all his nether man exposed to the biting blasts of the mountains. Still his wit was never frozen, nor his sunshiny temper beclouded; and his innumerable antics and practical jokes, while they quickened the circulation of his own blood, kept his companions in high good-humor.

So passed the first day after the departure from the patriarch's. The second day commenced in the same manner; the captain in the advance, the rest of the party following on slowly. She-wee-she, for the greater part of the time, trudged on foot over the snow, keeping himself warm by hard exercise, and all kinds of crazy capers. In the height of his foolery, the patriarchal colt, which, unbroken to the saddle, was suffered to follow on at large, happened to come within his reach. In a moment, he was on his back, snapping his fingers, and yelping with delight. The colt, unused to such a burthen, and half wild by nature, fell to prancing and rearing and snorting and plunging and kicking; and, at length, set off full speed over the most dangerous ground. As the route led generally along the steep and craggy sides of the hills, both horse and horseman were constantly in danger, and more than once had a hairbreadth escape from deadly peril. Nothing, however, could daunt this madcap savage. He stuck to the colt like a plaister, up ridges, down gullies; whooping and yelping with the wildest glee. Never did beggar on horseback display more headlong horsemanship. His companions followed him with their eyes, sometimes laughing, sometimes holding in their breath at his vagaries, until they saw the colt make a sudden plunge or start, and pitch his unlucky rider headlong over a precipice. There was a general cry of horror, and all hastened to the spot. They found the poor fellow lying among the rocks below, sadly bruised and mangled. It was almost a miracle that he had escaped with life. Even in this condition, his merry spirit was not entirely quelled, and he summoned up a feeble laugh at the alarm and anxiety of those who came to his relief. He was extricated from his rocky bed, and a messenger despatched to inform Captain Bonneville of the accident. The latter returned with all speed, and encamped the party at the first convenient spot. Here the wounded man was stretched upon buffalo skins, and the captain, who officiated on all occasions as doctor and surgeon to the party, proceeded to examine his wounds. The principal one was a long and deep gash in the thigh, which reached to the bone. Calling for a needle and thread, the captain now prepared to sew up the wound, admonishing the patient to submit to the operation with becoming fortitude. His gayety was at an end; he could no longer summon up even a forced smile; and, at the first puncture of the needle, flinched so piteously, that the captain was obliged to pause, and to order him a powerful dose of alcohol. This somewhat rallied up his spirit and warmed his heart; all the time of the operation, however, he kept his eyes riveted on the wound; with his teeth set; and a whimsical wincing of the countenance, that occasionally gave his nose something of its usual comic curl.

When the wound was fairly closed, the captain washed it with rum, and administered a second dose of the same to the patient, who was tucked in for the night, and advised to compose himself to sleep. He was restless and uneasy, however; repeatedly expressing his fears that his leg would be so much swollen the next day, as to prevent his proceeding with the party; nor could he be quieted, until the captain gave a decided opinion favorable to his wishes.

Early the next morning, a gleam of his merry humor returned, on finding that his wounded limb retained its natural proportions. On attempting to use it, however, he found himself unable to stand. He made several efforts to coax himself into a belief that he might still continue forward; but at length, shook his head despondingly, and said, that "as he had but one leg," it was all in vain to attempt the passage of the mountain.

Every one grieved to part with so boon a companion, and under such disastrous circumstances. He was once more clothed and equipped, each one making him some parting present. He was then helped on a horse, which Captain Bonneville presented to him; and after many parting expressions of good-will on both sides, set off on his return to his old haunts; doubtless, to be once more plucked by his affectionate but needy cousins.

Chapter XXXVI

CONTINUING their journey up the course of the Immahah, the travellers found, as they approached the head waters, the snow increased in quantity, so as to lie two feet deep. They were again obliged, therefore, to beat down a path for their horses, sometimes travelling on the icy surface of the stream. At length they reached the place where they intended to scale the mountain; and, having broken a pathway to the foot, were agreeably surprised to find that the wind had drifted the snow from off the side, so that they attained the summit with but little difficulty. Here they encamped, with the intention of beating a track through the mountains. A short experiment, however, obliged them to give up the attempt, the snow lying in vast drifts, often higher than the horses heads.

Captain Bonneville now took the two Indian guides, and set out to reconnoitre the neighborhood. Observing a high peak which overtopped the rest, he climbed it, and discovered from the summit a pass about nine miles long, but so heavily piled with snow, that it seemed impracticable. He now lit a pipe, and, sitting down with the two guides, proceeded to hold a consultation after the Indian mode. For a long while they all smoked vigorously and in silence, pondering over the subject matter before them. At length a discussion commenced, and the opinion in which the two guides concurred, was, that the horses could not possibly cross the snows. They advised, therefore, that the party should proceed on foot, and they should take the horses back to the village, where they would be well taken care of until Captain Bonneville should send for them. They urged this advice with great earnestness; declaring that their chief would be extremely angry, and treat them severely, should any of the horses of his good friends, the white men, be lost, in crossing under their guidance; and that, therefore, it was good they should not attempt it.

Captain Bonneville sat smoking his pipe, and listening to them with Indian silence and gravity. When they had finished, he replied to them in their own style of language.

"My friends," said he, "I have seen the pass, and have listened to your words; you have little hearts. When troubles and dangers lie in your way, you turn your backs. That is not the way with my nation. When great obstacles present, and threaten to keep them back, their hearts swell, and they push forward. They love to conquer difficulties. But enough for the present. Night is coming on: let us return to our camp."

He moved on, and they followed in silence. On reaching the camp, he found the men extremely discouraged. One of their number had been surveying the neighborhood, and seriously assured them, that the snow was at least a hundred feet deep. The Captain cheered them up, and diffused fresh spirit in them by his example. Still he was much perplexed how to proceed. About dark there was a slight drizzling rain. An expedient now suggested itself. This was to make two light sleds, place the packs on them, and drag them to the other side of the mountain, thus forming a road in the wet snow, which, should it afterwards freeze, would be sufficiently hard to bear the horses. This plan was promptly put into execution; the sleds were constructed, the heavy baggage was drawn backward and forward until the road was beaten, when they desisted from their fatiguing labor. The night turned out clear and cold, and by morning, their road was encrusted with ice sufficiently strong for their purpose. They now set out on their icy turnpike, and got on well enough, excepting that now and then a horse would sidle out of the track, and immediately sink up to the neck. Then came on toil and difficulty, and they would be obliged to haul up the floundering animal with ropes. One, more unlucky than the rest, after repeated falls, had to be abandoned in the snow. Notwithstanding these repeated delays, they succeeded, before the sun had acquired sufficient power to thaw the snow, in getting all the rest of their horses safely to the other side of the mountain.

Their difficulties and dangers, however, were not yet at an end. They had now to descend, and the whole surface of the snow was glazed with ice. It was necessary, therefore, to wait until the warmth of the sun should melt the glassy crust of sleet, and give them a foothold in the yielding snow. They had a frightful warning of the danger of any movement while the sleet remained. A wild young mare, in her restlessness, strayed to the edge of a declivity. One slip was fatal to her; she lost her balance, careered with headlong velocity down the slippery side of the mountain for more than two thousand feet, and was dashed to pieces at the bottom. When the travellers afterwards sought the carcass to cut it up for food, they found it torn and mangled in the most horrible manner.

It was quite late in the evening before the party descended to the ultimate skirts of the snow. Here they planted large logs below them to prevent their sliding down, and encamped for the night. The next day they succeeded in bringing down their baggage to the encampment; then packing all up regularly, and loading their horses, they once more set out briskly and cheerfully, and in the course of the following day succeeded in getting to a grassy region.

Here their Nez Percé guides declared that all the difficulties of the mountains were at an end, and their course was plain and simple, and needed no further guidance; they asked leave, therefore, to return home. This was readily granted, with many thanks and presents for their faithful services. They took a long farewell smoke with their white friends, after which, they mounted their horses and set off, exchanging many farewells and kind wishes.

On the following day, Captain Bonneville completed his journey down the mountain, and encamped on the borders of Snake River, where he found the grass in great abundance and eight inches in height. In this neighborhood, he saw on the rocky banks of the river several prismoids of basaltes, rising to the height of fifty or sixty feet.

Nothing particularly worthy of note occurred during several days as the party proceeded up along Snake River and across its tributary streams. After crossing Gun Creek, they met with various signs that white people were in the neighborhood, and Captain Bonneville made earnest exertions to discover whether they were any of his own people, that he might join them. He soon ascertained that they had been starved out of this tract of country, and had betaken themselves to the buffalo region, whither he now shaped his course. In proceeding along

Snake River, he found small hordes of Shoshonies lingering upon the minor streams, and living upon trout and other fish, which they catch in great numbers at this season in "fishtraps." The greater part of the tribe, however, had penetrated the mountains to hunt the elk, deer, and ahsahta or bighorn.

On the 12th of May, Captain Bonneville reached the Portneuf River, in the vicinity of which he had left the winter encampment of his company on the preceding Christmas day. He had then expected to be back by the beginning of March, but circumstances had detained him upwards of two months beyond the time, and the winter encampment must long ere this have been broken up. Halting on the banks of the Portneuf, he despatched scouts a few miles above, to visit the old camping ground and search for signals of the party, or of their whereabouts, should they actually have abandoned the spot. They returned without being able to ascertain any thing.

Being now destitute of provisions, the travellers found it necessary to make a short hunting excursion after buffalo. They made caches, therefore, in an island in the river, in which they deposited all their baggage, and then set out on their expedition. They were so fortunate as to kill a couple of fine bulls, and cutting up the carcasses, determined to husband this stock of provisions with the most miserly care, lest they should again be obliged to venture into the open and dangerous hunting grounds. Returning to their island on the 18th of May, they found that the wolves had been at the caches, scratched up the contents, and scattered them in every direction. They now constructed a more secure one, in which they deposited their heaviest articles, and then descended Snake River again, and encamped just above the American Falls. Here they proceeded to fortify themselves, intending to remain here, and give their horses an opportunity to recruit their strength with good pasturage, until it should be time to set out for the annual rendezvous in Bear River valley.

On the 1st of June, they descried four men on the other side of the river, opposite to the camp, and, having attracted their attention by the discharge of rifles, ascertained to their joy that they were some of their own people. From these men, Captain Bonneville learnt, that the whole party which he had left in the preceding month of December, were encamped on Blackfoot

River, a tributary of Snake River, not very far above the Portneuf. Thither he proceeded with all possible despatch, and in a little while had the pleasure of finding himself once more surrounded by his people, who greeted his return among them in the heartiest manner; for his long-protracted absence had convinced them that he and his three companions had been cut off by some hostile tribe.

The party had suffered much during his absence. They had been pinched by famine and almost starved, and had been forced to repair to the caches at Salmon River. Here they fell in with the Blackfeet bands, and considered themselves fortunate in being able to retreat from the dangerous neighborhood without sustaining any loss.

Being thus reunited, a general treat from Captain Bonneville to his men was a matter of course. Two days, therefore, were given up to such feasting and merriment as their means and situation afforded. What was wanting in good cheer was made up in good-will; the free trappers in particular, distinguished themselves on the occasion, and the saturnalia was enjoyed with a hearty holiday spirit, that smacked of the game flavor of the wilderness.

Chapter XXXVII

AFTER the two days of festive indulgence, Captain Bonneville broke up the encampment, and set out with his motley crew of hired and free trappers, half-breeds, Indians, and squaws, for the main rendezvous in Bear River valley. Directing his course up the Blackfoot River, he soon reached the hills among which it takes its rise. Here, while on the march, he descried from the brow of a hill, a war party of about sixty Blackfeet, on the plain immediately below him. His situation was perilous; for the greater part of his people were dispersed in various directions. Still, to betray hesitation or fear, would be to discover his actual weakness, and to invite attack. He assumed, instantly, therefore, a belligerant tone; ordered the squaws to lead the horses to a small grove of ashen trees, and unload and tie them; and caused a great bustle to be made by his scanty handful; the leaders riding hither and thither, and vociferating with all their might, as if a numerous force was getting under way for an attack.

To keep up the deception as to his force, he ordered, at night, a number of extra fires to be made in his camp, and kept up a vigilant watch. His men were all directed to keep themselves prepared for instant action. In such cases, the experienced trapper sleeps in his clothes, with his rifle beside him, the shotbelt and powderflask on the stock; so that, in case of alarm, he can lay his hand upon the whole of his equipment at once, and start up, completely armed.

Captain Bonneville was also especially careful to secure the horses, and set a vigilant guard upon them; for there lies the great object, and principal danger of a night attack. The grand move of the lurking savage, is to cause a panic among the horses. In such cases, one horse frightens another, until all are alarmed, and struggle to break loose. In camps where there are great numbers of Indians, with their horses, a night alarm of the kind is tremendous. The running of the horses that have broken loose; the snorting, stamping, and rearing of those which remain fast; the howling of dogs; the yelling of Indians; the scampering of white men, and red men, with their guns; the overturning of lodges, and trampling of fires by the horses; the flashes of the fires, lighting up forms of men and steeds dashing through the gloom; altogether make up one of the wildest scenes of confusion imaginable. In this way, sometimes, all the horses of a camp, amounting to several hundred, will be frightened off in a single night.

The night passed off without any disturbance; but there was no likelihood that a war party of Blackfeet, once on the track of a camp where there was a chance for spoils, would fail to hover around it. The captain, therefore, continued to maintain the most vigilant precautions; throwing out scouts in the advance, and on every rising ground.

In the course of the day, he arrived at the plain of white clay, already mentioned, surrounded by the mineral springs, called Beer Springs by the trappers.* Here, the men all halted to have a regale. In a few moments, every spring had its jovial knot of hard drinkers, with tin cup in hand, indulging in a mock carouse; quaffing, pledging, toasting, bandying jokes, singing drinking songs, and uttering peals of laughter, until it seemed as if their imaginations had given potency to the beverage, and cheated them into a fit of intoxication. Indeed, in the excitement of the moment, they were loud and extravagant in their commendations of "the mountain tap;" elevating it above

---

* In a manuscript journal of Mr. Nathaniel G. Wyeth, we find the following mention of this watering-place:

"There is here a soda spring; or, I may say, fifty of them. These springs throw out lime, which deposits and forms little hillocks of a yellowish colored stone. There is, also, here, a warm spring, which throws out water, with a jet; which is like bilge-water in taste. There are, also, here, peat beds, which sometimes take fire, and leave behind deep, light ashes; in which animals sink deep. * * * I ascended a mountain, and from it could see that Bear River took a short turn round Sheep Rock. There were, in the plain, many hundred mounds of yellowish stone, with a crater on the top, formed of the deposits of the impregnated water."

every beverage produced from hops or malt. It was a singular and fantastic scene; suited to a region where every thing is strange and peculiar:—These groups of trappers, and hunters, and Indians, with their wild costumes, and wilder countenances; their boisterous gayety, and reckless air; quaffing, and making merry round these sparkling fountains; while beside them lay their weapons, ready to be snatched up for instant service. Painters are fond of representing banditti, at their rude and picturesque carousals: but here were groups, still more rude and picturesque; and it needed but a sudden onset of Blackfeet, and a quick transition from a fantastic revel to a furious melée, to have rendered this picture of a trapper's life complete.

The beer frolic, however, passed off without any untoward circumstance; and, unlike most drinking bouts, left neither headache, nor heartache, behind. Captain Bonneville now directed his course up along Bear River; amusing himself, occasionally, with hunting the buffalo, with which the country was covered. Sometimes, when he saw a huge bull taking his repose in a prairie, he would steal along a ravine, until close upon him; then rouse him from his meditations with a pebble, and take a shot at him as he started up. Such is the quickness with which this animal springs upon his legs, that it is not easy to discover the muscular process by which it is effected. The horse rises first upon his fore legs; and the domestic cow, upon her hinder limbs; but the buffalo bounds at once from a couchant to an erect position, with a celerity that baffles the eye. Though from his bulk, and rolling gait, he does not appear to run with much swiftness; yet, it takes a staunch horse to overtake him, when at full speed on level ground: and a buffalo cow is still fleeter in her motion.

Among the Indians and half-breeds of the party, were several admirable horsemen and bold hunters; who amused themselves with a grotesque kind of buffalo bait. Whenever they found a huge bull in the plains, they prepared for their teasing and barbarous sport. Surrounding him on horseback, they would discharge their arrows at him in quick succession, goading him to make an attack; which, with a dexterous movement of the horse, they would easily avoid. In this way, they hovered round him, feathering him with arrows, as he reared and plunged about, until he was bristled all over like a porcupine. When they perceived in him signs of exhaustion, and he could no longer be provoked to make battle, they would dismount from their horses, approach him in the rear, and seizing him by the tail, jerk him from side to side, and drag him backwards; until the frantic animal, gathering fresh strength from fury, would break from them, and rush, with flashing eyes and a hoarse bellowing, upon any enemy in sight; but in a little while, his transient excitement at an end, would pitch headlong on the ground, and expire. The arrows were then plucked forth, the tongue cut out and preserved as a dainty, and the carcass left a banquet for the wolves.

Pursuing his course up Bear River, Captain Bonneville arrived, on the 13th of June, at the Little Snake Lake; where he encamped for four or five days, that he might examine its shores and outlets. The latter, he found extremely muddy, and so surrounded by swamps and quagmires, that he was obliged to construct canoes of rushes, with which to explore them. The mouths of all the streams which fall into this lake from the west, are marshy and inconsiderable; but on the east side, there is a beautiful beach, broken, occasionally, by high and isolated bluffs, which advance upon the lake, and heighten the character of the scenery. The water is very shallow, but abounds with trout, and other small fish.

Having finished his survey of the lake, Captain Bonneville proceeded on his journey, until on the banks of the Bear River, some distance higher up, he came upon the party which he had detached a year before, to circumambulate the Great Salt Lake, and ascertain its extent, and the nature of its shores. They had been encamped here about twenty days; and were greatly rejoiced at meeting once more with their comrades, from whom they had so long been separated. The first inquiry of Captain Bonneville, was about the result of their journey, and the information they had procured as to the Great Salt Lake, the object of his intense curiosity and ambition. The substance of their report will be found in the following chapter.

Chapter XXXVIII

IT WAS on the 24th of July, in the preceding year (1833), that the brigade of forty men set out from Green River valley, to explore the Great Salt Lake. They were to make the complete circuit of it, trapping on all the streams which should fall in their way, and to keep journals and make charts, calculated to impart a knowledge of the lake and the surrounding country. All the resources of Captain Bonneville had been tasked to fit out this favorite expedition. The country lying to the southwest of the mountains, and ranging down to California, was as yet almost unknown; being out of the buffalo range, it was untraversed by the trapper; who preferred those parts of the wilderness where the roaming herds of that species of animal gave him comparatively an abundant and luxurious life. Still it was said the deer, the elk, and the bighorn were to be found there, so that, with a little diligence and economy, there was no danger of lacking food. As a precaution, however, the party halted on Bear River and hunted for a few days, until they had laid in a supply of dried buffalo meat and venison, they then passed by the head waters of the Cassie River, and soon found themselves launched on an immense sandy desert. Southwardly, on their left, they beheld the Great Salt Lake, spread out like a sea, but they found no stream running into it. A desert extended around them and stretched to the southwest, as far as their eye could reach, rivalling the deserts of Asia and Africa in sterility. There was neither tree, nor herbage, nor spring, nor pool, nor running stream, nothing but parched wastes of sand, where horse and rider were in danger of perishing.

Their sufferings, at length, became so great that they abandoned their intended course, and made towards a range of snowy mountains, brightening in the north, where they hoped to find water. After a time, they came upon a small stream leading directly towards these mountains. Having quenched their burning thirst, and refreshed themselves and their weary horses for a time, they kept along this stream, which gradually increased in size, being fed by numerous brooks. After approaching the mountains, it took a sweep towards the southwest, and the travellers still kept along it, trapping beaver as they went, on the flesh of which they subsisted for the present, husbanding their dried meat for future necessities.

The stream on which they had thus fallen is called by some, Mary River, but is more generally known as Ogden's River, from Mr. Peter Ogden, an enterprising and intrepid leader of the Hudson's Bay Company, who first explored it. The wild and half desert region through which the travellers were passing, is wandered over by hordes of Shoshokoes, or Root Diggers, the forlorn branch of the Snake tribe. They are a shy people, prone to keep aloof from the stranger. The travellers frequently met with their trails, and saw the smoke of their fires rising in various parts of the vast landscape, so that they knew there were great numbers in the neighborhood, but scarcely ever were any of them to be met with.

After a time, they began to have vexatious proofs that, if the Shoshokoes were quiet by day, they were busy at night. The camp was dogged by these cavesdroppers; scarce a morning, but various articles were missing, yet nothing could be seen of the marauders. What particularly exasperated the hunters, was to have their traps stolen from the streams. One morning, a trapper of a violent and savage character, discovering that his traps had been carried off in the night, took a horrid oath to kill the first Indian he should meet, innocent or guilty. As he was returning with his comrades to camp, he beheld two unfortunate Diggers, seated on the river bank, fishing. Advancing upon them, he levelled his rifle, shot one upon the spot, and flung his bleeding body into the stream. The other Indian fled, and was suffered to escape. Such is the indifference with which acts of violence are regarded in the wilderness, and such the immunity an armed ruffian enjoys beyond the barriers of the laws, that the only punishment this desperado met with, was a rebuke from the leader of the party.

The trappers now left the scene of this infamous tragedy, and kept on westward, down the course of the river, which wound along with a range of mountains on the right hand, and a sandy, but somewhat fertile plain, on the left. As they proceeded, they beheld columns of smoke rising, as before, in various directions, which their guilty consciences now converted into alarm signals, to arouse the country and collect the scattered bands for vengeance.

After a time, the natives began to make their appearance, and sometimes in considerable numbers, but always pacific; the trappers, however, suspected them of deep laid plans to draw them into ambuscades; to crowd into and get possession of their camp, and various other crafty and daring conspiracies, which it is probable, never entered into the heads of the poor savages. In fact, they are a simple, timid, inoffensive race, unpractised in warfare, and scarce provided with any weapons, excepting for the chase. Their lives are past in the great sand plains and along the adjacent rivers; they subsist sometimes on fish, at other times on roots and the seeds of a plant, called the cat's-tail. They are of the same kind of people that Captain Bonneville found upon Snake River, and whom he found so mild and inoffensive.

The trappers, however, had persuaded themselves that they were making their way through a hostile country, and that implacable foes hung round their camp or beset their path, watching for an opportunity to surprise them. At length, one day they came to the banks of a stream emptying into Ogden's River, which they were obliged to ford. Here a great number of Shoshokoes were posted on the opposite bank. Persuaded they were there with hostile intent, they advanced upon them, levelled their rifles, and killed twenty-five of them upon the spot. The rest fled to a short distance, then halted and turned about, howling and whining like wolves, and uttering most piteous wailings. The trappers chased them in every direction; the poor wretches made no defence, but fled with terror;

neither does it appear from the accounts of the boasted victors, that a weapon had been wielded or a weapon launched by the Indians throughout the affair. We feel perfectly convinced that the poor savages had no hostile intention, but had merely gathered together through motives of curiosity, as others of their tribe had done when Captain Bonneville and his companions passed along Snake River.

The trappers continued down Ogden's River, until they ascertained that it lost itself in a great swampy lake, to which there was no apparent discharge. They then struck directly westward, across the great chain of Californian Mountains intervening between these interior plains and the shores of the Pacific.

For three and twenty days they were entangled among these mountains, the peaks and ridges of which are in many places covered with perpetual snow. Their passes and defiles present the wildest scenery, partaking of the sublime rather than the beautiful, and abounding with frightful precipices. The sufferings of the travellers among these savage mountains were extreme: for a part of the time they were nearly starved; at length, they made their way through them, and came down upon the plains of New California, a fertile region extending along the coast, with magnificent forests, verdant savannas, and prairies that look like stately parks. Here they found deer and other game in abundance, and indemnified themselves for past famine. They now turned towards the south, and passing numerous small bands of natives, posted upon various streams, arrived at the Spanish village and post of Monterey.

This is a small place, containing about two hundred houses, situated in latitude 37° north. It has a capacious bay, with indifferent anchorage. The surrounding country is extremely fertile, especially in the valleys; the soil is richer, the further you penetrate into the interior, and the climate is described as a perpetual spring. Indeed, all California, extending along the Pacific Ocean from latitude 19° 30' to 42° north, is represented as one of the most fertile and beautiful regions in North America.

Lower California, in length about seven hundred miles, forms a great peninsula, which crosses the tropics and terminates in the torrid zone. It is separated from the mainland by the Gulf of California, sometimes called the Vermilion Sea; into this gulf empties the Colorado of the West, the Seeds-ke-dee, or Green River, as it is also sometimes called. The peninsula is traversed by stern and barren mountains, and has many sandy plains, where the only sign of vegetation is the cylindrical cactus growing among the clefts of the rocks. Wherever there is water, however, and vegetable mould, the ardent nature of the climate quickens every thing into astonishing fertility. There are valleys luxuriant with the rich and beautiful productions of the tropics. There the sugar cane and indigo plant attain a perfection unequalled in any other part of North America. There flourish the olive, the fig, the date, the orange, the citron, the pomegranate, and other fruits belonging to the voluptuous climates of the south; with grapes in abundance, that yield a generous wine. In the interior are salt plains; silver mines and scanty veins of gold are said, likewise, to exist; and pearls of a beautiful water are to be fished upon the coast.

The peninsula of California was settled in 1698, by the Jesuits, who, certainly, as far as the natives were concerned, have generally proved the most beneficent of colonists. In the present instance, they gained and maintained a footing in the country without the aid of military force, but solely by religious influence. They formed a treaty, and entered into the most amicable relations with the natives, then numbering from twenty-five to thirty thousand souls, and gained a hold upon their affections, and a control over their minds, that effected a complete change in their condition. They built eleven missionary establishments in the various valleys of the peninsula, which formed rallying places for the surrounding savages, where they gathered together as sheep into the fold, and surrendered themselves and their consciences into the hands of these spiritual pastors. Nothing, we are told, could exceed the implicit and affectionate devotion of the Indian converts to the Jesuit fathers; and the Catholic faith was disseminated widely through the wilderness.

The growing power and influence of the Jesuits in the new world, at length excited the jealousy of the Spanish government, and they were banished from the colonies. The governor, who arrived at California to expel them, and to take charge of the country, expected to find a rich and powerful fraternity, with immense treasures hoarded in their missions, and an army of Indians ready to defend them. On the contrary, he beheld a few venerable silver-haired priests coming humbly forward to meet him, followed by a throng of weeping, but submissive natives. The heart of the governor, it is said, was so touched by this unexpected sight, that he shed tears; but he had to execute his orders. The Jesuits were accompanied to the place of their embarcation by their simple and affectionate parishioners, who took leave of them with tears and sobs. Many of the latter abandoned their hereditary abodes, and wandered off to join their southern brethren, so that, but a remnant remained in the peninsula. The Franciscans immediately succeeded the Jesuits, and subsequently the Dominicans; but the latter managed their affairs ill. But two of the missionary establishments are at present occupied by priests; the rest are all in ruins, excepting one, which remains a monument of the former power and prosperity of the order. This is a noble edifice, once the seat of the chief of the resident Jesuits. It is situated in a beautiful valley, about half way between the Gulf of California and the broad ocean, the peninsula being here about sixty miles wide. The edifice is of hewn stone, one story high, two hundred and ten feet in front, and about fifty-five feet deep. The walls are six feet thick, and sixteen feet high, with a vaulted roof of stone, about two feet and a half in thickness. It is now abandoned and desolate; the beautiful valley is without an inhabitant— not a human being resides within thirty miles of the place!

In approaching this deserted mission house from the south, the traveller passes over the mountain of San Juan, supposed to be the highest peak in the Californias. From this lofty eminence, a vast and magnificent prospect unfolds itself; the great Gulf of California, with the dark blue sea beyond, studded with islands; and in another direction, the immense lava plain of San Gabriel. The splendor of the climate gives an Italian effect to the immense prospect. The sky is of a deep blue color, and the sunsets are often magnificent beyond description. Such is a slight and imperfect sketch of this remarkable peninsula.

Upper California extends from latitude 31° 10′ to 42° on the Pacific, and inland, to the great chain of snow-capped mountains which divide it from the sand plains of the interior. There are about twenty-one missions in this province, most of which were established about fifty years since, and are generally under the care of the Franciscans. These exert a protecting sway over about thirty-five thousand Indian converts, who reside on the lands around the mission houses. Each of these houses has fifteen miles square of land allotted to it, subdivided into small lots, proportioned to the number of Indian converts attached to the mission. Some are enclosed with high walls; but in general they are open hamlets, composed of rows of huts, built of sunburnt bricks; in some instances whitewashed and roofed with tiles. Many of them are far in the interior, beyond the reach of all military protection, and dependant entirely on the good-will of the natives, which never fails them. They have made considerable progress in teaching the Indians the useful arts. There are native tanners, shoemakers, weavers, blacksmiths, stonecutters, and other artificers attached to each establishment. Others are taught husbandry, and the rearing of cattle and horses; while the females card and spin wool, weave, and perform the other duties allotted to their sex in civilized life. No social intercourse is allowed between the unmarried of the opposite sexes after working hours; and at night they are locked up in separate apartments, and the keys delivered to the priests.

The produce of the lands, and all the profits arising from sales, are entirely at the disposal of the priests; whatever is not required for the support of the missions, goes to augment a fund which is under their control. Hides and tallow constitute the principal riches of the missions, and, indeed, the main commerce of the country. Grain might be produced to an unlimited extent at the establishments, were there a sufficient market for it. Olives and grapes are also reared at the missions.

Horses and horned cattle abound throughout all this region; the former may be purchased at from three to five dollars, but they are of an inferior breed. Mules, which are here of a large size and of valuable qualities, cost from seven to ten dollars.

There are several excellent ports along this coast. San Diego, Santa Barbara, Monterey, the bay of San Francisco, and the northern port of Bondago; all afford anchorage for ships of the largest class. The port of San Francisco is too well known to require much notice in this place. The entrance from the sea is sixty-seven fathoms deep, and within, whole navies might ride with perfect safety. Two large rivers, which take their rise in mountains two or three hundred miles to the east, and run through a country unsurpassed for soil and climate, empty themselves into the harbor. The country around affords admirable timber for ship building. In a word, this favored port combines advantages which not only fit it for a grand naval depot, but almost render it capable of being made the dominant military post of these seas.

Such is a feeble outline of the Californian coast and country, the value of which is more and more attracting the attention of naval powers. The Russians have always a ship of war upon this station, and have already encroached upon the Californian boundaries, by taking possession of the port of Bondago, and fortifying it with several guns. Recent surveys have likewise been made, both by the Russians and the English; and we have little doubt, that at no very distant day, this neglected, and, until recently, almost unknown region, will be found to possess sources of wealth sufficient to sustain a powerful and prosperous empire. Its inhabitants, themselves, are but little aware of its real riches; they have not enterprise sufficient to acquaint themselves with a vast interior, that lies almost a terra incognita; nor have they the skill and industry to cultivate properly the fertile tracts along the coast; nor to prosecute that foreign commerce, which brings all the resources of a country into profitable action.

Chapter XXXIX

THE WANDERING BAND of trappers were well received at Monterey: the inhabitants were desirous of retaining them among them; and offered extravagant wages to such as were acquainted with any mechanic art. When they went into the country, too, they were kindly treated by the priests at the missions; who are always hospitable to strangers, whatever may be their rank or religion. They had no lack of provisions; being permitted to kill as many as they pleased of the vast herds of cattle that graze the country, on condition, merely, of rendering the hides to the owners. They attended bullfights, and horseraces; forgot all the purposes of their expedition; squandered away, freely, the property that did not belong to them; and, in a word, revelled in a perfect fool's paradise.

What especially delighted them, was the equestrian skill of the Californians. The vast number and the cheapness of the horses in this country, makes every one a cavalier. The Mexicans and half-breeds of California, spend the greater part of their time in the saddle. They are fearless riders; and their daring feats upon unbroken colts and wild horses, astonished our trappers; though accustomed to the bold riders of the prairies.

A Mexican horseman has much resemblance, in many points, to the equestrians of Old Spain; and especially to the vainglorious Caballero of Andalusia. A Mexican dragoon, for instance, is represented as arrayed in a round blue jacket, with red cuffs and collar; blue velvet breeches, unbuttoned at the knees to show his white stockings; bottinas of deer skin; a round-crowned Andalusian hat, and his hair queued. On the pommel of his saddle, he carries balanced a long musket, with fox skin round the lock. He is cased in a cuirass of double-fold deer skin, and carries a bull's hide shield: he is forked in a Moorish saddle, high before and behind: his feet are thrust into wooden-box stirrups, of Moorish fashion, and a tremendous pair of iron spurs, fastened by chains, jingle at his heels. Thus equipped, and suitably mounted, he considers himself the glory of California, and the terror of the universe.

The Californian horsemen seldom ride out without the laso; that is to say, a long coil of cord, with a slip noose; with which they are expert, almost to a miracle. The laso, now almost entirely confined to Spanish America, is said to be of great antiquity; and to have come, originally, from the east. It was used, we are told, by a pastoral people of Persian descent; of whom eight thousand accompanied the army of Xerxes. By the Spanish Americans, it is used for a variety of purposes; and among others, for hauling wood. Without dismounting, they cast the noose round a log, and thus drag it to their houses. The vaqueros, or Indian cattle-drivers, have also learnt the use of the laso from the Spaniards; and employ it to catch the half-wild cattle, by throwing it round their horns.

The laso is also of great use in furnishing the public with a favorite, though barbarous sport; the combat between a bear and a wild bull. For this purpose, three or four horsemen sally forth to some wood, frequented by bears, and, depositing the carcass of a bullock, hide themselves in the vicinity. The bears are soon attracted by the bait. As soon as one, fit for their purpose, makes his appearance, they run out, and with the laso, dexterously noose him by either leg. After dragging him at full speed until he is fatigued, they secure him more effectually; and tying him on the carcass of the bullock, draw him in triumph to the scene of action. By this time, he is exasperated to such frenzy, that they are sometimes obliged to throw cold water on him, to moderate his fury: and dangerous would it be, for horse and rider, were he, while in this paroxysm, to break his bonds.

A wild bull, of the fiercest kind, which has been caught and exasperated in the same manner, is now produced; and both animals are turned loose in the arena of a small amphitheatre. The mortal fight begins instantly; and always, at first, to the disadvantage of bruin; fatigued, as he is, by his previous rough riding. Roused, at length, by the repeated goring of the bull, he seizes his muzzle with his sharp claws, and clinging to this most sensitive part, causes him to bellow with rage and agony. In his heat and fury, the bull lolls out his tongue; this is instantly clutched by the bear: with a desperate effort he overturns his huge antagonist; and then despatches him without difficulty.

Beside this diversion, the travellers were likewise regaled with bullfights, in the genuine style of Old Spain; the Californians being considered the best bullfighters in the Mexican dominions.

After a considerable sojourn at Monterey, spent in these very edifying, but not very profitable amusements, the leader of this vagabond party set out with his comrades, on his return journey. Instead of retracing their steps through the mountains, they passed round their southern extremity, and, crossing a range of low hills, found themselves in the sandy plains south of Ogden's River; in traversing which, they again suffered, grievously, for want of water.

In the course of their journey, they encountered a party of Mexicans in pursuit of a gang of natives, who had been stealing horses. The savages of this part of California are represented as extremely poor, and armed only with stone-pointed arrows; it being the wise policy of the Spaniards not to furnish them with fire-arms. As they find it difficult, with their blunt shafts, to kill the wild game of the mountains, they occasionally supply themselves with food, by entrapping the Spanish horses. Driving them stealthily into fastnesses and ravines, they slaughter them without difficulty, and dry their flesh for provisions. Some they carry off, to trade with distant tribes: and in this way, the Spanish horses pass from hand to hand among the Indians, until they even find their way across the Rocky Mountains.

The Mexicans are continually on the alert, to intercept these marauders: but the Indians are apt to outwit them, and force them to make long and wild expeditions in pursuit of their stolen horses.

Two of the Mexican party just mentioned, joined the band of trappers, and proved themselves worthy companions. In the course of their journey through the country frequented by the poor Root Diggers, there seems to have been an emulation between them, which could inflict the greatest outrages upon the natives. The trappers still considered them in the light of dangerous foes; and the Mexicans, very probably, charged them with the sin of horsestealing: we have no other mode of accounting for the infamous barbarities of which, according to their own story, they were guilty; hunting the poor Indians like wild beasts, and killing them without mercy. The Mexicans excelled at this savage sport; chasing their unfortunate victims at full speed; noosing them round the neck with their lasos, and then dragging them to death!

Such are the scanty details of this most disgraceful expedition; at least, such are all that Captain Bonneville had the patience to collect: for he was so deeply grieved by the failure of his plans, and so indignant at the atrocities related to him, that he turned, with disgust and horror, from the narrators. Had he exerted a little of the Lynch law of the wilderness, and hanged those dexterous horsemen in their own lasos, it would but have been a well-merited and salutary act of retributive justice. The failure of this expedition was a blow to his pride, and a still greater blow to his purse. The Great Salt Lake still remained unexplored: at the same time, the means which had been furnished so liberally to fit out this favorite expedition, had all been squandered at Monterey; and the peltries, also, which had been collected on the way. He would have but scanty returns, therefore, to make this year, to his associates in the United States; and there was great danger of their becoming disheartened, and abandoning the enterprise.

Chapter XL

THE HORROR and indignation felt by Captain Bonneville at the excesses of the Californian adventurers, were not participated by his men: on the contrary, the events of that expedition were favorite themes in the camp. The heroes of Monterey bore the palm in all the gossipings among the hunters. Their glowing descriptions of Spanish bearbaits and bullfights especially, were listened to with intense delight; and had another expedition to California been proposed, the difficulty would have been, to restrain a general eagerness to volunteer.

The captain had not been long at the rendezvous when he perceived, by various signs, that Indians were lurking in the neighborhood. It was evident that the Blackfoot band, which he had seen when on his march, had dogged his party, and were intent on mischief. He endeavored to keep his camp on the alert; but it is as difficult to maintain discipline among trappers at a rendezvous, as among sailors when in port.

Buckeye, the Delaware Indian, was scandalized at this heedlessness of the hunters when an enemy was at hand, and was continually preaching up caution. He was a little prone to play the prophet, and to deal in signs and portents, which occasionally excited the merriment of his white comrades. He was a great dreamer, and believed in charms and talismans, or medicines; and could foretel the approach of strangers by the howling or barking of the small prairie wolf. This animal, being driven by the larger wolves from the carcasses left on the hunting grounds by the hunters, follows the trail of the fresh meat carried to the camp. Here the smell of the roast and broiled meat, mingling with every breeze, keeps them hovering about the neighborhood; scenting every blast, turning up their noses like hungry hounds, and testifying their pinching hunger by long whining howls, and impatient barkings. These are interpreted by the superstitious Indians into warnings that strangers are at hand; and one accidental coincidence, like the chance fulfilment of an almanac prediction, is sufficient to cover a thousand failures. This little, whining, feast-smelling animal, is, therefore, called among Indians the "medicine wolf;" and such was one of Buckeye's infallible oracles.

One morning early, the soothsaying Delaware appeared with a gloomy countenance. His mind was full of presentiments, whether from mysterious dreams, or the intimations of the medicine wolf, does not appear. "Danger," he said, "was lurking in their path, and there would be some fighting before sunset." He was bantered for his prophecy, which was attributed to his having supped too heartily, and been visited by bad dreams. In the course of the morning, a party of hunters set out in pursuit of buffalo, taking with them a mule, to bring home the meat they should procure. They had been some few hours absent, when they came clattering at full speed into camp, giving the war cry of Blackfeet! Blackfeet! Every one seized his weapon, and ran to learn the cause of the alarm. It appeared that the hunters, as they were returning leisurely, leading their mule, well laden with prime pieces of buffalo meat, passed close by a small stream overhung with trees, about two miles from the camp. Suddenly, a party of Blackfeet, who lay in ambush among the thickets, sprang up with a fearful yell, and discharged a volley at the hunters. The latter immediately threw themselves flat on their horses, put them to their speed, and never paused to look behind, until they found themselves in camp. Fortunately, they had escaped without a wound; but the mule, with all the "provant," had fallen into the hands of the enemy. This was a loss, as well as an insult, not to be borne. Every man sprang to horse, and with rifle in hand, galloped off to punish the Blackfeet, and rescue the buffalo beef. They came too late; the marauders were off, and all that they found of their mule were the dents of his hoofs, as he had been conveyed off at a round trot, bearing his savory cargo to the hills, to furnish the scampering savages with a banquet of roast meat at the expense of the white men.

The party returned to camp, balked of their revenge, but still more grievously balked of their supper. Buckeye, the Delaware, sat smoking by his fire, perfectly composed. As the hunters related the particulars of the attack, he listened in silence, with unruffled countenance, then pointing to the west, "The sun has not yet set," said he; "Buckeye did not dream like a fool!"

All present now recollected the prediction of the Indian at daybreak, and were struck with what appeared to be its fulfilment. They called to mind, also, a long catalogue of foregone presentiments and predictions made at various times by the Delaware, and, in their superstitious credulity, began to consider him a veritable seer; without thinking how natural it was to predict danger, and how likely to have the prediction verified in the present instance, when various signs gave evidence of a lurking foe.

The various bands of Captain Bonneville's company had now been assembled for some time at the rendezvous; they had had their fill of feasting, and frolicking, and all the species of wild and often uncouth merrimaking, which invariably take place on these occasions. Their horses, as well as themselves, had recovered from past famine and fatigue, and were again fit for active service; and an impatience began to manifest itself among the men once more to take the field, and set off on some wandering expedition.

At this juncture, Mr. Cerré arrived at the rendezvous at the head of a supply party, bringing goods and equipments from the states. This active leader, it will be recollected, had embarked the year previously in skin boats on the Bighorn, freighted with the year's collection of peltries. He had met with misfortunes in the course of his voyage: one of his frail barks being upset, and part of the furs lost or damaged.

The arrival of the supplies gave the regular finish to the annual revel. A grand outbreak of wild debauch ensued among the mountaineers; drinking, dancing, swaggering, gambling, quarrelling and fighting. Alcohol, which, from its portable qualities, containing the greatest quantity of fiery spirit in the smallest compass, is the only liquor carried across the mountains, is the inflammatory beverage at these carousals, and is dealt out to the trappers at four dollars a pint. When inflamed by this fiery beverage, they cut all kinds of mad pranks and gambols, and sometimes burn all their clothes in their drunken bravadoes. A camp, recovering from one of these riotous revels, presents a serio-comic spectacle; black eyes, broken heads, lacklustre visages. Many of the trappers have squandered in one drunken frolic the hard-earned wages of a year; some have run in debt, and must toil on to pay for past pleasure. All are sated with this deep draught of pleasure, and eager to commence another trapping campaign; for hardship and hard work, spiced with the stimulants of wild adventure, and topped off with an annual frantic carousal, is the lot of the restless trapper.

The captain now made his arrangements for the current year. Cerré and Walker, with a number of men who had been to California, were to proceed to St. Louis with the packages of furs collected during the past year. Another party, headed by a leader named Montero, was to proceed to the Crow country, trap upon its various streams; and among the Black Hills, and thence to proceed to the Arkansas, where he was to go into winter quarters.

The captain marked out for himself a widely different course. He intended to make another expedition, with twenty-three men, to the lower part of the Columbia River, and to proceed to the valley of the Multnomah; after wintering in those parts, and establishing a trade with those tribes, among whom he had sojourned on his first visit, he would return in the spring, cross the Rocky Mountains, and join Montero and his party in the month of July, at the rendezvous on the Arkansas; where he expected to receive his annual supplies from the states.

If the reader will cast his eye upon a map, he may form an idea of the contempt for distance which a man acquires in this vast wilderness, by noticing the extent of country comprised in these projected wanderings. Just as the different parties were about to set out on the 3d of July, on their opposite routes, Captain Bonneville received intelligence that Wyeth, the indefatigable leader of the salmon-fishing enterprise, who had parted with him about a year previously on the banks of the Bighorn, to descend that wild river in a bull boat, was near at hand, with a new levied band of hunters and trappers, and was on his way once more to the banks of the Columbia.

As we take much interest in the novel enterprise of this "eastern man," and are pleased with his pushing and persevering spirit; and as his movements are characteristic of life in the wilderness, we will, with the reader's permission, while Captain Bonneville is breaking up his camp and saddling his horses, step back a year in time, and a few hundred miles in distance, to the bank of the Bighorn, and launch ourselves with Wyeth in his bull boat: and though his adventurous voyage will take us many hundreds of miles further down wild and wandering rivers; yet such is the magic power of the pen, that we promise to bring the reader safe back to Bear River valley, by the time the last horse is saddled.

Chapter XLI

A Voyage in a Bull Boat

IT was about the middle of August (1833), that Mr. Nathaniel J. Wyeth, as the reader may recollect, launched his bull boat at the foot of the rapids of the Bighorn, and departed in advance of the parties of Campbell and Captain Bonneville. His boat was made of three buffalo skins, stretched on a light frame, stitched together, and the seams payed with elk tallow and ashes. It was eighteen feet long, and about five feet six inches wide, sharp at each end, with a round bottom, and drew about a foot and half of water; a depth too great for these upper rivers, which abound with shallows and sandbars. The crew consisted of two half-breeds, who claimed to be white men, though a mixture of the French Creole and the Shawnee and Potawattomie. They claimed, moreover, to be thorough mountaineers, and firstrate hunters—the common boast of these vagabonds of the wilderness. Besides these, there was a Nez Percé lad of eighteen years of age, a kind of servant of all work, whose great aim, like all Indian servants, was to do as little work as possible; there was, moreover, a half-breed boy of thirteen, named Baptiste, son of a Hudson's Bay trader by a Flathead beauty; who was travelling with Wyeth to see the world and complete his education. Add to these, Mr. Milton Sublette, who went as passenger, and we have the crew of the little bull boat complete.

It certainly was a slight armament with which to run the gauntlet through countries swarming with hostile hordes, and a slight bark to navigate these endless rivers, tossing and pitching down rapids, running on snags and bumping on sandbars; such, however, are the cockle-shells with which these hardy rovers of the wilderness will attempt the wildest streams; and it is surprising what rough shocks and thumps these boats will endure, and what vicissitudes they will live through. Their duration, however, is but limited; they require frequently to be hauled out of the water and dried, to prevent the hides from becoming water-soaked; and they eventually rot and go to pieces.

The course of the river was a little to the north of east; it ran about five miles an hour, over a gravelly bottom. The banks were generally alluvial, and thickly grown with cotton-wood trees, intermingled occasionally with ash and plumb trees. Now and then, limestone cliffs and promontories advanced upon the river, making picturesque headlands. Beyond the woody borders rose ranges of naked hills.

Milton Sublette was the Pelorus of this adventurous bark; being somewhat experienced in this wild kind of navigation. It required all his attention and skill, however, to pilot her clear of sandbars and snags, or sunken trees. There was often, too, a perplexity of choice, where the river branched into various channels, among clusters of islands; and occasionally the voyagers found themselves aground and had to turn back.

It was necessary, also, to keep a wary eye upon the land, for they were passing through the heart of the Crow country, and were continually in reach of any ambush that might be lurking on shore. The most formidable foes that they saw, however, were three grizzly bears, quietly promenading along the bank, who seemed to gaze at them with surprise as they glided by. Herds of buffalo, also, were moving about, or lying on the ground, like cattle in the pasture; excepting such inhabitants as these, a perfect solitude reigned over the land. There was no sign of human habitation; for the Crows, as we have already shown, are a wandering people, a race of hunters and warriors, who live in tents and on horseback, and are continually on the move.

At night they landed, hauled up their boat to dry, pitched their tent, and made a rousing fire. Then, as it was the first evening of their voyage, they indulged in a regale, relishing their buffalo beef with inspiring alcohol; after which, they slept soundly, without dreaming of Crows or Blackfeet. Early in the morning, they again launched their boat and committed themselves to the stream.

In this way, they voyaged for two days without any material occurrence, excepting a severe thunder storm, which compelled them to put to shore, and wait until it was past. On the third morning, they descried some persons at a distance on the river bank. As they were now, by calculation, at no great distance from Fort Cass, a trading post of the American Fur

Company, they supposed these might be some of its people. A nearer approach showed them to be Indians. Descrying a woman apart from the rest, they landed and accosted her. She informed them that the main force of the Crow nation, consisting of five bands, under their several chiefs, were but about two or three miles below, on their way up along the river. This was unpleasant tidings, but to retreat was impossible, and the river afforded no hiding place. They continued forward, therefore, trusting that, as Fort Cass was so near at hand, the Crows might refrain from any depredations.

Floating down about two miles further, they came in sight of the first band, scattered along the river bank, all well mounted; some armed with guns, others with bows and arrows, and a few with lances. They made a wildly picturesque appearance, managing their horses with their accustomed dexterity and grace. Nothing can be more spirited than a band of Crow cavaliers. They are a fine race of men, averaging six feet in height, lithe and active, with hawks' eyes and Roman noses. The latter feature is common to the Indians on the east side of the Rocky Mountains; those on the western side have generally straight or flat noses.

Wyeth would fain have slipped by this cavalcade unnoticed; but the river, at this place, was not more than ninety yards across; he was perceived, therefore, and hailed by the vagabond warriors, and, we presume, in no very choice language; for, among their other accomplishments, the Crows are famed for possessing a Billingsgate vocabulary of unrivalled opulence, and for being by no means sparing of it whenever an occasion offers. Indeed, though Indians generally are very lofty, rhetorical, and figurative in their language at all great talks, and high ceremonials, yet, if trappers and traders may be believed, they are the most unsavory vagabonds in their ordinary colloquies; they make no hesitation to call a spade a spade; and when they once undertake to call hard names, the famous pot and kettle, of vituperating memory, are not to be compared with them for scurrility of epithet.

To escape the infliction of any compliments of the kind, or the launching, peradventure, of more dangerous missiles, Wyeth landed with the best grace in his power, and approached the chief of the band. It was Arapooish, the quondam friend of

Rose the outlaw, and one whom we have already mentioned as being anxious to promote a friendly intercourse between his tribe and the white men. He was a tall stout man, of good presence, and received the voyagers very graciously. His people, too, thronged around them, and were officiously attentive after the Crow fashion. One took a great fancy to Baptiste, the Flathead boy, and a still greater fancy to a ring on his finger, which he transposed to his own with surprising dexterity, and then disappeared with a quick step among the crowd.

Another was no less pleased with the Nez Percé lad, and nothing would do but he must exchange knives with him; drawing a new knife out of the Nez Percé's scabbard, and putting an old one in its place. Another stepped up and replaced this old knife with one still older, and a third helped himself to knife, scabbard, and all. It was with much difficulty that Wyeth and his companions extricated themselves from the clutches of these officious Crows, before they were entirely plucked.

Falling down the river a little further, they came in sight of the second band, and sheered to the opposite side, with the intention of passing them. The Crows were not to be evaded. Some pointed their guns at the boat, and threatened to fire; others stripped, plunged into the stream, and came swimming across. Making a virtue of necessity, Wyeth threw a cord to the first that came within reach, as if he wished to be drawn to the shore.

In this way he was overhauled by every band, and by the time he and his people came out of the busy hands of the last, they were eased of most of their superfluities. Nothing, in all probability, but the proximity of the American trading post, kept these land pirates from making a good prize of the bull boat and all its contents.

These bands were in full march, equipped for war, and evidently full of mischief. They were, in fact, the very bands that overrun the land in the autumn of 1833; partly robbed Fitzpatrick of his horses and effects; hunted and harassed Captain Bonneville and his people; broke up their trapping campaigns, and in word, drove them all out of the Crow country. It has been suspected that they were set on to these pranks by some of the American Fur Company, anxious to defeat the plans of their rivals of the Rocky Mountain Company; for at this time, their competition was at its height, and the trade of the Crow country was a great object of rivalry. What makes this the more probable, is, that the Crows in their depredations, seemed by no means bloodthirsty, but intent chiefly on robbing the parties of their traps and horses, thereby disabling them from prosecuting their hunting.

We should observe that this year, the Rocky Mountain Company were pushing their way up the rivers, and establishing rival posts near those of the American Company; and that, at the very time of which we are speaking, Captain Sublette was ascending the Yellowstone with a keel boat, laden with supplies; so that there was every prospect of this eager rivalship being carried to extremities.

The last band of Crow warriors had scarce disappeared in the cloud of dust they had raised, when our voyagers arrived at the mouth of the river, and glided into the current of the Yellowstone. Turning down this stream, they made for Fort Cass, which is situated on the right bank, about three miles below the Bighorn. On the opposite side, they beheld a party of thirty-one savages, which they soon ascertained to be Blackfeet. The width of the river enabled them to keep at a sufficient distance, and they soon landed at Fort Cass. This was a mere fortification against Indians; being a stockade of about one hundred and thirty feet square, with two bastions at the extreme corners. Tulloch, an agent of the American Company, was stationed there with twenty men: two boats of fifteen tons burden, were lying here: but at certain seasons of the year a steamboat can come up to the fort.

They had scarcely arrived, when the Blackfeet warriors made their appearance on the opposite bank, displaying two American flags in token of amity. They plunged into the river, swam across, and were kindly received at the fort. They were some of the very men who had been engaged, the year previously, in the battle at Pierre's Hole, and a fierce-looking set of fellows they were; tall and hawk-nosed, and very much resembling the Crows. They professed to be on an amicable errand, to make peace with the Crows, and set off in all haste, before night, to overtake them. Wyeth predicted that they would lose their scalps, for he had heard the Crows denounce vengeance on them, for having murdered two of their warriors who had ventured among them on the faith of a treaty of peace. It is probable, however, that this pacific errand was all a pretence, and that the real object of the Blackfeet braves was to hang about the skirts of the Crow bands, steal their horses, and take the scalps of stragglers.

At Fort Cass, Wyeth disposed of some packages of beaver, and a quantity of buffalo robes. On the following morning (August 18th), he once more launched his bull boat, and proceeded down the Yellowstone, which inclined in an east-north-east direction. The river had alluvial bottoms, fringed with great quantities of the sweet cotton-wood, and interrupted occasionally by "bluffs" of sandstone. The current occasionally brings down fragments of granite and porphyry.

In the course of the day, they saw something moving on the bank among the trees, which they mistook for game of some kind; and, being in want of provisions, pulled towards shore. They discovered, just in time, a party of Blackfeet, lurking in the thickets, and sheered, with all speed, to the opposite side of the river.

After a time, they came in sight of a gang of elk. Wyeth was immediately for pursuing them, rifle in hand, but saw evident signs of dissatisfaction in his half-breed hunters; who considered him as trenching upon their province, and meddling with things quite above his capacity; for these veterans of the wilderness are exceedingly pragmatical on points of venery and woodcraft, and tenacious of their superiority; looking down with infinite contempt upon all raw beginners. The two worthies, therefore, sallied forth themselves, but after a time, returned empty handed. They laid the blame, however, entirely on their guns; two miserable old pieces with flint locks, which, with all their picking and hammering, were continually apt to miss fire. These great boasters of the wilderness, however, are very often exceeding bad shots, and fortunate it is for them when they have old flint guns to bear the blame.

The next day they passed where a great herd of buffalo were bellowing on a prairie. Again the Castor and Pollux of the wilderness sallied forth, and again their flint guns were at fault, and missed fire, and nothing went off but the buffalo.

Wyeth now found there was danger of losing his dinner if he depended upon his hunters; he took rifle in hand, therefore, and went forth himself. In the course of an hour, he returned laden with buffalo meat, to the great mortification of the two regular hunters, who were annoyed at being eclipsed by a greenhorn.

All hands now set to work to prepare the mid-day repast. A fire was made under an immense cotton-wood tree, that over-shadowed a beautiful piece of meadow land; rich morsels of buffalo hump were soon roasting before it; in a hearty and prolonged repast, the two unsuccessful hunters gradually re-covered from their mortification; threatened to discard their old flint guns as soon as they should reach the settlements, and boasted more than ever of the wonderful shots they had made, when they had guns that never missed fire.

Having hauled up their boat to dry in the sun, previous to making their repast, the voyagers now set it once more afloat, and proceeded on their way. They had constructed a sail out of their old tent, which they hoisted whenever the wind was fa-vorable, and thus skimmed along down the stream. Their voy-age was pleasant, notwithstanding the perils by sea and land, with which they were environed. Whenever they could, they encamped on islands, for the greater security. If on the main-land, and in a dangerous neighborhood, they would shift their camp after dark, leaving their fire burning, dropping down the river to some distance, and making no fire at their second en-campment. Sometimes they would float all night with the cur-rent; one keeping watch and steering while the rest slept: in such case, they would haul their boat on shore, at noon of the following day, to dry; for notwithstanding every precaution, she was gradually getting water soaked and rotten.

There was something pleasingly solemn and mysterious in thus floating down these wild rivers at night. The purity of the atmosphere in these elevated regions, gave additional splendor to the stars, and heightened the magnificence of the firma-ment. The occasional rush and laving of the waters; the vague sounds from the surrounding wilderness; the dreary howl, or rather whine, of wolves from the plains; the low grunting and bellowing of the buffalo, and the shrill neighing of the elk, struck the ear with an effect unknown in the daytime.

The two knowing hunters had scarcely recovered from one mortification, when they were fated to experience another. As the boat was gliding swiftly round a low promontory, thinly covered with trees, one of them gave the alarm of Indians. The boat was instantly shoved from shore, and every one caught up his rifle. "Where are they?" cried Wyeth.

"There—there! riding on horseback!" cried one of the hunters.

"Yes; with white scarfs on!" cried the other.

Wyeth looked in the direction they pointed, but descried nothing but two bald eagles, perched on a low dry branch, beyond the thickets, and seeming, from the rapid motion of the boat, to be moving swiftly in an opposite direction. The detection of this blunder in the two veterans, who prided themselves on the sureness and quickness of their sight, produced a hearty laugh at their expense, and put an end to their vauntings.

The Yellowstone, above the confluence of the Bighorn, is a clear stream; its waters were now gradually growing turbid, and assuming the yellow clay color of the Missouri. The current was about four miles an hour, with occasional rapids; some of them dangerous, but the voyagers passed them all without accident. The banks of the river were in many places precipitous, with strata of bituminous coal.

They now entered a region abounding with buffalo—that ever journeying animal, which moves in countless droves from point to point of the vast wilderness; traversing plains, pouring through the intricate defiles of mountains, swimming rivers—ever on the move; guided on its boundless migrations by some traditionary knowledge, like the finny tribes of the ocean, which, at certain seasons, find their mysterious paths across the deep, and revisit the remotest shores.

These great migratory herds of buffalo have their hereditary paths and highways, worn deep through the country, and making for the surest passes of the mountains, and the most practicable fords of the rivers. When once a great column is in full career, it goes straight forward, regardless of all obstacles; those in front being impelled by the moving mass behind. At such times, they will break through a camp, trampling down every thing in their course.

It was the lot of the voyagers, one night, to encamp at one of these buffalo landing places, and exactly on the trail. They had not been long asleep, when they were awakened by a great bellowing, and tramping, and the rush, and splash, and snorting of animals in the river. They had just time to ascertain that a buffalo army was entering the river on the opposite side, and making towards the landing place. With all haste they moved their boat and shifted their camp, by which time, the head of the column had reached the shore, and came pressing up the bank.

It was a singular spectacle, by the uncertain moonlight, to behold this countless throng making their way across the river, blowing, and bellowing, and splashing. Sometimes they pass in such dense and continuous column as to form a temporary dam across the river; the waters of which, rise and rush over their backs, or between their squadrons. The roaring and rushing sound of one of these vast herds crossing a river, may sometimes, in a still night, be heard for miles.

The voyagers now had game in profusion. They could kill as many buffalo as they pleased, and, occasionally, were wanton in their havoc; especially among scattered herds, that came swimming near the boat. On one occasion, an old buffalo bull approached so near, that the half-breeds must fain try to noose him, as they would a wild horse. The noose was successfully thrown around his head, and secured him by the horns, and they now promised themselves ample sport. The buffalo made a prodigious turmoil in the water, bellowing, and blowing, and floundering; and they all floated down the stream together. At length he found foothold on a sandbar, and taking to his heels, whirled the boat after him, like a whale when harpooned; so that the hunters were obliged to cast off their rope, with which strange headgear the venerable bull made off to the prairies.

On the 24th of August, the bull boat emerged, with its adventurous crew, into the broad bosom of the mighty Missouri. Here, about six miles above the mouth of the Yellowstone, the voyagers landed at Fort Union, the distributing post of the American Fur Company in the western country. It was a stockaded fortress, about two hundred and twenty feet square, pleasantly situated on a high bank. Here they were hospitably entertained by Mr. M'Kenzie, the superintendent, and re-mained with him three days, enjoying the unusual luxuries of bread, butter, milk, and cheese, for the fort was well supplied with domestic cattle, though it had no garden. The atmos-phere of these elevated regions is said to be too dry for the cul-ture of vegetables; yet the voyagers, in coming down the Yellowstone, had met with plumbs, grapes, cherries, and cur-rants, and had observed ash and elm trees. Where these grow, the climate cannot be incompatible with gardening.

At Fort Union, Wyeth met with a melancholy memento of one of his men. This was a powderflask, which a clerk had purchased from a Blackfoot warrior. It bore the initials of poor More, the unfortunate youth murdered the year previ-ously, at Jackson's Hole, by the Blackfeet, and whose bones had been subsequently found by Captain Bonneville. This flask had either been passed from hand to hand of the tribe, or, perhaps, had been brought to the fort by the very savage who slew him.

As the bull boat was now nearly worn out, and altogether unfit for the broader and more turbulent stream of the Mis-souri, it was given up, and a canoe of cotton-wood, about twenty feet long, fabricated by the Blackfeet, was purchased to supply its place. In this, Wyeth hoisted his sail, and bidding adieu to the hospitable superintendent of Fort Union, turned his prow to the east, and set off down the Missouri.

He had not proceeded many hours, before, in the evening, he came to a large keel boat, at anchor. It proved to be the boat of Captain William Sublette, freighted with munitions for carrying on a powerful opposition to the American Fur Com-pany. The voyagers went on board, where they were treated with the hearty hospitality of the wilderness, and passed a social evening, talking over past scenes and adventures, and especially the memorable fight at Pierre's Hole.

Here Milton Sublette determined to give up further voyag-ing in the canoe, and remain with his brother; accordingly, in the morning, the fellow voyagers took kind leave of each other, and Wyeth continued on his course. There was now no one on board of his boat that had ever voyaged on the Missouri; it was, however, all plain sailing down the stream, without any chance of missing the way.

All day the voyagers pulled gently along, and landed in the evening and supped; then re-embarking, they suffered the canoe to float down with the current; taking turns to watch and sleep. The night was calm and serene; the elk kept up a continual whinnying or squealing, being the commencement of the season when they are in heat. In the midst of the night, the canoe struck on a sandbar, and all hands were aroused by the rush and roar of the wild waters, which broke around her. They were all obliged to jump overboard, and work hard to get her off, which was accomplished with much difficulty.

In the course of the following day, they saw three grizzly bears at different times along the bank. The last one was on a point of land, and was evidently making for the river, to swim across. The two half-breed hunters were now eager to repeat the manœuvre of the noose; promising to entrap Bruin, and have rare sport in strangling and drowning him. Their only fear was, that he might take fright and return to land before they could get between him and the shore. Holding back, therefore, until he was fairly committed in the centre of the stream, they then pulled forward with might and main, so as to cut off his retreat, and take him in the rear. One of the worthies stationed himself in the bow, with the cord and slip-noose, the other, with the Nez Percé, managed the paddles. There was nothing further from the thoughts of honest Bruin, however, than to beat a retreat. Just as the canoe was drawing near, he turned suddenly round and made for it, with a horrible snarl, and a tremendous show of teeth. The affrighted hunter called to his comrades to paddle off. Scarce had they turned the boat, when the bear laid his enormous claws on the gunwale, and attempted to get on board. The canoe was nearly overturned, and a deluge of water came pouring over the gunwale. All was clamor, terror, and confusion. Every one bawled out—the bear roared and snarled—one caught up a gun; but water had rendered it useless. Others handled their paddles more effectually, and beating old Bruin about the head and claws, obliged him to relinquish his hold. They now plied their paddles with might and main, the bear made the best of his way to shore, and so ended the second exploit of the noose; the hunters determining to have no more naval contests with grizzly bears.

The voyagers were now out of the range of Crows and Black-feet; but they were approaching the country of the Rees, or Arickaras; a tribe no less dangerous: and who were, generally, hostile to small parties.

In passing through their country, Wycth laid by all day, and drifted quietly down the river at night. In this way, he passed on, until he supposed himself safely through the region of danger; when he resumed his voyaging in the open day. On the 3d of September, he had landed, at mid-day, to dine; and while some were making a fire, one of the hunters mounted a high bank, to look out for game. He had scarce glanced his eye round, when he perceived horses grazing on the opposite side of the river. Crouching down, he slunk back to the camp, and reported what he had seen. On further reconnoitring, the voyagers counted twenty-one lodges; and, from the number of horses, computed that there must be nearly a hundred Indians encamped there. They now drew their boat, with all speed and caution, into a thicket of water willows, and remained closely concealed all day. As soon as the night closed in, they re-embarked. The moon would rise early; so that they had but about two hours of darkness, to get past the camp. The night, however, was cloudy, with a blustering wind. Silently, and with muffled oars, they glided down the river, keeping close under the shore opposite to the camp; watching its various lodges and fires, and the dark forms passing to and fro between them. Suddenly, on turning a point of land, they found themselves close upon a camp on their own side of the river. It appeared that not more than one half of the band had crossed. They were within a few yards of the shore: they saw distinctly the savages—some standing, some lying round the fire. Horses were grazing around. Some lodges were set up, others had been sent across the river. The red glare of the fires upon these wild groups and harsh faces, contrasted with the surrounding darkness, had a startling effect, as the voyagers suddenly came upon the scene. The dogs of the camp perceived them, and barked; but the Indians, fortunately, took no heed of their clamor. Wyeth instantly sheered his boat out into the stream; when, unluckily, it struck upon a sandbar, and stuck fast. It was a perilous and trying situation; for he was fixed between the two camps, and within rifle range of both. All hands jumped out into the water, and tried to get the boat off; but as no one dared to give the word, they could not pull together, and their labor was in vain. In this way, they labored for a long time; until Wyeth thought of giving a signal for a general heave, by lifting his hat. The expedient succeeded. They launched their canoe again into deep water, and getting in, had the delight of seeing the camp fires of the savages soon fading in the distance.

They continued under way the greater part of the night; until far beyond all danger from this band: when they pulled to shore, and encamped.

The following day was windy; and they came near upsetting their boat, in carrying sail. Towards evening, the wind subsided, and a beautiful calm night succeeded. They floated along with the current throughout the night, taking turns to watch and steer. The deep stillness of the night was occasionally interrupted by the neighing of the elk; the hoarse lowing of the buffalo; the hooting of large owls, and the screeching of the small ones; now and then the splash of a beaver, or the gong-like sound of the swan.

Part of their voyage was extremely tempestuous; with high winds, tremendous thunder, and soaking rain; and they were repeatedly in extreme danger from drift wood and sunken trees. On one occasion, having continued to float at night, after the moon was down, they ran under a great snag, or sunken tree, with dry branches above the water. These caught the mast, while the boat swung round, broadside to the stream, and began to fill with water. Nothing saved her from total wreck, but cutting away the mast. She then drove down the stream; but left one of the unlucky half-breeds clinging to the snag, like a monkey to a pole. It was necessary to run in shore, toil up, laboriously, along the eddies, and to attain some distance above the snag, when they launched forth again into the stream, and floated down with it to his rescue.

We forbear to detail all the circumstances and adventures, of upwards of a month's voyage, down the windings and doublings of this vast river; in the course of which, they stopped, occasionally, at a post of one of the rival fur companies, or at a government agency for an Indian tribe. Neither shall we dwell upon the changes of climate and productions, as the voyagers

swept down from north to south, across several degrees of latitude; arriving at the regions of oaks and sycamores; of mul-
berry and basswood trees; of paroquets and wild turkeys. This
is one of the characteristics of the middle and lower part of
the Missouri: but still more so of the Mississippi; whose rapid
current traverses a succession of latitudes, so as in a few days
to float the voyager almost from the frozen regions to the
tropics.

The voyage of Wyeth shows the regular and unobstructed
flow of the rivers, on the east side of the Rocky Mountains, in
contrast to those of the western side; where rocks and rapids
continually menace and obstruct the voyager. We find him in a
frail bark of skins, launching himself in a stream at the foot of
the Rocky Mountains, and floating down from river to river, as
they empty themselves into each other: and so he might have
kept on, upwards of two thousand miles, until his little bark
should drift into the ocean. At present, we shall stop with him
at Cantonment Leavenworth, the frontier post of the United
States; where he arrived on the 27th of September.

Here, his first care was to have his Nez Percé Indian, and
his half-breed boy, Baptiste, vaccinated. As they approached
the fort, they were hailed by the sentinel. The sight of a soldier in full array, with what appeared to be a long knife glittering on the end of his musket, struck Baptiste with such
affright, that he took to his heels, bawling for mercy at the
top of his voice. The Nez Percé would have followed him,
had not Wyeth assured him of his safety. When they underwent the operation of the lancet, the doctor's wife and another lady were present: both beautiful women. They were
the first white women that they had seen, and they could not
keep their eyes off of them. On returning to the boat, they recounted to their companions all that they had observed at the
fort; but were especially eloquent about the white squaws,
who, they said, were white as snow, and more beautiful than
any human being they had ever beheld.

We shall not accompany Wyeth any further in his voyage;
but will simply state, that he made his way to Boston, where he
succeeded in organizing an association under the name of
"The Columbia River Fishing and Trading Company," for his
original objects of a salmon fishery and a trade in furs. A brig,

the May Dacres, had been despatched for the Columbia with supplies: and he was now on his way to the same point, at the head of sixty men, whom he had enlisted at St. Louis; some of whom were experienced hunters, and all more habituated to the life of the wilderness than his first band of "down-easters."

We will now return to Captain Bonneville and his party, whom we left, making up their packs and saddling their horses, in Bear River valley.

Chapter XLII

IT WAS the 3d of July, that Captain Bonneville set out on his second visit to the banks of the Columbia, at the head of twenty-three men. He travelled leisurely, to keep his horses fresh, until on the 10th of July, a scout brought word that Wyeth, with his band, was but fifty miles in the rear, and pushing forward with all speed. This caused some bustle in the camp; for it was important to get first to the buffalo ground, to secure provisions for the journey. As the horses were too heavily laden to travel fast, a cache was digged, as promptly as possible, to receive all superfluous baggage. Just as it was finished, a spring burst out of the earth at the bottom. Another cache was therefore digged, about two miles further on; when, as they were about to bury the effects, a line of horsemen, with packhorses, were seen streaking over the plain, and encamped close by.

It proved to be a small band in the service of the Hudson's Bay Company, under the command of a veteran Canadian; one of those petty leaders, who, with a small party of men, and a small supply of goods, are employed to follow up a band of Indians from one hunting ground to another, and buy up their peltries.

Having received numerous civilities from the Hudson's Bay Company, the captain sent an invitation to the officers of the party to an evening regale; and set to work to make jovial preparations. As the night air in these elevated regions is apt to be cold, a blazing fire was soon made, that would have done credit to a Christmas dinner, instead of a midsummer banquet. The parties met in high good-fellowship. There was abundance of such hunter's fare as the neighborhood furnished;

and it was all discussed with mountain appetites. They talked over all the events of their late campaigns: but the Canadian veteran had been unlucky in some of his transactions; and his brow began to grow cloudy. Captain Bonneville remarked his rising spleen, and regretted that he had no juice of the grape, to keep it down.

A man's wit, however, is quick and inventive in the wilderness: a thought suggested itself to the captain, how he might brew a delectable beverage. Among his stores, was a keg of honey but half exhausted. This he filled up with alcohol, and stirred the fiery and mellifluous ingredients together. The glorious result may readily be imagined: a happy compound, of strength and sweetness, enough to sooth the most ruffled temper, and unsettle the most solid understanding.

The beverage worked to a charm; the can circulated merrily: the first deep draught washed out every care from the mind of the veteran; the second, elevated his spirit to the clouds. He was, in fact, a boon companion; as all veteran Canadian traders are apt to be. He now became glorious; talked over all his exploits, his huntings, his fightings with Indian braves, his loves with Indian beauties; sang snatches of old French ditties, and Canadian boat songs; drank deeper and deeper, sang louder and louder; until, having reached a climax of drunken gayety, he gradually declined, and at length, fell fast asleep upon the ground. After a long nap, he again raised his head, imbibed another potation of the "sweet and strong," flashed up with another slight blaze of French gayety, and again fell asleep.

The morning found him still upon the field of action, but in sad and sorrowful condition; suffering the penalties of past pleasures, and calling to mind the captain's dulcet compound, with many a retch and spasm. It seemed as if the honey and alcohol, which had passed so glibly and smoothly over his tongue, were at war within his stomach; and that he had a swarm of bees within his head. In short, so helpless and wobegone was his plight, that his party proceeded on their march without him: the captain promising to bring him on in safety, in the after part of the day.

As soon as this party had moved off, Captain Bonneville's men proceeded to construct and fill their cache; and just as it was completed, the party of Wyeth was descried at a distance.

In a moment, all was activity to take the road. The horses were prepared and mounted; and being lightened of a great part of their burthens, were able to move with celerity. As to the worthy convive of the preceding evening, he was carefully gathered up from the hunter's couch on which he lay, repentant and supine, and, being packed upon one of the horses, was hurried forward with the convoy, groaning and ejaculating at every jolt.

In the course of the day, Wyeth, being lightly mounted, rode ahead of his party, and overtook Captain Bonneville. Their meeting was friendly and courteous: and they discussed, sociably, their respective fortunes since they separated on the banks of the Bighorn. Wyeth announced his intention of establishing a small trading post at the mouth of the Portneuf, and leaving a few men there, with a quantity of goods, to trade with the neighboring Indians. He was compelled, in fact, to this measure, in consequence of the refusal of the Rocky Mountain Fur Company to take a supply of goods, which he had brought out for them according to contract; and which he had no other mode of disposing of. He further informed Captain Bonneville, that the competition between the Rocky Mountain and American Fur Companies, which had led to such nefarious stratagems, and deadly feuds, was at an end; they having divided the country between them: allotting boundaries, within which each was to trade and hunt, so as not to interfere with the other.

In company with Wyeth, were travelling two men of science; Mr. Nuttall, the botanist; the same who ascended the Missouri, at the time of the expedition to Astoria; and Mr. Townshend, an ornithologist: from these gentlemen, we may look forward to important information concerning these interesting regions. There were three religious missionaries, also, bound to the shores of the Columbia, to spread the light of the gospel in that far wilderness.

After riding for some time together, in friendly conversation, Wyeth returned to his party, and Captain Bonneville continued to press forward, and to gain ground. At night, he sent off the sadly sober, and moralizing chief of the Hudson's Bay Company, under a proper escort, to rejoin his people; his route branching off in a different direction. The latter took a cordial leave of his host, hoping, on some future occasion, to repay his hospitality in kind.

In the morning, the captain was early on the march; throwing scouts out far ahead, to scour hill and dale, in search of buffalo. He had confidently expected to find game, in abundance, on the head waters of the Portneuf: but on reaching that region, not a track was to be seen.

At length, one of the scouts, who had made a wide sweep away to the headwaters of the Blackfoot River, discovered great herds quietly grazing in the adjacent meadows. He set out on his return, to report his discoveries; but night overtaking him, he was kindly, and hospitably entertained at the camp of Wyeth. As soon as day dawned, he hastened to his own camp with the welcome intelligence; and about ten o'clock of the same morning, Captain Bonneville's party were in the midst of the game.

The packs were scarcely off the backs of the mules, when the "runners," mounted on the fleetest horses, were full tilt after the buffalo. Others of the men were busied erecting scaffolds, and other contrivances, for jerking or drying meat; others were lighting great fires for the same purpose: soon, the hunters began to make their appearance, bringing in the choicest morsels of buffalo meat: these were placed upon the scaffolds, and the whole camp presented a scene of singular hurry and activity. At daylight the next morning, the runners again took the field, with similar success: and, after an interval of repose made their third and last chase, about twelve o'clock; for by this time, Wyeth's party was in sight. The game being now driven into a valley, at some distance, Wyeth was obliged to fix his camp there: but he came in the evening to pay Captain Bonneville a visit. He was accompanied by Captain Stewart, the amateur traveller; who had not yet sated his appetite for the adventurous life of the wilderness. With him, also, was a Mr. M'Kay, a half-breed; son of the unfortunate adventurer of the same name, who came out in the first maritime expedition to Astoria, and was blown up in the Tonquin. His son had grown up in the employ of the British fur companies; and was a prime hunter, and a daring partisan. He held, moreover, a farm, in the valley of the Wallamut.

The three visiters, when they reached Captain Bonneville's camp, were surprised to find no one in it but himself and three men; his party being dispersed in all directions, to make the most of their present chance for hunting. They remonstrated with him on the imprudence of remaining with so trifling a guard, in a region so full of danger. Captain Bonneville vindicated the policy of his conduct. He never hesitated to send out all his hunters, when any important object was to be attained: and experience had taught him that he was most secure, when his forces were thus distributed over the surrounding country. He then was sure that no enemy could approach, from any direction, without being discovered by his hunters; who have a quick eye for detecting the slightest signs of the proximity of Indians: and who would instantly convey intelligence to the camp.

The captain now set to work with his men, to prepare a suitable entertainment for his guests. It was a time of plenty in the camp; of prime hunters' dainties; of buffalo humps, and buffalo tongues; and roasted ribs, and broiled marrowbones: all these were cooked in hunters' style; served up with a profusion known only on a plentiful hunting ground, and discussed with an appetite that would astonish the puny gourmands of the cities. But above all, and to give a bacchanalian grace to this truly masculine repast, the captain produced his mellifluous keg of home-brewed nectar, which had been so potent over the senses of the veteran of Hudson's Bay. Potations, pottle deep, again went round; never did beverage excite greater glee, or meet with more rapturous commendation. The parties were fast advancing to that happy state, which would have ensured ample cause for the next day's repentance; and the bees were already beginning to buzz about their ears, when a messenger came spurring to the camp with intelligence, that Wyeth's people had got entangled in one of those deep and frightful ravines, piled with immense fragments of volcanic rock, which gash the whole country about the head waters of the Blackfoot River. The revel was instantly at an end: the keg of sweet and potent home-brewed was deserted; and the guests departed with all speed, to aid in extricating their companions from the volcanic ravine.

Chapter XLIII

A rapid march—A cloud of dust—Wild horsemen—"High jinks"—Horseracing and rifle shooting—The game of hand —The fishing season—Mode of fishing—Table lands—Salmon fishers—The captain's visit to an Indian lodge—The Indian girl—The pocket mirror—Supper—Troubles of an evil conscience

---

"UP and away!" is the first thought at daylight of the Indian trader, when a rival is at hand and distance is to be gained. Early in the morning, Captain Bonneville ordered the half-dried meat to be packed upon the horses, and leaving Captain Wyeth and his party to hunt the scattered buffalo, he pushed off rapidly to the east, to regain the plain of the Portneuf. His march was rugged and dangerous; through volcanic hills, broken into cliffs and precipices; and seamed with tremendous chasms, where the rocks rose like walls.

On the second day, however, he encamped once more in the plain, and as it was still early, some of the men strolled out to the neighboring hills. In casting their eyes round the country, they perceived a great cloud of dust rising in the south, and evidently approaching. Hastening back to the camp, they gave the alarm. Preparations were instantly made to receive an enemy; while some of the men, throwing themselves upon the "running horses" kept for hunting, galloped off to reconnoitre. In a little while, they made signals from a distance that all was friendly. By this time, the cloud of dust had swept on as if hurried along by a blast, and a band of wild horsemen came dashing at full leap into the camp, yelling and whooping like so many maniacs. Their dresses, their accoutrements, their mode of riding, and their uncouth clamor, made them seem a party of savages arrayed for war: but they proved to be principally half-breeds, and white men grown savage in the wilderness, who were employed as trappers and hunters in the service of the Hudson's Bay Company.

Here was again "high jinks" in the camp. Captain Bonneville's men hailed these wild scamperers as congenial spirits, or rather, as the very game birds of their class. They entertained them with the hospitality of mountaineers, feasting them at every fire. At first, there were mutual details of adventures and exploits, and broad joking mingled with peals of laughter. Then came on boasting of the comparative merits of horses and rifles, which soon engrossed every tongue. This naturally led to racing, and shooting at a mark: one trial of speed and skill succeeded another; shouts and acclamations rose from the victorious parties, fierce altercations succeeded, and a general melée was about to take place, when suddenly the attention of the quarrellers was arrested by a strange kind of Indian chant or chorus, that seemed to operate upon them as a charm. Their fury was at an end; a tacit reconciliation succeeded, and the ideas of the whole mongrel crowd; whites, half-breeds, and squaws; were turned in a new direction. They all formed into groups, and taking their places at the several fires, prepared for one of the most exciting amusements of the Nez Percés, and the other tribes of the Far West.

The choral chant, in fact, which had thus acted as a charm, was a kind of wild accompaniment to the favorite Indian game of "Hand." This is played by two parties drawn out in opposite platoons before a blazing fire. It is in some respects like the old game of passing the ring or the button, and detecting the hand which holds it. In the present game, the object hidden, or the *cache* as it is called by the trappers, is a small splint of wood, or other diminutive article, that may be concealed in the closed hand. This is passed backwards and forwards among the party "in hand," while the party "out of hand" guess where it is concealed. To heighten the excitement and confuse the guessers, a number of dry poles are laid before each platoon, upon which the members of the party "in hand" beat furiously with short staves, keeping time to the choral chant already mentioned, which waxes fast and furious as the game proceeds. As large bets are staked upon the game, the excitement is prodigious. Each party in turn bursts out in full chorus, beating, and yelling, and working themselves up into such a heat, that the perspiration rolls down their naked shoulders, even in the cold of a winter night. The bets are doubled and trebled as the game advances, the mental excitement increases almost to madness, and all the worldly effects of the gamblers are often hazarded upon the position of a straw.

These gambling games were kept up throughout the night; every fire glared upon a group that looked like a crew of maniacs at their frantic orgies; and the scene would have been kept up throughout the succeeding day, had not Captain Bonneville interposed his authority, and, at the usual hour, issued his marching orders.

Proceeding down the course of Snake River, the hunters regularly returned to camp in the evening laden with wild geese, which were yet scarcely able to fly, and were easily caught in great numbers. It was now the season of the annual fish-feast, with which the Indians in these parts celebrate the first appearance of the salmon in this river. These fish are taken in great numbers at the numerous falls of about four feet pitch. The Indians flank the shallow water just below, and spear them as they attempt to pass. In wide parts of the river, also, they place a sort of chevaux-de-frise, or fence, of poles interwoven with withes, and forming an angle in the middle of the current, where a small opening is left for the salmon to pass. Around this opening the Indians station themselves on small rafts, and ply their spears with great success.

The table lands so common in this region have a sandy soil, inconsiderable in depth, and covered with sage, or, more properly speaking, wormwood. Below this, is a level stratum of rock, riven occasionally by frightful chasms. The whole plain rises as it approaches the river, and terminates with high and broken cliffs; difficult to pass, and in many places so precipitous, that it is impossible, for days together, to get down to the water's edge, to give drink to the horses. This obliges the traveller occasionally to abandon the vicinity of the river, and make a wide sweep into the interior.

It was now far in the month of July, and the party suffered extremely from sultry weather and dusty travelling. The flies and gnats, too, were extremely troublesome to the horses; especially when keeping along the edge of the river where it runs between low sand banks. Whenever the travellers encamped in the afternoon, the horses retired to the gravelly shores and remained there, without attempting to feed until the cool of the evening. As to the travellers, they plunged into the clear and cool current, to wash away the dust of the road, and refresh themselves after the heat of the day. The nights were always cool and pleasant.

At one place where they encamped for some time, the river was nearly five hundred yards wide, and studded with grassy islands, adorned with groves of willow and cotton-wood. Here the Indians were assembled in great numbers, and had barricadoed the channels between the islands, to enable them to spear the salmon with greater facility. They were a timid race, and seemed unaccustomed to the sight of white men. Entering one of the huts, Captain Bonneville found the inhabitants just proceeding to cook a fine salmon. It is put into a pot filled with cold water, and hung over the fire. The moment the water begins to boil, the fish is considered cooked.

Taking his seat unceremoniously, and lighting his pipe, the captain awaited the cooking of the fish, intending to invite himself to the repast. The owner of the hut seemed to take his intrusion in good part. While conversing with him, the captain felt something move behind him, and turning round and removing a few skins and old buffalo robes, discovered a young girl, about fourteen years of age, crouched beneath, who directed her large black eyes full in his face, and continued to gaze in mute surprise and terror. The captain endeavored to dispel her fears, and drawing a bright riband from his pocket, attempted repeatedly to tie it round her neck. She jerked back at each attempt, uttering a sound very much like a snarl; nor could all the blandishments of the captain, albeit a pleasant, good looking, and somewhat gallant man, succeed in conquering the shyness of the savage little beauty. His attentions were now turned to the parents, whom he presented with an awl and a little tobacco, and having thus secured their goodwill, continued to smoke his pipe and watch the salmon. While thus seated near the threshold, an urchin of the family approached the door, but catching a sight of the strange guest, ran off screaming with terror, and ensconced himself behind the long straw at the back of the hut.

Desirous to dispel entirely this timidity, and to open a trade with the simple inhabitants of the hut, who, he did not doubt, had furs somewhere concealed; the captain now drew forth that grand lure in the eyes of the savage, a pocket mirror. The sight of it was irresistible. After examining it for a long time with wonder and admiration, they produced a muskrat skin, and offered it in exchange. The captain shook his head; but purchased the skin for a couple of buttons—superfluous trinkets! as the worthy lord of the hovel had neither coat nor breeches on which to place them.

The mirror still continued the great object of desire, particularly in the eyes of the old housewife, who produced a pot of parched flour and a string of biscuit roots. These procured her some trifle in return; but could not command the purchase of the mirror. The salmon being now completely cooked, they all joined heartily in supper. A bounteous portion was deposited before the captain by the old woman, upon some fresh grass, which served instead of a platter; and never had he tasted a salmon boiled so completely to his fancy.

Supper being over, the captain lighted his pipe and passed it to his host, who, inhaling the smoke, puffed it through his nostrils so assiduously, that in a little while his head manifested signs of confusion and dizziness. Being satisfied, by this time, of the kindly and companionable qualities of the captain, he became easy and communicative; and at length, hinted something about exchanging beaver skins for horses. The captain at once offered to dispose of his steed, which stood fastened at the door. The bargain was soon concluded, whereupon the Indian, removing a pile of bushes under which his valuables were concealed, drew forth the number of skins agreed upon as the price.

Shortly afterwards, some of the captain's people coming up, he ordered another horse to be saddled, and mounting it took his departure from the hut, after distributing a few trifling presents among its simple inhabitants. During all the time of his visit, the little Indian girl had kept her large black eyes fixed upon him, almost without winking, watching every movement with awe and wonder; and as he rode off, remained gazing after him, motionless as a statue. Her father, however, delighted with his new acquaintance, mounted his newly purchased horse, and followed in the train of the captain, to whom he continued to be a faithful and useful adherent during his sojourn in the neighborhood.

The cowardly effects of an evil conscience were evidenced in the conduct of one of the captain's men, who had been in the Californian expedition. During all their intercourse with the harmless people of this place, he had manifested uneasiness and anxiety. While his companions mingled freely and joyously with the natives, he went about with a restless, suspicious look; scrutinizing every painted form and face, and starting often at the sudden approach of some meek and inoffensive savage, who regarded him with reverence as a superior being. Yet this was ordinarily a bold fellow, who never flinched from danger, nor turned pale at the prospect of a battle. At length, he requested permission of Captain Bonneville to keep out of the way of these people entirely. Their striking resemblance, he said, to the people of Ogden's River, made him continually fear that some among them might have seen him in that expedition; and might seek an opportunity of revenge. Ever after this, while they remained in this neighborhood, he would skulk out of the way and keep aloof, when any of the native inhabitants approached. "Such," observes Captain Bonneville, "is the effect of self-reproach, even upon the roving trapper in the wilderness, who has little else to fear than the stings of his own guilty conscience."

Chapter XLIV

Outfit of a trapper—Risks to which he is subjected—Partner-
ship of trappers—Enmity of Indians—Distant smoke—A
country on fire—Gun Creek—Grand Rond—Fine pastures—
Perplexities in a smoky country—Conflagration of forests

I T HAD been the intention of Captain Bonneville, in descending along Snake River, to scatter his trappers upon
the smaller streams. In this way, a range of country is
"trapped," by small detachments from a main body. The outfit of a trapper is generally a rifle, a pound of powder, and four
pounds of lead, with a bullet mould, seven traps, an axe, a
hatchet, a knife and awl, a camp kettle, two blankets, and,
where supplies are plenty, seven pounds of flour. He has, generally, two or three horses, to carry himself, and his baggage
and peltries. Two trappers commonly go together, for the
purposes of mutual assistance and support; a larger party
could not easily escape the eyes of the Indians. It is a service
of peril, and even more so at present than formerly, for the Indians, since they have got into the habit of trafficking peltries
with the traders, have learnt the value of the beaver, and look
upon the trappers as poachers, who are filching the riches
from their streams, and interfering with their market. They
make no hesitation, therefore, to murder the solitary trapper,
and thus destroy a competitor, while they possess themselves
of his spoils. It is with regret we add, too, that this hostility
has in many cases been instigated by traders, desirous of injuring their rivals, but who have themselves often reaped the
fruits of the mischief they have sown.

When two trappers undertake any considerable stream,
their mode of proceeding is, to hide their horses in some
lonely glen, where they can graze unobserved. They then
build a small hut, dig out a canoe from a cotton-wood tree,
and in this, poke along shore silently, in the evening, and set
their traps. These, they revisit in the same silent way at daybreak. When they take any beaver, they bring it home, skin it,
stretch the skin on sticks to dry, and feast upon the flesh. The

body, hung up before the fire, turns by its own weight, and is roasted in a superior style; the tail is the trapper's titbit; it is cut off, put on the end of a stick, and toasted, and is considered even a greater dainty than the tongue or the marrowbone of a buffalo.

With all their silence and caution, however, the poor trappers cannot always escape their hawk-eyed enemies. Their trail has been discovered, perhaps, and followed up for many a mile; or their smoke has been seen curling up out of the secret glen, or has been scented by the savages, whose sense of smell is almost as acute as that of sight. Sometimes they are pounced upon when in the act of setting their traps; at other times, they are roused from their sleep by the horrid war whoop; or, perhaps, have a bullet or an arrow whistling about their ears, in the midst of one of their beaver banquets. In this way they are picked off, from time to time, and nothing is known of them, until, perchance, their bones are found bleaching in some lonely ravine, or on the banks of some nameless stream, which from that time is called after them. Many of the small streams beyond the mountains thus perpetuate the names of unfortunate trappers that have been murdered on their banks.

A knowledge of these dangers deterred Captain Bonneville, in the present instance, from detaching small parties of trappers as he had intended; for his scouts brought him word, that formidable bands of the Banneck Indians were lying on the Boisée and Payette Rivers, at no great distance, so that they would be apt to detect and cut off any stragglers. It behooved him, also, to keep his party together, to guard against any predatory attack upon the main body; he continued on his way, therefore, without dividing his forces. And fortunate it was that he did so; for in a little while, he encountered one of the phenomena of the western wilds, that would effectually have prevented his scattered people from finding each other again. In a word, it was the season of setting fire to the prairies. As he advanced, he began to perceive great clouds of smoke at a distance, rising by degrees, and spreading over the whole face of the country. The atmosphere became dry and surcharged with murky vapor, parching to the skin, and irritating to the eyes. When travelling among the hills, they could scarcely discern objects at the distance of a few paces; indeed, the least exertion of the vision was painful. There was evidently some vast conflagration in the direction toward which they were proceeding; it was as yet at a great distance, and during the day, they could only see the smoke rising in larger and denser volumes, and rolling forth in an immense canopy. At night, the skies were all glowing with the reflection of unseen fires; hanging in an immense body of lurid light, high above the horizon.

Having reached Gun Creek, an important stream coming from the left, Captain Bonneville turned up its course, to traverse the mountains and avoid the great bend of Snake River. Being now out of the range of the Bannecks, he sent out his people in all directions to hunt the antelope for present supplies; keeping the dried meats for places where game might be scarce.

During four days that the party were ascending Gun Creek, the smoke continued to increase so rapidly, that it was impossible to distinguish the face of the country and ascertain landmarks. Fortunately, the travellers fell upon an Indian trail, which led them to the head waters of the Fourche de glace or Ice River, sometimes called the Grand Rond. Here they found all the plains and valleys wrapped in one vast conflagration; which swept over the long grass in billows of flame, shot up every bush and tree, rose in great columns from the groves, and sent up clouds of smoke that darkened the atmosphere. To avoid this sea of fire, the travellers had to pursue their course close along the foot of the mountains; but the irritation from the smoke continued to be tormenting.

The country about the head waters of the Grand Rond, spreads out into broad and level prairies, extremely fertile, and watered by mountain springs and rivulets. These prairies are resorted to by small bands of the Skynses, to pasture their horses, as well as to banquet upon the salmon which abound in the neighboring waters. They take these fish in great quantities and without the least difficulty; simply taking them out of the water with their hands, as they flounder and struggle in the numerous long shoals of the principal stream. At the time the travellers passed over these prairies, some of the narrow deep streams by which they were intersected, were completely choked with salmon, which they took in great numbers. The wolves and bears frequent these streams at this season, to avail themselves of these great fisheries.

The travellers continued, for many days, to experience great difficulties and discomforts from this wide conflagration, which seemed to embrace the whole wilderness. The sun was for a great part of the time obscured by the smoke, and the loftiest mountains were hidden from view. Blundering along in this region of mist and uncertainty, they were frequently obliged to make long circuits, to avoid obstacles which they could not perceive until close upon them. The Indian trails were their safest guides, for though they sometimes appeared to lead them out of their direct course, they always conducted them to the passes.

On the 26th of August, they reached the head of the Way-lee-way River. Here, in a valley of the mountains through which this head water makes its way, they found a band of the Skynses, who were extremely sociable, and appeared to be well disposed, and as they spoke the Nez Percé language, an intercourse was easily kept up with them.

In the pastures on the bank of this stream, Captain Bonneville encamped for a time, for the purpose of recruiting the strength of his horses. Scouts were now sent out to explore the surrounding country, and search for a convenient pass through the mountains towards the Wallamut or Multnomah. After an absence of twenty days, they returned weary and discouraged. They had been harassed and perplexed in rugged mountain defiles, where their progress was continually impeded by rocks and precipices. Often they had been obliged to travel along the edges of frightful ravines, where a false step would have been fatal. In one of these passes, a horse fell from the brink of a precipice, and would have been dashed to pieces, had he not lodged among the branches of a tree, from which he was extricated with great difficulty. These, however, were not the worst of their difficulties and perils. The great conflagration of the country, which had harassed the main party in its march, was still more awful, the further this exploring party proceeded. The flames, which swept rapidly over the light vegetation of the prairies, assumed a fiercer character, and took a stronger hold amidst the wooded glens and ravines of the mountains. Some of the deep gorges and defiles sent up sheets of flame, and clouds of lurid smoke, and sparks and cinders, that in the night made them resemble the craters of volcanoes. The groves and forests, too, which crowned the cliffs, shot up their towering columns of fire, and added to the furnace glow of the mountains. With these stupendous sights were combined the rushing blasts caused by the rarefied air, which roared and howled through the narrow glens, and whirled forth the smoke and flames in impetuous wreaths. Ever and anon, too, was heard the crash of falling trees, sometimes tumbling from crags and precipices, with tremendous sounds.

In the daytime, the mountains were wrapped in smoke so dense and blinding, that the explorers, if by chance they separated, could only find each other by shouting. Often, too, they had to grope their way through the yet burning forests, in constant peril from the limbs and trunks of trees, which frequently fell across their path. At length they gave up the attempt to find a pass as hopeless, under actual circumstances, and made their way back to the camp to report their failure.

Chapter XLV

DURING the absence of this detachment, a sociable intercourse had been kept up between the main party and the Skynses, who had removed into the neighborhood of the camp. These people dwell about the waters of the Way-lee-way and the adjacent country, and trade regularly with the Hudson's Bay Company; generally giving horses in exchange for the articles of which they stand in need. They bring beaver skins, also, to the trading posts; not procured by trapping, but by a course of internal traffic with the shy and ignorant Shoshokoes and Too-el-icans, who keep in distant and unfrequented parts of the country, and will not venture near the trading houses. The Skynses hunt the deer and elk, occasionally; and depend, for a part of the year, on fishing. Their main subsistence, however, is upon roots, especially the kamash. This bulbous root is said to be of a delicious flavor, and highly nutritious. The women dig it up in great quantities, steam it, and deposit it in caches for winter provisions. It grows spontaneously, and absolutely covers the plains.

This tribe were comfortably clad and equipped. They had a few rifles among them, and were extremely desirous of bartering for those of Captain Bonneville's men; offering a couple of good running horses for a light rifle. Their firstrate horses, however, were not to be procured from them on any terms. They almost invariably use ponies; but of a breed infinitely superior to any in the United States. They are fond of trying their speed and bottom, and of betting upon them.

As Captain Bonneville was desirous of judging of the comparative merit of their horses, he purchased one of their racers, and had a trial of speed between that, an American, and a Shoshonie, which were supposed to be well matched. The race-course was for the distance of one mile and a half out, and back. For the first half mile, the American took the lead, by a few hands; but, losing his wind, soon fell far behind; leaving the Shoshonie and Skynse to contend together. For a mile and a half, they went head and head; but at the turn, the Skynse took the lead, and won the race with great ease: scarce drawing a quick breath when all was over.

The Skynses, like the Nez Percés and the Flatheads, have a strong devotional feeling, which has been successfully cultivated by some of the resident personages of the Hudson's Bay Company. Sunday is invariably kept sacred among these tribes. They will not raise their camp on that day, unless in extreme cases of danger or hunger: neither will they hunt, nor fish, nor trade, nor perform any kind of labor on that day. A part of it is passed in prayer and religious ceremonies. Some chief, who is, generally, at the same time what is called a "medicine man," assembles the community. After invoking blessings from the Deity, he addresses the assemblage; exhorting them to good conduct; to be diligent in providing for their families; to abstain from lying and stealing; to avoid quarrelling or cheating in their play, and to be just and hospitable to all strangers who may be among them. Prayers and exhortations are also made, early in the morning, on weekdays. Sometimes, all this is done by the chief, from horseback; moving slowly about the camp, with his hat on, and uttering his exhortations with a loud voice. On all occasions, the bystanders listen with profound attention; and at the end of every sentence, respond one word in unison; apparently equivalent to an amen. While these prayers and exhortations are going on, every employment in the camp is suspended. If an Indian is riding by the place, he dismounts, holds his horse, and attends with reverence until all is done. When the chief has finished his prayer, or exhortation, he says, "I have done;" upon which there is a general exclamation in unison.

With these religious services, probably derived from the white men, the tribes abovementioned, mingle some of their old Indian ceremonials: such as dancing to the cadence of a song or ballad; which is generally done in a large lodge, provided for the purpose. Besides Sundays, they likewise observe the cardinal holidays of the Roman Catholic Church.

Whoever has introduced these simple forms of religion among these poor savages, has evidently understood their characters and capacities, and effected a great melioration of their manners. Of this, we speak not merely from the testimony of Captain Bonneville, but, likewise, from that of Mr. Wyeth, who passed some months in a travelling camp of the Flatheads. "During the time I have been with them," says he, "I have never known an instance of theft among them; the least thing, even to a bead or pin, is brought to you, if found; and often, things that have been thrown away. Neither have I known any quarrelling, nor lying. This absence of all quarrelling the more surprised me, when I came to see the various occasions that would have given rise to it among the whites: the crowding together of from twelve to eighteen hundred horses, which have to be driven into camp at night, to be picketed; to be packed in the morning: the gathering of fuel in places where it is extremely scanty. All this, however, is done without confusion or disturbance.

"They have a mild, playful, laughing disposition; and this is portrayed in their countenances. They are polite, and unobtrusive. When one speaks, the rest pay strict attention: when he is done, another assents by 'yes,' or dissents by 'no;' and then states his reasons; which are listened to with equal attention. Even the children are more peaceable than other children. I never heard an angry word among them, nor any quarrelling; although there were, at least, five hundred of them together, and continually at play. With all this quietness of spirit, they are brave when put to the test; and are an overmatch for an equal number of Blackfeet."

The foregoing observations, though gathered from Mr. Wyeth as relative to the Flatheads, apply, in the main, to the Skynses, also. Captain Bonneville, during his sojourn with the latter, took constant occasion, in conversing with their principal men, to encourage them in the cultivation of moral and religious habits; drawing a comparison between their peaceable and comfortable course of life, and that of other tribes: and attributing it to their superior sense of morality and religion. He frequently attended their religious services, with his people; always enjoining on the latter the most reverential deportment;

and he observed that the poor Indians were always pleased to have the white men present.

The disposition of these tribes is evidently favorable to a considerable degree of civilization. A few farmers, settled among them, might lead them, Captain Bonneville thinks, to till the earth and cultivate grain: the country of the Skynses, and Nez Percés, is admirably adapted for the raising of cattle. A Christian missionary or two, and some trifling assistance from government, to protect them from the predatory and warlike tribes, might lay the foundation of a Christian people in the midst of the great western wilderness, who would "wear the Americans near their hearts."

We must not omit to observe, however, in qualification of the sanctity of this Sabbath in the wilderness, that these tribes, who are all ardently addicted to gambling and horseracing, make Sunday a peculiar day for recreations of the kind, not deeming them in any wise out of season. After prayers and pious ceremonials are over, there is scarce an hour in the day, says Captain Bonneville, that you do not see several horses racing at full speed; and in every corner of the camp, are groups of gamblers, ready to stake every thing upon the all-absorbing game of hand. The Indians, says Wyeth, appear to enjoy their amusements with more zest than the whites. They are great gamblers; and in proportion to their means, play bolder, and bet higher than white men.

The cultivation of the religious feeling, above noted, among the savages, has been, at times, a convenient policy, with some of the more knowing traders; who have derived great credit and influence among them, by being considered "medicine men:" that is, men gifted with mysterious knowledge. This feeling is, also, at times, played upon by religious charlatans; who are to be found in savage, as well as civilized life. One of these was noted by Wyeth, during his sojourn among the Flatheads. A new great man, says he, is rising in the camp, who aims at power and sway. He covers his designs under the ample cloak of religion: inculcating some new doctrines and ceremonials among those who are more simple than himself. He has already made proselytes of one-fifth of the camp; beginning by working on the women, the children, and the weak-minded. His followers are all dancing on the plain, to their own vocal music. The more knowing ones of the tribe look on and laugh; thinking it all too foolish to do harm: but they will soon find that women, children, and fools, form a large majority of every community; and they will have, eventually, to follow the new light, or be considered among the profane. As soon as a preacher, or pseudo prophet of the kind, gets followers enough, he either takes command of the tribe, or branches off and sets up for an independent chief and "medicine man."

Chapter XLVI

Scarcity in the camp—Refusal of supplies by the Hudson's Bay Company—Conduct of the Indians—A hungry retreat— John Day's River—The Blue Mountains—Salmon fishing on Snake River—Messengers from the Crow country—Bear River valley—Immense migration of buffalo—Danger of buffalo hunting—A wounded Indian—Eutaw Indians—A "surround" of antelopes

PROVISIONS were now growing scanty in the camp, and Captain Bonneville found it necessary to seek a new neighborhood. Taking leave, therefore, of his friends, the Skynses, he set off to the westward, and, crossing a low range of mountains, encamped on the head waters of the Ottolais. Being now within thirty miles of Fort Wallah-Wallah, the trading post of the Hudson's Bay Company, he sent a small detachment of men thither, to purchase corn for the subsistence of his party. The men were well received at the fort; but all supplies for their camp were peremptorily refused. Tempting offers were made them, however, if they would leave their present employ, and enter into the service of the company; but they were not to be seduced.

When Captain Bonneville saw his messengers return empty handed, he ordered an instant move, for there was imminent danger of famine. He pushed forward down the course of the Ottolais, which runs diagonal to the Columbia, and falls into it about fifty miles below the Wallah-Wallah. His route lay through a beautiful undulating country, covered with horses belonging to the Skynses, who sent them there for pasturage.

On reaching the Columbia, Captain Bonneville hoped to open a trade with the natives, for fish and other provisions, but to his surprise, they kept aloof, and even hid themselves on his approach. He soon discovered that they were under the influence of the Hudson's Bay Company, who had forbidden them to trade, or hold any communion with him. He proceeded along the Columbia, but it was everywhere the same; not an article of provisions was to be obtained from the natives, and he was, at length, obliged to kill a couple of his horses to sustain his famishing people. He now came to a halt, and consulted what was to be done. The broad and beautiful Columbia lay before them, smooth and unruffled as a mirror; a little more journeying would take them to its lower region; to the noble valley of the Wallamut, their projected winter quarters. To advance under present circumstances would be to court starvation. The resources of the country were locked against them, by the influence of a jealous and powerful monopoly. If they reached the Wallamut, they could scarcely hope to obtain sufficient supplies for the winter; if they lingered any longer in the country, the snows would gather upon the mountains and cut off their retreat. By hastening their return, they would be able to reach the Blue Mountains just in time to find the elk, the deer, and the bighorn; and after they had supplied themselves with provisions, they might push through the mountains, before they were entirely blocked up by snow. Influenced by these considerations, Captain Bonneville reluctantly turned his back a second time on the Columbia, and set off for the Blue Mountains. He took his course up John Day's River, so called from one of the hunters in the original Astorian enterprise. As famine was at his heels, he travelled fast, and reached the mountains by the 1st of October. He entered by the opening made by John Day's River; it was a rugged and difficult defile, but he and his men had become accustomed to hard scrambles of the kind. Fortunately, the September rains had extinguished the fires which recently spread over these regions; and the mountains, no longer wrapped in smoke, now revealed all their grandeur and sublimity to the eye.

They were disappointed in their expectation of finding abundant game in the mountains; large bands of the natives had passed through, returning from their fishing expeditions, and had driven all the game before them. It was only now and then that the hunters could bring in sufficient to keep the party from starvation.

To add to their distress, they mistook their route, and wandered for ten days among high and bald hills of clay. At length, after much perplexity, they made their way to the banks of Snake River, following the course of which, they were sure to reach their place of destination.

It was the 20th of October when they found themselves once more upon this noted stream. The Shoshokoes, whom they had met with in such scanty numbers on their journey down the river, now absolutely thronged its banks, to profit by the abundance of salmon, and lay up a stock for winter provisions. Scaffolds were everywhere erected, and immense quantities of fish drying upon them. At this season of the year, however, the salmon are extremely poor, and the travellers needed their keen sauce of hunger to give them a relish.

In some places, the shores were completely covered with a stratum of dead salmon, exhausted in ascending the river, or destroyed at the falls; the fetid odor of which, tainted the air.

It was not until the travellers reached the head waters of the Portneuf, that they really found themselves in a region of abundance. Here the buffalo were in immense herds; and here they remained for three days, slaying, and cooking, and feasting, and indemnifying themselves by an enormous Carnival, for a long and hungry Lent. Their horses, too, found good pasturage, and enjoyed a little rest after a severe spell of hard travelling.

During this period, two horsemen arrived at the camp, who proved to be messengers sent express for supplies, from Montero's party; which had been sent to beat up the Crow country and the Black Hills, and to winter on the Arkansas. They reported that all was well with the party, but that they had not been able to accomplish the whole of their mission, and were still in the Crow country, where they should remain until joined by Captain Bonneville in the spring. The captain retained the messengers with him until the 17th of November, when, having reached the caches on Bear River, and procured thence the required supplies, he sent them back to their party; appointing a rendezvous towards the last of June, following, on the forks of Wind River valley, in the Crow country.

He now remained several days encamped near the caches, and having discovered a small band of Shoshonies in his neighborhood, purchased from them lodges, furs, and other articles of winter comfort, and arranged with them to encamp together during the winter.

The place designed by the captain for the wintering ground, was on the upper part of Bear River, some distance off. He delayed approaching it as long as possible, in order to avoid driving off the buffalo, which would be needed for winter provisions. He accordingly moved forward but slowly, merely as the want of game and grass obliged him to shift his position. The weather had already become extremely cold, and the snow lay to a considerable depth. To enable the horses to carry as much dried meat as possible, he caused a cache to be made, in which all the baggage that could be spared was deposited. This done, the party continued to move slowly toward their winter quarters.

They were not doomed, however, to suffer from scarcity during the present winter. The people upon Snake River having chased off the buffalo before the snow had become deep, immense herds now came trooping over the mountains; forming dark masses on their sides, from which their deep-mouthed bellowing sounded like the low peals and mutterings from a gathering thunder cloud. In effect, the cloud broke, and down came the torrent thundering into the valley. It is utterly impossible, according to Captain Bonneville, to convey an idea of the effect produced by the sight of such countless throngs of animals of such bulk and spirit, all rushing forward as if swept on by a whirlwind.

The long privation which the travellers had suffered, gave uncommon ardor to their present hunting. One of the Indians attached to the party, finding himself on horseback in the midst of the buffaloes, without either rifle, or bow and arrows, dashed after a fine cow that was passing close by him, and plunged his knife into her side with such lucky aim as to bring her to the ground. It was a daring deed; but hunger had made him almost desperate.

The buffaloes are sometimes tenacious of life, and must be wounded in particular parts. A ball striking the shagged frontlet of a bull, produces no other effect than a toss of the head, and greater exasperation; on the contrary, a ball striking the forehead of a cow, is fatal. Several instances occurred during this great hunting bout, of bulls fighting furiously, after having received mortal wounds. Wyeth, also, was witness to an instance of the kind, while encamped with Indians. During a grand hunt of the buffalo, one of the Indians pressed a bull so closely, that the animal turned suddenly upon him. His horse stopped short, or started back, and threw him. Before he could rise, the bull rushed furiously upon him, and gored him in the chest, so that his breath came out at the aperture. He was conveyed back to the camp, and his wound was dressed. Giving himself up for slain, he called round him his friends, and made his will by word of mouth. It was something like a death chant, and at the end of every sentence, those around responded in concord. He appeared no ways intimidated by the approach of death. "I think," adds Wyeth, "the Indians die better than the white men; perhaps, from having less fear about the future."

The buffalo may be approached very near, if the hunter keeps to the leeward; but they are quick of scent, and will take the alarm and move off from a party of hunters, to the windward, even when two miles distant.

The vast herds which had poured down into the Bear River valley, were now snow bound, and remained in the neighborhood of the camp throughout the winter. This furnished the trappers and their Indian friends a perpetual Carnival; so that, to slay and eat seemed to be the main occupations of the day. It is astonishing what loads of meat it requires to cope with the appetite of a hunting camp.

The ravens and wolves soon came in for their share of the good cheer. These constant attendants of the hunter gathered in vast numbers as the winter advanced. They might be completely out of sight, but at the report of a gun, flights of ravens would immediately be seen hovering in the air, no one knew whence they came; while the sharp visages of the wolves would peep down from the brow of every hill, waiting for the hunter's departure, to pounce upon the carcass.

Beside the buffaloes, there were other neighbors snow bound in the valley, whose presence did not promise to be so advantageous. This was a band of Eutaw Indians, who were encamped higher up on the river. They are a poor tribe, that, in a scale of the various tribes inhabiting these regions, would rank between the Shoshonies and the Shoshokoes or Root Diggers; though more bold and warlike than the latter. They have but few rifles among them, and are generally armed with bows and arrows.

As this band and the Shoshonies were at deadly feud, on account of old grievances, and as neither party stood in awe of the other, it was feared some bloody scenes might ensue. Captain Bonneville, therefore, undertook the office of pacificator, and sent to the Eutaw chiefs, inviting them to a friendly smoke, in order to bring about a reconciliation. His invitation was proudly declined; whereupon he went to them in person, and succeeded in effecting a suspension of hostilities, until the chiefs of the two tribes could meet in council. The braves of the two rival camps sullenly acquiesced in the arrangement. They would take their seats upon the hill tops, and watch their quondam enemies hunting the buffalo in the plain below, and evidently repine, that their hands were tied up from a skirmish. The worthy captain, however, succeeded in carrying through his benevolent mediation. The chiefs met; the amicable pipe was smoked, the hatchet buried, and peace formally proclaimed. After this, both camps united and mingled in social intercourse. Private quarrels, however, would occasionally occur in hunting, about the division of the game, and blows would sometimes be exchanged over the carcass of a buffalo; but the chiefs wisely took no notice of these individual brawls.

One day, the scouts, who had been ranging the hills, brought news of several large herds of antelopes in a small valley at no great distance. This produced a sensation among the Indians, for both tribes were in ragged condition, and sadly in want of those shirts made of the skin of the antelope. It was determined to have "a surround," as the mode of hunting that animal is called. Every thing now assumed an air of mystic solemnity and importance. The chiefs prepared their medicines or charms, each according to his own method, or fancied inspiration, generally with the compound of certain simples; others consulted the entrails of animals which they had sacrificed, and thence drew favorable auguries. After much grave smoking and deliberating, it was at length proclaimed, that all who were able to lift a club, man, woman, or child, should muster for "the surround." When all had congregated, they moved in rude procession to the nearest point of the valley in question, and there halted. Another course of smoking and deliberating, of which the Indians are so fond, took place among the chiefs. Directions were then issued for the horsemen to make a circuit of about seven miles, so as to encompass the herd. When this was done, the whole mounted force dashed off, simultaneously, at full speed, shouting and yelling at the top of their voices. In a short space of time, the antelopes, started from their hiding places, came bounding from all points into the valley. The riders now gradually contracting their circle, brought them nearer and nearer to the spot, where the senior chief, surrounded by the elders, male and female, was seated in supervision of the chase. The antelopes, nearly exhausted with fatigue and fright, and bewildered by perpetual whooping, made no effort to break through the ring of the hunters, but ran round in small circles, until man, woman, and child, beat them down with bludgeons. Such is the nature of that species of antelope hunting, technically called "a surround."

Chapter XLVII

GAME continued to abound throughout the winter; and the camp was overstocked with provisions. Beef and venison, humps and haunches, buffalo tongues and marrowbones, were constantly cooking at every fire; and the whole atmosphere was redolent with the savory fumes of roast meat. It was, indeed, a continual "feast of fat things," and though there might be a lack of "wine upon the lees," yet, we have shown that a substitute was occasionally to be found in honey and alcohol.

Both the Shoshonies and the Eutaws conducted themselves with great propriety. It is true, they now and then filched a few trifles from their good friends, the Big Hearts, when their backs were turned; but then, they always treated them, to their faces, with the utmost deference and respect; and good-humoredly vied with the trappers in all kinds of feats of activity and mirthful sports. The two tribes maintained towards each other, also, a friendliness of aspect, which gave Captain Bonneville reason to hope that all past animosity was effectually buried.

The two rival bands, however, had not long been mingled in this social manner, before their ancient jealousy began to break out, in a new form. The senior chief of the Shoshonies was a thinking man, and a man of observation. He had been among the Nez Percés; listened to their new code of morality and religion received from the white men, and attended their devotional exercises. He had observed the effect of all this, in elevating the tribe in the estimation of the white men; and determined, by the same means, to gain for his own tribe a superiority over their ignorant rivals, the Eutaws. He accordingly assembled his people, and promulgated among them the mongrel doctrines and form of worship of the Nez Percés; recommending the same to their adoption. The Shoshonies were struck with the novelty, at least, of the measure, and entered into it with spirit. They began to observe Sundays and holidays, and to have their devotional dances, and chants, and other ceremonials; about which, the ignorant Eutaws knew nothing: while they exerted their usual competition in shooting and horseracing, and the renowned game of hand.

Matters were going on thus pleasantly and prosperously, in this motley community of white and red men, when, one morning, two stark free trappers, arrayed in the height of savage finery, and mounted on steeds as fine and as fiery as themselves, and all jingling with hawks' bells, came galloping, with whoop and halloo, into the camp.

They were fresh from the winter encampment of the American Fur Company, in the Green River valley; and had come to pay their old comrades of Captain Bonneville's company a visit. An idea may be formed from the scenes we have already given of conviviality in the wilderness, of the manner in which these game birds were received by those of their feather in the camp; what feasting; what revelling; what boasting; what bragging; what ranting and roaring, and racing and gambling, and squabbling and fighting, ensued among these boon companions. Captain Bonneville, it is true, maintained always a certain degree of law and order in his camp, and checked each fierce excess: but the trappers, in their seasons of idleness and relaxation, require a degree of license and indulgence, to repay them for the long privations, and almost incredible hardships of their periods of active service.

In the midst of all this feasting and frolicking, a freak of the tender passion intervened, and wrought a complete change in the scene. Among the Indian beauties in the camp of the Eutaws and Shoshonies, the free trappers discovered two, who had whilom figured as their squaws. These connexions frequently take place for a season; and sometimes, continue for years, if not perpetually; but are apt to be broken when the free trapper starts off, suddenly, on some distant and rough expedition.

In the present instance, these wild blades were anxious to regain their belles; nor were the latter loath once more to come under their protection. The free trapper combines, in the eye of an Indian girl, all that is dashing and heroic in a warrior of her own race, whose gait, and garb, and bravery he emulates, with all that is gallant and glorious in the white man. And then the indulgence with which he treats her; the finery in which he decks her out; the state in which she moves; the sway she enjoys over both his purse and person, instead of being the drudge and slave of an Indian husband: obliged to carry his pack, and build his lodge, and make his fire, and bear his cross humors and dry blows.—No; there is no comparison, in the eyes of an aspiring belle of the wilderness, between a free trapper and an Indian brave.

With respect to one of the parties, the matter was easily arranged. The beauty in question was a pert little Eutaw wench, that had been taken prisoner, in some war excursion, by a Shoshonie. She was readily ransomed for a few articles of trifling value; and forthwith figured about the camp in fine array, "with rings on her fingers, and bells on her toes," and a tossed-up, coquettish air, that made her the envy, admiration, and abhorrence, of all the leathern-dressed, hard-working squaws of her acquaintance.

As to the other beauty, it was quite a different matter. She had become the wife of a Shoshonie brave. It is true, he had another wife, of older date than the one in question; who, therefore, took command in his household, and treated his new spouse as a slave: but the latter was the wife of his last fancy, his latest caprice; and was precious in his eyes. All attempt to bargain with him, therefore, was useless: the very proposition was repulsed with anger and disdain. The spirit of the trapper was roused; his pride was piqued as well as his passion. He endeavored to prevail upon his quondam mistress to elope with him. His horses were fleet; the winter nights were long and dark: before daylight, they would be beyond the reach of pursuit; and once at the encampment in Green River valley, they might set the whole band of Shoshonies at defiance.

The Indian girl listened and longed. Her heart yearned after the ease and splendor of condition of a trapper's bride, and throbbed to be freed from the capricious control of the premier squaw; but she dreaded the failure of the plan, and the fury of a Shoshonie husband. They parted; the Indian girl in tears, and the madcap trapper more mad than ever, with his thwarted passion.

Their interviews had, probably, been detected, and the jealousy of the Shoshonie brave aroused: a clamor of angry voices was heard in his lodge, with the sound of blows, and of female weeping and lamenting. At night, as the trapper lay tossing on his pallet, a soft voice whispered at the door of his lodge. His mistress stood trembling before him. She was ready to follow whithersoever he should lead.

In an instant, he was up and out. He had two prime horses, sure, and swift of foot, and of great wind. With stealthy quiet, they were brought up and saddled; and, in a few moments, he and his prize were careering over the snow, with which the whole country was covered. In the eagerness of escape, they had made no provision for their journey: days must elapse before they could reach their haven of safety, and mountains and prairies be traversed, wrapped in all the desolation of winter. For the present, however, they thought of nothing but flight; urging their horses forward over the dreary wastes, and fancying, in the howling of every blast, they heard the yell of the pursuer.

At early dawn, the Shoshonie became aware of his loss. Mounting his swiftest horse, he set off in hot pursuit. He soon found the trail of the fugitives, and spurred on in hopes of overtaking them. The winds, however, which swept the valley, had drifted the light snow into the prints made by the horses' hoofs. In a little while, he lost all trace of them, and was completely thrown out of the chase. He knew, however, the situation of the camp toward which they were bound, and a direct course through the mountains, by which he might arrive there sooner than the fugitives. Through the most rugged defiles, therefore, he urged his course by day and night, scarce pausing until he reached the camp. It was some time before the fugitives made their appearance. Six days, had they been traversing the wintry wilds. They came, haggard with hunger and fatigue, and their horses faltering under them. The first object that met their eyes, on entering the camp, was the Shoshonie brave. He rushed, knife in hand, to plunge it in the heart that had proved false to him. The trapper threw himself before the cowering form of his mistress, and, exhausted as he was, prepared for a deadly struggle. The Shoshonie paused. His habitual awe of the white man checked his arm; the trapper's friends crowded to the spot, and arrested him. A parley ensued. A kind of *crim. con.* adjudication took place; such as frequently occurs in civilized life. A couple of horses were declared to be a fair compensation for the loss of a woman who had previously lost her heart: with this, the Shoshonie brave was fain to pacify his passion. He returned to Captain Bonneville's camp, somewhat crest-fallen, it is true; but parried the officious condolements of his friends, by observing, that two good horses were very good pay for one bad wife.

Chapter XLVIII

THE WINTER was now breaking up, the snows were melted from the hills, and from the lower parts of the mountains, and the time for decamping had arrived. Captain Bonneville despatched a party to the caches, who brought away all the effects concealed there, and on the 1st of April (1835), the camp was broken up, and every one on the move. The white men and their allies, the Eutaws and Shoshonies, parted with many regrets and sincere expressions of good-will, for their intercourse throughout the winter had been of the most friendly kind.

Captain Bonneville and his party passed by Ham's Fork, and reached the Colorado, or Green River, without accident, on the banks of which they remained during the residue of the spring. During this time, they were conscious that a band of hostile Indians were hovering about their vicinity, watching for an opportunity to slay or steal; but the vigilant precautions of Captain Bonneville baffled all their manœuvres. In such dangerous times, the experienced mountaineer is never without his rifle, even in camp. On going from lodge to lodge to visit his comrades, he takes it with him. On seating himself in a lodge, he lays it beside him, ready to be snatched up; when he goes out, he takes it up as regularly as a citizen would his walking staff. His rifle is his constant friend and protector.

On the 10th of June, the party were a little to the east of the Wind River Mountains, where they halted for a time in excellent pasturage, to give their horses a chance to recruit their strength for a long journey; for it was Captain Bonneville's intention to shape his course to the settlements; having already been detained by the complication of his duties, and by various losses and impediments, far beyond the time specified in his leave of absence.

While the party was thus reposing in the neighborhood of the Wind River Mountains, a solitary free trapper rode one day into the camp, and accosted Captain Bonneville. He belonged, he said, to a party of thirty hunters, who had just past through the neighborhood, but whom he had abandoned in consequence of their ill treatment of a brother trapper; whom they had cast off from their party, and left with his bag and baggage, and an Indian wife into the bargain, in the midst of a desolate prairie. The horseman gave a piteous account of the situation of this helpless pair, and solicited the loan of horses to bring them and their effects to the camp.

The captain was not a man to refuse assistance to any one in distress, especially when there was a woman in the case; horses were immediately despatched, with an escort, to aid the unfortunate couple. The next day, they made their appearance with all their effects: the man, a stalwart mountaineer, with a peculiarly game look; the woman, a young Blackfoot beauty, arrayed in the trappings and trinketry of a free trapper's bride.

Finding the woman to be quickwitted and communicative, Captain Bonneville entered into conversation with her, and obtained from her many particulars concerning the habits and customs of her tribe; especially their wars and huntings. They pride themselves upon being the "best legs of the mountains," and hunt the buffalo on foot. This is done in spring time, when the frosts have thawed and the ground is soft. The heavy buffalo then sink over their hoofs at every step, and are easily overtaken by the Blackfeet; whose fleet steps press lightly on the surface. It is said, however, that the buffalo on the Pacific side of the Rocky Mountains are fleeter and more active than on the Atlantic side; those upon the plains of the Columbia can scarcely be overtaken by a horse that would outstrip the same animal in the neighborhood of the Platte, the usual hunting ground of the Blackfeet. In the course of further conversation, Captain Bonneville drew from the Indian woman her whole story; which gave a picture of savage life, and of the drudgery and hardships to which an Indian wife is subject.

"I was the wife," said she, "of a Blackfoot warrior, and I served him faithfully. Who was so well served as he? Whose lodge was so well provided, or kept so clean? I brought wood in the morning, and placed water always at hand. I watched for his coming; and he found his meat cooked and ready. If he rose to go forth, there was nothing to delay him. I searched the thought that was in his heart, to save him the trouble of speaking. When I went abroad on errands for him, the chiefs and warriors smiled upon me, and the young braves spoke soft things, in secret; but my feet were in the straight path, and my eyes could see nothing but him.

"When he went out to hunt, or to war, who aided to equip him, but I? When he returned, I met him at the door; I took his gun; and he entered without further thought. While he sat and smoked, I unloaded his horses; tied them to the stakes; brought in their loads, and was quickly at his feet. If his moccasins were wet, I took them off, and put on others, which were dry and warm. I dressed all the skins he had taken in the chase. He could never say to me, why is it not done? He hunted the deer, the antelope, and the buffalo, and he watched for the enemy. Every thing else was done by me. When our people moved their camp, he mounted his horse and rode away; free as though he had fallen from the skies. He had nothing to do with the labor of the camp: it was I that packed the horses, and led them on the journey. When we halted in the evening, and he sat with the other braves and smoked, it was I that pitched his lodge; and when he came to eat and sleep, his supper and his bed were ready.

"I served him faithfully; and what was my reward? A cloud was always on his brow, and sharp lightning on his tongue. I was his dog; and not his wife.

"Who was it that scarred and bruised me? It was he. My brother saw how I was treated. His heart was big for me. He begged me to leave my tyrant, and fly. Where could I go? If retaken, who would protect me? My brother was not a chief; he could not save me from blows and wounds, perhaps death. At length, I was persuaded. I followed my brother from the village. He pointed the way to the Nez Percés, and bade me go and live in peace among them. We parted. On the third day I saw the lodges of the Nez Percés before me. I paused for a moment, and had no heart to go on; but my horse neighed, and I took it as a good sign, and suffered him to gallop forward. In a little while, I was in the midst of the lodges. As I sat silent on my horse, the people gathered round me, and inquired whence I came. I told my story. A chief now wrapped his blanket close around him, and bade me dismount.

I obeyed. He took my horse, to lead him away. My heart grew small within me. I felt, on parting with my horse, as if my last friend was gone. I had no words, and my eyes were dry. As he led off my horse, a young brave stepped forward. 'Are you a chief of the people?' cried he. 'Do we listen to you in council, and follow you in battle? Behold! a stranger flies to our camp from the dogs of Blackfeet, and asks protection. Let shame cover your face! The stranger is a woman, and alone. If she were a warrior, or had a warrior by her side, your heart would not be big enough to take her horse. But he is yours. By the right of war, you may claim him; but look!'—his bow was drawn, and the arrow ready:—'you never shall cross his back!' The arrow pierced the heart of the horse, and he fell dead.

"An old woman said she would be my mother. She led me to her lodge: my heart was thawed by her kindness, and my eyes burst forth with tears; like the frozen fountains in spring time. She never changed; but as the days passed away, was still a mother to me. The people were loud in praise of the young brave, and the chief was ashamed. I lived in peace.

"A party of trappers came to the village, and one of them took me for his wife. This is he. I am very happy; he treats me with kindness, and I have taught him the language of my people. As we were travelling this way, some of the Blackfeet warriors beset us, and carried off the horses of the party. We followed, and my husband held a parley with them. The guns were laid down, and the pipe was lighted; but some of the white men attempted to seize the horses by force, and then a battle began. The snow was deep; the white men sank into it at every step; but the red men, with their snowshoes, passed over the surface like birds, and drove off many of the horses in sight of their owners. With those that remained, we resumed our journey. At length, words took place between the leader of the party and my husband. He took away our horses, which had escaped in the battle, and turned us from his camp. My husband had one good friend among the trappers. That is he (pointing to the man who had asked assistance for them). He is a good man. His heart is big. When he came in from hunting, and found that we had been driven away, he gave up all his wages, and followed us, that he might speak good words for us to the white captain."

Chapter XLIX

A rendezvous at Wind River—Campaign of Montero and his brigade in the Crow country—Wars between the Crows and Blackfeet—Death of Arapooish—Blackfeet lurkers—Sagacity of the horse—Dependance of the hunter on his horse—Return to the settlements

O N THE 22D of June, Captain Bonneville raised his camp, and moved to the forks of Wind River; the appointed place of rendezvous. In a few days, he was joined there by the brigade of Montero, which had been sent, in the preceding year, to beat up the Crow country, and afterwards proceed to the Arkansas. Montero had followed the early part of his instructions; after trapping upon some of the upper streams, he proceeded to Powder River. Here he fell in with the Crow villages or bands, who treated him with unusual kindness, and prevailed upon him to take up his winter quarters among them.

The Crows, at that time, were struggling almost for existence with their old enemies, the Blackfeet; who, in the past year, had picked off the flower of their warriors in various engagements, and among the rest, Arapooish, the friend of the white men. That sagacious and magnanimous chief, had beheld with grief, the ravages which war was making in his tribe, and that it was declining in force, and must eventually be destroyed, unless some signal blow could be struck to retrieve its fortunes. In a pitched battle of the two tribes, he made a speech to his warriors, urging them to set every thing at hazard in one furious charge; which done, he led the way into the thickest of the foe. He was soon separated from his men, and fell covered with wounds, but his self-devotion was not in vain. The Blackfeet were defeated; and from that time the Crows plucked up fresh heart, and were frequently successful.

Montero had not been long encamped among them, when he discovered that the Blackfeet were hovering about the neighborhood. One day the hunters came galloping into the camp, and proclaimed that a band of the enemy was at hand. The Crows flew to arms, leaped on their horses, and dashed out in squadrons in pursuit. They overtook the retreating

944

enemy in the midst of a plain. A desperate fight ensued. The Crows had the advantage of numbers, and of fighting on horseback. The greater part of the Blackfeet were slain; the remnant took shelter in a close thicket of willows, where the horse could not enter; whence they plied their bows vigorously.

The Crows drew off out of bow shot, and endeavored by taunts and bravadoes, to draw the warriors out of their retreat. A few of the best mounted among them, rode apart from the rest. One of their number then advanced alone, with that martial air and equestrian grace for which the tribe is noted. When within an arrow's flight of the thicket, he loosened his rein, urged his horse to full speed, threw his body on the opposite side, so as to hang by but one leg, and present no mark to the foe; in this way, he swept along in front of the thicket, launching his arrows from under the neck of his steed. Then regaining his seat in the saddle, he wheeled round, and returned whooping and scoffing to his companions, who received him with yells of applause.

Another and another horseman repeated this exploit; but the Blackfeet were not to be taunted out of their safe shelter. The victors feared to drive desperate men to extremities, so they forebore to attempt the thicket. Towards night they gave over the attack, and returned all-glorious with the scalps of the slain. Then came on the usual feasts and triumphs; the scalp-dance of warriors round the ghastly trophies, and all the other fierce revelry of barbarous warfare. When the braves had finished with the scalps, they were, as usual, given up to the women and children, and made the objects of new parades and dances. They were then treasured up as invaluable trophies and decorations by the braves who had won them.

It is worthy of note, that the scalp of a white man, either through policy or fear, is treated with more charity than that of an Indian. The warrior who won it is entitled to his triumph if he demands it. In such case, the war party alone dance round the scalp. It is then taken down, and the shagged frontlet of a buffalo substituted in its place, and abandoned to the triumphs and insults of the million.

To avoid being involved in these guerrillas, as well as to escape from the extremely social intercourse of the Crows, which began to be oppressive, Montero moved to the distance of several miles from their camps, and there formed a winter cantonment of huts. He now maintained a vigilant watch at night. Their horses, which were turned loose to graze during the day, under heedful eyes, were brought in at night, and shut up in strong pens, built of large logs of cotton-wood.

The snows, during a portion of the winter, were so deep that the poor animals could find but little sustenance. Here and there a tuft of grass would peer above the snow; but they were in general driven to browse the twigs and tender branches of the trees. When they were turned out in the morning, the first moments of freedom from the confinement of the pen were spent in frisking and gamboling. This done, they went soberly and sadly to work, to glean their scanty subsistence for the day. In the meantime, the men stripped the bark of the cotton-wood tree for the evening fodder. As the poor horses would return towards night, with sluggish and dispirited air, the moment they saw their owners approaching them with blankets filled with cotton-wood bark, their whole demeanor underwent a change. A universal neighing and capering took place; they would rush forward, smell to the blankets, paw the earth, snort, whinny and prance round with head and tail erect, until the blankets were opened, and the welcome provender spread before them. These evidences of intelligence and gladness were frequently recounted by the trappers as proving the sagacity of the animal.

These veteran rovers of the mountains look upon their horses as in some respects gifted with almost human intellect. An old and experienced trapper, when mounting guard about the camp in dark nights and times of peril, gives heedful attention to all the sounds and signs of the horses. No enemy enters nor approaches the camp without attracting their notice, and their movements not only give a vague alarm, but it is said, will even indicate to the knowing trapper the very quarter whence danger threatens.

In the daytime, too, while a hunter is engaged on the prairie, cutting up the deer or buffalo he has slain, he depends upon his faithful horse as a sentinel. The sagacious animal sees and smells all round him, and by his starting and whinnying, gives notice of the approach of strangers. There seems to be a dumb communion and fellowship, a sort of fraternal sympathy, between the hunter and his horse. They mutually rely upon each other for company and protection; and nothing is more difficult, it is said, than to surprise an experienced hunter on the prairie, while his old and favorite steed is at his side.

Montero had not long removed his camp from the vicinity of the Crows, and fixed himself in his new quarters, when the Blackfeet marauders discovered his cantonment, and began to haunt the vicinity. He kept up a vigilant watch, however, and foiled every attempt of the enemy, who, at length, seemed to have given up in despair, and abandoned the neighborhood. The trappers relaxed their vigilance, therefore, and one night, after a day of severe labor, no guards were posted, and the whole camp was soon asleep. Towards midnight, however, the lightest sleepers were aroused by the trampling of hoofs; and, giving the alarm, the whole party were immediately on their legs, and hastened to the pens. The bars were down; but no enemy was to be seen or heard, and the horses being all found hard by, it was supposed the bars had been left down through negligence. All were once more asleep, when, in about an hour, there was a second alarm, and it was discovered that several horses were missing. The rest were mounted, and so spirited a pursuit took place, that eighteen of the number carried off were regained, and but three remained in possession of the enemy. Traps, for wolves, had been set about the camp the preceding day. In the morning, it was discovered that a Blackfoot was entrapped by one of them, but had succeeded in dragging it off. His trail was followed for a long distance, which he must have limped alone. At length, he appeared to have fallen in with some of his comrades, who had relieved him from his painful incumbrance.

These were the leading incidents of Montero's campaign in the Crow country. The united parties now celebrated the 4th of July, in rough hunters' style, with hearty conviviality; after which, Captain Bonneville made his final arrangements. Leaving Montero with a brigade of trappers to open another campaign, he put himself at the head of the residue of his men, and set off on his return to civilized life. We shall not detail his journey along the course of the Nebraska, and so, from point to point of the wilderness, until he and his band reached the frontier settlements on the 22d of August.

Here, according to his own account, his cavalcade might have been taken for a procession of tatterdemalion savages; for the men were ragged almost to nakedness, and had contracted a wildness of aspect during three years of wandering in the wilderness. A few hours in a populous town, however, produced a magical metamorphosis. Hats of the most ample brim and longest nap; coats with buttons that shone like mirrors, and pantaloons of the most liberal plenitude, took the place of the well-worn trapper's equipments; and the happy wearers might be seen strolling about in all directions, scattering their silver like sailors just from a cruise.

The worthy captain, however, seems by no means to have shared the excitement of his men, on finding himself once more in the thronged resorts of civilized life, but, on the contrary, to have looked back to the wilderness with regret. "Though the prospect," says he, "of once more tasting the blessings of peaceful society, and passing days and nights under the calm guardianship of the laws, was not without its attractions; yet to those of us whose whole lives had been spent in the stirring excitement and perpetual watchfulness of adventures in the wilderness, the change was far from promising an increase of that contentment and inward satisfaction most conducive to happiness. He who, like myself, has roved almost from boyhood among the children of the forest, and over the unfurrowed plains and rugged heights of the western wastes, will not be startled to learn, that notwithstanding all the fascinations of the world on this civilized side of the mountains, I would fain make my bow to the splendors and gayeties of the metropolis, and plunge again amidst the hardships and perils of the wilderness."

We have only to add, that the affairs of the captain have been satisfactorily arranged with the War Department, and that he is actually in service at Fort Gibson, on our western frontier; where we hope he may meet with further opportunities of indulging his peculiar tastes, and of collecting graphic and characteristic details of the great western wilds and their motley inhabitants.

We here close our picturings of the Rocky Mountains and their wild inhabitants, and of the wild life that prevails there;

These thread the rivers, traverse the plains, penetrate to the heart of the mountains, extend their enterprises northward, to the Russian possessions, and southward, to the confines of California. Their yearly supplies are received by sea, at Vancouver; and thence their furs and peltries are shipped to London. They likewise maintain a considerable commerce, in wheat and lumber, with the Pacific islands, and to the north, with the Russian settlements.

Though the company, by treaty, have a right to a participation only, in the trade of these regions, and are, in fact, but tenants on sufferance: yet have they quietly availed themselves of the original oversight, and subsequent supineness of the American government, to establish a monopoly of the trade of the river and its dependancies; and are adroitly proceeding to fortify themselves in their usurpation, by securing all the strong points of the country.

Fort George, originally Astoria, which was abandoned on the removal of the main factory to Vancouver, was renewed in 1830; and is now kept up as a fortified post and trading house. All the places accessible to shipping have been taken possession of, and posts recently established at them by the company.

The great capital of this association; their long established system; their hereditary influence over the Indian tribes; their internal organization, which makes every thing go on with the regularity of a machine; and the low wages of their people, who are mostly Canadians, give them great advantages over the American traders; nor is it likely the latter will ever be able to maintain any footing in the land, until the question of territorial right is adjusted between the two countries. The sooner that takes place, the better. It is a question too serious to national pride, if not to national interest, to be slurred over; and every year is adding to the difficulties which environ it.

The fur trade, which is now the main object of enterprise west of the Rocky Mountains, forms but a part of the real resources of the country. Beside the salmon fishery of the Columbia, which is capable of being rendered a considerable source of profit; the great valleys of the lower country, below the elevated volcanic plateau, are calculated to give sustenance to countless flocks and herds, and to sustain a great population of graziers and agriculturists.

Such, for instance, is the beautiful valley of the Wallamut; from which the establishment at Vancouver draws most of its supplies. Here, the company holds mills and farms; and has provided for some of its superannuated officers and servants. This valley, above the falls, is about fifty miles wide, and extends a great distance to the south. The climate is mild, being sheltered by lateral ranges of mountains; while the soil, for richness, has been equalled to the best of the Missouri lands. The valley of the river Des Chutes, is also admirably calculated for a great grazing country. All the best horses used by the company for the mountains, are raised there. The valley is of such happy temperature, that grass grows there throughout the year, and cattle may be left out to pasture during the winter. These valleys must form the grand points of commencement of the future settlement of the country; but there must be many such, enfolded in the embraces of these lower ranges of mountains; which, though at present they lie waste and uninhabited, and to the eye of the trader and trapper, present but barren wastes, would, in the hands of the skilful agriculturists and husbandmen, soon assume a different aspect, and teem with waving crops, or be covered with flocks and herds.

The resources of the country, too, while in the hands of a company restricted in its trade, can be but partially called forth: but in the hands of Americans, enjoying a direct trade with the East Indies, would be brought into quickening activity; and might soon realize the dream of Mr. Astor, in giving rise to a flourishing commercial empire.

———————

Wreck of a Japanese Junk on the Northwest Coast

The following extract of a letter which we received, lately, from Mr. Wyeth, may be interesting, as throwing some light upon the question as to the manner in which America has been peopled.

"Are you aware of the fact, that in the winter of 1833, a Japanese junk was wrecked on the northwest coast, in the neighborhood of Queen Charlotte's Island; and that all but two of the crew, then much reduced by starvation and disease, during a long drift across the Pacific, were killed by the natives? The two fell into the hands of the Hudson's Bay Company, and were sent to England. I saw them, on my arrival at Vancouver, in 1834."

―――――――

Instructions to Captain Bonneville from the Major General Commanding the Army of the United States.

Head Quarters of the Army, ⎫
WASHINGTON, August 3, 1831. ⎭

SIR,

The leave of absence which you have asked, for the purpose of enabling you to carry into execution your design of exploring the country to the Rocky Mountains and beyond, with a view of ascertaining the nature and character of the several tribes of Indians inhabiting those regions: the trade which might be profitably carried on with them: the quality of the soil, the productions, the minerals, the natural history, the climate, the geography and topography, as well as geology of the various parts of the country within the limits of the territories belonging to the United States, between our frontier and the Pacific,—has been duly considered and submitted to the War Department for approval, and has been sanctioned. You are, therefore, authorized to be absent from the army until October, 1833. It is understood that the government is to be at no expense in reference to your proposed expedition, it having originated with yourself; and all that you required was the permission from the proper authority to undertake the enterprise. You will, naturally, in preparing yourself for the expedition, provide suitable instruments, and especially the best maps of the interior to be found.

It is desirable, besides what is enumerated as the object of your enterprise, that you note particularly the number of warriors that may be in each tribe or nation that you may meet with; their alliances with other tribes, and their relative position as to a state of peace or war, and whether their friendly or warlike dispositions towards each other are recent or of long standing. You will gratify us by describing the manner of their making war; of the mode of subsisting themselves during a state of war, and a state of peace; their arms, and the effect of them; whether they act on foot or on horseback; detailing the discipline and manoeuvres of the war parties: the power of their horses, size, and general description: in short, every information which you may conceive would be useful to the government.

You will avail yourself of every opportunity of informing us of your position and progress, and at the expiration of your leave of absence, will join your proper station.

I have the honor to be, Sir,
Your obt. servant,
ALEXANDER MACOMB,
Major General, commanding the Army.

Capt. B. L. E. BONNEVILLE,
    7th Regt. of Infantry, New York.

Chronology

1783–86   Born April 3, 1783, at 131 William Street, New York City, youngest of eight surviving children of William Irving and Sarah Sanders Irving. (Father was born in 1731 on Shapinsay, in the Orkney Islands north of Scotland, the descendant of seamen, tradesmen, and shopkeepers. In 1761, while a petty officer in the Royal Navy, he married Sarah Sanders, born 1738, the granddaughter of an English curate, in Falmouth, England. They immigrated to New York in 1763, where father became successful merchant, with business at 75 William Street, and a Presbyterian deacon.) Mother names him Washington Irving in honor of George Washington. Within a few weeks after his birth, family moves across the street to 128 William Street. Baptized in 1784 in the Episcopal Church of St. Paul in a Presbyterian service. Father reads the Bible aloud to the family every evening, takes them to three sermons on Sundays, and makes the children study the catechism on Thursday afternoons. Irving feels close to his mother and is the favorite of his four brothers (William, Jr., b. 1766; Peter, b. 1772; Ebenezer, b. 1776; John Treat, b. 1778) and three sisters (Ann, b. 1770; Catharine, b. 1774; Sarah, b. 1780).

1787–89   Attends Mrs. Ann Kilmaster's kindergarten. On a walk in the summer of 1789, his Scottish nurse, Lizzie, sees President George Washington in a shop and asks him to bless his namesake, which he does.

1789–97   Attends school of Benjamin Romaine, a Revolutionary War veteran and strict disciplinarian. Reads romances and travel books, including *The World Displayed* (later writes that these volumes "were more delightful to me than a fairy tale and the plates by which they were illustrated are indelibly stamped on my reccollection"), John Bunyan's *Pilgrim's Progress*, Jonathan Swift's *Gulliver's Travels*, Daniel Defoe's *Robinson Crusoe*, and *Sinbad the Sailor*. Wanders among the wharves and watches ships sail out to sea. Begins attending theaters and pantomimes, sneaking out through the window and over the rooftop at night. Visitors to the Irving home include Archibald and Alexander Robertson, artists whose drawing academy at 135 William Street Irving attends, and the wood engraver Alexander Anderson and his brother John, in whose drawings Irving takes an interest.

1797–98   When Benjamin Romaine retires in the spring, Irving is sent by brothers to school of Josiah A. Henderson, author of *The Well-Bred Scholar* and an authority on theater; in December 1797, his brothers send him to Jonathan Fiske's school, where he studies Latin. Against his father's wishes, attends dancing school, takes long walks in the country, and hunts squirrels along the Hudson River.

1799   Unlike his brothers Peter and John, does not attend Columbia College. Enters law offices of Henry Masterson, for whom John also clerked, in preference to the family import business.

1800   Takes first extended trip up the Hudson River to visit sisters Ann and Catharine, now living with their families in Johnstown, near Albany (later writes, "of all the scenery of the Hudson, the Kaatskill Mountains had the most witching effect on my boyish imagination").

1801   Moves in summer to office of prominent attorney Brockholst Livingston, a Revolutionary War veteran and Jeffersonian Anti-Federalist.

1802   After Livingston is named to the state supreme court, Irving transfers to offices of Judge Josiah Hoffman, former attorney general of New York, a leading New York Federalist, and a wealthy landowner and real estate speculator. Becomes an intimate of Hoffman's family. In November, begins publishing letters under pseudonym "Jonathan Oldstyle, Gent." in the *Morning Chronicle*, edited by brother Peter; they attract generally favorable notice.

1803   Accompanies Hoffman, lawyer Ludlow Ogden, and members of their families on a trip through upstate New York in the summer. Visits Albany, Ballston, Johnstown, Utica, and Oswegatchie, where Ogden and Hoffman own land and plan to lay out a town (later Ogdensburg), before going on to Montreal. Travels through forests and across unbridged rivers and streams, participates in a deer hunt for the first time, and encounters Indians. Keeps journal for part of trip. In Montreal, meets Henry Brevoort of New York, who becomes a close friend.

1804   Writes in March and April for *The Corrector*, a newssheet supporting Aaron Burr's campaign for governor of New York, anonymously published by Peter, who is running for the assembly on Burr's ticket (neither Burr nor Peter is elected). Brothers William and Ebenezer, worried that Irving is becoming consumptive, finance trip to Europe, and he embarks for Bordeaux on May 19. Keeps journal of his travels through France and Italy. Successfully hides his money when his ship, bound for Sicily, is robbed by pirates.

1805   Watches the *Victory* and other ships of Admiral Nelson's fleet sail through the Strait of Messina in January. Participates in social life of Americans and English abroad. Explores Naples and surroundings (including Pompeii and Herculaneum) with Virginians Joseph Cabell and Colonel John Mercer. Departs on March 24 with Cabell for Rome, where he begins lifelong friendship with American artist Washington Allston and briefly considers becoming a painter; introduced to French writer Madame de Staël by Baron Wilhelm von Humboldt, the Prussian minister at Rome. Travels through Switzerland to Paris with Cabell, arriving May 24. Leaves on September 22 for London, via Belgium and Holland. Attends theaters throughout his travels, especially in England. Joins crowds in London mourning death of Admiral Nelson during the British victory at Trafalgar on October 21.

1806   Irving sails for New York on January 17, arriving March 24. Returns to Hoffman law offices. Becomes a member of "lads of Kilkenny" or "nine worthies," a social and literary club with brothers William, Peter, and Ebenezer, James Kirke Paulding (William's brother-in-law), Henry Brevoort, Henry Ogden, Peter and Gouverneur Kemble, David Porter, and Richard McCall. Assists brother Peter and George Caines in translating a French travel account by François Depons (published as *A Voyage to the Eastern Part of Terra Firma, or the Spanish Main in*

South-America). Continues to visit the Hoffman household and falls in love with 15-year-old Matilda Hoffman. Passes bar examination November 21; shares an office with brother John at 3 Wall Street.

1807   Co-authors *Salmagundi* with William Irving and James Kirke Paulding (published serially by David Longworth from January 24, 1807, to January 25, 1808); the pieces receive much praise. Among friends is Mary Fairlie ("Miss Sophy Sparkle" of *Salmagundi*). Attends the trial for treason of Aaron Burr in Richmond on an informal retainer from a friend of Burr's who hoped Irving might write in Burr's favor. (Irving privately writes to Mrs. Josiah Hoffman, "though opposed to him in political principles, yet I consider him as a man so fallen, so shorn of the power to do national injury, that I feel no sensation remaining but compassion for him," but is not known to have written publicly about the case.) Meets Congressman John Randolph, the foreman of the grand jury that indicted Burr; visits his Virginia friends from European travels, Colonel John Mercer and Joseph Cabell. Makes periodic visits to Philadelphia and becomes friends with merchant Michael Gratz and family, especially his children Rebecca, a close friend of Matilda Hoffman's, and Joseph. Father dies on October 25.

1808   Begins work on a burlesque historical guidebook to New York, originally conceived in collaboration with brother Peter as a parody of Samuel L. Mitchill's *The Picture of New-York; or The Traveller's Guide through the Commercial Metropolis of the United States* (1807). Travels with Peter to Montreal in May; prevented by President Jefferson's embargo from taking the $9,000 in silver he is carrying into Canada, Irving buys cashier's receipts in Burlington, Vermont, hoping to exchange them for cash in Montreal. Sister Ann Dodge dies May 10. Makes a second trip to Montreal in December.

1809   Returns to New York in January. Develops friendship with 18-year-old John Howard Payne, actor and author. Matilda Hoffman dies of tuberculosis on April 26. Irving retires in mourning to Kinderhook, the country home of William P. Van Ness (Burr's second in his duel with Alexander Hamilton). Works on *A History of New York*.

Returns to New York in mid-June and spends late summer at Ravenswood, Judge Hoffman's farm in upper Manhattan. Travels to Philadelphia in October to put *A History* through the press. Perpetrates with Paulding and Brevoort a newspaper hoax concerning the disappearance of "Diedrich Knickerbocker," the fictitious author of the parody. *A History of New York* published on December 6 by Bradford and Inskeep in Philadelphia, where it had been printed to keep its contents a secret in New York until publication; it becomes an instant success.

1810   Travels to Albany in an unsuccessful attempt to obtain a clerkship in the state courts. Visits the Hoffmans, travels in the Hudson Valley, keeps notebooks. After being approached by the brother of Scottish poet Thomas Campbell, arranges for a selection of Campbell's poems to be published in the United States by Charles I. Nicholas, and writes a brief biographical introduction. Brothers Peter and Ebenezer make him inactive partner in a new import business, P. & E. Irving, based in Liverpool and New York, giving him one-fifth interest. Enjoys being a literary celebrity in New York.

1811   Sent to Washington by brothers William and Ebenezer to lobby Congress for the interests of New York merchants. Stays with the family of John P. Van Ness, brother of William; attends, without invitation, a ball given by President Madison's wife, Dolly, but is well-received, meets the President, and becomes friends with Dolly Madison. Participates in Washington social life, meets naval officer Captain Stephen Decatur and Senator Henry Clay. Secretary of State Robert Smith suggests his name as secretary of legation to France, under Joel Barlow as minister; Irving correctly predicts that Barlow will not choose him. Returns to New York in May and moves from family home to share living quarters with Henry Brevoort at 16 Broadway. *Salmagundi* published in book form in London by J. M. Richardson, with introduction by John Lambert but otherwise unsigned.

1812   Corrects *A History of New York* for a new printing by Bradford and Inskeep. Congress declares war on Great Britain on June 18 and renews 1811 Nonimportation Act barring entry of British goods. Firm of P. & E. Irving, unaware of outbreak of war and believing that the 1811 act lapsed with the repeal on June 17 of British Orders in Council restricting American trade, brings ship laden with British imports to New York, where cargo is confiscated until firm posts bond. Irving returns to Washington in November as member of committee of merchants petitioning for remission of bonds. Moses Thomas, a Philadelphia bookseller, buys the magazine *Select Reviews*, and Irving accepts his offer to edit it, for which he is "handsomely paid" (salary $1,500 a year).

1813   Irving and Thomas change the name of *Select Reviews* to *Analectic Magazine*; Irving writes a regular column, biographical sketches of naval heroes, and literary criticism, but dislikes editing. Walter Scott praises *A History* in a letter to Brevoort, who had presented him with a copy while visiting Britain. Brother William wins special election to the U.S. House of Representatives (serves in Congress from January 22, 1814, to March 3, 1819).

1814   Moves in the summer with Brevoort to new lodgings at the corner of Greenwich and Rector streets (Stephen Decatur and his wife are among the other lodgers). His patriotism aroused by British burning of Washington in August, Irving becomes aide-de-camp to Governor Daniel Tompkins of New York, with rank of colonel. Serves on the Canadian frontier but does not see action. Writes Moses Thomas in November that he intends to resign as editor of *Analectic Magazine* at the end of the year. David Longworth publishes revised edition of *Salmagundi* with woodcuts and plates by Irving's old friend Alexander Anderson.

1815   When Moses Thomas is financially hurt by the failure of Bradford and Inskeep, Irving assists with arrangements that permit *Analectic Magazine* to continue, but resigns as editor, and swears never to edit again. Peace treaty with Great Britain is ratified February 16; Irving, feeling restless, resolves to travel abroad and leaves May 25. Arrives in Liverpool in late June on the *Mexico* after a rough passage ("mewed up together for thirty days in dirty cabins"). Sees brother Peter, now suffering from rheumatism and erysipelas, for the first time in seven years. Visits sister Sarah Van Wart and her family in Birmingham; travels to

London in July to view the celebrations following the British victory at Waterloo on June 18. Travels through the English countryside and visits Wales with engineer James Renwick (who marries Brevoort's sister in 1816) for the first two weeks in August. Irving abandons further plans to travel to France, Italy, and possibly Greece when he discovers that Peter's health is worsening; goes to Liverpool in late August to take over the business while Peter convalesces in Birmingham. Forms friendship with English historian William Roscoe.

1816   Visits Van Warts in Birmingham from mid-January to early April. Firm of P. & E. Irving is increasingly troubled by lack of demand for British goods and by Peter's over-purchasing; Irving returns to Liverpool in effort to help redeem the firm's debts and the family's name ("anxious days and sleepless nights"); borrows from James Renwick to pay firm's debts. Tours Derbyshire with Peter in August for two weeks; Peter returns to Liverpool, while Irving travels along Welsh border before returning to stay with Van Warts in Birmingham.

1817   Returns to Liverpool February 23 to be with Peter to help "relieve the loneliness of his life." Resolves to return to New York to visit his mother, but then learns that she died April 9. In June, Virginian William Campbell Preston arrives in Liverpool and joins Irving and Peter on a walking tour in Wales. Irving takes lodgings in London in early August on Cockspur Lane, Westminster, and begins work on *The Sketch Book of Geoffrey Crayon, Gent.* ("to raise myself from the degradation into which I considered myself fallen," he later writes). Visits Thomas Campbell in Sydenham and tries through Brevoort to arrange an American lecture tour for the poet (Campbell later declines to go). Dines with publisher John Murray II, who introduces him to writer Isaac D'Israeli (father of Benjamin Disraeli) and publisher John Miller. Visits poet Samuel Taylor Coleridge. Renews friendships with James Oglivie (a teacher of oratory, whom Irving met at the Burr trial) and American artists Washington Allston and Charles Leslie, who are working on illustrations for *A History of New York* for Murray, and becomes friends with American artist Gilbert Stuart Newton. Interrupts work on *The Sketch Book* to travel to Scotland on August 25.

Visits Francis Jeffrey, editor of the *Edinburgh Review*, and meets Walter Scott at Abbotsford, where he is invited to stay for a few days. Irving is amazed at "being under the roof of Scott . . . in the very centre of that region which had for some time past been the favorite scene of romantic fiction." Scott reads aloud from *Le Morte d'Arthur* and introduces him to German legend and literature. Tours Scottish Highlands with Preston. Returns to Liverpool in September but takes occasional trips to London. Learns of Brevoort's marriage to Laura Elizabeth Carson; in his congratulations Irving says the news makes him more "melancholy than glad" for "marriage is the grave of Bachelors intimacy." Brother William attempts unsuccessfully, through Henry Clay, to have Irving appointed as secretary to the American legation in London; Irving asks William to seek positions for Peter or Ebenezer instead.

1818   Irving and Peter appear before the Commissioners of Bankruptcy between January 27 and March 14, and their bankruptcy is allowed in June (writes to Brevoort on January 28, " . . . my mind is made up to any thing that will extricate me from this loathsome entanglement in which I have so long been involved"). Immerses himself in his notebooks, and studies German ("day & night by way of driving off horrid thoughts"). Leaves Liverpool and visits the Van Warts in Birmingham, before taking the waters at Leamington with sister Sarah. Returns to London in August, lodging at 21 Edward Street, Portland Place. Tries to dissuade Allston from returning to America, but Allston departs on August 10. Visits often with Newton and Leslie; meets the wealthy banker and writer Samuel Rogers. Declines position in Washington as first clerk in Navy Department that William has arranged (salary $2,500) to devote himself to writing.

1819   *The Sketch Book of Geoffrey Crayon, Gent.* is published in America in seven installments by C. S. Van Winkle in New York (June 1819–Sept. 1820); several selections appear in British newspapers, but Murray declines to publish the book in England. (American publication is arranged by Brevoort and brother Ebenezer, who continue to act as Irving's agents.) James Paulding brings out second series of *Salmagundi* on his own (May–Sept. 1820), displeasing

Irving, who now considers the original "a juvenile pro-
duction . . . full of errors, puerilities & impertinen-
cies." Turns down editorship of an "Anti-Jacobin weekly"
offered by Scott (salary £500).

1820   First volume of *The Sketch Book* published by John Miller
in London in February at Irving's expense (Miller's business fails within two months, and Murray buys Miller's
unbound sheets and reissues them with a new title page).
Enthusiastic reviews on both sides of the Atlantic establish Irving as the first American man of letters with an
international reputation; sales give him financial independence. Irving attends afternoon gatherings at his publisher Murray's home, where he meets many of the
writers and reviewers of the day, including critic William
Gifford, editor of the *Quarterly Review*, Italian writer
Ugo Foscolo, and English poets Robert Southey and
Henry Hart Milman. Dines out frequently in the homes
of fashionable London society; meets the Duke of
Wellington. Murray publishes second volume of *The
Sketch Book* on July 15. Travels with Peter to France in late
August. Irving invests $5,000 in a steamboat venture on
the Seine between Le Havre and Rouen with Reuben
Beasley, American consul at Le Havre, who has already
started a successful service between Le Havre and Hon-
fleur. Takes out $2,000 in drafts on William and writes to
him that he wishes to give Peter employment as an agent
for the line. To Irving's dismay, William refuses to honor
the drafts, thinking the investment unwise. (Irving eventually accepts $2,000 loan from Brevoort and uses literary
earnings to pay the remainder of the money owed
Beasley.) Takes lodgings in Paris at 4 Rue du Mont Tha-
bor, near the Tuileries; dines often with Albert Gallatin,
American minister in Paris, and John Jacob Astor and his
family; meets and becomes friends with Irish poet
Thomas Moore and Lord John Russell, a Whig member
of Parliament (later prime minister and foreign secretary).
Sales of *The Sketch Book* so exceed Murray's expectations
that he sends Irving more money and tries to persuade
him to publish his works under his own name; Murray
also tells Irving that Byron praised *The Sketch Book*, and
arranges for Leslie to illustrate a new edition of *A History
of New York*.

1821   Continues active social life; is introduced to English critic
              Sidney Smith by future foreign secretary George Can-
              ning, a close friend of Sir Walter Scott; through John
              Howard Payne, meets actor François Joseph Talma; intro-
              duced by Thomas Moore to Lord and Lady Holland and
              the playwright James Kenney. Visited by young American
              George Bancroft (later a historian and secretary of the
              navy). Begins writing *Bracebridge Hall* and returns to
              England in July by way of Brussels to work on it and
              arrange publication. Arrives in London on the day before
              the coronation of George IV, and views the procession
              with Newton and Leslie. Tries unsuccessfully to bring
              Payne's *The Borrower* to the stage in London. Visits the
              home of Lord and Lady Holland, a gathering place of lit-
              erary and political figures in London. Awarded honorary
              master of arts by Columbia College. Travels with Leslie to
              the Van Warts in Birmingham in September, visiting
              Oxford, Stratford-on-Avon, Warwick, and Kenilworth en
              route. Suffers from severely inflamed ankles during his
              stay in Birmingham whole preparing *Bracebridge Hall* for
              press. Two of sister Catharine's four daughters die; soon
              afterward, learns of death of brother William Irving of
              tuberculosis on November 9, and calls it "one of the dis-
              mallest events" of his life, saying William "was like a father
              to the family." Returns to London on December 26.

1822   Is enlisted by Charles Wiley, James Fenimore Cooper's
              American publisher, to help arrange publication by Mur-
              ray of Cooper's *The Spy*, but Murray declines to publish it
              on the advice of William Gifford. Irving asks Murray for
              £1,575 for *Bracebridge Hall*, but accepts his counter-offer
              of £1,050. *Bracebridge Hall by Geoffrey Crayon, Gent.*
              published on May 21 by C. S. Van Winkle in New York
              and in London by Murray on May 23. Worried by the re-
              curring inflammations on his legs, leaves England on July
              6 and travels through Holland to the spas at Aachen, in-
              tending to make a short trip through Germany before go-
              ing to Paris in the fall. Finds the treatments helpful, and
              takes baths for two weeks in Wiesbaden and three weeks
              in Mainz. Goes to Koblenz, visits the fair in Frankfurt,
              and spends two weeks taking baths at Heidelberg, before
              visiting Karlsruhe, Baden-Baden, Strasbourg, Ulm, Mu-
              nich, Salzburg, and Vienna, where he spends four weeks

exploring the city and surroundings. Travels through Moravia and Bohemia to Prague, then goes to Dresden. Finds that with parts of *The Sketch Book* already published in German and *Bracebridge Hall* being translated (published in Berlin in 1823), his presence is hailed as an event in Dresden when he arrives in late November.

1823   Becomes close friends with Mrs. Amelia Foster of England and her family, with whom he acts in amateur theatricals. Grows deeply attached to 18-year-old Emily Foster. Takes lessons in German (from two tutors), Italian (from Mrs. Foster), and French (from Emily Foster). Becomes a favorite of the court of Frederick Augustus I, King of Saxony. Meets the author and critic Ludwig Tieck. Attends theater often, seeing plays by Heinrich von Kleist and Friedrich Schiller. Hears the music of Beethoven and Mozart, and listens to Carl Maria von Weber performing his own piano music in Dresden. Together with Barham John Livius, translates and adapts Weber's operas *Abu Hassan* and *Der Freischütz* (attends performances of the latter in four cities during his travels in Germany). Leaves on May 20 in the company of British artillery officer Lieutenant John Cockburn for a tour of Bohemia and Silesia, arriving in Prague on May 28; plans to stay only a few days there, but Cockburn develops scarlet fever and they remain until June 24 before returning to Dresden. Travels with the Fosters to Rotterdam in July on their way back to England, then returns to Paris to write, arriving August 3. Visits Peter in Le Havre for two weeks in late September, where he again has problems with inflamed ankles. Moves into Payne's rooms at 89 Rue Richelieu, a five-minute walk from the national library, on his return to Paris on October 3. Begins collaboration on plays with Payne, but insists on anonymity. Leads active social life with Moore, Payne, the painter David Wilkie, the American merchant Thomas Wentworth Storrow and family, Pierre François Guestier (Reuben Beasley's brother-in-law), Talma, Prince Frederick Augustus of Saxony (later King Frederick Augustus II), and many others. Takes care of two nephews (sons of the Van Warts) who are going to school in Paris, and looks after Irving Van Wart when he has smallpox. Peter moves in with Irving in November.

1824   Writes Payne in January that he can no longer afford to collaborate on plays but must devote himself to his own writing, though he continues to offer help. Begins period of intense work that produces most of *Tales of a Traveller*. Tells Murray in March that he has abandoned plans for additional volumes of *The Sketch Book* in favor of *Tales*; rejects Murray's offer of £1,260 and asks for £1,574, which Murray later agrees to pay. Arrives in England on May 28, in time to see second night's performance of *Charles II*, a play written in collaboration with Payne. Introduced by Payne to Mary Wollstonecraft Shelley. Corrects proofs of *Tales*, writes additional material to fill two octavo volumes. Travels to Auteuil, outside Paris, to visit the Storrows for a month before going to the city. *Tales of a Traveller by Geoffrey Crayon, Gent.* published by Carey & Lea of Philadelphia in four parts (appearing Aug. 24–Oct. 9); published in London by Murray on August 25; receives mixed reviews in both countries, with some calling it imitative, indecent, and sycophantic. Depressed by criticism, visits friends in Paris. Takes nine-day trip through the Loire Valley (Orléans, Tours) with Peter in October.

1825   Studies Spanish for distraction. Reads dramatist and poet Pedro Calderón de la Barca, dramatist Lope de Vega, and Spanish history. Invests £1,150 in Mexican and Peruvian copper mines (his hopes for an immediate return are disappointed and in 1829 he will ask that the stocks be forfeited to prevent further costs). Goes to Le Havre in mid-June to visit Peter, returning to Paris on July 9. Visits Compiègne with the Storrows in early September. Leaves Paris with Peter on September 21 to visit friends in and around Bordeaux; stays at the Hôtel de France, with the Guestiers at the Château Beychevelle, then takes lodgings at 24 Rue Rolland in late October to save money. Realizes he must write to earn money, as his investments are unproductive.

1826   Decides to go to Spain. Writes in January to Alexander H. Everett, American minister in Madrid, accepting Everett's previous offer of a diplomatic passport for protection amid civil unrest; becomes an attaché to the American legation in Madrid without official duties. Everett suggests that Irving translate Martín Fernández de Navarrete's two-volume work on Columbus' voyages. Arrives with Peter in Madrid on February 15, where he lives and works in the house of Obadiah Rich, acting secretary of the American legation, using Rich's extensive private library. Decides for artistic and financial reasons not to do a direct translation of Navarrete's scholarly work, but to write instead a popular biography of Columbus. Presented to King Ferdinand VII of Spain by Everett on March 18. Visited for two weeks by nephew Pierre Munro Irving, 24-year-old son of William. Begins planning *Conquest of Granada* in August and works on it until mid-November, when he returns to *Columbus.* Meets American naval officer Alexander Slidell (later known as Alexander Slidell Mackenzie) in November. Regularly attends bullfights in Madrid.

1827   Concentrates on his work, researching and writing *Columbus,* using Navarrete's books. Asks nephew Pierre Munro Irving to help see *Columbus* through the press in London (because of delays in preparing the manuscript, task is eventually done by Thomas Aspinwall, the American consul in London, who becomes Irving's English agent). Frequently visits the home of Pierre D'Oubril, Russian minister at Madrid, where he becomes friends with Prince Dmitri I. Dolgorouki, Russian diplomat and son of the poet Ivan M. Dolgorouki. Irving is visited in March by 20-year-old Henry Wadsworth Longfellow, who remains in Madrid until September. Sends first volume of *Columbus* to Murray on July 29, asking £3,150 for it; Murray is delighted with the book and accepts his terms. Works on stories with Spanish themes, and begins a life of the prophet Mohammed in November. David Wilkie arrives in Madrid on October 10.

1828   *Life and Voyages of Columbus,* which appears under Irving's own name, published by Murray in London on February 8 and by Carvill in New York on March 15. Irving leaves Madrid on March 1 with two Russian diplomats for a tour of southern Spain; visits Cordova, Granada, Málaga, Gibraltar, Cádiz, and Seville, where he takes up residence in mid-April. Explores Seville and vicinity with Wilkie during the later half of April. Begins correcting first edition of *Columbus* in May. Carey & Lea buys the

rights to *A History, The Sketch Book, Bracebridge Hall,*
and *Tales* for seven years at $600 a year. In July, Irving
moves to a cottage ("Casa de Cera") outside of Seville
with John Nader Hall, a consumptive young Englishman
living in Spain for his health. Sends corrected copies of
Columbus to England and America on August 5. Goes
with Hall to Puerto de Santa Maria, on the Bay of Cádiz,
in late August. Visits with German scholar Johann Niko-
laus Böhl von Faber, manager of a winery in Puerto de
Santa Maria, whom Irving met in Seville. Sends final portion of *Grenada* to Murray in London and Ebenezer in
New York on October 19. Declines Murray's offers of
£1,000 a year to edit a new periodical Murray is establishing, plus £105 for any articles for the *Quarterly Review* (writes to Everett that the *Review* "has been so
hostile to our country, that I cannot think of writing a
line for it"). Works on *Voyages and Discoveries of the Companions of Columbus.* Returns to Seville on November 3
to work in the cathedral, where the personal library of
Fernando Columbus is kept. Completes abridged version
of *Columbus* in 19 days after hearing from Peter on November 18 that a pirated abridgment was being planned in
America (Carvill buys rights to both corrected edition
and abridgment of *Columbus* for five years for $6,000;
Murray receives abridgment "gratis"). Learns in late November of the death of John Nader Hall at Puerto de
Santa Maria. Elected to Spanish Royal Academy of History in December.

1829   Continues studying Spanish history and legend, working
on *Companions of Columbus, The Legends of the Conquest
of Spain* (completed in June), *The Alhambra,* and *Mahomet. A Chronicle of the Conquest of Granada by Fray
Antonio Agapida* published in Philadelphia on April 20
by Carey & Lea ($4,750 for five years) and in London on
May 23 by Murray (Irving receives £2,100, but is annoyed
that Murray placed Irving's name on the title page, and
not only that of the fictional narrator, as he wished).
Book is praised by Coleridge. In April, Prince Dolgorouki
arrives from Madrid and Irving shows him Seville and
vicinity. Their plan to visit North Africa ("to get a peep at
the turbaned infidels in their own towns") is hindered by
the Austrian bombardment of Tangiers, but in May they
travel to the Alhambra palace in Granada, where they are

met by Ebenezer's son Edgar. Remains in the Alhambra after Edgar and Dolgorouki leave in mid-May ("It absolutely appears to me like a dream; or as if I am spell bound in some fairy palace"). Feels more and more homesick and plans to return to America, but accepts instead appointment as first secretary at the American legation in London under Minister Louis McLane (salary $2,000) at the urging of his friends and brothers. Leaves Granada on July 28, traveling in the company of Ralph Sneyd, a young Englishman, through Alicante, Valencia, and Catalonia, leaving Spain "with feelings of great regret" on August 23. Meets Peter in Paris and visits Rouen with him. Arrives in London on September 19, taking lodgings on Chandos Street, Cavendish Square, across the street from McLane. Learns that Sneyd, who had fallen ill during the trip, died on his return to London.

1830   Irving's wide friendships in English society are helpful to McLane, who is negotiating a new Anglo-American trade agreement covering the West Indies. Moves to 8 Argyll Street. Learns that the Royal Society of Literature voted to present him with a gold medal. Sees Louis Philippe crowned king of France on a visit to Paris in August. Visits Van Warts in Birmingham in October and sees much of Prince Dolgorouki, who is now attached to the Russian embassy in London. Sees John Randolph, who has resigned his post as American minister to Russia, during Randolph's stay in London. Invests $5,000 in New York iron works and loans money to nephew Pierre P. Irving, son of Ebenezer, to establish a brewery. *Voyages and Discoveries of the Companions of Columbus* published on December 30 by Murray in London (published in Philadelphia by Carey & Lea on March 7, 1831).

1831   Goes to Birmingham for a month, hoping to write, but is unproductive. Arranges for Murray to publish Alexander Slidell's *A Year in Spain*, revises and edits it, and reviews it in the *Quarterly Review*. Receives honorary doctorate of civil law from Oxford. McLane sails in June for the United States, where he assumes duties as secretary of the treasury in August. Irving is acting chargé d'affaires until Martin Van Buren, the new minister, arrives on September 13. Attends coronation of William IV on September 8. Resigns his position at legation in late September to devote himself to writing. Dines on September 27 with Sir Walter Scott, who is on his way to Italy (their last meeting before Scott's death in 1832). Irving visits the Van Warts in Birmingham, his nephew Irving Van Wart in Sheffield, and the Reverend C. R. Reaston Rodes at Barlborough Hall in Derbyshire, from where he makes an excursion to Newstead Abbey, ancestral home of Lord Byron. Returns to London on November 1. Sends first part of *Mahomet* to Murray in October with the understanding that he will receive £525 for it and £1,050 for *The Alhambra*; Murray balks at price, citing losses sustained on earlier books and the uncertain literary market. Irving takes Van Buren and his son on a three-week excursion, visiting Oxford, Stratford-on-Avon, Kenilworth, and the Van Warts in Birmingham, arriving on Christmas Eve at Barlborough Hall, where they spend two weeks before going on to Newstead Abbey.

1832   Irving remains after the Van Burens return to London, "visiting the haunts of Lord Byron and Robin Hood," sleeping in Byron's bed at Newstead Abbey, and dining with Duke of Sussex, brother to the king. Commiserates with Van Buren when his appointment as minister is not confirmed by the Senate. Unable to persuade Murray to publish William Cullen Bryant's poetry, Irving convinces John Andrews to bring out an English edition, sees it through the press, and writes preface in the form of a dedicatory letter to Samuel Rogers (is later criticized for having changed a line in "The Song of Marion's Men" that Andrews felt might injure British pride). Spends a week in Le Havre with Peter, who is too ill to travel. Leaves on the *Havre* for America, April 11. On board meets Englishman Charles Joseph Latrobe and Swiss count Albert-Alexander de Pourtalès, as well as John Schell, an 11-year-old German boy whom Irving employs as a servant. (In 1835 Schell and his father move to Quincy, Illinois, and receive a $100 loan from Irving, which Schell eventually turns into an estate worth $70,000.) *The Alhambra* published in England by Colburn and Bentley on May 4 (Irving and Murray are unable to come to terms) and in America by Carey, Lea & Blanchard on June 11. Arrives in New York, May 21, after a 17-year absence, to an enthusiastic reception. Enjoys official dinner in his honor on May 30, but declines invitations to ceremonies in Philadelphia, Baltimore, and other cities. Dines in Washington with President Andrew Jackson and Van Buren, now the vice-presidential nominee on Jackson's ticket. Visits Clay, Jackson's National Republican opponent in the 1832 election. Takes steamboat trip up the Hudson with Latrobe and Pourtalès to visit Gouverneur Kemble at West Point and the Catskill Mountains. Sees Gilbert Stuart Newton and his fiancée in Boston, continues on to the White Mountains in New Hampshire with Latrobe and Pourtalès, then goes alone to Tarrytown, where he considers buying the property and cottage adjacent to his nephew Oscar's home. Rejoins Latrobe and Pourtalès at Saratoga Springs in early August; in September they accompany Commissioner of Indian Affairs Henry Ellsworth on his trip west to superintend removal of Indians. Sees defeated Sauk chief Black Hawk at Jefferson Barracks outside St. Louis. Travels west by land into Indian Territory (now Oklahoma), living "almost Indian style"; hunts buffalo and wolf, fords rivers, eats skunk, and is exhilarated by the adventure. Parts with Latrobe and Pourtalès at Fort Gibson, Indian Territory, on November 11 and travels by steamboat down the Arkansas and Mississippi rivers to New Orleans, where he spends several days. Travels by mail coach through Mississippi, Alabama, Georgia, South Carolina (where he dines with William C. Preston, with whom he toured Wales and Scotland), North Carolina, and Virginia, reaching Washington in mid-December. Stays with McLane and sees Gouverneur Kemble.

1833   Attends congressional debates on the tariff bill, states' rights, and nullification, in which Daniel Webster, Henry Clay, and John C. Calhoun speak (writes to Peter, "I became so deeply interested in the debates of Congress, that I almost lived in the capitol"). Leaves Washington in early March and spends three weeks in Baltimore, where he visits writer John Pendleton Kennedy, who becomes a close friend. Arrives in New York in late March. Lives with Ebenezer at 3 Bridge Street. Receives diploma for honorary doctor of laws degree conferred on him by Harvard University while he was traveling in 1832. Takes trip up the Hudson to the Catskills with Van Buren in September. Begins writing *A Tour on the Prairies* in October.

1834   John Jacob Astor suggests that Irving write a history of
        Astor's fur trade in Oregon and the Northwest; Irving
        agrees and enlists nephew Pierre Munro Irving to help
        organize the materials. (Astor pays Pierre $3,000 for his
        work, to which Irving later adds $1,000, but Irving re-
        ceives no money from Astor for the book.) Completes *A
        Tour on the Prairies* in November.

1835   *The Crayon Miscellany* published in three volumes by
        Murray in London and by Carey, Lea & Blanchard in
        Philadelphia: *A Tour on the Prairies* appears in England in
        March and in America in April; *Abbotsford and Newstead
        Abbey* in May; and *Legends of the Conquest of Spain* in Oc-
        tober (America) and December (England). Irving receives
        £900 and $4,500 for the three works. Carey, Lea buys the
        American rights to all of Irving's previous works (except
        the abridgment of *Columbus*) for seven years at $1,150 a
        year. Irving buys a "neglected cottage" and ten acres
        along the Hudson two miles south of Tarrytown (the
        property he had looked at in 1832), and begins renovating
        cottage. Begins writing *Astoria*, history of fur trade, in
        May. Helps nephew John Treat Irving publish *Indian
        Sketches*. Moves into Hell Gate, Astor estate in Manhat-
        tan, to work on *Astoria*. Meets western explorer Captain
        Benjamin Bonneville at Hell Gate and purchases his
        papers.

1836   Completes *Astoria* in February. Peter arrives from France
        in June; stays with Ebenezer until cottage is ready. Irving
        moves into it with Peter in September (household later
        includes Ebenezer, five nieces, and visiting relatives) and
        calls new home "Wolfert's Roost," after the original
        owner, Wolfert Acker. Grows especially fond of Sarah
        Paris, 23-year-old daughter of sister Catharine. *Astoria*
        published on October 28 by Carey, Lea & Blanchard in
        Philadelphia; Irving receives $4,000 for 5,000-copy print-
        ing, and £500 for later English edition. Engages in several
        western land speculations that fail to yield returns he
        hopes for. Begins work on account of Bonneville's travels,
        based on his journals.

1837   Irving enjoys family life at Tarrytown cottage. Visited in
        the spring by Charles Louis Napoleon Bonaparte (later

Napoleon III). *Adventures of Captain Bonneville, U.S.A.* published in London by Bentley in May and by Carey, Lea, & Blanchard in June as *The Rocky Mountains: Or, Scenes, Incidents and Adventures in the Far West; Digested from the Journal of Captain B.L.E. Bonneville, of the Army of the United States, and Illustrated from Various Other Sources,* Irving receives £900 and $3,000.

1838   Declines Tammany Hall nomination for mayor of New York and Van Buren's offer to appoint him secretary of the navy. Judge John Treat Irving dies in March and Peter, Irving's closest brother, in June. Worries about lack of funds to support his household, because too much of his money is invested in unprofitable western lands. Begins work in the fall on a history of the conquest of Mexico, but abandons it with regret when he hears that William Prescott is working on the same project.

1839   Writes letters that help get nephew Pierre Munro Irving job as notary at the New York Bank of Commerce. Becomes regular contributor to *Knickerbocker* at $2,000 a year (30 of his essays, tales, and sketches appear between March 1839 and October 1841). Praises Edgar Allan Poe's story "William Wilson" in a letter to Poe in November.

1840   Writes letter to editor of *Knickerbocker* in support of international copyright law. Concerned that Ebenezer's business is failing, writes Van Buren, Kemble, and other politically influential people in attempt to have Ebenezer appointed to new subtreasury in New York. Angry over Van Buren's lack of response, Irving supports Whig slate of William Henry Harrison and John Tyler in the presidential election. Edits *Life and Works of Oliver Goldsmith* in two volumes for Harper & Brothers School District Library, reworking his three previous introductions to Goldsmith's works into a new biographical essay.

1841   Writes life of the young poet Margaret Miller Davidson (1823–38), using memoranda supplied by her mother. (*Biography and Poetical Remains of the Late Margaret Miller Davidson* published by Lea & Blanchard in June, with the profits going to the Davidson family.) Responds warmly to Charles Dickens after receiving an admiring letter from him. Takes trip through the Highlands of the Hudson in July and August to visit Brevoort and Gouverneur Kemble. Ebenezer, unemployed, lives at the Tarrytown cottage (which Irving now calls "Sunnyside"). Irving gathers materials and begins work on a life of George Washington.

1842   Appointed minister to Spain by President John Tyler, at the recommendation of Secretary of State Daniel Webster, with salary of $9,000. Spends time with Dickens when he visits America, but "breaks down" when he tries to give a speech at dinner in Dickens' honor on February 18. Irving offers Lea & Blanchard the rights to revised edition of his collected works, including works never before published, for $3,000 a year (they reject his offer, citing the depressed market for literature, as well as Irving's second offer to extend the present contract for two years). Submits petition to Congress in support of international copyright law. Travels to Washington in March to discuss position at legation. Dines with William Preston, now a U.S. senator from South Carolina. Makes provisions for Sunnyside and his nieces there and collects materials for his life of Washington before leaving on April 10 for England. Presented to Queen Victoria by American minister Edward Everett on May 4. Sees old friends Rogers, Leslie, Moore, and Murray, and attends dinner of the Literary Fund with Prince Albert presiding on May 11. Arrives in Paris on May 24 and is presented by American minister Lewis Cass to King Louis Philippe at his palace at Neuilly. Goes to Madrid and takes over his predecessor Aaron Vail's lodgings at 112 Calle de Alcalá, Plazuela de la Villa. Finds himself well-known and well-received ("all welcome me as a 'friend of Spain'"). Spain is in political turmoil, with many factions seeking control of the regency of 12-year-old Isabella II, daughter of the exiled former consort María Christina; Irving maneuvers skillfully among the contenders. Writes dispatches to Webster (the first of five secretaries of state he will serve under in the next four years) describing the political situation in which ministers are "transient functionaries." Moves into Calle Victor Hugo in mid-September to be nearer the public promenades and theaters. Works on Spanish-American trade relations.

1843   Falls ill with herpetic inflammation in legs (similar to 1822 attack) that spreads over his entire body, accompanied by intermittent fever, and is forbidden to write by his physician. Several insurrections break out in June against the regency of General Baldomero Fernández Espartero and Madrid is briefly besieged by rebel forces in July. Irving hears sound of skirmishing outside city gates, and recommends that the diplomatic corps go to the palace to protect Isabella II in case Madrid is stormed (offer is rejected by the Spanish). Espartero is defeated by General Ramón María Narváez and goes into exile. Feeling sick and lonely, Irving leaves Madrid on September 7 to visit Sarah in France. Despite incomplete recovery, returns to Madrid to follow continuing political turmoil; arrives on November 30, shortly after Isabella II is declared of age and crowned.

1844   Feels somewhat better and takes greater part in social life. María Christina returns from exile in March. Marriage plans for Isabella II become main topic of debate among the various factions; Irving continues to closely follow fate of "the little Queen." Begins revising his works for new edition. Learns that nephew Pierre Munro Irving, who holds Irving's power of attorney in America, has received some money for him from his previously unproductive land investments in Green Bay, Wisconsin. Irving leaves Madrid on June 25 for Barcelona, where the court has gone for the summer, to deliver two official letters from President Tyler to Isabella II. Granted leave for reasons of health. Takes Spanish steamer to Marseilles on July 29, travels up the Rhone to Lyons, then continues by coach to Paris. Sees Sarah at Versailles for a week, then visits Beasley for a few days at Le Havre before leaving on August 21 for Birmingham. Spends three weeks with the Van Warts before returning to Paris to take baths. Visits King Louis Philippe at St. Cloud in October with William King, American minister at Paris. Returns to Madrid on November 17.

1845   Resumes writing. Reports to Secretary of State John C. Calhoun on debate in the Spanish parliament over new penal law against the slave trade (legislation is result of British pressure; Calhoun suspects that Britain's anti-

slavery efforts mask intention to seize Cuba). Irving tries
to further American trade interests in Cuba. Begins discus-
sions with publisher George Putnam about planned revised edition. Still troubled by herpetic malady, takes
leave in September. Travels through Bordeaux, Nantes,
and Orléans, on his way to visit Sarah in Paris. McLane,
who is again serving as minister to Britain, requests Irving's help in November as Anglo-American dispute over
the Oregon border intensifies. Irving writes letter of res-
ignation as minister to Spain on December 12.

1846   Goes to London to help McLane with Oregon negotiations (treaty setting border along the 49th parallel is
signed in May and ratified in June). Breakfasts with John
Murray III (who inherited his father's firm in 1843) and
Gansevoort Melville, secretary of the American legation
in London; Melville reads from the manuscript of his
brother Herman's forthcoming book *Typee*, which Irving
praises. Goes to Paris in February to see Sarah, who is
planning a trip to America, then returns to Madrid on
March 6 to await the arrival of Romulus M. Saunders, his
replacement. Has special audience with the Queen and her
mother on March 14. Explains American position in Mexican War to Spanish government. To the regret of Spanish court and government, leaves Spain permanently early
in August. Visits Paris, Birmingham, and London, before
sailing in early September on a steamer to Boston. Arrives
on September 18 and goes the following day to Sunnyside. Begins work on repairs and improvements to his
property, adding a tower to his "snuggery" to accommodate guests and family. Lives with nieces and brother
Ebenezer.

1847   Inflammation of eyes and recurrence of inflammation in
ankles slow work on revised edition. Revises several un-
published works on Spanish themes (published post-
humously in *Spanish Papers* in 1866). Resumes work on life
of Washington in September. Moves to New York in mid-
December, staying with various relatives.

1848   Spends most of the year in New York, visiting Astor and
other friends, attending opera and theater, and working
on *Washington* and the revised edition of his works. Receives $3,500 from company that plans to build railroad

along Hudson River through his property (later complains of noise). Acts as pallbearer for John Jacob Astor, who died March 29, and is made one of six executors of his will (eventually receives $10,592 for his role) and president of the trustees of the Astor Library (which later becomes part of the New York Public Library). Irving signs with Putnam on July 26 for complete edition of his works (15 volumes appear over the next two years; Irving receives 12.5 percent of the retail price of all copies sold, and earns over $88,000 from Putnam by the time of his death).

1849   Visits former Irving family home at 128 William Street with nephew Pierre Munro Irving before it is torn down. *A Book of the Hudson. Collected from the Various Works of Diedrich Knickerbocker* published in April. Returns to Sunnyside in summer, making regular trips to New York for meetings of the executors of Astor's estate and the trustees of the Astor Library, and to work on the revised edition. First volume of *Mahomet and His Successors* published on December 15.

1850   Second volume of *Mahomet and His Successors* published on April 15. Supports John Murray III in struggle over the British copyrights for his writings. Meets Henry James, Sr., and his seven-year-old son Henry, Jr., on steamboat to Long Island in August and tells them that Margaret Fuller has drowned in a shipwreck off Fire Island.

1851   Works on *Washington*, using 25 years of notes and Jared Sparks's earlier 12-volume edition of Washington's writings. Writer Donald G. Mitchell (Ik Marvel) visits Sunnyside. Writes public letter correcting "erroneous statement" by explorer and historian of American Indians Henry Schoolcraft that Irving had received $5,000 from Astor for writing *Astoria*.

1852   Writes to Nathaniel Hawthorne in January, praising his work. Continues to see returns from his western land investments. Irving is chairman of memorial committee formed in honor of James Fenimore Cooper (who died September 14, 1851) and makes short remarks at public meeting held in New York on February 25, with Daniel Webster presiding and William Cullen Bryant delivering the eulogy. English writer William Makepeace Thackeray visits Sunnyside in November, accompanied by *Knicker-bocker* contributor Frederick Cozzens.

1853   Irving is amazed by news of marriage of Eugenia de Montijo, whom he knew in Spain, and Napoleon III, who visited him at Tarrytown in 1837. Encounters Thackeray by chance at the ferry in New York and rides with him as far as Philadelphia, where Thackeray is delivering a series of lectures. Irving goes on to Baltimore, where he visits Edward Gray, John Pendleton Kennedy's father-in-law, with whom he becomes friends. Continues to Washington to stay with Kennedy, now secretary of the navy. Develops friendship with President and Mrs. Millard Fillmore. Does research on Washington in archives and visits Mount Vernon in January and February. Attends inauguration of President Franklin Pierce on March 4 and speaks with him afterwards; is favorably impressed when Pierce tells him that he is giving Hawthorne a consular post. Returns to Sunnyside in early March. Has Pierre Munro Irving read his *Washington* manuscript and is reassured when his nephew praises it. Travels with Kennedy through western Virginia, visiting Cassilis (estate near Harpers Ferry owned by Kennedy's brother Andrew), examining Washington manuscripts and sites, and taking baths at Berkeley Springs. Returns to Sunnyside on July 12, then leaves on August 1 for Saratoga Springs, where he rejoins the Kennedys and Edward Gray. Goes with Kennedy by boat up Lake Champlain to Plattsburg and then by train to Ogdensburg, where he visits the old French fort he stayed at on his 1803 trip with the Hoffman and Ogden families. Continues by steamer to Lake Ontario and Lewiston, then by carriage to Niagara Falls. After difficult trip in hot weather, returns to Sunnyside August 17, very ill with fever, chills, and delirium. Irving prepares family plot in cemetery of Sleepy Hollow Church and has his parents' remains moved there.

1854   Sick with fever in April; continued poor health often prevents him from writing. Dearman, the village and railroad station adjacent to Sunnyside, changes its name to Irvington in April. Nephew William Irving, son of Ebenezer, dies of overdose of morphine on July 28. Writes reminiscence of Washington Allston for Evert Duyckinck's *Cyclopedia of American Literature* (published 1855).

1855   *Wolfert's Roost*, a miscellany from the *Knickerbocker* which Irving calls "garret trumpery," published in February by Putnam and is well-received by readers. Irving is badly bruised and in bed for a few days in April after being thrown from a horse. First volume of *Life with George Washington* published by Putnam in May. Visits Martin Van Buren in early September at his Kinderhook home (where Irving wrote part of *A History of New York*, when it belonged to the Van Ness family). Second volume of *Washington* published by Putnam in December. Hires Pierre Munro Irving as his literary assistant (formally authorizes salary of $135 a month in February 1856).

1856   With Pierre's help, continues work on *Washington*. Often ill, Irving seldom leaves Sunnyside, where he receives stream of admiring visitors. Third volume of *Washington* published in July.

1857   Fourth volume of *Washington* published in May. Now comfortable financially, negotiates new contract and buys plates for entire edition from Putnam, which needs cash due to national economic depression.

1858   Health deteriorates. Works intermittently on last volume of *Washington*. Visits New York on September 1 to take part in celebrations of the laying of the Atlantic telegraph cable. Pierre Munro Irving and his wife, Helen, move to Sunnyside in December (will stay with Irving for the rest of his life). Writer Oliver Wendell Holmes, Sr., visits Sunnyside on December 20, accompanied by Frederick Cozzens.

1859   Pierre often reads aloud to him, to calm his nerves. Alexander Slidell's *A Year in Spain* is among his favorites. Finishes fifth and final volume of *Washington* March 15. Pierre does final revisions and sees it through the press; it is published by Putnam in April. Irving dies of heart attack at Sunnyside at 10:30 P.M. on November 28, surrounded by his family, and is buried at Sleepy Hollow Cemetery on December 1.

Note on the Texts

This volume contains the three books Washington Irving wrote about the American West: *A Tour on the Prairies* (1835); *Astoria, Or, Anecdotes of an Enterprize Beyond the Rocky Mountains* (1836); and *The Adventures of Captain Bonneville* (1837).

The texts of the three works presented here are those established in *The Complete Works of Washington Irving* under the general editorship of Henry A. Pochmann and his successor Herbert L. Kleinfeld, with Edwin T. Bowden as textual editor, and published by Twayne Publishers in, respectively, 1979, 1976, and 1977. These texts received the approval of the Center for American Authors or its successor, the Center for Scholarly Editions, of the Modern Language Association of America (see *The Center for Scholarly Editions: An Introductory Statement*, 1977).

In the fall of 1833, most likely in October, Irving began writing *A Tour on the Prairies*, his account of a month spent traveling through Indian territory in what is now eastern Oklahoma in October–November 1832. Working from notes recorded in his journal during the trip, Irving spent more than a year creating a narrative of the tour, completing a first draft in late November 1834. After taking a few weeks to revise his draft, he recruited several copyists to prepare a printer's copy from the manuscript for publication in England, where he hoped to see his book published before the appearance of the account written by his traveling companion, Charles Joseph Latrobe. Because of the time necessary to send the manuscript to London, the printer's copy for the English edition had to be completed first. Although most of his revisions and additions made during the preparation of the English printer's copy appear in both the English and American editions of *A Tour on the Prairies*, Irving continued to make changes after a 424-page version of the narrative was mailed to his agent in London in early January 1835; the most extensive late alterations were made in Chapter XXXII, "A republic of prairie dogs," and in the final chapter. For the American edition Irving also included a more extensive introduction. *A Tour on the Prairies* was published in London by John Murray on March 2, 1835, and, as the first book of the three-volume set *The Crayon Miscellany*, by Carey, Lea, and Blanchard in Philadelphia on April 10, 1835. The *New York Mirror* excerpted two chapters from the book, "The honey camp" and "A bee hunt," on April 4, 1835. *A Tour on the Prairies* was favorably received and sold well; by the year's end two more editions, based on the English text, had been published in Paris, and within two years *A Tour on the Prairies* was translated into Dutch, French, German, Russian, and Italian. In 1849, *The Crayon Miscellany* was published by George P. Putnam in New York as Volume IX of *The Works of Washington Irving*, Author's Revised Edition. Irving supervised this edition through the press, correcting errors and in a few instances altering the work (the introduction, for example, is considerably shorter).

Proof sheets for the 1835 John Murray and the 1835 Carey, Lea, and Blanchard editions are not known to be extant. The Twayne edition, edited by Dahlia Kirby Terrell, bases its text of *A Tour on the Prairies* on the American printer's-copy manuscript. This manuscript does not survive for the first paragraph of Chapter I and the passage from "crowned by a broad and smoking dish" [161.5–6] through "again pushed forward" [161.40]; in these instances the Twayne edition bases its text on the printer's-copy manuscript prepared for the English edition. The text of the "Introduction," for which there is no printer's-copy manuscript, is taken from the first printing of the 1835 Carey, Lea, and Blanchard edition.

Astoria, Or, Anecdotes of an Enterprize Beyond the Rocky Mountains is Irving's history of John Jacob Astor's attempt to establish a commercial empire in the Pacific Northwest. The project was initiated by Astor, with whom Irving had been friendly for many years, shortly after Irving's return from his tour of eastern Oklahoma. After agreeing to write the book, Irving engaged his nephew, the lawyer Pierre Munro Irving, to work as a research assistant and to prepare a summary of the relevant manuscripts and reports. Irving himself began writing *Astoria* in May 1835, consulting his own books and notes, Pierre Irving's report, and various documents provided by Astor. He also solicited information from eyewitnesses and incorporated material about the region from secondary sources. Much of *Astoria* was written at Astor's country estate in the upper part of Manhattan, where Irving stayed as a guest from the summer of 1835 through the following year. He began sending his manuscript to the printer in the spring of 1836 while continuing to revise and add to the text. *Astoria, Or, Anecdotes of an Enterprize Beyond the Rocky Mountains* was published by Carey, Lea, and Blanchard on October 28, 1836. The London firm of Richard Bentley published an English edition at about the same time using proof sheets from the American edition; the book appeared with a slightly changed title (*Astoria, Or, Enterprise Beyond the Rocky Mountains*), prompting Irving to complain of Bentley's taking "unwarranted liberties with my mss. altering my title pages." The Bentley edition was the basis for two additional English-language editions published in Paris in 1836.

Translations soon appeared in French, German, Dutch, and Swedish. In 1849, *Astoria* was included as Volume VIII of the Author's Revised Edition of Irving's works. Unlike some of the volumes in the series, Irving made few alterations to *Astoria*; the most significant change is the addition of the paragraph at 597.19–26.

The Twayne edition of *Astoria*, edited by Richard Dilworth Rust, bases its text on the printer's-copy manuscript for the 1836 Carey, Lea, and Blanchard edition; according to the editor, "manuscript for approximately 90 percent of the *Astoria* text has been made available for use in determining Washington Irving's original intentions." In passages where the manuscript has not been made available, the 1836 Carey, Lea, and Blanchard edition provides the basis of the Twayne edition's text. The Twayne edition also includes the paragraph Irving added in the Author's Revised Edition and incorporates several readings adopted from this version of *Astoria*.

Of the two trips U.S. Army Captain Benjamin L. E. Bonneville made to the Rocky Mountains, the second, longer expedition (May 1, 1832–August 22, 1835) provided the raw material for *The Adventures of Captain Bonneville*. The two men met shortly after the captain's return from the West, while Irving was working on *Astoria* at the estate of John Jacob Astor. After an aborted attempt to write his own book, Bonneville sold a manuscript containing an account of the expedition based on his notes to Irving, who began adapting the manuscript into *The Adventures of Captain Bonneville* almost immediately after the publication of *Astoria* in October 1836. Because Bonneville's manuscript does not survive, the full extent of Irving's reliance on Bonneville's account is not clear. In a letter dated February 8, 1837, Irving wrote to Thomas Aspinwall, the American Consul in London who was acting as his agent with British publishers, that the book "is *all true*, being based on journals furnished me by individuals who have been among the mountains, and on oral accounts which I have gathered from various sources. It is full of adventure, description, and stirring incident; with occasional passages of humor. Were it all my own narration, I would speak of it with diffidence, but, knowing how I have been interested and delighted with my materials in their crude state, I am led to believe they will be very taking when properly dressed up." Irving completed the book in about four months. Although the manuscript was sent to the printer in early 1837, the publication of the American edition by the Philadelphia firm of Carey, Lea, and Blanchard was delayed, perhaps to allow time for the inclusion of a map of Bonneville's journey. An English edition, brought out by Richard Bentley in London, was published in May 1837 under the title *The Adventures of Captain Bonneville; Or, Scenes Beyond the Rocky Moun-*

tains of the Far West; this edition included several changes not authorized by Irving. The following month, the American edition of the book was published by Carey, Lea, and Blanchard under the title *The Rocky Mountains: Or, Scenes, Incidents, and Adventures in the Far West; Digested from the Journal of Captain B. L. E. Bonneville, of the Army of the United States, and Illustrated from Various Other Sources.* Two English-language editions appeared in Paris later in the year, as well as a German translation published in Frankfurt.

In 1849, Irving included the book in *The Complete Works of Washington Irving,* Author's Revised Edition, published in New York by George P. Putnam. According to the Twayne edition of *Adventures of Captain Bonneville,* edited by Robert A. Rees and Alan Sandy, Irving did not "extensively or consistently" revise the 1837 Carey, Lea, and Blanchard text for this publication; the Twayne edition uses the Carey, Lea, and Blanchard edition as copy-text and incorporates emendations from the Author's Revised Edition "in those instances where we are convinced Irving made a change or where he apparently approved a change." The Twayne editors go on to explain that the "changes in the copy-text attributed to Irving are, generally, those in which he 1) simplified his text, 2) toned down his style, 3) sought for greater precision, 4) corrected grammar, and 5) strove to avoid repetition and redundancy."

This volume presents the texts of the printings chosen for inclusion here, but it does not attempt to reproduce nontextual features of their typographic design. The texts are presented without change, except for the correction of typographical errors. Spelling, punctuation, and capitalization are often expressive features and are not altered, even when inconsistent or irregular. The following is a list of typographical errors corrected, cited by page and line number: 23.26, longed; 27.5, pie / bald; 30.37, trial; 84.38, riffle; 88.30, as us; 169. 20, *Manual;* 174.29, *tavelling;* 257.31, squardon; 307.29, Papillon; 340.23, flowerly; 348.5, intercourse.; 383.22, described; 397.20, approching; 405.14, accompanned; 450.2, valor;; 581.39, management; 821.31, precicipes.

Notes

In the notes below, the reference numbers denote page and line of the present volume (the line count includes chapter headings). No note is made for material included in standard desk-reference books such as Webster's *Ninth New Collegiate* and *Biographical* dictionaries. Biblical quotations are keyed to the King James Version. Quotations from Shakespeare are keyed to *The Riverside Shakespeare*, ed. G. Blakemore Evans (Boston: Houghton Mifflin, 1974). The most extensively annotated scholarly editions of these works are: *A Tour on the Prairies* (Norman: University of Oklahoma Press, 1956), ed. John Francis McDermott; *Astoria* (Norman: University of Oklahoma Press, 1964), ed. Edgeley W. Todd; *The Adventures of Captain Bonneville* (Norman: University of Oklahoma Press, 1961), ed. Edgeley W. Todd. John Francis McDermott's edition of *The Western Journals of Washington Irving* (Norman: University of Oklahoma Press, 1944) is especially important for evaluating *A Tour on the Prairies*. For additional notes, references to other studies, and general histories of the fur trade and western exploration, see also John L. Allen, "The Invention of the American West: Fur Trade Exploration, 1821–1839," in *North American Exploration. Volume 3: A Continent Comprehended*, ed. J. L. Allen (Lincoln: University of Nebraska Press, 1997), pp. 132–89; Bernard DeVoto, *Across the Wide Missouri* (Cambridge, Mass.: Houghton, Mifflin, 1947); James R. Gibson, *Otter Skins, Boston Ships, and China Goods: The Maritime Fur Trade of the Northwest Coast, 1785–1841* (Seattle: University of Washington Press, 1992); William H. Goetzmann, *Exploration and Empire: The Explorer and the Scientist in the Winning of the American West* (New York: Alfred A. Knopf, 1966); Fred R. Gowans, *Rocky Mountain Rendezvous* (Provo, Utah: Brigham Young University Press, 1976); LeRoy R. Hafen, ed., *The Mountain Men and the Fur Trade of the Far West*, 10 vols. (Glendale, California: Arthur H. Clark Company, 1965–1972); D. W. Meinig, *The Great Columbia Plain: A Historical Geography, 1805–1910* (Seattle: University of Washington Press, 1968); Dale L. Morgan, *Jedediah Smith and the Opening of the West* (Indianapolis: Bobbs-Merrill, 1953); Dale L. Morgan, *The West of William H. Ashley* (Denver: Old West Publishing Company, 1964); Paul C. Phillips, *The Fur Trade*, 2 vols. (Norman: University of Oklahoma Press, 1961); James P. Ronda, *Astoria and Empire* (Lincoln: University of Nebraska Press, 1990); Robert M. Utley, *A Life*

Wild and Perilous: Mountain Men and the Paths to the Pacific (New York: Henry Holt, 1997); Carl I. Wheat, *Mapping the Transmississippi West, 1540–1861*, 5 vols. in 6 (San Francisco: Institute for Historical Cartography, 1957–1963); David J. Wishart, *The Fur Trade of the American West, 1807–1840* (Lincoln: University of Nebraska Press, 1979). The present editor gratefully acknowledges the pioneering work on Irving's western writings done by Edgeley W. Todd and John Francis McDermott.

A TOUR ON THE PRAIRIES

8.10–11   "treading . . . dalliance,"] Cf. Shakespeare, *Hamlet*, I.iii.50.

9.21   my native city] Irving returned to New York City in 1832.

13.4   *Gil Blas*] Hero of the picaresque novel *Histoire de Gil Blas de Santillane* (1715–35) by Alain-René Lesage (1668–1747).

14.21   leader of our little band] Henry L. Ellsworth (1791–1858), one of three government commissioners selected to investigate lands set aside for Indians removed by federal legislation. Ellsworth was the only commissioner to make such a journey.

14.31   Mr. L—] Charles J. Latrobe (1801–75), tutor and traveling companion of Albert-Alexandre Pourtalès, comte de Pourtalès (1812–61), the "young Swiss Count" at 15.6–7. Latrobe's account of the 1832 western tour was published in 1836 as *The Rambler in North America, 1832–1833*. Irving sometimes called Latrobe "the Amateur" or "the Virtuoso."

15.15   Antoine] Antoine Deshetres (1791–1854).

17.28–29   company of mounted rangers] A unit of military rangers commanded by Captain Jesse Bean.

20.5   Col. Choteau] Auguste Pierre Choteau; more commonly spelled Chouteau (1786–1838).

21.26   Antoine] Antoine Lombard (b. 1810). Irving calls this Antoine by his proper first name while using "Tonish" for Antoine Deshetres.

21.40   Pierre Beatte] A renowned frontier guide.

25.8   west bank of the Arkansas] The expedition was actually on the left or north side of the river.

34.11   the banks of the Arkansas] The expedition was now at the site of present-day Tulsa, Oklahoma.

39.11   Old Ryan] John and William Ryan, described as father and son, were part of the ranger company; which man was "Old Ryan" remains unclear.

40.28   "a land flowing with milk and honey;"]   The land of Canaan as described in Exodus 3:8.

44.19–20   the Doctor]   Dr. Daniel Holt, a civilian physician assigned to Bean's ranger company.

44.26–27   the Cross Timber]   A dense thicket of brush and trees in present-day east-central Oklahoma and extending into Texas.

44.35   Red Fork]   The Cimarron River.

47.7   Covenanters]   A reference to those who signed the covenants of the Scottish Presbyterian church in the seventeenth century.

47.9–10   Praise God Barebones]   Religious radical (c. 1596–1679) and Member of Parliament during the English Civil War.

47.16   Charley]   Ranger Charles Nelson.

55.17   wise men . . . bowl]   Cf. the English nursery rhyme: "Three wise men of Gotham / Went to sea in a bowl; / If the bowl had been stronger / My song would have been longer."

60.31–32   Pawnees worship . . . it]   The Pawnee Morning Star or Captive Girl Sacrifice ritual is performed to ensure fertile soil and a bountiful corn harvest.

60.35   the sergeant]   Isaac Bean, Captain Bean's brother.

73.9   Sawyer]   Latrobe identifies this man as William Sawyer of Spadra, Arkansas.

75.15   Nestor]   The wisest and oldest of the Greeks at the siege of Troy.

80.1   Konza tribe]   Kansa Indians.

84.18   Lieutenant King's]   Robert King.

90.23   Brasis]   Brazos River in present-day Texas.

102.29   Clements]   Irving identifies him as Jeremiah C. Clements.

108.14   the boundary line of Texas]   The expedition was in fact some one hundred miles away from the boundary at the Red River.

112.14   north fork of the Red river]   More properly, the North Fork of the Canadian River.

116.14   through a valley]   The party was near present-day Oklahoma City, Oklahoma.

117.28   Grand Canadian]   The main stem of the Canadian River.

120.4–5   encamping . . . land]   The expedition was near present-day Norman, Oklahoma.

122.4   One of the anecdotes]   The story was an early version of an event in the life of mountain man Hugh Glass.

123.29   Requa]   William R. Requa (1795–1886). Irving's party visited Requa on October 6 at Hopefield Mission on the Neosho River.

131.5–6   "The Great Prairie"]   The travelers were now in broad, open country in present-day south-central Oklahoma.

138.13   the Amateur]   Latrobe.

149.28–29   a lieutenant]   First Lieutenant Joseph Pentecost.

153.14–15   "Canst thou . . . Orion?"]   Cf. Job 38:31: "Canst thou bind the sweet influences of Pleiades, or loose the bands of Orion?"

158.17   commanding a wide prospect]   The party was now near present-day Okmulgee, Oklahoma.

161.25   Apicius]   Marcus Gavius Apicius (b. 25 BCE), culinary expert for Roman emperors Augustus and Tiberius.

ASTORIA

179.4   North West Fur Company]   The North West Company, established in 1779 by Canadian fur traders and British supply merchants.

179.29   John Jacob Astor]   New York fur-trade entrepreneur (1763–1848) and founder of both the Pacific Fur Company and the American Fur Company.

180.34–37   published journals . . . Cox]   *Travels in the Interior of America, in the Years 1809, 1810, and 1811* (London, 1817) by the Scottish naturalist John Bradbury (1768–1823); Henry Marie Brackenridge, *Journal of a Voyage up the River Missouri* (Baltimore, 1815); Edwin James, comp., *Account of an Expedition from Pittsburgh to the Rocky Mountains, Performed in the Years 1819, 1820 . . . under the Command of Major Stephen H. Long*, 2 vols., (Philadelphia, 1823); Gabriel Franchère, *Relation d'un voyage à la Côte du Nord-ouest de l'Amérique Septentrionale* (Montreal, 1820); Ross Cox, *Adventures on the Columbia River* (London, 1831). Bradbury, Breckenridge, Franchère, and Cox were participants in various parts of the Astoria enterprise.

184.38   an old French writer]   Baron Louis Armand de Lahontan (1666–1715) served in New France and wrote *Nouveaux voyages . . . dans l'Amérique Septentrionale* (Paris, 1703).

188.17–18   treacherous and bloody affairs . . . Michilimackinac]   These British posts were attacked by Indians in 1763 during Pontiac's War.

191.9   the Grand Portage]   Canoe and merchandise-carrying point in the fur trade at the western tip of Lake Superior.

196.28   a treaty with Great Britain]   The Jay Treaty, 1795–1796.

200.12   a company] The Russian-American Company, established in 1799.

201.27   Captain Jonathan Carver] Explorer (1710–80) and author of *Travels through the Interior Parts of North America* (London, 1778).

202.13   Straits of Annian] Legendary part of the Northwest Passage.

202.29–30   an account] *Voyages from Montreal . . . to the Frozen and Pacific Oceans* (London, 1801).

204.17–18   The Russian establishment] Headquarters for the Russian-American Company at Sitka, Alaska.

206.12–13   New Caledonia] Present-day British Columbia.

208.10   Wilson Price Hunt] Hunt (1783?–1842), Astor's chief lieutenant in the West and leader of the second American expedition across the West.

210.30   our Tripolitan war] A reference to naval engagements against Tripoli and the Barbary States, 1801–5.

220.21   the elder Stuart] David Stuart (1765–1853), a partner in Astor's Pacific Fur Company.

228.7   Tamaahmaah] Kamehameha I (1737?–1819).

231.5   bay of Tocaigh] Kailua Bay.

234.12   Waititi] Honolulu.

246.4   Wappatoo] An edible plant described by the Lewis and Clark Expedition.

251.17   within Point George] Now Astoria, Oregon.

257.8   Lewis River] Snake River.

259.10   parallel ridges of mountains] The Cascade Mountains.

260.22   Falls or Rapids of the Columbia] Celilo Falls.

261.4   "The Long Narrows."] The Dalles.

262.2   Quamash] Camas, an edible plant.

276.11   the trading post] The North West Company's Spokane House, near present-day Spokane, Washington.

279.37   Donald M'Kenzie] Donald Mackenzie (1783–1851), prominent Canadian fur trader and a partner in Astor's Pacific Fur Company.

284.31–32   Ramsay Crooks] Noted fur trader (1787–1859) and longtime Astor associate in both business and politics.

288.2–3   Manuel Lisa] Energetic St. Louis fur trader (1772?–1820) and one of Astor's principal western rivals.

288.8   Mr. Henry] Andrew Henry (1775–1833), fur-trade explorer and a partner in many western fur ventures.

292.14   Fort Osage] Military post on the Missouri River established in 1808 by General William Clark.

295.39   John Bradbury] See note 180.34–37.

296.2–5   Mr. Nuttall . . . Plants."] Thomas Nuttall (1786–1859), botanist and author of *Journal of Travels into Arkansas Territory, 1818–1820* (Philadelphia, 1821) and *The Genera of North American Plants, and a Catalogue of the Species, to the Year 1817* (London, 1818).

325.4   "The Bloody Ground."] A reference to the violent encounters between white settlers and Indians in Kentucky during the late eighteenth century.

331.35   carottes] Twists of tobacco commonly used in the fur trade.

333.2   *The great bend*] The Great Bend of the Missouri River in present-day South Dakota.

336.23   the Arickara town] The Arikara earth-lodge villages around the Grand River in present–day South Dakota.

340.24–25   scriptural descriptions . . . hills."] See Psalm 50:10.

343.18   an interpreter] Joseph Gravelines, a fur trader who spoke Arikara.

344.24–25   "The left handed"] An Arikara civil chief, also known as Le Gauche.

349.17   Big Man] An influential Arikara war chief.

357.25   passage of Scripture] Jeremiah 31:15.

358.20–21   "The Great American desert."] A geographic image of the Great Plains advanced by explorers Lieutenant Zebulon Montgomery Pike and Major Stephen H. Long.

360.3–6   "A great company . . . goods."] Cf. Ezekiel 38:12, 15.

364.15   Big River] Grand River in present-day north-central South Dakota.

368.26   Edward Rose] Noted African-American mountain man (d. 1832 or 1833).

383.26   a chain of mountains] The Big Horn Mountains.

393.36   "horse . . . wear,"] *King Lear*, III.iv.137.

394.32   the second Big Horn Ridge] Irving's geography is vague here: the Astorians were about to enter the Big Horn Basin in present-day Wyoming.

396.1   head waters of the Columbia] A confused reference to the Snake River.

396.15   three mountain peaks] The Grand Tetons.

396.36   Spanish River] The Green River.

400.15–16   Mad River] The Snake River.

408.40   a dangerous strait] Idaho Falls on the Snake River.

412.21   "The Caldron Linn."] Named by Astorian Robert Stuart (1785–1848) on his eastbound journey in August 1812.

423.1–2   a beautiful little stream] The Boise River.

425.17   Sciatogas] Probably the Cayuse Indians.

429.19   small rivers] The Payette, Weiser, and Boise rivers.

445.5–6   Lewis, and Clarke rivers] The Snake River and that portion of the Columbia River above the confluence with the Snake.

470.12   Euryalus] A warrior in Homer's *Iliad*.

475.24–25   a confidential agent] Astor's son-in-law, Adrian Benjamin Bentzon.

476.33   New Archangel] Sitka, Alaska.

491.20   one much shorter and easier] This information led Robert Stuart to discover South Pass, which was essential in the development of the Oregon Trail.

493.12   Lake Bonneville] Now called the Great Salt Lake, this lake had formerly been named for Captain Benjamin L. E. Bonneville, the subject of Irving's *The Adventures of Captain Bonneville*.

509.38   craters in a state of eruption] One of Irving's fictional touches. Stuart was looking at mountains that were part of the Bitterroot Range.

523.5–6   an extensive low country] The valley of the Sweetwater River.

524.11   the river] The North Platte River.

537.11   first intelligence] News of Stuart's arrival was first announced in the St. Louis, Missouri *Gazette*, May 8, 1813. A subsequent report entitled "American Enterprize" was widely circulated and prompted considerable interest in the western fur trade.

567.21–22   Count Baranoff] Alexander Baranov (1747–1819), field manager for the Russian-American Company in Alaska.

568.25   "potations pottle deep."] *Othello*, II.iii.54.

578.25   Tahoorowa] Maui.

604.26   Buenaventura] Mythical western river; the reference here is probably to the Sacramento River.

604.38–39   Rio del Norte] Mythical western river; the reference here is probably to the Rio Grande.

605.7   Grand river] Ottawa River.

610.9   James's Peak] Pike's Peak.

THE ADVENTURES OF CAPTAIN BONNEVILLE

617.2   CAPTAIN BONNEVILLE] Captain Benjamin Louis Eulalie de Bonneville (1796–1878), army officer, explorer, and fur trader.

631.1   Mr. Alfred Seton] Participant in the Astoria enterprise and author of an account of his western adventures published in *American Monthly Magazine* in 1835.

631.26   Corporal Trim] A character in Sterne's *Tristram Shandy.*

632.27   a mass of manuscript] Irving purchased Bonneville's papers (now lost) for one thousand dollars in March 1836.

636.30   General Ashley] William H. Ashley (1778–1838), St. Louis explorer, fur-trade entrepreneur, and politician.

637.26–27   Smith . . . Sublette] Jedediah Smith (1798–1831); Thomas Fitzpatrick (1799–1854); Jim Bridger (1804–81); Robert Campbell (1804–79); William Sublette (1799–1845). All were major figures in the Rocky Mountain fur trade.

637.38   "Bloody Ground."] See note 325.4.

643.2   *Fort Osage*] See note 292.14.

644.4–5   J. R. Walker . . . M. S. Cerré] Joseph Reddeford Walker (1798–1876), noted fur trapper and frontier scout. Michel Sylvestre Cerré (1804–60), St. Louis–based trader in both the Rocky Mountains and Santa Fe.

644.28   Pierre's Hole] Located in the Teton Basin in present-day Idaho and site of the 1832 fur trade rendezvous.

646.27–28   General Clark . . . traveller] An odd mistake for Irving to make since William Clark was superintendent for Indian affairs in the West.

651.1   Red River] The Vermillion River in present-day eastern Kansas and Nebraska.

651.11   Great Island] Grand Island, Nebraska.

651.37   the fork of the Nebraska] Present-day North Platte, Nebraska.

653.17   the chimney] Chimney Rock, a prominent feature in present-day western Nebraska on what became the Oregon Trail.

658.37   The Black Hills]   The foothills or Laramie Range of the Rockies, not to be confused with today's Black Hills of South Dakota.

659.6–7   Dolland reflecting telescope]   More properly the Dolland refracting telescope, named for London instrument maker George Dolland (1774–1856).

661.27   Powder River Mountains]   More properly the Big Horn Mountains.

666.16   a low and very rocky ridge]   South Pass, at the Continental Divide in present-day Wyoming.

667.26   Mr. Fontenelle]   Lucien Fontenelle (1800?–1840), St. Louis trader working for the American Fur Company.

670.10–11   one of their tribe . . . Lewis]   Lewis's scouting party killed two Piegan Blackfeet in late July 1806 on the Two Medicine River in present-day north-central Montana.

672.27   Nathaniel J. Wyeth]   Boston adventurer and fur trade promoter (1802–56).

690.14   Vanderburgh and Dripps]   William H. Vanderburgh (c.1798–1832); Andrew Dripps (1789–1860).

692.24–25   summit of a mountain]   Teton Pass, near present-day Jackson Hole, Wyoming.

694.18–19   his winter quarters]   North of present-day Salmon, Idaho, on the Salmon River.

702.1   Racine Amère]   The Bitterroot River.

726.10   *feu de joie*]   A gunfire salute.

729.35   Godin's River]   The Big Lost River.

750.40   Cottonois Indians]   The Kutenai Indians.

751.2–3   a resident trader]   Francis Ermatinger (1798–1858).

765.37   several large streams]   The Weber, Jordan, and Bear rivers.

770.39–40   General Atkinson . . . Missouri]   General Henry Atkinson (1782–1842) commanded the Atkinson-O'Fallon Expedition to treat with Indians on the upper Missouri.

775.40   Colter]   John Colter (c. 1774–c. 1813), member of the Lewis and Clark expedition, fur trader, and explorer of present-day western Wyoming.

776.29   Captain Stewart]   William Drummond Stewart (1796–1871), Scottish adventurer and sportsman who traveled with many mountain men in the 1830s.

787.12   up the left bank]   Bonneville was now near present-day Riverton, Wyoming.

792.6–7   Mr. Thompson]   David Thompson (1770–1857), Canadian explorer and cartographer.

799.16–17   a defile]   Union Pass, at the Continental Divide near present-day Dubois, Wyoming.

806.10   Hane's Fork]   Ham's Fork of the Green River, site of four important fur-trade rendezvous.

818.7   Cassié]   The Raft River.

820.30   Powder River]   Now known as the Bruneau River.

827.15   "Grand Rond,"]   The Grand Ronde Valley.

828.23   a mere chasm]   The Grand Canyon of the Snake River.

840.25   Way-lee-way]   The Grand Ronde River.

845.3   Big Wyer]   Present-day Owyhee River in eastern Oregon.

850.36   O-push-y-e-cut]   Principal Nez Perce chief.

853.17   He-mim-el-pilp]   Nez Perce village chief.

854.3   *Mr. Pambrun*]   Pierre C. Pambrun (1792–1841), chief factor at Fort Walla Walla.

854.28   Skynses]   The Tenino Indians.

874.14   Little Snake Lake]   Present-day Bear Lake.

876.17   Mary River . . . Ogden's River]   Present-day Humboldt River.

878.9   great swampy lake]   The Humboldt and Carson Sinks in present-day northwestern Nevada.

878.11   Californian Mountains]   The Sierra Nevada Mountains.

890.21   Multnomah]   The Willamette River

893.8   Pelorus]   Hannibal's navigator on his return from Italy.

897.38   Castor and Pollux]   Twin sons of Zeus and Leda.

901.1   Mr. M'Kenzie]   Kenneth McKenzie (1801–61), chief factor at the American Fur Company's Fort Union.

909.28–29   Mr. Nuttall . . . Mr. Townshend]   Thomas Nuttall, see note 296.2–5. John Kirk Townsend (1809–51), naturalist and author of *Narrative of a Journey Across the Rocky Mountains to the Columbia River* (Philadelphia, 1839).

911.26   Potations, pottle deep]   See note 568.25.

920.9   Gun Creek]   Present-day Powder River in eastern Oregon.

928.13   Ottolais]   The Umatilla Indians.

935.11–12   "feast . . . lees,"]   Cf. Isaiah 25:6.

939.1–2   *crim. con.*]   Criminal conversation.

951.16   Wappatoo Island]   Present-day Sauvie Island, near the confluence
of the Columbia and Willamette rivers.

953.9   by treaty]   The Treaty of Joint Occupation (1818, 1827) between
Great Britain and the United States.

Library of Congress Cataloging-in-Publication Data

Irving, Washington, 1783–1859.
    Three western narratives / Washington Irving.
        p. cm. — (The Library of America; 146)
    Includes bibliographical references.
    Contents: A tour on the prairies—Astoria, or Anecdotes of an
enterprize beyond the Rocky Mountains—The adventures of
Captain Bonneville.
    ISBN 1–931082–53–7 (alk. paper)
        1. West (U.S.)—History—To 1848. 2. West (U.S.)—Description
and travel. 3. Oklahoma—Description and travel. 4. Indians of
North America—Oklahoma—History—19th century. 5. Astoria
(Or.)—History. 6. Overland journeys to the Pacific. 7. Astor,
John Jacob, 1763–1848. 8. Fur trade—West (U.S.)—History—19th
century. 9. Bonneville, Benjamin Louis Eulalie de, 1796–1878.
10. Explorers—West (U.S.)—Biography. I. Title: 3 western narra-
tives. II. Title: Tour on the prairies. III. Title: Astoria.
IV. Title: Adventures of Captain Bonneville. V. Title:
VI. Series.

F592.174 2004
978'.02—dc21   2003044202

THE LIBRARY OF AMERICA SERIES

The Library of America fosters appreciation and pride in America's literary heritage by publishing, and keeping permanently in print, authoritative editions of America's best and most significant writing. An independent nonprofit organization, it was founded in 1979 with seed money from the National Endowment for the Humanities and the Ford Foundation.

This book is set in 10 point Linotron Galliard,
a face designed for photocomposition by Matthew Carter
and based on the sixteenth-century face Granjon. The paper
is acid-free Domtar Literary Opaque and meets the requirements
for permanence of the American National Standards Institute. The
binding material is Brillianta, a woven rayon cloth made by
Van Heek-Scholco Textielfabrieken, Holland. Composition
by Dedicated Business Services. Printing and binding
by R.R.Donnelley & Sons Company.
Designed by Bruce Campbell.